Writing as Revision

Third Edition

Beth Alvarado
Barbara Cully

Learning Solutions

New York   Boston   San Francisco
London   Toronto   Sydney   Tokyo   Singapore   Madrid
Mexico City   Munich   Paris   Cape Town   Hong Kong   Montreal

Pearson Learning Solutions, 501 Boylston Street, Suite 900, Boston, MA 02116
A Pearson Education Company
www.pearsoned.com

Printed in the United States of America

1 2 3 4 5 6 7 8 9 10 XXXX 15 14 13 12 11 10

000200010270562311

NM/SC

ISBN 10: 0-558-71433-1
ISBN 13: 978-0-558-71433-8

Acknowledgments Report

Grateful acknowledgment is made to the following sources for permission to reprint material copyrighted or controlled by them:

"When We Dead Awaken: Writing as Re-Vision," by Adrienne Rich, reprinted from *On Lies, Secrets, and Silence: Selected Prose 1966–1978* (1979), W.W. Norton & Company.

"Disliking Books at an Early Age," by Gerald Graff, reprinted from *Beyond the Culture Wars: How Teaching the Conflicts Can Revitalize American Education* (1992), by permission of W.W. Norton & Company.

"Mother Tongue," by Amy Tan, reprinted from *The Threepenny Review* (1990), Sandra Dijkstra Literary Agency.

"Coming Into Language," by Jimmy Baca, reprinted from *Working in the Dark* (1992), Red Crane Books.

"A Good Crot is Hard to Find," reprinted from *Rhetoric Review 3*, January 1995, by permission of Rhetoric Review.

"Memory and Imagination," by Patricia Hampl, reprinted from *The Dolphin Reader II*, edited by Douglas Hunt (1985), Marly Rusoff & Associates, Inc.

"She Had Some Horses: the Education of a Poet," reprinted from *Teachers & Writers* (March–April 1995), by permission of Teachers & Writers magazine.

"She Had Some Horses," "September Moon," and "Anchorage"," by Joy Harjo (1983), reprinted by permission from W.W. Norton & Company.

"It's Just a Movie: A Teaching Essay for Introductory Media Classes," by Greg Smith, reprinted from *Cinema Journal* (fall 2001), by permission of University of Texas Press.

"Die Hard: The American Mythos," by Peter Parshall, reprinted from *Journal of Popular Film and Television* (summer 1990), Heldref Publications.

"Seduction and Betrayal," by bell hooks, reprinted from *Visions Magazine* (fall 1993).

"Disney's Sub/Version of Anderson's 'The Little Mermaid'," by Roberta Trites, reprinted from *Journal of Popular Film and Television*, (winter 1991), Heldref Publications.

"Crash Course: Race, Class and Context," by Christine Farris, (March 2007), by permission of College English.

"Alice's Little Sister: Exploring Pan's Labyrinth," by Kim Edwards, reprinted from *Screen Education* Australian Teachers of Media.

"Gender and Romance," by Meagan Lehr.

"The Yellow Wallpaper," by Charlotte Gilman, reprinted from *The Yellow Wallpaper* (March 13, 1905).

"The Story of an Hour," by Kate Chopin, reprinted from *Literature and its Writers: An Introduction to Fiction, Poetry, and Drama* (1894).

"Floating" by Karen Brennan, reprinted from *Wild Desire*.

"First Ed," by Terry Castle, reprinted from *The Apparitional Lesbian* (1995), by permission of Columbia University Press.

"Pass," by Boyer Rickel, reprinted from *Taboo* (1999), University of Wisconsin Press.

"Girl," by Jamaica Kincaid, reprinted from *At the Bottom of the River* (1983), Farrar, Straus & Giroux.

"Hairbrush," reprinted from *One Hundred Histories* Trident Media Group.

"Mascara," by Aurelie Sheehan, reprinted from *One Hundred Histories* Trident Media Group.

"Purse," by Aurelie Sheehan, reprinted from *One Hundred Histories* Trident Media Group.

"To Reduce Your Likelihood of Murder," by Ander Monson, reprinted from *Other Electricities* (2005), by permission of Sarabande Books.

"She Wasn't Soft," by T.C. Boyle, reprinted from *The New Yorker*, September 18, 1995, Penguin Group, Inc.

"Tell Him about Brother John," by Manuel Munoz, reprinted from *The Faith Healer of Olive Avenue*, Algonquin Books of Chapel Hill.

"Jealous Husband Returns in Form of Parrot," by Robert Butler, reprinted from *Tabloid Dreams* (1996), Henry Holt & Company.

"Jon," by George Saunders, reprinted from *The New Yorker*, January 27, 2003.

"The Necessity of Certain Behaviors," by Shannon Cain, reprinted from *New England Review*, New England Review.

"How to Date a Browngirl, Blackgirl, Whitegirl, or Halfie," by Junot Diaz, reprinted from *Drown* (1996), Riverhead Books.

"Persephone Speaks," by Alison Hawthorne Deming, reprinted from *Rope* (2009), Penguin Group, Inc.

"Zeus," by Alison Hawthorne Deming, reprinted from *Rope* (2009), Penguin Group, Inc.

"Translator's Note, What I Love by Odysseas Elytis," by Olga Broumas, reprinted from *What I Love*, edited by Odysseas Elytis (1978), by permission of Copper Canyon Press.

"The Monogram," by Odysseas Elytis, reprinted from *What I love*, edited by Odysseas Elytis (1986), by permission of Copper Canyon Press.

"Black Holes, Black Stockings," by Jane Miller and Olga Broumas, reprinted from *Memory at These Speeds*, edited by Jane Miller (1996), by permission of Wesleyan University Press.

"In an Open View," by Barbara Cully, reprinted from *The New Intimacy* (1997), Penguin Group, Inc.

"Maybe It's Cold Outside," by Barbara Cully, reprinted from *The New Intimacy* (1997), Penguin Group, Inc.

"The New Colossus: Exploring the Idea of a Border," by John Washington.

"The Homeland, Azlan/El Otro Mexico," by Gloria Anzaldua, reprinted from *Borderlands/La Frontera: the New Mestiza* (1987), Aunt Lute Books.

"The Space In Between," by Kimi Eisele.

"Letter to Mexico," by Eula Biss, reprinted from *Notes from No Man's Land* (2009), Frances Goldin Literary Agency.

"Sifting Through the Trash," by Luis Urrea, Anchor Books, a division of Random House.

"The Border Patrol State," by Leslie Silko, reprinted from *The Nation* (October 1994), Wylie Agency.

"Yellow Woman," by Leslie Silko, reprinted from *Storyteller* (1981), Seaver Books.

"Emily's Exit," by Beth Alvarado, by permission of New Rivers Press.

"The Bus to Veracruz," by Richard Shelton, reprinted from *The Other Side of the Story* (1987), by permission of University of Pittsburgh Press.

"What I Am," by Luci Tapahonso, reprinted from *Saani Dahataal: The Women Are Singing* (1993), by permission of University of Arizona Press.

"The Moths," by Helena Viramontes, reprinted from *The Moths and Other Stories* (1986), Arte Publico Press.

"What They Say about Glass Houses," by Aisha Sabatini Sloan.

"The Necessity to Speak," by Sam Hamill, reprinted from *A Poet's Work*.

"So Much Water So Close to Home," by Raymond Carver, reprinted from *Furious Seasons* (1977).

"A New Kind of Gravity," by Andrew Foster Altschul, reprinted from *Story Quarterly - The Literary Magazine of Rutgers University — Camden* (2005), Rutgers University-Camden.

"Tall Tales from the Mekong Delta," by Kate Braverman, reprinted from *Squandering the Blue* (1989), Ballantine Books, a division of Random House.

"Because my Father Always Said He was the Only Indian who Saw Jimmy Hendrix Play 'The Star-Spangled Banner' at Woodstock," by Alexie Sherman, reprinted from *The Lone Ranger and Tonto Fistfight in Heaven* (1994), by permission of Grove/Atlantic.

"Sonny's Blues," by James Baldwin, reprinted from *Going to Meet the Man* (1965), by permission of James Baldwin Estate.

"Birth of the Cool," by Aisha Sabatini Sloan, reprinted from *Identity Theory* (August 3, 2009), Identity Theory.

"Where Are You Going, Where Have You Been?" by Joyce Oates, reprinted from *The Wheel of Love* (1970), by permission of John Hawkins & Associates, Inc.

"The Fourth State of Matter," by Jo Ann Beard, June 24, 1996, reprinted from *The New Yorker*.

"Introduction to Against Forgetting: Twentieth Century Poetry of Witness," by Carolyn Forche, reprinted from *Against Forgetting: Twentieth Century Poetry of Witness* (1993), by permission of W.W. Norton & Company.

"The Colonel," by Carolyn Forche, reprinted from *The Country Between Us* (1980), HarperCollins.

"On the Subway," by Sharon Olds, reprinted from *The Gold Cell* Alfred A. Knopf, a division of Random House.

"A Litnany for Survival," by Audre Lorde, reprinted from *The Black Unicorn* (1978), by permission of W.W. Norton & Company.

"How to Watch your Brother Die," by Michael Lassell, reprinted from *Decade Dance* (1990), Lassell, Michael.

"Charlie Howard's Descent," by Mark Doty, reprinted from *Turtle, Swan* (1980), David R. Godine, Publisher, Inc.

"How to Tell a True War Story," by Tim O'Brien, reprinted from *The Things They Carried* (1991), Houghton Mifflin Harcourt Publishing Company.

"What Saves Us," by Bruce Weigl, reprinted from *What Saves Us* (1992), Northwestern University Press.

"The Way of Tet" and "Song of Napalm," by Bruce Weigl, reprinted from *Song of Napalm* (1988), by permission of Grove/Atlantic.

"What Every Soldier Should Know," by Brian Turner, reprinted from *Here, Bullet* (2005), Alice James Books.

"Here Bullet," by Brian Turner, reprinted from *Here, Bullet* (2005), Alice James Books.

"AB Negative (The Surgeon's Poem)," by Brian Turner, reprinted from *Here, Bullet* (2005), Alice James Books.

"Night in Blue," by Brian Turner, reprinted from *Here, Bullet* (2005), Alice James Books.

Kathryn Alvarado created, collected, and/or formatted all of the images for *Writing as Re-Vision* as part of an internship for Arizona International College, where she was a Liberal Studies major with an emphasis in photography. In addition to photographing public art for the Tucson Pima Arts Council, she has published one other cover photo and had her work displayed in two exhibits.

Daniel Cardis self-identifies as a redneck, hillbilly mixed media artist from West Virginia. Although he's been known to ride some of the best half pipes in the nation, he currently resides in Incline Village, Nevada where he does custom woodworking to support his snowboarding habit.

Re-vision—the act of looking back, of seeing with fresh eyes, of entering an old text from a new critical direction—is more . . . than a chapter in cultural history: it is an act of survival.

—Adrienne Rich

—toward the end, only revision mattered: to look
Again, more deeply, harder, clearer, the one
Redemption granted us to ask.

—Jane Hirshfield

Writing as Revision

3rd Edition; Editors: Beth Alvarado, Barbara Cully

Table of Contents

Preface for Instructors and Students

Peter Elbow in his essay "The War between Reading and Writing—And How to End It" argues that one of the main difficulties in teaching composition stems from the fact that "reading has dominance over writing in the academic or school culture" (5). For instance, in English classes in high schools "students spend less than 3 percent" of their time writing and in most college courses, "reading is more central than writing" (10). Still, Elbow believes that we can "create a better balance and relationship between reading and writing. To do so," he argues, "we will need to give more emphasis to writing in our teaching and our curricular structures and use writing in more imaginative ways. When we achieve this productive balance, even reading will benefit" (5). Our task, then, is to shift the emphasis from reading towards writing in order to create a balance between the two.

We have designed *Writing as Revision* to facilitate this shift in emphasis. First of all, the various chapter introductions recognize, and encourage students to see, that reading and writing are reciprocal processes—when we read a text we are "writing our own reading" of it; in writing, we are re-reading; we must re-read and re-envision our own texts in order to effectively write them. We want to encourage students to practice this kind of active reading by keeping a writer's journal where they can have a running dialog with the texts. Not only should the writer's journal give them a place where they can begin a close reading of the texts they might analyze for their papers, but it should be a place where they feel free to respond, react, question, agree, disagree—and then inquire into their own responses and the assumptions behind them.

We have made the selections in these chapters with an eye towards engendering this process of inquiry. Janice Lauer, in her article "Writing as Inquiry: Some Questions for Teachers," defines inquiry in several ways. First of all, it is "the ability to go beyond the known" and its goal is "the discovery of insight"– the creation of knowledge rather than to acquire it. She points out that

> These views of writing as epistemic suggest that when students raise meaningful questions about incongruities in their own worlds, they gain genuine motivation and direction for writing, and that when students discover new understandings through writing, the writing becomes valuable to them and worth sharing with readers.

The question, then, for teachers of writing, is how can we create conditions conducive to inquiry, where students become active learners who use reading and writing as tools for discovery? Drawing on her research in philosophy and psychology, Lauer suggests that the catalyst for inquiry is disequilibrium or "cognitive dissonance," a state which springs from the perception of a gap between a current set of beliefs or values and some new experience or idea that seems to violate or confound those beliefs. This clash engenders puzzlement, curiosity, a sense of enigma, sometimes of wonder, a pressure to restore equilibrium. While some people suppress such tension, the inquirer, the learner, strives to resolve it by searching for new understanding, by going beyond the known.

Our first assumption, then, is that if we present students with texts that challenge their assumptions, that present them with a new experience or with a novel way of seeing a familiar topic, we can motivate them to explore the text and their responses to it. Our second assumption is that we are *not* teaching what the text "means." In other words, we are not teaching them to read the text the way that we might read it or in the way that others have read it. This is not a literature class. Rather, we're presenting them with ways to engage with the texts themselves – through writing and therefore through re-reading and re-writing. As Gerald Graff might say, we're introducing students to controversies that texts are inherently a part of. We could say that this book presumes an activist pedagogy, and it does, if our definition of activist is to activate our students to think critically, to re-see, to revise, and even to reaffirm. Our goal, then, is not that students come away from the text changed, but that they come away more aware of complexities and challenged to enter the conversation in the classroom and in their own writing.

The title of the book, *Writing as Revision*, suggests that re-vision is integral to the act of writing. This references Adrienne Rich who, in her essay, "When We Dead Awaken: Writing as Re-vision," defines revision as "the act of looking back, of seeing with fresh eyes, of entering an old text from a new critical direction." Each chapter introduction sets up central concepts that can be used by the instructor as critical lenses students can use to examine the texts; further, these concepts will enable students to see connections among texts and thus facilitate their movement from analysis to synthesis as the course progresses. The concepts are not meant to limit the ways the text might be read, but instead to provide entry points for reading and writing. The chapter introductions foreground ways that the readings of the chapter interrogate and/or reflect the central theme of the chapter.

Just as we believe that readings that challenge students' assumptions can motivate their process of inquiry, we also believe that teaching a number of short interrelated texts can help balance the reading and writing in the classroom. First of all, this approach can allow students more time for the incubation and exploration of their ideas in writing and give the teacher more time to help them with their development and arrangement. According to Lonergan, the process of inquiry is "cumulative and organic" or recursive in nature: "later stages presuppose and build on earlier ones" (as cited in Lauer). For this reason, each of the chapters is meant to constitute a "unit" of related readings. Further, we have seen in teaching these materials that the chapters themselves create either a thematic or conceptual context for each author's work as well as for the students' own writing.

Along with the fiction and poetry, we have included quite a bit of creative non-fiction in order to facilitate the study of writing, not only because it provides students with various models of writing in the "real world"—rhetorical analysis, interpretive analysis, cultural critique, autobiography, and reader response—but also because it provides a cultural site for discussions of a cross-disciplinary nature. Of course, it is also entirely possible to choose readings from all or several of the chapters based on your own theme or approach. To facilitate this, we provide the following synopsis of each chapter:

Chapter One: Writing as Re-Vision Please note that the chapter one introduction serves as an introduction to the whole book and that it can also serve as an introduction to the course. This chapter is compiled of essays that invite students to think about their relationship to literature and language and, specifically, to reading and writing. We placed these essays in the beginning of the book because they situate students in the course by introducing them to issues they may not have considered before: the connections between language, reading, and writing and identity; the idea that whole cultural conversations surround texts; and the premise that writing can be used to explore ideas as well as express them. One or more of these essays could be used to begin the course, to facilitate a discussion of these issues as they arise in the classroom, or to look back over the readings studied. Each piece also presents provocative ideas and controversies within academic and cultural discourses that invite students to hone their reading strategies and critical perspectives.

Chapter Two: Rereading Hollywood provides students with essays that situate readings of films within particular genres and conventions; many of these essays read films as a way of rereading the cultures that produced them. These essays can be paired thematically with readings from other chapters; they also provide students with excellent models of rhetorical analysis and/or cultural critique. An instructor may choose to teach films as texts and these essays will provide students with the vocabulary they will need to analyze them.

Chapters Three through Five are each designed as a set of thematic readings for a course, and each of these chapters contains a mix of genres. The introductory essay at the beginning of each chapter provides a theoretical lens through which to view the subsequent readings. Each of the chapters creates a cultural conversation that the students are asked to analyze and to join—through discussions in the classroom, through their own writing, and through their evaluation of one another's work. Finally, the chapter introductions and the essays within chapters are worthy of serious study and, in addition, provide students with models for their own writing.

After all, the primary text in any composition course is the on-going text of the students' writing: students continually write—journal entries, drafts of papers, responses to one another's work—in order to explore and express their ideas about what they have learned and to make connections to their own contexts as readers. It is our hope that Writing as Revision will both invite them into the cultural conversation and support instructors in their efforts to create courses that balance reading and writing. These "fifty-fifty" courses, as Elbow calls them, "are probably the most natural and fruitful place for reading and writing mutually to enhance each other; courses where we go back and forth constantly between reading and writing and neither activity is felt as simply a handmaiden to the other one" (19).

Works Cited

Elbow, Peter. "The War between Reading and Writing—and How to End It." *Rhetoric Review*. Vol. 12, No. 1, Fall 1993. 5-24.

Lauer, Janice M. "Writing as Inquiry: Some Questions for Teachers." *College Composition and Communication*, Vol. 33, No. 1, February 1982. 89-93.

Rich, Adrienne. "When We Dead Awaken: Writing as Re-Vision." *On Lies, Secrets, and Silence: Selected Prose 1966-1978*. New York: Norton and Company, 1979.

Acknowledgments

We would like to thank many people for their help in the revision of this anthology and in the creation of the two editions that preceded it, including Dr. Anne-Marie Hall, Dr. Jun Liu, Dr. Tilly Warnock, Dr. Larry Evers, Dr. Thomas P. Miller and Dr. Rudolph Troike. We'd also like to acknowledge the chapter editors of the first two editions, whose work provided a foundation for this edition: Michael Robinson, Joanna Hearne, Debra White-Stanley, Amanda Brobbel, Jocelyn White, Damla Isik, Wendy Weise-Smith, Jillian Cantor, Leta McGaffey Sharp, Ute Haker, Sharon Wright, Deborah Margolis, Patty Malesh, Josh Carney Mary Beth Callie, Jonathan Dryden, Alesia Garcia, James Livingston, and Maureen Salzer. Their collaborative efforts and insight made for a range of readings otherwise not possible.

We'd also like to thank the many graduate student teachers, teaching supervisors, and adjunct lecturers who provided feedback and suggested readings. Special thanks to Meagan Lehr and John Washington for their insightful writing and assistance in finalizing this new edition. Finally, we'd like to thank our editor, Gretchen Anderson, who always gave us helpful advice and timely responses.

Beth Alvarado
Barbara Cully
Tucson, April 3, 2010

Elizabeth

"J"

The light that shines from friendships eye
In its pure native glows of Heaven
Can change life's stormy, wintry sky
To summers mild and quiet Even

Can pour a flood of ^2 pangless joy
In ev'ry breast by anguish riven
And turn from sorrows sad employ
To the sweet work of praise to Heaven

May Friendships ^3 pure as this be thine
To cheer the darkest hours of life
And cause the sun of peace to shine
Till earthly storms shall cease this life

Montgomery June – 1854   L. R.

1

Writing as Re-Vision

Barbara Cully

Whenever we take note of the world in any form, be it by writing something down, typing it into a computer or recording audio, video, or film, we create a text to which others may respond. These responses in turn are texts that add to the conversation—the cultural discourse—that is saved and re-read and re-viewed. All writing and research stem from these simple beginnings in the act of "taking note." For me, the human worth of such note taking is entwined with my memories of my cousin Dirk.

Dirk died at the age of 24 of a rattlesnake bite on Mt. Palomar near San Diego in 1971 when I was fifteen. Dirk left behind a journal on three cassette tapes that document his thoughts about whether to stay in college, whether to live in the city or the wilderness. They recorded his projections into the future regarding his girl-friend at the time, and some thoughts about conversations he had had with a close male friend while hiking the edges of the Grand Canyon. His tapes include an oral delivery of a paper he wrote on population control for one of his anthropology classes at San Diego State University and a conversation he had with his grand-mother while watching the TV broadcast of the Apollo 12 moon landing in the summer of 1969. I have listened to Dirk's tapes twice, once just as I turned 21, nearing the age he was when he died, and again later at the age of 39. One obvious irony, and oddity, is that Dirk's age has remained the same while I have reached and then surpassed his age. Despite his ability to hold still in death, what I hear in his voice, his ideas and his emotions, have changed with time. A paradox opens here: My cousin is unchanged yet growing younger as I listen to him from my own altering circumstances. Before, he was a role model way ahead of me in life, going to college, reading Walt Whitman, studying anthropology, writing poems. Now he resembles more the students I teach, with their uncertainties about the future, their love of both technology and the wilderness, and their unsullied spiritual power. At each review the character of Dirk's record is transformed. What will Dirk's tapes sound like to my nieces and nephews as they approach the age I was when Dirk died? Is there anything in his reflections that will help them grapple with questions they will face when they become Dirk's age at 24?

In her essay "When We Dead Awaken: Writing as Re-Vision (in chapter one)," Adrienne Rich defines re-vision as "the act of looking back, of seeing with fresh eyes, of entering an old text from a new critical direction . . . an act of survival." Like Dirk's tapes, every literary text, provides an opportunity to listen anew from various vantage points and contexts. This philosophy of rereading and rewriting provides the overall conceptual framework for this anthology. The book is designed to invite you, as students and initiates, into the process of revision first as readers then, most importantly, as writers. It is designed to help us all—students and teachers, since we will explore these texts together—"see with fresh eyes," and enter texts, both familiar and alien, "from a new critical direction" that is of our own making. The chapters are set up to emphasize that rereading and revision are the keys to this making, that analysis can lead to the writing of new texts for new times and circumstances. At the center of this course is the premise that mastering these reading and research components of the writing process is essential for you as university students. These skills and habits of mind will help you achieve critical literacy, which is one of the primary goals of a composition course.

What we learn from classical rhetoric is that human discourse and the art of persuasion take place in realms of uncertainty where speculation, wonder and attempts at understanding abound and clash and vie for ascendance. For this reason, I have taken many lessons from Janice Lauer's essay, "Writing as Inquiry: Some Questions for Teachers" where she offers an alternative to argumentation, rebuttal, and debate. As a departure from and an extension of these modes of thought, she offers a scholarly pursuit of "going beyond the known." She explains that the "cognitive dissonance"—the disconnect between what we think we believe and what we think a text is asking us to believe—is resolved not in coming to final terms but in conducting open-ended research and meditation. Her methods allow us a chance to come into insight and to develop informed perspectives on texts of all kinds, about social and scientific conflicts, about the political and personal themes of love and war, the stuff of education and of life.

Gerald Graff, who writes under the title "Disliking Books at an Early Age" (in chapter one), confesses that reading and writing assignments in school left him cold and unengaged. That is, until he understood that interpretations could be contested, that any reading of a text was in fact up for grabs, that in fact very few readers agree completely. His moment of insight came when he understood he had permission to read for the controversies and to enter the fray. He found then that he had energy for deciding where he stood and enthusiasm for demanding in forceful prose of his own that others prick up their ears and hear him out. His victory over boredom, his ability (like radar) to locate the dramas of the texts he scans and enters becomes a model for us. He challenges us to be the next ones to read and speak—*from* our generations and *to* the generations—about classic works like Mark Twain's *Huckleberry Finn* but also about last night's headlines depicting suicide bombings in Israel and Israel's invasions of Palestinian homes, and this morning's terrifying "breaking news" still full of ghosts and armed forces in the aftermath of September 11th 2001.

We humans love stories and we love music; that is why we fill the airways with a raucous popular culture that is full of stories, full of song. These manic/tender lyrics and twisting plots allow us to celebrate while we drive and shop, work and eat. They offer us tragicomic dramas that are larger than life. They offer us the glitz and buzz of lovers and heroes that remind us, thankfully, that life, on the other hand, is larger than us. It is for this reason, I think, that University of Arizona Professor Emeritus N. Scott Momaday asserts in his essay "The Man Made of Words" that it is through language that human beings create themselves. He says we become fully human when ideas are embodied in literature in its "broadest sense," by which he means texts of all kinds—songs, stories, poems, memoirs, movies, documentaries, and websites. As a Native American, his training is in knowing, through stories, what it is to be human across time. He states, "Only when he is embodied in an idea and the idea is realized in language, can man take possession of himself."

Similarly, but out of radically different circumstances, author Amy Tan speaks of coming into personal power and identity through the acquistion of a second language. Her essay "Mother Tongue" (in chapter one) narrates the story of her mother's struggle with English as a Chinese immigrant. We see her mother's humiliations in restaurants and her inability to get anyone at her bank to take her seriously. Ultimately, Tan offers us a vision (a revision?) of English for native speakers of it: She asserts that there are many Englishes, not just the familiar English we think we know, and that her Chinese mother is the author—whenever she picks up the phone or opens her mouth—of one of them.

What are the implications of ideas such as these for you? One of our authors in chapter eight, Audre Lorde, states plainly that she is a black lesbian feminist speaking in the face of a racist, patriarchal and anti-erotic society. It will be up to you as the student reader-writer to decide what you speak *as* and what you speak *in the face of*. In this, of course, Lorde is encouraging us to think about our content; whereas Tita French Baumlin, in her essay "A Good Crot is Hard to Find" (in chapter one) asks us to free our style, to experiment with language nonlinearly, ungrammatically, and in fragments:

> A crot is an old-fashioned word for "bit" or "fragment." Like a stanza is to poetry. Like a note is to music is a crot to my work. Free your crots. Let them stand alone. Long, or short, let your crots be crots. Without connecting tissue Like this . . . a crot without transition is like a new scent wafted on the breeze of the imagination.

As you read this chapter, indeed this whole book, you will notice that you are being invited into a conversation that started long before you were born and that this conversation relies upon you in order to continue. My advice amid this complex, often challenging atmosphere is simply to take in as much as you can and to respond honestly in ways that imitate the strategies—of voice, analysis, story-telling, and research—these author-teachers have demonstrated for you. They are gathered here as at a table to speak to you. Think of it as a dinner party without food? Think of the ideas *as* the food? In any case, you are invited. I hope you arrive hungry with flowers in your hands.

Adrienne Rich

Adrienne Rich (b. 1929) is among the most prominent poets of the century. Her first book of poetry was a Yale Series of Younger Poets selection in 1951, the same year she graduated from Radcliffe College. Rich has since published many volumes of poetry and non-fiction, each formally and thematically distinct. Her work has been translated into eight languages, and she has received several honors and awards, including Guggenheim Fellowships (1952 and 1961), a National Book Award (1974) for Diving into the Wreck, *and a Fund for Human Dignity Award from the National Gay and Lesbian Task Force (1981). This essay was first delivered, in slightly different form, as a speech. It was published, in 1976, in its present form.*

When We Dead Awaken: Writing as Re-Vision

The Modern Language Association is both marketplace and funeral parlor for the professional study of Western literature in North America. Like all gatherings of the professions, it has been and remains a "procession of the sons of educated men" (Virginia Woolf): a congeries of old-boys' networks, academicians rehearsing their numb canons in sessions dedicated to the literature of white males, junior scholars under the lash of "publish or perish" delivering papers in the bizarrely lit drawing-rooms of immense hotels: a ritual competition veering between cynicism and desperation.

However, in the interstices of these gentlemanly rites (or, in Mary Daly's words, on the boundaries of this patriarchal space), some feminist scholars, teachers, and graduate students, joined by feminist writers, editors, and publishers, have for a decade been creating more subversive occasions, challenging the sacredness of the gentlemanly canon, sharing the rediscovery of buried works by women, asking women's questions, bringing literary history and criticism back to life in both senses. The Commission on the Status of Women in the Profession was formed in 1969, and held its first public event in 1970. In 1971 the Commission asked Ellen Peck Killoh, Tillie Olsen, Elaine Reuben, and myself, with Elaine Hedges as moderator, to talk on "The Woman Writer in the Twentieth Century." The essay that follows was written for that forum, and later published, along with the other papers from the forum and workshops, in an issue of *College English*

Reprinted from *On Lies, Secrets, and Silence: Selected Prose, 1966–1978,* by Adrienne Rich (1979), W.W. Noorton & Company.

edited by Elaine Hedges ("Women Writing and Teaching," vol. 34, no. 1, October 1972.) With a few revisions, mainly updating, it was reprinted in *American Poets* in 1976, edited by William Heyen (New York: Bobbs-Merrill, 1976). That later text is the one published here.

The challenge flung by feminists at the accepted literary canon, at the methods of teaching it, and at the biased and astigmatic view of male "literary scholarship," has not diminished in the decade since the first Women's Forum: it has become broadened and intensified more recently by the challenges of black and lesbian feminists pointing out that feminist literary criticism itself has overlooked or held back from examining the work of black women and lesbians. The dynamic between a political vision and the demand for a fresh vision of literature is clear: without a growing feminist movement, the first inroads of feminist scholarship could not have been made; without the sharpening of a black feminist consciousness, black women's writing would have been left in limbo between misogynist black male critics and white feminists still struggling to unearth a white women's tradition: without an articulate lesbian/feminist movement, lesbian writing would still be lying in that closet where many of us used to sit reading forbidden books "in a bad light."

Much, much more is yet to be done; and university curricula have of course changed very little as a result of all this. What *is* changing is the availability of knowledge, of vital texts, the visible effects on women's lives of seeing, hearing our wordless or negated experience affirmed and pursued further in language.

Ibsen's *When We Dead Awaken* is a play about the use that the male artist and thinker—in the process of creating culture as we know it—has made of women, in his life and in his work; and about a woman's slow struggling awakening to the use to which her life has been put. Bernard Shaw wrote in 1900 of this play:

> [Ibsen] shows us that no degradation ever devised or permitted is as disastrous as this degradation; that through it women can die into luxuries for men and yet can kill them; that men and women are becoming conscious of this; and that what remains to be seen as perhaps the most interesting of all imminent social developments is what will happen "when we dead awaken."[1]

It's exhilarating to be alive in a time of awakening consciousness; it can also be confusing, disorienting, and painful. This awakening of dead or sleeping consciousness has already affected the lives of millions of women, even those who don't know it yet. It is also affecting the lives of men, even those who deny its claims upon them. The argument will go on whether an oppressive economic class system is responsible for the oppressive nature of male/female relations, or whether, in fact, patriarchy—the domination of males—is the original model of oppression on which all others are based. But in the last few years the women's movement has drawn inescapable and illuminating connections between our sexual lives and our political institutions. The sleepwalkers are coming awake, and for the first time this awakening has a collective reality; it is no longer such a lonely thing to open one's eyes.

Re-vision—the act of looking back, of seeing with fresh eyes, of entering an old text from a new critical direction—is for women more than a chapter in cultural history: it is an act of survival. Until we can understand the assumptions in which we are drenched we cannot know ourselves. And this drive to self-knowledge, for women, is more than a search for identity: it is part of our refusal of the self-destructiveness of male-dominated society. A radical critique of literature, feminist in its impulse, would take the work first of all as a clue to how we live, how we have been living, how we have been led to imagine ourselves, how our language has trapped as well as liberated us, how the very act of naming has been till now a male prerogative, and how we can begin to see and name—and therefore live—afresh. A change in the concept of sexual identity is essential if we are not going to see the old political order reassert itself in every new revolution. We need to know the writing of the past, and know it differently than we have ever known it; not to pass on a tradition but to break its hold over us.

For writers, and at this moment for women writers in particular, there is the challenge and promise of a whole new psychic geography to be explored. But there is also a difficult and dangerous walking on the ice, as we try to find language and images for a consciousness we are just coming into, and with little in the past to support us. I want to talk about some aspects of this difficulty and this danger.

Jane Harrison, the great classical anthropologist, wrote in 1914 in a letter to her friend Gilbert Murray:

> By the by, about "Women," it has bothered me often—why do women never want to write poetry about Man as a sex—why is Woman a dream and a terror to man and not the other way around? . . . Is it mere convention and propriety, or something deeper?[2]

I think Jane Harrison's question cuts deep into the myth-making tradition, the romantic tradition; deep into what women and men have been to each other; and deep into the psyche of the woman writer. Thinking about that question, I began thinking of the work of two twentieth-century women poets, Sylvia Plath and Diane Wakoski. It strikes me that in the work of both Man appears as, if not a dream, a fascination and a terror; and that the source of the fascination and the terror is, simply, Man's power—to dominate, tyrannize, choose, or reject the woman. The charisma of Man seems to come purely from his power over her and his control of the world by force, not from anything fertile or life-giving in him. And, in the work of both these poets, it is finally the woman's sense of *herself*—embattled, possessed—that gives the poetry its dynamic charge, its rhythms of struggle, need, will, and female energy. Until recently this female anger and this furious awareness of the Man's power over her were not available materials to the female poet, who tended to write of Love as the source of her suffering, and to view that victimization by Love as an almost inevitable fate. Or, like Marianne Moore and Elizabeth Bishop, she kept sexuality at a measured and chiseled distance in her poems.

One answer to Jane Harrison's question has to be that historically men and women have played very different parts in each others' lives. Where woman has been a luxury for man, and has served as the painter's model and the poet's muse, but also as comforter, nurse, cook, bearer of his seed, secretarial assistant, and copyist of manuscripts, man has played a quite different role for the female artist. Henry James repeats an incident which the writer Prosper Mérimée described, of how, while he was living with George Sand,

> he once opened his eyes, in the raw winter dawn, to see his companion, in a dressing-gown, on her knees before the domestic hearth, a candlestick beside her and a red *madras* round her head, making bravely, with her own hands the fire that was to enable her to sit down betimes to urgent pen and paper. The story represents him as having felt that the spectacle chilled his ardor and tried his taste; her appearance was unfortunate, her occupation an inconsequence, and her industry a reproof—the result of which was a lively irritation and an early rupture.[3]

The specter of this kind of male judgment, along with the misnaming and thwarting of her needs by a culture controlled by males, has created problems for the woman writer: problems of contact with herself, problems of language and style, problems of energy and survival.

In rereading Virginia Woolf's *A Room of One's Own* (1929) for the first time in some years, I was astonished at the sense of effort, of pains taken, of dogged tentativeness, in the tone of that essay. And I recognized that tone. I had heard it often enough, in myself and in other women. It is the tone of a woman almost in touch with her anger, who is determined not to appear angry, who is *willing* herself to be calm, detached, and even charming in a roomful of men where things have been said which are attacks on her very integrity. Virginia Woolf is addressing an audience of women, but she is acutely conscious—as she always was—of being overheard by men: by Morgan and Lytton and Maynard Keynes and for that matter by her father, Leslie Stephen.[4] She drew the language out into an exacerbated thread in her determination to have her own sensibility yet protect it from those masculine presences. Only at rare moments in that essay do you hear the passion in her voice; she was trying to sound as cool as Jane Austen, as Olympian as Shakespeare, because that is the way the men of the culture thought a writer should sound.

No male writer has written primarily or even largely for women, or with the sense of women's criticism as a consideration when he chooses his materials, his theme, his language. But to a lesser or greater extent, every woman writer has written for men even when, like Virginia Woolf, she was supposed to be addressing women. If we have come to the point when this balance might begin to change, when women can stop being haunted, not only by "convention and propriety" but by internalized fears of being and saying themselves, then it is an extraordinary moment for the woman writer—and reader.

I have hesitated to do what I am going to do now, which is to use myself as an illustration. For one thing, it's a lot easier and less dangerous to talk about other women writers. But there is something else. Like Virginia Woolf, I am aware of the women who are not with us here because they are washing the dishes and looking after the children. Nearly fifty years after she spoke, that fact remains largely unchanged. And I am thinking also of women whom she left out of the picture altogether—women who are washing other people's dishes and caring for other people's children, not to mention women who went on the streets last night in order to feed their children. We seem to be special women here, we have liked to think of ourselves as special, and we have known that men would tolerate, even romanticize us as special, as long as our words and actions didn't threaten their privilege of tolerating or rejecting us and our work according to *their* ideas of what a special woman ought to be. An important insight of the radical women's movement has been how divisive and how ultimately destructive is this myth of the special woman, who is also the token woman. Every one of us here in this room has had great luck—we are teachers, writers, academicians; our own gifts could not have been enough, for we all know women whose gifts are buried or aborted. Our struggles can have meaning and our privileges—however precarious under patriarchy—can be justified only if they can help to change the lives of women whose gifts—and whose very being—continue to be thwarted and silenced.

My own luck was being born white and middle-class in a house full of books, with a father who encouraged me to read and write. So for about twenty years I wrote for a particular man, who criticized and praised me and made me feel I was indeed "special." The obverse side of this, of course, was that I tried for a long time to please him, or rather, not to displease him. And then of course there were other men—writers, teachers—the Man, who was not a terror or a dream but a literary master and a master in other ways less easy to acknowledge. And there were all those poems about women, written by men: it seemed to be a given that men wrote poems and women frequently inhabited them. These women were almost always beautiful, but threatened with the loss of beauty, the loss of youth—the fate worse than death. Or, they were beautiful and died young, like Lucy and Lenore. Or, the woman was like Maud Gonne, cruel and disastrously mistaken, and the poem reproached her because she had refused to become a luxury for the poet.

A lot is being said today about the influence that the myths and images of women have on all of us who are products of culture. I think it has been a peculiar confusion to the girl or woman who tries to write because she is peculiarly susceptible to language. She goes to poetry or fiction looking for *her* way of being in the world, since she too has been putting words and images together; she is looking eagerly for guides, maps, possibilities; and over and over in the "words' masculine persuasive force" of literature she comes up against something that negates everything she is about: she meets the image of Woman in books written by men. She finds a terror and a dream, she finds a beautiful pale face, she finds La Belle Dame Sans Merci, she finds Juliet or Tess or Salomé, but precisely what she does not find is that absorbed, drudging, puzzled, sometimes inspired creature, herself, who sits at a desk trying to put words together.

So what does she do? What did I do? I read the older women poets with their peculiar keenness and ambivalence: Sappho, Christina Rossetti, Emily Dickinson,

Elinor Wylie, Edna Millay, H. D. I discovered that the woman poet most admired at the time (by men) was Marianne Moore, who was maidenly, elegant, intellectual, discreet. But even in reading these women I was looking in them for the same things I had found in the poetry of men, because I wanted women poets to be the equals of men, and to be equal was still confused with sounding the same.

I know that my style was formed first by male poets: by the men I was reading as an undergraduate—Frost, Dylan Thomas, Donne, Auden, MacNiece, Stevens, Yeats. What I chiefly learned from them was craft.[5] But poems are like dreams: in them you put what you don't know you know. Looking back at poems I wrote before I was twenty-one, I'm startled because beneath the conscious craft are glimpses of the split I even then experienced between the girl who wrote poems, who defined herself in writing poems, and the girl who was to define herself by her relationships with men. "Aunt Jennifer's Tigers" (1951), written while I was a student, looks with deliberate detachment at this split.[6]

> Aunt Jennifer's tigers stride across a screen,
> Bright topaz denizens of a world of green.
> They do not fear the men beneath the tree;
> They pace in sleek chivalric certainty.
>
> Aunt Jennifer's fingers fluttering through her wool
> Find even the ivory needle hard to pull.
> The massive weight of Uncle's wedding band
> Sits heavily upon Aunt Jennifer's hand.
>
> When Aunt is dead, her terrified hands will lie
> Still ringed with ordeals she was mastered by.
> The tigers in the panel that she made
> Will go on striding, proud and unafraid.

In writing this poem, composed and apparently cool as it is, I thought I was creating a portrait of an imaginary woman. But this woman suffers from the opposition of her imagination, worked out in tapestry, and her life-style, "ringed with ordeals she was mastered by." It was important to me that Aunt Jennifer was a person as distinct from myself as possible—distanced by the formalism of the poem, by its objective, observant tone—even by putting the woman in a different generation.

In those years formalism was part of the strategy—like asbestos gloves, it allowed me to handle materials I couldn't pick up bare-handed. A later strategy was to use the persona of a man, as I did in "The Loser" (1958):

> *A man thinks of the woman he once loved: first, after the wedding,*
> *and then nearly a decade later.*
>
> I
> I kissed you, bride and lost, and went
> home from that bourgeois sacrament,
> your cheek still tasting cold upon

my lips that gave you benison
with all the swagger that they knew—
as losers somehow learn to do.

Your wedding made my eyes ache; soon
the world would be worse off for one
more golden apple dropped to ground
without the least protesting sound,
and you would windfall lie, and we
forget your shimmer on the tree.

Beauty is always wasted: if
not Mignon's song sung to the deaf,
at all events to the unmoved.
A face like yours cannot be loved
long or seriously enough.
Almost, we seem to hold it off.

II

Well, you are tougher than I thought.
Now when the wash with ice hangs taut
this morning of St. Valentine,
I see you strip the squeaking line,
your body weighed against the load,
and all my groans can do no good.

Because you are still beautiful,
though squared and stiffened by the pull
of what nine windy years have done.
You have three daughters, lost a son.
I see all your intelligence
flung into that unwearied stance.

My envy is of no avail.
I turn my head and wish him well
who chafed your beauty into use
and lives forever in a house
lit by the friction of your mind.
You stagger in against the wind.

I finished college, published my first book by a fluke, as it seemed to me, and broke off a love affair. I took a job, lived alone, went on writing, fell in love. I was young, full of energy, and the book seemed to mean that others agreed I was a poet. Because I was also determined to prove that as a woman poet I could also have what was then defined as a "full" woman's life, I plunged in my early twenties into marriage and had three children before I was thirty. There was nothing overt in the environment to warn me: these were the fifties, and in reaction to the earlier wave of feminism, middle-class women were making careers of domestic perfection, working to send their husbands through professional schools, then

11

retiring to raise large families. People were moving out to the suburbs, technology was going to be the answer to everything, even sex; the family was in its glory. Life was extremely private; women were isolated from each other by the loyalties of marriage. I have a sense that women didn't talk to each other much in the fifties—not about their secret emptinesses, their frustrations. I went on trying to write; my second book and first child appeared in the same month. But by the time that the book came out I was already dissatisfied with those poems, which seemed to me mere exercises for poems I hadn't written. The book was praised, however, for its "gracefulness"; I had a marriage and a child. If there were doubts, if there were periods of null depression or active despairing, these could only mean that I was ungrateful, insatiable, perhaps a monster.

About the time my third child was born, I felt that I had either to consider myself a failed woman and a failed poet, or to try to find some synthesis by which to understand what was happening to me. What frightened me most was the sense of drift, of being pulled along on a current which called itself my destiny, but in which I seemed to be losing touch with whoever I had been, with the girl who had experienced her own will and energy almost ecstatically at times, walking around a city or riding a train at night or typing in a student room. In a poem about my grandmother I wrote (of myself): "A young girl, thought sleeping, is certified dead" ("Halfway"). I was writing very little, partly from fatigue, that female fatigue of suppressed anger and loss of contact with my own being; partly from the discontinuity of female life with its attention to small chores, errands, work that others constantly undo, small children's constant needs. What I did write was unconvincing to me; my anger and frustration were hard to acknowledge in or out of poems because in fact I cared a great deal about my husband and my children. Trying to look back and understand that time I have tried to analyze the real nature of the conflict. Most, if not all, human lives are full of fantasy—passive day-dreaming which need not be acted on. But to write poetry or fiction, or even to think well, is not to fantasize, or to put fantasies on paper. For a poem to coalesce, for a character or an action to take shape, there has to be an imaginative transformation of reality which is in no way passive. And a certain freedom of the mind is needed—freedom to press on, to enter the currents of your thought like a glider pilot, knowing that your motion can be sustained, that the buoyancy of your attention will not be suddenly snatched away. Moreover, if the imagination is to transcend and transform experience it has to question, to challenge, to conceive of alternatives, perhaps to the very life you are living at that moment. You have to be free to play around with the notion that day might be night, love might be hate; nothing can be too sacred for the imagination to turn into its opposite or to call experimentally by another name. For writing is re-naming. Now, to be maternally with small children all day in the old way, to be with a man in the old way of marriage, requires a holding-back, a putting-aside of that imaginative activity, and demands instead a kind of conservatism. I want to make it clear that I am *not* saying that in order to write well, or think well, it is necessary to become unavailable to others, or to become a devouring ego. This has been the myth of the masculine artist and thinker; and I do not accept it. But to be a female human being trying to fulfill traditional female functions in a traditional way *is* in direct conflict with the subversive function of the imagination. The word traditional is important here. There must be ways, and we will be finding out more and more about them, in which the energy of creating and the energy of relation can be united. But in those years I always felt the conflict as a failure of love in myself. I had thought I was choosing a full life: the life available to most men, in which sexuality, work, and parenthood could coexist. But I felt, at twenty-nine, guilt toward the people closest to me, and guilty toward my own being.

I wanted, then, more than anything, the one thing of which there was never enough: time to think, time to write. The fifties and early sixties were years of rapid revelations: the sit-ins and marches in the South, the Bay of Pigs, the early anti-war movement, raised large questions—questions for which the masculine world of the academy around me seemed to have expert and fluent answers. But I needed to think for myself—about pacifism and dissent and violence, about poetry and society, and about my own relationship to all these things. For about ten years I was reading in fierce snatches, scribbling in notebooks, writing poetry in fragments; I was looking desperately for clues, because if there were no clues then I thought I might be insane. I wrote in a notebook about this time:

> Paralyzed by the sense that there exists a mesh of relationships—
> e.g., between my anger at the children, my sensual life, pacifism,
> sex (I mean sex in its broadest significance, not merely sexual de-
> sire)—an interconnectedness which, if I could see it, make it valid,
> would give me back myself, make it possible to function lucidly
> and passionately. Yet I grope in and out among these dark webs.

I think I began at this point to feel that politics was not something "out there" but something "in here" and of the essence of my condition.

In the late fifties I was able to write, for the first time, directly about experiencing myself as a woman. The poem was jotted in fragments during children's naps, brief hours in a library, or at 3:00 A.M. after rising with a wakeful child. I despaired of doing any continuous work at this time. Yet I began to feel that my fragments and scraps had a common consciousness and a common theme, one which I would have been very unwilling to put on paper at an earlier time because I had been taught that poetry should be "universal," which meant, of course, non-female. Until then I had tried very much *not* to identify myself as a female poet. Over two years I wrote a ten-part poem called "Snapshots of a Daughter-in-Law" (1958–1960), in a longer, looser mode than I'd ever trusted myself with before. It was an extraordinary relief to write that poem. It strikes me now as too literary, too dependent on allusion; I hadn't found the courage yet to do without authorities, or even to use the pronoun "I"—the woman in the poem is always "she." One section of it, No. 2, concerns a woman who thinks she is going mad; she is haunted by voices telling her to resist and rebel, voices which she can hear but not obey.

2.

Banging the coffee-pot into the sink
she hears the angels chiding, and looks out

past the raked gardens to the sloppy sky.
Only a week since They said: *Have no patience.*

The next time it was: *Be insatiable.*
Then: *Save yourself; others cannot save.*
Sometimes she's let the tapstream scald her arm,
a match burn to her thumbnail,

or held her hand above the kettle's snout
right in the woolly steam. They are probably angels,
since nothing hurts her anymore, except
each morning's grit blowing into her eyes.

The poem "Orion," written five years later, is a poem of reconnection with a part of myself I had felt I was losing—the active principle, the energetic imagination, the "half-brother" whom I projected, as I had for many years, into the constellation Orion. It's no accident that the words "cold and egotistical" appear in this poem, and they applied to myself.

Far back when I went zig-zagging
through tamarack pastures
you were my genius, you
my cast-iron Viking, my helmed
lion-heart king in prison.
Years later now you're young

my fierce half-brother, staring
down from that simplified west
your breast open, your belt dragged down
by an old-fashioned thing, a sword
the last bravado you won't give over
though it weighs you down as you stride

and the stars in it are dim
and maybe have stopped burning.
But you burn, and I know it;
as I throw back my head to take you in
an old transfusion happens again:
divine astronomy is nothing to it.

Indoors I bruise and blunder,
break faith, leave ill enough
alone, a dead child born in the dark.
Night cracks up over the chimney,
pieces of time, frozen geodes
come showering down in the grate.

A man reaches behind my eyes
and finds them empty
a woman's head turns away

> from my head in the mirror
> children are dying my death
> and eating crumbs of my life.
>
> Pity is not your forte.
> Calmly you ache up there
> pinned aloft in your crow's nest,
> my speechless pirate!
> You take it all for granted
> and when I look you back
>
> it's with a starlike eye
> shooting its cold and egotistical spear
> where it can do least damage.
> Breathe deep! No hurt, no pardon
> out here in the cold with you
> you with your back to the wall.

The choice still seemed to be between "love"—womanly, maternal love, altruistic love—a love defined and ruled by the weight of an entire culture; and egotism—a force directed by men into creation, achievement, ambition, often at the expense of others, but justifiably so. For weren't they men, and wasn't that their destiny as womanly, selfless love was ours? We know now that the alternatives are false ones—that the word "love" is itself in need of revision.

There is a companion poem to "Orion," written three years later, in which at last the woman in the poem and the woman writing the poem become the same person. It is called "Planetarium," and it was written after a visit to a real planetarium, where I read an account of the work of Caroline Herschel, the astronomer, who worked with her brother William, but whose name remained obscure as his did not.

> *Thinking of Caroline Herschel, 1750–1848, astronomer, sister of William; and others*
>
> A woman in the shape of a monster
> a monster in the shape of a woman
> the skies are full of them
>
> a woman   "in the snow
> among the Clocks and instruments
> or measuring the ground with poles"
>
> in her 98 years to discover
> 8 comets
>
> she whom the moon rules
> like us

levitating into the night sky
riding the polished lenses

Galaxies of women, there
doing penance for impetuousness
ribs chilled
in those spaces   of the mind

An eye,
        "virile, precise and absolutely certain"
        from the mad webs of Uranisborg
                        encountering the NOVA

every impulse of light exploding
from the core
as life flies out of us

        Tycho whispering at last
        "Let me not seem to have lived in vain"

What we see, we see
and seeing is changing

the light that shrivels a mountain
and leaves a man alive

Heartbeat of the pulsar
heart sweating through my body

The radio impulse
pouring in from Taurus

        I am bombarded yet   I stand
I have been standing all my life in the
direct path of a battery of signals
the most accurately transmitted most
untranslateable language in the universe
I am a galactic cloud so deep   so involuted that a light wave could take 15
years to travel through me   And has
taken   I am an instrument in the shape
of a woman trying to translate pulsations
into images   for the relief of the body
and the reconstruction of the mind.

In closing I want to tell you about a dream I had last summer. I dreamed I was asked to read my poetry at a mass women's meeting, but when I began to read, what came out were the lyrics of a blues song. I share this dream with you because it seemed to me to say something about the problems and the future of the woman writer, and probably of women in general. The awakening of consciousness is not like the crossing of a frontier—one step and you are in another country. Much of woman's poetry has been of the nature of the blues song: a cry of pain, of victimization, or a lyric of seduction.[7] And today, much poetry by women—and prose for that matter—is charged with anger. I think we need to go through that anger, and we will betray our reality if we try, as Virginia Woolf was trying, for an objectivity, a detachment, that would make us sound more like Jane Austen or Shakespeare. We know more than Jane Austen or Shakespeare knew: more than Jane Austen because our lives are more complex, more than Shakespeare because we know more about the lives of women—Jane Austen and Virginia Woolf included.

Both the victimization and the anger experienced by women are real, and have real sources, everywhere in the environment, built into society, language, the structures of thought. They will go on being tapped and explored by poets, among others. We can neither deny them, nor will we rest there. A new generation of women poets is already working out of the psychic energy released when women begin to move out towards what the feminist philosopher Mary Daly has described as the "new space" on the boundaries of patriarchy.[8] Women are speaking to and of women in these poems, out of a newly released courage to name, to love each other, to share risk and grief and celebration.

To the eye of a feminist, the work Western male poets are now writing reveals a deep, fatalistic pessimism as to the possibilities of change, whether societal or personal, along with a familiar and threadbare use of women (and nature) as redemptive on the one hand, threatening on the other, and a new tide of phallocentric sadism and overt woman-hating which matches the sexual brutality of recent films. "Political" poetry by men remains stranded amid the struggles for power among male groups; in condemning U.S. imperialism or the Chilean junta the poet can claim to speak for the oppressed while remaining, as male, part of a system of sexual oppression. The enemy is always outside the self, the struggle somewhere else. The mood of isolation, self-pity, and self-imitation that pervades "nonpolitical" poetry suggests that a profound change in masculine consciousness will have to precede any new male poetic—or other—inspiration. The creative energy of patriarchy is fast running out; what remains is its self-generating energy for destruction. As women, we have our work cut out for us.

Notes

1. G. B. Shaw, *The Quintessence of Ibsenism* (New York: Hill & Wang, 1922), p. 139.
2. J. G. Stewart, *Jane Ellen Harrison: A Portrait from Letters* (London: Merlin, 1959), p. 140.
3. Henry James, "Notes on Novelists," in *Selected Literary Criticism of Henry James*, Morris Shapira, ed. (London: Heinemann, 1963), pp. 157–58.
4. A. R., 1978: This intuition of mine was corroborated when, early in 1978 I read the correspondence between Woolf and Dame Ethel Smyth (Henry W. and Albert A. Berg Collection, The New York Public Library, Astor, Lenox and Tilden Foundations); in a letter dated June 8, 1933, Woolf speaks of having kept her own personality out of *A Room of One's Own* lest she not be taken seriously: ". . . how personal, so will they say, rubbing their hands with glee, women always are; *I even hear them as I write.*" (Italics mine.)

5. A. R., 1978: Yet I spent months, at sixteen, memorizing and writing imitations of Millay's sonnets; and in notebooks of that period I find what are obviously attempts to imitate Dickinson's metrics and verbal compression. I knew H. D. only through anthologized lyrics; her epic poetry was not then available to me.

6. A. R., 1978: Texts of poetry quoted herein can be found in A. R., *Poems Selected and New: 1950–1974* (New York: Norton, 1975).

7. A. R., 1978: When I dreamed that dream, was I wholly ignorant of the tradition of Bessie Smith and other women's blues lyrics which transcended victimization to sing of resistance and independence?

8. Mary Daly, *Beyond God the Father: Towards a Philosophy of Women's Liberation* (Boston: Beacon, 1971), pp. 40–41.

Gerald Graff

Gerald Graff, born in Chicago in 1937, was educated in the public school system. He earned his B.A. from the University of Chicago and his Ph.D. from Stanford. His first books are iconoclastic, attacking the deficiencies of popular theory. Literature Against Itself: Literary Ideas in Modern Society *(1979), Graff's second book, is a rebuttal against structuralism and deconstruction. It is with his third book* Professing Literature: An Institutional History *(1987) that Graff becomes a national figure. In this book he addresses the hostility among professors of literature who stand their ground in contrasting schools of thought. Stacey D'Erasmo of the* Village Voice *notes that "Graff wants to move these struggles [between literary schools of thought] out of the convention and into the classroom." Graff is a co-founder of Teachers for a Democratic Culture, a Center-left coalition of scholars who are organized to combat conservative assault against the universities. The following essay originally appeared in the September/October 1992 issue of* Lingua Franca *and is reprinted in slightly different form in his book,* Beyond the Culture Wars: How Teaching the Conflicts Can Revitalize American Education *(1992).*

Disliking Books at an Early Age

I like to think I have a certain advantage as a teacher of literature because when I was growing up I disliked and feared books. My youthful aversion to books showed a fine impartiality, extending across the whole spectrum of literature, history, philosophy, science, and what was known by then (the late 1940s) as social studies. But had I been forced to choose, I would have singled out literature and history as the reading I disliked most. Science at least had some discernible practical use, and you could have fun solving the problems in the textbooks with their clear-cut answers. Literature and history had no apparent application to my experience, and any boy in my school who had cultivated them—I can't recall one who did—would have marked himself as a sissy.

As a middle-class Jew growing up in an ethnically mixed Chicago neighborhood, I was already in danger of being beaten up daily by rougher working-class boys. Becoming a bookworm would only have given them a decisive reason for beating me up. Reading and studying were more permissible for girls, but they,

Reprinted from *Beyond the Culture Wars: How Teaching the Conflicts Can Revitalize American Education*, (1992), W.W. Norton & Company.

too, had to be careful not to get too intellectual, lest they acquire the stigma of being "stuck up."

In *Lives on the Boundary,* a remarkable autobiography of the making of an English teacher, Mike Rose describes how the "pain and confusion" of his working-class youth made "school and knowledge" seem a saving alternative. Rose writes of feeling "freed, as if I were untying fetters," by his encounters with certain college teachers, who helped him recognize that "an engagement with ideas could foster competence and lead me out into the world." Coming at things from my middle-class perspective, however, I took for granted a freedom that school, knowledge, and engagement with ideas seemed only to threaten.

My father, a literate man, was frustrated by my refusal to read anything besides comic books, sports magazines, and the John R. Tunis and Clair Bee sports novels. I recall his once confining me to my room until I finished a book on the voyages of Magellan, but try as I might, I could do no better than stare bleakly at the pages. I could not, as we would later say, "relate to" Magellan or to any of the other books my father brought home—detective stories, tales of war and hero- ism, adventure stories with adolescent heroes (the Hardy Boys, *Hans Brinker,* or *The Silver Skates*), stories of scientific discovery (Paul de Kruif's *The Microbe Hunters*), books on current events. Nothing worked.

It was understood, however, that boys of my background would go to college and that once there we would get serious and buckle down. For some, "getting serious" meant pre-law, pre-med, or a major in business to prepare for taking over the family business. My family did not own a business, and law and medicine did not interest me, so I drifted by default into the nebulous but conveniently non- committal territory of the liberal arts. I majored in English.

At this point the fear of being beaten up if I were caught having anything to do with books was replaced by the fear of flunking out of college if I did not learn to deal with them. But though I dutifully did my homework and made good grades (first at the University of Illinois, Chicago branch, then at the University of Chicago, from which I graduated in 1959), I continued to find "serious" reading painfully difficult and alien. My most vivid recollections of college reading are of assigned classics I failed to finish: *The Iliad* (in the Richmond Lattimore transla- tion); *The Autobiography of Benvenuto Cellini,* a major disappointment after the paperback jacket's promise of "a lusty classic of Renaissance ribaldry"; E. M. Forster's *A Passage to India,* sixty agonizing pages of which I managed to slog through before giving up. Even Hemingway, Steinbeck, and Fitzgerald, whose contemporary world was said to be "close to my own experience," left me cold. I saw little there that did resemble my experience.

Even when I had done the assigned reading, I was often tongue-tied and embarrassed when called on. What was unclear to me was what I was supposed to *say* about literary works, and why. Had I been born a decade or two earlier, I might have come to college with the rudiments of a literate vocabulary for talking about culture that some people older than I acquired through family, high school, or church. As it was, "cultured" phrases seemed effete and sterile to me. When I was able to produce the kind of talk that was required in class, the intellectualism of it came out sounding stilted and hollow in my mouth. If *Cliffs Notes* and other such crib sheets for the distressed had yet come into existence, with their ready-to-copy summaries of widely taught literary works, I would have been an excellent customer. (As it was, I did avail myself of the primitive version then in existence called *Masterplots*.)

What first made literature, history, and other intellectual pursuits seem attractive to me was exposure to critical debates. There was no single conversion experience, but a gradual transformation over several years, extending into my first teaching positions, at the University of New Mexico and then Northwestern University. But one of the first sparks I remember was a controversy over *The Adventures of Huckleberry Finn* that arose in a course during my junior year in college. On first attempt, Twain's novel was just another assigned classic that I was too bored to finish. I could see little connection between my Chicago upbringing and Huck's pre-Civil War adventures with a runaway slave on a raft up the Mississippi.

My interest was aroused, however, when our instructor mentioned that the critics had disagreed over the merits of the last part of the novel. He quoted Ernest Hemingway's remark that "if you read [the novel] you must stop where the nigger Jim is stolen by the boys. This is the real end. The rest is cheating." According to this school of thought, the remainder of the book trivializes the quest for Jim's freedom that has motivated the story up to that point. This happens first when Jim becomes an object of Tom Sawyer's slapstick humor, then when it is revealed that unbeknownst to Huck, the reader, and himself, Jim has already been freed by his benevolent owner, so that the risk we have assumed Jim and Huck to be under all along has really been no risk at all.

Like the critics, our class divided over the question: Did Twain's ending vitiate the book's profound critique of racism, as Hemingway's charge of cheating implied? Cheating in my experience up to then was something students did, an unthinkable act for a famous author. It was a revelation to me that famous authors were capable not only of mistakes but of ones that even lowly undergraduates might be able to point out. When I chose to write my term paper on the dispute over the ending, my instructor suggested I look at several critics on the opposing sides—T. S. Eliot and Lionel Trilling, who defended the ending, and Leo Marx, who sided with Hemingway.

Reading the critics was like picking up where the class discussion had left off, and I gained confidence from recognizing that my classmates and I had had thoughts that, however stumbling our expression of them, were not too far from the thoughts of famous published critics. I went back to the novel again and to my surprise found myself rereading it with an excitement I had never felt before with a serious book. Having the controversy over the ending in mind, I now had some issues *to watch out for* as I read, issues that reshaped the way I read the earlier chapters as well as the later ones and focused my attention. And having issues to watch out for made it possible not only to concentrate, as I had not been able to do earlier, but to put myself into the text—to read with a sense of personal engagement that I had not felt before. Reading the novel with the voices of the critics running through my mind, I found myself thinking things that I might say about what I was reading, things that may have belonged partly to the critics but also now belonged to me. It was as if having a stock of things to look for and to say about a literary work had somehow made it possible for me to read one.

One of the critics had argued that what was at issue in the debate over *Huckleberry Finn* was not just the novel's value but its cultural significance: If *Huckleberry Finn* was contradictory or confused in its attitude toward race, then what did that say about the culture that had received the novel as one of its representative cultural documents and had made Twain a folk hero? This critic had also made the intriguing observation—I found out only later that it was a critical commonplace at the time—that judgments about the novel's aesthetic value could not be separated from judgments about its moral substance. I recall taking in both this critic's arguments and the cadence of the phrases in which they were couched; perhaps it would not be so bad after all to become the sort of person who talked about "cultural contradictions" and the "inseparability of form and content." Perhaps even mere literary-critical talk could give you a certain power in the real world. As the possibility dawned on me that reading and intellectual discussion might actually have something to do with my real life, I became less embarrassed about using intellectual formulas.

It was through exposure to such critical reading and discussion over a period of time that I came to catch the literary bug, eventually choosing the vocation of teaching. This was not the way it is supposed to happen. In the standard story of academic vocation that we like to tell ourselves, the germ is first planted by an early experience of literature itself. The future teacher is initially inspired by some primary experience of a great book and only subsequently acquires the secondary, derivative skills of critical discussion. A teacher may be involved in instilling this inspiration, but only a teacher who seemingly effaces himself or herself before the text. Any premature or excessive acquaintance with secondary critical discourse, and certainly with its sectarian debates, is thought to be a corrupting danger, causing one to lose touch with the primary passion for literature.

This is the charge leveled against the current generation of literature teachers, who are said to have become so obsessed with sophisticated critical theories that they have lost the passion they once had for literature itself. They have been seduced by professionalism, drawn away from a healthy absorption in literature to the sickly fascination with analysis and theory and to the selfish advancement of their careers.

This hostility to recent theory would not have been so powerful, however, if it were not overlaid on an older set of resentments that long predate the rise of deconstruction and poststructuralism, resentments at literature's having become an academic "field" to begin with. Today's attacks on literary theory are often really attacks on literary criticism, or at least on criticism of the intensely analytic kind that academics practice, which has always been suspected of coming between readers (and students) and the primary experience of literature itself. This resentment is rooted in anxieties about the increasing self-consciousness of modern life, which often leaves us feeling that we are never quite living but only endlessly talking about it, too often in some abstract professional vocabulary. The anxieties are expressed in our romantic literary tradition, which protests against the urban forms of sophistication that, it is believed, cause us to lose touch with the innocence of childhood and our creative impulses.

To those who have never reconciled themselves to the academicization of literature, the seeming overdevelopment of academic criticism with its obtrusive methodology and its endless disputes among interpretations and theories seems a betrayal not just of literature and the common reader but of the professor's own original passion for literature. In a recent letter to an intellectual journal one writer suggests that we should be concerned less about the oft-lamented common reader whom academic critics have deserted than about "the souls of the academics and literati themselves, who, as a result of social and professional pressures, have lost touch with the inner impulses that drew them to the world of books in the first place." What the writer of this letter cannot imagine is that someone might enter academic literary study because he actually *likes* thinking and talking in an analytical or theoretical way about books and that such a person might see his acceptance of "professional pressures" not as a betrayal of the "inner impulses" that drew him "to the world of books in the first place" but as a way to fulfill those impulses.

The standard story ascribes innocence to the primary experience of literature and sees the secondary experience of professional criticism as corrupting. In my case, however, things had evidently worked the other way around: I had to be corrupted first in order to experience innocence. It was only when I was introduced to a critical debate about *Huckleberry Finn* that my helplessness in the face of the novel abated and I could experience a personal reaction to it. Getting into immediate contact with the text was for me a curiously triangular business; I could not do it directly but needed a conversation of other readers to give me the issues and terms that made it possible to respond.

As I think back on it now, it was as if the critical conversation I needed had up to then been withheld from me, on the ground that it could only interfere with my direct access to literature itself. The assumption was that leaving me alone with literary texts themselves, uncontaminated by the interpretations and theories of professional critics, would enable me to get on the closest possible terms with those texts. But being alone with the texts only left me feeling bored and helpless, since I had no language with which to make them mine. On the one hand, I was being asked to speak a foreign language—literary criticism—while on the other hand, I was being protected from that language, presumably for my own safety.

The moral I draw from this experience is that our ability to read well depends more than we think on our ability to *talk well* about what we read. Our assumptions about what is "primary" and "secondary" in the reading process blind us to what actually goes on. Many literate people learned certain ways of talking about books so long ago that they have forgotten they ever had to learn them. These people therefore fail to understand the reading problems of the struggling students who have still not acquired a critical vocabulary.

The standard story of how we learn to read provides little help in dealing with such problems. Seeing criticism (and critical debate) as a distraction from the "primary" experience of literature itself, the standard story implies that the business of teaching is basically simple: Just put the student in front of a good book, provide teachers who are encouraging and helpful, and the rest presumably will take care of itself. The traditional maxim that sums up this view is that a good book "essentially teaches itself." The great teacher is one who knows how to let the book teach itself. And it is true that in the spell cast by such a teacher, it often *seems* as if the work is itself speaking directly to the student without intervention from the teacher's interpretations and theories. But this spell is an illusion. If books really taught themselves, there would be no reason to attend classes; students could simply stay home and read them on their own.

Nevertheless, the standard story remains seductive. Much of the appeal of Allan Bloom's *The Closing of the American Mind* lies in its eloquent restatement of the standard story, with its reassuringly simple view of reading and teaching: "a liberal education means reading certain generally recognized classic texts, just reading them, letting them dictate what the questions are and the method of approaching them—not forcing them into categories we make up, not treating them as historical products, but trying to read them as their authors wished them to be read." What has gone wrong, Bloom suggests, is that instead of letting the texts themselves dictate the questions we ask about them, a generation of overly professionalized teachers has elevated its own narcissistic interests over those of the author and the students. These teachers, as Bloom puts it, engage in "endless debates about methods—among them Freudian criticism, Marxist criticism, New Criticism, Structuralism and Deconstructionism, and many others, all of which have in common the premise that what Plato or Dante had to say about reality is unimportant."

It sounds so commonsensical that only a desiccated academic could disagree. What could be more obvious than the difference between "just" reading books, as ordinary readers have always done, and imposing theories and isms on books, as methodology-crazed academics do? The question, however, is whether anyone ever "just" reads a book the way Bloom describes. We need go no further than Bloom's own quoted statements to see that he himself does not practice the doctrine he preaches. When Bloom invokes the names of Plato and Dante, he does *not* let these authors dictate the questions that govern his discussion but "forces" them into categories he, Allan Bloom, with his twentieth-century preoccupations, has "made up." After all, what did Plato and Dante know about Freudians, Marxists, cultural relativists, and the other contemporary targets of Bloom's polemic? In using Plato and Dante to attack the intellectual and educational trends of his own time, Bloom is not reading these writers as they wished to be read but is *applying* them to a set of contexts they did not and could not have anticipated. This is not to say that Bloom is unfaithful to Plato's text, only that he does not passively take dictation from Plato's text but actively selects from it for his own purposes—just as he accuses theorists of doing.

The philosopher Richard Rorty has succinctly pointed out the trouble with Bloom's "just read the books" theory. Rorty acknowledges that interpreters are obliged "to give authors a run for their money," respecting "an author's way of talking and thinking, trying to put ourselves in her shoes." He argues, however, that "it is not clear how we can avoid forcing books into 'categories we make up. . . .'" We cannot help reading books, Rorty says, "with questions in mind— not questions dictated by the books—but questions we have previously, if vaguely, formulated." Rorty's point is not that reading is merely subjective but that it is inevitably *selective*. It is not that any reading of Plato is as good as any other but that even the most reliable reading has to select certain aspects of the text to emphasize, and the selection will be conditioned by the contingent situations in which the text is read. I would restate Rorty's point this way: As readers we are necessarily concerned with *both* the questions posed by the text and the questions we bring to it from our own differing interests and cultural backgrounds. Bloom thinks he can choose between "just reading" Plato and Dante and applying a "method" to them as do academic Freudians and Marxists. But Bloom's way of reading, which is influenced by his mentor the philosopher Leo Strauss, is as much a "method" as any other, bringing its special set of interests and principles of selection that are not dictated by Plato or Dante.

In teaching any text, one necessarily teaches an interpretation of it. This seems so obvious as to be hardly worth restating, but what follows from it is not obvious and is resisted violently by many who oppose the spread of theory. It follows that what literature teachers teach is not literature but criticism, or literature as it is filtered through a grid of analysis, interpretation, and theory. "Remarks are not literature," said Gertrude Stein in a now-celebrated observation, and Stein was right: Teachers cannot avoid interposing "remarks" between literature and their students—remarks, we hope, that illuminate the works and help our students take personal possession of them, but remarks nevertheless.

If teachers cannot avoid translating the literature they teach into some critical language or other, neither can students, for criticism is the language students are expected to speak and are punished for not speaking well. Inevitably the students who do well in school and college are those who learn to talk more or less like their teachers, who learn to produce something resembling intellectualspeak.

By what process do we imagine students will learn this language? The assumption seems to be that it will happen by a kind of osmosis, as students internalize the talk that goes on in class until they are able to produce a reasonable facsimile of it. However, as a recent textbook writer, Gordon Harvey, points out, not all students "can make this translation, since it requires that they intuit a whole set of intellectual moves and skills . . . too basic for experienced writers to notice themselves carrying out." The polite fiction that students will learn to make the "intellectual moves" by being in the presence of them for several hours a week is usually just that, a polite fiction.

Again, the problem is that what students are able to say about a text depends not just on the text but on their relation to a critical community of readers, which over time has developed an agenda of problems, issues, and questions with respect to both specific authors and texts and to culture generally. When students are screened from this critical community and its debates, or when they experience only the fragmentary and disconnected versions of it represented by a series of courses, they are likely to either be tongue-tied in the face of the text itself or to respond in a limited personal idiom, like the student who "relates to" Hamlet because he, too, had a mean stepfather.

In short, reading books with comprehension, making arguments, writing papers, and making comments in a class discussion are *social* activities. They involve entering into a cultural or disciplinary conversation, a process not unlike initiation into a social club. We obscure this social dimension when we conceive of education as if it were a process of contemplating important truths, values, and "cultural literacy" information in a vacuum and consequently treat such student tasks as reading assignments, making arguments, writing papers, and entering class discussions as if they were a matter of performing abstract procedures in a social void. Choose a topic that interests you, freshman writers are told; organize your paper logically around a central idea, and remember to support your thesis with specific illustration and evidence. Such advice is usually more paralyzing than helpful because it factors out the social conversation that reading, writing, and arguing must be part of in order to become personally meaningful.

Choosing a topic that interests you or making an effective argument depends on having a sense of what *other people* are saying, of what the state of the discussion is. Before my exposure to the critical debate on *Huckleberry Finn*, I had been trying to generate that discussion out of myself, something I did not know how to do. Exposure to the debate made me less of an outsider, provided me with a social community that gave my reading stimulus and direction. I could now discover what my teachers meant by "enjoying literature" because this had ceased to be a matter of vainly struggling to achieve some mysterious and rarefied experience. Relation to a community made the intimacy of literary experience possible.

Amy Tan

Amy Tan was born in Oakland, California in 1952; her parents were both born in China. Her father was an engineer, educated in Beijing and her mother left China in 1949, just before the communist revolution. Tan is best known as a fiction writer. Her first book, The Joy Luck Club, *(1989) was nominated for a National Book Award and was later the basis for the film of the same title. She has since published several other novels, including* The Kitchen God's Wife *(1991),* The Hundred Secret Senses *(1995) and* The Bonesetter's Daughter *(2001). This essay, "Mother Tongue," was chosen for inclusion in* Best American Essays 1991.

Mother Tongue

I am not a scholar of English or literature. I cannot give you much more than personal opinions on the English language and its variations in this country or others.

I am a writer. And by that definition, I am someone who has always loved language. I am fascinated by language in daily life. I spend a great deal of my time thinking about the power of language—the way it can evoke an emotion, a visual image, a complex idea, or a simple truth. Language is the tool of my trade. And I use them all—all the Englishes I grew up with.

Recently, I was made keenly aware of the different Englishes I do use. I was giving a talk to a large group of people, the same talk I had already given to half a dozen other groups. The nature of the talk was about my writing, my life, and my book, *The Joy Luck Club*. The talk was going along well enough, until I remembered one major difference that made the whole talk sound wrong. My mother was in the room. And it was perhaps the first time she had heard me give a lengthy speech, using the kind of English I have never used with her. I was saying things like, "The intersection of memory upon imagination" and "There is an aspect of my fiction that relates to thus-and-thus"—a speech filled with carefully wrought grammatical phrases, burdened, it suddenly seemed to me, with nominalized forms, past perfect tenses, conditional phrases, all the forms of standard English that I had learned in school and through books, the forms of English I did not use at home with my mother.

Just last week, I was walking down the street with my mother, and I again found myself conscious of the English I was using, the English I do use with her. We were talking about the price of new and used furniture and I heard myself

Reprinted from *The Threepenny Review*, (1990), by permission of the author and Sandra Dijkstra Literary Agency. Copyright © 1990 by Amy Tan.

saying this: "Not waste money that way." My husband was with us as well, and he didn't notice any switch in my English. And then I realized why. It's because over the twenty years we've been together I've often used that same kind of English with him, and sometimes he even uses it with me. It has become our language of intimacy, a different sort of English that relates to family talk, the language I grew up with.

So you'll have some idea of what this family talk I heard sounds like, I'll quote what my mother said during a recent conversation which I videotaped and then transcribed. During this conversation, my mother was talking about a political gangster in Shanghai who had the same last name as her family's, Du, and how the gangster in his early years wanted to be adopted by her family, which was rich by comparison. Later, the gangster became more powerful, far richer than my mother's family, and one day showed up at my mother's wedding to pay his respects. Here's what she said in part:

"Du Yusong having business like fruit stand. Like off the street kind. He is Du like Du Zong—but not Tsung-ming Island people. The local people call putong, the river east side, he belong to that side local people. That man want to ask Du Zong father take him in like become own family. Du Zong father wasn't look down on him, but didn't take seriously, until that man big like become a mafia. Now important person, very hard to inviting him. Chinese way, came only to show respect, don't stay for dinner. Respect for making big celebration, he shows up. Mean gives lots of respect. Chinese custom. Chinese social life that way. If too important won't have to stay too long. He come to my wedding. I didn't see, I heard it. I gone to boy's side, they have YMCA dinner. Chinese age I was nineteen."

You should know that my mother's expressive command of English belies how much she actually understands. She reads the *Forbes* report, listens to *Wall Street Week*, converses daily with her stockbroker, reads all of Shirley MacLaine's books with ease—all kinds of things I can't begin to understand. Yet some of my friends tell me they understand 50 percent of what my mother says. Some say they understand 80 to 90 percent. Some say they understand none of it, as if she were speaking pure Chinese. But to me, my mother's English is perfectly clear, perfectly natural. It's my mother tongue. Her language, as I hear it, is vivid, direct, full of observation and imagery. That was the language that helped shape the way I saw things, expressed things, made sense of the world.

Lately, I've been giving more thought to the kind of English my mother speaks. Like others, I have described it to people as "broken" or "fractured" English. But I wince when I say that. It has always bothered me that I can think of no other way to describe it other than "broken," as if it were damaged and needed to be fixed, as if it lacked a certain wholeness and soundness. I've heard other terms used, "limited English," for example. But they seem just as bad, as if everything is limited, including people's perceptions of the limited English speaker.

I know this for a fact, because when I was growing up, my mother's "limited" English limited *my* perception of her. I was ashamed of her English. I believed that her English reflected the quality of what she had to say. That is, because she expressed them imperfectly her thoughts were imperfect. And I had plenty of empirical evidence to support me: the fact that people in department stores, at banks, and at restaurants did not take her seriously, did not give her good service, pretended not to understand her, or even acted as if they did not hear her.

My mother has long realized the limitations of her English as well. When I was fifteen, she used to have me call people on the phone to pretend I was she. In this guise, I was forced to ask for information or even to complain and yell at people who had been rude to her. One time it was a call to her stockbroker in New York. She had cashed out her small portfolio and it just so happened we were going to go to New York the next week, our very first trip outside California. I had to get on the phone and say in an adolescent voice that was not very convincing, "This is Mrs. Tan."

And my mother was standing in the back whispering loudly, "Why he don't send me check, already two weeks late. So mad he lie to me, losing me money."

And then I said in perfect English, "Yes, I'm getting rather concerned. You had agreed to send the check two weeks ago, but it hasn't arrived."

Then she began to talk more loudly. "What he want, I come to New York tell him front of his boss, you cheating me?" And I was trying to calm her down, make her be quiet, while telling the stockbroker, "I can't tolerate any more excuses. If I don't receive the check immediately, I am going to have to speak to your manager when I'm in New York next week." And sure enough, the following week there we were in front of this astonished stockbroker, and I was sitting there red-faced and quiet, and my mother, the real Mrs. Tan, was shouting at his boss in her impeccable broken English.

We used a similar routine just five days ago, for a situation that was far less humorous. My mother had gone to the hospital for an appointment, to find out about a benign brain tumor a CAT scan had revealed a month ago. She said she had spoken very good English, her best English, no mistakes. Still, she said, the hospital did not apologize when they said they had lost the CAT scan and she had come for nothing. She said they did not seem to have any sympathy when she told them she was anxious to know the exact diagnosis, since her husband and son had both died of brain tumors. She said they would not give her any more information until the next time and she would have to make another appointment for that. So she said she would not leave until the doctor called her daughter. She wouldn't budge. And when the doctor finally called her daughter, me, who spoke in perfect English—lo and behold—we had assurances the CAT scan would be found, promises that a conference call on Monday would be held, and apologies for any suffering my mother had gone through for a most regrettable mistake.

I think my mother's English almost had an effect on limiting my possibilities in life as well. Sociologists and linguists probably will tell you that a person's developing language skills are more influenced by peers. But I do think that the language spoken in the family, especially in immigrant families which are more insular, plays a large role in shaping the language of the child. And I believe that it affected my results on achievement tests, IQ tests, and the SAT. While my English skills were never judged as poor, compared to math, English could not be considered my strong suit. In grade school I did moderately well, getting perhaps B's, sometimes B-pluses, in English and scoring perhaps in the sixtieth or seventieth percentile on achievement tests. But those scores were not good enough to override the opinion that my true abilities lay in math and science, because in those areas I achieved A's and scored in the ninetieth percentile or higher.

This was understandable. Math is precise; there is only one correct answer. Whereas, for me at least, the answers on English tests were always a judgment call, a matter of opinion and personal experience. Those tests were constructed around items like fill-in-the-blank sentence completion, such as "Even though Tom was _____, Mary thought he was _____." And the correct answer always seemed to be the most bland combinations of thoughts, for example, "Even though Tom was shy, Mary thought he was charming," with the grammatical structure "even though" limiting the correct answer to some sort of semantic opposites, so you wouldn't get answers like, "Even though Tom was foolish, Mary thought he was ridiculous." Well, according to my mother, there were very few limitations as to what Tom could have been and what Mary might have thought of him. So I never did well on tests like that.

The same was true with word analogies, pairs of words in which you were supposed to find some sort of logical, semantic relationship—for example, "*Sunset* is to *nightfall* as _____ is to _____." And here you would be presented with a list of four possible pairs, one of which showed the same kind of relationship: *red* is to *stoplight*, *bus* is to *arrival*, *chills* is to *fever*, *yawn* is to *boring*. Well, I could never think that way. I knew what the tests were asking, but I could not block out of my mind the images already created by the first pair, "*sunset* is to *nightfall*"— and I would see a burst of colors against a darkening sky, the moon rising, the lowering of a curtain of stars. And all the other pairs of words—red, bus, stoplight, boring—just threw up a mass of confusing images, making it impossible for me to sort out something as logical as saying: "A sunset precedes nightfall" is the same as "a chill precedes a fever." The only way I would have gotten that answer right would have been to imagine an associative situation, for example, my being disobedient and staying out past sunset, catching a chill at night, which turns into feverish pneumonia as punishment, which indeed did happen to me.

I have been thinking about all this lately, about my mother's English, about achievement tests. Because lately I've been asked, as a writer, why there are not more Asian Americans represented in American literature. Why are there few Asian Americans enrolled in creative writing programs? Why do so many Chinese students go into engineering? Well, these are broad sociological questions I can't begin to answer. But I have noticed in surveys—in fact, just last week—that Asian students, as a whole, always do significantly better on math achievement tests than in English. And this makes me think that there are other Asian-American students whose English spoken in the home might also be described as "broken" or "limited." And perhaps they also have teachers who are steering them away from writing and into math and science, which is what happened to me.

Fortunately, I happen to be rebellious in nature and enjoy the challenge of disproving assumptions made about me. I became an English major my first year in college, after being enrolled as pre-med. I started writing nonfiction as a freelancer the week after I was told by my former boss that writing was my worst skill and I should hone my talents toward account management.

But it wasn't until 1985 that I finally began to write fiction. And at first I wrote using what I thought to be wittily crafted sentences, sentences that would finally prove I had mastery over the English language. Here's an example from the first draft of a story that later made its way into *The Joy Luck Club,* but without this line: "That was my mental quandary in its nascent state." A terrible line, which I can barely pronounce.

Fortunately, for reasons I won't get into today, I later decided I should envision a reader for the stories I would write. And the reader I decided upon was my mother, because these were stories about mothers. So with this reader in mind—and in fact she did read my early drafts—I began to write stories using all the Englishes I grew up with: the English I spoke to my mother, which for lack of a better term might be described as "simple": the English she used with me, which for lack of a better term might be described as "broken"; my translation of her Chinese, which could certainly be described as "watered down"; and what I imagined to be her translation of her Chinese if she could speak in perfect English, her internal language, and for that I sought to preserve the essence, but neither an English nor a Chinese structure. I wanted to capture what language ability tests can never reveal: her intent, her passion, her imagery, the rhythms of her speech, and the nature of her thoughts.

Apart from what any critic had to say about my writing, I knew I had succeeded where it counted when my mother finished reading my book and gave me her verdict: "So easy to read."

Jimmy Santiago Baca

Today, Jimmy Santiago Baca (b. 1952) is recognized as a leading Chicano writer. He is a poet and essayist, and has written screenplays and a memoir, A Place to Stand: The Making of a Poet. *His list of awards is distinguished: Pushcart Prize, National Endowment of Poetry Award, Vogelstein Foundation Award, National Hispanic Heritage Award, Berkeley Regents Award, Southwest Book Award, and American Book Award. He has been a poet in residence at the University of California, Berkeley, and at Yale University.*

Yet, at the age of twenty-one Baca was illiterate and incarcerated. He had been sentenced to five years in a maximum-security prison for selling drugs. In prison, Baca became determined to change his life. He spent long hours studying grammar books and teaching himself to read and write. Soon he was writing letters and poems for other prisoners in exchange for cigarettes and coffee. Baca used poetry to work through the pain of his traumatic childhood in Santa Fe, New Mexico, his adolescence spent in orphanages and detention centers, and his experiments with crime and dealing drugs. His poetry is a product of his efforts to heal and make sense of a life filled with poverty, struggle, and betrayal.

Coming into Language

On weekend graveyard shifts at St. Joseph's Hospital I worked the emergency room, mopping up pools of blood and carting plastic bags stuffed with arms, legs, and hands to the outdoor incinerator. I enjoyed the quiet, away from the screams of shotgunned, knifed, and mangled kids writhing on gurneys outside the operating rooms. Ambulance sirens shrieked and squad car lights reddened the cool nights, flashing against the hospital walls: gray—red, gray—red. On slow nights I would lock the door of the administration office, search the reference library for a book on female anatomy and, with my feet propped on the desk, leaf through the illustrations, smoking my cigarette. I was seventeen.

One night my eye was caught by a familiar-looking word on the spine of a book. The title was *450 Years of Chicano History in Pictures*. On the cover were black-and-white photos: Padre Hidalgo exhorting Mexican peasants to revolt against the Spanish dictators; Anglo vigilantes hanging two Mexicans from a tree; a young Mexican woman with rifle and ammunition belts crisscrossing her breast;

Reprinted from *Working in the Dark*, (1992), Red Crane Books.

César Chávez and field workers marching for fair wages; Chicano railroad workers laying creosote ties; Chicanas laboring at machines in textile factories; Chicanas picketing and hoisting boycott signs.

From the time I was seven, teachers had been punishing me for not knowing
my lessons by making me stick my nose in a circle chalked on the blackboard.
Ashamed of not understanding and fearful of asking questions, I dropped out of
school in the ninth grade. At seventeen I still didn't know how to read, but those
pictures confirmed my identity. I stole the book that night, stashing it for safety
under the slopsink until I got off work. Back at my boardinghouse, I showed the
book to friends. All of us were amazed; this book told us we were alive. We, too,
had defended ourselves with our fists against hostile Anglos, gasping for breath in
fights with the policemen who outnumbered us. The book reflected back to us our
struggle in a way that made us proud.

Most of my life I felt like a target in the cross hairs of a hunter's rifle. When
strangers and outsiders questioned me I felt the hang-rope tighten around my
neck and the trapdoor creak beneath my feet. There was nothing so humiliating as
being unable to express myself, and my inarticulateness increased my sense of
jeopardy, of being endangered. I felt intimidated and vulnerable, ridiculed and
scorned. Behind a mask of humility, I seethed with mute rebellion.

Before I was eighteen, I was arrested on suspicion of murder after refusing to
explain a deep cut on my forearm. With shocking speed I found myself hand-
cuffed to a chain gang of inmates and bused to a holding facility to await trial.
There I met men, prisoners, who read aloud to each other the works of Neruda,
Paz, Sabines, Nemerov, and Hemingway. Never had I felt such freedom as in that
dormitory. Listening to the words of these writers, I felt that invisible threat from
without lessen—my sense of teetering on a rotting plank over swamp water where
famished alligators clapped their horny snouts for my blood. While I listened to
the words of the poets, the alligators slumbered powerless in their lairs. Their language was the magic that could liberate me from myself, transform me into
another person, transport me to other places far away.

And when they closed the books, these Chicanos, and went into their own
Chicano language, they made barrio life come alive for me in the fullness of its
vitality. I began to learn my own language, the bilingual words and phrases
explaining to me my place in the universe. Every day I felt like the paper boy taking delivery of the latest news of the day.

Months later I was released, as I had suspected I would be. I had been guilty
of nothing but shattering the windshield of my girlfriend's car in a fit of rage.

Two years passed. I was twenty now, and behind bars again. The federal mar-
shals had failed to provide convincing evidence to extradite me to Arizona on a
drug charge, but still I was being held. They had ninety days to prove I was guilty.
The only evidence against me was that my girlfriend had been at the scene of the
crime with my driver's license in her purse. They had to come up with something
else. But there was nothing else. Eventually they negotiated a deal with the actual
drug dealer, who took the stand against me. When the judge hit me with a million-
dollar bail, I emptied my pockets on his booking desk: twenty-six cents.

One night in my third month in the county jail, I was mopping the floor in front of the booking desk. Some detectives had kneed an old drunk and hand-cuffed him to the booking bars. His shrill screams raked my nerves like a hacksaw on bone, the desperate protest of his dignity against their inhumanity. But the detectives just laughed as he tried to rise and kicked him to his knees. When they went to the bathroom to pee and the desk attendant walked to the file cabinet to pull the arrest record, I shot my arm through the bars, grabbed one of the attendant's university textbooks, and tucked it in my overalls. It was the only way I had of protesting.

It was late when I returned to my cell. Under my blanket I switched on a pen flashlight and opened the thick book at random, scanning the pages. I could hear the jailer making his rounds on the other tiers. The jangle of his keys and the sharp click of his boot heels intensified my solitude. Slowly I enunciated the words . . . p-o-n-d, ri-pple. It scared me that I had been reduced to this to find comfort. I always had thought reading a waste of time, that nothing could be gained by it. Only by action, by moving out into the world and confronting and challenging the obstacles, could one learn anything worth knowing.

Even as I tried to convince myself that I was merely curious, I became so absorbed in how the sounds created music in me and happiness, I forgot where I was. Memories began to quiver in me, glowing with a strange but familiar intimacy in which I found refuge. For a while, a deep sadness overcame me, as if I had chanced on a long-lost friend and mourned the years of separation. But soon the heartache of having missed so much of life, that had numbed me since I was a child, gave way, as if a grave illness lifted itself from me and I was cured, innocently believing in the beauty of life again. I stumblingly repeated the author's name as I fell asleep, saying it over and over in the dark: Words–worth, Words–worth.

Before long my sister came to visit me, and I joked about taking her to a place called Kubla Khan and getting her a blind date with this *vato* named Coleridge who lived on the seacoast and was *malías* on morphine. When I asked her to make a trip into enemy territory to buy me a grammar book, she said she couldn't. Bookstores intimidated her, because she, too, could neither read nor write.

Days later, with a stub pencil I whittled sharp with my teeth, I propped a Red Chief notebook on my knees and wrote my first words. From that moment, a hunger for poetry possessed me.

Until then, I had felt as if I had been born into a raging ocean where I swam relentlessly, flailing my arms in hope of rescue, of reaching a shoreline I never sighted. Never solid ground beneath me, never a resting place. I had lived with only the desperate hope to stay afloat; that and nothing more.

But when at last I wrote my first words on the page, I felt an island rising beneath my feet like the back of a whale. As more and more words emerged, I could finally rest: I had a place to stand for the first time in my life. The island grew, with each page, into a continent inhabited by people I knew and mapped with the life I lived.

I wrote about it all—about people I had loved or hated, about the brutalities and ecstasies of my life. And, for the first time, the child in me who had witnessed and endured unspeakable terrors cried out not just in impotent despair, but with the power of language. Suddenly, through language, through writing, my grief and my joy could be shared with anyone who would listen. And I could do this all alone; I could do it anywhere. I was no longer a captive of demons eating away at me, no longer a victim of other people's mockery and loathing, that had made me clench my fist white with rage and grit my teeth to silence. Words now pleaded back with the bleak lucidity of hurt. They were wrong, those others, and now I could say it.

Through language I was free. I could respond, escape, indulge; embrace or reject earth or the cosmos. I was launched on an endless journey without boundaries or rules, in which I could salvage the floating fragments of my past, or be born anew in the spontaneous ignition of understanding some heretofore concealed aspect of myself. Each word steamed with the hot lava juices of my primordial making, and I crawled out of stanzas dripping with birth-blood, reborn and freed from the chaos of my life. The child in the dark room of my heart, that had never been able to find or reach the light switch, flicked it on now; and I found in the room a stranger, myself, who had waited so many years to speak again. My words struck in me lightning crackles of elation and thunderhead storms of grief.

When I had been in the county jail longer than anyone else, I was made a trustee. One morning, after a fist fight, I went to the unlocked and unoccupied office used for lawyer-client meetings, to think. The bare white room with its fluorescent tube lighting seemed to expose and illuminate my dark and worthless life. And yet, for the first time, I had something to lose—my chance to read, to write; a way to live with dignity and meaning, that had opened for me when I stole that scuffed, second-hand book about the Romantic poets. In prison, the abscess had been lanced.

"I will never do any work in this prison system as long as I am not allowed to get my G.E.D." That's what I told the reclassification panel. The captain flicked off the tape recorder. He looked at me hard and said, "You'll never walk outta here alive. Oh, you'll work, put a copper penny on that, you'll work."

After that interview I was confined to deadlock maximum security in a subterranean dungeon, with ground-level chickenwired windows painted gray. Twenty-three hours a day I was in that cell. I kept sane by borrowing books from the other cons on the tier. Then, just before Christmas, I received a letter from Harry, a charity house samaritan who doled out hot soup to the homeless in Phoenix. He had picked my name from a list of cons who had no one to write to them. I wrote back asking for a grammar book, and a week later received one of Mary Baker Eddy's treatises on salvation and redemption, with Spanish and English on opposing pages. Pacing my cell all day and most of each night, I grappled with grammar until I was able to write a long true-romance confession for a con to send to his pen pal. He paid me with a pack of smokes. Soon I had a thriving barter business, exchanging my poems and letters for novels, commissary pencils, and writing tablets.

One day I tore two flaps from the cardboard box that held all my belongings and punctured holes along the edge of each flap and along the border of a ream of state-issue paper. After I had aligned them to form a spine, I threaded the holes with a shoestring, and sketched on the cover a hummingbird fluttering above a rose. This was my first journal.

Whole afternoons I wrote, unconscious of passing time or whether it was day or night. Sunbursts exploded from the lead tip of my pencil, words that grafted me into awareness of who I was; peeled back to a burning core of bleak terror, an embryo floating in the image of water, I cracked out of the shell wide-eyed and insane. Trees grew out of the palms of my hands, the threatening otherness of life dissolved, and I became one with the air and sky, the dirt and the iron and concrete. There was no longer any distinction between the other and I. Language made bridges of fire between me and everything I saw. I entered into the blade of grass, the basketball, the con's eye and child's soul.

At night I flew. I conversed with floating heads in my cell, and visited strange houses where lonely women brewed tea and rocked in wicker rocking chairs listening to sad Joni Mitchell songs.

Before long I was frayed like a rope carrying too much weight, that suddenly snaps. I quit talking. Bars, walls, steel bunk and floor bristled with millions of poem-making sparks. My face was no longer familiar to me. The only reality was the swirling cornucopia of images in my mind, the voices in the air. Mid-air a cactus blossom would appear, a snakeflame in blinding dance around it, stunning me like a guard's fist striking my neck from behind.

The prison administrators tried several tactics to get me to work. For six months, after the next monthly prison board review, they sent cons to my cell to hassle me. When the guard would open my cell door to let one of them in, I'd leap out and fight him—and get sent to thirty-day isolation. I did a lot of isolation time. But I honed my image-making talents in that sensory-deprived solitude. Finally they moved me to death row, and after that to "nut-run," the tier that housed the mentally disturbed.

As the months passed, I became more and more sluggish. My eyelids were heavy, I could no longer write or read. I slept all the time.

One day a guard took me out to the exercise field. For the first time in years I felt grass and earth under my feet. It was spring. The sun warmed my face as I sat on the bleachers watching the cons box and run, hit the handball, lift weights. Some of them stopped to ask how I was, but I found it impossible to utter a syllable. My tongue would not move, saliva drooled from the corners of my mouth. I had been so heavily medicated I could not summon the slightest gesture. Yet inside me a small voice cried out, I am fine! I am hurt now but I will come back! I am fine!

Back in my cell, for weeks I refused to eat. Styrofoam cups of urine and hot water were hurled at me. Other things happened. There were beatings, shock therapy, intimidation.

Later, I regained some clarity of mind. But there was a place in my heart where I had died. My life had compressed itself into an unbearable dread of being. The strain had been too much. I had stepped over that line where a human being has lost more than he can bear, where the pain is too intense, and he knows he is changed forever. I was now capable of killing, coldly and without feeling. I was empty, as I have never, before or since, known emptiness. I had no connection to this life.

But then, the encroaching darkness that began to envelop me forced me to re-form and give birth to myself again in the chaos. I withdrew even deeper into the world of language, cleaving the diamonds of verbs and nouns, plunging into the brilliant light of poetry's regenerative mystery. Words gave off rings of white energy, radar signals from powers beyond me that infused me with truth. I believed what I wrote, because I wrote what was true. My words did not come from books or textual formulas, but from a deep faith in the voice of my heart.

I had been steeped in self-loathing and rejected by everyone and everything— society, family, cons, God and demons. But now I had become as the burning ember floating in darkness that descends on a dry leaf and sets flame to forests. The word was the ember and the forest was my life.

I was born a poet one noon, gazing at weeds and creosoted grass at the base of a telephone pole outside my grilled cell window. The words I wrote then sailed me out of myself, and I was transported and metamorphosed into the images they made. From the dirty brown blades of grass came bolts of electrical light that jolted loose my old self; through the top of my head that self was released and reshaped in the clump of scrawny grass. Through language I became the grass, speaking its language and feeling its green feelings and black root sensations. Earth was my mother and I bathed in sunshine. Minuscule speckles of sunlight passed through my green skin and metabolized in my blood.

Writing bridged my divided life of prisoner and free man. I wrote of the emotional butchery of prisons, and of my acute gratitude for poetry. Where my blind doubt and spontaneous trust in life met, I discovered empathy and compassion. The power to express myself was a welcome storm rasping at tendril roots, flooding my soul's cracked dirt. Writing was water that cleansed the wound and fed the parched root of my heart.

I wrote to sublimate my rage, from a place where all hope is gone, from a madness of having been damaged too much, from a silence of killing rage. I wrote to avenge the betrayals of a lifetime, to purge the bitterness of injustice. I wrote with a deep groan of doom in my blood, bewildered and dumbstruck; from an indestructible love of life, to affirm breath and laughter and the abiding innocence of things. I wrote the way I wept, and danced, and made love.

Tita French Baumlin

Tita French Baumlin, who has a Ph.D. in English with concentrations in British Renaissance Literature and Rhetoric, teaches at Southwest Missouri State University. She wrote this essay and carried out this class exercise during the spring semester of 1984 when she was doing her graduate work at Texas Christian University.

A Good Crot Is Hard to Find

With a copy of Winston Weathers' "The Grammars of Style: New Options in Composition" (*Freshman English News*, Winter, 1976) firmly in hand, I recently resolved to make a fresh attempt at presenting my second semester freshmen with a new exploratory assignment: write a composition using what Weathers calls "Grammar B." I briefly outlined in class some of the significant features of this new style—sentence fragments and/or long and convoluted sentences, word repetitions, odd orthographic devices, and a total disregard for transition between divisions of material. I also offered the students some brief samples from my file, such as Weathers' essay on William Blake (contained in his article) and some inventive newspaper articles; I even brought out my dog-eared, personal (and precious) copy of *Tristram Shandy*. I suggested some possible topics and most of the students left the room with those unmistakable this-is-going-to-be-easy smiles on their faces: *You mean I'm allowed to write incomplete sentences?*

By noon the following day, however, I began to realize that these students, far from complacent, were now in the early stages of panic, having gone home and contemplated their options. One after another, they left notes in my mailbox, sought me in my office, in the library, in the departmental office, in the hallway, all asking the same question: "What is it that you WANT?" Again and again, I smiled and said, "Relax. Have fun with it. See what happens." But my freshmen would not be moved.

I decided that some additional material from Winston Weathers' textbook, *An Alternate Style* (Rochelle Park, N.J.: Hayden Book Company, Inc., 1980), couldn't hurt. I had also decided earlier that I would write this assignment along with my class, not only to show them that it could be done, but also (and most of all) to give *myself* what I believed this assignment promised the students: a liberation from the conventions that, allowed to reign too long at a time, can stifle the creativity on which most of us have an all too tenuous hold. I had not yet hit upon any particular topic for my paper when I sat down at the typewriter, but thumbing through *An Alternate Style* worked its magic on me, and within four hours I had

Reprinted from *Rhetoric Review* 3, January 1995.

produced the following essay, a piece which I hoped would combine a discussion of the significant features of "Grammar B," examples of suggested techniques, an open letter to my composition class, and my own response to the assignment.

"Just Tell Me What You Want"

You listen. And you smile. Try to act eager. Try to BE EAGER. You go home. Write. TRY to write. Pen the words, pencil the words, type the words, anywayyoucan the words, curse the words you use like steel files to try to scrape your way out of prison. Try to free your soul from the bondage of freshman comp. I and II. Free your mind from the bondage of A*B*C*D*F. Why not an E and a G? An F-sharp? Take an A-flat on your next paper. Or a G.

But you traipse into my office. Streams of freshmen YOU CAN ALWAYS TELL THE FRESHMEN THEY'RE THE ONES WITH THE fffffffur-rrrrowwwwwwwed brows AND ANXIOUS EYES and you

```
say
    Just
        tell
            me
                what
                    you
                        want,
                            Miss
                                French
                                    and
                                    I
                                will
                            do
                        it
                    OKAY
                ??
```

I don't know what I want. On your blank page.
Because I'm not you.
But. Now that I have your attention. I'll tell you what I want.

CHAPTER 1

What Miss French Wants

I want your smiling face in my classroom every time class meets. I want to know you'll be there to read the crazy pieces I stay up until four a.m. writing for you. I want to know your drafts will be clutched in sweaty hands not because you are afraid of poor grades and punishment but because you are thirsting for the good stuff that only we can give you. Your class. Mates.

I want to never again have to reply to ARE WE DOING ANYTHING IMPORTANT TODAY CAUSE IF WE AREN'T I HAVE TO GO TO***** I HAVE A DOCTOR'S APPOINTMENT***** I HAVE A JOB INTERVIEW *****I HAVE OTHER CLASSES / DEMANDING PROFS / LABS / REHEARS-ALS / PRACTICES / WORKOUTS / DON'T WORRY IT'S AN EXCUSED ABSENCE . . . Not that I believe my every word is Golden. It's just that you never know when the Magic will strike.

Maybe now.

And if you miss it

It may not come again. Come again?

CHAPTER 2

What MISS FRENCH really WANTS

Magic. Free the P*O*Ws of the mind/little bits of grey matter held hostage by the POWERS THAT BE/i.e., THOSE WHO TELL YOU

Please do not write in this area.

Fill out forms in triplicate.

Press hard you are making five copies.

Office use only.

Past due after

Do not fold, staple, or mutilate.

DO NOT

Do not combine process analysis with compare/contrast.

Do not use 2nd person.

Do NOT use 1st person. On pain of death.

Put your thesis statement

HERE.

/victims of the wars your mommas and daddies didn't even know they served in. Liberate slave labor!!! Let judgment come rolling down like waters and righteousness like a mighty stream of words, a torrent of words, a flood of words, of passion, of electric love like you've never known before, of magic that comes from that part of you that holds on to words like a lifeline in a typhoon.

Do you not know that your native tongue is a gift? beyond compare? That what I write and what you read here

EVEN

HERE

makes us human? makes us mankind? makes us man? kind?

AND GOD SAID, LET US MAKE MAN IN OUR IMAGE, AFTER OUR LIKENESS: AND LET THEM HAVE DOMINION OVER THE FISH OF THE SEA, AND OVER THE FOWL OF THE AIR, AND OVER THE CATTLE, AND OVER ALL THE EARTH,

AND OVER EVERY CREEPING THING THAT CREEPETH
UPON THE EARTH. SO GOD CREATED MAN IN HIS *OWN*
IMAGE, IN THE IMAGE OF GOD CREATED HE HIM.

And, behold. It was very good.

don'tforgetdon'tforgetdon'tforgetdon'tforgetdon'tforget:

Tricks of the Trade

A. What to play with.

1. *Crots.* A crot is an old-fashioned word for "bit" or "fragment." Like a stanza is to poetry. Like a note is to music is a crot to my work. Free your crots. Let them stand alone. Long or short, let your crots be crots. Without connecting tissue. Like this.

Brevity. In brief, a short crot can be like a proverb. A crot without transition is like a new scent wafted on the breeze of the imagination.

> Dear Students,
>
> Longer crots are quite acceptable, as well. The trick is to present your crots in nearly random sequence or in sequences that finally (at last!) suggest a circular pattern. Impose no other kind of order on your crots than the flow of your mind. Use your crots like good snapshots of the wonderful orderly disorder that is your mind.
>
> Very truly, etc.,

Give Your Crots Titles, If You Like

An effective title sometimes says more than the text you put after it.

2. *The Labyrinthine Sentence and the Sentence Fragment.* Give you two kinds of sentences to play with. The Labyrinthine Sentence is just what it sounds like: a long, involuted sentence like a LABYRINTH that flows along, has nooks and crannies, twists, turns, snips, snags, and oh! that fluidity that sings like water slipping and slurrrrppping down the thirsty, rocky, dry creekbeds of our minds; for instance, if you are speaking of eternity, you may want to mention the height of the bluest distances between mountains (gasp!) or perhaps the deepest part of the rolling, moaning, foaming, pitching, roaring ocean, but if you are talking about a misunderstanding—how did it get this way?—between friends, you may need—how did this ever come to pass?—to intersperse your sentence with (pardon me, while I remember and pause to choose my words carefully) the kinds of pauses that such a story might call for, might actually WANT.

On the other hand.

A fragment. Often a single word. Alone. Or a very short phrase. Very. Suggests a far greater awareness of separation. Fragmentation. Not entanglement. But isolation. It can be emphatic. Pointed. Get the point?

3. *The List.* Basically, there are at least two or three ways to create a list.

If you want to suggest the illusion that the items you are listing are all there, all present in the mind or in the vision, all at once, then you may want to list them in a paragraph of continuous prose, words, phrases, non-*sense* phrases, crots, blips, blobs, bits, bytes, all in one block.

On the other hand, you may want to suggest a catalog. An orderly picture.

A Set of Words That Bounce Off Each Other

One word	Versus another
And yet here	Can be
Another	Well placed
Beside one	Another
Here	And there

Or you may want to list them all in one short vertical list.

Eternity
Wants
Needs
Kindness
Mankindness

Or a list of short phrases
Like bits you might write on a blackboard
Careless as to length, with
Individual phrases free to be very very long
Or short
You thus may say to your reader
I'm keeping my mouth shut
YOU look at these items
YOU make up your own @/*# mind
Add them up
Evaluate them
In your own reality, for
Your reality is
Different from mine.

4. *The Double Voice.*
I would use this technique to present
my material as though I were running
two compositions down two sides of
the page.

I want to try to suggest that I COULD
say this OR that about my subject, and
in a way I'd like to say both.

I'm dealing with ambiguous realities.

I'm presenting information and FACTS.

I'm commenting upon the facts in such a way that I can help the reader distinguish between the two roles that I can play when I write, as fact-giver AND/or as interpreter/commentator.

Straight line double voice *Like this when I have something* is harder *else to say* with a conventional typewriter *in between the phrases* because I don't have access to italics which is *to seem like I'm carrying on* easier *a conversation with myself* to say the least *to indicate confusion, maybe, or mixed emotions.*

5. *Repetitions/Refrains.* Hurry! Hurry! I'm almost finished! You find a key word Faster! Faster! or a key phrase and you repeat it. As D. H. Lawrence does here:

Doom.

Doom! Doom! Doom! Something seems to whisper it in the very dark trees of America. Doom!

Doom of what?

Doom of our white day. We are doomed, doomed. And the doom is in America. The doom of our white day. (Want more? Go see "Herman Melville's *Moby Dick*," in *Studies in Classic American Literature,* London: Heinemann, 1924, okay?)

6. *Language Variegation: Orthographic Schemes and the Foreign Word.*

You might want to play with word spelling, MISSpellings to you, ma'am, to inject some laughs, or to oPUN the door to playing with language and alternate meanings. You can make up words, like Lewis Carroll's Jabjabjabjabjabberwocky, for as James Joyce says, "A nod to the nabir is better than a wink to the wabsanti." Such play can signal "fun" and "play" to the reader, help articulate the philosophy and presence of *homo ludens* (thank you, Winston Weathers), or remind your reader how delightfully complex language is. Sometimes the tragic flaw of a piece is that there's no comic relief.

Or you might consider sound effects. Winston Weathers told us about Blake's Tygrrrrrrr, remember? Or how about someone who is speeeeeeeaking slooooowly? Just be playYAYful, if you know what I mean.

Or how about a foreign phrase? Not necessarily to be high-brow, *per se,* but maybe just to indicate "a deliberate spilling over and outside the boundaries of English" (thanks again, W. W.).

Deo gratias!

I'm almost finished!

B. There is no B in this outline. A polite (?) thumb-to-nose at the ones who say DO NOT have an A without a B in an outline.

I say, Let X equal X (thank you, Laurie Anderson) and let the crots fall where they may. *E pluribus unum.*

This isn't easy. It's taken me HOURS to do this first draft. But I had fun. And I have something to work with now. So that I can try to do justice to this assignment. Justice is not just ice, you know. And a good, crot is hard to find.

Just try to mix these different tricks for different effects. Try not to get stuck in one long list or one long unbroken line of prose, unless, of course, you want to. It's just more fun to try on different hats, *Hütte, chapeaux, cappelli,* as it were. Try them ALL on.

You might like what you see in the mirror when you do.

> *C'est finis!*
>
> > *What?*
>
> *É finita!*
>
> > Hold the phone.
>
> *Es ist zu Ende!*
>
> > er, um
>
> *Consummatum est!*
>
> > Bingo!
>
> > > theend.

FOOTNOTE: Most of the above information (Just the facts, ma'am) and much of the inspiration was GREATfully absorbed from Winston Weathers, *An Alternate Style* (Rochelle Park, N. J.: Hayden Book Company, Inc., 1980). Only the syntax was changed to protect the innocent.
FOOTNOTE: Keep on your toes. . . .

After distributing copies of this essay and explaining its origin, I discussed my paper with the class. One student remarked that he noticed a union of form and content in the paper; several others responded by saying they thought it was funny, while it got the point across, as well. At least when our class period was over, they seemed to have clearer ideas of directions to take in their own papers. Perhaps the best result of this essay was that the students seemed energized and inspired to find their own ways to explore this assignment, rather than frustrated and daunted with the intimidation that usually accompanies the instructor's presentation of his or her own "model essay." This essay WAS a model of the kind of paper I expected from them, but in serving the primary function of informing the class of possible techniques and "tricks of the trade," this paper doubled as a mere class handout, ordinary, innocuous, and informative. Further, the students' classroom responses indicated that they did not dismiss this essay as just another teacher's attempt to "show off." On the contrary, my own creativity seemed to spark similar creativity in the students, urges which pushed each student to explore his or her own unique topic in increasingly unique ways. Best of all, my paper's "topic" was not one which encouraged imitation and thus it did not produce insurmountable mental blocks when these students went about finding suitable topics.

Our first workshop session surprised me. Not one of the students had picked one of my "suggested topics" for the essay, but rather each and every class member had found a subject that had personal meaning in his or her own life, and the resulting wide range of topics added a new dimension of adventure to our first workshop. Furthermore, even though each paper was highly and uniquely personal, this workshop group offered more constructive criticism and suggestions for improvement than ever before. The major phrase for the day became: "Why don't you play with that section and see what happens?" The critics were eager to suggest a playfulness in revision, as were the recipients playful in their responses.

On a practical level, this workshop might have proceeded more smoothly if I had been able to have several drafts duplicated ahead of time so that we could see the visual effects; instead, the authors here had to explain as they read aloud. Still, these authors didn't seem to mind stopping and explaining what each passage was supposed to accomplish—in fact, they seemed to enjoy hashing out their own reasoning behind the techniques they had chosen, and it occurred to me that this was perhaps the first time that the class as a whole had begun to operate on the overt assumption that any given technique must be a careful, rational choice. It is this discovery that leads me to consider that this exercise might work very well for some instructors if it is strategically placed early in the semester, allowing students to discover the value of rationally planning one's rhetoric and of finding union of form and content, then building upon that discovery throughout the remainder of the semester.

On the other hand, saving this assignment for at least mid-semester has its advantages, because, though wildly liberating, such an exercise is simultaneously frustrating in that it demands both creativity and self-consciousness more overtly than do other types of expository writing; a particular group may have to create a certain level of dynamics before it can attempt this venture. Many students reported that this assignment was the most difficult one they faced all year, simply because it is so difficult to break out of the prisons of traditions: sometimes the slaves find out they don't want to be released! Knowing one another well may have helped us voice our frustrations, fears, and discoveries with greater ease, may have helped us support and nurture the growth that such an assignment demanded among us.

In any case, these authors' final drafts astounded me. Every paper showed playful incorporations of the techniques I had offered them, but, best of all, each essay also showed innovations and discoveries that my model essay had not displayed. One chemistry major wrote about the terrors of chemistry class and, while describing her frustration with a particularly esoteric ion, she constructed word pictures that visually displayed the chemical bond. Another student used a word association technique that allowed him to stop in mid-sentence, taking a different direction based upon an alternate meaning of a pivotal word; the final effect was a kind of zipping from crot to crot with little verbal links, suggesting a deeper theme of the complexities of communication in language. A computer science major wrote an entertaining and informative paper about her relationship with computers; she submitted her final draft typed on discarded computer paper. A very fine paper about the subliminal influence of television on our minds showed the subtle, tempting voice of "*t*v*" as a magical, almost imperceptible whisper that interrupts our every thought; the most humorous essay in this group attempted to translate a polite exchange between professor and student into each participants' *real* thoughts through a quadruple voice technique—a dialogue within a dialogue.

The two best papers in the class were perhaps the most dissimilar. A Mexican-American student wrote a fine and fun essay about the frustrations of trying to write this assignment, but he emphasized the double voice technique and created a delightful interplay between his serious and fearful "English" student-self and his free and easy "Mexican" alter ego: the student-self feared that his usage of his second language would always be inferior, stifling any creativity he might ever muster, while the confident alter ego bounced happily between both languages, offering encouragement to forget about pleasing anybody but himself. The alter ego became an impish voice, tempting the student to let out all his frustrations by skipping this assignment altogether. This "I can't write this paper"/"Forget it; have a cigarette, *amigo*" dialogue resulted in a delightful essay that not only produced a wry and ironic "nonessay," but also underscored the deeper poignant struggles of our classmate in his complex, bilingual world. We laughed, but we were also touched by the vulnerability he shared with us; we all felt that some kind of bridge had been crossed.

The other paper was as serious and moving as its partner was funny and profane, proving that this new style is not necessarily most effective in a comic tone. The essay explored the gradual unfolding of the doom of the Jews in Nazi Germany; each page of the essay displayed a different step in the Nazi philosophy, but the words and statistics, nicely interwoven with German phrases, formed a separate arm of the swastika on each page. By the end of the essay, a final page was produced through reductive photocopying so that the previous arms assembled the insignia just as the final edict for extermination was announced, a chilling and sobering progression from mere inflation on page one to genocide on page five. The paper was well researched and artfully produced, but most meaningful to me was the fact that this student sought me in my office *before* the class due date, personally to place his paper into my hands; it was the first time in nearly two semesters that this particular student had handed in an assignment on time.

The mutual admiration among us was at its greatest peak during this entire assignment, but the levels of frustration and bewilderment were highest here, too. Still, aren't the most exhilarating victories usually the hardest won? I, too, shared the sense of pride in looking at this wide range of excellence in these final products that included my own little essay, because we all knew that this particular accomplishment had been so slow in development. One final commentary is perhaps the best summary of the results of this experiment: "You know, at first I thought this assignment was going to be so easy," one student remarked, "but it was hard, one of the hardest papers I've ever written. It was so *hard* to stop writing regular, boring sentences. I never knew I was so locked into traditions. And I never knew that how I write what I want to say could matter so much to me." This student had clearly encountered and explored the limitations both she and conventional English had previously placed on her creativity. And she, like the rest of us, had learned to explore her own unique writer's self in a way that encouraged her to be different, to be stunning, to have fun with her own words and ideas. The students learned that writing well can be both exhausting and exhilarating, frustrating and rewarding. I learned that an instructor's own enthusiasm and creativity is not only contagious but absolutely intrinsic to our students' discovery of creativity and the fun of composition. And we all learned a truth that is demonstrable in Grammar A as well as in Grammar B or any other: a good crot is hard to find.

Patricia Hampl

Patricia Hampl (1946-) is the author of several works of creative nonfiction and has received multiple awards as a memoirist. These titles include, A Romantic Education *(1999),* Blue Arabesque: A Search for the Sublime *(2007),* Virgin Time: In Search of the Contemplative Life *(2005), and most recently* The Florist's Daughter *(2009). She has published two collections of poetry,* Woman before an Aquarium *(1978) and* Resort and Other Poems *(1983). The essay "Memory and Imagination" was first published in* The Anatomy of Memory: An Anthology *(1996) and later in her collection of essays,* I Could Tell You Stories: Sojourns in the Land of Memory *(2000). She currently teaches in the MFA program at the University of Minnesota.*

Memory and Imagination

When I was seven, my father, who played the violin on Sundays with a nicely tortured flair which we considered artistic, led me by the hand down a long, unlit corridor in St. Luke's School basement, a sort of tunnel that ended in a room full of pianos. There many little girls and a single sad boy were playing truly tortured scales and arpeggios in a mash of troubled sound. My father gave me over to Sister Olive Marie, who did look remarkably like an olive.

Her oily face gleamed as if it had just been rolled out of a can and laid on the white plate of her broad, spotless wimple. She was a small, plump woman; her body and the small window of her face seemed to interpret the entire alphabet of olive: her face was a sallow green olive placed upon the jumbo ripe olive of her black habit. I trusted her instantly and smiled, glad to have my hand placed in the hand of a woman who made sense, who provided the satisfaction of being what she was: an Olive who looked like an olive.

My father left me to discover the piano with Sister Olive Marie so that one day I would join him in mutually tortured piano-violin duets for the edification of my mother and brother who sat at the table meditatively spooning in the last of their pineapple sherbet until their part was called for: they put down their spoons and clapped while we bowed, while the sweet ice in their bowls melted, while the music melted, and we all melted a little into each other for a moment.

But first Sister Olive must do her work. I was shown middle C, which Sister seemed to think terribly important. I stared at middle C and then glanced away for a second. When my eye returned, middle C was gone, its slim finger lost in the complicated grasp of the keyboard. Sister Olive struck it again, finding it with laughable ease. She emphasized the importance of middle C, its central position, a sort of North Star of sound. I remember thinking, "Middle C is the belly button of the piano," an insight whose originality and accuracy stunned me with pride. For the first time in my life I was astonished by metaphor. I hesitated to tell the kindly Olive for some reason; apparently I understood a true metaphor is a risky business, revealing of the self. In fact, I have never, until this moment of writing it down, told my first metaphor to anyone.

Sunlight flooded the room; the pianos, all black, gleamed. Sister Olive, dressed in the colors of the keyboard, gleamed; middle C shimmered with meaning and I resolved never—never—to forget its location: it was the center of the world.

Then Sister Olive, who had had to show me middle C twice but who seemed to have drawn no bad conclusions about me anyway, got up and went to the windows on the opposite wall. She pulled the shades down, one after the other. The sun was too bright, she said. She sneezed as she stood at the windows with the sun shedding its glare over her. She sneezed and sneezed, crazy little convulsive sneezes, one after another, as helpless as if she had the hiccups.

"The sun makes me sneeze," she said when the fit was over and she was back at the piano. This was odd, too odd to grasp in the mind. I associated sneezing with colds, and colds with rain, fog, snow and bad weather. The sun, however, had caused Sister Olive to sneeze in this wild way, Sister Olive who gleamed benignly and who was so certain of the location of the center of the world. The universe wobbled a bit and became unreliable. Things were not, after all, necessarily what they seemed. Appearance deceived: here was the sun acting totally out of character, hurling this woman into sneezes, a woman so mild that she was named, so it seemed, for a bland object on a relish tray.

I was given a red book, the first Thompson book, and told to play the first piece over and over at one of the black pianos where the other children were crashing away. This, I was told, was called practicing. It sounded alluringly adult, practicing. The piece itself consisted mainly of middle C, and I excelled, thrilled by my savvy at being able to locate that central note amidst the cunning camouflage of all the other white keys before me. Thrilled too by the shiny red book that gleamed, as the pianos did, as Sister Olive did, as my eager eyes probably did. I sat at the formidable machine of the piano and got to know middle C intimately, preparing to be as tortured as I could manage one day soon with my father's violin at my side.

But at the moment Mary Katherine Reilly was at my side, playing something at least two or three lessons more sophisticated than my piece. I believe she even struck a chord. I glanced at her from the peasantry of single notes, shy, ready to pay homage. She turned toward me, stopped playing, and sized me up.

Sized me up and found a person ready to be dominated. Without introduction she said, "My grandfather invented the collapsible opera hat."

I nodded, I acquiesced, I was hers. With that little stroke it was decided between us—that she should be the leader, and I the sidekick. My job was admiration. Even when she added, "But he didn't make a penny from it. He didn't have a patent"—even then, I knew and she knew that this was not an admission of powerlessness, but the easy candor of a master, of one who can afford a weakness or two.

With the clairvoyance of all fated relationships based on dominance and submission, it was decided in advance: that when the time came for us to play duets,

I should always play second piano, that I should spend my allowance to buy her the Twinkies she craved but was not allowed to have, that finally, I should let her copy from my test paper, and when confronted by our teacher, confess with convincing hysteria that it was I, I who had cheated, who had reached above myself to steal what clearly belonged to the rightful heir of the inventor of the collapsible opera hat. . . .

There must be a reason I remember that little story about my first piano lesson. In fact, it isn't a story, just a moment, the beginning of what could perhaps become a story. For the memoirist, more than for the fiction writer, the story seems already *there*, already accomplished and fully achieved in history ("in reality," as we naively say). For the memoirist, the writing of the story is a matter of transcription.

That, anyway, is the myth. But no memoirist writes for long without experiencing an unsettling disbelief about the reliability of memory, a hunch that memory is not, after all, *just* memory. I don't know why I remembered this fragment about my first piano lesson. I don't, for instance, have a single recollection of my first arithmetic lesson, the first time I studied Latin, the first time my grandmother tried to teach me to knit. Yet these things occurred too, and must have their stories.

It is the piano lesson that has trudged forward, clearing the haze of forgetfulness, showing itself bright with detail more than thirty years after the event. I did not choose to remember the piano lesson. It was simply there, like a book that has always been on the shelf, whether I ever read it or not, the binding and title showing as I skim across the contents of my life. On the day I wrote this fragment I happened to take that memory, not some other, from the shelf and paged through it. I found more detail, more event, perhaps a little more entertainment than I had expected, but the memory itself was there from the start. Waiting for me.

Or was it? When I reread what I had written just after I finished it, I realized that I had told a number of lies. I *think* it was my father who took me the first time for my piano lesson—but maybe he only took me to meet my teacher and there was no actual lesson that day. And did I even know then that he played the violin— didn't he take up his violin again much later, as a result of my piano playing, and not the reverse? And is it even remotely accurate to describe as "tortured" the musicianship of a man who began every day by belting out "Oh What a Beautiful Morning" as he shaved?

More: Sister Olive Marie did sneeze in the sun, but was her name Olive? As for her skin tone—I would have sworn it was olive-like; I would have been willing to spend the better part of an afternoon trying to write the exact description of imported Italian or Greek olive her face suggested: I wanted to get it right. But now, were I to write that passage over, it is her intense black eyebrows I would see, for suddenly they seem the central fact of that face, some indicative mark of her serious and patient nature. But the truth is, I don't remember the woman at all. She's a sneeze in the sun and a finger touching middle C. That, at least, is steady and clear.

Worse: I didn't have the Thompson book as my piano text. I'm sure of that because I remember envying children who did have this wonderful book with its pictures of children and animals printed on the pages of music.

As for Mary Katherine Reilly. She didn't even go to grade school with me (and her name isn't Mary Katherine Reilly—but I made that change on purpose). I met her in Girl Scouts and only went to school with her later, in high school. Our relationship was not really one of leader and follower; I played first piano most of the time in duets. She certainly never copied anything from a test paper of mine: she was a better student, and cheating just wasn't a possibility with her. Though her grandfather (or someone in her family) did invent the collapsible opera hat and I remember that she was proud of that fact, she didn't tell me this news as a deft move in a childish power play.

So, what was I doing in this brief memoir? Is it simply an example of the curious relation a fiction writer has to the material of her own life? Maybe. That may have some value in itself. But to tell the truth (if anyone still believes me capable of telling the truth), I wasn't writing fiction. I was writing memoir—or was trying to. My desire was to be accurate. I wished to embody the myth of memoir: to write as an act of dutiful transcription.

Yet clearly the work of writing narrative caused me to do something very different from transcription. I am forced to admit that memoir is not a matter of transcription, that memory itself is not a warehouse of finished stories, not a static gallery of framed pictures. I must admit that I invented. But why?

Two whys: why did I invent, and then, if a memoirist must inevitably invent rather than transcribe, why do I—why should anybody—write memoir at all?

I must respond to these impertinent questions because they, like the bumper sticker I saw the other day commanding all who read it to QUESTION AUTHORITY, challenge my authority as a memoirist and as a witness.

It still comes as a shock to realize that I don't write about what I know: I write in order to find out what I know. Is it possible to convey to a reader the enormous degree of blankness, confusion, hunch and uncertainty lurking in the act of writing? When I am the reader, not the writer, I too fall into the lovely illusion that the words before me (in a story by Mavis Gallant, an essay by Carol Bly, a memoir by M. F. K. Fisher), which *read* so inevitably, must also have been *written* exactly as they appear, rhythm and cadence, language and syntax, the powerful waves of the sentences laying themselves on the smooth beach of the page one after another faultlessly.

But here I sit before a yellow legal pad, and the long page of the preceding two paragraphs is a jumble of crossed-out lines, false starts, confused order. A mess. The mess of my mind trying to find out what it wants to say. This is a writer's frantic, grabby mind, not the poised mind of a reader ready to be edified or entertained.

I sometimes think of the reader as a cat, endlessly fastidious, capable, by turns, of mordant indifference and riveted attention, luxurious, recumbent, and ever poised. Whereas the writer is absolutely a dog, panting and moping, too eager for an affectionate scratch behind the ears, lunging frantically after any old stick thrown in the distance.

The blankness of a new page never fails to intrigue and terrify me. Sometimes, in fact, I think my habit of writing on long yellow sheets comes from an atavistic fear of the writer's stereotypic "blank white page." At least when I begin writing, my page isn't utterly blank; at least it has a wash of color on it, even if the absence of words must finally be faced on a yellow sheet as truly as on a blank white one. Well, we all have our ways of whistling in the dark.

If I approach writing from memory with the assumption that I know what I wish to say, I assume that intentionality is running the show. Things are not that simple. Or perhaps writing is even more profoundly simple, more telegraphic and immediate in its choices than the grating wheels and chugging engine of logic and rational intention. The heart, the guardian of intuition with its secret, often fearful intentions, is the boss, its commands are what a writer obeys—often without knowing it. Or, I do.

That's why I'm a strong adherent of the first draft. And why it's worth pausing for a moment to consider what a first draft really is. By my lights, the piano lesson memoir is a first draft. That doesn't mean it exists here exactly as I first wrote it. I like to think I've cleaned it up from the first time I put it down on paper. I've cut some adjectives here, toned down the hyperbole there, smoothed a transition, cut a repetition—that sort of housekeeperly tidying-up. But the piece remains a first draft because I haven't yet gotten to know it, haven't given it a chance to tell me anything. For me, writing a first draft is a little like meeting someone for the first time. I come away with a wary acquaintanceship, but the real friendship (if any) and genuine intimacy—that's all down the road. Intimacy with a piece of writing, as with a person, comes from paying attention to the revelations it is capable of giving, not by imposing my own preconceived notions, no matter how well-intentioned they might be.

I try to let pretty much anything happen in a first draft. A careful first draft is a failed first draft. That may be why there are so many inaccuracies in the piano lesson memoir: I didn't censor, I didn't judge. I kept moving. But I would not publish this piece as a memoir on its own in its present state. It isn't the "lies" in the piece that give me pause, though a reader has a right to expect a memoir to be as accurate as the writer's memory can make it. No, it isn't the lies themselves that makes the piano lesson memoir a first draft and therefore "unpublishable."

The real trouble: the piece hasn't yet found its subject; it isn't yet about what it wants to be about. Note: what *it* wants, not what I want. The difference has to do with the relation a memoirist—any writer, in fact—has to unconscious or half-known intentions and impulses in composition.

Now that I have the fragment down on paper, I can read this little piece as a mystery which drops clues to the riddle of my feelings, like a culprit who wishes to be apprehended. My narrative self (the culprit who has invented) wishes to be discovered by my reflective self, the self who wants to understand and make sense of a half-remembered story about a nun sneezing in the sun. . . .

We only store in memory images of value. The value may be lost over the passage of time (I was baffled about why I remembered that sneezing nun, for example), but that's the implacable judgment of feeling: *this*, we say somewhere deep within us, is something I'm hanging on to. And of course, often we cleave to things because they possess heavy negative charges. Pain likes to be vivid.

Over time, the value (the feeling) and the stored memory (the image) may become estranged. Memoir seeks a permanent home for feeling and image, a habitation where they can live together in harmony. Naturally, I've had a lot of experiences since I packed away that one from the basement of St. Luke's School; that piano lesson has been effaced by waves of feeling for other moments and episodes. I persist in believing the event has value—after all, I remember it—but in writing the memoir I did not simply relive the experience. Rather, I explored the mysterious relationship between all the images I could round up and the even more impacted feelings that caused me to store the images safely away in memory. Stalking the relationship, seeking the congruence between stored image and hidden emotion—that's the real job of memoir.

By writing about that first piano lesson, I've come to know things I could not know otherwise. But I only know these things as a result of reading this first draft. While I was writing, I was following the images, letting the details fill the room of the page and use the furniture as they wished. I was their dutiful servant—or thought I was. In fact, I was the faithful retainer of my hidden feelings which were giving the commands.

I really did feel, for instance, that Mary Katherine Reilly was far superior to me. She was smarter, funnier, more wonderful in every way—that's how I saw it. Our friendship (or she herself) did not require that I become her vassal, yet perhaps in my heart that was something I wanted; I wanted a way to express my feeling of admiration. I suppose I waited until this memoir to begin to find the way.

Just as, in the memoir, I finally possess that red Thompson book with the barking dogs and bleating lambs and winsome children. I couldn't (and still can't) remember what my own music book was, so I grabbed the name and image of the one book I could remember. It was only in reviewing the piece after writing it that I saw my inaccuracy. In pondering this "lie," I came to see what I was up to: I was getting what I wanted. At last.

The truth of many circumstances and episodes in the past emerges for the memoirist through details (the red music book, the fascination with a nun's name and gleaming face), but these details are not merely information, not flat facts. Such details are not allowed to lounge. They must work. Their work is the creation of symbol. But it's more accurate to call it the *recognition* of symbol. For meaning is not "attached" to the detail by the memoirist; meaning is revealed. That's why a first draft is important. Just as the first meeting (good or bad) with someone who later becomes the beloved is important and is often reviewed for signals, meanings, omens, and indications.

Now I can look at that music book and see it not only as "a detail," but for what it is, how it *acts*. See it as the small red door leading straight into the dark room of my childhood longing and disappointment. That red book *becomes* the palpable evidence of that longing. In other words, it becomes symbol. There is no symbol, no life-of-the-spirit in the general or the abstract. Yet a writer wishes— indeed all of us wish—to speak about profound matters that are, like it or not, general and abstract. We wish to talk to each other about life and death, about love, despair, loss, and innocence. We sense that in order to live together we must learn to speak of peace, of history, of meaning and values. Those are a few.

We seek a means of exchange, a language which will renew these ancient concerns and make them wholly and pulsingly ours. Instinctively, we go to our store of private images and associations for our authority to speak of these weighty issues. We find, in our details and broken and obscured images, the language of symbol. Here memory impulsively reaches out its arms and embraces imagination. That is the resort to invention. It isn't a lie, but an act of necessity, as the innate urge to locate personal truth always is.

All right. Invention is inevitable. But why write memoir? Why not call it fiction and be done with all the hashing about, wondering where memory stops and imagination begins? And if memoir seeks to talk about "the big issues," about history and peace, death and love—why not leave these reflections to those with expert and scholarly knowledge? Why let the common or garden variety memoirist into the club? I'm thinking again of that bumper sticker: why Question Authority?

My answer, of course, is a memoirist's answer. Memoir must be written because each of us must have a created version of the past. Created: that is, real, tangible, made of the stuff of a life lived in place and in history. And the down side of any created thing as well: we must live with a version that attaches us to our limitations, to the inevitable subjectivity, of our points of view. We must acquiesce to our experience and our gift to transform experience into meaning and value. You tell me your story, I'll tell you my story.

If we refuse to do the work of creating this personal version of the past, someone else will do it for us. That is a scary political fact. "The struggle of man against power," a character in Milan Kundera's novel *The Book of Laughter and Forgetting* says, "is the struggle of memory against forgetting." He refers to willful political forgetting, the habit of nations and those in power (Question Authority!) to deny the truth of memory in order to disarm moral and ethical power. It's an efficient way of controlling masses of people. It doesn't even require much bloodshed, as long as people are entirely willing to give over their personal memories. Whole histories can be rewritten. As Czeslaw Milosz said in his 1980 Nobel Prize lecture, the number of books published that seek to deny the existence of the Nazi death camps now exceeds one hundred.

What is remembered is what *becomes* reality. If we "forget" Auschwitz, if we "forget" My Lai, what then do we remember? And what is the purpose of our remembering? If we think of memory naively, as a simple story, logged like a documentary in the archive of the mind, we miss its beauty but also its function. The beauty of memory rests in its talent for rendering detail, for paying homage to the senses, its capacity to love the particles of life, the richness and idiosyncrasy of our existence. The function of memory, on the other hand, is intensely personal and surprisingly political.

Our capacity to move forward as developing beings rests on a healthy relation with the past. Psychotherapy, that widespread method of mental health, relies heavily on memory and on the ability to retrieve and organize images and events from the personal past. We carry our wounds and perhaps even worse, our capacity to wound, forward with us. If we learn not only to tell our stories but to listen to what our stories tell us—to write the first draft and then return for the second draft—we are doing the work of memoir.

Memoir is the intersection of narration and reflection, of story-telling and essay-writing. It can present its story *and* reflect and consider the meaning of the story. It is a peculiarly open form, inviting broken and incomplete images, half-recollected fragments, all the mass (and mess) of detail. It offers to shape this confusion—and in shaping, of course it necessarily creates a work of art, not a legal document. But then, even legal documents are only valiant attempts to consign the truth, the whole truth and nothing but the truth to paper. Even they remain versions.

Locating touchstones—the red music book, the olive Olive, my father's violin playing—is deeply satisfying. Who knows why? Perhaps we all sense that we can't grasp the whole truth and nothing but the truth of our experience. Just can't be done. What can be achieved, however, is a version of its swirling, changing wholeness. A memoirist must acquiesce to selectivity, like any artist. The version we dare to write is the only truth, the only relationship we can have with the past. Refuse to write your life and you have no life. At least, that is the stern view of the memoirist.

Personal history, logged in memory, is a sort of slide projector flashing images on the wall of the mind. And there's precious little order to the slides in the rotating carousel. Beyond that confusion, who knows who is running the projector? A memoirist steps into this darkened room of flashing, unorganized images and stands blinking for a while. Maybe for a long while. But eventually, as with any attempt to tell a story, it is necessary to put something first, then something else. And so on, to the end. That's a first draft. Not necessarily the truth, not even *a* truth sometimes, but the first attempt to create a shape.

The first thing I usually notice at this stage of composition is the appalling inaccuracy of the piece. Witness my first piano lesson draft. Invention is screamingly evident in what I intended to be transcription. But here's the further truth: I feel no shame. In fact, it's only now that my interest in the piece truly quickens. For I can see what isn't there, what is shyly hugging the walls, hoping not to be seen. I see the filmy shape of the next draft. I see a more acute version of the episode or—this is more likely—an entirely new piece rising from the ashes of the first attempt.

The next draft of the piece would have to be a true re-vision, a new seeing of the materials of the first draft. Nothing merely cosmetic will do—no rouge buffing up the opening sentence, no glossy adjective to lift a sagging line, nothing to attempt covering a patch of gray writing. None of that. I can't say for sure, but my hunch is the revision would lead me to more writing about my father (why was I so impressed by that ancestral inventor of the collapsible opera hat? Did I feel I had nothing as remarkable in my own background? Did this make me feel inadequate?). I begin to think perhaps Sister Olive is less central to this business than she is in this draft. She is meant to be a moment, not a character.

And so I might proceed, if I were to undertake a new draft of the memoir. I begin to feel a relationship developing between a former self and me.

And, even more compelling, a relationship between an old world and me. Some people think of autobiographical writing as the precious occupation of a particularly self-absorbed person. Maybe, but I don't buy that. True memoir is written in an attempt to find not only a self but a world.

The self-absorption that seems to be the impetus and embarrassment of autobiography turns into (or perhaps always was) a hunger for the world. Actually, it begins as hunger for *a* world, one gone or lost, effaced by time or a more sudden brutality. But in the act of remembering, the personal environment expands, resonates beyond itself, beyond its "subject," into the endless and tragic recollection that is history.

We look at old family photographs in which we stand next to black, boxy Fords and are wearing period costumes, and we do not gaze fascinated because there we are young again, or there we are standing, as we never will again in life, next to our mother. We stare and drift because there we are . . . historical. It is the dress, the black car that dazzle us now and draw us beyond our mother's bright arms which once caught us. We reach into the attractive impersonality of something more significant than ourselves. We write memoir, in other words. We accept the humble position of writing a version rather than "the whole truth."

I suppose I write memoir because of the radiance of the past—it draws me back and back to it. Not that the past is beautiful. In our communal memoir, in history, the death camps *are* back there. In intimate life too, the record is usually pretty mixed. "I could tell you stories . . . " people say and drift off, meaning terrible things have happened to them.

But the past is radiant. It has the light of lived life. A memoirist wishes to touch it. No one owns the past, though typically the first act of new political regimes, whether of the left or the right, is to attempt to re-write history, to grab the past and make it over so the end comes out right. So their power looks inevitable.

No one owns the past, but it is a grave error (another age would have said a grave sin) not to inhabit memory. Sometimes I think it is all we really have. But that may be a trifle melodramatic. At any rate, memory possesses authority for the fearful self in a world where it is necessary to have authority in order to Question Authority.

There may be no more pressing intellectual need in our culture than for people to become sophisticated about the function of memory. The political implications of the loss of memory are obvious. The authority of memory is a personal confirmation of selfhood. To write one's life is to live it twice, and the second living is both spiritual and historical, for a memoir reaches deep within the personality as it seeks its narrative form and also grasps the life-of-the-times as no political treatise can.

Our most ancient metaphor says life is a journey. Memoir is travel writing, then, notes taken along the way, telling how things looked and what thoughts occurred. But I cannot think of the memoirist as a tourist. This is the traveller who goes on foot, living the journey, taking on mountains, enduring deserts, marveling at the lush green places. Moving through it all faithfully, not so much a survivor with a harrowing tale to tell as a pilgrim, seeking, wondering.

Sherman Alexie

Sherman Alexie (1966-) grew up on the Spokane Indian reservation in Washington state and is a member of the Spokane and Coeur D'Alene tribes. Since 1992, Alexie has published several novels, as well as collections of poetry and short stories. The film Smoke Signals *(Chris Eyre, 1998) was based on Alexie's short story collection* The Lone Ranger and Tonto Fistfight in Heaven *(1993). The article "She Had Some Horses: The Education of a Poet," based on the poet Joy Harjo's influence on Alexie's own work, first appeared in the journal* Teachers & Writers *in 1995. Alexie currently lives in Seattle and is at work on a documentary film.*

She Had Some Horses:
The Education of a Poet

I grew up on the Spokane Indian Reservation—Wellpinit was the name of the town. I grew up poor, but not real poor. We had to go on commodity food only every once in a while, the lights were off only once in a while, and sometimes we'd get a phone: that was our vacation. We'd call our next-door neighbors, even though we could have yelled to them just as well. That's how I grew up, in that poverty, with alcoholic parents, an alcoholic older sister, and most of my cousins and other relatives either alcoholics or recovering alcoholics. Like many kids in that situation, I learned to retreat into myself. From the beginning I was good at dropping into my imagination and being absent from things going on around me—I'm still good at it. Like sometimes when I'm giving a reading and it's not going well, I drop into my imagination. In that sense I've always been a "storyteller."

But in terms of reading material, when I was growing up on the reservation, nobody ever told me that Indians wrote. I went up through eighth grade at a tribal school on the reservation and not once did anyone ever tell me that Indians wrote books. We did get a lot of books, though, those Indian books written by non-Indians, in which everyone was hunting buffalo, everyone was in warpaint, everyone was running across the Great Plains. It was always about the Plains Indians or the Navahos. There never were any books about Spokane Indians. I guess we weren't glamorous enough: we didn't hunt buffalo, except once every couple of years. We were essentially a fishing tribe, and I don't think salmon fishing translates well to the big screen. *Dances with Salmon?* [From the audience: "Salmon Bill Cody!"] Ha ha, that's good! I'll have to remember that one! But I never saw any positive representation of Indians: Tonto, "F Troop." Even in tribal school they were teaching us that Columbus discovered America.

We had white teachers, white *missionary* teachers usually, which amounted to torture. Even at that age I challenged teachers a lot. I challenged one teacher, who got mad at me and made me hold a math book in one hand, a Bible in the other, and stand eagle-armed for an hour in front of the classroom. In terms of self-image or self-esteem, I thought Indians were either the stuff going on in the books, the TV shows, and the movies—the idea of being beaten because you're an Indian. That was my whole image of being Indian.

Then I started going to a white school just off the reservation. But nobody told me that Indians wrote there either. It was the same stuff over and over again.

Then I got into college, Gonzaga University in Spokane, a Jesuit University. I wonder why I went there: they were always chasing me around, trying to save me. The original mission of the school was to educate Indians. I'd skip class and they'd call me and ask, "Why are you skipping class?" I'd answer, "Because I'm sleeping in," and they'd go on and on and on. I'd have nightmares about being chased around by priests who'd lift up their cassocks and they'd be wearing Nikes and I'd have boots on or cheap K Mart fall-aparts. Finally I left the school. Nobody there had told me that Indians wrote stories. So I didn't know.

I transferred to Washington State. I started out in pre-med, because I was very good in chemistry and science. But you have to take human anatomy classes, and the first time I walked in, there was a cadaver, and I fainted. The professor told me that people do that all the time, and to come back. The second time I was fine, but when the professor reached in and pulled out something that looked like meatloaf, I fainted again. The professor said, "That happens. People have fainted twice and gone on to become doctors. Don't worry about it." So I went back for the third time, and I worked on the body. I was doing really well. At one point—we were working in the evening to get me caught up—the professor asked if I was thirsty. I went to the fridge to get us a Coke. In the fridge was an "iso-organ," which is short for "isolated organ." In this case, it was an arm, and the two Cokes were there in the crook of the arm. And I fainted again. So I needed a career change.

Creative writing was the only course that fit into my schedule: once a week on Tuesday afternoon. I got into class and I sat down with 50 other students and the teacher, Alex Kuo, said, "OK, I'm going to call out your names and look at you and tell you what grade you will get in this class. I've been doing this for 15 years and I run about 90 percent accurate." The next time the class met, there were 20 of us. He scared everybody! I was getting a little scared.

The first assignment was to write five poems and turn them in next week. I had taken a lot of English classes and my whole idea of poetry was informed by Keats and Yeats and Eliot and Pound, but I had never read anything past "The Waste Land." But I went home and sat down and wrote. In the first poems I wrote, the linebreaks were pretty much determined by how long I could say them without running out of breath. I found out later that that was called a breath unit and that Robert Creeley and other poets had been doing it for a long time. I turned in the poems the next day, and just before class the teacher called me outside and asked me what I was planning on doing with the rest of my life. I said that had no idea. He said, "I think you should write." Being malleable at that point, I said, "OK."

Then he brought me an anthology of contemporary Native-American poetry called *Songs from This Earth on Turtle's Back*, and said, "I think you should read this." I took it home and opened it up and—I expected more of what I had been reading: the four directions, corn pollen, eagle feather all that kind of "Indian" stuff—but it had all this amazing stuff. Back then I loved it all. I've become more discriminating now, but back then it was amazing to me. The first time I saw the phrase *commodity cheese* in a poem, it was some sort of an epiphany for me! To have someone write about commodity foods, about drunkenness . . .

The first person whose work really got to me in that book was Joy Harjo. I wish I could remember exactly what was that got to me so strongly, but I'm not really sure what it was. Probably the first thing was her use of repetition, the chantlike quality of her work. The first poem of hers I read was "She Had Some Horses":

> She had some horses.
>
> She had horses who were bodies of sand.
> She had horses who were maps drawn of blood.
> She had horses who were skins of ocean water.
> She had horses who were blue air of sky.
> She had horses who were fur and teeth.
> She had horses who were clay and would break.
> She had horses who were splintered red cliff.
> She had some horses.
>
> She had horses with long, pointed breasts.
> She had horses with full, brown thighs.
> She had horses who laughed too much.
> She had horses who threw rocks at glass houses.
> She had horses who licked razor blades.
>
> She had some horses.
>
> She had horses who danced in their mothers' arms.
> She had horses who thought they were the sun and their
>   bodies shone and burned like stars.
> She had horses who waltzed nightly on the moon.
> She had horses who were much too shy, and kept quiet in
>   stalls of their own making.
>
> She had some horses.
>
> She had horses who liked Creek Stomp Dance songs.
> She had horses who cried in their beer.
> She had horses who spit at male queens who made them
>   afraid of themselves.
> She had horses who said they weren't afraid.
> She had horses who lied.
> She had horses who told the truth, who were stripped bare of
>   their tongues.

She had some horses.

She had horses who called themselves "horse."
She had horses who called themselves "spirit," and kept their
voices secret and to themselves.
She had horses who had no names.
She had horses who had books of names.

She had some horses.

She had horses who whispered in the dark, who were afraid
to speak.
She had horses who screamed out of fear of the silence, who
carried knives to protect themselves from ghosts.
She had horses who waited for destruction.
She had horses who waited for resurrection.

She had some horses.

She had horses who got down on their knees for any saviour.
She had horses who thought their high price had saved them.
She had horses who tried to save her, who climbed in her bed
at night and prayed as they raped her.

She had some horses.

She had some horses she loved.
She had some horses she hated.

These were the same horses.

And I read that and I said, "Whoa!" My first thought was: I know horses exactly like that. And I did something I had never done before, either in class or out: I read the poem loud. It made me feel it aloud. I sat there reading that poem and others of hers aloud. The music of it started, but it wasn't the music I'd been taught about in poetry: iambic pentameter, end-rhyme, or alliteration. Hers was a different kind of music. It was really the first time I identified with poetry, and the first time I had a positive representation of what it means to be Native American. So it was great! I started going crazy. I write a lot now, but back then I was *really* crazy. I'd stay up all night long writing poems, churn out 20, 30 pages of poems a night, for weeks on end. It was like a huge opening. It was as if I had pulled out a plug and spilled out this big mess. It was messy and accidental.

At that time, Joy Harjo had published just one little book, which I read over and over. And I wrote her a letter—my teacher had her address—and sent her a few poems. I get those letters now, and I wonder if I sounded to her the way people sound to me now: sort of fawning and desperate? I know I did. And I love the letters I get, that have that big "search" quality. And I always write back. I don't care who or where they are, I always write back.

I remember the feeling I had, a few weeks after writing to her, when I went down to the mailbox and pulled out a letter that said "Joy Harjo" up in the corner, in the return address. It was thick letter. I started shaking. I walked up to my apartment, clutching the letter the whole way back. I wanted to stop and read it, but I kept walking, my heart beating like crazy. I sat down in my student apartment with no furniture, a black and white TV hooked up to a TV dinner tray so I could get better reception, milk crates, no phone. The letter started off, "I like your poems," and I stayed on that sentence for a long time. Because I expected the next sentence to begin, "But . . ." or "However. . . ." But instead it was a wonderful letter. I still have it at home. I get it out and read it once in a while, especially whenever I get discouraged. It talked about poetry, about growing up, and about being Indian, and she gave me some advice. She said, "A writing career is about writing." You don't hear that very much. Writers tend to be self-important and egotistical, throwing out terms like "muse" and using a huge vocabulary about what it means to be a writer. All of which is true, but it was way out there for me: I didn't know what they meant. But she said simply, "Writing is about writing." Which I understood. Because I was a guy up until three or four in the morning, and then skipping the class the next day because I had spent the whole night writing. And she said, "Writing is about ink."

And the next big news I got was that she was coming to Pullman to read, in about three months. So I had to prepare!

I'm going to admit some funny things. Joy Harjo is a very beautiful woman: I could tell by the photographs. So I had these huge dreams about her, which I never wrote about, because I get these letters now from fans who dream the same kind of things and which I don't really care to know about! I suppose at the beginning I deified her, way above where I could ever be or do. In my fantasy she would come off the plane and we'd fall in love and run away together. I had carried this dream around with me for a week or so when Alex, my teacher, who was a friend of hers, told me she is lesbian. Well, there went my dream! But that got me thinking again: she is a lesbian writer. I had to reevaluate everything. Not that I didn't know any lesbians or gays. It was just that I had never read any work knowing the author was lesbian or gay. So I asked Alex, "Who else is?"

He looked at his bookshelves and said, "He is and he is and she is and she is and he is," and on and on and on, with me saying, "Oh, really?"

So I had to go back and read her again: brand new interpretation. My new knowledge changed this poem of hers, called "September Moon":

> Last night she called and told me
> about the moon over San Francisco Bay.
> Here in Albuquerque it is mirrored
> in a cool, dark, Sandia sky.
> The reflection is within all of us.
> Orange, and almost the harvest
> moon. Wind and the chill of the colder
> months coming on. The children and I
> watched it, crossed San Pedro and Central
> coming up from the state fair.
> Wind blowing my hair was caught
> in my face. I was fearful of traffic,

trying to keep my steps and the moon was east,
ballooning out of the mountain ridge, out of smokey clouds
out of any skin that was covering her. Naked.
Such beauty.

Look.

We are alive. The woman of the moon looking
at us, and we looking at her, acknowledging
each other.

All this started me thinking about where we write out of. OK, she's Indian, I understood that. She's writing out of being Indian, out of being disadvantaged, out of oppression, out of the pain of that, pain inflicted and self-inflicted. That was my first concept of her writing. It was only when I thought of her writing as that of a lesbian that I thought of her writing as a woman. Poetry wasn't as simple as I thought. I was one of those arrogant guys who start out as pretty good writers to begin with, but think they're a lot better than they are. So I was humbled by that experience.

And now that she was coming in a couple of months, I had to re-prepare. Alex gave me a reading list and I went to the library for three or four anthologies of gay writing, which I read over and over. It was at this time that I had my first poem accepted for publication, in *Hanging Loose*.

I started to look more closely at how poetry works, such as the use of line-breaks. I was writing free verse randomly—wherever it felt like I should break the line, I broke it. And gave it no thought. But then I realized that there were all these different ways to do lines: not only can you write out of your own situation, you can break lines in your own way too. Then Alex showed me a movie in which Robert Creeley talked about linebreaks, and I understood.

The thought then occurred to me: How do you write poems in English? You're an Indian, you should be writing in your own language. The whole half-breed thing started getting to me. How can I be honest? "Anchorage," a poem of Joy's, helped me. By the way, a good thing about Joy's poems (and poems by others, of course) is that they're dedicated to people, or use epigraphs from people I've never heard of. It makes me go search their work out. She dedicated this poem to Audre Lorde, which led me to Audre Lorde's work (I could go on about that for an hour, too). Here's "Anchorage":

This city is made of stone, of blood, and fish,
There are Chugatch Mountains to the east
and whale and seal to the west.
It hasn't always been this way, because glaciers
who are ice ghosts create oceans, carve earth
and shape this city here, by the sound.
They swim backwards in time.

Once a storm of boiling earth cracked open
the streets, threw open the town.
It's quiet now, but underneath the concrete

is the cooking earth,
and above that, air
which is another ocean, where spirits we can't see
are dancing   joking   getting full
on roasted caribou, and the praying
goes on, extends out.

Nora and I go walking down 4th Avenue
and know it is all happening.
On a park bench we see someone's Athabascan
grandmother, folded up, smelling like 200 years
of blood and piss, her eyes closed against some
unimagined darkness, where she is buried in an ache
in which nothing makes

                             sense.

We keep on breathing, walking, but softer now.
the clouds whirling in the air above us.
What can we say that would make us understand
better than we do already?
Except to speak of her home and claim her
as out own history, and know that our dreams
don't end here, two blocks away from the ocean
where our hearts still batter away at the muddy shore.

And I think of the 6th Avenue jail, of mostly Native
and Black men, where Henry told about being shot at
eight times outside a liquor store in L.A., but when
the car sped away he was surprised he was alive,
no bullet holes, man, and eight cartridges strewn
on the side walk

                        all around him.

Everyone laughed at the impossibility of it,
but also the truth. Because who would believe
the fantastic and terrible story of all of our survival
those who were never meant

                         to survive?

So then I caught on. *Survive*! It was as if she had used that word 15 times in this poem. *Survive, survive.* So just when I figure that I understood what was going on technically, I realized that it all goes back to survival. OK, I understood how she used linebreaks, how she writes about being an Indian, a woman, a lesbian, a poor person. But I kept trying to understand it all together, as if I could own it, as if I could reach in and grab it.

So I was deifying her. And then she shows up. Gets of the plane. I meet her at the gate—it was my job. She didn't fall in love with me! But the first thing she said when we go in the car was, "I like your poems."

I was being calm: "Thanks." But inside I'm going, "Yes, yes!" And I started asking her questions, like, "Why did you do such-and-such a linebreak?" "What made you write this?" "Why did you move those lines all the way over to the side of the page?" On and on and on.

She answered them. Since then I've seen her interviewed by people like Bill Moyers, and thought to myself, "Oh, I asked her those same dumb questions!" I didn't know how to ask her the right questions. I don't even know what the right questions might have been. But when her reading started, I realized, there aren't any answers. She's a good reader, but she stumbled a few times, lost her place, even read a few new poems I didn't think were very good. She talked about how she was having a difficult time with the memoir she was working on, and about the fact that she was writing short stories and finding it to be a problem. Sitting in the audience there, I realized that it's all about *questions* . . . .

The biggest effect Joy Harjo had on me was that she was the first writer who gave me permission to write. We all need that, because we think we need it.

I'll finish with this poem, called "Song":

> Brown-skinned women
> I dreamed of you
> long before
> any of you decided
> to dream about me.
> I slept on the top bunk
> of my U.S. Army Surplus bed

and pretended one of you was asleep on the bottom bunk beneath me.
Too young to fully understand what that physical presence would've
meant, I still knew it was what I needed. But like anything believed too
hard, those dreams always failed me. I remember all your names. Indian
girls I loved, Dawn, Loretta, Michelle, Jana, Go-Go, LuLu, all of you
Spokane Indian princesses who never asked me to slow dance

> to the music
> that always found its way
> into the Tribal School
> and it wasn't only drums
> we heard, you know?
> The reservation has a symphony
> complicated as any
> and we all practiced
> the fingering
> on the piano, on the pine trees
> on the secondhand trumpets

but I was always outside the chords, just a little too short for the melody,
and too skinny for the tempo. Oh, I loved it all from a distance, from
inches and miles away, from a generation removed it seemed. And I
loved you all, crazy and brave, in your young Indian arrogance

and I love you still
when I see any of you
all these years later
often broken
and defeated by this reservation
by alcohol

when I see you in the bars, your faces scarred and scared. Sometimes, I
think I love you because your failures validate mine and because my
successes move me beyond the same boundaries that stop you. I can be
as selfish as any white or Indian man. Sometimes, I think I love you
because you all still slow dance with the next Indian man who might
save you. I can hear your bar voice crack into questions. *What tribe are
you? Are you married? How long have you been sober/drunk?* Sometimes,
I think I love you

because it's always easiest
to love the unloved
to dream
about the dreamless
to watch an Indian woman
just this side
of beautiful
slow dance
to a sad song
and never have to worry
about making her any promises

because this distance I've created is perfect. I can never be hurt. Don't
you see? I am afraid; I am not afraid. Don't you understand? I know
some of you will die in car wrecks. I know some of you will die of cirrhosis.
I know some of you will die of a broken heart. But more than
that, I know some of you will live, will learn how to breathe this
twentieth-century oxygen

and learn how
to dance a new dance
with the rhythm
only Indians possess
with the rhythm
innate
practiced
beautiful

and I can hope you'll find your new warriors. Believe me, the Indian
men are rising from the alleys and doorways, rising from self-hatred and
self-pity, rising up on horses of their own making. Believe me, the warriors
are coming back

to take their place beside you
rising
beyond the "just surviving"
singing
those new songs
that sound
exactly
like the old ones.

2

Rereading Hollywood

Mary Beth Callie

lens: a shape of transparent material (usually glass) with either or both sides curved to gather and focus light rays. Most camera and projector lenses place a series of lenses within a metal tube to form a compound lens.

filter: a piece of glass or gelatin placed in front of the camera or printer lens to alter the quality or quantity of light striking the film in the aperture.

David Bordwell and Kristin Thompson, *Film Art*

It is Wednesday night and you need a break from a rough day. You and your new roommate decide to camp out at Gallagher Theater to see *Legends of the Fall*. After a several-hour wait you make it into the theater, get some popcorn and Red Vines, settle into your seats, and pull out your glasses. The movie begins, and you are immersed in a frontier world eighty years and a thousand miles from the university. . . . Two-and-a-half hours later the lights go up and everyone starts filing out as the credits roll behind them. When you remark, "That was great!" your friend responds, "I don't know, I thought it was pretty sappy at times." . . . While Siskel and Ebert have mixed opinions, M. Scot Skinner of the *Arizona Daily Star* thinks very little of the movie. He compared it to *Bonanza*. You begin to doubt whether you had all seen the same movie. . . .

Why did you all see *Legends of the Fall* so differently? In a sense, each person had put on a different pair of glasses, each equipped with different sorts of lenses and filters. These lenses and filters shaped how each person made sense of the story. Like all storytelling, Hollywood movies have the power to entertain, to horrify, to thrill; they can touch us emotionally, help us see the world differently, perpetuate or challenge stereotypes, or be the most boring way you've spent two hours in a long time. The complex interaction of producers' motives and financial interests, standardized processes, and collaborative artistry make movies multilayered and their reception a complicated process.

The entertainment industry is a billion-dollar, multinational business. Media companies like Time-Warner, Turner Entertainment and Disney do not just make and distribute movies and TV programs—they also own publishing companies, magazines, record labels, chain stores, theme parks and cable networks. These media companies have become the world's most pervasive storytellers. Stories shape how we look at the world, history and social problems. Through the images and narrative patterns of film, social norms and values become entrenched to the point that they seem natural and inevitable.

Movies are often the focus of our leisure time and the topic of national conversation. In the average day you may come across a good deal of writing and talk about the movies. Magazines such as *Premiere and Entertainment* Weekly and TV shows such as *Entertainment Tonight* and the cable network *E!* offer behind-the-scenes news and reviews for the general public. We often hear reports on box office grosses or on how much a movie cost to make. This conversation is driven by marketing, which sets parameters on the ways that we learn to see movies.

Movie reviewers and scholars provide readers or viewers with certain ways of seeing. Standard movie reviews found in mainstream magazines and newspapers ask us to focus on the plot and actors' performances. For example, one reviewer might claim that while *Legends* is too contrived and Brad Pitt too glamorized, Anthony Hopkins is perfect in the role of the father and the cinematography is spectacular. On the other end of the spectrum, specialized academic journals, such as *Wild Angle* and *Screen*, offer more developed analyses of individual films, genres, periods and film-makers. Some scholars might examine the film as a Western or epic and question its depiction of history, of the frontier, of contact between Native Americans and pioneers. Their writings advocate a certain perspective and study.

This chapter provides essays that fit between the promotional hype and specialized scholarly analyses. Depending on your reading experiences, you may or may not have come across this type of writing before. These film essays, written by journalists and scholars and found in the pages of magazines, journals, and newspapers such as *Film Comment, Sight and Sound, Journal of Popular Film and Television*, and *The New York Times*, offer challenging yet accessible readings to a wide range of readers. The essays provide models for your own viewing and writing. As you read the developed and often highly researched analyses, consider what questions are at the root of each writer's particular interpretation or reading. What enables a writer to see what he/she sees? Imagine that we all are wearing invisible glasses, whether we know it or not. A first step in becoming a perceptive writer is becoming aware of the effects of your own glasses. Though socialization an individual inherits the glasses of a whole culture, subculture, and school of thought. These predict and shape the way we perceive and make sense of the world. Yet, time, history and a unique combination of lived experience also ensure variety and nuances of perception. A writer's "reading glasses" are developed over a whole lifetime. Life experiences and rigorous academic study grind and polish the lenses. The lenses in these glasses allow these writers to see what may have gone unrecognized or unnoticed before.

Yet, why do these writers, and why should we, pull out reading glasses and closely examine movies and our own responses to movies? Some people within and outside the media industry argue that movies and TV shows are *just* entertainment: "We shouldn't read into them too much." However, these very claims paradoxically carry within them the most urgent calls to write about movies. The articles in this chapter springboard from the fact that films *are* designed to be entertaining and popular. Certainly some genres—Westerns like *Tombstone* or *Dances with Wolves*; action-adventures like *Terminator II*; romantic comedies like *While You Were Sleeping*—can provide escape or help us deal with today's social conflicts and anxieties. The fact that these genres perform certain social functions leads to further questions:

- How do film-makers provide escape?
- What does it take for a film to be "entertaining"?
- What can we learn about our culture when we consider what is entertaining and popular?
- How can many films work to confirm preexisting perceptions and stereotypes while others can provide the viewer with a fresh way of understanding and relating to the world and others?
- How are the films more complicated and multi-voiced than they first appear? How are they often contradictory collaborative efforts?
- How can movies work on multiple levels—depending on how the viewer "sees" the film?

This chapter offers examples of how to examine and write critically about the cultural workings of Hollywood and alternative movies. All these writers are essentially modeling "reader response," "rhetorical" and "contextual analysis"— the same types of writing you are learning in English 101. You can also take questions about "social context" and the relations between "authors" and "audiences" and apply them to other academic, professional and daily experiences. By examining these writers closely and critically you can begin to build your own repertoire of choices and strategies. For example:

- What makes the writings and similar to or different from what you've read before? What makes the reading difficult, interesting or questionable?
- How does their analysis depend on an understanding of how films are put together?
- How is each writer's understanding of the film as craft shaped by an underlying ideological perspective? How does the lens hold the essay together?
- How do some of the writers move from general, more theoretical claims to closer, detailed analysis of individual scenes and shots?

- What is the tone and style of the writing: is it presented as documented analysis or as more spontaneous and reflective?
- How do the writers develop sustained analyses based on particular "readings" of how a film represents gender, race or ethnicity?

What unites these writers is that they read against the grain of market-driven or topical responses. To do so, their writing draws on broad historical, cultural and mythic contexts, and also pays close attention to the details and complexities. Many place individual films in the context of whole genres in order to question how and why genres work and change. They demonstrate how today's films build on, adapt and/or perpetuate existing cultural myths. Whereas the heroine of *The Little Mermaid* was widely celebrated as Disney's new positive role model for girls, Roberta Trites' comparison of the movie with its folk tale source suggests otherwise. Whereas many viewers left *Natural Born Killers* confused or disturbed, Gavin Smith's interview with director Oliver Stone explores the movie's rhetorical and satiric strategies.

Implicit in the writers' analyses is that they read film as narrative. This standard lens leads them to assume that films are unified and that they use storytelling devices in order to deal with basic human conflicts. As the craft emerged one hundred years ago, early film-makers borrowed techniques of other media and genres. Like ancient myths, short stories, plays and novels, films have basic structural and thematic features. All the parts should work towards a whole. In *Film Art: An Introduction*, David Bordwell and Kristin Thompson explain that a distinctive narrative form came to dominate cinema; they refer to this mode as "classical Hollywood cinema." In this form, individuals—not nature or society—are assumed to be central "causal agents." In a Hollywood movie, characters make decisions and choices as they try to fulfill their "desire" and attain a primary "goal."

A narrative develops as a character faces small goals and "counter forces," or conflicts, along the way. Thus, while *Legends of the Fall* may appear to be a sweeping historical epic, it is more deeply the story of Tristan (Brad Pitt). In the beginning of the movie he desires to be wild and explore the world—thus he leaves behind the woman he loves. Seeing the film through this lens helps us to see through the comments and understand the critiques of many reviewers. For example, while Leonard Klad of *Variety* recognized that the screen adapters detail "the forces—internal and external—that erode the family unit," many other reviewers flippantly compared the movie to the father and sons of the 1970's television Western *Bonanza*.

Some argue that this reductive comparison blinded reviewers to the complexities and layers of Legends. Others might say that the similarities reveal the film for what it is: a formula star vehicle for Brad Pitt that mechanically blends epic and melodramatic elements but is at its core a Western about rugged men. Martin Peretz, a writer for *The New Republic*, describes how he began to see through reviewers' perceptions:

> I saw Edward Zwicks's *Legends of the Fall* last weekend. The first time out, I went just to see it. This time I went to understand why a few movie critics, including Stanley Kauffman, didn't like it. My impression is that they were so rattled by its epic aspects that they

didn't see it for what it was: an intimate tale with classical, or to be more precise, biblical resonance. (43)

Based on his own re-viewing, Peretz speculates that reviewers had seen the film through a filter that made them blind to the mythic qualities of the story. Changing the lens and filter changes the evaluation: perhaps reviewers were so busy with the sweeping epic views that they paid little attention to the "classical" father/son story and possible complexities of character and relationships.

As you experiment with new reading glasses and develop your own writing, you too will begin to see more layers on the screen and see into viewers' responses. Most discussions about particular movies or genres will discuss how the film is crafted—characters, actors, photography, editing, and so forth. However, how a writer interprets the meaning of these elements depends on his/her ideological perspective and how it is developed. For example, when Brian D. Wilson of *Mac-Clean's* sees the main characters of *Nobody's Fool* and *Legends of the Fall* as fantasy "renegade males," we might recognize that he perceives the film and its maker's intentions through a sociological lens. When Stanley Kauffman of *The New Republic* proclaims that the Western story centers on males and "the few women in the film are props for male actors" we might realize that he is using the lenses of gender and genre. When James Bowman of *The American Spectator* comments that the film is "Harlequin romance brought to the screen as a vehicle for the teen heartthrob, Brad Pitt," we can see that his understanding is based in comparison and a knowledge of how films are cast and marketed for audiences. When Christopher Miller compares *Legends of the Fall* and *Little Women*, we see that he is focusing on how film-makers use voice-over in literary adaptations. These writers focus their attention on certain features of the movie. Each sees a film's craft through a certain ideological perspective.

Movies and audiences are complex and multifaceted. By considering how a Hollywood narrative and genres work, and how audiences are socialized to "see" films in certain kinds of ways, we can begin to examine and write about how the different layers and complexities work together. In the above responses to *Legends of the Fall*, the writers touched on certain analyses, but because of the constraints of time and space, style and perspective, only went so far. Your own writing can employ the lenses and strategies modeled in this chapter in order to develop substantial analysis. As Timothy Corrigan explains in *A Short Guide to Writing About Film*:

> To write an intelligent, perceptive analysis of the stories and characters in the movies, you must be prepared to see them as constructed according to certain forms and styles that arise from many different historical influences. This is what analysis of the movies is fundamentally about: examining how a subject has been framed to mean something specific through the power of art, technology, and commerce. (22–23)

Use these essays to help you examine the films and themes that you might be studying in your English 101 course. You can explore how a movie or whole genre uses cultural myth and narrative strategies. You can see how the seemingly unified final cut that appears on the movie or television screen is shaped by forms and styles, technology and commerce. If you want to consider issues of violence and war you might take a look at essays on the action-adventure or war genres. You could think about issues of gender and how they intersect with race and history. You can examine *Legends of the Fall*, or countless other films, as Hollywood blockbusters or explore how a low-budget, independent film compares to and contrasts with a Hollywood film. Like the writers in this chapter you can "see" deeply into what you may have not seen or glossed over before.

This discussion of how *Legends of the Fall* has been and can be re-viewed and written about is only one example of countless applications. Like the writers in this chapter, I have witnessed the way my own reading glasses have changed since I saw my first movie, *Cinderella*. Studying history, literature, political economy and filmmaking have helped me to see movies on multiple levels. As a child I saw just the plot and actors; now I question how a film is presented and what has been emphasized or left out. Nonetheless, at times I am as emotionally affected by certain films and genres as I have always been. Sometimes a movie is so overpowering that I will not begin to make sense of its complexities or implications until later or until after a second or third viewing. Sometimes a movie is so layered that I will recognize new elements at each viewing. Other times new knowledge and experience—for example when I studied editing and then made my own movie—allow me to see the effects of certain techniques in a new way. My friends and I have gone to movies and found them much more interesting and complicated than reviewers make them out to be. On the other hand, I may not get to see much in a film if I do not have the necessary background or if I never have been a fan of its genre or cast. Even though I will know on one level that a movie is formulaic and has a lot of flaws, I will sometimes be drawn in by other elements. As you read the essays in this chapter and the others, reflect on how your own lenses change and develop; as you see movies in class or late one Wednesday night, experiment with and reflect on your own ways of seeing.

And now, our feature presentations. . . .

Greg M. Smith

Greg M. Smith teaches in the Communications department at Carlow College in Pittsburgh, PA. He is finishing his dissertation at the University of Wisconsin-Madison on film and emotion. He has published several essays in Cinema Journal, *the journal for the Society for Cinema Studies, and an edited collection entitled* On a Silver Platter: CD-ROMs and the Promise of a New Technology *(1999).* Cinema Journal *is published by the Society for Cinema Studies and is one of the major journals in academic film and television studies.*

"It's Just a Movie": A Teaching Essay for Introductory Media Classes

The question arises almost every semester. My introductory film class and I will be hip deep in analyzing the details of a film and a hand will creep up, usually from the back: "Aren't we reading too much into this? After all, it's just a movie." Taking a deep breath, I launch into a spirited defense of our analytic activity. After five or ten minutes, the student usually has a shell-shocked, what-did-I-do-to-deserve-this look on her face.

I have never been pleased with my spur-of-the-moment justifications of film analysis, which tend to come across as a bit defensive. Worst of all, they do not deal fully with the question, which I believe is very profound. Why are we spending so much time finding new meanings in something as insignificant as a movie? Aren't we just "reading into" the film? The student's question deserves a fuller answer, or, rather, it deserves several answers. As a way of finding those answers, this essay extends the dialogue started by that series of brave, inquiring students in my classes.

Leaving Nothing to Chance.

"All right, do you really think that every little thing in the film is there for a reason?"

Lots of things in our everyday world are there by accident. If I trip over a stone, causing me to bump into someone, the encounter is probably not part of a higher design. Random occurrences happen all the time, with no enormous significance. There is a temptation to treat a film in a similar manner, as if everything occurs by chance. Nothing could be further from the truth.

Reprinted from *Cinema Journal*, Fall 2001.

A Hollywood film is one of the most highly scrutinized, carefully constructed, least random works imaginable. Of course, we know this, having seen *Entertainment Tonight*. We all know that it takes thousands of people to create a blockbuster movie: directors, actors, grips, and gaffers. We know that producing a film is a highly coordinated effort by dedicated professionals, but to most people it is a bit of a mystery what all these people do. When we start watching a film, we are encouraged to forget about all that mysterious collective labor. A Hollywood film usually asks us to get caught up in the story, in the world that has been created, so that we are not aware of the behind-the-scenes effort. We tend to forget the thousands of minute decisions that consciously construct the artificial world that has been created.

When I put on a shirt in the morning, I do so with very little thought (as my students will tell you). By contrast, a movie character's shirt is chosen by a professional whose job it is to think about the shirt this character would wear. Similar decisions are made for props, sound, cuts, and so on. Filmmakers work hard to exclude the random from their fictional worlds. Sets are built so that the filmmaker can have absolute control over the environment. Crews spend a great deal of time and expense between shots adjusting the lighting so that each shot will look as polished as possible. When filmmakers do want something to appear random, they carefully choreograph it. For instance, extras who are merely walking by the main characters are told where to go and what to do to appear "natural."

"But what about directors who do not sanitize the film set, who try to let bits of the real world into their films (from the Italian neorealists to Kevin Smith, director of Clerks *[1994])? What about actors like Dustin Hoffman and Robin Williams who like to improvise? What about documentary filmmakers who do not script what happens in front of the camera? Don't these directors and actors let a little bit of chance creep into film?"* Not really. These strategies may allow some chance occurrences to make it into the raw footage. However, the filmmaker and the editor watch the collected footage over and over, deciding which portions of which takes they will assemble into the final cut of a movie. They do so with the same scrutiny that was applied to the actual filming. Even if something occurred on film without their planning for it, they make a conscious choice whether to include that chance occurrence. What was chance in the filming becomes choice in editing.

"Come on, do film professionals from editors to set designers really *spend all that time scrutinizing such details?"* Think of it this way: A Hollywood blockbuster may cost up to $200 million. If you were to make something that costs that much, wouldn't you scrutinize every tiny detail? Even a "low-budget" movie can cost $10 million or so. With so much money riding on a film, there needs to be enormous scrutiny, and this extends to all levels. Of course this process, like all human effort, is fallible; mistakes sometimes creep in (for example, extras in a film set in ancient Rome may be seen wearing wristwatches). All too often, beginning film scholars have a tendency to assume that odd moments in a film are mistakes, when the opposite is more likely to be true. Nothing in a final film is there unless scores of professionals have carefully examined it. You can trust that if something is in a film, it is there for a reason.

A Movie Is Not a Telegram.

"Okay, so the director really cares about the details. But do you think your interpretation is what she really meant to say?"

In high school English classes, you may have been taught to look for the meaning of a literary work, a single sentence that summarizes what the author was trying to convey. So you might have boiled Shakespeare's *Macbeth* down to a single sentence that reveals the moral lesson of the play (perhaps "Greed for power corrupts people"). Similarly, one can reduce a film to its message, which makes the game of interpretation fairly simple. All we have to do is figure out what the author/director was trying to say.

Some filmmakers scoff at the idea that their movies contain messages. Hollywood producer Samuel Goldwyn, for example, is alleged to have said, "If I wanted to send a message, I would've called Western Union." What is at issue here is the conception of what communication is. The traditional understanding of speech considers a sender trying to relay a message to a receiver (often called the S-M-R model). A sender has a clear intention of what she wants to get across to the receiver, but she may not present her message particularly clearly. The receiver tries to understand the message, but she may misunderstand the sender for a variety of reasons. By comparing the sender's intention with the receiver's understanding, one can discover how effective the communication was. For example, if a receiver gets a telegram asking for bail money and then starts collecting the necessary cash, then a successful instance of communication has taken place.

It is tempting to conceptualize a film as communicating a message in a similar way. To find out if a film is effective, one can compare the filmmaker's intentions with our interpretations and see if we "got" it. If a viewer did not receive the message, then perhaps the film is poorly made or perhaps the viewer is not very savvy.

Films, plays, and novels, however, are not telegrams; they are infinitely more complicated. One of the first traps that the budding critic should avoid is thinking that a film can be understood as having a single message that we either "get" or don't get. To think this way is to treat a film like a telegram. The cinema is a richer form of communication than can be conceptualized as sender-message-receiver.

"Okay, so perhaps the filmmaker isn't just sending a single message. Maybe she's sending several messages. If we can figure out what those messages are, then we've got it, yes?"

First of all, there is a thorny question of who the film's "author" is. Unlike a book, hundreds of people put their work into a major film. If all of them are trying to convey meaning, do we have to consider all of their combined intentions? Or if some people's contributions are more important than others (screenwriter, actors, director, cinematographer, producer), then can we understand a film as the sum total of their intentions?

Let's make it easy on ourselves. Assume that the author/filmmaker of a movie is the person who is in charge of coordinating all the decisions in the shooting process: the director. If we can figure out what the director intends, then we've got it, right? If we could interview Hitchcock and gain an understanding of what was going through his mind when he made *Vertigo* (1958), we would have a pretty solid hold on the film, yes?

But can we reduce the film to what the director consciously intended? At times we all express the beliefs, attitudes, and assumptions of our times without necessarily being conscious of doing so. Did Hitchcock fully understand his attitude toward blonde women, or was he propagating a widely held belief? Sometimes the ideology of our day speaks through us with little awareness on our part. In addition, we can unconsciously express personal issues as well as social attitudes. Many believe that the unconscious seeks to express painful things that we have repressed and buried within ourselves. These tensions can emerge in our everyday lives through dreams, Freudian slips, and artwork. Perhaps Hitchcock was unconsciously working through an obsession with cool, aloof women in ways that he did not even understand when he made *Vertigo*. Since human beings cannot be reduced to their conscious thoughts, films should not be reduced to the director's conscious intentions.

"Okay, so if we get a sense of what the director's conscious intentions are, what ideological beliefs she gained from her socialization, and what her unconscious issues are (admittedly a difficult process), then we've arrived at a well-grounded, comprehensive description of what the film is trying to communicate, right?" We have, if we stay within the sender-message-receiver model. But let's step outside that paradigm. Why should we limit the viewer to arriving at only those meanings that come directly from the sender/filmmaker? If I get meaning out of a film and apply it to my life, why should I have to check with the filmmaker to see if it's the right meaning? In other words, why should the filmmaker have more authority over my interpretation of the film than I do?

"Because she's the filmmaker. It's her movie," you may reply. I would respond, "You are the audience. It is your movie, too." If you let go of the notion that the filmmaker is trying to convey a message, then the activity of viewers is to interpret the film according to their lives, their experiences, their tastes—not the filmmaker's. That activity is just as valid as the filmmaker's. The meaning of a movie does not lie solely within the film itself but in the interaction of the film and the audience.

As we learn more and more about how audiences interpret movies, we discover the striking range of interpretations people make. If we consider those "readings" to be somehow less valid than the filmmaker's, then we lose much of the complexity of how movies work, make meaning, and provide pleasure in our society.

"Reading Into" Films.

"But those audiences are just reading things into the movie, right?"

Let's think about what "reading into" a movie is. "That's simple," you might reply. "It's when an audience puts things into the movie that aren't there." That certainly seems straightforward enough. But is it?

Picture yourself watching a horror film in which a group of teenagers are staying at a spooky cabin deep in the woods. It is midnight. A couple sneaks off to a back bedroom and has sex. The attractive young woman then gets up, decides that she is going to take a shower, and says that she will be right back.

You know that this woman will be toast in a matter of minutes.

But how do you know? There is nothing in the film itself that says this woman will die. The same incident (romantic rural location, sexy couple) could take place in a romantic film, and the shower would not raise any hackles. No, the knowledge of her imminent death comes from you, the experienced horror film viewer. You have "read into" the scene.

Like the characters in *Scream* (1996), you know that horror films operate according to a set of rules or conventions that have been established by previous films in the genre. The filmmaker depends on you to know these conventions. She knows that by sending the woman to the shower, she can create tension in the audience ("No! Don't go, you crazy girl!"). The filmmaker can toy with the audience, delaying the inevitable, because she knows that we expect the girl to be slashed. It is our job as audience members to read into the scene; filmmakers count on that.

Movies rely on the audience to supply information that is only hinted at in the film, like the shower convention in horror films. This "reading into" occurs even at the simplest levels of filmmaking. When we see a shot of someone getting into a car and driving away, followed by a shot of the car pulling into another driveway, we understand that the driver drove from one place to another. We understand this without the film actually showing us the drive. If we were limited to what was explicitly laid out in the film, if we did not read into it, then we would not be able to make basic sense out of the movie. There is really no choice of whether to read into a film or not; audiences always do.

This is not to say that you can read a movie in any way you want. Certain pieces of information are established beyond dispute. If you do not think that *Raiders of the Lost Ark* (1981) is about an explorer/archaeologist looking for the Ark of the Covenant, then you have missed something. If you believe that it is about Arctic beekeeping, you are doing a remarkably perverse bit of reading.

Between a pedestrian reading (the driving example, which some would call an inference or expectation) and the ludicrous kind (*Raiders* as about Arctic beekeeping), a wide range of readings are possible. You may find some of them too much of a stretch. What I would ask is that you remain open to the possibility that some of these readings may be interesting. Do not close down your mind simply because an interpretation involves "reading into" a movie, because all film viewings involve this active process. Instead, look at the movie with an open mind and see if there is evidence to support a particular interpretation. If someone says that *Raiders* is really about finding God, Freudian revenge on the father, or Ronald Reagan, see if there is corroborating material.[1] Based on the film, decide if there is a case to be made for one of those interpretations.

Just a Movie.

"Okay, maybe I see the value of coming up with new interpretations of Hamlet *or* Citizen Kane, *but* Raiders? *Or* Evil Dead 2 *(1987)? Come on. Aren't you taking all this a bit too seriously? After all, it's just a movie."*

You would not say, "Why are you analyzing *Hamlet*? After all, it's just Shakespeare." Why is it okay to analyze Shakespeare and not *Evil Dead 2*? The answer has as much to do with the social status of these works as it does with the works themselves.

There was a time when the study of Shakespeare would have been questionable as being not serious enough. At first, scholars in the West did not think that anything written in English was as worthy of study as the classics written in Greek. Homer, Sophocles, and Aristotle were the serious writers whose works were taught in school, not Shakespeare's plays or Dickens's novels. Lawrence Levine has traced how the status of Shakespeare's work has changed in America, from rather lowbrow in vaudeville productions to its current highbrow status.[2] Dickens's novels, now clearly considered classics, were serialized in newspapers as pulp fiction. In their day, to argue that Dickens's work should be taught in schools would have seemed almost scandalous. Such trash obviously could not withstand the scrutiny applied to great works like Homer's *Odyssey*, or so it seemed.

Instead of relying purely on our society's understanding of what artworks are good enough to be taken seriously, we should instead look to the artworks themselves. If we look for rich interpretations of a work, we may find them, or we may not. The point is not to dismiss the process outright simply because it is "just a movie." The proof is in the pudding, as the old saying goes. If your analysis produces insightful, well-grounded interpretations of a film, then it is definitely fruitful for analyzing, even if it is titled *Evil Dead 2*.

No one will argue that all media works are equally rich for analysis. Probably *Hamlet* is a more complex text than *Evil Dead 2*. But that should not lead us to neglect a text that is "just a movie." You should take insight where you can get it. And even if a film is not particularly complex, it can still provide hints about the society that produced it. Events do not have to be overtly complicated to yield knowledge.

For example, Robert Darnton analyzes a particularly unpromising-sounding phenomenon: a mock trial and execution of some cats by the apprentices and journeymen in a Parisian printing shop in the 1730s.[3] What could this bizarre, sadistic, and unusual ritual possibly tell us about eighteenth-century French society? Reading closely, Darnton shows how this odd ceremony reveals much about the relationship between workers and bosses, the sexual and class structures of the society, and the tradition of a craft. His essay demonstrates that even slight cultural artifacts bear the imprint of the society that made them. Examining a film can give us clues about the meanings and assumptions shared by the members of a culture. If a mock trial of cats can reveal social interrelationships, then an uncomplicated film that does not appear to warrant much aesthetic scrutiny can be examined for its social insights. All cultural products carry cultural meaning.

Ruining the Movie.

Part of the resistance to applying analytic tools to a film like *Evil Dead 2* is the belief that such analysis will kill the pleasure of watching the movie. After all, movies are intended to be "mere entertainment." We have already dealt with the question of the filmmaker's intention, so let's not deal further with whether we should be limited to the filmmaker's conception of the film as "mere entertainment." Instead, let's deal with the fear that analyzing a film will destroy the simple pleasure of watching it.

Sometimes it seems that the surest way to ruin a good book is to have to read it for a class. English classes are supposed to make you read things that you would not normally pick up yourself. They force you to read Chaucer or James Joyce, and the hope is that in the process of analyzing these works you'll gain insight into your life. But that is very different from reading Michael Crichton or John Grisham. In the latter case, reading is an escape. If we start thinking too hard about airport novels or mainstream films, doesn't it ruin them?

When people learn that I study the media for a living, they frequently ask, "Are you ever able to just sit back and enjoy a movie, or are you always analyzing it?" The question never rings true because it is phrased as either/or. For me, it is not a matter of substituting cerebral analysis for visceral pleasure; I experience both simultaneously. I can still root for the good guy while admiring a film's editing and thinking about the plot's social ramifications. Similarly, after taking media studies classes, students should be able to add the pleasures of analysis to the pleasures of moviegoing.

I realize that as you are taking an introductory film analysis class, there may not seem to be much pleasure in analysis. It probably seems more like tedious, difficult work. At first, it may seem that you are losing the pleasurable experience of the movie as you dissect it, but as you get better at film analysis, you will be able to recombine those activities. The end result, I believe, is a richer kind of pleasure. I believe that I respond more fully to movies than I did before I started analyzing them. I now feel joy at a well-composed shot, a tautly constructed narrative structure, and an innovative social commentary, as well as the simpler pleasure of finding out whodunit. The outcome we hope for in a film analysis class is not to ruin film watching but to increase the complexity of enjoyment.

"Why do that? Why tinker with the simple pleasure of watching a movie?" This question goes to the foundation of what education is. The basic faith underlying education is that an examined life is better, richer, and fuller than an unexamined life. How do we really know that self-examination is better than the bliss of simple ignorance? Like most statements of faith, there is no way to prove it. But by being in a college classroom, you have allied yourself with those of us who believe that if you do not examine the forces in your life, you will become subject to them. You can go through life merely responding to movies, but if you are an educated person, you will also think about them, about what they mean, and how they are constructed. In so doing, you may experience pleasures and insights that you could not have obtained any other way. This is the promise of the educated life in reading, in living, and in watching movies.

Notes

Thanks to David Bordwell, Henry Jenkins, and Pamela Wilson for their helpful comments on an earlier version of this essay.

1. The idea that Indiana Jones is an avatar of Ronald Reagan is found in Frank P. Tomasulo, "Mr. Jones Goes to Washington: Myth and Religion in *Raiders of the Lost Ark,*" *Quarterly Review of Film Studies* 7, no. 4 (fall 1982): 331–40.
2. Lawrence Levine, *Highbrow/Lowbrow: The Emergence of a Cultural Hierarchy in America* (Cambridge: Harvard University Press, 1990).
3. Robert Darnton, "Workers Revolt: The Great Cat Massacre of the Rue Saint-Séverin," in *The Great Cat Massacre and Other Episodes in French Cultural History* (New York: Random House, 1985), 9–72.

Peter Parshall

Peter Parshall, a professor of comparative literature and film, teaches at the Rose-Hulman Institute of Technology in Indiana. His writings have appeared in Literature/Film Quarterly, Film Criticism, *and* Perspectives on Contemporary Literature. *This essay on the film* Die Hard *was published in the* Journal of Popular Film and Television. *Contributors to this journal tend to be scholars or graduate students who examine films and genres from a socio-cultural perspective. The journal concentrates on commercial film and television and appeals to both academics and a general readership.*

Die Hard: *The American Mythos*

"Ah, take one consideration with another, / A policeman's lot is not a happy one." Such was the opinion of the Sergeant of Police in Gilbert and Sullivan's *The Pirates of Penzance*. His unhappiness stemmed from the fact that he and his timorous band of officers were ordered to apprehend a blood-thirsty gang of pirates. True to his misdoubts, the pirates quickly captured *them*. In contemporary times, the policeman's lot has become considerably unhappier, an unequal contest with the well-financed armies of the drug lords. As the law officer himself certainly recognizes, the problems he faces are symptoms of a sickness in the heart of society, which he can at best contain and cannot remedy. And yet, simply because he is in the front lines of the struggle, he is often cast in the role of the doctor who must find society's cure.

The most popular version of the policeman as hero is the rogue cop in the Dirty Harry mold, who takes over where the Western hero left off and inherits many traits from him. Robert B. Ray in *A Certain Tendency of the Hollywood Cinema* has argued for the centrality of the "outlaw hero" role in American film, typified in the cowboy loner, such as Shane, who rides into town and is persuaded to side temporarily with law and order before riding off again.[1] Variations of the role are found in other films from *Casablanca* to *Star Wars*. Ray suggests that such films show a struggle between the desire for law and order and profound mistrust of a legal establishment felt to be corrupt or impotent. In general, these films support the idea that the individual knows better than the group, that one's gut instincts about right and wrong are truer than society's laws, and that violence is often the best way to solve a problem. As Ray argues, these values typify American heroes back to Huckleberry Finn. The wave of popular

Reprinted from *Journal of Popular Film and Television*, Summer 1990, pp. 14–17, by permission of The Helen Dwight Reid Educational Foundation. Published by Heldref Publications.

support for Ollie North demonstrates that these values still enjoy widespread currency in America.

We may mourn the shallowness of the rogue cop and his ilk whose solution to the presence of human evil is to find the villain and gun him down. The higher the caliber of weapons used, the better. However, this very simplicity suggests an archetype at work, relating him to the epic hero, whose major task was "combat with an uncivilized monster (like the Cyclops or Grendel or Satan), an outsider who embodies the forces of anarchy."[2] While the epic simplified the problem by drawing a neat contrast between the hero and the chaos-monster from outside the society, the Greeks quickly discovered that those forces existed within the civilized citizenry as well. As Joseph Campbell suggests in *The Hero With a Thousand Faces*, the mythic hero's journey into the underworld to battle with dark forces represents an interior voyage to struggle with his own nature. King Minos of Crete kept for himself the bull sent by Poseidon for sacrifice, thus putting personal gain above public good. That bull engenders the Minotaur, but Minos is its symbolic father (as its name indicates), for it is the visible symbol of his corrupt rule. Theseus undertakes the task of defeating it to prove himself worthy to run Athens. The labyrinth he enters is a figuration of his own soul; the Minotaur he defeats is his own selfishness, for he risks his life to save others.[3] Heroes such as Theseus show the human spirit winning through to higher possibilities and returning to the ordinary world to manifest this potential to others.

Our current cultural heroes, typified more by macho toughness than depth of character, may seem to lack the inner struggle. However, we must remember that epics from the *Iliad* on were designed first and foremost to entertain, and their heroes have generally been known more for action than introspection. The hero's conflict may indeed be against inner forces, but these are typically personified as external monsters to which he must take sword or Uzi. Further, the hero is not without human failings: "He has a human heart and therefore a dimension of vulnerability and the possibility of failing."[4] Thus, Achilles and Roland were flawed by pride, and Lancelot betrayed his king. These flaws link us to the hero, suggesting that we may share his shortcomings and, like him, can overcome them.

One contemporary hero who battles both external and internal monsters and thus fits the archetypal mode is John McClane, the New York policeman in John McTiernan's 1988 film *Die Hard*. The success of the film—it tied for seventh in 1988 with a gross of $35 million[5] and spawned a big budget sequel—suggests that McClane personifies some of the heroic traits our culture finds most appealing. He arrives in Los Angeles to meet his wife Holly at the Nakatomi Corporation's Christmas party, taking place on the thirtieth floor of the Nakatomi Tower. John no sooner joins her and begins to argue about her putting her career before their marriage when the tower is invaded by a group of quasi-terrorists who take the partygoers hostage and set to work to crack the Nakatomi vault. The terrorists kill the Nakatomi security officers in cold blood, then the Los Angeles director, Mr. Takagi, and finally Harry Ellis, Holly's co-worker, who tries to bargain with them. John escapes to wage guerilla warfare against the terrorists from the upper floors of the unfinished building, receiving little help from the regulation-bound police and even less from the FBI. His major ally is a sympathetic patrolman, Sgt. Al Powell, to whom he talks via a captured walkie-talkie. One by one, John dispatches the villains. Their leader, Hans Gruber, tries to escape using Holly as a shield, but John finally outwits him and sends him falling to his death from a building window. Holly and John are then driven away in the Nakatomi limo by Argyle, the chauffeur who brought John from the airport in the beginning.

In many regards, *Die Hard*'s story is an age-old one: A hero conquers the villains. Typical of Ray's "outlaw hero," John brings about justice single-handedly, trusting his own instincts rather than following official procedures. Indeed, the film makes a running joke of John as cowboy hero, culminating in the final shootout where John neatly plugs Hans and his remaining accomplice with his last two bullets and then, blowing imaginary smoke from his gun barrel, says, "Happy trails, Hans." Beyond its stereotypic dispatching of the villains, however, *Die Hard* functions on two additional levels. First, its hero attacks villains who personify major cultural problems and, second, he confronts problems in his own nature. As Campbell states, "The first work of the hero is to retreat from the world of secondary effects to those causal zones of the psyche where the difficulties really reside . . . [and] eradicate them." By wrestling with these problems, the hero presents a vision of how they may be dealt with by the larger society.

Christmas and the Family

According to Campbell, the hero's story begins with the "call to adventure"[7] that pulls him from his accustomed life. "The familiar life horizon has been outgrown; the old concepts, ideals, and emotional patterns no longer fit; the time for the passing of a threshold is at hand."[8] The film does not show the call that sets John McClane on his journey, but he has left the familiar territory of New York to come to Los Angeles. The hero must remedy society's blight, and California does appear blighted, for the action occurs on Christmas Eve and the holiday seems all wrong in this climate; there is no snow and the limousine radio is playing Christmas rap tunes instead of "Jingle Bells." Christmas is used as a benchmark throughout the film, with the good guys shown to be pro-Christmas and pro-family and the bad guys anti-Christmas and hence anti-family. John McClane is first seen dragging around a giant teddy bear he is bringing to his children as a Christmas present. He also declines Argyle's invitation to meet some "mama bears" because he's married. Al Powell, the black policeman, is first seen buying snacks for his pregnant wife and singing "Let It Snow" along with the store's Muzak. Al also has a Christmas ornament hanging from the mirror of his squad car. Obviously, he too is pro-family and pro-Christmas. Holly Gennero McClane (whose very name—Holly—links her to Christmas) is first seen fending off the advances of her fellow worker Ellis. She reminds him, "Harry, it's Christmas Eve. Family. Stockings. Chestnuts. Rudolf and Frosty. Any of these things ring a bell?" He responds: "Actually, I was thinking more of a mulled wine, a nice aged Brie, a roaring fireplace. You know what I'm saying?" She thinks of Christmas as a time for family; he thinks of it as a time for sex.

If Ellis flunks the Christmas test, so does the Nakatomi Corporation, whose values he represents. It is Christmas Eve, but instead of being home with their children, the employees are at the office Christmas party. They are isolated on the thirtieth floor, the only people left in the building. Holly has to phone her children since she can't be there with them. John wanted to hear Christmas music and instead, when he walks into the party, the orchestra is playing Bach's Sixth Brandenburg Concerto. He is kissed by a man who may just be friendly but who may be homosexual—another suggestion that the corporate life is anti-family. This is suggested again by the couple found making out in an empty office. Further, the spirit of Christmas at Nakatomi is corrupted by the continual intrusion of business elements. Mr. Takagi, the head of the Los Angeles branch, thanks his employees "for making this one of the greatest years in the history of Nakatomi Corporation" and then wishes them a Merry Christmas. John is surprised that the Japanese celebrate Christmas and Takagi responds, "We're flexible. Pearl Harbor didn't work out, so we got you with tape decks." It's a joke, but one that subtly suggests the party is part of the Japanese business invasion. Ellis chimes in that the party is also a celebration of a successful business deal. Hollywood films like to set things right, and this film announces from the start that Christmas in the corporate world is all wrong. As Holly suggests to her co-worker Ginny, she feels like Ebeneezer Scrooge.

The terrorists also show themselves to be anti-Christmas and hence anti-family by their constant cynical remarks. Hans, the leader, promises Theo, the black computer wizard, that he will open the safe: "It's Christmas, Theo, the time of miracles. So be of good cheer." And when the safe finally does open, Theo says, "Merry Christmas." Also, when Theo is using the building security system to monitor the attacking police forces, he alerts his fellow conspirators by saying "T'was the night before Christmas and all through the house, not a creature was stirring . . . except the four assholes coming in the rear in standard two by two cover formation." The point is that John McClane is defending more than the Nakatomi employees: He is defending Christmas and, hence, traditional societal values.

The Role of Women

When the hero sets out to remedy society's problems, he often discovers that the illness that plagues society is also found within him. For example, when King Oedipus hears the chorus tell of a blight that has struck the city, he is unaware that he himself caused and contains the blight. In John McClane's case, he is forced to confess to Argyle, the limousine driver, that he has come to Los Angeles to win back his estranged wife. Thus, the loss of traditional values in the external world parallels his personal situation. On the social level, the film wrestles with a continuing problem in modern society—the changing structure of the family. American films have dealt with this problem from their inception, since the Industrial Revolution caused dramatic changes in the family, with fathers working in factories rather than on farms, and families moving from small towns to the city. By setting its action on Christmas Eve, possibly the most important time of the year for families to be together, *Die Hard* emphasizes that John and Holly McClane are *not* together. The major thrust of the film becomes to remove the barriers that keep this couple apart—a fairly typical Hollywood structure.

The film's concern with the changing nature of the family leads directly to a related issue, the changing role of women, which is a major dissonance in American culture at present. Women in the film are generally portrayed as empty-headed—the broadcaster Gail Wallens and the female police dispatcher—or as stereotypic sex objects, including the blonde girl whom the terrorists drag out of an office with her blouse off, the pin-up posters that John pats as he runs through the construction area, and Holly herself at the end as Hans's prisoner, with several buttons of her blouse undone. More specifically, the film criticizes the corporate woman as a poor mother. When Holly's pregnant co-worker Ginny heads to the party and asks if the baby can "handle a little sip," Holly replies, "That baby is ready to tend bar." Behind the joke, the implication is clear that corporate mothers are better at downing cocktails than in caring for their unborn offspring. Holly herself, the film suggests, has been "corrupted" by corporate thinking. Although she is portrayed positively in the film's opening, fending off Ellis' advances and showing concern for her children, she has put her career ahead of her family and her husband and she denies her married status. (She has retained her maiden name—Gennero—so as not to impede her career.) She says to her maid Pauline on the phone, "What would I do without you?"—suggesting that she cannot raise the children without help. The film's major project, second only to dispatching the terrorists, is thus to re-educate Holly.

It does so, first of all, by reducing this busy executive, first seen briskly walking the corporate corridors, to a passive victim, waiting to be rescued. It is true that she confronts Hans bravely and asks for a couch for the pregnant Ginny and trips to the bathroom for other employees. But that is female work: taking care of others. The important job of rescuing everyone is left to John. And when Hans asks, "What idiot put you in charge?" she replies, "You did. When you murdered my boss." It's a nice joke on Hans but also a reminder that women only receive authority when men choose to delegate it to them. The contrasting male/female roles are echoed in the methods of filming that follow Mulvey's well-known formulation that men do the looking and women are the object of the gaze.[9] When the terrorists first invade the thirtieth floor and begin rounding up employees, Holly is seen in one brief medium-closeup shot, looking around for John. The closeup shot traps her in the frame, giving her no space to move. Further, she is looking for John to help her, rather than running for an exit on her own. John is portrayed just the opposite. Hearing the commotion, he jumps to the door to peer out, and the camera does a 180° dolly around him, emphasizing the space he has and also adopting his point of view. With gun in hand, he sizes up the situation and spots the exit he will run to. Throughout the film, similarly, John is the active one: The camera has to pan and track frantically to keep up with him as he runs, shoots, dodges, dives for cover, leaps over parapets, swings from hoses, and smashes through windows. By contrast, Holly is filmed passively. There are eighteen closeup reaction shots of her, since the female's role is to express emotion and not to take action. Especially at the end, when Hans tries to use her as a shield, the film is filled with closeups of her face with his pistol jammed against her head.

The film implies that Holly reaccepts the "standard" feminine role because, surrounded by terrorists, she comes to appreciate John's courage and initiative. She also reevaluates her own role, shown in her reaction to her daughter, Lucy, talking on television. Prodded by the newscaster Thornburg to say something to her parents, Lucy looks into the camera and says, "Come home." That is followed immediately with two reaction shots of Holly watching wide-eyed. Clearly, the message "come home" is addressed to her. Lucy spoke those same words when she talked to her mother on the telephone at the very beginning of the film: "When are you coming home?" The film thus emphasizes that Holly has abandoned her family, as she has abandoned her married name. This may also explain the film's brutal and early murder of her boss, Takagi. He serves as Holly's alternative "husband," standing behind her as John first embraces her at the party saying, "She was made for the business. Tough as nails." The film seeks to break down the image of her toughness, to derail her career as an independent woman, and to return her to the accepted female role: weak and dependent. Takagi must be blown away so that John can step back into the picture and reestablish the traditional male/female roles. This is made very clear at the end when Hans nearly pulls Holly out the window with him. John saves her by unfastening the Rolex watch, symbol of her corporate success, allowing Hans to fall to his death.

Thus, on the social level, *Die Hard* seems to fall away from the true mythic journey. As Campbell suggests, "schism in the soul, schism in the body social, will not be resolved by any scheme to return to the good old days." Rather, the hero must be "reborn."[10] *Die Hard* dodges such a revolutionary step and reaffirms the traditional nuclear family and "standard" male/female roles. This is nicely encapsulated in the closing scene when John and Holly emerge slowly from the wreckage of the building. The black leather policeman's jacket she is wearing covers her suit and signals that her major role is now policeman's wife rather than corporate executive. She is no longer above John, sealed off on the thirtieth floor by security guards but has come down to his level. The woman Takagi described as "tough as nails" now leans on her husband and stares at him adoringly as he leads her to safety. When he introduces her to Al Powell as "Holly Gennero," she corrects it to "Holly McClane." At the end, she and John are driven away together, satisfying the film's drive to restore the family and to reestablish the male as its head.

The Terrorists and the Corporation

In *Die Hard*'s attack on forces separating John and Holly, one obvious obstacle to their reunion is the corporate world; a second is the terrorists, and it takes only a moment's thought to realize that the two overlap to a considerable degree. The fact that Hans clings so tightly to Holly's Rolex watch suggests a connection between him and the corporate world it represents. Most obviously, the terrorists are not terrorists at all—they are businessmen, seeking a profit, and using the latest technology to carry out their plan. Ellis, flashing the same insincere smile at Hans, treats him as a compatriot, saying, "Business is business. You use a gun, I use a fountain pen. What's the difference?" Other references tie the terrorists even more specifically to the Nakatomi Corporation. When Hans confronts the Nakatomi employees, herded together into the main room, his first words are, "Ladies and Gentlemen," exactly the words Joe Takagi first used when he appeared on the balcony to wish the employees a Merry Christmas. The links between Hans and Takagi continue: As they ride up in the elevator together, the camera cuts between closeups of the two, portraying them as equals. Hans compliments Takagi on his London-tailored suit and says, "I have two myself." Hans also hums the "Ode to Joy" theme, which the party orchestra had been playing a few moments earlier when the terrorists first emerged from the elevator. That theme is associated with the terrorists throughout the film—first played when they enter the basement of the Nakatomi Tower, notably evident at the moment the safe finally opens, and occurring in the final credits. The fact that the theme is also played by the Nakatomi orchestra serves to emphasize the overlap in the two groups. The point is that, exactly as Ellis suggests, this is a "hostile takeover," with one organization co-opting another. The terrorists are a magnified, darker version of the corporate world.

One of the major traits of the terrorists is their robot-like mechanicality, which mirrors the conformity of the corporate world. When the truck first enters the garage and backs up to the loading dock, its ramp extends like a robot arm and its metal door flies up, both emphasized by the mechanical noise on the sound track. There are more mechanical sounds as Tony cuts open the telephone boxes in the basement and as his brother, Karl, flipping down his plastic visor, cuts through all the phone trunks with a chainsaw. Later on, there are shots of Theo with goggles on, drilling through the safe locks, the mechanical noises as the terrorists assemble the anti-tank gun, and the steam and noise of the roof compressors where the terrorists plant their explosives. This mechanicality is reflected even in the way they move in trained commando fashion. Particularly noteworthy is the teamwork of the three terrorists who attack John on the roof as he is broadcasting his appeal for help. Two of them chase him backward while, up above, Karl advances smoothly and stealthily to ambush him, his weapon ready, a deadly killing machine. Karl's machine-like qualities are emphasized also by the contrast with John's fighting style when the two battle near the end. John throws himself passionately into the fight, whereas Karl circles and kicks, a precise, detached, efficient karate robot.

These same traits—coldness, mechanicality, rigidity—are characteristic of the corporate world as symbolized by the Nakatomi Tower itself: its echoing marble lobby, its computers, its security guards and surveillance cameras, its automatic grills that clang down, its glaring stainless steel elevators, and all its glass. The geometric Nakatomi logo, found throughout the building, is a nice reminder of how the corporation invades every aspect of life. The terrorists are perfectly at home here and set up operations at desks in the corporate offices. John, who opposes this rigidity, operates in the upper floors still under construction where he has room to run and duck and improvise.

Terrence Rafferty in *The New Yorker* commented: "The most entertaining thing about this movie is the sheer joy it takes in destruction."[11] True. The film takes as much delight in John's demolishing the building as in his polishing off the terrorists. Scene after scene shows shot-up computers, overturned desks, smashed windows, and machine-gun fire sprayed in all directions. Particularly spectacular are the explosions when John blows out the entire third floor and when Hans detonates the roof. By the final scenes, the building has been reduced to shambles, suggesting considerable antagonism to the corporate values it represents. The building is a gigantic concrete and steel trap that tries to imprison John. It symbolizes the corporate life that captures people and squeezes them into its mold. The film is determined to break out of this cage, just as Argyle does at the end, crashing his limo through the grate that trapped him in the garage to take John and Holly home.

What the film is dealing with, then, is another major conflict in American culture: the individual versus corporate life. John represents the individual who chafes under bureaucracy and the need to work as a team member. He is at the other end of the spectrum from the corporate person. The film's first shot of him shows his hand clenched on the armrest of the plane seat. He is not a frequent flyer. He carries a duffel bag rather than a briefcase. He is more comfortable riding in the front seat of the limo with Argyle rather than in the back. In contrast to the yuppies who want to get as high up in the building as possible, he hates heights. Where the corporate workers wear suit and tie, he wears an open-collared sport shirt. In fairly short order, he is wearing even less, waging his guerrilla war barefoot and eventually barechested. In the final shootout, Hans still has on his suit and tie, whereas John, grimy and bloody, looks like some kind of primitive beast. That shootout is the showdown between the modern corporate leader and the ordinary individual. Hans has had "the benefit of a classical education"; he speaks several languages and talks polished English; he has an organization of a dozen professionals at his command. John is ordinary American, working class by speech and dress, uncomfortable in the cosmopolitan world, his only assets guts and determination and a quick mind. Where Hans uses anti-tank guns and computers, John uses a screwdriver, a cigarette lighter, and a roll of package tape. And he wins.

Evaluating the Values

Die Hard resolves the cultural problems portrayed by a return to traditional values, exalting the nuclear family and attacking the corporate world. Its portrayal of the terrorists as brutal thieves is especially disturbing, ruling out more complex cross-cultural values and implying that all terrorist actions may have similar venal motivation. It further simplifies the problem by suggesting that violence is the only way to deal with such people. Ellis' fate gives the film's judgment of those who try negotiation. The emphasis on violence and vigilante justice is reaffirmed in the conclusion when the terrorist Karl bursts from the building, threatening to kill John and Holly, and is shot by Al Powell. The film emphasizes the significance of this moment—arguably the most important outside of the killing of Hans—by three closeups of Al's gun firing and then a fourth slow rack focus from the gun to his face. There is also a shot of John looking at Al, giving his official hero's approval to his act, and the soundtrack swells with triumphant music. By this action, the film, after exalting the renegade cop throughout, cleverly turns law enforcement back over to the legitimate cop. Al is a goodhearted person who would prefer not to shoot because of his accidental killing of a thirteen-year-old boy. However, now he must do so to protect others. Besides exalting violence, this moment also suggests that we should trust immediate instinct rather than thought. The film reinforces this message a second later by having Holly punch out Thornburg, which the audience heartily applauds. He has been shown as sleazy throughout, invading the McClane home and endangering both John and Holly, so violence against him is perfectly acceptable. Besides, any man who can be punched out by a woman deserves to be laughed at. In sum, the film's value system is a distressingly common portrayal of vigilante justice.

Despite this superficial exploration of social problems, the fact that they are present at all may explain in part why *Die Hard* is more successful than the average rogue cop film. That is, Grendel gains resonance as the villain in *Beowolf* because he exemplifies the outer chaos that threatens to take over civilized society. The villains in *Die Hard*, likewise, personify the invasion of foreign concerns as well as American corporate life and are "stealing" Christmas as well as bearer bonds. Hence, they are all the more threatening. Most important, the social conflicts embodied in the film affect all of us. How does one resolve the conflicting demands of career and family? With both parents expending the majority of their effort at making a living, how do they remain caring, communicating human beings? The tensions caused by exactly such daily problems are conveniently personified in the film and then blown away—a satisfying fantasy that temporarily reduces the pressure and gives us the hope that the problems can indeed be overcome.

John McClane as Cultural Hero

On the personal level, the film's hero shares in these societal problems and his victory is over inner limitations as much as outer ones. Although not transfigured like a Buddha or a Christ, not able to discuss the inner truths he has discovered, John McClane's battles have important symbolic dimensions. In the first place, the person he kills at the end, Hans Gruber, is partly his own evil double. They both "crash" the Nakatomi party, they talk to one another at several points, and they even speak the same lines: John says "Trust me" to his seat mate on the plane who spots his Beretta pistol, and Hans says the same thing to Theo, promising to open the safe. Hans tries to trick John by pretending to be a frightened corporate executive when found near the roof compressors. John does the same thing more skillfully at the end as he also plays helpless, throwing his machine gun away and surrendering himself to Hans.

Hans represents the dark side of John, in particular, because he is a loner. Although part of a gang, he works only for himself, as when he blows up the roof at the end even though his own men are on it. Hans stands for isolation: The first act of the terrorists when they invade Nakatomi is to lock the doors, bring down the gates, and cut all the phone lines. Hans does not communicate with his underlings: He does not explain his plan for opening the final lock on the safe until the FBI has cut the power that will do it. John, too, is isolated and uncommunicative. He has absented himself from his family for six months and plays the loner's game throughout the film. In the opening scenes, we note his reluctance to speak of his fear of flying to his seat mate on the plane and a similar reluctance to discuss his family situation with Argyle. He is a stranger at the Nakatomi party, observing the festivities without really participating. Most important, he and Holly no longer communicate well. He did not call before he took the flight and he blunders his attempt to talk with her in the executive washroom.

Somehow this loner learns communication. The first positive sign is that he leaves his world, New York, and journeys to Los Angeles to meet Holly on her territory. After allowing Holly to separate herself for six months, he now bends every effort to defeat the forces keeping them apart. He tells his alter ego Al Powell that he should have supported her and, in contrast to his joking with Argyle about the relationship, shows real feeling. (Typical of male adventure films, John discusses his marital relations more successfully with other men than with Holly herself. He does at least make his confession in a washroom, reminiscent of the executive washroom where he bungled his first conversation with Holly.) John has come to recognize her importance in his life, just as she comes to realize the importance of his police career. By the end of the film, John is reduced to some primitive, bloody creature, but still he mutters "Hang in here, honey" as he prepares his final assault on Hans, and calls out to her, "Hi, honey," as he limps forward out of the shambles of the building to the showdown. After operating as a loner throughout the film, he kills Hans—symbol of isolation—and emerges from the jungle of the Nakatomi Tower to rejoin Holly, his family, and civilization.

Linked to his closer connection with Holly is a key confrontation with himself: his fear of heights. The first shot of the film shows a plane landing, and the second shot shows John's hand clutching the armrest of his seat. John's fear of high places and his inability to accept Holly's career are related; he cannot accept the fact that she is above him. This is symbolized by the imposing height of the Nakatomi Tower, which he keeps glancing at as he rides with Argyle. This fear of heights becomes a major motif in the film, and John must confront it again and again. He hangs from a gun strap (in a shot that pays homage to *Vertigo*) and nearly falls to his death when the strap comes loose. The four times he goes to the roof all put him in danger: He is chased by three terrorists the first time, encounters Hans and three more terrorists the second time, and must fight to the death with Karl the third time. The fourth time—trying to herd the hostages out of danger—he is fired at by the FBI helicopter and must leap over the edge of the building, using a fire hose as a rappelling line. He breaks in through a window, but then the empty reel falls past and nearly pulls him to his death. The climax comes when he must leap to a window to keep Holly from being pulled out by Hans and let Hans take the death that had been stalking him all along. The terror of this fate is emphasized by the long tilting shot that follows Hans as he falls thirty stories to land with a crunch that makes the policemen below wince. Because John can confront his fear of high places he can accept his wife's position and introduce her as Holly Gennero to Al Powell at the end. Hence, John's actions suggest that a cultural solution to the new feminine roles requires men to overcome their fears of inadequacy and to ascend new heights themselves.

Sequel and Conclusion

Die Hard 2: Die Harder has even more action than its predecessor and yet is not as satisfying because it has lost the mythic resonance of the first film. The script is clever, but the jokes do not contain subtext messages as consistently as *Die Hard*.

The film is set at Christmas again, but there is less sense of the villains being opposed to it and John a defender of it. There is little treatment of John and Holly's relationship and hence of male/female role conflicts. Her role becomes even more passive than in the first film as she sits on an airplane circling the airport, unable to do anything except beat on Thornburg the reporter one more time. John is fighting bureaucracy again, as one would expect of the rogue cop, but the airport hierarchy is a far less satisfying surrogate for corporate values. In particular, there is no sense of John fighting any internal battles—he never hesitates in his pursuit of the villains or doubts his abilities. The film's one interesting dimension is that John's two major opponents, Colonel Stuart and Captain Grant, are traitorous operatives, hinting at the dangers of the renegade cop's role if he adopts purely selfish ends.

Both films are simplistic in many ways. The complex global problems facing us cannot really be gunned down like villains in the Old West. Trusting gut instinct doesn't always work. The nuclear family will inevitably change. The earlier film, however, is able to make simplicity a virtue, transforming its story into something near myth. Myths reassure us that the culture will survive the changes it is undergoing (cf. Levi-Strauss[12]) because the mythic hero shows that the monsters within us can be defeated and a way out of the labyrinth can be found. Society may survive if we set personal concerns aside and throw Hans, symbol of selfishness, out the window. The family may endure if we have the confidence to assail the heights that daunt us and the sensitivity to communicate to those who love us. Perhaps most important, myth brings us a message of hope. We should all continue to be of good cheer, to expect miracles, and to believe in heroes. We should believe in Santa Claus, personified in John McClane, who whistles "Here Comes Santa Claus" when first entering the Nakatomi Tower and whose final words in the film are "Merry Christmas." Hans, the Scrooge figure, the man who would kill to amass wealth, has been dispatched. Hans, the killjoy, the man who smiles with mirth at Takagi before shooting him in cold blood, has been replaced by John, who can joke with Hans and Al Powell, talking about Twinkies and flat feet and cowboys. This joking Santa not only gets Mommy and Daddy together again, he actually brings Christmas to Nakatomi Land with bearer bonds drifting down through the sky as Vaughn Monroe sings "Let It Snow." Greed has been replaced by the spirit of giving; love and laughter have overcome violence; and we can have a white Christmas, even in L.A.

Acknowledgments

I would like to express my appreciation to the Lilly Endowment for granting me an Open Faculty Fellowship for sabbatical study at the University of Wisconsin 1988–1989. This paper was originally prepared as part of a sabbatical report for that year.

Notes

1. Robert B. Ray, *A Certain Tendency of the Hollywood Cinema, 1930–1980* (Princeton: Princeton University Press, 1985).

2. Beverle Houston and Marsha Kinder, *Self and Cinema* (Pleasantville, NY: Redgrave, 1980), p. 152.
3. Joseph Campbell, *The Hero With a Thousand Faces* (Cleveland: World Publishing, 1956), p. 15.
4. P. L. Travers, "The World of the Hero." *Parabola,* No. 1 (Winter 1976), pp. 46–47.
5. "Big Rental Films of '88 in U.S.-Canada," *Variety,* 11–17 January 1989, p. 16.
6. Campbell, p. 17.
7. Campbell, p. 51.
8. Campbell, p. 51.
9. Laura Mulvey, "Visual Pleasure and Narrative Cinema." *Screen* 16, No. 3 (Autumn 1975), pp. 6–19.
10. Campbell, pp. 16–17.
11. Terrence Rafferty "Current Cinema." *The New Yorker,* 8 August 1988, p. 79.
12. Claude Levi-Strauss, "The Structural Study of Myth." In Clair Jacobson and Brooke G. Schoepf, trans., *Structural Anthropology* (New York: Basic Books, 1963).

bell hooks

bell hooks is an internationally known cultural critic and scholar. In addition to her many books, hooks frequently contributes essays to various popular magazines. Her writings, which examine issues of race and gender, include Black Looks: Race and Representation *and* Teaching to Transgress: Education as the Practice of Freedom. *This essay, "Seduction and Betrayal," which originally appeared in* Visions Magazine *in the fall of 1993, compares the representations of African American female protagonists in films of two different genres.*

Seduction and Betrayal

Two recent films—Hollywood's *The Bodyguard* and the independent *The Crying Game*—highlight relationships that cross boundaries. *The Crying Game* explores the boundaries of race, gender, and nationality; *The Bodyguard*, boundaries of race and class. Within their particular genres, both films have been major box office successes. Yet critics acclaimed *The Crying Game* and overwhelmingly trashed *The Bodyguard*. Though *The Crying Game* was certainly a better film by artistic standards (superior acting, more complex plot, good screenwriting), it is more similar to *The Bodyguard* in the elements that make it work for audiences than it is different: both are romances that look at "desire" deemed taboo and exploit the theme of love on the edge.

At a time when critical theory and cultural criticism call us to interrogate the politics of race, nationality, and gender, these films locate reconciliation and redemption in the realm of desire, not politics. And while both exploit race as subject matter, both directors deny the significance of race in these films. Until *The Bodyguard*, American audiences had never seen a Hollywood film in which a major white star chooses a black female lover, yet the publicity for the film insisted that race was not important. In an interview in the black magazine *Ebony*, Kevin Costner insisted: "I don't think race is an issue here. The film is about a relationship between two people, and it would have been a failure if it became a film about interracial relationships." Similarly, in interviews about *The Crying Game*, director Neil Jordan identifies the female character only as "the woman," never as black. In his interview with Lawrence Chua in *Bomb* magazine, for example, Jordan says, "Fergus thinks the woman is one thing and he finds out she is something different." Their assertions expose the extent to which neither white male has interrogated his position. As progressive feminist thinkers and cultural

Reprinted from *Visions Magazine*, Fall 1993, by permission of the publisher.

critics have long noted, white supremacy allows those who exercise white privilege to behave as though race does not matter even as they help establish and maintain fixed and absolute racial hierarchies.

Both *The Crying Game* and *The Bodyguard* get their edge from the racial identity of the heroine. Long before the viewers of *The Crying Game* know that Dil is a transvestite, they are intrigued by her exoticism—marked by her race. Not just any ol' black woman, she/he embodies the "tragic mulatto" persona that has always characterized sexually desirable mixed-black female characters in Hollywood films. Kevin Costner's insistence that *The Bodyguard* is not about interracial relationships seems ludicrously arrogant when masses of viewers—including black women—flocked to see this film because it depicted a relationship between a black woman and a white man, portrayed by "big stars" Whitney Houston and Costner. Previously, the politics of racism and white supremacy in Hollywood had blocked the portrayal of such a relationship. And since the female lead is so often romantically linked with the male lead, this meant that black women were rarely given the female lead in movies.

The characters of Dil (Jaye Davidson) in *The Crying Game* and Rachel Marron (Whitney Houston) in *The Bodyguard* were portrayed unconventionally only in that they were the love objects of white men. Otherwise, they were stereotypically oversexed, aggressive, sexually experienced women—'ho's. Though Dil works as a hair stylist and Marron makes her money as an entertainer, their lure is in the realm of the sexual. As white racist and sexist stereotypes in mass media teach audiences, if you scratch the surface of any black woman's sexuality, you'll find a 'ho—someone sexually available, apparently indiscriminate, incapable of commitment, and likely to seduce and betray. Neither Dil nor Marron bothers to get to know the individual white male she falls in love with. In both cases, it is love—or should I say, lust—at first sight. Both films suggest that actual knowledge of the "other" would destroy the sexual mystery, the pleasure and danger caused by unknowing. Though Fergus (Stephen Rea) has sought Dil, she quickly becomes the sexual initiator, servicing him. Similarly, Marron seduces the bodyguard she has hired, Frank Farmer (Kevin Costner). Both films suggest that the sexual allure of these black females is so intense that the vulnerable white males lose all will to resist (even when Fergus must face the fact that Dil is not biologically female).

Before slavery was abolished in the United States, white government officials who supported sending black folks back to Africa warned of the danger of sexual relations between decent white men and licentious black females, asking specifically that the government "remove this temptation from us." They wanted the state to check their lust lest it get out of hand. Uncontrollable lust between white men and black women is not taboo. It becomes taboo only to the extent that such lust leads to the development of a committed relationship.

The Bodyguard assures its audience that no matter how magical, sexy, and thrilling the love between Rachel Marron and Frank Farmer is, it will not work. And should we dare to imagine otherwise, the powerful theme song sets us straight. Though the refrain declares, "I will always love you," other lyrics suggest that this relationship has been doomed from the start. "Bittersweet memories [are] all I am taking with me," the parting lover declares, since "We both know I am not what you need." Audiences can only presume that the unspoken, denied subject of interracial romance makes this love impossible. Conventionally, then, *The Bodyguard* promises a fulfilling romance between a white male and a black female only to declare that relationship doomed. Xenophobic and racist moviegoers who want to be titillated by taboo are thus comforted by having the status quo restored in the end.

In keeping with a colonizing mind set, the bodies of black men and women in these films are the playing field where white men work out their longing for tran-scendence. In Fergus's eyes, the black male prisoner Jody (Forest Whitaker) embodies the humanity his white comrades have lost. Though a grown man, Jody is childlike, innocent, a neo-primitive who, like Dil (another primitive), is not cut off from feeling or sensuality, and Fergus relates to him, according to Jordan, "like a mother." Jody alters the power relationship between himself and Fergus by emotionally seducing Fergus. Though, at the film's end, Jordan attempts to reverse his depiction of blacks as childlike and in need of white parents/protectors by turning Dil into Fergus's caretaker, he instead reinscribes racial stereotypes.

Fergus "eats the other" when he consumes Jody's life story, then usurps his place in Dil's affections. As the film ends, Fergus has not only cannibalized Jody but appropriated Jody's narrative to claim possession of Dil. As Jordan asserts, "his obsession with the man leads him to reshape her in the image of the guy he's lost." Black bodies, then, are like clay, to be shaped into anything the white man wants them to be. This paradigm romanticizes again the white colonizer's occupy-ing of black territory, possessing it in a way that affirms his identity. Fergus never fully acknowledges Dil's race or sex. Like the real-life Costner and Jordan, he can make black bodies the site of his political and cultural "radicalism" without hav-ing to respect those bodies.

Few critical reviews of *The Crying Game* discussed race; indeed, most suggested that the film's power lies in its insistence that race and gender finally do not matter; what counts is what's inside. Yet, this message is undermined by the fact that all the people subordinated to white power are black. Even though the film (like *The Body-guard*) seduces by suggesting that crossing boundaries, accepting difference, can be pleasurable, it does not disrupt conventional representations of subordination and domination. Black people allow white men to remake them in the film. And Dil's transvestism becomes less radical when she gives up her "womanly identity" to sat-isfy Fergus—whose actions are clearly paternalistic and patriarchal—without ask-ing for an explanation. With her Billie Holiday "hush, now; don't explain" kind of love, Dil acts in complicity with Fergus's appropriation of Jody.

The Crying Game disrupts many of our conventional notions about identity. The British soldier is black. His girlfriend turns out to be a transvestite. Fergus readily abandons his role as an IRA freedom fighter (a group simplistically por-trayed as only terrorists) to become an average working man. Much of this film invites us to interrogate the limits of identity politics by showing us how desire and feelings can disrupt fixed notions of who we are and what we stand for. Yet in the final scenes of the film, Fergus and Dil seem primarily concerned with fulfilling racist and sexist gender roles. He reverts to the passive, silent, unemotional, "rational" white man, an identity he earlier sought to escape. And Dil, no longer bold or defiant, becomes the "black woman" taking care of her white man; the "little woman" waiting for her man. Suddenly, heterosexism is evoked as the ideal relationship—so much for difference and ambiguity. Complex readings of identity are abandoned and everything is back in its place. No wonder mainstream viewers find this film so acceptable.

In a culture that systematically devalues black womanhood, that sees our presence as meaningful only to the extent that we serve others, it is not surprising that audiences would love a film that symbolically reinscribes us in this role. I say symbolically because the fact that Dil is really a black man suggests that in an ideal white supremacist, capitalist, patriarchal, imperialist world, females are not needed, women can be erased (no need for a real black woman) or annihilated (let the black man murder the white woman, not because she is a fascist terrorist but because she is biologically female). Ultimately, despite some magical transgressive moments, much of this film is conservative-reactionary. Crudely put, it suggests that transvestites hate and want to destroy "real" women; that straight white men want black mammies so badly that they will invent them, willingly vomiting up their own homophobia and entering a relationship with a black man to get that down-home service only a "black female" can give; that real homosexual men batter; and ultimately that the world would be a better place if we would forget about articulating race, gender, and sexual issues and become conventional white heterosexual couples. These reactionary messages echo *The Bodyguard's* conservative messages regarding difference.

Critics' rejection of *The Bodyguard* seems somehow fitting in a white supremacist, capitalist patriarchy. For despite its conventional plot, its representation of blackness in general and black femaleness in particular are far more radical than any image in *The Crying Game*. It disrupts, for example, Hollywood's conventional casting of black females in the role of servant. In fact, Rachel Marron is wealthy, and Frank Farmer is hired to serve her. However utopian this inversion is, it does challenge stereotypical assumptions about race, class, and gender hierarchies. When Frank Farmer acts to protect the life of Marron (how many films do we see in the United States in which black female life is deemed valuable, worth protecting or saving?), he takes her "home" to his white patriarchal father, who embraces her. Again, this representation breaks radically with racist stereotypes. It cannot be dismissed as mere coincidence that critics should trash a film that breaks significantly with racist and sexist norms in its representation of black womanhood even as they extol as more meaningful another film that reinscribes racist and sexist representations. Even though *The Bodyguard* conservatively suggests that interracial relationships are doomed, it still offers meaningful disruptions in the representation of race.

Despite flaws, both *The Crying Game* and *The Bodyguard* are daring works that evoke much beyond the screen dialogue about issues of race and gender, about difference and identity. Unfortunately, both films resolve the tensions of difference, of shifting roles and identity, by affirming the status quo. Both suggest that "otherness" can be the place where white folks—in both cases, white men—work through their troubled identity, their longing for transcendence. In this way they perpetuate white cultural imperialism and colonialism. Though compelling in those moments when they celebrate the possibility of accepting difference, of growing by shifting one's location, ultimately they seduce and betray.

Roberta Trites

Roberta Seelinger Trites was named Distinguished Lecturer at Illinois State University in 2010 and teaches children's and adolescent literature. She has published several scholarly books including, Disturbing the Universe: Power and Repression in Adolescent Literature *(2000), which was a winner of the Children's Literature Association Book Award. Her scholarly article, "Disney's Sub/Version of Andersen's* Little Mermaid*" was first published in the* Journal of Popular Film and Television *in 1991.*

Disney's Sub/Version of Andersen's The Little Mermaid

Although Hans Christian Andersen's "The Little Mermaid," published in 1837, contains many patronizing nineteenth-century attitudes toward women, a value system that at least acknowledges the legitimacy of femininity shapes the fairytale. Unfortunately, Walt Disney's 1989 film version of "The Little Mermaid" eliminates the values that affirm femininity in the original story. Disney's changes result in characters, images, and conflicts that rob women of integrity, making the movie even more sexist than the original story.

In both versions of the story, the little mermaid is the youngest, and loveliest, of the mer-king's daughters, but her motivation for wanting to become human in the original tale differs significantly from her controlling motivation in the movie. In Andersen's tale, when the mermaid does not understand her own dissatisfaction with mer-life, she turns to her grandmother, a wise mer-woman who serves as the mermaid's role model. The grandmother tells the little mermaid that mermaids live 300 years but have no immortal souls. Mermaids do not go to heaven after they die; they dissolve into sea foam. According to the grandmother, the only way the mermaid can gain a soul is for a human to love the mermaid so much that part of his soul flows into her and creates a soul within her. After listening to her grandmother, the little mermaid realizes that she has been discontent because she does not have an immortal soul. Thus, Andersen's mermaid quests for a soul, but Disney's mermaid, Ariel, quests for a mate.

Early in the movie, Ariel is characterized as being obsessed with humans. Mermaids are forbidden contact with anything human, a stricture that Ariel's father, the sea-king Triton, reiterates specifically to Ariel. Collecting human artifacts becomes a way for Ariel to rebel against this parental repression. But the more Ariel rebels against her father, the more dissatisfied she becomes with her own identity. Ariel repudiates the voice of acceptance, the crab Sebastian, when he counsels her to enjoy life "under the sea," because she believes humans have identities that allow them more freedom than she does. She yearns for legs so that she might dance as humans do without recognizing that she is herself dancing a uniquely mermaid dance. Disney's message is obvious: If children are needlessly repressed, they may rebel by developing obsessive behaviors that cause them to reject their identity. This didacticism is directed more to adults than it is to children, which is a recurring tendency in Disney movies.[1]

The original mermaid in the Andersen tale, unlike Ariel, is allowed the freedom of the surface once she turns 15. She is never forbidden contact with humans. She experiences no parental repression because the story centers not around the mermaid's growth to maturity but around her quest for a soul. The original mermaid does not even consider becoming human until she sees the prince and discovers from her grandmother that through their mutual love she might gain heaven. Ariel—who already possesses a soul that she is willing to wager with Ursula, the sea-witch—wants to become human before she ever falls in love because she "just [doesn't] see how a world that can make such wonderful things can be bad." She sings about the "neat stuff" that to her represents mankind. Ariel's original motivation to become human seems very materialistic.

Ariel's materialistic motivation diminishes once she falls in love-at-first-sight with Prince Eric. Ariel then interprets being forbidden contact with anything human as being forbidden both love and an identity separate from her father. When Triton decides to teach Ariel a lesson by displaying in full force the tyrannical power with which any parent can dominate a child, Ariel does not assert herself. Instead, she hides behind a statue of Eric. Once she leaves this shelter behind the figure of a human male, Triton reminds Ariel that his strength is greater than this other man's by destroying the statue. Ariel feels that her father has betrayed her.

The value system that controls the plot has been established: Ariel must choose between these two men. Ariel never considers running away to a life that does not include male protection; she rejects her father's culture to embrace Eric's culture. She seems intelligent, resourceful, and courageous but incapable of autonomy. Disregarding the motivation of Andersen's original mermaid, who wants human form so that she can gain an eternal identity, Disney has its mermaid take human form so that her identity can be defined by mortal love. The underlying message creates a startling incongruity: Children, especially girls, can gain an identity independent from their parents by becoming dependent on someone else.

To the Andersen mermaid, love is a means to an end rather than an end in itself. Three times in the story the mermaid predicates gaining an immortal soul on gaining the prince's love: She decides she will risk everything "to win him and an immortal soul"[2] when the enchantress names the terms of the spell that will make the mermaid human, the mermaid bolsters her courage by thinking about "her prince and how she would win an immortal soul"[3]; and when she finally has human form, the mermaid dreams "of human happiness and an immortal soul."[4] The mermaid equates the ideas of "love" and "soul" because she believes immortality depends on first gaining human love. In all three instances that "love" and "soul" are coordinated, the soul is placed last, in the climactic position, because the mermaid considers happiness in eternity more important than happiness on earth.

Ariel, on the other hand, wants only to gain marriage, which she equates with love, so she channels all of her strength and energy into pursuing marriage as a goal. This establishes the movie's superficial values regarding marriage. Before Ariel sees Eric, she is obsessed with the entire human culture, but love narrows her focus to just one member of that culture. Ariel's new obsession becomes the type of worship that makes the individual seem somehow larger than life and better than the rest of humanity. This implies that the only beings worth marrying are those who are perfect and that perfection is not only somehow attainable but is actually necessary for a man to be loveable. The collapse of Ariel's obsession with human artifacts into the pursuit of one perfect man indicates, moreover, that no goal matters as much as hunting for a mate. Furthermore, Ariel is manipulative and dishonest in pursuing this goal. For example, after she has landed on shore in human form, she clings dependently to Eric while grinning and winking back at her friends in the sea to show that she is faking her weakness for the sake of the prince's ego. Even worse than presenting a spouse as someone who is ensnared through guile, the movie presents marriage as a goal to be achieved rather than a process to be experienced, as if once a female has bonded with a male, her life is complete. Because Ariel perceives herself as being somehow incomplete without a man's love, Ariel thinks Eric is the panacea that will make her life perfect. She therefore considers any means by which she can entrap him to be legitimate.

The terms of the bargain that the mermaid makes with the sea-witch to become human reinforce the opposing values each story promotes. In the original version, the mermaid can live as a human until the prince marries someone else. She has the leisure to develop her love slowly into an intimate relationship. The mermaid's reward will come only if the prince marries her. Disney, however, turns the process of human love into a rushed affair that requires only three days. Ariel will be rewarded if the prince kisses her within that time, which reduces love to no more than physical sexuality. The Disney witch blatantly equates love with sexuality, telling Ariel the prince must "fall in love with you—that is—kiss you." Disney's representation of love lacks the basic integrity imbued in Andersen's representation of it.

The contrasts between the male love interests in the Andersen and Disney versions further illustrate the differing values in each of the stories. The two princes' motivations for marrying differ drastically. The Andersen prince is never aware that a mermaid has rescued him from the shipwreck. When the prince awakens onshore after the wreck, he is discovered by a young girl at a convent. This is the girl with whom the prince falls in love, but because he believes she is a novitiate at the convent, he considers her inaccessible. (She is, in actuality, a princess who is only at the convent to be educated.) The triangle that forms the plot's blocking action is thus completed by a character with an existence separate from the enchantress, yet the little mermaid is not competitively jealous of this woman. Validating the prince's values, the mermaid admires the human princess's delicacy and gentleness, even though this princess has displaced her in the prince's affections. That the mermaid can admire the princess makes the prince's decision seem sound.

In contrast, the third person in the Disney story's triangle is essentially an illusion. Eric falls in love with his memory of the physical beauty and the voice of the maiden who rescues him. Eric never considers this girl's personality. Since Eric's infatuation is so shallowly based on beauty rather than on personality, he is easily deceived by Ursula's disguising herself as the raven-headed ingénue who possesses the little mermaid's voice. Eric loves the imposter as he has loved the image in his mind: for her physical attributes and for nothing more. Eric's motivation for love is as superficial as Ariel's reason for wanting to become human.

Not only does Disney weaken the values that determine the dramatic motivations of the Andersen characters, Disney also massacres Andersen's strong imagery. Much of Andersen's imagery symbolizes the mermaid's burgeoning sexuality. The little mermaid has been slowly preparing for human sexuality, for she alone of all the daughters in her family has cultivated a garden of red flowers. These red flowers are a standard image; they prefigure the human genitalia the mermaid will seek. The enchantress educates the mermaid about human sexuality using similar images. When naming the terms of the spell, the enchantress tells the little mermaid that she will be subjected to great pain: "every time your foot touches the ground it will feel as though you were walking on knives so sharp that your blood must flow."[5] The enchantress's image of flowing blood prepares the girl for menarche, while the image of knife-like pain warns the girl about the potentially hymen-breaking phallus. All of these images indicate that the mermaid must be a menstruating adult before she will be given a chance to realize her love, unlike the Disney counterpart, who seems to grow up precisely because she has experienced love. Andersen depicts human love as a product of maturity, whereas Disney depicts it as a cause of maturity.

The Andersen mermaid's becoming human is in itself an important image. She makes a simple decision to seek out the sea-witch, unprovoked by any manipulation on the enchantress's part, with the hope that the enchantress can assist her. Andersen's enchantress thinks the mermaid's decision is foolish but helps the maid anyway. The mermaid irrevocably trades her tail for human feet in order to be with the prince, and she suffers the resulting pain willingly because she hopes to gain eternal life by self-denial in this life. Andersen's mermaid is no stranger to suffering. The physical pain of humans is contrasted to the emotional pain of mer-life. "mermaids can't weep and that makes their suffering even deeper and greater."[6] Because physical pain is described as less devastating than emotional pain, the self-inflicted physical pain the mermaid endures is not simply a stereotypical image of women as masochistic. The pain is something the mermaid chooses as the only way she knows to gain an immortal soul. Her pain has a purpose. Through her suffering she will earn an eternal identity. Disney's mermaid, however, makes pain-free sacrifices so that she can become attractive to a man.

Much of Disney's imagery focuses on demonstrating Ariel's malleability. This is especially apparent in her decision to become human. No beguiling temptress entices the Andersen mermaid; her decision to become human is self-determined. But Ariel depends on characters who are stronger than she to shape her destiny for her. This enables Ursula to tempt Ariel in an allusively Miltonic style. Contact with humans has already been established as Ariel's "forbidden fruit," and Ursula's eels evoke the tempting snake in the Garden of Eden. Ursula has the same revenge motive that Satan has: Just as Satan is jealous of God's power in *Paradise Lost*, Ursula covets Triton's power. Ursula scornfully comments on how different life is at Triton's palace than it was when she lived there, much like Satan comments on heaven after he has fallen. No explanation is ever given as to why Ursula has been displaced from her former home, but clearly she has had a falling out with Triton and has decided she would rather rule in the hell she has created than serve in Triton's "heaven." Ursula has the same interest in seeing Ariel fall that Satan has in Adam's fall. Ursula hopes that Ariel's downfall will be "the key to Triton's undoing," just as Satan hopes that tempting Adam will injure Adam's father. Furthermore, Ursula will be able to keep Ariel's soul in her hellish garden, just as Satan gathers souls for hell from mankind. Ursula's predatory nature provides the perfect foil for Ariel's weakness.

Frighteningly Freudian images proliferate in Ursula's castle, further typifying mature women as predatory. Whereas the palaces of Triton and Eric are built of many juxtaposed long, cylindrical towers, Ursula's place of power is cavernous. Ursula's palace is entered through the mouth opening of a skeletal animal, and the swimming entrant must traverse the long neck of the animal before penetrating the womb-like inner chamber where Ursula resides. In the rear of this inner chamber is a conch shell, its lips spread open to reveal a gaping hole leading to some unknown place. This gynophobic image is a grotesque parody of the female anatomy.

Ursula's breasts, too, figure prominently in the bargain scene. One especially memorable sequence involves a "zoom-in" on Ursula's cleavage, so that her ponderous bosom occupies the entire screen. Ursula's breasts seem suffocating, rather than nurturing, which is a perversion of the biological function of breasts. Disney portrays the mature female body as ominously menacing.

Disney makes Ursula's personality even more threatening than her body. Ursula is devious, cruel, and manipulative. In order to gain power over Ariel, Ursula must convince the young girl that she is in need of the witch's services, so Ursula capitalizes on the mermaid's immature motivation for loving Eric. Twice Ursula sways Ariel's decision by evoking the face of Eric—once when Ursula's eels flick the almost-shattered visage of Eric's statue toward the grieving girl and again in the smoke over the enchantress's crucible. It is as if Ariel is not firmly resolved to pursue love and so a reminder of her love must be provided for her. Ariel accepts these physical reminders as tangible evidence of her love because, like Eric, she bases her love on physical attributes rather than on personality. When Ariel agonizes over the conflict of choosing between Eric and her family, Ursula agrees that the choices are "tough" and placates the maid by consoling her: "at least you'll have your man." Ursula uses the same logic to convince Ariel to give up her voice: "she who holds her tongue gets her man."[7] The sea-witch's comments are calculatedly self-serving, despite her spurious claims to the contrary.

Disney gives its sea-witch an interest in the mermaid's relationship with the prince that the original witch does not have. Ariel's love affords Ursula an opportunity to compete with Ariel for the possession of the mermaid's soul, which Ursula perceives as a weapon to use against Triton. Therefore, whereas the plot of the Disney version centers around Ariel's motivation to gain a man, the subplot centers around Ursula's motivation to gain the power of a man. And Ursula seems to think the only way she can gain power over Triton is by callously using another female. In contrast to Ursula, Andersen's enchantress has only the power to take the little mermaid's voice. She does this mechanically rather than magically by cutting out the mermaid's tongue. After the bargain is made, the Andersen enchantress plays only a minor role in the remainder of the story because she has no stake in either the mermaid's success or failure. The Andersen sea-witch's tacit support of the little mermaid delineates a bond between women entirely absent from the movie. Disney's witch has far greater involvement in the story than in the original because Disney always relies on women to create the conflict between good and evil in feature-length fairytales. The conflict in *The Little Mermaid*—as in Disney's other feature-length fairytales *Snow White, Cinderella,* and *Sleeping Beauty*—pits one woman against another.

The Disney-constructed conflict in *The Little Mermaid* is between an over-weight, ugly woman and a doe-eyed heroine with a figure less realistic than a Barbie doll's. Once Ursula transforms herself into a rival love-interest for the prince, the conflict is between a dark-haired anorexic and a fairer one. The stereotyping of evil as dark and good as fair is traditional, but only recently has Disney associated corpulence with evil. Disney's villainesses before the 1970s look predatory because they are so thin: Snow White's and Cinderella's stepmothers, Maleficient the Magnificent, and Cruella deVille are all emaciated. In the 1970s, Disney begins to reflect the cultural emphasis on weight consciousness. Ursula, with her delusions that she is "practically starving," is much like the overweight villainess in *The Rescuers*. Ursula's portrait of "poor souls" (who are both impoverished and pitiful) reemphasizes the movie's weight consciousness; the poor souls Ursula paints in the smoke over her cauldron are an underweight male and an overweight female who have been granted well-toned bodies. The movie's portrayal of good as fairer and thinner than evil presents a bigoted distortion of the human body.

There is no conflict between good and evil in the Andersen tale, but in the Disney version, predictably, the conflict centers on evil's attempt to usurp the power of the good. Ursula is power hungry; she wants to rob Triton of his power, just as the Medusa, a woman with snakes growing out of her head, robs men of power by turning them to stone. Distinguished from other mer-folk by a lower body made of eight tentacles, Ursula seems to be an inverse Medusa figure. The snake-like appendages also make Ursula a perversion of femininity; her tentacles could be interpreted as eight phalluses. That Disney considers the myth of Medusa to be a story about power-robbing, "unsexed" woman is clear; Ursula's overweight predecessor in *The Rescuers* is named Madame Medusa.

The final confrontation between good and evil in the movie version defines male power as positive and female power as negative. Evil comes in the form of a woman who covets the power of the male phallus. Ursula lovingly caresses Triton's trident while he is holding it. Her penis envy is stereotypical. Once Ursula gains possession of the trident, the phallic symbol of Triton's power, she grows to monstrous proportions. Her potency is represented as if she herself has become a mighty phallus, emerging erect from the water. Her voice becomes heavy and masculine as she sadistically toys with the trapped Ariel, zapping the mermaid with ejaculatory bolts from the middle prong of the usurped trident and sarcastically taunting the mermaid, "So much for 'true love.'" The prince then kills Ursula by aiming for the sea-witch's groin with a long, jagged beam that protrudes from a sailing ship. The beam is aimed first for the area of traditional male vulnerability, but because Ursula is not male, at the moment just prior to penetration, the thrust of the prince's phallic symbol is diverted to the area just beneath Ursula's gargantuan breast. Despite the G-rating, the movie is very sexual in its sexism.

Even though the Disney mermaid has suffered much more at the hands of the sea-witch than the prince has, it is the prince who kills the witch. This is Disney's most annoying reworking of Andersen's plot. If Disney must insert a good versus evil conflict into every feature-length fairytale, why—since the studio rewrites the whole story anyway—can't the maid kill the witch herself? The answer: because nice girls are not supposed to have that much power.

After the Disney hero has slaughtered the Satanic woman, he and Ariel still cannot be united. Ariel has reverted to her mermaid form because Eric did not kiss her within the allotted time. Watching Eric forlornly, Ariel sits on a rock in the pose of the little mermaid statue in Copenhagen harbor. She despairs. Because she looks so defeated, Triton finally takes pity on his daughter. "She really does love him," the sea-king admits. His counsellor agrees with him: "Children got to be free to live their own lives."

The counsellor's statement is as admirable as it is accurate; unfortunately, in this context, it is hypocritical. Triton does not grant Ariel human form simply because Ariel is interested in humans and wants to explore their culture; the king only "frees" Ariel to "live her own life" so that she may live under Eric's power. The final scene, as Triton kisses his daughter goodbye and she turns with subservient awe to Eric, carries overt approval of female dependency.

Compare the cliché-ridden ending of the movie with the conclusion of Andersen's original story. After the princess from the convent reappears, the prince marries her. The little mermaid is supposed to die, but the allegedly irrevocable spell is made revocable at the last moment. The mermaid's sisters have sold their hair to the enchantress to buy a knife. If the mermaid will use the knife to kill the prince on his wedding night, the original enchantment will be broken and she can assume a mermaid's body again. But accepting responsibility for her own actions, the mermaid chooses instead to die herself.

As the dying mermaid is dissolving into sea foam, the "daughters of the air" come to her and tell her that they, too, do not have souls, but they can acquire souls by performing good deeds, such as cooling children who suffer from heat. The little mermaid then becomes a part of the wind. For the first time she can cry, indicating that her emotional suffering has come to an end. She kisses the forehead of the prince and smiles at his bride, minimizing the conflict between women.

The overtones of Christian allegory are strong in Andersen's tale. The original little mermaid discovers that grace through man's love is not the only means to salvation. Although it takes longer, salvation can also be achieved through the self-sacrifice of good works. Andersen clearly wants the mermaid to gain a soul by her own efforts instead of relying on someone else to bestow a soul upon her. Andersen wrote to a friend in 1837: "I have not . . . allowed the mermaid's acquiring of an immortal soul to depend upon an alien creature, upon the love of a human being . . . I have permitted my mermaid to follow a more natural, more divine path."[8] Andersen offers women several paths toward self-realization, so the message to children is much more far-sighted than Disney's limited message that only through marriage can a woman be complete.

Disney attempts to define self-realization as resulting from the archetypal separation of the adolescent from the parent. Disney shows both a male and female authority figure who abuse their power. The negative figure that Bruno Bettelheim might label the "female Oedipal figure" is permanently destroyed, while the positive parental figure becomes less threatening when Triton accepts

Ariel's maturity.[9] Moreover, the adolescent's archetypal initiation into adulthood is presented in beautiful birth imagery as Ariel emerges in human form from the water.

But Disney's use of the fairytale as an initiation myth eventually falls apart. Berland accurately defines the structure of a fairytale: "overall fairytales present a character with a problem of conflict that character must overcome. As the character masters the situation, he or she grows up."[10] Since Eric kills the witch for Ariel and since Triton makes her marriage possible, Ariel does not solve her own problems. Ariel is not really initiated into adulthood because she is not self-empowered. She does not earn independence; her father only grants her the right to transfer her dependence to another man.

Even though the Andersen tale does not focus on growing up, the story's many positive female figures provide a more accurate portrait of what it is to be a woman than the movie does.[11] Remember, for example, that in the original tale the grandmother serves as a source of information and as a positive role model for the little mermaid. In the Disney version, this role model is replaced by a male bird who misinforms the maid. Second, unlike the Disney witch, the Andersen enchantress supports the little mermaid's search for an immortal soul; she never attempts to foil the mermaid's plans and even contributes blood from her own breast to make the potion that transforms the mermaid into a human. Third, the sisters of the mermaid in the original story sacrifice their only treasure to help their sister; Ariel's sisters do nothing. Fourth, the prince's beloved is someone whose femininity the little mermaid respects. Finally, femininity gets its ultimate affirmation from the daughters of the air. They teach the little mermaid about charity, and they exist only as females. The grandmother, the enchantress, the princess, the sisters, and the daughters of the air are all strong, beautiful, supportive, and feminine. But by changing their gender, by making their motivations anti-feminine, or by editing their function from the story, Disney destroys all of these characters.

Disney's most destructive changes, however, involve the characterization of the little mermaid. Both the Andersen and the Disney mermaids agree to be voiceless, to give up their physical forms, and to separate themselves from their cultures, although their motivations for doing so differ significantly. Both of them believe that they can gain love by suppressing their true identities. But because they have no verbal communication skills and are illiterate, they can express their personalities only by relying on their appearances. In the Andersen version, since the mermaid has forfeited her ability to articulate her identity, the prince regards her as an object of beauty rather than as a person to be loved. The mermaid is so self-effacing that she cannot win love, but she redeems herself by earning for herself the capacity for an eternal identity. Disney subverts the little mermaid's process of self-actualization. Ariel effaces herself and wins. She gets her man.

In a 1987 issue of *Children's Literature Association Quarterly*, Lucy Rollin writes that critics fear Disney because the studio rewrites the fairytale to reflect American values.[12] This is precisely what is so frightening about Disney's The *Little Mermaid*, the movie depicts women as either self-effacing or evil, incapable of creating their own responsible power without either depending on men or stealing power from them. Thus, Disney's interpretation of Andersen's story perpetrates sexist values by teaching those values to a new generation.

Acknowledgment

The author gratefully acknowledges the ideas of Stuart Kenny that are contained in this paper.

Notes

1. David I. Berland discusses this tendency in "Disney and Freud: Walt Meets the Id." *Journal of Popular Culture* 15 (1982), pp. 93–104.
2. All references to Hans Christian Andersen's "The Little Mermaid" are taken from *The Complete Fairy Tales and Stories*, trans. Erik Christian Haugaard (New York: Doubleday, 1974), pp. 57–76.
3. Andersen, p. 69.
4. Andersen, p. 72.
5. Andersen, p. 68.
6. Andersen, p. 61.
7. Although some viewers might perceive those of Ursula's statements that capitalize on Ariel's inexperience as ironic and as an intended tribute to feminism, these comments are voiced in the midst of too much gynophobic imagery to honestly promote feminism.
8. As quoted in *Tales and Stories by Hans Christian Andersen*, ed. and trans. Patricia L. Conroy and Sven H. Rossel (Seattle: University of Washington Press, 1980), pp. 250–251.
9. Bruno Bettelheim, *The Uses of Enchantment: The Meaning and Importance of Fairy Tales* (New York: Knopf, 1976), pp. 66–75.
10. Berland, p. 101.
11. Disney invariably erases positive figures of women from its feature-length fairytales; women are either reduced to the status of servants (e.g., the servant who is the only human woman in *The Little Mermaid*) or else they are elevated to an unattainable position above humanity by their possession of magical powers (e.g., Cinderella's fairy-godmother).
12. Lucy Rollin, "Fear of Faerie: Disney and the Elitist Critics." *Children's Literature Association Quarterly* 12 (1987), pp. 90–93.

Christine Farris

Christine Farris is a professor and Director of Composition at Indiana University, Bloomington. Her most recent book is called Integrating Literature and Writing Instruction: First-Year English, Humanities Core Courses, Seminars, *edited with Judith H. Anderson (2007). The article "Crash Course: Race, Class, and Context" was published in* College English *in 2007.*

Crash *Course: Race, Class, and Context*

> The only way to break down barriers is to have everything out in the open.
>
> Simon Green, Ashton Kutcher's character in *Guess Who*

As most everyone knows by now, the 2006 Academy Award Winner for Best Picture, *Crash*, directed and co-written by Paul Haggis, screenwriter of *Million Dollar Baby* and of drama shows for television like *Thirtysomething*, consists of eight racialized incidents in contemporary Los Angeles, involving characters whose fates intersect. When I first became aware of the buzz surrounding the release of *Crash*, I imagined it would be a good film to teach. Anyone who uses film in writing or literature courses for undergraduates looks for films that will spark lively classroom conversation and perhaps even serious debate.

Often I have first-year writing students analyze representations of race in Hollywood films. I've put films like *Do the Right Thing* and *Grand Canyon* (also set in Los Angeles) in "conversation" and asked students to use the ideas of cultural critics like W. E. B. Du Bois, Michael Omi, and bell hooks as lenses for examining how race narratives intersect with other cultural narratives. More recently, we've been working with "remakes" of classic Hollywood films, investigating how shifting historical contexts and social values account for the different ways in which race, class, gender, and sexuality are represented in the original and recent versions of films like *Guess Who's Coming to Dinner, King Kong, The Stepford Wives,* and *The Manchurian Candidate.*

Prior to its release, it seemed that *Crash* might resist the Hollywood formulae my students and I have encountered again and again that would have us believe that racism is no longer a problem—because Morgan Freeman and Jessica Tandy (*Driving Miss Daisy*) or Danny Glover and Mel Gibson (*Lethal Weapon 1, 2* and *3*) or Danny Glover and Kevin Kline (*Grand Canyon*) can somehow manage to get past race, or because Bernie Mac and Ashton Kutcher (*Guess Who*) can get over race and teach each other about women and the tango. Unlike those films in which black-white friendship works to distract and conceal American racial and class politics (see Benjamin DeMott's "Put on a Happy Face"), *Crash* promised to keep it real.

In an early review, Roger Ebert claimed that rather than sugarcoat race, *Crash* "presumes that most people feel prejudice and resentment against members of other groups, and observes the consequences of those feelings." "Along the way," according to Ebert, "these people say exactly what they are thinking, without the filters of political correctness." *Crash*'s multiple plotlines intersect, permitting all sorts of racial, ethnic, and class prejudice to collide. It sounded promising. A sort of L.A. "contact zone," a cinematic version of Mary Louise Pratt's social space "where cultures meet, clash, and grapple with each other, often in contexts of highly asymmetrical relations of power" (34). As *if* . . .

My first reaction upon seeing *Crash* was to take issue with Ebert's and other reviewers' claims that the dialogue, characters, and events in this contact zone were somehow more realistic than usual. While certainly not putting a P.C. or a "happy face" on race relations, *Crash*'s efforts to keep it real rely on the very racial stereotypes that the film's overall project wants to deconstruct—all the while presuming in its opening voiceover (delivered by Don Cheadle) a universal "we" (people of color as well as whites), who supposedly need to come out "from behind this metal and glass" and "crash into each other" to feel bigotry.

Contributing to the faux honesty and stereotyping is Haggis's narrative structure. Rather than creating a logical and sequential narrative orientation for viewers, Haggis uses discontinuous editing of short, tense vignettes in which all the characters say what's on their minds, eventually revealing both their racist and their redeeming qualities. Haggis combines these Tarantino- and Altman-like "short cuts" with broadly drawn characters and hardboiled sound bites characteristic of episodic TV drama. Need to get a bead on Rick, Brendan Fraser's character? He's the DA running for office who's calculating how not to alienate the minority vote. His wife, Jean, played by Sandra Bullock? She's the uptight rich racist white bitch. If you didn't read the signs as Anthony (Ludacris) did when she clutched her husband's arm at the sight of two young black men in Brentwood, you get it when she "realistically" yells "exactly what she's thinking" in earshot of Daniel, the Latino locksmith (Michael Peña), whom she believes to be a gangbanger likely to sell his friends her housekeys. More troubling is the racist stereotyping of Anthony and Peter, whose habit of carjacking seems to go without saying and, in the case of Anthony, whose political views are a source of comic relief more than they are of character development and change. The racist representation of Asians is even more naturalized: just-off-the-boat people from Thailand or Cambodia are released into the LA land of opportunity after their imprisonment by a Korean couple engaged in the trafficking of sweatshop labor. Unlike the film's other characters, the Koreans don't even get a "good side," nor do they get "saved," unless you count Anthony and Peter's delivery of the husband to the emergency room after they've run him over.

Haggis seemingly uses narrative experimentation to give the film's antiracist message more weight: he opens with a minor fender bender at a murder scene and then backs up to reveal the preceding day's backstory and unravel the causal chain and cosmic interconnectedness of the characters, some of whom are at the scene. But as film scholar David Bordwell has pointed out, such experimentation is often accompanied by very conventional tropes, which, as viewers, we use to make sense of narratives with scrambled time schemes and plots based on converging fates or social networks. At the same time that such strategies intrigue and interest us, says Bordwell, they "exploit the redundancy built into the classical norms [. . .] and rely on our acquaintance with story schemas circulating in popular culture at large" (82). Haggis relies on the easy sentimentalism of Hollywood and television drama in his treatment of David, the falsely maligned Latino locksmith, who we learn is actually a gentle and loving father to a young girl terrified of drive-by shootings, one of which she magically survives. Other myths abound, including the misguided love of the Don Cheadle character's drug-addicted mother for her wayward son rather than for the one who's a successful provider.

Perhaps we are meant to think of these segments not as stories with the complexities of motivation, development, cause, and effect, but as what Ebert calls "parables" of hope, because "as the characters crash into one other, they learn things, mostly about themselves." If so, then *Crash*'s most disturbing lesson seems to be that everybody—even a mean, sadistic cop like Matt Dillon's character—has a good side and reasons for his or her racist acts, for which he or she can be forgiven.

Because his father (who lost his janitor business when government bids went to minority-owned businesses) can't get his HMO to cover the medical procedure he desperately needs, Officer Ryan (Matt Dillon) goes on a racist tirade in several conversations with Shaniqua, a black HMO administrator played by Loretta Devine. He takes his hatred out further on Cameron (Terrence Howard), an upscale TV director, and Cameron's wife Christine (Thandie Newton), a woman who must endure not just the racial profiling of a needless traffic stop but also a sexualized body search. Later, however, Ryan comes to Christine's rescue when she is trapped in her overturned car, and by saving her, the film suggests, he is redeemed.

The problem with parables is this: the intended lesson is not always the lesson learned. Rather than analyze the heterogeneity of experiences among members of various races and ethnicities, ultimately the film invites viewers to supply what's missing in the stories by looking to their own experience. This "hopeful" treatment of racism seems especially designed to appeal to white audiences, for whom the film is an opportunity to rearrange what Krista Rateliffe calls a "guilt/blame logic" (91) rather than to examine the systemic causes and effects of a racist patriarchal system. Viewers might take comfort in the notion that everyone is a little bit racist, and that they would never criticize the housekeeper like that, much less shoot the locksmith. I am reminded of the student in one of my introductory literature classes who, while reading Toni Morrison's *The Bluest* Eye, was relieved that Pecola, the little girl who goes mad from abuse, was shunned by her black neighbors. "That lets white people off the hook," the student wrote.

So *Crash* is not the film I thought it was going to be. Does this mean I would not teach it? No, on the contrary. When *Crash* came out on DVD, I went ahead and paired it with John Singleton's *Higher Learning* and with Spike Lee's *Do the Right Thing*, chiefly to examine the different uses that filmmakers make of stereotypes to critique stereotypes.

Now that I've seen Spike Lee's documentary on Hurricane Katrina, *When the Levees Broke*, I can imagine a way to work with students on the differences between Lee's and Haggis's approach to antiracist projects. There's an important distinction to be made between the rhetorical strategies of the two films. *Crash* makes the same point over and over—intolerance is human, but humans aren't all bad—at the same level of generality. Causal connections for actions are unexplored or thin, and, in the end, every protagonist has a realization of more or less equal weight. In *Writing Analytically* David Rosenwasser and Jill Stephen call this approach "1 on 10," observing that it's what weaker writers do when they make the same point with about ten examples but fail to analyze any of them in depth. In contrast, Spike Lee's (admittedly lengthy) documentary is an instance of what Rosenwasser and Stephen call "10 on 1": an approach that makes ten related points on a single subject, thereby engaging "in prolonged scrutiny of evidence" rather than settling for one idea and applying it mechanically over and over (33). Spike Lee, I might point out to students, is concerned in his "four acts" with expansion and complication of the thesis that what happened to New Orleans was an avoidable horrific disaster. While Lee also brings together a cast of black and white victims of devastating trauma, his episodes do not add up to four hours of making exactly the same point. Rather, the anger of the characters we get to know through his interviews is woven into a larger narrative that includes a much wider context, an intersection of systemic factors that, when threaded with racism, worsened the Katrina tragedy for New Orleans. We learn in the four hours of the effects of local versus state and federal politics, Democrats versus Republicans, Bush's indifference to a state and citizens he didn't need to court, the incompetence of FEMA and of the Army Corps of Engineers, and the greed of insurance companies who weasel out of the claims submitted by property owners. All of this is contextualized within the history of New Orleans as a site for slave trading, a connection not lost on Lee's subjects, who recount tales of post-Katrina family separation and displacement across forty-six states. Lee manages to find common ground among Katrina victims that does not render them interchangeable, while insisting on the function of geography, economics, power, and language as well as race.

A film like *Crash* also points to racial and cultural differences and to common ground with regard to racism. But, as Jay Jordan has said of multicultural composition textbooks, it leaves relatively unquestioned "the various structures that determine what those differences mean" (171). In teaching with *Crash*, we should heed what Pratt said about the curriculum of "Culture, Ideas, Values," the revised Stanford Western civilization course that got her thinking about contact zones as pedagogical sites: "One had to work in the knowledge that whatever one said was going to be systematically received in radically heterogeneous ways that we were neither able nor entitled to prescribe" (39). Those who experience racism on a daily basis don't see it as something they can choose to invoke or not, depending on the sort of day they're having. While Paul Haggis may believe his film has represented racism in a balanced, equal-opportunity fashion, *Crash* does not speak to all viewers in the same way. As Michael Dyson has pointed out about so-called multicultural projects, any mainstream packaging of diversity that categorizes the other as "interchangeable" obfuscates the fact that in real cultural space not all voices are getting to tell the truth; "we're not all participating equally at the table" (Dobrin 93).

Although both *Crash* and *When the Levees Broke* can be considered improvements upon the usual celebratory packaging of diversity in most Hollywood films and multicultural college textbooks, merely acknowledging differences and racism is often not enough to get students who write about racism beyond agree/disagree, us/them, or off-the-hook positions, if the various structures and events that determine where those differences come from and what they mean in our culture are not also explored. Spike Lee's project on Hurricane Katrina and New Orleans might be further seen, then, as a model for reconstructing with our students a history and system of beliefs and institutional practices so as to deepen their analysis.

Works Cited

Bordwell, David. *The Way Hollywood Tells It: Story and Style in Modern Movies.* Berkeley: U of California P, 2006.

DeMott, Benjamin. "Put On a Happy Face: Masking the Differences between Blacks and Whites." *Signs of Life in the USA.* 5th ed. Ed. Sonia Maasik and Jack Solomon. Boston: Bedford, 2006, 567–77.

Dobrin, Sidney L. "Race and the Public Intellectual: An Interview with Michael Eric Dyson." *Race, Rhetoric and the Postcolonial.* Ed. Gary A. Olson and Lynn Worsham. Albany: SUNY P., 1999, 81–126.

Ebert, Roger. Rev. of *Crash, Chicago Sun-Times* 5 May 2006. 4 Sept. 2006 http://rogerebert.suntimes.com/apps/pbes.dll/article?AID=/20050505/REVIEWS/50502001.

Haggis, Paul, dir. *Crash*, 2004. DVD. Lions Gate, 2006.

Jordan, Jay. "Rereading the Multicultural Reader: Toward More 'Infectious' Practices in Multicultural Composition." College English (2005): 168–85.

Lee, Spike, dir. *When the Levees Broke: A Requiem in Four Acts.* HBO, 2006.

Morrison, Toni. *The Bluest Eye.* New York: Holt, 1970.

Pratt, Mary Louise. "Arts of the Contact Zone." *Profession 91.* New York: MLA, 1991, 33–40.

Rateliffe, Krista. *Rhetorical Listening: Identification, Gender, Whiteness.* Carbondale: Southern Illinois UP, 2005.

Rosenwasser, David, and Jill Stephen. *Writing Analytically.* 4th ed. Boston: Thomson, 2006.

Kim Edwards

Kim Edwards is a film scholar and has published several articles in the Australian magazine *Screen Education*, including "Alice's Little Sister: Exploring *Pan's Labyrinth*" (2008). *Screen Education* is published by the Australian Teachers of Media (ATOM) and *Screen Australia*. The quarterly magazine is aimed at educators and students, for the enhancement of primary and secondary school curricula.

Alice's Little Sister: Exploring Pan's Labyrinth

> *We're all mad here.*
> – The Cheshire Cat to Alice[1]

The first draft of Lewis Carroll's iconic text was called *Alice's Adventures Under Ground*, and recalling this early title unearths some fascinating metaphors. Consider: Alice's journey was, quite literally, groundbreaking in positing a child heroine in a subterranean fantasy world, where the surreal clashed with overt real-world satire and nonsense was imbued with disturbing meaning. The creation of an imaginary realm that is indeed 'below the surface' invites exploration of the language we need to describe such a space. In being subterranean, an underground world is 'subtext' made manifest: it is the secret place under the world/word that explains reality in subtle ways, the buried meaning for which one must dig. By its very location it is subversive because it truly *undermines* the real world.

While Alice's adventures have permeated fantasy fiction since they were first published, cinematic fantasy and science fiction have been particularly enamoured with Carroll's literary heroine in the last few decades. She is all grown up in *The Matrix* (Andy and Larry Wachowski, 1999, 2003, 2003) and *Resident Evil* (Paul W.S. Anderson, 2002, 2004, 2007) series and reinvented for *Labyrinth* (Jim Henson, 1986), *MirrorMask* (Dave McKean, 2005) and *Tideland* (Terry Gilliam, 2005). Recently *Pan's Labyrinth* (Guillermo del Toro, 2006) is particularly conscious of its sororal relationship with Alice and its re-imagining of a W(under)land, and with the way events below the surface of the world and the text inform reality and meaning.

Feminizing the underworld

In classical mythology, traditional depictions of an Underworld were emphatically masculine and adult space: Hades was the land of the dead, named for the Greek

111

god who ruled over it. To journey there was a descent into hell and thus the central and climactic destination for questing heroes from epic poetry. In contrast, Alice's Wonderland is emphatically matriarchal, feminized (with tea parties, croquet and poetry) and anthropomorphically lively. From the outset, *Pan's Labyrinth* also usurps the traditional male space of the Underworld, displaces it, and designates it a female realm: the questing hero is the runaway princess Ofelia (Ivana Baquero); lies, pain and 'death' occur outside its borders; and the ultimate desire is to return to this netherworld as home rather than brave its perils and escape from it. The visual impact of the fantasy world is Freudian in its gendering – from the downward wipe through the mother Carmen's (Ariadna Gil) swollen belly into the fairytale landscape, the imagery is continually organic and uterine, with warm rich colours, earthy cavernous spaces and the recurring curved feminine shapes reminiscent of the Faun's horns.

In its affiliation with nature and the natural, this 'underland' is not divorced from abjectness or from danger and darkness, such as the horrors of the child-eating Pale Man (Doug Jones) and the slimy glutinous toad in the bowels of the dead tree or the moral ambiguities of the Faun (Doug Jones). But it is more a place of life and rebirth than a land of the dead. Like the opening image of Ofelia's death being reversed, as the blood flows backwards, the underground realm teems with moist, breathing, growing life. Even Ofelia's descent down a relative 'rabbit-hole' into the Labyrinth is heralded with the stick insect metamorphosing into a carnivorous nature-green fairy, and her three life-affirming quests are to resurrect the dead tree, escape a reanimated monster and preserve her baby brother. Moreover, this world seems to value energy and action and extols rebellion, disobedience and freedom of choice. Ofelia succeeds in her quests by disobeying her mother and destroying her dress while hunting the toad, by ignoring the fairies and choosing a different door to unlock, and by refusing absolutely to shed her brother's blood to return to her kingdom.

This fecund, earthy and maternal underland is juxtaposed with scenes in the 'real' world of fascist Spain in 1944, with their steely military colours and sharp cold lines and shapes. Ofelia's stepfather, Captain Vidal (Sergi López), parodies the White Rabbit of Wonderland with his beloved pocket watch and his desire for order, precision and unfailing obedience. Yet his controlling, mechanical, cog-driven world is in overt opposition to the fairytale realm. This 'fatherland' is ruthlessly and sadistically masculine and death-dealing, where men are in power, in action and inexplicable. The adult politics underpinning the war are beyond Ofelia's comprehension, the violence and punishments are widespread and unremitting, and universally women and children are seen and not heard. In this environment, Carmen's one admirable quality is that she is pretty to look at; Mercedes' (Maribel Verdú) lullaby is an indication of her quiet rebellion against servile silence; and Ofelia is reduced to marginalized spaces: the liminal Labyrinth, the kitchens, under the bed and up in the attic.

Thus, like the original Hades, locations become macrocosms of their inhabitants, for not only is the underland presented as a feminized space in contrast to the male-dominated real world, but it is also designated a child's space in reaction to the adult world. It is hidden and contained, but opens out into vast possibilities.

Like the obsession with getting bigger and smaller in Alice's Wonderland, this fantasy world actually grows around the figure of the child: the Faun gets younger, the magic gets stronger, and, like the protagonist herself, portals are physically right under the adults' noses as well as under their feet.

Clashing dichotomies

The Labyrinth exists between the two worlds and, expressing a number of binary oppositions, acknowledges aspects of both. The Faun too is a signifier for the Labyrinth; thus it appears as a force of nature that is both creative and destructive.

Furthermore, it is androgenous and morally ambiguous, and not only does it occupy a largely undefined position between male and female and evil and good, it also literally embodies these binaries by being both the human and the animal, the man and the monster, and the child and the adult.

These clashing dichotomies extend beyond the figure of the Faun and the confines of the Labyrinth when the fantasy invades the real world, as rich colours, female power and nature encroach upon the unrest between the military and the rebels. This merging of the worlds is also an organic and growing phenomenon that begins with the relatively insignificant appearance of an insect and the existence of the portal to the Labyrinth. It develops into the perhaps coincidental incursion into the dead tree that destroys the Alice dress and the 'miracle' cure of the mother after the arrival of the mandrake baby. It finally culminates in the undisputable evidence of the chalk – for how did Ofelia escape from a guarded room to reach the Captain's study if not for a magic door?

> Pan's Labyrinth usurps the traditional male space of the Underworld, displaces it, and designates it a female realm.

Ofelia's mother dismisses fairytales as the stuff of childhood, and even sympathetic Mercedes says she herself outgrew such fantasies. But Ofelia's underground realm grows in validity and power and becomes increasingly indistinguishable from reality. Meanwhile, the cold imagery and logical action in the 'real' world begin to disintegrate into gothic horrors (such as the bloodied death of the mother and birth of the brother) and macabre and fractured violence (from the tortured rebel's split hand to the Captain's split face).

In challenging their respective boundaries as the two worlds collide, the doubling motif that both compares and contrasts realism and the imaginary becomes more apparent. As in Alice's adventures, great significance is attached to unlocking doors and magical keys (in themselves, potently gendered symbols). In Ofelia's realm, there is the toad quest and the booty from the Pale Man, and in the real world the power of possession over the storeroom keys and the horrors of torture and childbirth that happen behind closed doors.

This mirroring is also seen in the significance of the two knives that both become symbols of sacrifice and freedom rather than violence. While the male weapons of choice are guns and grenades and the Captain's blunt instruments of torture, the knives are inherently female as tools of the kitchen and the relics of the underland. Mercedes' little paring knife is not lethal, but her attack on the Captain in self-defence ensures her escape and freedom.

Ofelia's magic quest object becomes her final test when she rejects the knife, and the pain and self-interest it represents, thus proving her purity of soul and allowing her to transcend death and return home.

The parody of the Mad Hatter's tea party in the dual dining rooms is perhaps the most revealing parallel drawn between the worlds: the hypocritical, greedy, devouring adults at the Captain's dinner table are visualty doubled with the luxurious and horrific temptations of the Pale Man's banquet hall, complete with the two hosts at the head of the tables framed by fireplaces with leaping hell flames.

Fantasy and reality

The fairytale realm – that submerged sub-text – therefore becomes an insightful commentary on war and the rules of society and gender in the real world: it undermines the authority of the fascists and the dictates of the Captain by exhuming that which has been hidden and silenced. The horror of the Pale Man's dining room is literally contained within the space of the Captain's house; rather than a parallel universe, the underland is inside reality, like a kernel of truth or an essence made manifest. As in Wonderland, the creatures in *Pan's Labyrinth* function as distorted reflections of and satirical commentary on adults in the real world: monstrous as the Pale Man is, his propensity for horrendous violence is limited by magical rules and literally pales next to the sadistic, unchecked war and domestic crimes of the Captain. The visual comparison of the two as brooding demons in hellish dining rooms relocates the site of true horror, for the war atrocities we witness are far more distressing than the fantasy monsters, and the Captain is revealed to be far more frightening and deadly to Ofelia than anything she faces underground.

Actor Doug Jones plays both the Pale Man and the Faun. While this character doubling reiterates the dark and dangerous side of the latter, the Faun's subsequent comparison to the Captain reveals where Ofelia herself locates the site of evil. After the actions of her merciless stepfather, the Faun's reappearance to forgive her for her mistakes and give her a second chance is greeted with outstretched arms. When a monster inspires more affection and displays more paternal care than a man, we are ourselves forced to reassess what we demonize.

Strangely, though, the extent to which the fantasy world both overgrows and undermines the real world is problematized by the film's climax: 'curiouser and curiouser,' as Alice might say. The two worlds finally unite in the underland's rosy but violent explosions of colour and light. They are the life-affirming marks of rebellion and disobedience, but are exacted by the real-world rebels attacking the military base: war is hell, but freedom demands sacrifice. However, the bittersweet death/rebirth of Ofelia into her 'true' role is curiously tainted by re-establishing binary structures. For Greek epic heroes, the descent into the Underworld also functions as a personal inner journey of self-discovery – to locate one's fears and outgrow them, to lose one's identity and find it again, to travel within yourself to establish your place in the outer/upper world.

> The fairytale realm – that submerged sub-text – becomes an insightful commentary on war and the rules of society and gender in the real world: it undermines the authority of the fascists and the dictates of the Captain by exhuming that which has been hidden and silenced.

The coming-of-age journey by the child heroine is particularly appealing because of the perceived double vulnerability of both age and gender. This sentimentalized role is menaced, however, by rude, rebellious, malicious, arrogant Alice, for example, who is more self-aware and in control than any of the parodied adults, and more powerful than any of the male figures in Wonderland. Ofelia begins her quest as an equally defiant heroine and iconoclastic adventurer, but her position is paradoxically diminished by the close of the film. With the loss of her mother, she is obliged to take on the traditional and gendered role of surrogate mother in caring for her brother. Indeed, it is interesting to note the film's thematic concern with siblings; the ties of brothers and sisters are revealed as far stronger than those of lovers or of children and their parents. The self-effacing and self-sacrificing role of mothering, as represented by Carmen, has already been established as ruled and defined by men. Indeed, the motif of women saving and nurturing dangerous, difficult and demanding males can be seen from Carmen (with both the Captain and the son that killed her) to Mercedes (with her rebel brother), and in this 'growing up' or coming-of-age fable, the same relinquishing of life and freedom to uphold the male line is demanded of Ofelia.

> It is unsettling that such an active, rebellious and subversive heroine is finally reduced to a traditionally passive female role.

Ofelia's final return home?

In a text so concerned with unearthing and empowering the repressed, it is unsettling that such an active, rebellious and subversive heroine is finally reduced to a traditionally passive female role: like her Shakespearean namesake, Ofelia becomes the pawn, the sacrifice, the paraclete. Even her return 'home' beyond her death is problematic: her underland, where children have power and females are action heroes, has been usurped by yet another god-like and dictatorial adult male. However romanticized the imagery or benevolent the replacement father, Ofelia finally returns underground only to find another patriarchy established, where men rule and women are holy mothers (or sacred sisters or passive daughters) who are to sit beside and below the king and wear beautiful clothes and nurture male heirs. Rather than the fantasy realm undermining and subverting the real world, it is ultimately the gendered and adult values of the world above that seem to have permeated down into the underland – as Alice herself sorrowfully noted, 'there's no room to grow up any more *here*.'[2] Perhaps our only consolation down at the end of *Pan's Labyrinth* is that, despite her gender, her age and her royal lineage, Ofelia is finally able to actively and heroically choose her role rather than being born – or indeed, falling – into it.

Endnotes

1   Lewis Carroll, *Alice's Adventures in Wonderland*, W.W. Norton & Co, New York & London, [1865] 1992, p.51.
2   Ibid., p.29.

3

Gender and Romance

Meagan Lehr

I want your love and
I want your revenge
You and me could write a bad romance

—Lady Gaga, "Bad Romance"

Of those we have let go . . . how many of their departures do we still
suffer under a different name or delusion . . . in the morning light, the
tamp of plastic awning and in the evening clack of roof tile, the living we
divine by imagining.
and Olga Broumas, "Black Holes, Black Stockings"

—Jane Miller

Campus life often seems like an incubated social experiment; at any moment
researchers in white lab coats will pop out of library stacks and take our vital signs.
Or maybe they are music video dancers dressed in shiny pleather jumpsuits, wearing Frankenstein masks and 5 inch heels. Even still, they are paparazzi shouting
and flashing hundreds of bulbs in our faces, as if each us were Tiger Woods apolo-
gizing on national television. These exaggerated moments in our media culture are
metaphors for the hyperbolic world of the college student; you are judged, you are
ogled, you are admired, you are objectified. Perhaps nowhere else in our country
do humans engage on a daily basis with their own desires, anxieties, dreams, and

attractions than the college campus. Students, professors, and administrators alike are faced (or tested) by their reactions to the opposite sex as much as their own.

Questions on the hypothetical researchers' survey might include: Who do you intentionally flirt with? Who do you unintentionally flirt with? What is consensual sex? What does the phrase *loving relationship* mean? What does it look like? How do you imagine yourself in the eyes of men? Of women? Of those who are transgendered? We need look no further than our own campus environment to observe representations of romantic love and gendered roles, how these representations have developed, and how they are shifting.

When I reentered the university community after taking a few years off in between undergraduate and graduate degrees, I immediately began *rereading* campus life. Before, I had been aware of the built-in social systems on campus, and had willingly participated in events, organizations, and relationships as a product of that environment. Still, coming back to campus seemed hyper-real at first; had those two years away from school pushed me so far out of touch? The systems seemed to be in place more firmly. Students and instructors were assessing, understanding, desiring, and dreaming based upon standards cultivated by the American university social situation. At the same time, campus was more colorful, more open. The conversations I heard while waiting for classes (and in those classes) were controversial, progressive, shocking, and therefore, interesting.

What would it mean to take social situations at the University of Arizona—club meetings, music events, protests on the mall, classroom discussions—and examine them through the lenses of these theoretical researchers? How does a university environment instill or echo our traditional views about romantic love as a closed union of male and female? How are straight, gay, bisexual and transgendered faculty, students and staff challenged to identify themselves on a campus? How do we reconcile what we hear through the media about love, sex, same-sex marriage, rape, or pornography with what we learn in the classroom and in the dorm room? These are not the kinds of questions we can immediately answer, but they do provoke awareness. Enacting this awareness in our shared atmosphere is complex and fascinating. What makes learning and teaching in this environment worthwhile is an inevitable diversity; the inevitable opportunity to engage and challenge our roles as humans with the capacity to be involved with others. In other words, the campus environment feeds our obsessions with romance and gender.

The shapes of these human obsessions—finding love, being loved, having intercourse, feeling wanted—are malleable. Our world takes advantage of this malleability. If romance is shaped by outside influences, our ideals and definitions of love reflect social and cultural consciousness. For example, consider your reaction when one of the country's most watched athletes, Tiger Woods, admitted to extramarital affairs. Varied phrases blazed on the headlines: "Fall from Grace," "Sex Addict!" "Cheater!!." Without having any knowledge of Woods' personal relationships with his wife, children, or mistresses, we as a mass audience felt the authority to judge his indiscretions. This certainly reflects upon the largely American perceptions that a husband should remain faithful to his wife, should publicly and dutifully apologize for his wrongs, and should remain out of sight until tensions have cooled. Regardless of our individual reactions to Woods, we have cultivated these standards of marriage and fidelity as a collective audience.

One of the epigraphs that open this essay is drawn from the lyrics of pop star Lady Gaga, who plays on and challenges these standards. After viewing the video for the song "Bad Romance" as part of a class lesson, one of my former students questioned whether the artist was a hermaphrodite. A lively discussion ensued, but another student said he wasn't as perturbed by that bit of information, but rather by the explicit images of Lady Gaga erotically licking the shoe of one of the other actors in the video. Most of the students hailed Gaga as an artist of our times. "She's bizarre," they said; "She's doing something original." Is originality linked to sexuality, to controversy? Eighties icon Madonna provoked media attention by way of what was considered blasphemy and explicit eroticism long before Gaga. Who is original? What is originality when it comes to identity? Can we think of an original image of love, sex, or attraction?

To study these grand terms is essentially to study language. Labels are the inertia of social concepts. We are shaped by our surroundings, but we are influenced even more by the way we discuss these surroundings. Consider the markers that we hear on campus every day: dude, girl, kid, dick, chick, whore, slut, hook-up, sext (sex + text), fag, dyke, etc. These words are complicated to analyze. They are used in colloquial speech. Romance and gender appear to have fixed meanings, yet we must accept that these meanings are constantly in flux. Meanings shift with experience. Our ideas of "romance"—the web of connotations behind that word on the page—are intricate and socialized and personal. To address romance is to address gender. These two concepts are linked because gender awareness is a distinctly human cognition (whether you abide by constructs or not), just as it is human to form ideals of romantic connection (feeling beyond procreation). When you imagine a lover, you imagine their gender. That glaringly abstract word, *love*, is altered and internalized by our encounters with one another and in talking or writing about those encounters. This is the way we process creativity and meaning.

The authors in this chapter both examine and reconceptualize the human preoccupation with love. They take on the abstractions that love, sex, and gender have become, and seek to establish specific (but still complicated) claims to their meaning. For centuries, humans have relied on the artists of their generation to produce works that speak to the nature of love and attraction. Our tragedies and joys are preserved and celebrated through the artists that represented them. Though artists still seek the same tragic celebration, as readers we are obliged to constantly rethink, reexamine, and interrogate. These writers take risks to push the limits of what Jane Miller calls *divined imaginings*. By divining imagination, we accept that gender and romance are terms that can and will be altered. It is an acceptance of our imagination. These artists move beyond the researchers' questions and probe their inner lives to create tangible statements that, in turn, prompt our own investigations. When reading and analyzing the following texts, pay close attention to your reactions. Where do these texts disrupt your previous imaginings? Why? Who do you love? Why? Most importantly, where and how does love manifest in our times? This chapter is about our interactions, how we perceive one another, and how we imagine ourselves.

Charlotte Perkins Gilman

Charlotte Perkins Gilman (1860–1935) was born in Hartford, Connecticut. Shortly after she was born, her father deserted the family and provided her mother with little financial support. She was raised by her mother and studied art at the Rhode Island School of Design. She became a very important figure as a prominent lecturer and a writer on feminism and the labor movement.

The Yellow Wallpaper

It is very seldom that mere ordinary people like John and myself secure ancestral halls for the summer.

A colonial mansion, a hereditary estate, I would say a haunted house and reach the height of romantic felicity—but that would be asking too much of fate!

Still I will proudly declare that there is something queer about it.

Else, why should it be let so cheaply? And why have stood so long untenanted?

John laughs at me, of course, but one expects that.

John is practical in the extreme. He has no patience with faith, an intense horror of superstition, and he scoffs openly at any talk of things not to be felt and seen and put down in figures.

John is a physician, and *perhaps*—(I would not say it to a living soul, of course, but this is dead paper and a great relief to my mind)—*perhaps* that is one reason I do not get well faster.

You see, he does not believe I am sick! And what can one do?

If a physician of high standing, and one's own husband, assures friends and relatives that there is really nothing the matter with one but temporary nervous depression—a slight hysterical tendency—what is one to do?

My brother is also a physician, and also of high standing, and he says the same thing.

So I take phosphates or phosphites—whichever it is—and tonics, and air and exercise, and journeys, and am absolutely forbidden to "work" until I am well again.

Personally, I disagree with their ideas.

Personally, I believe that congenial work, with excitement and change, would do me good.

But what is one to do?

I did write for a while in spite of them; but it *does* exhaust me a good deal—having to be so sly about it, or else meet with heavy opposition.

I sometimes fancy that in my condition, if I had less opposition and more society and stimulus—but John says the very worst thing I can do is to think about my condition, and I confess it always makes me feel bad.

So I will let it alone and talk about the house.

The most beautiful place! It is quite alone, standing well back from the road, quite three miles from the village. It makes me think of English places that you read about, for there are hedges and walls and gates that lock, and lots of separate little houses for the gardeners and people.

There is a *delicious* garden! I never saw such a garden—large and shady, full of box-bordered paths, and lined with long grape-covered arbors with seats under them.

There were greenhouses, but they are all broken now.

There was some legal trouble, I believe, something about the heirs and co-heirs; anyhow, the place has been empty for years.

That spoils my ghostliness, I am afraid, but I don't care—there is something strange about the house—I can feel it.

I even said so to John one moonlight evening, but he said what I felt was a draught, and shut the window.

I get unreasonably angry with John sometimes. I'm sure I never used to be so sensitive. I think it is due to this nervous condition.

But John says if I feel so I shall neglect proper self-control; so I take pains to control myself—before him, at least, and that makes me very tired.

I don't like our room a bit. I wanted one downstairs that opened onto the piazza and had roses all over the window, and such pretty old-fashioned chintz hangings! But John would not hear of it.

He said there was only one window and not room for two beds, and no near room for him if he took another.

He is very careful and loving, and hardly lets me stir without special direction.

I have a schedule prescription for each hour in the day; he takes all care from me, and so I feel basely ungrateful not to value it more.

He said he came here solely on my account, that I was to have perfect rest and all the air I could get. "Your exercise depends on your strength, my dear," said he, "and your food somewhat on your appetite; but air you can absorb all the time." So we took the nursery at the top of the house.

It is a big, airy room, the whole floor nearly, with windows that look all ways, and air and sunshine galore. It was nursery first, and then playroom and gymnasium, I should judge, for the windows are barred for little children, and there are rings and things in the walls.

The paint and paper look as if a boys' school had used it. It is stripped off—the paper—in great patches all around the head of my bed, about as far as I can reach, and in a great place on the other side of the room low down. I never saw a worse paper in my life. One of those sprawling, flamboyant patterns committing every artistic sin.

It is dull enough to confuse the eye in following, pronounced enough constantly to irritate and provoke study, and when you follow the lame uncertain curves for a little distance they suddenly commit suicide—plunge off at outrageous angles, destroy themselves in unheard-of contradictions.

The color is repellent, almost revolting: a smouldering unclean yellow, strangely faded by the slow-turning sunlight. It is a dull yet lurid orange in some places, a sickly sulphur tint in others.

No wonder the children hated it! I should hate it myself if I had to live in this room long.

There comes John, and I must put this away—he hates to have me write a word.

We have been here two weeks, and I haven't felt like writing before, since that first day.

I am sitting by the window now, up in this atrocious nursery, and there is nothing to hinder my writing as much as I please, save lack of strength.

John is away all day, and even some nights when his cases are serious.

I am glad my case is not serious!

But these nervous troubles are dreadfully depressing.

John does not know how much I really suffer. He knows there is no reason to suffer, and that satisfies him.

Of course it is only nervousness. It does weigh on me so not to do my duty in any way!

I meant to be such a help to John, such a real rest and comfort, and here I am a comparative burden already!

Nobody would believe what an effort it is to do what little I am able—to dress and entertain, and order things.

It is fortunate Mary is so good with the baby. Such a dear baby!

And yet I *cannot* be with him, it makes me so nervous.

I suppose John never was nervous in his life. He laughs at me so about this wallpaper!

At first he meant to repaper the room, but afterward he said that I was letting it get the better of me, and that nothing was worse for a nervous patient than to give way to such fancies.

He said that after the wallpaper was changed it would be the heavy bedstead, and then the barred windows, and then that gate at the head of the stairs, and so on.

"You know the place is doing you good," he said, "and really, dear, I don't care to renovate the house just for a three months' rental."

"Then do let us go downstairs," I said. "There are such pretty rooms there."

Then he took me in his arms and called me a blessed little goose, and said he would go down cellar, if I wished, and have it whitewashed into the bargain.

But he is right enough about the beds and windows and things.

It is as airy and comfortable a room as anyone need wish, and, of course, I would not be so silly as to make him uncomfortable just for a whim.

I'm really getting quite fond of the big room, all but that horrid paper.

Out of one window I can see the garden—those mysterious deep-shaded arbors, the riotous old-fashioned flowers, and bushes and gnarly trees.

Out of another I get a lovely view of the bay and a little private wharf belonging to the estate. There is a beautiful shaded lane that runs down there from the house. I always fancy I see people walking in these numerous paths and arbors, but John has cautioned me not to give way to fancy in the least. He says that with my imaginative power and habit of story-making, a nervous weakness like mine is sure to lead to all manner of excited fancies, and that I ought to use my will and good sense to check the tendency. So I try.

I think sometimes that if I were only well enough to write a little it would relieve the press of ideas and rest me.

But I find I get pretty tired when I try.

It is so discouraging not to have any advice and companionship about my work. When I get really well, John says we will ask Cousin Henry and Julia down for a long visit; but he says he would as soon put fireworks in my pillow-case as to let me have those stimulating people about now.

I wish I could get well faster.

But I must not think about that. This paper looks to me as if it *knew* what a vicious influence it had!

There is a recurrent spot where the pattern lolls like a broken neck and two bulbous eyes stare at you upside down.

I get positively angry with the impertinence of it and the everlastingness. Up and down and sideways they crawl, and those absurd unblinking eyes are everywhere. There is one place where two breadths didn't match, and the eyes go all up and down the line, one a little higher than the other.

I never saw so much expression in an inanimate thing before, and we all know how much expression they have! I used to lie awake as a child and get more entertainment and terror out of blank walls and plain furniture than most children could find in a toy-store.

I remember what a kindly wink the knobs of our big old bureau used to have, and there was one chair that always seemed like a strong friend.

I used to feel that if any of the other things looked too fierce I could always hop into that chair and be safe.

The furniture in this room is no worse than inharmonious, however, for we had to bring it all from downstairs. I suppose when this was used as a playroom they had to take the nursery things out, and no wonder! I never saw such ravages as the children have made here.

The wallpaper, as I said before, is torn off in spots, and it sticketh closer than a brother—they must have had perseverance as well as hatred.

Then the floor is scratched and gouged and splintered, the plaster itself is dug out here and there, and this great heavy bed, which is all we found in the room, looks as if it had been through the wars.

But I don't mind it a bit—only the paper.

There comes John's sister. Such a dear girl as she is, and so careful of me! I must not let her find me writing.

She is a perfect and enthusiastic housekeeper, and hopes for no better profession. I verily believe she thinks it is the writing which made me sick!

But I can write when she is out, and see her a long way off from these windows.

There is one that commands the road, a lovely shaded winding road, and one that just looks off over the country. A lovely country, too, full of great elms and velvet meadows.

This wallpaper has a kind of sub-pattern in a different shade, a particularly irritating one, for you can only see it in certain lights, and not clearly then.

But in the places where it isn't faded and where the sun is just so—I can see a strange, provoking, formless sort of figure that seems to skulk about behind that silly and conspicuous front design.

There's sister on the stairs!

Well, the Fourth of July is over! The people are all gone, and I am tired out. John thought it might do me good to see a little company, so we just had Mother and Nellie and the children down for a week.

Of course I didn't do a thing. Jennie sees to everything now.

But it tired me all the same.

John says if I don't pick up faster he shall send me to Weir Mitchell[1] in the fall.

But I don't want to go there at all. I had a friend who was in his hands once, and she says he is just like John and my brother, only more so!

Besides, it is such an undertaking to go so far.

I don't feel as if it was worthwhile to turn my hand over for anything, and I'm getting dreadfully fretful and querulous.

I cry at nothing, and cry most of the time.

Of course I don't when John is here, or anybody else, but when I am alone.

And I am alone a good deal just now. John is kept in town very often by serious cases, and Jennie is good and lets me alone when I want her to.

So I walk a little in the garden or down that lovely lane, sit on the porch under the roses, and lie down up here a good deal.

I'm getting really fond of the room in spite of the wallpaper. Perhaps *because* of the wallpaper.

It dwells in my mind so!

I lie here on this great immovable bed—it is nailed down, I believe—and follow that pattern about by the hour. It is as good as gymnastics, I assure you. I start, we'll say, at the bottom, down in the corner over there where it has not been touched, and I determine for the thousandth time that I *will* follow that pointless pattern to some sort of a conclusion.

I know a little of the principle of design, and I know this thing was not arranged on any laws of radiation, or alternation, or repetition, or symmetry, or anything else that I ever heard of.

It is repeated, of course, by the breadths, but not otherwise.

Looked at in one way, each breadth stands alone; the bloated curves and flourishes—a kind of "debased Romanesque" with delirium tremens go waddling up and down in isolated columns of fatuity.

But, on the other hand, they connect diagonally, and the sprawling outlines run off in great slanting waves of optic horror, like a lot of wallowing sea-weeds in full chase.

The whole thing goes horizontally, too, at least it seems so, and I exhaust myself trying to distinguish the order of its going in that direction.

They have used a horizontal breadth for a frieze, and that adds wonderfully to the confusion.

There is one end of the room where it is almost intact, and there, when the crosslights fade and the low sun shines directly upon it, I can almost fancy radiation after all—the interminable grotesque seems to form around a common center and rush off in headlong plunges of equal distraction.

It makes me tired to follow it. I will take a nap, I guess.

I don't know why I should write this.

I don't want to.

I don't feel able.

And I know John would think it absurd. But I *must* say what I feel and think in some way—it is such a relief!

But the effort is getting to be greater than the relief.

Half the time now I am awfully lazy, and lie down ever so much. John says I mustn't lose my strength, and has me take cod liver oil and lots of tonics and things, to say nothing of ale and wines and rare meat.

Dear John! He loves me very dearly, and hates to have me sick. I tried to have a real earnest reasonable talk with him the other day, and tell him how I wish he would let me go and make a visit to Cousin Henry and Julia.

But he said I wasn't able to go, nor able to stand it after I got there; and I did not make out a very good case for myself, for I was crying before I had finished.

It is getting to be a great effort for me to think straight. Just this nervous weakness, I suppose.

And dear John gathered me up in his arms, and just carried me upstairs and laid me on the bed, and sat by me and read to me till it tired my head.

He said I was his darling and his comfort and all he had, and that I must take care of myself for his sake, and keep well.

He says no one but myself can help me out of it, that I must use my will and self-control and not let any silly fancies run away with me.

There's one comfort—the baby is well and happy, and does not have to occupy this nursery with the horrid wallpaper.

If we had not used it, that blessed child would have! What a fortunate escape! Why, I wouldn't have a child of mine, an impressionable little thing, live in such a room for worlds.

I never thought of it before, but it is lucky that John kept me here after all; I can stand it so much easier than a baby, you see.

Of course I never mention it to them any more—I am too wise—but I keep watch for it all the same.

There are things in the wallpaper that nobody knows about but me, or ever will.

Behind that outside pattern the dim shapes get clearer every day.

It is always the same shape, only very numerous.

And it is like a woman stooping down and creeping about behind that pattern. I don't like it a bit. I wonder—I begin to think—I wish John would take me away from here!

It is so hard to talk with John about my case, because he is so wise, and because he loves me so.

But I tried it last night.

It was moonlight. The moon shines in all around just as the sun does.

I hate to see it sometimes, it creeps so slowly, and always comes in by one window or another.

John was asleep and I hated to waken him, so I kept still and watched the moonlight on that undulating wallpaper till I felt creepy.

The faint figure behind seemed to shake the pattern, just as if she wanted to get out.

I got up softly and went to feel and see if the paper *did* move, and when I came back John was awake.

"What is it, little girl?" he said. "Don't go walking about like that—you'll get cold."

I thought it was a good time to talk, so I told him that I really was not gaining here, and that I wished he would take me away.

"Why, darling!" said he. "Our lease will be up in three weeks, and I can't see how to leave before.

"The repairs are not done at home, and I cannot possibly leave town just now. Of course, if you were in any danger, I could and would, but you really are better, dear, whether you can see it or not. I am a doctor, dear, and I know. You are gaining flesh and color, your appetite is better, I feel really much easier about you."

"I don't weigh a bit more," said I, "nor as much; and my appetite may be better in the evening when you are here but it is worse in the morning when you are away!"

"Bless her little heart!" said he with a big hug. "She shall be as sick as she pleases! But now let's improve the shining hours by going to sleep, and talk about it in the morning!"

"And you won't go away?" I asked gloomily.

"Why, how can I, dear? It is only three weeks more and then we will take a nice little trip for a few days while Jennie is getting the house ready. Really, dear, you are better!"

"Better in body perhaps—" I began, and stopped short, for he sat up straight and looked at me with such a stern, reproachful look that I could not say another word.

"My darling," said he, "I beg you, for my sake and for our child's sake, as well as for your own, that you will never for one instant let that idea enter your mind! There is nothing so dangerous, so fascinating, to a temperament like yours. It is a false and foolish fancy. Can you trust me as a physician when I tell you so?"

So of course I said no more on that score, and we went to sleep before long. He thought I was asleep first, but I wasn't, and lay there for hours trying to decide whether that front pattern and the back pattern really did move together or separately.

On a pattern like this, by daylight, there is a lack of sequence, a defiance of law, that is a constant irritant to a normal mind.

The color is hideous enough, and unreliable enough, and infuriating enough, but the pattern is torturing.

You think you have mastered it, but just as you get well under way in following, it turns a back-somersault and there you are. It slaps you in the face, knocks you down, and tramples upon you. It is like a bad dream.

The outside pattern is a florid arabesque, reminding one of a fungus. If you can imagine a toadstool in joints, an interminable string of toadstools, budding and sprouting in endless convolutions—why, that is something like it.

That is, sometimes!

There is one marked peculiarity about this paper, a thing nobody seems to notice but myself, and that is that it changes as the light changes.

When the sun shoots in through the east window—I always watch for that first long, straight ray—it changes so quickly that I never can quite believe it.

That is why I watch it always.

By moonlight—the moon shines in all night when there is a moon—I wouldn't know it was the same paper.

At night in any kind of light, in twilight, candlelight, lamplight, and worst of all by moonlight, it becomes bars! The outside pattern, I mean, and the woman behind it is as plain as can be.

I didn't realize for a long time what the thing was that showed behind, that dim sub-pattern, but now I am quite sure it is a woman.

By daylight she is subdued, quiet. I fancy it is the pattern that keeps her so still. It is so puzzling. It keeps me quiet by the hour.

I lie down ever so much now. John says it is good for me, and to sleep all I can.

Indeed he started the habit by making me lie down for an hour after each meal.

It is a very bad habit, I am convinced, for you see, I don't sleep.

And that cultivates deceit, for I don't tell them I'm awake—oh, no!

The fact is I am getting a little afraid of John.

He seems very queer sometimes, and even Jennie has an inexplicable look.

It strikes me occasionally, just as a scientific hypothesis, that perhaps it is the paper!

I have watched John when he did not know I was looking, and come into the room suddenly on the most innocent excuses, and I've caught him several times *looking at the paper!* And Jennie too. I caught Jennie with her hand on it once.

She didn't know I was in the room, and when I asked her in a quiet, a very quiet voice, with the most restrained manner possible, what she was doing with the paper, she turned around as if she had been caught stealing, and looked quite angry—asked me why I should frighten her so!

Then she said that the paper stained everything it touched, that she had found yellow smooches on all my clothes and John's and she wished we would be more careful!

Did not that sound innocent? But I know she was studying that pattern, and I am determined that nobody shall find it out but myself!

Life is very much more exciting now than it used to be. You see, I have something more to expect, to look forward to, to watch. I really do eat better, and am more quiet than I was.

John is so pleased to see me improve! He laughed a little the other day, and said I seemed to be flourishing in spite of my wallpaper.

I turned it off with a laugh. I had no intention of telling him it was *because* of the wallpaper—he would make fun of me. He might even want to take me away.

I don't want to leave now until I have found it out. There is a week more, and I think that will be enough.

I'm feeling so much better!

I don't sleep much at night, for it is so interesting to watch developments; but I sleep a good deal during the daytime.

In the daytime it is tiresome and perplexing.

There are always new shoots on the fungus, and new shades of yellow all over it. I cannot keep count of them, though I have tried conscientiously.

It is the strangest yellow, that wallpaper! It makes me think of all the yellow things I ever saw—not beautiful ones like buttercups, but old, foul, bad yellow things.

But there is something else about that paper—the smell! I noticed it the moment we came into the room, but with so much air and sun it was not bad. Now we have had a week of fog and rain, and whether the windows are open or not, the smell is here.

It creeps all over the house.

I find it hovering in the dining-room, skulking in the parlor, hiding in the hall, lying in wait for me on the stairs.

It gets into my hair.

Even when I go to ride, if I turn my head suddenly and surprise it—there is that smell!

Such a peculiar odor, too! I have spent hours in trying to analyze it, to find what it smelled like.

It is not bad—at first—and very gentle, but quite the subtlest, most enduring odor I ever met.

In this damp weather it is awful. I wake up in the night and find it hanging over me.

It used to disturb me at first. I thought seriously of burning the house—to reach the smell.

But now I am used to it. The only thing I can think of that it is like is the *color* of the paper! A yellow smell.

There is a very funny mark on this wall, low down, near the mopboard. A streak that runs round the room. It goes behind every piece of furniture, except the bed, a long, straight, even *smooch*, as if it had been rubbed over and over.

I wonder how it was done and who did it, and what they did it for. Round and round and round—round and round and round—it makes me dizzy!

I really have discovered something at last.

Through watching so much at night, when it changes so, I have finally found out.

The front pattern *does* move—and no wonder! The woman behind shakes it!

Sometimes I think there are a great many women behind, and sometimes only one, and she crawls around fast, and her crawling shakes it all over.

Then in the very bright spots she keeps still, and in the very shady spots she just takes hold of the bars and shakes them hard.

And she is all the time trying to climb through. But nobody could climb through that pattern—it strangles so; I think that is why it has so many heads.

They get through and then the pattern strangles them off and turns them upside down, and makes their eyes white!

If those heads were covered or taken off it would not be half so bad.

I think that woman gets out in the daytime!

And I'll tell you why—privately—I've seen her!

I can see her out of every one of my windows!

It is the same woman, I know, for she is always creeping, and most women do not creep by daylight.

I see her in that long shaded lane, creeping up and down. I see her in those dark grape arbors, creeping all around the garden.

I see her on that long road under the trees, creeping along, and when a carriage comes she hides under the blackberry vines.

I don't blame her a bit. It must be very humiliating to be caught creeping by daylight!

I always lock the door when I creep by daylight. I can't do it at night, for I know John would suspect something at once.

And John is so queer now that I don't want to irritate him. I wish he would take another room! Besides, I don't want anybody to get that woman out at night but myself.

I often wonder if I could see her out of all the windows at once.

But, turn as fast as I can, I can only see out of one at one time.

And though I always see her, she *may* be able to creep faster than I can turn! I have watched her sometimes away off in the open country, creeping as fast as a cloud shadow in a wind.

If only that top pattern could be gotten off from the under one! I mean to try it, little by little.

I have found out another funny thing, but I shan't tell it this time! It does not do to trust people too much.

There are only two more days to get this paper off, and I believe John is beginning to notice. I don't like the look in his eyes.

And I heard him ask Jennie a lot of professional questions about me. She had a very good report to give.

She said I slept a good deal in the daytime.

John knows I don't sleep very well at night, for all I'm so quiet!

He asked me all sorts of questions too, and pretended to be very loving and kind.

As if I couldn't see through him!

Still, I don't wonder he acts so, sleeping under this paper for three months.

It only interests me, but I feel sure John and Jennie are affected by it. Hurrah! This is the last day, but it is enough. John is to stay in town over night, and won't be out until this evening.

Jennie wanted to sleep with me—the sly thing; but I told her I should undoubtedly rest better for a night all alone.

That was clever, for really I wasn't alone a bit! As soon as it was moonlight and that poor thing began to crawl and shake the pattern, I got up and ran to help her.

I pulled and she shook. I shook and she pulled, and before morning we had peeled off yards of that paper.

A strip about as high as my head and half around the room.

And then when the sun came and that awful pattern began to laugh at me, I declared I would finish it today!

We go away tomorrow, and they are moving all my furniture down again to leave things as they were before.

Jennie looked at the wall in amazement, but I told her merrily that I did it out of pure spite at the vicious thing.

She laughed and said she wouldn't mind doing it herself, but I must not get tired.

How she betrayed herself that time!

But I am here, and no person touches this paper but Me—not *alive!*

She tried to get me out of the room—it was too patent! But I said it was so quiet and empty and clean now that I believed I would lie down again and sleep all I could, and not to wake me even for dinner—I would call when I woke.

So now she is gone, and the servants are gone, and the things are gone, and there is nothing left but that great bedstead nailed down, with the canvas mattress we found on it.

We shall sleep downstairs tonight, and take the boat home tomorrow.

I quite enjoy the room, now it is bare again.

How those children did tear about here!

This bedstead is fairly gnawed!

But I must get to work.

I have locked the door and thrown the key down into the front path.

I don't want to go out, and I don't want to have anybody come in, till John comes.

I want to astonish him.

I've got a rope up here that even Jennie did not find. If that woman does get out, and tries to get away, I can tie her!

But I forgot I could not reach far without anything to stand on!

This bed will *not* move!

I tried to lift and push it until I was lame, and then I got so angry I bit off a little piece at one corner—but it hurt my teeth.

Then I peeled off all the paper I could reach standing on the floor. It sticks horribly and the pattern just enjoys it! All those strangled heads and bulbous eyes and waddling fungus growths just shriek with derision!

I am getting angry enough to do something desperate. To jump out of the window would be admirable exercise, but the bars are too strong even to try.

Besides I wouldn't do it. Of course not. I know well enough that a step like that is improper and might be misconstrued.

I don't like to *look* out of the windows even—there are so many of those creeping women, and they creep so fast.

I wonder if they all come out of that wallpaper as I did?

But I am securely fastened now by my well-hidden rope—you don't get *me* out in the road there!

I suppose I shall have to get back behind the pattern when it comes night, and that is hard!

It is so pleasant to be out in this great room and creep around as I please!

I don't want to go outside. I won't, even if Jennie asks me to.

For outside you have to creep on the ground, and everything is green instead of yellow.

But here I can creep smoothly on the floor, and my shoulder just fits in that long smooch around the wall, so I cannot lose my way.

Why, there's John at the door!

It is no use, young man, you can't open it!

How he does call and pound!

Now he's crying to Jennie for an axe.

It would be a shame to break down that beautiful door!

"John, dear!" said I in the gentlest voice. "The key is down by the front steps, under a plantain leaf!"

That silenced him for a few moments.

Then he said, very quietly indeed, "Open the door, my darling!"

"I can't," said I. "The key is down by the front door under a plantain leaf!" And then I said it again, several times, very gently and slowly, and said it so often that he had to go and see, and he got it of course, and came in. He stopped short by the door.

"What is the matter?" he cried. "For God's sake, what are you doing!"

I kept on creeping just the same, but I looked at him over my shoulder.

"I've got out at last," said I, "in spite of you and Jane. And I've pulled off most of the paper, so you can't put me back!"

Now why should that man have fainted? But he did, and right across my path by the wall, so that I had to creep over him every time!

Note

1. American neurologist who treated Gilman.

Kate Chopin

Katherine O'Flaherty Chopin (1851–1904) was born and raised in St. Louis, Missouri. In 1870 she married a Louisiana Creole and it was only after her husband's death that she started to write about her experiences. She was almost forty when she published her first novel, At Fault *(1890). Her novel did not receive that much praise or recognition; however, her short stories (she wrote more than 100) brought her fame and acclaim. In 1899, Chopin published her most famous piece,* The Awakening, *which was highly condemned in her time because of its sexual frankness.*

The Story of an Hour

Knowing that Mrs. Mallard was afflicted with a heart trouble, great care was taken to break to her as gently as possible the news of her husband's death.

It was her sister Josephine who told her, in broken sentences; veiled hints that revealed in half concealing. Her husband's friend Richards was there, too, near her. It was he who had been in the newspaper office when intelligence of the railroad disaster was received, with Brently Mallard's name leading the list of "killed." He had only taken the time to assure himself of its truth by a second telegram, and had hastened to forestall any less careful, less tender friend in bearing the sad message.

She did not hear the story as many women have heard the same, with a paralyzed inability to accept its significance. She wept at once, with sudden, wild abandonment, in her sister's arms. When the storm of grief had spent itself she went away to her room alone. She would have no one follow her.

There stood, facing the open window, a comfortable, roomy armchair. Into this she sank, pressed down by a physical exhaustion that haunted her body and seemed to reach into her soul.

She could see in the open square before her house the tops of trees that were all aquiver with the new spring life. The delicious breath of rain was in the air. In the street below a peddler was crying his wares. The notes of a distant song which someone was singing reached her faintly, and countless sparrows were twittering in the eaves.

There were patches of blue sky showing here and there through the clouds that had met and piled one above the other in the west facing her window.

She sat with her head thrown back upon the cushion of the chair, quite motionless, except when a sob came up into her throat and shook her, as a child who had cried itself to sleep continues to sob in its dreams.

She was young, with a fair, calm face, whose lines bespoke repression and even a certain strength. But now there was a dull stare in her eyes, whose gaze was fixed away off yonder on one of those patches of blue sky. It was not a glance of reflection, but rather indicated a suspension of intelligent thought.

There was something coming to her and she was waiting for it, fearfully. What was it? She did not know; it was too subtle and elusive to name. But she felt it, creeping out of the sky, reaching toward her through the sounds, the scents, the color that filled the air.

Now her bosom rose and fell tumultuously. She was beginning to recognize this thing that was approaching to possess her, and she was striving to beat it back with her will—as powerless as her two white slender hands would have been.

When she abandoned herself a little whispered word escaped her slightly parted lips. She said it over and over under her breath: "free, free, free!" The vacant stare and the look of terror that had followed it went from her eyes. They stayed keen and bright. Her pulses beat fast, and the coursing blood warmed and relaxed every inch of her body.

She did not stop to ask if it were or were not a monstrous joy that held her. A clear and exalted perception enabled her to dismiss the suggestion as trivial.

She knew that she would weep again when she saw the kind, tender hands folded in death; the face that had never looked save with love upon her, fixed and gray and dead. But she saw beyond that bitter moment a long procession of years to come that would belong to her absolutely. And she opened and spread her arms out to them in welcome.

There would be no one to live for her during those coming years: she would live for herself. There would be no powerful will bending hers in that blind persistence with which men and women believe they have a right to impose a private will upon a fellow-creature. A kind intention or a cruel intention made the act seem no less a crime as she looked upon it in that brief moment of illumination.

And yet she had loved him—sometimes. Often she had not. What did it matter! What could love, the unsolved mystery, count for in face of this possession of self-assertion which she suddenly recognized as the strongest impulse of her being!

"Free! Body and soul free!" she kept whispering.

Josephine was kneeling before the closed door with her lips to the keyhole, imploring for admission. "Louise, open the door! I beg; open the door—you will make yourself ill. What are you doing, Louise? For heaven's sake open the door."

"Go away. I am not making myself ill." No; she was drinking in a very elixir of life through that open window.

Her fancy was running riot along those days ahead of her. Spring days, and summer days, and all sorts of days that would be her own. She breathed a quick prayer that life might be long. It was only yesterday she had thought with a shudder that life might be long.

She arose at length and opened the door to her sister's importunities. There was a feverish triumph in her eyes, and she carried herself unwittingly like a goddess of Victory. She clasped her sister's waist, and together they descended the stairs. Richards stood waiting for them at the bottom.

Some one was opening the front door with a latchkey. It was Brently Mallard who entered, a little travel-stained, composedly carrying his gripsack and umbrella. He had been far from the scene of accident, and did not even know there had been one. He stood amazed at Josephine's piercing cry; at Richards' quick motion to screen him from the view of his wife.

But Richards was too late.

When the doctors came they said she had died of heart disease—of joy that kills.

Karen Brennan

Karen Brennan, who received her Ph.D. from the University of Arizona, is Professor at the University of Utah, where she teaches creative writing and critical and feminist theories. Having published in a variety of genres, her work includes Here on Earth, *a book of poems;* Wild Desire, *a collection of short stories and winner of the prestigious Associated Writers Program Award for Fiction; and* Being with Rachel, *a memoir.*

Floating

In the morning I levitated for the first time. I woke up and heard a tiny sound coming from the back of the house. It was a baby. She was wrapped in a white windbreaker and her face was raw from the cold. But she was ok. I unwrapped her and though she was wet, she was fine. I changed her diaper and even her little undershirt. She had all the plumpness of a baby; dimpled knees and folds around the wrists; pale baby skin. She had been crying for two days straight and had survived.

In my own room I realized I could float, simply by willing it. I ascended from the ground and spread my arms like an archangel's. Then I turned on my back and deadman's-floated parallel to the ceiling. My toes touched the plaster, I was wearing my new black boots that look like nun's bowling shoes according to my husband.

My husband was in the living room. I said, Look what I can do! and I floated up, I clasped my knees in my arms and floated across as if I was sitting on a rug. My husband shook his head. He wasn't shocked, but annoyed. He took off his glasses and rubbed the bridge of his nose. I said, Isn't it amazing? But it didn't amaze him.

In the supermarket there are intriguing headlines: *Woman Meets Satan Face-to-Face.* Underneath is a picture of a monster done in fanciful swirls, reminiscent of an eighteenth-century tapestry. The woman said she had been out mowing the lawn. She had spread out a green plastic tarp and as she was heaving the first forkful (interesting that she used a pitchfork, I thought), Satan appeared on a cloud. Terrified, she ran inside to phone the police. Satan followed, opened her refrigerator, took out some of that Boursin cheese and fixed himself a snack. Then she snapped his picture with her Canon-Sure-Shot.

I wish I could float in the supermarket or even outside beneath the stars, over the treetops which would be so attractive from this angle. But I can only float through the rooms of my own house. I float like Chagall's bridal couple, slantwise, past the huge oak mirror my grandmother bequeathed me where I catch a glimpse of myself floating, hair swept back on one side as if there were a breeze. I smile to see myself this way, so uncharacteristically glamorous in this position.

Thinking back on my life as I float through these rooms, I try to remember what it was like before I could do this: How it was walking through rooms the regular way, picking up objects from the coffee table, dusting them, replacing them. A shell. A blue bowl made by my friend Eileen. An octagonal map of the world. I used to value these objects, their arrangement on my coffee table graceful but unpretentious, I thought, giving just the right sort of clue to my personality. A stone found in a Vermont creek; a number two pencil called Thor; a picture of my mother in a cloche hat smoking a cigarette.

My husband says: Come down now. It's six o'clock. This is no longer amusing. But it's a miracle! I say. I wonder if he knows about the baby, the other miracle. I wonder if she is sleeping or shivering. The back room where we store old photographs and old note-books from law school and old clothes that are out of fashion, the back room is so cold. There is one cracked window where someone shot a beebee. I tacked a sheet over it and now, in addition to being cold, there is only the frailest light seeping through; no view of the mountain or even of the peach tree outside, or the apricot tree which is in bloom now, tiny white blossoms with pink centers and black needles like a bee's anten-nae. I put the baby in a drawer lined with dark blue velvet. I had imagined satin thick as cream but I could only find this dark blue velvet which belonged to my mother. The baby smiles at me as I float past; she lifts her hand as if to say *take it easy, have a great time*. She is very beautiful and around her chin which had been raw from the cold, little yellow flowers have sprung up. This is a secret baby: the baby of my after hours.

No one, especially my husband, would understand this. In the kitchen he is boil-ing water for the pasta, *spaghetti verdi*. My job is the sauce but from such a height he won't trust me with the garlic; I wish I had the nerve to go outside, I tell him. He grunts as if nothing was out of the ordinary. He peels an onion by himself, then puts a can of tomatoes in the Cuisinart. If I went outside I might go up and up, there might be no stopping me, I say.

How do we get this way? I was a perfectly ordinary girl. I went to sixteen years of Catholic school. I read three volumes of Thomas Aquinas's *Summa Theologica*. I made my debut on the St. Regis Roof in New York City. I imitated Ella Fitzgerald in a Boston nightclub called The Alibi. I married a nice responsible man who loved me. He gave me my first umbrella.

But now, what does it mean to be able to float through all these rooms? To roll over and over in sheer invisible air? I yell down to my husband, Watch this, it's a miracle! It's better than The Loaves and Fishes and The Marriage Feast at Cana. I love you, I yell down. He is straining the pasta in the colander. I could use some help, he says.

It took Satan hours to leave the woman's house. He ate cheese and crackers, bit the top off a bottle of Chablis and forced the woman to recite her life's story. So I had to, she told reporters. I began with my birth and worked my way up to this very minute. I never felt so embarrassed. Satan sat on the sofa and drank wine out of the broken Chablis bottle without cutting his mouth. He wore green cowboy boots and a turquoise ring. The woman remembers an eerie feeling whenever Satan would address her, as if his voice were resounding in an echo chamber. It gave me the creeps, said the woman, I will never forget that voice.

In the bedroom, the baby breathes in and out so softly I have to swoop down and touch her forehead to make sure she's alive. Her eyelids are like beautiful stones, but she is surviving. Nestled in dark blue velvet like a string of pearls or a magic good-luck stone, she is still breathing, and in each breath or rather between breaths, riding on that infinitesimal gap, I hear her thoughts. She is thinking about me. I let myself slowly down beside her, hold her in my arms, sing to her in almost a whisper. Then my husband opens the door. Dinner's served, he says sarcastically. I am kneeling over the baby in the drawer, but luckily he doesn't see. He turns on the light and kicks a pile of magazines across the room. What a mess, he says. Dust flies up and softly wafts to the ground and this reminds me of myself and my newfound power.

I float through the room, I float to the door on my stomach and push it open. My husband is angry but from this height his anger is so small; his footsteps which shake the floor and rattle the bric-a-brac on the shelves are so far away now. I feel sorry for him walking to the dining room, ladling our food into bowls, sitting down. So pathetic. I am way up here and will he be amazed? Will he believe in this extraordinary power? No. Nothing can impress him.

The woman confessed to reporters that at the end she had developed a kind of feeling for Satan. That he had been charming. He had listened to her stories about herself, even encouraged her to speak more openly. She confessed she found him attractive, sexually attractive.

No one knows about this baby and I'm not sure how long I can keep her. Sooner or later she'll want to fly off, just like me, only outside, over the trees, higher than the world. I hear her thinking to herself, making plans. . . . I wish her well, a good, intelligent baby with no crimp in her vision—for her the way is as clear as water, right through the clouds, like rain or tears. But no one owns anyone or owes anyone anything, I tell my husband as I float upside down over the dinner table, a long piece of spaghetti dangling from my mouth to tantalize him. Spaghetti kiss? I say. Because I want us to be friends, to be affectionate with one another. But he just looks down.

Terry Castle

Terry Castle (b. 1953) is a prize-winning essayist and a professor of English at Stanford University. She won the William Riley Parker Prize of the Modern Language Association in 1985 and the Crompton-Noll Prize of the Lesbian and Gay Caucus of the Modern Language Association in 1993. She has also been nominated for the PEN Spielvogel-Diamondstein Award for the Art of the Essay. She has written five books including Clarissa's Ciphers: Meaning and Disruption in Richardson's 'Clarissa' *(1982)* Masquerade and Civilization: The Carnivalesque in Eighteenth-Century English Culture and Fiction *(1986), and* The Female Thermometer: Eighteenth-Century Culture and the Invention of the Uncanny *(1995).*

First Ed

First, Ed—who, for all the sense of drama her memory evokes, is surrounded with a certain haze, a nimbus of uncertainty. Did our encounter, the one I remember, take place in 1963 or 1964? It must, I think, have been 1964, if only because the Dixie Cups' "Chapel of Love" (a crucial clue) was on the radio that summer, lilting out of dashboards all over San Diego, along with "Don't Worry Baby," "Pretty Woman," and "I Want to Hold Your Hand." It was the summer that my father's large brown and white Oldsmobile got a cracked block from the heat, and his hair, which had gone gray after my mother divorced him, went completely white, like Marie Antoinette's. A few months later the Dodgers, resplendent with Koufax, won the Series, and I and my fellow sixth-graders, transistors in hand, celebrated with loud huzzahs on the rough gravel playgrounds of Whittier Elementary School.

All during the long hot months of vacation, I went once a week for a swimming lesson at the old YWCA downtown at 10th and C Street. We had recently returned (my mother, my younger sister, and I) from two years on the English coast, where we had lived in a gloomy village near Dover. My British-born mother had taken us there—in a flurry of misguided nostalgia and emotional confusion—immediately after her divorce in 1961, and we had stayed on, in a strange state of immobility and shared melancholia, until mid-1963. In the summer of 1964, however, things seemed better. While my sister and I reaccustomed ourselves to the unfamiliar sunshine, my mother exulted in being back in California, in living as a "bachelorette" (with two children) in the pink Buena Vista apartments, and in the hope—not yet dashed by various Jamesian revelations—of her imminent

Reprinted from *The Apparitional Lesbian: Female Homosexuality and Modern Culture*, (1995), Columbia University Press.

marriage to the handsome Chuck, the mustachioed ensign in the Navy with whom she had committed the sweetest of adulteries before her divorce.

My mother had been a swimming instructor for the Y during the ten years she had been married to my father, and the organization kept her loyalty, being associated with water, freedom, light, pools, and "living in San Diego"—with everything, indeed, that she had dreamed of as a teenager working for the gasworks in St. Albans. She herself had taken a number of classes at the downtown Y: the intermediate and advanced swim course, synchronized swimming, and beginning and advanced lifeguard training, during which she learned to divest herself of numerous layers of clothing, including laced snow boots, while submerged in eight feet of water. Despite my mother's demonstrated aquatic skills, however, I adamantly refused to let her teach me any of them, and remained, at the relatively advanced age of ten, a coy nonswimmer. After several abortive sessions at the bathroom sink, during which she tried to make me open my eyes under water, it became clear that I was not going to learn anything under her tutelage, but would require instruction from some more neutral party. Hence my introduction to the Y, the children's evening swim program, and the delicious orchestrated flutterings of breast, elbow, and ankle.

The YWCA was an antiquated building by southern California standards—Julia Morganish, from the teens or twenties, though not a work of her hand. It preserved the dowdy grandeur of turn-of-the-century California women's buildings, manifest in its square white facade, Mission-style touches, and cool, cavernous interior. Of the actual decor of the building, I remember little: only, vaguely, some seedy fifties leatherette furniture parked at odd angles in the reception area, peeling bulletin boards, the ancient candy machine expelling Paydays and Snickers with a frightful death rattle, and the small front office staffed—inevitably—by a middle aged, short-haired woman in slacks. The place had an interesting air of desolation: various lost or ill-fitting souls lingered in the front area especially—off-duty sailors, people speaking Spanish, Negroes and Filipinas, mysterious solitary women. I never saw any of the guest rooms, and did not know that they existed: it would not have occurred to me that anyone might actually live there.

The indoor pool was deep in the netherworld of the building, seemingly underground—a greenish, Bayreuthian extravagance, reeking of chlorine and steam. Entering from the women's locker room, one found oneself immediately at one of the pool's deep-end corners. A wobbly diving board jutted out here in dangerous invitation, while at the opposite end a set of pale scalloped steps beckoned to the less adventurous. Running around the pool on all sides was an ornate white tile gutter, cheerfully decorated—by the same wayward deco hand, presumably, that had done the steps—with tiny mosaic flowers and swastikas. The water itself was cloudy, awash with dead moths and floating Band-Aids, but nonetheless, in its foggy Byzantine way, also warm-seeming and attractive. A slippery tiled walkway, inset with more flowers and swastikas and the imprinted words DO NOT RUN, completed the scene. Along this elevated platform our blond-haired teacher, an athletic woman named Pam, would slap up and down in bathing suit and bare feet, calling out instructions in a plaintive Midwestern tongue.

We were five or six in all, a sprinkling of little girls in cotton suits with elastic waists, and one or two even smaller boys in minuscule trunks. Under Pam's guidance we soon mastered the basics: the dog paddle, a variety of elementary crawls and backstrokes, flapping sidestrokes, "sculling" and "treading water"—all with much gasping and excitement. It was on one of these occasions, while struggling to float on my back without inhaling water, that I must first have seen Ed. The ceiling over the pool was high up, some thirty or forty feet, with tall windows of opaque glass near the roof line, through which a few dim green rays of evening sunlight would sometimes penetrate to the fluorescent fog below. A dusty balcony overhung the pool at this level, stacked with seldom-used folding chairs for the spectators who came to observe the water ballet displays put on by the synchronized swimming class. Ed stood up there aloft, along with a few seamen in whites, waiting for the adult free swim hour that immediately followed our class.

Even from my unusual angle I could see that Ed was spectacularly good-looking—in a hoodish fifties way that had not yet, by mid-1964, been utterly superseded by the incoming styles of the era. I might grace my bedroom bulletin board with the toothy images of John, Paul, George, and Ringo, but Ed's "look" (as I knew even then) was far more compelling. Indeed I felt oddly giddy those times when she met my gaze—as though our positions had reversed, water and air had changed places, and I was the one looking down from above. She wore men's clothes of a decade earlier, Sears and Roebuck style, the tightest of black pants (with a discreet fly), a dark leather belt and white shirt, a thin striped tie, and, as I saw later, the same pointy-toed black dress shoes worn by the Mexican "bad boys" at Clairemont High School, down the street from the Buena Vista apartments. Her hair was excessively, almost frighteningly groomed into a narrow scandalous pompadour, and had been oiled with brilliantine to a rich black-brown, against which her face stood out with stark and ravishing paleness. She appeared to be in her late twenties or early thirties—definitely "old" to me—though something about the drastic formality of her costume also gave her the look of a teenage boy, one dressed up, perhaps, for a senior prom. She spoke to no one, smoked a cigarette, and seemed, despite her great beauty, consumed by sadness. She had a thin face of the sort I would later find irresistible in women.

One evening, more sultry than usual, my mother, who normally dropped me off and picked me up after class in the front foyer, was unable to collect me, owing to some sudden disorder in the radiator of our bulbous green Studebaker. My teacher, Pam, and her mother, the gamy old Peg, a short tanned woman who wore pants and also taught swimming classes at the Y, agreed to drive me home to Clairemont in their car. As soon as they had closed up the office we were to leave.

I had already finished changing and sat by myself in the locker room, waiting for my ride, when Ed came in. The other little girls were long gone. The floor was still wet with the footprints of the departed; the thick damp air hung about like a dream. At the same time everything seemed to open up, as if I—or she and I together—had suddenly entered a clearing in a forest. Ed said nothing, yet seemed, in some distant way, to recognize me. I sat still, not knowing where to go. She scrutinized me ambiguously for a few moments. Then, as if some complex agreement had been reached between us, she began to strip away, vertiginously, the emblems of her manhood.

Ed, Ed, my first, my only undressing. She moved gracefully, like a Pierrot, her pallid face a mask in the dim light. She removed her jacket and unbuckled her belt first, laying them carefully on the bench next to me. Then she slipped off her shoes and socks. I gazed down at her bare feet. Her eyes met mine and looked away. Then she loosened her tie with one hand, and pulled it off, followed by her heavy cuff links. Glancing again in my direction, she began to unbutton her shirt, twisting her torso in an uneasy fashion as she did so. She wore, heart-stoppingly, a woman's white brassiere. This she unhooked slowly from behind, and watching me intently now, let her breasts fall forward. Her breasts were full and had dark nipples. She stopped to flick back some wet-looking strands of hair that had come down, Dion-like, over her brow. Then rather more quickly, with a practiced masculine gesture, she began to undo her fly. She removed her trousers, revealing a pair of loose Jockey shorts. She hesitated a moment before uncovering the soft hairiness beneath—that mystery against which I would thrust my head, blindly, in years to come. I stared childishly at the curly black V between her legs. She took off her watch, a man's gold Timex, last of all.

Her transfiguration was not complete, of course: now she took out a rusty-looking woman's swimsuit from a metal locker and began, uncannily, stepping into it. She became a woman. Then she folded up her clothes neatly and put them away. Still she did not speak—nor, it seemed, did she ever remove her eyes from mine.

I am aware, too late, how almost painfully sexy Ed was—and perhaps, at the level of hallucination, intended to be. Even now I seem to see the disquieting movement of her chest and shoulders as she leaned over the bench between us, the damp pressed-in look of her thighs when she began to pull the resistant nylon swimsuit up her body, her breasts poignantly hanging, then confined, with the aid of diffident fingers, in the suits's stiff built-in cups. Indeed, I seem to be assisting her, leaning into her, even (slyly) inhaling her. She bends slightly at the knees, balances herself with one hand against the locker, begins to hold me around the neck—but this is a fantasy of the present. In that moment my feelings were of a far more polite, delicate, even sentimental nature. Astonishment gave way to, resolved into, embarrassment. When at last Ed drew on, over the dark crown of her head, a flowered Esther Williams-style bathing cap—the final clownish touch of femininity—I felt, obscurely, the pathos of her transformation: she had become somehow less than herself. But her eyes, with their mute, impassive challenge, never faltered. They seemed to say, I own you now. And I realized too, though I had no words for it at the time, how much I adored her, and what tumult lay ahead.

The other women came and got me soon enough—Ed must have gone—for the next thing I remember is sitting deep in the well of the backseat of my teacher's Plymouth, the warm night breeze blowing in my face, and the lights of downtown glinting in the background as we drove away. Pam and her mother talked in a desultory, friendly way in the front seat. They used slang with each other and swore softly—almost as if I weren't there, or were much older, which I enjoyed. I looked at the back of their heads, at Pam's blond nape and her mother's cropped gray thatch, while the sounds of the radio—KCBQ—wafted sweetly through the summer air:

> We're going to the chapel
> And we're
> Gonna get ma-a-a-rried
>
> Going to the Chapel of Love

Then, as we wound our way down 101 through Balboa Park, under the tall bridge by the zoo, the two of them began—as if to the music—to talk about Ed. They seemed to know her; they spoke almost tenderly, referring to her by name. Ed looked more like a guy than ever, my teacher remarked. The words hung about softly in the air. I began listening hard, as I did at school. Her mother, Peg, reflected for a moment, then glanced back and smiled at me in the dark, enigmatically, before murmuring in reply, "Yeah, but she don't have the superior plumbing system." And into the night we sped away.

Many years later, when I had just turned twenty-two, and lay in bed with a much older woman with whom I was greatly in love, I told the story of Ed, this story, for the first time. I was already getting on Helen's nerves by that point; she tried to find the fastest way through my postcoital maunderings. Ed was, she concluded, "just an externalization." As she often reminded me, Helen had spent fifty thousand dollars a year for eight years of psychoanalysis in Chicago. She wore her hair in a long braid down her back to represent, she told me, her "missing part." She was thin and dark, and, when she wasn't teaching, wore a man's watch and lumberman's jacket. My mother, she said, "sounded like a hysteric." A lot of things happened later, and I finally got to resenting Helen back, but that's a winter, not a summer story.

Boyer Rickel

Boyer Rickel, a recent National Endowment for the Arts fellow, is the author of a collection of poetry, arreboles *(Wesleyan University Press, 1991) and a collection of autobiographical essays,* Taboo *(The University of Wisconsin Press, 1999). His work has appeared in* Poetry, Ploughshares, Iowa Review, Puerto del Sol, *and many other literary magazines. Recent poetry titles include* Remanance *(Parlor Press, 2008) and* Reliquary *(Kitchen Press, 2009).*

Pass

Born in 1951, I was reared in Tempe, Arizona, fifty years ago a mix of family farms, small businesses on a short, hooked main drag, Mill Avenue, and a state college where my father taught on the piano faculty. Tempe then was of a knowable dimension, one bank, one drugstore, one haberdashery. And even more important for my early boyhood formation, one place for the flat-top haircut I preferred, Ray's Barbershop. A low, narrow structure, Ray's was just down from the newspaper office on Mill, and marked by a revolving barber pole, the red stripe spinning forever down or up, I couldn't decide. At age five and six, propped on a smooth board laid across the arms of the barber chair, a white smock fanning out from my neck, I'd fuss—I hated the buzzing clippers, and being confined—till some treat, usually a piece of Dentyne gum, could be found to pacify me.

Entering Ray's, to the right one saw three black leather swivel chairs that rose and turned on pedestals like carnival rides; to the left, against the wall, a line of five or six green naugahyde-covered chairs with chrome tube arm-rests. These waiting chairs I loved because their surfaces stung with coolness the skin on my arms and bare legs in the many hot months of the year. Having used up the cool of one spot, I'd lift my legs and shift my arms to a new position—enjoying even the unsticking sound—and use up the cool in the new location.

Despite the chairs, each time we neared Ray's those first few years, my fingers wrapped in my father's hand, I felt an odd sense of dread. Ray's was a world of men, men without women. If a mother had the job of seeing to her son's haircut, she'd usher him through the door, ask Ray to keep an eye out till she got some other errand done, and be on her way. This charged the atmosphere in some way that made me uncomfortable. Though the talk was generally good-natured, it took on the quality of a public competition, voices chiming in from all parts of the room, the volume rising and falling and rising again quickly.

And the talk seemed to follow a pattern. Whether a man agreed or disagreed with what had just been said—"What a lousy baseball team the college has this

Reprinted from *Taboo*, (1999), University of Wisconsin Press, by permission of the author.

year," or "We need to pass those road bonds"—he'd have to up the ante, speaking more loudly, making a point, or countering a point, with greater intensity. A break in the build-up and he was out.

What made me most uneasy, though, was how my father, stepping through Ray's door, became someone else; how he suddenly treated me as an other, to be discussed as if not present, located in the third-person: "I hope he's not too much trouble today, Ray." My father's voice would dip to a lower register, sounding flat and less gentle.

"A bad time to be in the stock market, Ray?" he'd ask, chin raised. I could see his shoulders, even beneath the smock, flatten against the chair back—my father, who was otherwise noticeably round-shouldered. I could see that rather than take part in the actual contest, my father asked questions, deferring somewhat to the others. I was puzzled by the changes that took place in him; I was embarrassed by his awkwardness.

Some years later, as a member of the high school tennis team, I'd stand with about a dozen naked boys every day after practice in the open showers, the air thick with steam and the stink of gym clothes.

—"What a fuck-up Jimmy was in his match Thursday."

—"It'd serve that asshole right if Sally didn't let him touch her for a month."

—"Hey, Jimmy, she let you do stuff to her with that little wang of yours?"

Though we made our points with quick insults and sarcasm, the pattern was the same as in Ray's, each comment an attempt to top the one before.

Without calling too much attention to myself, I discovered how to add in a sentence here and there, not unlike my father's practice of posing questions. I'd snort at the appropriate moments, and find safe places (the splintered foot of an old wooden bench, a pile of discarded towels) to direct my gaze—away, always, from what interested and confused me most: the other boys' bodies.

By age twelve I visited Ray's alone, riding my bike downtown after school or on Saturday. Not only had I begun to figure out what made me uncomfortable there, I was becoming a student of character, intrigued by the manners of speech and dress and movement that gave adults their distinctive places in my small universe. Ray's was no good for this, the cast changing too quickly for long observation. But just a few blocks up and across the street, I found in another men's place, The Q, a pool hall, a cast of characters who daily arrived to take up their roles. Allowed, perhaps encouraged, to watch—these men knew how to play to an audience—I'd rent a table for half an hour, then sit with a cherry coke at a distance to observe the drama.

The Q was cavernous, a huge open rectangle with lights like giant plungers hanging down over the green felt-covered tables. Entering through the heavy glass door at one end of the storefront, you were met by a squinty little man with stringy dark hair and a stringy body, a body dried and smoked like beef jerky, and a few fading tattoos on his forearms. He sat at the register at the near-end of a long snack counter. From any of the high stools along this counter one could turn and watch the nearby tables. The real action, though, was usually at a back corner snooker table, where the older characters—the Mex, Doc, Walter—would mix it up with the younger hustlers like Smitty and the Rail—and my brother, Richard.

Richard, four years my senior and in high school already, was friends with Smitty and the others; he could hold his own at this table. Always voluble, and tall, with a broad smile and crisp flat-top haircut like mine, he could smoke and curse and talk about sex in conspiratorial ways with the other guys, hinting at conquests, winking, cigarette jittering between his lips, breaking into a growling laugh. All this carried off as he sighted along his cue to make a shot. Between turns he sat with three or four others in high plastic scooped chairs along the wall. They'd slouch in their seats, sticks standing straight up and held with both hands between their legs, comments floating side to side, heads rolling back and forth along the cool painted cinder-block.

I was his kid brother, OK as long as he said so; he said so as long as I never made a point of being his brother. For hours I'd lurk outside the circle, witness to the give and take of men—from late adolescents like my brother, through the older unemployed or retired ones, some of them drunks, noses red and porous from years on the bottle.

Walter and the Mex were the lords of this latter group. Though Walter was light and the Mex dark, their bodies matched in almost every other way, paunches overlapping their belts, skin puffy and creased, brown eyes bloodshot as if they never slept. And their voices were ragged. Walter barked out phrases in hoarse bursts, tugging at his pants from the belt-loops to emphasize a point. The Mex, quieter, was more inclined to ribbing Walter and the others than telling whole stories. "Better pull hard, my friend," he'd wheeze, "you got no ass to hold those pants up." They always looked and acted so settled, small grins and chuckles punctuating their remarks, I figured they had some secret to life.

The younger men handled themselves differently. If the rumpled Walter approached the snooker table like a respectful lover, deliberately considering each shot, gently placing the bridge-hand on the felt, his elbow coming to rest in one slow graceful motion, the young ones said with their bodies they would dominate. Volatile, loud, with quick eyes that knifed in anger or pleasure, Smitty charged the table, swiftly finding the desired angle, pulling the cue back in precise but sudden preliminary jerks. Missing an important shot, Rail, nicknamed both for his skill with bank shots and his skinny frame, would slam the butt of his cue against a wall, spitting a curse. And there were actual fights—over debts (these games were played for money), over occasional insults (about little peckers and never getting laid, or somebody's dumpy girlfriend). Sometimes I couldn't see the explosion coming. There'd be the thud of bodies against a table, arms and grunts and teeth in a blur, and then five or six men rushing in to pull the bodies apart. Those of us just watching would scatter to the walls like so many water droplets shaken from a rag.

I was scared almost to trembling each time I walked into The Q—and excited by my fear. But it wasn't because of the fights. It had to do with my role as a watcher. I felt no kinship with either group, the fiery young hustlers or their blowsy elders, though both I found fascinating. I knew I was a spy, an imposter. I was terrified some comment or some stupid stumbling gesture would show them who and what I was. And though I didn't know what that would be, I felt certain something fundamental in my nature would be different, and to these men, to my brother, even, unacceptable. And so I held myself in absolute, nearly frozen, reserve. If I was blank, I thought, if I didn't try to show I was anybody, if I simply watched, smiled, smirked, laughed at the right moments, slouched down in my chair, I'd pass.

Jamaica Kincaid

Jamaica Kincaid, whose original name was Elaine Potter Richardson, (b. 1949) was born in St. John's, Antigua, in the West Indies, and educated there in government schools. She left Antigua at the age of 16 and worked as an au pair in Manhattan. In 1973, she took the name Jamaica Kincaid, and began submitting articles to The New Yorker *magazine, where she became a staff member in 1976. Her essays and stories were published in other magazines as well. In 1983, Kincaid published her first book,* At the Bottom of the River, *which was a collection of short stories and reflections.*

Girl

Wash the white clothes on Monday and put them on the stone heap; wash the color clothes on Tuesday and put them on the clothesline to dry; don't walk barehead in the hot sun; cook pumpkin fritters in very hot sweet oil; soak your little cloths right after you take them off; when buying cotton to make yourself a nice blouse, be sure that it doesn't have gum on it, because that way it won't hold up well after a wash; soak salt fish overnight before you cook it; is it true that you sing benna in Sunday school?; always eat your food in such a way that it won't turn someone else's stomach; on Sundays try to walk like a lady and not like the slut you are so bent on becoming; don't sing benna in Sunday school; you mustn't speak to wharf-rat boys, not even to give directions; don't eat fruits on the street—flies will follow you; *but I don't sing benna on Sundays at all and never in Sunday school;* this is how to sew on a button; this is how to make a buttonhole for the button you have just sewed on; this is how to hem a dress when you see the hem coming down and so to prevent yourself from looking like the slut I know you are so bent on becoming; this is how you iron your father's khaki shirt so that it doesn't have a crease; this is how you iron your father's khaki pants so that they don't have a crease; this is how you grow okra—far from the house, because okra tree harbors red ants; when you are growing dasheen, make sure it gets plenty of water or else it makes your throat itch when you are eating it; this is how you sweep a corner; this is how you sweep a whole house; this is how you sweep a yard; this is how you smile to someone you don't like too much; this is how you smile to someone you don't like at all; this is how you smile to someone you like completely; this is how you set a table for tea; this is how you set a table for dinner; this is how you set a table for dinner with an important guest; this is how you

Reprinted from *At the Bottom of the River*, (1983), by permission of Farrar, Straus & Giroux.

set a table for lunch; this is how you set a table for breakfast; this is how to behave in the presence of men who don't know you very well, and this way they won't recognize immediately the slut I have warned you against becoming; be sure to wash every day, even if it is with your own spit; don't squat down to play marbles—you are not a boy, you know; don't pick people's flowers—you might catch something; don't throw stones at blackbirds, because it might not be a blackbird at all; this is how to make a bread pudding; this is how to make dou-kona; this is how to make pepper pot; this is how to make a good medicine for a cold; this is how to make a good medicine to throw away a child before it even becomes a child; this is how to catch a fish; this is how to throw back a fish you don't like, and that way something bad won't fall on you; this is how to bully a man; this is how a man bullies you; this is how to love a man, and if this doesn't work there are other ways, and if they don't work don't feel too bad about giving up; this is how to spit up in the air if you feel like it and this is how to move quick so that it doesn't fall on you; this is how to make ends meet; always squeeze bread to make sure it's fresh; *but what if the baker won't let me feel the bread?;* you mean to say that after all you are really going to be the kind of woman who the baker won't let near the bread?

Aurelie Sheehan

Aurelie Sheehan teaches fiction and is the director of the MFA program in creative writing at the University of Arizona. She is the author of two novels, History Lesson for Girls *(2006) and* The Anxiety of Everyday Objects *(2004), as well as a short story collection,* Jack Kerouac Is Pregnant *(1994). She has received a Camargo Fellowship, the Jack Kerouac Literary Award, and an Artists Projects Award from the Arizona Commission on the Arts. The pieces included in this anthology are from the series, "One Hundred Histories."*

Excerpts from One Hundred Histories

Hairbrush

Two girls, though at thirteen and fourteen they consider themselves—not women, exactly, because woman connotes a thickness around the waist and head—but big girls, certainly, girls as in *girlfriend*, as in *hey girl*, and not little children—sit on a queen size bed in suburban America. One sits with her eyes focused just above the brass rails, legs crossed. The other sits behind her, one bare leg hanging off the bed, the other tucked underneath her. She has a hairbrush in her hand.

The girl getting her hair brushed is holding back tears. She doesn't know, quite, where this feeling comes from. It's as if the pull of the brush—not exactly painful, but certainly there, here, in this world—activates some kind of nerve endings in her scalp that attach like threads to her heart, to her private spiritual heart, not the blood pumping one. She feels like she's been wearing her blue and white bandanna (side folded over to form a triangle, ends tucked in and tied at her neck) all her life, or that she's been in a dark cellar all her life and then suddenly someone opens the door and it's great, all the light, but you have to blink and blink. The headboard is made of brass rails, eleven of them, and the top of each has a little head, except for one, which is missing.

"I couldn't move, even though I wanted to," were the disembodied words from her best friend. "I knew Chris would be so pissed, and I don't even *like* him that much, for God's sake. For one thing, he smells like the inside of a chimney, he smokes so much . . . "

Her friend first brushes the very ends of the girl's wet brown hair, little nips and tucks. They'd read once about doing this—about minimizing hair breakage—and now they did it religiously. The magazines were very important. The magazines, even if they seemed out of whack, were always right. The brush felt like an animal nibbling on her bra strap.

"Did he say something first, or just—?" she asked.

"Oh yeah, he said a lot. You wouldn't believe what he was saying. He even said he loved me, for God's sake."

Now that the little creature had finished eating his snack, she felt the longer strokes of the brush, careful but firm, and, fast following, the warm palm of her friend, like a fist in a sock, like the way she imagines the curry comb feeling on the horse's back.

She swallowed, then said, "Was that before, or—"

"Before?"

"Yeah, y'know, before—"

"Before, during and after. He kept talking like crazy. Maybe he was drunk or something."

Then, she felt a little breath against her wet hair and her ear and heard the whispered words, "Can I tell you *everything* he said?"

"Tell me everything."

"He said I was beautiful, and that he had never seen eyes as big as mine. Then he said, when I just looked at him the other day in the hall—when he was with Peter, y'know? After tennis practice?—he got a hard on. I can't *believe* he said that to me."

"A little crass."

"Yeah, but don't you love it?"

The feeling of someone brushing your hair. The wallpaper was striped with roses in the middle. She thought it was a color called "dusty rose," and it matched the quilt, too, and the bed covers. She and her friend often spent the night together, on this bed, it was big enough for two. They'd talk for literally hours, until the pauses, longer and longer between question and answer, grew into hours, into sleep and dream and the next morning, when she'd use her friend's shampoo (always salon shampoo and other good stuff—her mom worked at a hairdresser's) and borrow a fresh shirt and they'd start their day, maybe go into town for pizza or shopping.

"I guess." It wasn't as if she knew from first-hand experience. There was the time when the man leaned out his car window and said, "Nice tushy, little girl." She was shocked and exhilarated. She'd even looked at her ass in the mirror that night, using the little hand-held mirror she used almost every week to see how long her hair had grown. She and her friend were both growing their hair long. They trimmed off the ends for each other. The tip was in *Glamour*, but also it was just common knowledge: you need to trim often so you don't get split ends. It was funny, though. Cut your hair and it grows faster.

Was life like that?

"C'mon, Mel, you know you'd love that."

"Yeah, maybe."

"What if Mark said that to you? What would you do?"

"I'd cream my pants," she said and laughed and her friend laughed, too.

"Told you."

Now the knots were out, and she was using a comb, and it seemed to take as long as a plane ride from New York to Paris for her to journey from the scalp, pin pricks of sensation, down the slide to the end, a little leap and release.

"Guys can be so—I don't know. It just gives me the shivers," her friend said as she stroked.

She closed her eyes.

"I don't know what I'll do if he is at the game tonight. But, if I feel as horny as I did last night—"

Her friend put the comb down and with both hands gathered the other girl's hair away from the shoulders, bare except for a bright green tank top and a bead necklace, and then she put her hands on each one of her shoulders and said, "Straighten up."

"All right," the girl said. She didn't feel like crying anymore. She was okay. She fell silent again, waiting for the first cut.

Mascara

She showered. She used the shampoo that smelled like bubble gum, but was really an exotic combination of rosemary and mint, and she used the conditioner that went with it. She used nectarine soap. She lathered her body with it, carefully. And then she scrubbed herself with a puff of plastic. And then she shaved her legs, all the way up the leg, back and front, and her armpits. And then she dried off. And then she sprayed some other conditioner/detangler on her hair. And then she clipped her toenails. And then she spread face moisturizer on her face and then she rubbed body moisturizer over the rest of her body. And then she combed her hair. And then she sat down and cut her toenails. And then she put special moisturizing cream on her feet. And then she tweezed her eyebrows and the one stray hair under her chin. And then she cleaned her ears with a Q-tip. And then she brushed her teeth. And then she used mouthwash. And then she flossed. And then she put on her underpants and bra. And then she rubbed a cream of some kind into her hair, and started drying it. It took a long time to dry, as she dried it thoroughly, and as she had two different brushes she used, a round one and a flat one. And when it was dry she combed a part in her hair. And then she sprayed something else in her hair. And then she put on a blouse and shorts. And then she stood by the mirror and placed her makeup bag on the sink, behind the faucets. And then she sloughed her skin with something. And then she applied foundation to her skin. And then she applied eye shadow to her eyes. And then she applied eyeliner to her eyes. And then she applied mascara to her eyes. And then she applied blush to her cheeks. And then she applied concealer under her eyes. And then she applied sparkly gel around her eyes. And then she applied lip pencil. And then she applied lipstick. And then she applied perfume. And then she brushed her hair a little more. And then she smoothed her hand over her leg. And then she applied a little more moisturizing cream to her elbows, knees, and her feet again. And then she inspected her toes. And then she noted that her toenail polish had chipped. And then she applied a dab of toenail polish on two toes. And then she put on her sandals. And then she looked in the full-length mirror. And then she turned to the side to look from a different angle. And then she realized she had forgotten to weigh herself, so she took her sandals off and weighed herself. And then she put her sandals back on and looked back in the mirror, one side, other side, front. And then she picked up her sunglasses. And then she put them on and looked in the mirror. And then she put them up on her head and looked in the mirror. And then she shrugged. And then she picked up her car keys and her purse. And then she went to him.

Purse

She wants him to care about it. She wants him to notice the lines of it, and the stitching. He is vacillating between looking at her eyes, which are crackling with imminently combustible anger, and what is in her hand: a purse from the vendor.

He'd only called her again because he was lonely and needed company, not because he in particular needed *her* company. Even a mall can be the site of spiritual compromises of the most complex and life-altering kind.

Still, he knows her: knows her body, knows her moods. He knows a little about how she dresses. He tries to employ some of this knowledge in this situation: does he like this black, square-ish purse more than the more narrow, floppier black purse, or does he like the small red purse?

Good fucking God, he doesn't care.

"I don't know, like I said. But this one is, you know, it's cool. It's . . . pretty," he says.

"Yeah, but, do you think it's, like, too clunky for just walking around?"

"No." Shrug.

"I don't know, it seems too much like my old one. You know. Maybe it's time for a change."

"Yeah, maybe. That sounds good."

"Although, on the other hand, I *like* my old one."

"So why not keep your old one?"

Now she shrugs. "I don't know, I'm kind of bored with it."

"Oh, okay."

"So do you like this one? As much as the one I have now?"

"Sure. Yeah."

"What do you mean, 'Sure'?"

"What do you mean what do I mean?"

"Well, you sound doubtful."

Jesus. "Look, I think it's nice. I mean it."

The young woman considers this purse for another thirty seconds, and then lets it fall down to the crook of her arm, and she regards the other purse—the small red one.

"This one is so cute, though."

"Yeah, it is," he says. Looking around.

"This one would go nice with my red pants, too."

"Yeah, you'd be all red," he says. It sounds more sarcastic than he means it to.

"That was a fucked up thing to say."

"What the—" he starts, and then says, "Look, I only meant it would go with your red pants, just like you said."

"Yeah, it would, but the way you said it sounded, like, I don't know—like you were making fun of me or something." She looks at the purse vendor, an Asian man sitting on a stool reading a magazine, and then at another shopper, a middle-aged woman with one hand on a stroller.

"Look, Jules, as far as I'm concerned, they're all nice purses. You know? Like they are all such nice purses that *who the fuck cares* which one you take anyway?"

The young woman starts putting all three purses, one after the other, kind of roughly, back on the pegs.

"What are you doing? C'mon, aren't you getting one?"

"No. I am *not* getting one."

"Why not? Get the red one. I like the red one."

"I don't even give a shit what you like. You're so clueless when it comes to these things." She is pretty much hissing the words and he knows that this is going to fuck up at least a good part of the afternoon, in fact, the afternoon already feels long gone, and he'd had hopes. Plans.

"Jules, Julie. I'm sorry. I'm so sorry." He holds onto her arm as she starts walking toward The Gap.

Julie puts her head down. She doesn't speak.

"Jules, honeybabe? C'mon, I'm sorry. It's just that to me—to me—I like care about you but I don't care as much about the purses, all right? I trust your judgment about what purse is the right one, okay?"

"I just, I just want to, you know, get taken seriously when I ask you a question. And, and, I want to look good for you."

"You always look good to me, Jules, no matter what purse you've got on your arm. You look better if the purse has a couple grand in it, but other than that—"

He smiles at her and leans his head in, touches her chin with his cupped hand. She's grinning now, at the mall floor. Then she looks back up at him, her eyes lit with expectation.

Ander Monson

Ander Monson writes fiction, poetry, and essays. His books include, Safety Features *(1999),* Other Electricities *(2005),* Vacationland *(2005),* Neck Deep and Other Predicaments: Essays *(2007), and* Our Aperture *(2008). He is the editor of the literary magazine* DIAGRAM *and teaches creative writing at the University of Arizona. His story "To Reduce Your Likelihood of Murder" was previously anthologized in* Flash Fiction Forward: 80 Very Short Stories *(2006) and is included in* Other Electricities.

To Reduce Your Likelihood of Murder

Do not go outside. Do not go outside, on dates, or to the store, alone. Do not go on dates with men. Do not go on dates with men who drive. Do not drive yourself to dates, because that may anger the man you are dating who may wonder if you're too good to step foot in his new custom chrome *baby-baby* car. Do not date men who sit in or lean on cars. Do not sit in cars or sprawl yourself against the seat, or lean up against the metal skin of the door while you are being kissed. Do not date at night. Do not walk at night. Do not walk at night alone. Do not be alone. Walk with a girlfriend or someone else. A man you trust? Do not spend time with men, men friends, or boys. Do not spend time with any kind of men at all. Do not spend time with friends at all. Most women are killed by someone they know. Most women are killed by someone they know intimately.

Install alarm systems on every window, every doorway in your house. Better, do not live in a house. Go apartment. Go co-op. Go someplace where you can be heard, where someone can hear you scream. Do not venture out in public (at night, alone). Do not stay at home. Do not wear black. Do not wear the dress your boyfriend likes so much. Do not date your boyfriend whom you like so much. Do not like so much. Do not say *like* so much. Everyone is a potential murderer. And murderee. You are the murderee. You are single, seventeen, and thin. You are a thing made for television, for the nights of drama crime. Do not watch crime shows on TV or DVD. Do not open the door for anyone. Do not tell your mother that you don't know when you'll be back. Do not frustrate. Do not comply. You must lie somewhere in-between.

Do not sleep deeply.

Do carry mace, or pepper spray, or a bowie knife. Do carry guns if you can get them. A crossbow. A blowgun. Do subscribe to the *Shotgun News* and carry it wherever you go. It will be a totem, will keep you safe from harm. Armor yourself:

plate mail, chain mail, studded leather armor. Helms and chain-link gloves. Keep away from the windows at all times. You must be surprising: Always travel in a crowd, in a cloud of smoke. Cover all your tracks. Keep an eye behind. Switch cabs. Duck into dead-end streets and wait for cars to pass.

Still you will be killed. You're born for it. Your life is a tree meant to be torn apart by weather and electricity.

T.C. Boyle

T. Coraghessan Boyle (1948-) is an award-winning fiction writer. His several titles include, After the Plague *(2001),* Drop City *(2003),* The Inner Circle *(2004),* Tooth and Claw *(2005),* The Human Fly *(2005),* Talk Talk *(2006), and most recently,* The Women *(2009). He teaches in the English Department at the University of Southern California in Los Angeles. The story, "She Wasn't Soft," first appeared in the* The New Yorker *in 1995.*

She Wasn't Soft

She wasn't tender, she wasn't soft, she wasn't sweetly yielding or coquettish, and she was nobody's little woman and never would be. That had been her mother's role, and look at the sad sack of neuroses and alcoholic dysfunction she'd become. And her father. He'd been the pasha of the living room, the sultan of the kitchen, and the emperor of the bedroom, and what had it got him? A stab in the chest, a tender liver, and two feet that might as well have been stumps. Paula Turk wasn't born for that sort of life, with its domestic melodrama and greedy sucking babies—no, she was destined for something richer and more complex, something that would define and elevate her, something great. She wanted to compete and she wanted to win—always, shining before her like some numinous icon was the glittering image of triumph. And whenever she flagged, whenever a sniffle or the flu ate at her reserves and she hit the wall in the numbing waters of the Pacific or the devilish winds at the top of San Marcos Pass, she pushed herself through it, drove herself with an internal whip that accepted no excuses and made no allowances for the limitations of the flesh. She was twenty-eight years old, and she was going to conquer the world.

On the other hand, Jason Barre, the thirty-three-year-old surf-and-dive shop proprietor she'd been seeing pretty steadily over the past nine months, didn't really seem to have the fire of competition in him. Both his parents were doctors (and that, as much as anything, had swayed Paula in his favor when they first met), and they'd set him up in his own business, a business that had continuously lost money since its grand opening three years ago. When the waves were breaking, Jason would be at the beach, and when the surf was flat he'd be stationed behind the counter on his tall swivel stool, selling wax remover to bleached-out adolescents who said things like "gnarly" and "killer" in their penetrating adenoidal tones. Jason liked to surf, and he liked to breathe the cigarette haze in sports bars, a permanent sleepy-eyed, widemouthed California grin on his face,

157

flip-flops on his feet, and his waist encircled by a pair of faded baggy shorts barely held in place by the gentle sag of his belly and the twin anchors of his hipbones.

That was all right with Paula. She told him he should quit smoking, cut down on his drinking, but she didn't harp on it. In truth, she really didn't care all that much—one world-beater in a relationship was enough. When she was in training, which was all the time now, she couldn't help feeling a kind of moral superiority to anyone who wasn't—and Jason most emphatically wasn't. He was no threat, and he didn't want to be—his mind just didn't work that way. He was cute, that was all, and just as she got a little frisson of pleasure from the swell of his paunch beneath the oversized T-shirt and his sleepy eyes and his laid-back ways, he admired her for her drive and the lean, hard triumph of her beauty and her strength. She never took drugs or alcohol—or hardly ever—but he convinced her to try just a puff or two of marijuana before they made love, and it seemed to relax her, open up her pores till she could feel her nerve ends poking through them, and their love-making was like nothing she'd ever experienced, except maybe breaking the tape at the end of the twenty-six-mile marathon.

It was a Friday night in August, half past seven, the sun hanging in the window like a piñata, and she'd just stepped out of the shower after a two-hour tuneup for Sunday's triathlon, when the phone rang. Jason's voice came over the wire, low and soft. "Hey, babe," he said, breathing into the phone like a sex maniac (he always called her babe, and she loved it, precisely because she wasn't a babe and never would be—it was their little way of mocking the troglodytes molded into the barstools beside him). "Listen, I was just wondering if you might want to join me down at Clubber's for a while. Yeah, I know, you need your sleep and the big day's the day after tomorrow and Zinny Bauer's probably already asleep, but how about it. Come on. It's my birthday."

"Your birthday? I thought your birthday was in December?"

There was the ghost of a pause during which she could detect the usual wash of background noise, drunken voices crying out as if from the netherworld, the competing announcers of the six different games unfolding simultaneously on the twelve big-screen TVs, the insistent pulse of the jukebox thumping faintly beneath it all. "No," he said, "my birthday's today, August twenty-sixth—it is. I don't know where you got the idea it was in December ... but come on, babe, don't you have to load up on carbohydrates?"

She did. She admitted it. "I was going to make pancakes and penne," she said, "with a little cheese sauce and maybe a loaf of that brown-and-serve bread. ... "

"I'll take you to the Pasta Bowl, all you can eat—and I swear I'll have you back by eleven." He lowered his voice. "And no sex, I know—I wouldn't want to drain you or anything."

She wasn't soft because she ran forty-five miles a week, biked two hundred and fifty, and slashed through fifteen thousand yards of the crawl in the Baños del Mar pool. She was in the best shape of her life, and Sunday's event was nothing, less than half the total distance of the big one—the Hawaii Ironman—in October. She wasn't soft because she'd finished second in the women's division last year in Hawaii and forty-fourth over all, beating out a thousand three hundred and fifty other contestants, twelve hundred of whom, give or take a few, were men. Like Jason. Only fitter. A whole lot fitter.

She swung by Clubber's to pick him up—he wasn't driving, not since his last D.U.I., anyway—and though parking was no problem, she had to endure the stench of cigarettes and the faint sour odor of yesterday's vomit while he finished his cocktail and wrapped up his ongoing analysis of the Dodgers' chances with an abstract point about a blister on somebody or other's middle finger. The guy they called Little Drake, white-haired at thirty-six and with a face that reminded her of one of those naked drooping dogs, leaned out of his Hawaiian shirt and into the radius of Jason's gesticulating hands as if he'd never heard such wisdom in his life. And Paula? She stood there at the bar in her shorts and Lycra halter top, sucking an Evian through a straw while the sports fans furtively admired her pecs and lats and the hard hammered musculature of her legs, for all the world a babe. She didn't mind. In fact, it made her feel luminous and alive, not to mention vastly superior to all those pale lumps of flesh sprouting out of the corners like toadstools and the sagging abrasive girlfriends who hung on their arms and tried to feign interest in whatever sport happened to be on the tube.

But somebody was talking to her, Little Drake, it was Little Drake, leaning across Jason and addressing her as if she were one of them. "So Paula," he was saying. "Paula?"

She swivelled her head toward him, hungry now, impatient. She didn't want to hang around the bar and schmooze about Tommy Lasorda and O.J. and Proposition 187 and how Phil Aguirre had broken both legs and his collarbone in the surf at Rincon; she wanted to go to the Pasta Bowl and carbo-load. "Yes?" she said, trying to be civil, for Jason's sake.

"You going to put them to shame on Sunday, or what?"

Jason was snubbing out his cigarette in the ashtray, collecting his money from the bar. They were on their way out the door—in ten minutes she'd be forking up fettucine or angel hair with black olives and sun-dried tomatoes while Jason regaled her with a satiric portrait of his day and all the crazies who'd passed through his shop. The little man with the white hair didn't require a dissertation, and besides, he couldn't begin to appreciate the difference between what she was doing and the ritualistic farce of the tobacco-spitting, crotch-grabbing "athletes" all tricked out in their pretty unblemished uniforms up on the screen over his head, so she just smiled, like a babe, and said, "Yeah."

Truly, the race was nothing, just a warm-up, and it would have been less than nothing but for the puzzling fact that Zinny Bauer was competing. Zinny was a professional, from Hamburg, and she was the one who'd cranked past Paula like some sort of machine in the final stretch of the Ironman last year. What Paula couldn't fathom was why Zinny was bothering with this small-time event when there were so many other plums out there. On the way out of Clubber's, she mentioned it to Jason. "Not that I'm worried," she said, "just mystified."

It was a fine, soft, glowing night, the air rich with the smell of the surf, the sun squeezing the last light out of the sky as it sank toward Hawaii. Jason was wearing his faded-to-pink 49ers jersey and a pair of shorts so big they made his legs look like sticks. He gave her one of his hooded looks, then got distracted and tapped at his watch twice before lifting it to his ear and frowning. "Damn thing stopped," he said. It wasn't until they were sliding into the car that he came back to the subject of Zinny Bauer. "It's simple, babe," he said, shrugging his shoulders and letting his face go slack. "She's here to psych you out."

He liked to watch her eat. She wasn't shy about it—not like the other girls he'd dated, the ones on a perpetual diet who made you feel like a two-headed hog every time you sat down to a meal, whether it was a Big Mac or the Mexican Plate at La Fondita. No "salad with dressing on the side" for Paula, no butterless bread or child's portions. She attacked her food like a lumberjack, and you'd better keep your hands and fingers clear. Tonight she started with potato gnocchi in a white sauce puddled with butter, and she ate half a loaf of crusty Italian bread with it, sopping up the leftover sauce till the plate gleamed. Next it was the fettucine with Alfredo sauce, and on her third trip to the pasta bar she heaped her plate with mostaccioli marinara and chunks of hot sausage—and more bread, always more bread.

He ordered a beer, lit a cigarette without thinking, and shovelled up some spaghetti carbonara, thick on the fork and sloppy with sauce. The next thing he knew, he was staring up into the hot green gaze of the waitperson, a pencil-necked little fag he could have snapped in two like a breadstick if this weren't California and everything so copacetic and laid back. It was times like this when he wished he lived in Cleveland, even though he'd never been there, but he knew what was coming and he figured people in Cleveland wouldn't put up with this sort of crap.

"You'll have to put that out," the little fag said.

"Sure, man," Jason said, gesturing broadly so that the smoke fanned out around him like the remains of a pissed-over fire. "Just as soon as I"—puff, puff—"take another drag and"—puff, puff—"find me an ashtray somewhere . . . you wouldn't happen"—puff, puff—"to have an ashtray, would you?"

Of course the little fag had been holding one out in front of him all along, as if it were a portable potty or something, but the cigarette was just a glowing stub now, the tiny fag end of a cigarette—fag end, how about that?—and Jason reached out, crushed the thing in the ashtray and said, "Hey, thanks, dude—even though it really wasn't a cigarette but just the *fag* end of one."

And then Paula was there, her fourth plate of the evening mounded high with angel hair, three-bean salad, and wedges of fruit in five different colors. "So what was that all about? Your cigarette?"

Jason ignored her, forking up spaghetti. He took a long swig of his beer and shrugged. "Yeah, whatever," he said finally. "One more fascist doing his job."

"Don't be like that," she said, using the heel of her bread to round up stray morsels on her plate.

"Like what?"

"You know what I mean. I don't have to lecture you."

"Yeah?" He let his eyes droop. "So what do you call this then?"

She sighed and looked away, and that sigh really irritated him, rankled him, made him feel like flipping the table over and sailing a few plates through the window. He was drunk. Or three-quarters drunk anyway. Then her lips were moving again. "Everybody in the world doesn't necessarily enjoy breathing through a tube of incinerated tobacco, you know," she said. "People are into health."

"Who? You maybe. But the rest of them just want to be a pain in the ass. They just want to abrogate my rights in a public place"—abrogate, now where did that come from?—"and then rub my nose in it." The thought soured him even more, and when he caught the waitperson pussyfooting by out of the corner of his eye he snapped his fingers with as much pure malice as he could manage. "Hey, dude, another beer here, huh? I mean, when you get a chance."

It was then that Zinny Bauer made her appearance. She stalked through the door like something crossbred in an experimental laboratory, so rangy and hollow-eyed and fleshless she looked as if she'd been pasted onto her bones. There was a guy with her—her trainer or husband or whatever—and he was right out of an X-Men cartoon, all head and shoulders and great big beefy biceps. Jason recognized them from Houston—he'd flown down to watch Paula compete in the Houston Ironman, only to see her hit the wall in the run and finish sixth in the women's while Zinny Bauer, the Amazing Bone Woman, took an easy first. And here they were, Zinny and Klaus—or Olaf or whoever—here in the Pasta Bowl, carbo-loading like anybody else. His beer came, cold and dependable, green in the bottle, pale amber in the glass, and he downed it in two gulps. "Hey, Paula," he said, and he couldn't keep the quick sharp stab of joy out of his voice—he was happy suddenly and he didn't know why. "Hey, Paula, you see who's here?"

The thing that upset her was that he'd lied to her, the way her father used to lie to her mother, the same way—casually, almost as a reflex. It wasn't his birthday at all. He'd just said that to get her out because he was drunk and he didn't care if she had to compete the day after tomorrow and needed her rest and peace and quiet and absolutely no stimulation whatever. He was selfish, that was all, selfish and unthinking. And then there was the business with the cigarette—he knew as well as anybody in the state that there was an ordinance against smoking in public places as of January last, and still he had to push the limits like some cocky immature chip-on-the-shoulder surfer. Which is exactly what he was. But all that was forgivable—it was the Zinny Bauer business she just couldn't understand.

Paula wasn't even supposed to be there. She was supposed to be at home, making up a batch of flapjacks and penne with cheese sauce and lying inert on the couch with the remote control. This was the night before the night before the event, a time to fuel up her tanks and veg out. But because of him, because of her silver-tongued hero in the baggy shorts, she was at the Pasta Bowl, carbo-loading in public. And so was Zinny Bauer, the last person on earth she wanted to see.

That was bad enough, but Jason made it worse, far worse—Jason made it into one of the most excruciating moments of her life. What happened was purely crazy, and if she hadn't known Jason better she would have thought he'd planned it. They were squabbling over his cigarette and how unlaid-back and uptight the whole thing had made him—he was drunk, and she didn't appreciate him when he was drunk, not at all—when his face suddenly took on a conspiratorial look and he said, "Hey, Paula, you see who's here?"

"Who?" she said, and she shot a glance over her shoulder and froze: it was Zinny Bauer and her husband Armin. "Oh, shit," she said, and she lowered her head and focussed on her plate as if it were the most fascinating thing she'd ever seen. "She didn't see me, did she? We've got to go. Right now. Right this minute."

Jason was smirking. He looked happy about it, as if he and Zinny Bauer were old friends. "But you've only had four plates, babe," he said. "You sure we got our money's worth? I could go for maybe just a touch more pasta—and I haven't even had any salad yet."

"No joking around, this isn't funny." Her voice withered in her throat. "I don't want to see her. I don't want to talk to her. I just want to get out of here, okay?"

His smile got wider. "Sure, babe, I know how you feel—but you're going to beat her, you are, no sweat. You don't have to let anybody chase you out of your favorite restaurant in your own town—I mean, that's not right, is it? That's not in the spirit of friendly competition."

"Jason," she said, and she reached across the table and took hold of his wrist. "I mean it. Let's get out of here. Now."

Her throat was constricted, as if everything she'd eaten was about to come up. Her legs ached, and her ankle—the one she'd sprained last spring—felt as if someone had driven a nail through it. All she could think of was Zinny Bauer, with her long muscles and the shaved blond stubble of her head and her eyes that never quit. Zinny Bauer was behind her, at her back, right there, and it was too much to bear. "*Jason,*" she hissed.

"Okay, okay," he was saying, and he tipped back the dregs of his beer and reached into his pocket and scattered a couple of rumpled bills across the table by way of a tip. Then he rose from the chair with a slow drunken grandeur and gave her a wink as if to indicate that the coast was clear. She got up, hunching her shoulders as if she could compress herself into invisibility and stared down at her feet as Jason took her arm and led her across the room—if Zinny saw her, Paula wouldn't know about it because she wasn't going to look up, and she wasn't going to make eye contact, she wasn't.

Or so she thought.

She was concentrating on her feet, on the black-and-white checked pattern of the floor tiles and how her running shoes negotiated them as if they were attached to somebody else's legs, when all of a sudden Jason stopped and her eyes flew up and there they were, hovering over Zinny Bauer's table like casual acquaintances, like neighbors on their way to a P.T.A. meeting. "But aren't you Zinny Bauer?" Jason said, his voice gone high and nasal as he shifted into his Valley Girl imitation. "The great triathlete? Oh, God, yes, yes, you are, aren't you? Oh, God, could I have your autograph for my little girl?"

Paula was made of stone. She couldn't move, couldn't speak, couldn't even blink her eyes. And Zinny—she looked as if her plane had just crashed. Jason was playing out the charade, pretending to fumble through his pockets for a pen, when Armin broke the silence. "Why don't you just fock off," he said, and the veins stood out in his neck.

"Oh, she'll be so thrilled," Jason went on, his voice pinched to a squeal. "She's so adorable, only six years old, and, oh, my God, she's not going to believe this—"

Armin rose to his feet. Zinny clutched at the edge of the table with bloodless fingers, her eyes narrow and hard. The waiter—the one Jason had been riding all night—started toward them, crying out, "Is everything all right?" as if the phrase had any meaning.

And then Jason's voice changed, just like that. "Fuck you too, Jack, and your scrawny fucking bald-headed squeeze."

Armin worked out, you could see that, and Paula doubted he'd ever pressed a cigarette to his lips, let alone a joint, but still Jason managed to hold his own—at least until the kitchen staff separated them. There was some breakage, a couple of chairs overturned, a whole lot of noise and cursing and threatening, most of it from Jason. Every face in the restaurant was drained of color by the time the kitchen staff came to the rescue, and somebody went to the phone and called the police, but Jason blustered his way out the door and disappeared before they arrived. And Paula? She just melted away and kept on melting until she found herself behind the wheel of the car, cruising slowly down the darkened streets, looking for Jason.

She never did find him.

When he called the next morning he was all sweetness and apology. He whispered, moaned, sang to her, his voice a continuous soothing current insinuating itself through the line and into her head and right on down through her veins and arteries to the unresisting core of her. "Listen, Paula, I didn't mean for things to get out of hand," he whispered, "you've got to believe me. I just didn't think you had to hide from anybody, that's all."

She listened, her mind gone numb, and let his words saturate her. It was the day before the event, and she wasn't going to let anything distract her. But then, as he went on, pouring himself into the phone with his penitential, self-pitying tones as if he were the one who'd been embarrassed and humiliated, she felt the outrage coming up in her: didn't he understand, didn't he know what it meant to stare into the face of your own defeat? And over a plate of pasta, no less? She cut him off in the middle of a long digression about some surfing legend of the fifties and all the adversity he'd had to face from a host of competitors, a blood-sucking wife and a fearsome backwash off Newport Beach.

"What did you think," she demanded, "that you were protecting me or something? Is that it? Because if that's what you think, let me tell you I don't need you or anybody else to stand up for me—"

"Paula," he said, his voice creeping out at her over the wire, "Paula, I'm on your side, remember? I love what you're doing. I want to help you." He paused. "And yes, I want to protect you too."

"I don't need it."

"Yes, you do. You don't think you do but you do. Don't you see: I was trying to psych her."

"Psych her? At the Pasta Bowl?"

His voice was soft, so soft she could barely hear him: "Yeah." And then, even softer: "I did it for you."

It was Saturday, seventy-eight degrees, sun beaming down unmolested, the tourists out in force. The shop had been buzzing since ten, nothing major—cords, tube socks, T-shirts, a couple of illustrated guides to South Coast hot spots that nobody who knew anything needed a book to find—but Jason had been at the cash register right through lunch and on into the four-thirty breathing spell when the tourist mind tended to fixate on ice-cream cones and those pathetic sidecar bikes they pedalled up and down the street like the true guppies they were. He'd even called Little Drake in to help out for a couple of hours there. Drake didn't mind. He'd grown up rich in Montecito and gone white-haired at twenty-seven, and now he lived with his even whiter-haired old parents and managed their two rental properties downtown—which meant he had nothing much to do except prop up the bar at Clubber's or haunt the shop like the thinnest ghost of a customer. So why not put him to work?

"Nothing to shout about," Jason told him, over the faint hum of the oldies channel. He leaned back against the wall on his high stool and cracked the first beer of the day. "Little stuff, but a lot of it. I almost had that one dude sold on the Al Merrick board—I could taste it—but something scared him off. Maybe mommy took away his Visa card, I don't know."

Drake pulled contemplatively at his beer and looked out the window on the parade of tourists marching up and down State Street. He didn't respond. It was that crucial hour of the day, the hour known as cocktail hour, two for one, the light stuck on the underside of the palms, everything soft and pretty and winding down toward dinner and evening, the whole night held out before them like a promise. "What time's the Dodger game?" Drake said finally.

Jason looked at his watch. It was a reflex. The Dodgers were playing the Mets at five-thirty, Astacio against the Doc, and he knew the time and channel as well as he knew his A.T.M. number. The Angels were on Prime Ticket, seven-thirty, at home against the Orioles. And Paula—Paula was at home too, focussing (do not disturb, thank you very much) for the big one with the Amazing Bone Woman the next morning. "Five-thirty," he said, after a long pause.

Drake said nothing. His beer was gone, and he shuffled behind the counter to the little reefer for another. When he'd cracked it, sipped, belched, scratched himself thoroughly, and commented on the physique of an overweight Mexican chick in a red bikini making her way up from the beach, he ventured an opinion on the topic under consideration: "Time to close up?"

All things being equal, Jason would have stayed open till six, or near six anyway, on a Saturday in August. The summer months accounted for the lion's share of his business—it was like the Christmas season for everybody else—and he tried to maximize it, he really did, but he knew what Drake was saying. Twenty to five now, and they had to count the receipts, lock up, stop by the night deposit at the B. of A., and then settle in at Clubber's for the game. It would be nice to be there, maybe with a tall tequila tonic and the sports section spread out on the bar, before the game got under way. Just to settle in and enjoy the fruits of their labor. He gave a sigh, for form's sake, and said, "Yeah, why not?"

And then there was cocktail hour and he had a couple of tall tequila tonics before switching to beer, and the Dodgers looked good, real good, red hot, and somebody bought him a shot. Drake was carrying on about something—his girlfriend's cat, the calluses on his mother's feet—and Jason tuned him out, ordered two soft chicken tacos, and watched the sun do all sorts of amazing pink and salmon things to the storefronts across the street before the gray finally settled in. He was thinking he should have gone surfing today, thinking he'd maybe go out in the morning, and then he was thinking of Paula. He should wish her luck or something, give her a phone call at least. But the more he thought about it, the more he pictured her alone in her apartment, power-drinking her fluids, sunk into the shell of her focus like some Chinese Zen master, and the more he wanted to see her.

They hadn't had sex in a week. She was always like that when it was coming down to the wire, and he didn't blame her. Or yes, yes, he did blame her. And he resented it too. What was the big deal? It wasn't like she was playing ball or anything that took any skill, and why lock him out for that? She was like his overachieving, straight-arrow parents, Type A personalities, early risers, joggers, let's go out and beat the world. God, that was anal. But she had some body on her, as firm and flawless as the Illustrated Man's—or Woman's, actually. He thought about that and about the way her face softened when they were in bed together, and he stood at the pay phone seeing her in the hazy soft-focus glow of some made-for-TV movie. Maybe he shouldn't call. Maybe he should just . . . surprise her.

She answered the door in an oversized sweatshirt and shorts, barefooted, and with the half-full pitcher from the blender in her hand. She looked surprised, all right, but not pleasantly surprised. In fact, she scowled at him and set the pitcher down on the bookcase before pulling back the door and ushering him in. He didn't even get the chance to tell her he loved her or to wish her luck before she started in on him. "What are you doing here?" she demanded. "You know I can't see you tonight, of all nights. What's with you? Are you drunk? Is that it?"

What could he say? He stared at the brown gloop in the pitcher for half a beat and then gave her his best simmering droopy-eyed smile and a shrug that radiated down from his shoulders to his hips. "I just wanted to see you. To wish you luck, you know?" He stepped forward to kiss her, but she dodged away from him, snatching up the pitcher full of gloop like a shield. "A kiss for luck?" he said.

She hesitated. He could see something go in and out of her eyes, the flicker of a worry, competitive anxiety, butterflies, and then she smiled and pecked him a kiss on the lips that tasted of soy and honey and whatever else was in that concoction she drank. "Luck," she said, "but no excitement."

"And no sex," he said, trying to make a joke of it. "I know."

She laughed then, a high girlish tinkle of a laugh that broke the spell. "No sex," she said. "But I was just going to watch a movie if you want to join me—"

He found one of the beers he'd left in the refrigerator for just such an emergency as this and settled in beside her on the couch to watch the movie—some inspirational crap about a demi-cripple who wins the hurdle event in the Swedish Special Olympics—but he was hot, he couldn't help it, and his fingers kept wandering from her shoulder to her breast, from her waist to her inner thigh. At least she kissed him when she pushed him away. "Tomorrow," she promised, but it was only a promise, and they both knew it. She'd been so devastated after the Houston thing she wouldn't sleep with him for a week and a half, strung tight as a bow every time he touched her. The memory of it chewed at him, and he sipped his beer moodily. "Bullshit," he said.

"Bullshit what?"

"Bullshit you'll sleep with me tomorrow. Remember Houston? Remember Zinny Bauer?"

Her face changed suddenly and she flicked the remote angrily at the screen and the picture went blank. "I think you better go," she said.

But he didn't want to go. She was his girlfriend, wasn't she? And what good did it do him if she kicked him out every time some chickenshit race came up? Didn't he matter to her, didn't he matter at all? "I don't want to go," he said.

She stood, put her hands on her hips, and glared at him. "I have to go to bed now."

He didn't budge. Didn't move a muscle. "That's what I mean," he said, and his face was ugly, he couldn't help it. "I want to go to bed too."

Later, he felt bad about the whole thing. Worse than bad. He didn't know how it happened exactly, but there was some resentment there, he guessed, and it just snuck up on him—plus he was drunk, if that was any excuse. Which it wasn't. Anyway, he hadn't meant to get physical, and by the time she'd stopped fighting him and he got her shorts down he hadn't even really wanted to go through with it. This wasn't making love, this wasn't what he wanted. She just lay there beneath him like she was dead, like some sort of zombie, and it made him sick, so sick he couldn't even begin to apologize or excuse himself. He felt her eyes on him as he was zipping up, hard eyes, accusatory eyes, eyes like claws, and he had to stagger into the bathroom and cover himself with the noise of both taps and the toilet to keep from breaking down. He'd gone too far. He knew it. He was ashamed of himself, deeply ashamed, and there really wasn't anything left to say. He just slumped his shoulders and slouched out the door.

And now here he was, contrite and hungover, mooning around on Ledbetter Beach in the cool hush of 7:00 A.M., waiting with all the rest of the guppies for the race to start. Paula wouldn't even look at him. Her mouth was set, clamped shut, a tiny little line of nothing beneath her nose, and her eyes looked no farther than her equipment—her spidery ultra-lightweight bike with the triathlon bars and her little skullcap of a helmet and water bottles and what-not. She was wearing a two-piece swimsuit, and she'd already had her number—23—painted on her upper arms and the long burnished muscles of her thighs. He shook out a cigarette and stared off past her, wondering what they used for the numbers: Magic Marker? Greasepaint? Something that wouldn't come off in the surf, anyway—or with all the sweat. He remembered the way she looked in Houston, pounding through the muggy haze in a sheen of sweat, her face sunk in a mask of suffering, her legs and buttocks taut, her breasts flattened to her chest in the grip of the clinging top. He thought about that, watching her from behind the police line as she bent to fool with her bike, not an ounce of fat on her, nothing, not even a stray hair, and he got hard just looking at her.

But that was short-lived, because he felt bad about last night and knew he'd have to really put himself through the wringer to make it up to her. Plus, just watching the rest of the four hundred and six fleshless masochists parade by with their Gore-Tex T-shirts and Lycra shorts and all the rest of their paraphernalia was enough to make him go cold all over. His stomach felt like a fried egg left out on the counter too long, and his hands shook when he lit the cigarette. He should be in bed, that's where he should be—enough of this seven o'clock in the morning. They were crazy, these people, purely crazy, getting up at dawn to put themselves through something like this—one mile in the water, thirty-four on the bike, and a ten-mile run to wrap it up, and this was a walk compared to the Ironman. They were all bone and long, lean muscle, like whippet dogs or something, the women indistinguishable from the men, stringy and titless. Except for Paula. She was all right in that department, and that was genetic—she referred to her breasts as her fat reserves. He was wondering if they shrank at all during the race, what with all that stress and water loss, when a woman with big hair and too much makeup asked him for a light.

She was milling around with maybe a couple hundred other spectators—or sadists, he guessed you'd have to call them—waiting to watch the crazies do their thing. "Thanks," she breathed, after he'd leaned in close to touch the tip of his smoke to hers. Her eyes were big wet pools, and she was no freak, no bone woman. Her lips were wet too, or maybe it was his imagination. "So," she said, the voice caught low in her throat, a real smoker's rasp, "here for the big event?"

He just nodded.

There was a pause. They sucked at their cigarettes. A pair of gulls flailed sharply at the air behind them and then settled down to poke through the sand for anything that looked edible. "My name's Sandra," she offered, but he wasn't listening, not really, because it was then that it came to him, his inspiration, his moment of grace and redemption: suddenly he knew how he was going to make it up to Paula. He cut his eyes away from the woman and through the crowd to where Paula bent over her equipment, the take-no-prisoners look ironed into her face. And what does she want more than anything? he asked himself, his excitement so intense he almost spoke the words aloud. What would make her happy, glad to see him, ready to party, celebrate, dance till dawn and let bygones be bygones?

To win. That was all. To beat Zinny Bauer. And in that moment, even as Paula caught his eye and glowered at him, he had a vision of Zinny Bauer, the Amazing Bone Woman, coming into the final stretch with her legs and arms pumping, in command, no problem, and the bright green cup of Gatorade held out for her by the smiling volunteer in the official volunteer's cap and T-shirt—yes—and Zinny Bauer refreshing herself, drinking it down in mid-stride, running on and on until she hit the wall he was already constructing.

Paula pulled the red bathing cap down over her ears, adjusted her swim goggles, and strode across the beach, her heartbeat as slow and steady as a lizard's. She was focussed, as clearheaded and certain as she'd ever been in her life. Nothing mattered now except leaving all the hotshots and loudmouths and macho types behind in the dust—and Zinny Bauer too. There were a couple of pros competing in the men's division and she had no illusions about beating them, but she was going to teach the rest of them a hard lesson, a lesson about toughness and endurance and will. If anything, what had happened with Jason last night was something she could use, the kind of thing that made her angry, that made her wonder what she'd seen in him in the first place. He didn't care about her. He didn't care about anybody. That was what she was thinking when the gun went off and she hit the water with the great thundering herd of them, the image of his bleary apologetic face burning into her brain—date rape, that's what they called it—and she came out of the surf just behind Zinny Bauer, Jill Eisen, and Tommy Roe, one of the men's pros.

All right. Okay. She was on her bike now, through the gate in a flash and driving down the flat wide concourse of Cabrillo Boulevard in perfect rhythm, effortless, as if the blood were flowing through her legs and into the bike itself. Before she'd gone half a mile she knew she was going to catch Zinny Bauer and pass her to ride with the men's leaders and get off first on the run. It was preordained, she could feel it, feel it pounding in her temples and in the perfect engine of her heart. The anger had settled in her legs now, a bitter, hot-burning fuel. She fed on the air, tucked herself into the handlebars, and flew. If all this time she'd raced for herself, for something uncontainable inside her, now she was racing for Jason, to show him up, to show him what she was, what she really was. There was no excuse for him. None. And she was going to win this event, she was going to beat Zinny Bauer and all those hundreds of soft, winded, undertrained, crowing, chest-thumping jocks too, and she was going to accept her trophy and stride right by him as if he didn't exist, because she wasn't soft, she wasn't, and he was going to find that out once and for all.

By the time he got back to the beach Jason thought he'd run some sort of race himself. He was breathing hard—got to quit smoking—and his tequila headache was heating up to the point where he was seriously considering ducking into Clubber's and slamming a shot or two, though it was only half past nine and all the tourists would be there buttering their French toast and would you pass the syrup please and thank you very much. He'd had to go all the way out to Drake's place and shake him awake to get the Tuinal—one of Drake's mother's six thousand and one prescriptions to fight off the withering aches of her seventy-odd years. Tuinal, Nembutal, Dalmane, Darvocet: Jason didn't care, just so long as there was enough of it. He didn't do barbiturates anymore—probably hadn't swallowed a Tooey in ten years—but he remembered the sweet numb glow they gave him and the way they made his legs feel like tree trunks planted deep in the ground.

The sun had burned off the fog by now, and the day was clear and glittering on the water. They'd started the race at seven-thirty, so that gave him a while yet—the first men would be crossing the finish line in just under three hours, and the women would be coming in at three-ten, three-twelve, something like that. All he needed to do now was finesse himself into the inner sanctum, pick up a stray T-shirt and cap, find the Gatorade and plant himself about two miles from the finish. Of course there was a chance the Amazing Bone Woman wouldn't take the cup from him, especially if she recognized him from the other night, but he was going to pull his cap down low and hide behind his Ray-Bans and show her a face of devotion. One second, that's all it would take. A hand coming out of the crowd, the cup beaded with moisture and moving right along beside her so she didn't even have to break stride—and what was there to think about? She drinks and hits the wall. And if she didn't go for it the first time, he'd hop in the car and catch her a mile farther on.

He'd been watching one of the security volunteers stationed outside the trailer that served as a command center. A kid of eighteen maybe, greasy hair, an oversized cross dangling from one ear, a scurf of residual acne. He was a carbon copy of the kids he sold wetsuits and Killer Beeswax to—maybe he was even one of them. Jason reminded himself to tread carefully. He was a businessman, after all, one of the pillars of the downtown community, and somebody might recognize him. But then so what if they did? He was volunteering his time, that was all, a committed citizen doing his civic best to promote tourism and everything else that was right in the world. He ducked under the rope. "Hey, bro," he said to the kid, extending his hand for the high five—which the kid gave him. "Sorry I'm late. Jeff around?"

The kid's face opened up in a big beaming half-witted grin. "Yeah, sure—I think he went up the beach a ways with Everardo and Linda and some of the press people, but I could maybe look if you want—"

Jeff. It was a safe bet—no crowd of that size, especially one consisting of whippets, bone people and guppies, would be without a Jeff. Jason gave the kid a shrug. "Nah, that's all right. But hey, where's the T-shirts and caps at?"

Then he was in his car, and forget the D.U.I., the big green waxed cup cold between his legs, breaking Tuinal caps and looking for a parking space along the course. He pulled in under a huge Monterey pine that was like its own little city and finished doctoring the Gatorade, stirring the stuff in with his index fingers. What would it take to make her legs go numb and wind up a Did Not Finish without arousing suspicion? Two? Three? He didn't want her to pass out on the spot or take a dive into the bushes or anything, and he didn't want to hurt her, either, not really. But four—four was a nice round number, and that ought to do it. He sucked the finger he'd used as a swizzle stick to see if he could detect the taste, but he couldn't. He took a tentative sip. Nothing. Gatorade tasted like such shit anyway, who could tell the difference?

He found a knot of volunteers in their canary-yellow T-shirts and caps and stationed himself a hundred yards up the street from them, the ice rattling as he swirled his little green time bomb around the lip of the cup. The breeze was soft, the sun caught in the crowns of the trees and reaching out to finger the road here and there in long, slim swatches. He'd never tell Paula, of course, no way, but he'd get giddy with her, pop the champagne cork, and let her fill him with all the ecstasy of victory.

A cheer from the crowd brought him out of his reverie. The first of the men was cranking his way round the long bend in the road, a guy with a beard and wraparound sunglasses—the Finn. He was the one favored to win, or was it the Brit? Jason tucked the cup behind his back and faded into the crowd, which was pretty sparse here, and watched the guy propel himself past, his mouth gaping black, the two holes of his nostrils punched deep into his face, his head bobbing on his neck as if it wasn't attached right. Another guy appeared round the corner just as the Finn passed by, and then two others came slogging along behind him. Somebody cheered, but it was a pretty feeble affair.

Jason checked his watch. It would be five minutes or so, and then he could start watching for the Amazing Bone Woman, tireless freak that she was. And did she fuck Klaus, or Olaf, or whoever he was, the night before the big event, or was she like Paula, all focus and negativity and no, no, no? He fingered the cup lightly, reminding himself not to damage or crease it in any way—it had to look pristine, fresh-dipped from the bucket—and he watched the corner at the end of the street till his eyes began to blur from the sheer concentration of it all.

Two more men passed by, and nobody cheered, not a murmur, but then suddenly a couple of middle-aged women across the street set up a howl, and the crowd chimed in: the first woman, a woman of string and bone with a puffing heaving puppetlike frame, was swinging into the street in distant silhouette. Jason moved forward. He tugged reflexively at the bill of his hat, jammed the rims of the shades back into his eyesockets. And he started to grin, all his teeth on fire, his lips spread wide: Here, take me, drink me, have me!

As the woman closed, loping, sweating, elbows flailing and knees pounding, the crowd getting into it now, cheering her, cheering this first of the women in a man's event, the first Iron-woman of the day, he began to realize that this wasn't Zinny Bauer at all. Her hair was too long, and her legs and chest were too full—and then he saw the number clearly, No. 23, and looked into Paula's face. She was fifty yards from him, but he could see the toughness in her eyes and the tight little frozen smile of triumph and superiority. She was winning. She was beating Zinny Bauer and Jill Eisen and all those pathetic jocks laboring up the hills and down the blacktop streets behind her. This was her moment, this was it.

But then, and he didn't stop to think about it, he stepped forward, right out on the street where she could see him, and held out the cup. He heard her feet beating at the pavement with a hard merciless slap, saw the icy twist of a smile and the cold, triumphant eyes. And he felt the briefest fleeting touch of her flesh as the cup left his hand.

Manuel Muñoz

Manuel Muñoz (1972-) is the author of two collections of short stories: Zigzagger *(2003) and* The Faith Healer of Olive Avenue *(2007), which is where the story, "Tell Him about Brother John," is collected. He is a recipient of a 2008 Whiting Writers' Award and a 2009 PEN/O. Henry Award. Muñoz received his MFA in creative writing from Cornell University and now teaches fiction in the University of Arizona's Creative Writing Program.*

Tell Him about Brother John

Every trip back from Over There is a wreck of anxiety. Every trip back, I used to be welcomed home eagerly and with open arms, but today it is only my father, subdued, babysitting the nephews. Over There is "Allá," the way my father says it and then tips his chin at the horizon. Right there. As if the place he means to talk about is either across the street or too far away to imagine. My mother is Over There: she packed her belongings and left with another man, headed for a big city. It's a different Allá, a different Over There, but the way my father tips his chin is the same. It isn't here. I love my mother still, but I wish she would come home sometimes, just so she knows how this feels, this coming back, this answering for the way things are.

My father takes care of the nephews, and they start immediately with too many questions about living Over There, the romanticizing of its danger, its enormity. My nephews watch old Charles Bronson movies on television, still popular on the local stations in the midafternoon. They ask me if my life is like this: stolen drugs and brutalized girlfriends and guns illuminating the night streets. My oldest nephew is only ten years old.

I started saying Allá, too, because I was embarrassed about it. "Here," I say, giving one of the lighter suitcases to my oldest nephew. "Put that in the bedroom for me." It pains me to hear my nephews ask such stupid questions, the way their young hearts believe that I'm lying to them and holding back the details of a life filled with excitement and anticipations. My life is this: I'm broke, cramped in my apartment, on edge in the late night—early morning hours, convinced I'm missing out on some unimaginable vitality somewhere in the city. I say nothing to my nephews or my father about my job, but then again they hardly ever ask.

Every year, when the tiny plane descends, bringing me back into the flat arid interior of the Valley, back to the house I grew up in on this street, when my nephews climb on my every limb to welcome me home, I think I might be yearning. But then a fear comes over me, a feeling of being fooled and hypnotized by nostalgia. Sometimes I imagine Gold Street as a living being, an entity with arms waiting. Sometimes I imagine waking up Over There, parting my curtains, and seeing not the shadowy city streets but the plum blossoms and the Chinese elms, the paperboys tossing the morning news, cycling down Gold Street at the point in the neighborhood where you can do a U-turn and not a three-point. All of that imagining gives me a tight, constricted feeling.

"So who's called?" I ask my father, and try to shoo the boys away.

"Your cousin Oscar, your tía Carolina. Your grandpa Eugenio. Your sister wants to show you the new baby." My father shakes his head. "Can you believe it? Seven boys and still no girl."

My nephews run back down the hallway toward me, all of their tiny hands grabbing at a basketball, ready for a game on the dirt driveway. My father has built them a hoop out of a large plastic bucket and a piece of plywood. "Not now," I say, sending them out. "Maybe later." I send them out even though there isn't much to say to my father. My father, as if he knows this, too, goes over to the phone and starts making a spate of calls, announcing my safe arrival.

I wait patiently on the couch, looking around at the house, which is becoming more unfamiliar, bit by bit, with every trip home. At the back of the kitchen, where the door opens out onto the garage and the dirt driveway, one of my nephews bounds back inside. I can hear his voice, already breathless and heated. I can hear the refrigerator door open, the sound of thirst being quenched. He's drinking cherry punch—some things do not change. I can hear my nephew's voice, but I'm embarrassed to admit that I cannot tell which one it is. My father is still on the telephone, but my nephew asks him anyway, "Did you tell him about Brother John?"

Brother John isn't my brother. He isn't anyone's brother, though all of us on Gold Street claim him as one of ours. This is why, whenever I come home, I'm obligated to see him.

Brother John, then and now, is the same person he has always been. He was the boy in town with no parents, no family. He had been held under the care of various aunts and uncles in some of the other small towns, always being shuttled back and forth between Orange Cove and Sanger and Parlier and even Pixley, his clothes carried in a single paper sack. Everyone on Gold Street watched from behind window curtains whenever he was brought back to the neighborhood to stay with the Márquez family, everyone shaking their heads about how poorly dressed he was, how underfed. Long after the Márquez family moved away— back to Mexico, some said—the car with Brother John came back and stopped at the empty house. The two women who had driven Brother John there knocked on the door; then one of them went back to the car and beeped the horn. They kept honking until one of the neighbors came over, told them that no one was living there, and then claimed Brother John, just like that. Our next-door neighbors, in fact. The car that brought Brother John drove away, and from then on, we were all instructed to treat Brother John as if he were one of our own.

I was too young then to know about legalities and I'm too old now to ask something so improper, something that is none of my business. Rumors about

Brother John flew all around, but they were not mean spirited. They were things we asked only among ourselves, and it was understood that we were never to mention our questioning to him. Was he from Mexico? Did his parents abandon him? Were his parents dead? Why didn't his aunts or uncles want him? Was he sick? Did our neighbors get money from the government to keep him? Had we all noticed how the neighbors drove new cars every couple of years, ever since they had taken in Brother John? Why didn't he look like anybody in town, where cousins lived around almost every corner? Did his parents love him?

"You should go next door," my father says to me, "and see if Brother John is home."

I try to think of some excuse to delay the obligatory visit, but there is no avoiding it, not with my father. Even though my mother left him, my father is still a well-respected man in town. He is a war veteran; he marches in all the town parades, holding the American flag. He attends Saturday breakfasts at the Iglesia de San Pedro, where the town elders raise funds. He sits on the town council and reviews applications for new businesses: always yes to franchise restaurants, always no to the new liquor stores. I can wait only so long before I have to go next door to see Brother John. It's expected, because of who my father is, that I not be arrogant.

I can hear my nephews arguing in the driveway. They are still young. I wonder when my father will start coming down on them.

I knock on the heavy black security door and I hear shuffling in the living room. "Who is it?" says Doña Paulina in her broken English, and when I call out to her that it's me, she parts the curtain as if to make sure. She opens the door and motions me in, but she isn't smiling—I've never liked her. I point to my car next door, as if it were running and ready to go. "Brother John?"

"¡Juanito!" she calls out, holding the door open, wiping one hand clean on her apron. The living room looks much smaller than I remember it.

"Hey," Brother John says, emerging from the hallway. His room is in the back, the same room. We're twenty-six now, both of us, and it flashes through me: why is he still here, when he had a chance to get away? He got away, actually—to Oklahoma—but he came back. "Your dad told me you were coming to visit."

"Yeah," I tell him. "Hey, do you want to get a bite to eat? Just here in town?"

Doña Paulina stands staring at both of us. I know she understands what we're saying, and even though I've never liked the woman, I respect her. Brother John is no one's flesh and blood, not on this street, but she raised him when she didn't have to.

"Sure," Brother John says, walking to the door without gathering anything, as if he had been expecting the invitation. He extends his hand and I shake it; it's thick and hot. Neither of us lets go, and I'm almost afraid to: it's as if my father were in the room and not next door. I can imagine the town elders talking to my father on Saturday morning: "¿Y tu hijo? When is he coming home?"

The trip home from Over There will be only a week long. I will visit my ailing grandfather Eugenio between his afternoon naps and then drive back to my father's house feeling guilty about my grandpa's health. I will supervise my nephews as my father escapes with relief from this daily task my brothers and sisters put on him, knowing he feels too guilty to say no to their demands. My brothers and sisters will go to work, grateful for the savings in day care, but won't say thank you. It will mean an uncomfortable session with my father, a sitting-in-silence that means nothing except that my father is still thinking about my mother and how she abandoned him. Luckily, my high school friends Willy and Al will invite me over to Willy's place for beer and then me driving the car home drunk. It will mean, one morning at the grocery store, running into the girl who had a crush on me in high school—Lily still not married, still idling in the cul-de-sacs of the men she now wants, parking outside their houses and waiting through nothing. It will mean opening my town's thin paper and whistling at how much property you can get for only five figures and what a pushover I am for living Over There. During the week, I will have to nurse a pulled and aching hamstring from playing basketball with my nephews. They know the small dips and holes in the dirt driveway better than I do. It will mean resting on the sofa with my hamstring wrapped, leg raised, the house quiet, and next door Brother John, and the story he told me unable to be taken back.

Brother John knows where the new places are and he directs me to one of the franchise restaurants in town, along the new strip mall that has sprouted on the east side, the painted stucco bright against the fresh parking lot, the cars eager with patrons. Everyone in town comes here now, avoiding the dilapidated downtown and its struggling stores. The strip mall is wide, neon lit, smooth tarred, convenient, sparely landscaped with fledgling trees and shrubs. I would never find a place like this Over There, and part of me is grateful for the proximity of all this, the wide space, the cleanliness and the order and the newness of everything in sight, everything an enormous city could never offer.

At the restaurant, we sit in a booth with comfortable cloth-covered seats, etched glass, and spacious tables. The young waiters circle quickly with hot dishes. I think of all my friends Over There and how they would deny that they come from such places. They feel a particular shame, I think, about coming from towns like this. But I'm glad for it: I think of my father and the town elders planning and hoping, counting the jobs at this restaurant, at the video store across the way, at the giant supermarket and the pharmacy. I wish I could be a little more like them or Doña Paulina, looking out for other people.

Brother John studies the menu, and while his eyes are downcast, I study him: he seems smaller, his shoulders narrowed, his chest caved. Because I've been Over There and know more than just Mexican faces, I see the mystery of his parents through his face. He has the wide face that we all have, and the dark skin, but his hair is fine—fine and brown. I don't remember it being brown. Beautiful, actually, the length of it creeping past his neck. With his face down, his eyes not showing, he could be a white boy, but I have never even tried to imagine who his parents could have been. None of the stories have ever convinced me.

"You look tired," I say to him.

Brother John sighs and closes the menu. "Tough lately." He looks up at me. "Being here." His eyes lock on mine. It's only Over There that people look me in the eye—that I feel okay about looking someone in the eye.

I look back down at my menu and don't say anything to Brother John. Our waiter takes a long time to come to our table, and I put on an act of not knowing what to order. For a while, it works; Brother John has little to say. But as soon as the waiter has come and taken our order, Brother John starts up, naming names, the people we went to school with. As with my friends Over There, I try to keep as much to myself as possible, only nod my head, try to avoid contributing to conjecture. It doesn't faze Brother John. He tells me that Agustina had a baby a year after high school and could never determine the father. "And word is, Ginger— that teacher's daughter—she had a baby, too, but no one knew about it and she gave it up for adoption. Beto and Patsy got married and then divorced, because Beto was having an affair with Carla—remember her? Carla Ysleta? Now Beto and Carla are married and Patsy's alone with no kids."

Brother John says all this without keeping his voice down, and I can sense people are cocking their ears for gossip. People know people in this town. People know.

"Violeta, of all the ones, never got married or had kids, but word was she couldn't have any and had depression for years. That happened to her sister, Sofia. Remember her? That's why a lot of people think she killed herself. And Emilio Rentería—he hurt himself so bad on night shift at the paper mill that he can't work anymore. But you can see him at the Little League games. He coaches the kids, even though he uses a wheelchair."

A friend of my father's passes by our table on his way out and extends his hand. "Good to see you," Señor Treviño says. He beams proudly at me, and behind his smile I can almost hear my father telling his lies to the old men at the Iglesia de San Pedro. "Say hello to your father." Brother John says nothing to him, does not meet his eyes, and it surprises me that Señor Treviño simply goes on his way, giving Brother John only a slight nod.

"What's that about?" I ask Brother John when the old man leaves the restaurant. "He knows you."

Brother John sniffs. "He thinks he does."

"What do you mean?"

"They're making me pay back the scholarship. Remember that?"

I do remember it. I remember the envy, the luck I thought he had, how the Iglesia de San Pedro had silently pushed their bake sales and Saturday breakfasts and tithing to present Brother John a check to attend a school in Oklahoma. My father had reprimanded me one night when I said something about how unfair it was: "You think about what that kid has been through. All his life. Who does he have to turn to except these people right here at the church?" My mother had been sitting on the couch watching her telenovela. She had rolled her eyes in disgust. That was the year before she left.

"Why are they making you pay it back?"

"I didn't finish," says Brother John, and he looks back down. His brown hair falls a little, but I can still see his face, and for the first time—maybe because I'm old enough now—I recognize what a sad life he has had, all the things he does not know. At least my mother, even though she is not with my father anymore, calls me. "Why are you Over There anyway?" she pleads, and right now, as I think of her and see Brother John's downcast eyes, her pleading is not a nuisance.

The waiter comes with the food, the plates hot, and I shovel the food in. I can sense it coming from Brother John, the need to say something, and I feel sorry for having asked him out to eat. He does not touch his food.

Finally, when I'm halfway through my plate, he picks up his fork and starts eating. "Did you think I was praying?" he asks.

I laugh nervously. I remember the school he was sent to, a religious school smack in the middle of Oklahoma.

His voice hushes a little and I have to lean in to hear him. He starts telling me, even while he's eating, but I can understand him. He doesn't swallow the words. "I got there, to Oklahoma, and I had that money. But I ran out real quick after I bought books and stuff, and I couldn't afford the dorms. So I found this room from a family that lived in the middle of town. When I told them I was a student down at the school, they let me stay real cheap. The room was upstairs, like an attic, and I had my own stairwell that ran above the garage. I had to be real careful in the rain. Or the snow. They had used this real cheap glossy paint on the wood and it was slippery. But they never bothered me. I still needed money, though, so I started tending bar without telling them, just to make some extra. Things were going fine for a long time, and then . . . "

I resist saying, *What?* My food is nearly gone, but Brother John takes his time. He pushes the fork around on his plate, takes a few small bites.

"I met someone," he says very quietly. "One of my classmates. He was from South Carolina."

He is telling me this because I'm living Over There; he thinks anywhere but here will let you live a life never allowed. He thinks Over There is full of people falling in love, people waiting to listen to you while you do the falling. He sees right through me, my moving Over There. But I still say nothing.

"His name was Gary. Gary Lee Brown. I met him and started seeing him a lot. And a few months later I lied to that family and told them that Gary needed help and could he stay with me, and they said yes. The father even helped us move Gary's bed up to that room, even though we never used it. We just set it up in case the family came upstairs, but they never did. The hard thing was, Gary was real religious. He believed it, I mean, and even after we'd been together like that for a year, he kept telling me that what we were doing was wrong, that it was a sin. He'd scare me sometimes, the things he'd say, like driving out in the middle of the wheat fields and just sitting, thinking about killing himself. 'You're just out there, thinking?' I would ask him when he'd come home late, real late—two in the morning, sometimes. And that's what would scare me, all those hours, being alone at night when I knew what he was thinking. You remember going out to the orchards at night, drinking, how you can see the stars all out? It's pretty when you're with other people, but when you're by yourself . . . And Oklahoma's flat. Flat, flat—flatter than here."

"He didn't kill himself, did he?" I ask him, because the way he's talking is making me nervous, the anticipation of terrible news.

"Nah, he didn't," Brother John says, pursing his lips. "We went on like that for a long time. A long time. Then one day I came home from school and Gary's things were gone—his clothes, even the bed. He left me a note taped to the mirror in the bathroom, explaining how it wasn't right, saying he went back to South Carolina. Back to his little town."

This is where the tears start, and the waiter comes by as if he's been listening the whole time. "Everything all right?" he asks. He must be sixteen or seventeen, young, and he looks like one of the Ochoa brothers.

"Some bad news is all," I tell him, and Brother John holds his head in his hands, and I'm grateful that the waiter walks away before Brother John begins again.

"I loved Gary. I really did. And I ran out of money and couldn't concentrate on the studying anymore, so I just came back home," he says, sobbing softly, and if only it weren't here in this restaurant, I would listen. But it's difficult. "It's been real hard to keep inside, ever since I came back. But I don't have anywhere else to go. I don't have family. I only had him. And I remember telling myself, all those times walking home from the bar in that little town, *This is it, this is it.* How could he go like that? I just couldn't believe it when I read that note, and I haven't heard from him since."

The waiter comes back with a coffeepot and two cups, even though we didn't ask for it. I'm too speechless to refuse him, and Brother John is too busy wiping away his tears, so the cups come down, and this means more that I have to sit through, waiting for the coffee to cool down, waiting for the check.

"For the longest time, I thought about going to South Carolina, to his little town, to find him. Call him out in the street in front of all his people and ask him why. But then I think about somebody doing that to me here and I know it would just be mean. At least he didn't kill himself, I hope."

I pour some sugar into my coffee, some of the warm milk, and slide the little condiment tray over to Brother John. He takes it calmly, the story out of him, and I figure maybe what he wants is a story in exchange. He wants to know about Over There, what you do when you feel like this Over There, where there isn't an empty wheat field to cry in. So I tell him a little bit, just to say something. But I just talk circles. I say that Over There is tall buildings. Over There is restaurants and the people who eat in them. I say that Over There is long, high windows by clean dining tables, and bright candles for the patrons. Over There is side streets with doors always open to the restaurant kitchens, the cooks sitting on the steps to get air. How there are enough restaurants Over There to employ actors and dancers who bend like Ls over the tables, enough work for the Mexican busboys and the dishwashers, how they all split the tips between cigarettes at the end of the long shift. Living Over There is cars and taxis, vans and too many horns, a bus to get you from one side of the city to the other whenever you needed.

I don't offer much more, and Brother John sips his coffee, quiet, not asking for more. What city doesn't have those things—tall buildings, too many cars, immigrants in the kitchen, actors and dancers eager for the spotlight? His face is done crying and it settles into resignation—he doesn't bother looking me in the eye.

The waiter brings the check, and both of us reach for our wallets. I don't want to do the dance of who pays, so I let Brother John put the money down when he insists and get up to leave. We walk out to the car, past families going in to eat, the smell of the brand-new tar of the parking lot in the air. When he shuts the car door, before I turn the ignition, Brother John clears his throat. He wants to revive the life in himself, and he says, "I loved that guy. Gary Lee Brown. I still love him . . . ," but I interrupt him.

"No more," I say apologetically. And then, "Keep it to yourself."

During the rest of the week, I think about Brother John next door, and I feel bad about how I left things with him. I nurse my aching hamstring in the quiet of the house, all of my nephews outside playing basketball, tireless. They'll come in filthy later, and it takes a long time to get all of them to wash their hands. I am lying on the couch and I close my eyes, hoping they'll stay out there until my brothers and sisters come back to collect them.

I keep wondering if I did the right thing by not telling Brother John my story, even though I knew he wanted to hear it. But I learned a long time ago to keep things simple. Don't tell much. Don't tell everything. Don't reveal what people don't need or want to know. It makes it easier all around.

Of my father: say no more of what happened to end the marriage. Of my brothers and sisters: nothing of the spider-cracks in their own unions. Of my tía Carolina: nothing of the money she stole from her job as the cashier of the mini-mart. Look at the people we went to school with: Agustina, though she knew the father of her baby, never brought him up. Ginger, whose mother worked with the school superintendent, wore big sweaters to hide the pregnancy. Maybe credit should have gone, then, to Ginger's mother for saving reputations all around. Beto and Carla married at the Iglesia de San Pedro, and no one raised a fuss, not even Patsy, alone and with no kids to show for her time with Beto. Violeta never talks about what is wrong with her insides, never takes her older sister Sofía's tragedy and brings it under the wing of her own misery. Emilio never admits that the accident at the paper mill might have been his fault, might have been caused by the sips of whiskey and the pot during his long breaks at four in the morning. *No one needs to know the whole story*, I wish I could tell Brother John. No one wants to know what Lily does in her car while she waits outside the houses of the men she loves. No one wants to know about Gary Lee Brown.

But I can't explain it to Brother John without telling him about the Actor. Take the Actor: when the Actor told me he was an actor, I had wanted to know what kind, because *actor* didn't differentiate him from any of the other actors Over There—stage actors, musical theater actors, dancers who did some acting because there were more opportunities to act than to dance, improv players, experimental and fringe performers, porn stars, soap actors, commercial hounds, film extras. But it had become apparent that I didn't need to know. All that I needed to know was the Actor's last hour at the bar, that the flirtations with the customers were nothing more than a way to get bigger tips, and that neither of us had to admit that this would be nothing more than a few brief months of small arguments and jealousies, caught hours and inconsequence. There would be no telling each other where we grew up and who our last boyfriend was and why it didn't work out. I learned to keep it to sitting at the bar, having two drinks, watching the Actor bend elegantly down, watching the customers admire that elegance. For all his story, Brother John got nothing; I left out my part about the Actor, about dating the Actor, then loving him, sitting at the bar and waiting for the end of his shift, watching as he stretched over a table to deliver drinks, a sharp L as the customers peered up at him.

"You shouldn't go on the plane like that, hurt and everything," my father says. His voice surprises me, and I open my eyes to see him standing over the couch. "Why don't you stay until you get better?"

"I have only a couple of vacation days," I tell him. "I have to go back." I put my hand over my eyes, as if I have a headache, but really it's to ward him off. We have not had our usual session of just the two of us sitting in a room, quiet, until he asks the questions that still eat away at him, the questions about my mother. Each and every time, I refuse to answer. I stay quiet and let him ponder on his own because I don't know how to relieve his exasperation.

"Why are you Over There anyway?" my father asks me.

"Dad, lay off," I say, sighing, and I rub my hamstring as if he's irritating it. My hand is still over my eyes, but I don't have to look at him to realize that our usual session is here, the two of us quiet. I think about the difficulty of easing anyone's pain after a sudden departure, the lack of reasons, the loss of hope. I can see Brother John in a small room in the wide plains of Oklahoma, the weather battering the thin glass of the windows of his attic apartment, him standing there and trying to ease his own confusion. It makes it easier to picture my father in this house on the first night after my mother's departure, how Brother John's story has allowed me to imagine. But then I realize my father has let go of those questions and those hurts, at least temporarily.

After a long while, I speak. "Dad," I ask, "why did you send me over to Brother John?" I keep my hand over my eyes, my other hand rubbing at my hamstring.

He does not answer. He stands at the foot of the couch. I can hear the clock ticking above the television set, the boys outside arguing, the ball bouncing against the dirt driveway. I still have my hand over my eyes, blind to my father's reaction, and the longer he stays silent, the more I want the pain in my leg to stay fiery and fierce, my hand over my eyes like a blindfold.

Robert Olen Butler

Robert Olen Butler's (1945-) work is celebrated and widely published. He has written several novels and short story collections. One of these collections, A Good Scent from a Strange Mountain, *won the 1993 Pulitzer Prize for Fiction. His most recent collection of short short stories is* Intercourse *(2008). He is the Francis Eppes Distinguished Professor of Creative Writing at Florida State University.*

Jealous Husband Returns in Form of Parrot

I never can quite say as much as I know. I look at other parrots and I wonder if it's the same for them, if somebody is trapped in each of them paying some kind of price for living their life in a certain way. For instance, "Hello," I say, and I'm sitting on a perch in a pet store in Houston and what I'm really thinking is Holy shit. It's you. And what's happened is I'm looking at my wife.

"Hello," she says, and she comes over to me and I can't believe how beautiful she is. Those great brown eyes, almost as dark as the center of mine. And her nose—I don't remember her for her nose but its beauty is clear to me now. Her nose is a little too long, but it's redeemed by the faint hook to it.

She scratches the back of my neck.

Her touch makes my tail flare. I feel the stretch and rustle of me back there. I bend my head to her and she whispers, "Pretty bird."

For a moment I think she knows it's me. But she doesn't, of course. I say "Hello" again and I will eventually pick up "pretty bird." I can tell that as soon as she says it, but for now I can only give her another hello. Her fingertips move through my feathers and she seems to know about birds. She knows that to pet a bird you don't smooth his feathers down, you ruffle them.

But of course she did that in my human life, as well. It's all the same for her. Not that I was complaining, even to myself, at that moment in the pet shop when she found me like I presume she was supposed to. She said it again, "Pretty bird," and this brain that works like it does now could feel that tiny little voice of mine ready to shape itself around these sounds. But before I could get them out of my beak there was this guy at my wife's shoulder and all my feathers went slick flat like to make me small enough not to be seen and I backed away. The pupils of my eyes pinned and dilated and pinned again.

He circled around her. A guy that looked like a meat packer, big in the chest and thick with hair, the kind of guy that I always sensed her eyes moving to when

I was alive. I had a bare chest and I'd look for little black hairs on the sheets when I'd come home on a day with the whiff of somebody else in the air. She was still in the same goddamn rut.

A "hello" wouldn't do and I'd recently learned "good night" but it was the wrong suggestion altogether, so I said nothing and the guy circled her and he was looking at me with a smug little smile and I fluffed up all my feathers, made myself about twice as big, so big he'd see he couldn't mess with me. I waited for him to draw close enough for me to take off the tip of his finger.

But she intervened. Those nut-brown eyes were before me and she said, "I want him."

And that's how I ended up in my own house once again. She bought me a large black wrought-iron cage, very large, convinced by some young guy who clerked in the bird department and who took her aside and made his voice go much too soft when he was doing the selling job. The meat packer didn't like it. I didn't either. I'd missed a lot of chances to take a bite out of this clerk in my stay at the shop and I regretted that suddenly.

But I got my giant cage and I guess I'm happy enough about that. I can pace as much as I want. I can hang upside down. It's full of bird toys. That dangling thing over there with knots and strips of rawhide and a bell at the bottom needs a good thrashing a couple of times a day and I'm the bird to do it. I look at the very dangle of it and the thing is rough, the rawhide and the knotted rope, and I get this restlessness back in my tail, a burning thrashing feeling, and it's like all the times when I was sure there was a man naked with my wife. Then I go to this thing that feels so familiar and I bite and bite and it's very good.

I could have used the thing the last day I went out of this house as a man. I'd found the address of the new guy at my wife's office. He'd been there a month in the shipping department and three times she'd mentioned him. She didn't even have to work with him and three times I heard about him, just dropped into the conversation. "Oh," she'd say when a car commercial came on the television, "that car there is like the one the new man in shipping owns. Just like it." Hey, I'm not stupid. She said another thing about him and then another and right after the third one I locked myself in the bathroom because I couldn't rage about this anymore. I felt like a damn fool whenever I actually said anything about this kind of feeling and she looked at me like she could start hating me real easy and so I was working on saying nothing, even if it meant locking myself up. My goal was to hold my tongue about half the time. That would be a good start.

But this guy from shipping. I found out his name and his address and it was one of her typical Saturday afternoons of vague shopping. So I went to his house, and his car that was just like the commercial was outside. Nobody was around in the neighborhood and there was this big tree in the back of the house going up to a second floor window that was making funny little sounds. I went up. The shade was drawn but not quite all the way. I was holding on to a limb with arms and legs wrapped around it like it was her in those times when I could forget the others for a little while. But the crack in the shade was just out of view and I crawled on along till there was no limb left and I fell on my head. Thinking about that now, my wings flap and I feel myself lift up and it all seems so avoidable. Though I know I'm different now. I'm a bird.

Except I'm not. That's what's confusing. It's like those times when she would tell me she loved me and I actually believed her and maybe it was true and we clung to each other in bed and at times like that I was different. I was the man in her life. I was whole with her. Except even at that moment, holding her sweetly, there was this other creature inside me who knew a lot more about it and couldn't quite put all the evidence together to speak.

My cage sits in the den. My pool table is gone and the cage is sitting in that space and if I come all the way down to one end of my perch I can see through the door and down the back hallway to the master bedroom. When she keeps the bedroom door open I can see the space at the foot of the bed but not the bed itself. That I can sense to the left, just out of sight. I watch the men go in and I hear the sounds but I can't quite see. And they drive my crazy.

I flap my wings and I squawk and I fluff up and I slick down and I throw seed and I attack that dangly toy as if it was the guy's balls, but it does no good. It never did any good in the other life either, the thrashing around I did by myself. In that other life I'd have given anything to be standing in this den with her doing this thing with some other guy just down the hall and all I had to do was walk down there and turn the corner and she couldn't deny it anymore.

But now all I can do is try to let it go. I sidestep down to the opposite end of the cage and look out the big sliding glass doors to the backyard. It's a pretty yard. There are great placid maple trees with good places to roost. There's a blue sky that plucks at the feathers on my chest. There are clouds. Other birds. Fly away. I could just fly away.

I tried once and I learned a lesson. She forgot and left the door to my cage open and I climbed beak and foot, beak and foot, along the bars and curled around to stretch sideways out the door and the vast scene of peace was there at the other end of the room. I flew.

And a pain flared through my head and I fell straight down and the room whirled around and the only good thing was she held me. She put her hands under my wings and lifted me and clutched me to her breast and I wish there hadn't been bees in my head at the time so I could have enjoyed that, but she put me back in the cage and wept awhile. That touched me, her tears. And I looked back to the wall of sky and trees. There was something invisible there between me and that dream of peace. I remembered, eventually, about glass, and I knew I'd been lucky, I knew that for the little fragile-boned skull I was doing all this thinking in, it meant death.

She wept that day but by the night she had another man. A guy with a thick Georgia truck-stop accent and pale white skin and an Adam's apple big as my seed ball. This guy has been around for a few weeks and he makes a whooping sound down the hallway, just out of my sight. At times like that I want to fly against the bars of the cage, but I don't. I have to remember how the world has changed.

She's single now, of course. Her husband, the man that I was, is dead to her. She does not understand all that is behind my "hello." I know many words, for a parrot. I am a yellow-nape Amazon, a handsome bird, I think, green with a splash of yellow at the back of my neck. I talk pretty well, but none of my words are adequate. I can't make her understand.

And what would I say if I could? I was jealous in life. I admit it. I would admit it to her. But it was because of my connection to her. I would explain that. When we held each other, I had no past at all, no present but her body, no future but to lie there and not let her go. I was an egg hatched beneath her crouching body, I entered as a chick into her wet sky of a body, and all that I wished was to sit on her shoulder and fluff my feathers and lay my head against her cheek, my neck exposed to her hand. And so the glances that I could see in her troubled me deeply, the movement of her eyes in public to other men, the laughs sent across a room, the tracking of her mind behind her blank eyes, pursuing images of others, her distraction even in our bed, the ghosts that were there of men who'd touched her, perhaps even that very day. I was not part of all those other men who were part of her. I didn't want to connect to all that. It was only her that I would fluff for but these others were there also and I couldn't put them aside. I sensed them inside her and so they were inside me. If I had the words, these are the things I would say.

But half an hour ago there was a moment that thrilled me. A word, a word we all knew in the pet shop, was just the right word after all. This guy with his cowboy belt buckle and rattlesnake boots and his pasty face and his twanging words of love trailed after my wife, through the den, past my cage, and I said, "Cracker." He even flipped his head back a little at this in surprise. He'd been called that before to his face, I realized. I said it again. "Cracker." But to him I was a bird and he let it pass. "Cracker," I said. "Hello, cracker." That was even better. They were out of sight through the hall doorway and I hustled along the perch and I caught a glimpse of them before they made the turn to the bed and I said, "Hello, cracker," and he shot me one last glance.

It made me hopeful. I eased away from that end of the cage, moved toward the scene of peace beyond the far wall. The sky is chalky blue today, blue like the brow of the blue-front Amazon who was on the perch next to me for about a week at the store. She was very sweet, but I watched her carefully for a day or two when she first came in. And it wasn't long before she nuzzled up to a cockatoo named Gordo and I knew she'd break my heart. But her color now in the sky is sweet, really. I left all those feelings behind me when my wife showed up. I am a faithful man, for all my suspicions. Too faithful, maybe. I am ready to give too much and maybe that's the problem.

The whooping began down the hall and I focused on a tree out there. A crow flapped down, his mouth open, his throat throbbing, though I could not hear his sound. I was feeling very odd. At least I'd made my point to the guy in the other room. "Pretty bird," I said, referring to myself. She called me "pretty bird" and I believed her and I told myself again, "Pretty bird."

But then something new happened, something very difficult for me. She appeared in the den naked. I have not seen her naked since I fell from the tree and had no wings to fly. She always had a certain tidiness in things. She was naked in the bedroom, clothed in the den. But now she appears from the hallway and I look at her and she is still slim and she is beautiful, I think—at least I clearly remember that as her husband I found her beautiful in this state. Now, though, she seems too naked. Plucked. I find that a sad thing. I am sorry for her and she goes by me and she disappears into the kitchen. I want to pluck some of my own feathers, the feathers from my chest, and give them to her. I love her more in that moment, seeing her terrible nakedness, than I ever have before.

And since I've had success in the last few minutes with words, when she comes back I am moved to speak. "Hello," I say, meaning, You are still connected to me, I still want only you. "Hello," I say again. Please listen to this tiny heart that beats fast at all times for you.

And she does indeed stop and she comes to me and bends to me. "Pretty bird," I say and I am saying, You are beautiful, my wife, and your beauty cries out for protection. "Pretty." I want to cover you with my own nakedness. "Bad bird," I say. If there are others in your life, even in your mind, then there is nothing I can do. "Bad." Your nakedness is touched from inside by the others. "Open," I say. How can we be whole together if you are not empty in the place that I am to fill?

She smiles at this and she opens the door to my cage. "Up," I say, meaning, Is there no place for me in this world where I can be free of this terrible sense of others?

She reaches in now and offers her hand and I climb onto it and I tremble and she says, "Poor baby."

"Poor baby," I say. You have yearned for wholeness too and somehow I failed you. I was not enough. "Bad bird," I say. I'm sorry.

And then the cracker comes around the corner. He wears only his rattlesnake boots. I take one look at his miserable, featherless body and shake my head. We keep our sexual parts hidden, we parrots, and this man is a pitiful sight. "Peanut," I say. I presume that my wife simply has not noticed. But that's foolish, of course. This is, in fact, what she wants. Not me. And she scrapes me off her hand onto the open cage door and she turns her naked back to me and embraces this man and they laugh and stagger in their embrace around the corner.

For a moment I still think I've been eloquent. What I've said only needs repeating for it to have its transforming effect. "Hello," I say. "Hello. Pretty bird. Pretty. Bad bird. Bad. Open. Up. Poor baby. Bad bird." And I am beginning to hear myself as I really sound to her. "Peanut." I can never say what is in my heart to her. Never.

I stand on my cage door now and my wings stir. I look at the corner to the hallway and down at the end the whooping has begun again. I can fly there and think of things to do about all this.

But I do not. I turn instead and I look at the trees moving just beyond the other end of the room. I look at the sky the color of the brow of a blue-front Amazon. A shadow of birds spanks across the lawn. And I spread my wings. I will fly now. Even though I know there is something between me and that place where I can be free of all these feelings, I will fly. I will throw myself there again and again. Pretty bird. Bad bird. Good night.

George Saunders

George Saunders (1958-) is best known as a short story writer and essayist. He is widely published in magazines such as The New Yorker, *where his short story, "Jon," appeared in 2003. He teaches in the Syracuse University Creative Writing Program. Saunders' books of fiction include* CivilWarLand in Bad Decline *(1996),* Pastoralia *(2000),* The Very Persistent Gappers of Frip *(2000),* The Brief and Frightening Reign of Phil *(2005), and* In Persuasion Nation *(2006). He also has a collection of essays,* The Braindead Megaphone *(2007).*

Jon

Back in the time of which I am speaking, due to our Coördinators had mandated us, we had all seen that educational video of "It's Yours to Do With What You Like!" in which teens like ourselfs speak on the healthy benefits of getting off by oneself and doing what one feels like in terms of self-touching, which what we learned from that video was, there is nothing wrong with self-touching, because love is a mystery but the mechanics of love need not be, so go off alone, see what is up, with you and your relation to your own gonads, and the main thing is, just have fun, feeling no shame!

And then nightfall would fall and our facility would fill with the sounds of quiet fast breathing from inside our Privacy Tarps as we all experimented per the techniques taught us in "It's Yours to Do With What You Like!" and what do you suspect, you had better make sure that that little gap between the main wall and the sliding wall that slides out to make your Gender Areas is like really really small. Which guess what, it wasn't.

That is all what I am saying.

Also all what I am saying is, who could blame Josh for noting that gap and squeezing through it snakelike in just his Old Navy boxers that Old Navy gave us to wear for gratis, plus who could blame Ruthie for leaving her Velcro knowingly un-Velcroed? Which soon all the rest of us heard them doing what the rest of us so badly wanted to be doing, only we, being more mindful of the rules than them, just laid there doing the self-stuff from the video, listening to Ruth and Josh really doing it for real, which believe me, even that was pretty fun.

And when Josh came back next morning so happy he was crying, that was a further blow to our morality, because why did our Coördinators not catch him on their supposedly nighttime monitors? In all of our hearts was the thought of,

O.K., we thought you said no boy-and-girl stuff, and yet here is Josh, with his Old Navy boxers and a hickey on his waist, and none of you guys is even saying boo?

Because I for one wanted to do right, I did not want to sneak through that gap, I wanted to wed someone when old enough (I will soon tell who) and relocate to the appropriate facility in terms of demographics, namely Young Marrieds, such as Scranton, PA, or Mobile, AL, and then along comes Josh doing Ruthie with imperity, and no one is punished, and soon the miracle of birth results and all our Coördinators, even Mr. Delacourt, are bringing Baby Amber stuffed animals? At which point every cell or chromosome or whatever it was in my gonads that had been holding their breaths was suddenly like, Dude, slide through that gap no matter how bad it hurts, squat outside Carolyn's Privacy Tarp whispering, Carolyn, it's me, please un-Velcro your Privacy opening!

Then came the final straw that broke the back of my saying no to my gonads, which was I dreamed I was that black dude on MTV's "Hot and Spicy Christmas" (around like Location Indicator 34412, if you want to check it out) and Carolyn was the oiled-up white chick, and we were trying to earn the Island Vacation by miming through the ten Hot 'n' Nasty Positions before the end of "We Three Kings," only then, sadly, during Her on Top, Thumb in Mouth, her Elf Cap fell off, and as the Loser Buzzer sounded she bent low to me, saying, Oh, Jon, I wish we did not have to do this for fake in front of hundreds of kids on Spring Break doing the wave but instead could do it for real with just each other in private.

And then she kissed me with a kiss I can only describe as melting.

So imagine that is you, you are a healthy young dude who has been self-practicing all those months, and you wake from that dream of a hot chick giving you a melting kiss, and that same hot chick is laying or lying just on the other side of the sliding wall, and meanwhile in the very next Privacy Tarp is that sleeping dude Josh, who a few weeks before a baby was born to the girl he had recently did it with, and nothing bad happened to them, except now Mr. Slippen sometimes let them sleep in.

What would you do?

Well, you would do what I did, you would slip through, and when Carolyn un-Velcroed that Velcro wearing her blue Guess kimono, whispering, Oh my God, I thought you'd never ask, that would be the most romantic thing you had ever underwent.

And though I had many times seen LI 34321 for Honey Grahams, where the stream of milk and the stream of honey enjoin to make that river of sweet-tasting goodness, I did not know that, upon making love, one person may become like the milk and the other like the honey, and soon they cannot even remember who started out the milk and who the honey, they just become one fluid, this like honey/milk combo.

Well, that is what happened to us.

Which is why soon I had to go to Mr. Slippen hat in hand and say, Sir, Baby Amber will be having a little playmate if that is O.K. with you, to which he just rolled his eyes and crushed the plastic cup in his hand and threw it at my chest, saying, What are we running in here, Randy, a freaking play school?

Then he said, Well, Christ, what am I supposed to do, lose two valuable team members because of this silliness? All right all right, how soon will Baby Amber be out of that crib or do I have to order your kid a whole new one?

Which I was so happy, because soon I would be a father and would not even lose my job.

A few days later, like how it was with Ruthie and Josh, Mr. Delacourt's brother the minister came in and married us, and afterward barbecue beef was catered, and we danced at our window while outside pink and purple balloons were released, and all the other kids were like, Rock on, you guys, have a nice baby and all!

It was the best day of our lifes thus far for sure.

But I guess it is true what they say at LI 11006 about life throwing us not only curves and sliders but sometimes even worse, as Dodger pitcher Hector Jones throws from behind his back a grand piano for Allstate, because soon here came that incident with Baby Amber, which made everybody just loony.

Which that incident was, Baby Amber died.

Sometimes it was just nice and gave one a fresh springtime feeling to sit in the much coveted window seat, finalizing one's Summary while gazing out at our foliage strip, which sometimes slinking through it would be a cat from Rustic Village Apartments, looking so cute that one wished to pet or even smell it, with wishful petting being the feeling I was undergoing on the sad day of which I am telling, such as even giving the cat a tuna chunk and a sip of my Diet Coke! If cats even like soda. That I do not know.

And then Baby Amber toddled by, making this funny noise in her throat of not being very happy, and upon reaching the Snack Cart she like seized up and tumped over, giving off this sort of shriek.

At first we all just looked at her, like going, Baby Amber, if that is some sort of new game, we do not exactly get it, plus come on, we have a lot of Assessments to get through this morning, such as a First-Taste Session for Diet GingerCoke, plus a very critical First View of Dean Witter's Preliminary Clip Reel for their campaign of "Whose Ass Are You Kicking Today?"

But then she did not get up.

We dropped our Summaries and raced to the Observation Window and began pounding, due to we loved her so much, her being the first baby we had ever witnessed living day after day, and soon the paramedics came and took her away, with one of them saying, Jesus, how stupid are you kids, anyway, this baby is burning up, she is like 107 with meningitis.

So next morning there was Carolyn all freaked out with her little baby belly, watching Amber's crib being dismantled by Physical Plant, who wiped all facility surfaces with Handi Wipes in case the meningitis was viral, and there was the rest of us, just like thrashing around the place kicking things down, going like, This sucks, this is totally fucked up!

Looking back, I commend Mr. Slippen for what he did next, which was he said, Christ, folks, all our hearts are broken, it is not just yours, do you or do you not think I have Observed this baby from the time she was born, do you or do you not think that I, too, feel like kicking things down while shouting, This sucks, this is totally fucked up? Only what would that accomplish, would that bring Baby Amber back? I am at a loss, in terms of how can we best support Ruth and Josh in this sad tragic time, is it via feeling blue and cranky, or via feeling refreshed and hopeful and thus better able to respond to their needs?

So that was a non-brainer, and we all voted to accept Mr. Slippen's Facility Morale Initiative, and soon were getting our Aurabon® twice a day instead of once, plus it seemed like better stuff, and I for one had never felt so glad or stress-free, and my Assessments became very nuanced, and I spent many hours doing and enjoying them and then redoing and reënjoying them, and it was during this period that we won the McDorland Prize for Excellence in Assessing in the Midwest Region in our demographic category of White Teens.

The only one who failed to become gladder was Carolyn, who due to her condition of pregnant could not join us at the place in the wall where we hooked in for our Aurabon®. And now whenever the rest of us hooked in she would come over and say such negative things as, Wake up and smell the coffee, you feel bad because a baby died, how about honoring that by continuing to feel bad, which is only natural, because a goddam baby died, you guys?

At night in our shared double Privacy Tarp in Conference Room 11, which our Coördinators had gave us so we would feel more married, I would be like, Honey, look, your attitude only sucks because you can't hook in, once baby comes all will be fine, due to you'll be able to hook in again, right? But she always blew me off, like she would say she was thinking of never hooking in again and why was I always pushing her to hook in and she just didn't know who to trust anymore, and one night when the baby kicked she said to her abdomen, Don't worry, angel, Mommy is going to get you Out.

Which my feeling was: Out? Hello? My feeling was: Hold on, I like what I have achieved, and when I thought of descending Out to somewhere with no hope of meeting luminaries such as actress Lily Farrell-Garesh or Mark Belay, chairperson of Thatscool.com, descending Out to, say, some lumberyard like at LI 77656 for Midol, merely piling lumber as cars rushed past, cars with no luminaries inside, only plain regular people who did not know me from Adam, who, upon seeing me, saw just some mere guy stacking lumber having such humdrum thoughts as thinking, Hey, I wonder what's for lunch, duh—I got a cold flat feeling in my gut, because I did not want to undergo it.

Plus furthermore (and I said this to Carolyn) what will it be like for us when all has been taken from us? Of what will we speak of? I do not want to only speak of my love in grunts! If I wish to compare my love to a love I have previous knowledge of, I do not want to stand there in the wind casting about for my metaphor! If I want to say like, Carolyn, remember that RE/MAX one where as the redhead kid falls asleep holding that Teddy bear rescued from the trash, the bear comes alive and winks, and the announcer goes, Home is the place where you find yourself suddenly no longer longing for home (LI 34451)—if I want to say to Carolyn, Carolyn, LI 34451, check it out, that is how I feel about you—well, then, I want to say it! I want to possess all the articulate I can, because otherwise there we will be, in non-designer clothes, no longer even on TrendSetters & TasteMakers gum cards with our photos on them, and I will turn to her and say, Honey, uh, honey, there is a certain feeling but I cannot name it and cannot cite a precedent-type feeling, but trust me, dearest, wow, do I ever feel it for you, right now. And what will that be like, that stupid standing there, just a man and a woman and the wind, and nobody knowing what nobody is meaning?

Just then the baby kicked my hand, which at that time was on Carolyn's stomach.

And Carolyn was like, You are either with me or agin me.

Which was so funny, because she was proving my point! Because you are either with me or agin me is what the Lysol bottle at LI 12009 says to the scrubbing sponge as they approach the grease stain together, which is making at them a threatening fist while wearing a sort of Mexican bandolera!

When I pointed this out, she removed my hand from her belly.

I love you, I said.

Prove it, she said.

So next day Carolyn and I came up to Mr. Slippen and said, Please, Mr. Slippen, we hereby Request that you supply us with the appropriate Exit Paperwork.

To which Mr. Slippen said, Guys, folks, tell me this is a joke by you on me.

And Carolyn said softly, because she had always liked Mr. Slippen, who had taught her to ride a bike when small in the Fitness Area, It's no joke.

And Slippen said, Holy smokes, you guys are possessed of the fruits of the labors of hundreds of thousands of talented passionate men and women, some of whom are now gone from us, they poured forth these visions in the prime of their lives, reacting spontaneously to the beauty and energy of the world around them, which is why these stories and images are such an unforgettable testimony to who we are as a nation! And you have it all within you! I can only imagine how thrilling that must be. And now, to give it all up? For what? Carolyn, for what?

And Carolyn said, Mr. Slippen, I did not see you raising your babies in such a confined environment.

And Slippen said, Carolyn, that is so, but also please note that neither I nor my kids have ever been on TrendSetters & TasteMakers gum cards and believe me, I have heard a few earfuls vis-à-vis that, as in: Dad, you could've got us In but no, and now, Dad, I am merely another ophthalmologist among millions of ophthalmologists. And please do not think that is not something that a father sometimes struggles with. In terms of coulda shoulda woulda.

And Carolyn said, Jon, you know what, he is not even really listening to us.

And Slippen said, Randy, since when is your name Jon?

Because by the way my name is really Jon. Randy is just what my mother put on the form the day I was Accepted, although tell the truth I do not know why.

It is one thing to see all this stuff in your head, Carolyn said. But altogether different to be out in it, I would expect.

And I could see that she was softening into a like daughter role, as if wanting him to tell her what to do, and up came LI 27493 (Prudential Life), where, with Dad enstroked in the hospital bed, Daughter asks should she marry the guy who though poor has a good heart, and we see the guy working with inner-city kids via spray-painting a swing set, and Dad says, Sweetie, the heart must lead you. And then later here is Dad all better in a tux, and Daughter hugging the poor but good dude while sneaking a wink at Dad, who raises his glass and points at the groom's shoe, where there is this little smudge of swing-set paint.

I cannot comment as to that, Slippen said. Everyone is different. Nobody can know someone else's experiences.

Larry, no offense but you are talking shit, Carolyn said. We deserve better than that from you.

And Slippen looked to be softening, and I remembered when he would sneak all of us kids in doughnuts, doughnuts we did not even need to Assess but could simply eat with joy with jelly on our face before returning to our Focussed Purposeful Play with toys we would Assess by coloring in on a sheet of paper either a smiling duck if the toy was fun or a scowling duck if the toy bit.

And Slippen said, Look, Carolyn, you are two very fortunate people, even chosen people. A huge investment was made in you, which I would argue you have a certain responsibility to repay, not to mention, with a baby on the way, there is the question of security, security for your future that I—

Uncle, please, Carolyn said, which was her trumpet cart, because when she was small he had let her call him that and now she sometimes still did when the moment was right, such as at Christmas Eve when all of our feelings was high.

Jesus, Slippen said. Look, you two can do what you want, clearly. I cannot stop you kids, but, golly, I wish I could. All that is required is the required pre-Exit visit to the Lerner Center, which as you know you must take before I can give you the necessary Exit Paperwork. When would you like to take or make that visit?

Now, Carolyn said.

Gosh, Carolyn, when did you become such a pistol? Mr. Slippen said, and called for the minivan.

The Lerner Center, even when reached via a blackened-window minivan, is a trip that will really blow one's mind, due to all the new sights and sounds one experiences, such as carpet on floor is different from carpet on facility floor, such as smoke smell from the minivan ashtrays, whereas we are a No Smoking facility, not to mention, wow, when we were led in blindfolded for our own protection, so many new smells shot forth from these like sidewalkside blooms or whatever that Carolyn and I were literally bumping into each other like swooning.

Inside they took our blindfolds off, and, yes, it looked and smelled exactly like our facility, and like every facility across the land, via the PervaScent® system, except in other facilities across the land a lady in blue scrubs does not come up to you with crossed eyes, sloshing around a cup of lemonade, saying in this drunk voice like, A barn is more than a barn it is a memory of a time when you were cared for by a national chain of caregivers who bring you the best of life with a selfless evening in Monterey when the stars are low you can be thankful to your Amorino Co broker!

And then she burst into tears and held her lemonade so crooked it was like spilling on the Foosball table. I had no idea what Location Indicator or Indicators she was even at, and when I asked, she didn't seem to even know what I meant by Location Indicator, and was like, Oh, I just don't know anymore what is going on with me or why I would expose that tenderest part of my baby to the roughest part of the forest where the going gets rough, which is not the accomplishment of any one man but an entire team of dreamers who dream the same dreams you dream in the best interests of that most important system of all, your family!

Then this Lerner Center dude came over and led her away, and she slammed her hand down so hard on the Foosball table that the little goalie cracked and his head flew over by us, and someone said, Good one, Doreen. Now there's no Foosball.

At which time luckily it was time for our Individual Consultation.

Who we got was this Mid-Ager from Akron, OH, who, when I asked my first question off of my Question Card they gave us, which was, What is it like in terms of pain, he said, There is no pain except once I poked myself in my hole with a coffee stirrer and, Jesus, that smarted, but otherwise you can't really even feel it.

So I was glad to hear it, although not so glad when he showed us where he had poked his hole with the stirrer, because I am famous as a wimp among my peers in terms of gore, and he had opted not to use any DermaFill®, and you could see right in. And, wow, there is something about observing up close a raw bloody hole at the base of somebody's hair that really gets one thinking. And though he said, in Question No. 2, that his hole did not present him any special challenges in terms of daily maintenance, looking into that hole, I was like, Dude, how does that give you no challenges, it is like somebody blew off a firecracker inside your freaking neck!

And when Carolyn said Question No. 3, which was, How do you now find your thought processes, his brow darkened and he said, Well, to be frank, though quite advanced, having been here three years, there are, if you will, places where things used to be when I went looking for them, brainwise, but now, when I go there, nothing is there, it is like I have the shelving but not the cans of corn, if you get my drift. For example, looking at you, young lady, I know enough to say you are pretty, but when I direct my brain to a certain place, to find there a more vivid way of saying you are pretty, watch this, some words will come out, which I, please excuse me, oh dammit—

Then his voice changed to this announcer voice and he was like, These women know that for many generations entrenched deep in this ancient forest is a secret known by coffeegrowers since the dawn of time man has wanted one thing which is to watch golf in peace will surely follow once knowledge is dispersed and the World Book is a super bridge across the many miles the phone card can close the gap!

And his eyes were crossing and he was sputtering, which would have been funny if we did not know that soon our eyes would be the crossing eyes and out of our mouths would the sputter be flying.

Then he got up and fled from the room, hitting himself hard in the face.

And I said to Carolyn, Well, that about does it for me.

And I waited for her to say that about did it for her, but she only sat there looking conflicted with her hand on her belly.

Out in the Common Room, I took her in my arms and said, Honey, I do not really think we have it all that bad, why not just go home and love each other and our baby when he or she comes, and make the best of all the blessings that we have been given?

And her head was tilted down in this way that seemed to be saying, Yes, sweetie, my God, you were right all along.

But then a bad decisive thing happened, which was this old lady came hobbling over and said, Dear, you must wait until Year Two to truly know, some do not thrive but others do, I am Year Two, and do you know what? When I see a bug now, I truly see a bug, when I see a paint chip I am truly seeing that paint chip, there is no distraction and it is so sweet, nothing in one's field of vision but what one opts to put there via moving one's eyes, and also do you hear how well I am speaking?

Out in the minivan I said, Well I am decided, and Carolyn said, Well I am too. And then there was this long dead silence, because I knew and she knew that what we had both decided was not the same decision, not at all, that old crony had somehow rung her bell!

And I said, How do you know what she said is even true?

And she said, I just know.

That night in our double Privacy Tarp, Carolyn nudged me awake and said, Jon, doesn't it make sense to make our mistakes in the direction of giving our kid the best possible chance at a beautiful life?

And I was like, Chick, please take a look in the Fridge, where there is every type of food that must be kept cold, take a look on top of the Fridge, where there is every type of snack, take a look in our Group Closet, which is packed with gratis designerwear such as Baby Gap and even Baby Ann Taylor, whereas what kind of beautiful life are you proposing with a Fridge that is empty both inside and on top, and the three of us going around all sloppenly, because I don't know about you but my skill set is pretty limited in terms of what do I know how to do, and if you go into the Fashion Module for Baby Ann Taylor and click with your blinking eyes on Pricing Info you will find that they are not just giving that shit away.

And she said, Oh, Jon, you break my heart, that night when you came to my Tarp you were like a lion taking what he wanted but now you are like some bunny wiffling his nose in fright.

Well, that wasn't nice, and I told her that wasn't nice, and she said, Jesus, don't whine, you are whining like a bunny, and I said I would rather be a bunny than a rag, and she said maybe I better go sleep somewhere else.

So I went out to Boys and slept on the floor, it being too late to check out a Privacy Tarp.

And I was pissed and sad, because no dude likes to think of himself as a rabbit, because once your girl thinks of you as a rabbit, how will she ever again think of you as a lion? And all of the sudden I felt very much like starting over with someone who would always think of me as a lion and never as a rabbit, and who really got it about how lucky we were.

Laying there in Boys, I did what I always did when confused, which was call up my Memory Loop of my mom, where she is baking a pie with her red hair up in a bun, and as always she paused in her rolling and said, Oh, my little man, I love you so much, which is why I did the most difficult thing of all, which was part with you, my darling, so that you could use your exceptional intelligence to do that most holy of things, help other people. Stay where you are, do not get distracted, have a content and productive life, and I will be happy too.

Blinking on End, I was like, Thanks, Mom, you have always been there for me, I really wish I could have met you in person before you died.

In the morning Slippen woke me by giving me the light shock on the foot bottom which was sometimes useful to help us arise if we had to arise early and were in need of assistance, and said to please accompany him, as we had a bit of a sticky wicket in our purview.

Waiting in Conference Room 6 were Mr. Dove and Mr. Andrews and Mr. Delacourt himself, and at the end of the table Carolyn, looking small, with both hands on her pile of Exit Paperwork and her hair in braids, which I had always found cute, her being like that milkmaid for Swiss Rain Chocolate (LI 10003), who suddenly throws away her pail and grows sexy via taking out her braids, and as some fat farm ladies line up by a silo and also take out their braids to look sexy, their thin husbands look dubious and run for the forest.

Randy, Mr. Dove said, Carolyn here has evinced a desire to Exit. What we would like to know is, being married, do you have that same desire?

And I looked at Carolyn like, You are jumping to some conclusion because of one little fight, when it was you who called me the rabbit first, which is the only reason I called you rag?

It's not because of last night, Jon, Carolyn said.

Randy, I sense some doubt? Mr. Dove said.

And I had to admit that some doubt was being felt by me, because it seemed more than ever like she was some sort of malcontentish girl who would never be happy, no matter how good things were.

Maybe you kids would like some additional time, Mr. Andrews said. Some time to talk it over and be really sure.

I don't need any additional time, Carolyn said.

And I said, You're going no matter what? No matter what I do?

And she said, Jon, I want you to come with me so bad, but, yes, I'm going.

And Mr. Dove said, Wait a minute, who is Jon?

And Mr. Andrews said, Randy is Jon, it is apparently some sort of pet name between them.

And Slippen said to us, Look, guys, I have been married for nearly thirty years and it has been my experience that, when in doubt, take a breath. Err on the side of being together. Maybe, Carolyn, the thing to do is, I mean, your Paperwork is complete, we will hold on to it, and maybe Randy, as a concession to Carolyn, you could complete your Paperwork, and we'll hold on to it for you, and when you both decide the time is right, all you have to do is say the word and we will—

I'm going today, Carolyn said. As soon as possible.

And Mr. Dove looked at me and said, Jon, Randy, whoever, are you prepared to go today?

And I said no. Because what is her rush, I was feeling, why is she looking so frantic with furrowed anxious brow like that Claymation chicken at LI 98473, who says the sky is falling the sky is falling and turns out it is only a Dodge

Ramcharger, which crushes her from on high and one arm of hers or wing sticks out with a sign that says March Madness Daze?

And Slippen said, Guys, guys, I find this a great pity. You are terrific together. A real love match.

Carolyn was crying now and said, I am so sorry, but if I wait I might change my mind, which I know in my heart would be wrong.

And she thrust her Exit Paperwork across at Mr. Slippen.

Then Dove and Andrews and Delacourt began moving with great speed, as if working directly from some sort of corporate manual, which actually they were, Mr. Dove had some photocopied sheets, and, reading from the sheets, he asked was there anyone with whom she wished to have a fond last private conversation, and she said, Well, duh, and we were both left briefly alone.

She took a deep breath while looking at me all tender and said, Oh Gadzooks. Which that broke my heart, Gadzooks being what we sometimes said at nice privacy moments in our Privacy Tarp when overwhelmed by our good luck in terms of our respective bodies looking so hot and appropriate, Gadzooks being from LI 38492 for Zookers Gum, where the guy blows a bubble so Zookified that it ingests a whole city and the city goes floating up to Mars.

At this point her tears were streaming down and mine also, because up until then I thought we had been so happy.

Jon, please, she said.

I just can't, I said.

And that was true.

So we sat there quiet with her hands against my hands like Colonel Sanders and wife at LI 87345, where he is in jail for refusing to give up the recipe for KFC Haitian MiniBreasts, and then Carolyn said, I didn't mean that thing about the rabbit, and I scrinkled up my nose rabbitlike to make her laugh.

But apparently in the corporate manual there is a time limit on fond last private conversations, because in came Kyle and Blake from Security, and Carolyn kissed me hard, like trying to memorize my mouth, and whispered, Someday come find us.

Then they took her away, or she took them away rather, because she was so far in front they had to like run to keep up as she clomped loudly away in her Kenneth Cole boots, which by the way they did not let her keep those, because that night, selecting my pajamas, I found them back in the Group Closet.

Night after night after that I would lay or lie alone in our Privacy Tarp, which now held only her nail clippers and her former stuffed dog Lefty, and during the days Slippen let me spend many unbillable hours in the much coveted window seat, just scanning some images or multiscanning some images, and around me would be the other facility Boys and Girls, all Assessing, all smiling, because we were still on the twice-a-day Aurabon®, and thinking of Carolyn in those blue scrubs, alone in the Lerner Center, I would apply for some additional Aurabon® via filling out a Work-Affecting Mood-Problem Notification, which Slippen would always approve, because he felt so bad for me.

And the Aurabon® would make things better, as Aurabon® always makes things better, although soon what I found was, when you are hooking in like eight or nine times a day, you are always so happy, and yet it is a kind of happy like chewing on tinfoil, and once you are living for that sort of happy, you soon cannot be happy enough, even when you are very very happy and are even near tears due to the beauty of the round metal hooks used to hang your facility curtains, you feel this intense wish to be even happier, so you tear yourself away from the beautiful curtain hooks, and with shaking happy hands fill out another Work-Affecting Mood-Problem Notification, and then, because nothing in your facility is beautiful enough to look at with your new level of happiness, you sit in the much coveted window seat and start lendelling in this crazy uncontrolled way, calling up, say, the Nike one with the Hanging Gardens of Babylon (LI 89736), and though it is beautiful, it is not beautiful enough, so you scatter around some Delicate Secrets lingerie models from LI 22314, and hang fat Dole oranges and bananas in the trees (LI 76765), and add like a sky full of bright stars from LI 74638 for Crest, and from the Smell Palate supplied by the anti-allergen Capaviv® you fill the air with jasmine and myrrh, but still that is not beautiful enough, so you blink on End and fill out another Work-Affecting Mood-Problem Notification, until finally one day Mr. Dove comes over and says, Randy, Jon, whatever you are calling yourself these days—a couple of items. First, it seems to us that you are in some private space not helpful to you, and so we are cutting back your Aurabon® to twice a day like the other folks, and please do not sit in that window seat anymore, it is hereby forbidden to you, and plus we are going to put you on some additional Project Teams, since it is our view that idle hands are the devil's work area. Also, since you are only one person, it is not fair, we feel, for you to have a whole double Privacy Tarp to yourself, you must, it seems to us, rejoin your fellow Boys in Boys.

So that night I went back with Rudy and Lance and Jason and the others, and they were nice, as they are always nice, and via No. 10 cable Jason shared with me some Still Photos from last year's Christmas party, of Carolyn hugging me from behind with her cute face appearing beneath my armpit, which made me remember how after the party in our Privacy Tarp we played a certain game, which it is none of your beeswax who I was in that game and who she was, only, believe me, that was a memorable night, with us watching the snow fall from the much coveted window seat, in which we sat snuggling around midnight, when we had left our Tarp to take a break for air, and also we were both sort of sore.

Which made it all that much more messed up and sad to be sleeping once again alone in Boys.

When the sliding wall came out to make our Gender Areas, I noticed that they had fixed it so nobody could slide through anymore, via five metal rods. All we could do was, by putting our mouths to the former gap, say good night to the Girls, who all said good night back from their respective Privacy Tarps in this sort of muffled way.

But I did not do that, as I had nobody over there I wished to say good night to, they all being like merely sisters to me, and that was all.

So that was the saddest time of my life thus far for sure.

Then one day we were all laying or lying on our stomachs playing Hungarian Headchopper for GameBoy, a new proposed one where you are this dude with a scythe in your mother's garden, only what your mother grows is heads, when suddenly a shadow was cast over my game by Mr. Slippen, which freaked up my display, and I harvested three unripe heads, but the reason Mr. Slippen was casting his shadow was, he had got a letter for me from Carolyn!

And I was so nervous opening it, and even more nervous after opening it, because inside were these weird like marks I could not read, like someone had hooked a pen to the back leg of a bird and said, Run, little bird, run around this page and I will mail it for you. And the parts I could read were bumming me out even worse, such as she had wrote all sloppenly, Jon a abbot is a cove, a glen, it is something with prayerful guys all the livelong day in silence as they move around they are sure of one thing which is the long-term stability of a product we not only stand behind we run behind since what is wrong with taking a chance even if that chance has horns and hoofs and it is just you and your worst fear in front of ten thousand screaming supporters of your last chance to be the very best you can be?

And then thank God it started again looking like the pen on the foot of the running bird.

I thought of how hot and smart she had looked when doing a crossword with sunglasses on her head in Hilfiger cutoffs, I thought of her that first night in her Privacy Tarp, naked except for her La Perla panties in the light that came from the Exit sign through the thin blue Privacy Tarp, so her flat tummy and not-flat breasts and flirty smile were all blue, and then all of the sudden I felt like the biggest jerk in the world, because why had I let her go? It was like I was all of the sudden waking up! She was mine and I was hers, she was so thin and cute, and now she was at the Lerner Center all alone? Shaking and scared with a bloody hole in her neck and our baby in her belly, hanging out with all those other scared shaking people with bloody holes in their necks, only none of them knew her and loved her like I did? I had done such a dumb-shit thing to her, all the time thinking it was sound reasoning, because isn't that how it is with our heads, when we are in them it always makes sense, but then later, when you look back, we sometimes are like, I am acting like a total dumb-ass!

Then Brad came up and was like, Dude, time to hook in.

And I was like, Please, Brad, do not bother me with that shit at this time.

And I went to get Slippen, only he was at lunch, so I went to get Dove and said, Sir, I hereby Request my appropriate Exit Paperwork.

And he said, Randy, please, you're scaring me, don't act rash, have a look out the window.

I had a look, and tell the truth it did not look that good, such as the Rustic Village Apartments, out of which every morning these bummed-out-looking guys in the plainest non-designer clothes ever would trudge out and get in their junky cars. And was someone joyfully kissing them goodbye, like saying when you come home tonight you will get a big treat, which is me? No, the person who should have been kissing them with joy was yelling, or smoking, or yelling while smoking, and when the dudes came home they would sit on their stoops with heads in hand, as if all day long at work someone had been pounding them with clubs on their heads, saying they were jerks.

Then Dove said, Randy, Randy, why would a talented young person like yourself wish to surrender his influence in the world and become just another lowing cattle in the crowd, don't you know how much people out there look up to you and depend on you?

And that was true. Because sometimes kids from Rustic Village would come over and stand in our lava rocks with our Tastemakers & Trendsetters gum cards upheld, pressing them to our window, and when we would wave to them or strike the pose we were posing on our gum cards, they would race back all happy to their crappy apartments, probably to tell their moms that they had seen the real actual us, which was probably like the high point of their weeks.

But still, when I thought of those birdlike markings of Carolyn's letter, I don't know, something just popped, I felt I was at a distinct tilt, and I blurted out, No, no, just please bring me the freaking Paperwork, I am Requesting, and I thought when I Requested you had to do it!

And Dove said sadly, We do, Randy, when you Request, we have to do it.

Dove called the other Coördinators over and said, Larry, your little pal has just Requested his Paperwork.

And Slippen said, I'll be damned.

What a waste, Delacourt said. This is one super kid.

One of our best, Andrews said.

Which was true, with me five times winning the Coöperative Spirit Award and once even the Denny O'Malley Prize, Denny O'Malley being this Assessor in Chicago, IL, struck down at age ten, who died with a smile on his face of leukemia.

Say what you will, it takes courage, Slippen said. Going after one's wife and all.

Yes and no, Delacourt said. If you, Larry, fall off a roof, does it help me to go tumbling after you?

But I am not your wife, Slippen said. Your pregnant wife.

Wife or no, pregnant or no, Delacourt said. What we then have are two folks not feeling so good in terms of that pavement rushing up. No one is helped. Two are crushed. In effect three are crushed.

Baby makes three, Andrews said.

Although anything is possible, Slippen said. You know, the two of them together, the three of them, maybe they could make a go of it—

Larry, whose side are you on? Dove said.

I am on all sides, Slippen said.

You see this thing from various perspectives, Andrews said.

Anyway, this is academic, Delacourt said. He has Requested his Paperwork and we must provide it.

His poor mother, Dove said. The sacrifices she made, and now this.

Oh, please, Slippen said. His mother.

Larry, sorry, did you say something? Dove said.

Which mother did he get? Slippen said.

Larry, please go to that Taste-and-Rate in Conference Room 6, Delacourt said. See how they are doing with those CheezWands.

Which mother did we give him? Slippen said. The redhead baking the pie? The blonde in the garden?

Larry, honestly, Dove said. Are you freaking out?

The brunette at prayer? Slippen said. Who, putting down her prayer book, says, Stay where you are, do not get distracted, have a content and productive life, and I will be happy too?

Larry has been working too hard, Andrews said.

Plus taking prescription pills not prescribed to him, Delacourt said.

I have just had it with all of this, Slippen said, and stomped off to the Observation Room.

Ha ha, that Larry! Dove said. He did not even know your mom, Randy.

Only we did, Andrews said.

Very nice lady, Delacourt said.

Made terrific pies, Dove said.

And I was like, Do you guys think I am that stupid, I know something is up, because how did Slippen know my mom was a redhead making a pie and how did he know her exact words she said to me on my private Memory Loop?

Then there was this long silence.

And Delacourt said, Randy, when you were a child, you thought as a child. Do you know that one?

And I did know that one, it being LI 88643 for Trojan Ribbed.

Well, you are not a child anymore, he said. You are a man. A man in the middle of making a huge mistake.

We had hoped it would not come to this, Dove said.

Please accompany us to the Facility Cinema, Delacourt said.

So I accompanied them to the Facility Cinema, which was a room off of Dining, with big-screen plasma TV and Pottery Barn leather couch and de-luxe Orville Redenbacher Corn Magician.

Up on the big-screen came this old-fashioned-looking film of a plain young girl with stringy hair, smoking a cigarette in a house that looked pretty bad.

And this guy unseen on the video said, O.K., tell us precisely why, in your own words.

And the girl said, Oh, I dunno, due to my relation with the dad, I got less than great baby interest?

O.K., the unseen voice said. And the money is not part?

Well, sure, yeah, I can always use money, she said.

But it is not the prime reason? the voice said. It being required that it not be the prime reason, but rather the prime reason might be, for example, your desire for a better life for your child?

O.K., she said.

Then they pulled back and you could see bashed-out windows with cardboard in them and the counters covered with dirty dishes and in the yard a car up on blocks.

And you have no objections to the terms and conditions? the voice said. Which you have read in their entirety?

It's all fine, the girl said.

Have you read it? the voice said.

I read in it, she said. O.K., O.K., I read it cover to freaking cover.

And the name change you have no objection to? the voice said.

O.K., she said. Although why Randy?

And the No-Visit Clause you also have no objection to? the voice said.

Fine, she said, and took a big drag.

Then Dove tapped on the wall twice and the movie Paused.

Do you know who that lady is, Randy? he said.

No, I said.

Do you know that lady is your mom? he said.

No, I said.

Well, that lady is your mom, Randy, he said. We are sorry you had to learn it in this manner.

And I was like, Very funny, that is not my mom, my mom is pretty, with red hair in a bun.

Randy, we admit it, Delacourt said. We gave some of you stylized mothers, in your Memory Loops, for your own good, not wanting you to feel bad about who your real mothers were. But in this time of crisis we must give you the straight skinny. That is your real mother, Randy, that is your real former house, that is where you would have been raised had your mother not answered our ad all those years ago, that is who you are. So much in us is hardwired! You cannot fight fate without some significant help from an intervening entity, such as us, such as our resources, which we have poured into you in good faith all these years. You are a prince, we have made you a prince. Please do not descend back into the mud.

Reconsider, Randy, Dove said. Sleep on it.

Will you? Delacourt said. Will you at least sleep on it?

And I said I would.

Because tell the truth that thing with my mom had freaked me out, it was like my foundation had fallen away, like at LI 83743 for Advil, where the guy's foundation of his house falls away and he thunks his head on the floor of Hell and thus needs a Advil, which the Devil has some but won't give him any.

As he left, Dove unhit Pause, and I had time to note many things on that video, such as that lady's teeth were not good, such as my chin and hers were similar, such as she referred to our dog as Shit Machine, which what kind of name was that for a dog, such as at one point they zoomed in on this little baby sitting on the floor in just a diaper, all dirty and looking sort of dumb, and I could see very plain it was me.

Just before Dinner, Dove came back in.

Randy, your Paperwork, per your Request, he said. Do you still want it?

I don't know, I said. I'm not sure.

You are making me very happy, Dove said.

And he sent in Tony from Catering with this intense Dinner of steak au poivre and our usual cheese tray with Alsatian olives, and a milkshake in my monogrammed cup, and while I watched "Sunset Terror Home" on the big-screen, always a favorite, Bedtime passed and nobody came and got me, them letting me stay up as late as I wanted.

Later that night in my Privacy Tarp I was wakened by someone crawling in, and, hitting my Abercrombie & Fitch night-light, I saw it was Slippen.

Randy, I am so sorry for my part in all of this, he whispered. I just want to say you are a great kid and always have been since Day One and in truth I at times have felt you were more of a son than my own personal sons, and likewise with Carolyn, who was the daughter I never had.

I did not know what to say to that, it being so personal and all, plus he was like laying or lying practically right on top of me and I could smell wine on his breath. We had always learned in Religion that if something is making you uncomfortable you should just say it, so I just said it, I said, Sir, this is making me uncomfortable.

You know what is making me uncomfortable? he said. You lying here while poor Carolyn sits in the Lerner Center all alone, big as a house, scared to death. Randy, one only has one heart, and when that heart is breaking via thinking of what is in store for poor Carolyn, one can hardly be blamed for stepping in, can one? Can one? Randy, do you trust me?

He had always been good to me, having taught me so much, like how to hit a Wiffle and how to do a pushup, and once had even brought in this trough and taught me and Ed and Josh to fish, and how fun was that, all of us laughing and feeling around on the floor for the fish we kept dropping during those moments of involuntary blindness that would occur as various fish-related LIs flashed in our heads, like the talking whale for Stouffer's FishMeals (LI 38322), like the fish and loafs Jesus makes at LI 83722 and then that one dude goes, Lord, this bread is dry, can you not summon up some ButterSub?

I trust you, I said.

Then come on, he said, and crawled out of my Privacy Tarp.

We crossed the Common Area and went past Catering, which I had never been that far before, and soon were standing in front of this door labelled Caution Do Not Open Without Facility Personnel Accompaniment.

Randy, do you know what is behind this door? Slippen said.

No, I said.

Take a look, he said.

And smiling a smile like that mother on Christmas morning at LI 98732 for Madpets.com, who throws off the tablecloth to reveal a real horse in their living room chewing on the rug, Slippen threw open that door.

Looking out, I saw no walls and no rug and no ceiling, only lawn and flowers, and above that a wide black sky with stars, which all of that made me a little dizzy, there being no glass between me and it.

Then Slippen very gently pushed me out.

And I don't know, it is one thing to look out a window, but when you are Out, actually Out, that is something very powerful, and how embarrassing was that, because I could not help it, I went down flat on my gut, checking out those flowers, and the feeling of the one I chose was like the silk on that Hermès jacket I could never seem to get Reserved because Vance was always hogging it, except the flower was even better, it being very smooth and built in like layers? With the outside layer being yellow, and inside that a white thing like a bell, and inside the white bell-like thing were fifteen (I counted) smaller bell-like red things, and inside each red thing was an even smaller orange two-dingly-thing combo.

Which I was like, Dude, who thought this shit up? And though I knew very well from Religion it was God, still I had never thought so high of God as I did just then, seeing the kind of stuff He could do when He put His or Her mind to it.

Also amazing was, laying there on my gut, I was able to observe very slowly some grass, on a blade basis! And what I found was, each blade is its total own blade, they are not all exact copies as I had always thought when looking at the Rustic Village Apartment lawn from the much coveted window seat, no, each blade had a special design of up-and-down lines on it, plus some blades were wider than others, and some were yellow, with some even having little holes that I guessed had been put there via bugs chewing them?

By now as you know I am sometimes a kidder, with Humor always ranked by my peers as one of my Principal Positives on my Yearly Evaluation, but being totally serious? If I live one million years I will never forget all the beautiful things I saw and experienced in that kickass outside yard.

Isn't it something? Slippen said. But look, stand up, here is something even better.

And I stood up, and here came this bland person in blue scrubs, which my first thought was, Ouch, why not accentuate that killer bone structure with some makeup, and also what is up with that dull flat hair, did you never hear of Bumble & Bumble Plasma Volumizer?

And then she said my name.

Not my name of Randy but my real name of Jon.

Which is how I first got the shock of going, Oh my God, this poor washed-out gal is my Carolyn.

And wow was her belly bigger!

Then she touched my face very tender and said, The suspense of waiting is over and this year's Taurus far exceeds expectations already high in this humble farming community.

And I was like, Carolyn?

And she was like, The beauty of a reunion by the sea of this mother and son will not soon again be parted and all one can say is amen and open another bag of chips, which by spreading on a thin cream on the face strips away the harsh effect of the destructive years.

Then she hugged me, which is when I saw the gaping hole in her neck where her gargadisk had formerly been.

But tell the truth, even with DermaFilled® neckhole and nada makeup and huge baby belly, still she looked so pretty, it was like someone had put a light inside her and switched it on.

But I guess it is true what they say at LI 23005, life is full of ironic surprises, where that lady in a bikini puts on sunscreen and then there is this nuclear war and she takes a sip of her drink only she has been like burned to a crisp, because all that time Out not one LI had come up, as if my mind was stymied or holding its breath, but now all of the sudden here came all these LIs of Flowers, due to I had seen those real-life flowers, such as talking daisies for Polaroid (LI 101119), such as that kid who drops a jar of applesauce but his anal mom totally melts when he hands her a sunflower (LI 22365), such as the big word PFIZER that as you pan closer is made of roses (LI 88753), such as LI 73486, where as you fly over wildflowers to a Acura Legend on a cliff the announcer goes, Everyone is entitled to their own individual promised land.

And I blinked on Pause but it did not Pause, and blinked on End but it did not End.

Then up came LIs of Grass, due to I had seen that lawn, such as an old guy sprinkling grass seed while repetitively checking out his neighbor girl who is sunbathing, and then in spring he only has grass in that one spot (LI 11121), such as LI 76567, with a sweeping lawn leading up to a mansion for Grey Poupon, such as (LI 00391) these grass blades screaming in terror as this lawnmower approaches but then when they see it is a Toro they put on little party hats.

Randy, can you hear me? Slippen said. Do you see Carolyn? She has been waiting out here an hour. During that hour she has been going where she wants, looking at whatever she likes. See what she is doing now? Simply enjoying the night.

And that was true. Between flinches and blinks on End I could dimly persee her sitting cross-legged near me, not flinching, not blinking, just looking pretty in the moonlight with a look on her face of deep concern for me.

Randy, this could all be yours, Slippen was saying. This world, this girl!

And then I must have passed out.

Because when I came to I was sitting inside that door marked Caution Do Not Open Without Facility Personnel Accompaniment, with my Paperwork in my lap and all my Coördinators standing around me.

Randy, Dove said. Larry Slippen here claims that you wish to Exit. Is this the case? Did you in fact Request your Paperwork, then thrust it at him?

O.K., I said. Yes.

So they rushed me to Removals, where this nurse Vivian was like, Welcome, please step behind that screen and strip off, then put these on.

Which I did, I dropped my Calvin Klein khakis and socks and removed my Country Road shirt as well as my Old Navy boxers, and put on the dreaded blue scrubs.

Best of luck, Randy, Slippen said, leaning in the door. You'll be fine.

Out out out, Vivian said.

Then she gave me this Patient Permission Form, which the first question was, Is patient aware of risk of significantly reduced postoperative brain function?

And I wrote, Yes.

And then it said, Does patient authorize Dr. Edward Kenton to perform all procedures associated with a complete gargadisk removal, including but not limited to e-wire severance, scar-tissue removal, forceful Kinney Maneuver (if necessary to fully disengage gargadisk), suturing, and postoperative cleansing using the Foreman Vacuum Device, should adequate cleaning not be achievable via traditional methods?

And I wrote, Yes.

I have been here since Wednesday, due to Dr. Kenton is at a wedding.

I want to thank Vivian for all this paper, and Mr. Slippen for being the father I never had, and Carolyn for not giving up on me, and Dr. Kenton, assuming he does not screw it up.

(Ha ha, you know, Dr. Kenton, I am just messing with you, even if you do screw it up, I know you tried your best. Only please do not screw it up, ha ha ha!)

Last night they let Carolyn send me a fax from the Lerner Center, and it said, I may not look my best or be the smartest apple on the applecart but, believe me, in time I will again bake those ninety-two pies.

And I faxed back, However you are is fine with me, I will see you soon, look for me, I will be the one with the ripped-up neck, smacking himself in the head!

No matter what, she faxed, at least we will now have a life, that life dreamed of by so many, living in freedom with all joys and all fears, bring it on, I say, the balloon of our excitement will go up up up, to that land which is the land of true living, we will not be denied!

I love you, I wrote.

I love you too, she wrote.

Which I thought that was pretty good, it being so simple and all, and it gave me hope.

Because maybe we can do it.

Maybe we can come to be normal, and sit on our porch at night, the porch of our own house, like at LI 87326, where the mom knits and the dad plays guitar and the little kid works very industrious with his Speak & Spell, and when we talk, it will make total sense, and when we look at the stars and moon, if choosing to do that, we will not think of LI 44387, where the moon frowns down at this dude due to he is hiding in his barn eating Rebel CornBells instead of proclaiming his SnackLove aloud, we will not think of LI 09383, where this stork flies through some crying stars who are crying due to the baby who is getting born is the future Mountain Dew Guy, we will not think of that alien at LI 33081 descending from the sky going, Just what is this thing called a Cinnabon?

In terms of what we will think of, I do not know. When I think of what we will think of, I draw this like total blank and get scared, so scared my Peripheral Area flares up green, like when I have drank too much soda, but tell the truth I am curious, I think I am ready to try.

Shannon Cain

Shannon Cain is a Tucson-based fiction writer. She received a Pushcart Prize in 2009 and a fellowship from the National Endowment for the Arts in 2006. She is the co-editor, with Lisa Bowden, of Powder: Writing by Women in the Ranks, from Vietnam to Iraq *(2008) and is the fiction editor at Kore Press. She teaches at the Gotham Writers' Workshop, UCLA Extension, and Arizona State University. Her short story, "The Necessity of Certain Behaviors," was published in* The New England Review *and received the 2008 O. Henry Prize.*

The Necessity of Certain Behaviors

To escape from the hot city and the people in it, Lisa goes on an ecotourism trek in the mountains of a foreign country. To get there she endures a long airplane ride. There is the usual business of camping equipment and protein bars and local guides in odd headgear carrying packs containing tea and dried meat. One day she becomes separated from her group of Americans, and after trudging half a day on a narrow path that doesn't look all that well-traveled, she comes to a village.

Lisa is thirsty, and relieved to have stumbled across civilization. She spent the last hour considering the possibility that when night fell the mountain goats could become aggressive. She'd read a novel set in Wyoming in which a wild sheep attacks a tourist on a motorcycle. She is teary and grateful when a woman comes out of a hut and gives her a bowl with water in it. With a great deal of kindness the woman watches her drink, and then takes her by the hand. She brings Lisa into the hut and feeds her a stew of meat and a starchy root vegetable, flavored with sweetish spices and featuring pleasant pungency caused, Lisa guesses, by someone having aged, or possibly smoked, a key ingredient. She thinks of a wedge of stinky cheese dredged in honey and almonds that someone bought to an office party.

Their stools sit six inches off the dirt floor. Lisa smiles and points at the food. She flashes a thumbs-up to the woman, who clearly doesn't understand. The woman is young, about Lisa's age, with muscular arms. She has a straight long nose and black eyes and moves with economy around her little hut. The woman points to a mat on the floor and Lisa removes her two hundred-dollar hiking boots and falls asleep.

When she wakes up it is still dark, and the woman is at the other side of the hut. She is washing herself, sitting cross-legged on an animal skin rug with a bowl of water in front of her. A single candle burns, illuminating her brown body. It occurs to Lisa that the woman might know she's being watched.

In the city where she's from Lisa knew a man named Bennett with full Greek eyelids, a cynical urban grin and unappeasable curiosity about Lisa's feelings. Some mornings while she showered they'd pretend she wasn't aware he was watching her through the vinyl curtain, which was clear but tinted a flattering pink. Her selection of the curtain was deliberate. In the city where she is from, people in love understand the necessity of certain behaviors.

The woman's name is unpronounceable, but Lisa tries: 'Hee-nara," she says. They laugh at her. Now, in the morning, there is another woman in the hut, someone who appears to have stopped by for the purposed of staring. Her hair is braided and piled on top of her head in a complicated arrangement. She wears a skirt made of a soft animal skin and a red cowboy shirt. She and Heenara sit with thighs touching, talking in low voices and looking at Lisa. They seem to be very close, like sisters. The woman leans over and deposits a long kiss on Heenara's lips. Lisa realizes she was wrong about the sister thing. They look at Lisa, aparently for a reaction. To put them at ease, she smiles.

Heenara and her girlfriend take Lisa for a walk in the village. People emerge from their huts and look at her. Each hut seems to contain only one person. Everyone is young and robust-looking. All in all, this is a very attractive tribe, or clan, or whatever.

In the parlance of the city she is from, Lisa does not "identify" as bisexual. She is a straight girl who on occasion will take a woman home. After having spent some time in her early twenties thinking about the issue, she settled on the strategy of refusing to adopt a label with regards to her sexuality. This train of thought has not rumbled unprovoked into Lisa's head. Heenara has received another visitor, this time a man, who like the other men of the village, walks around bare-chested and has a shiny mane of black hair. With this guy Heenara repeats the show of kissing. They take a break and regard Lisa, who offers what she believes to be an encouraging expression. Heenara throws back her head and laughs. Her neck is both soft and muscular. The man's name sounds something like Luck. He smiles brilliantly when she tries to pronounce it. Lisa wonder show he keeps his teeth so white.

The villagers are exceptionally good cooks. Lisa sees no children and no old people. Their language sounds like a stream over stones.

Lisa becomes the village guest. She spends a night or two in the huts of a dozen different people, each cheerful and attentive. One afternoon, she is helping her latest host prepare a batch of root stew and it occurs to her to wonder whether anyone has been feeding her dog. His name is Digit, and he's a fairly good-natured animal, considering the fact he lives in a six hundred square foot box five stories above the ground. The man named Bennett was particularly fond of him. If he could speak, Digit would be the kind of dog who wouldn't mind being pressed to reveal information, at any given moment, on his current state of mind.

If the villagers experienced curiosity about Lisa, it now appears to be satisfied. Although the language barrier is undoubtedly a factor in their failure to inquire where she's from, Lisa suspects even if she could talk with them freely they would not be particularly interested about her place of origin or whether she plans to return. Their unconditional acceptance feels both welcoming and indifferent, like a warm hug from an uncle who keeps forgetting your name. But what would be the point of going home? Only twenty or so people will have even noticed she's gone, if you count her co-workers, her doorman and the super. During her years in the city Lisa has failed to work toward establishing a circle of friends, a practice that seems important to other city dwellers. Here in the village, a community has made itself available to her, with practically no effort on her part. Sticking around feels logical, plus the people are sexy.

She makes Heenara understand, through a comic series of gestures, that she's evolved past the guest phase and wants a hut of her own. Twenty villagers show up to build for her. There is no mention of how or whether Lisa will pay for building materials, which mostly consist of mud and fronds and such. During construction they sing slow, melodic songs in a companionable harmony. Lisa experiences a frothy happiness. An unusually tall woman with a high forehead teaches Lisa how to weave her roof from strands of ropy grass. In two days the hut is finished, and people come by with gifts for her: a rug, some wool for her mattress, a candle. The emergency supplies in her backpack now seem foreign and useless: waterproof matches, freeze-dried chicken noodle soup, a flare gun.

One night Heenara and Luck drop by for a visit. Heenara has been crying. Drawing stick figures in the dirt floor, Heenara explains that she and the woman with complicated hair are no longer together. Luck makes a sympathetic face and puts his arm around Heenara's shoulder. Lisa is impressed with his ability to conceal his pleasure at this development. She serves them bowls of a fermented plum beverage brought as a housewarming present. They pass the time attempting to teach Lisa more of their impossible language and after they're all fairly drunk, Lisa draws two stick figures in her dirt floor meant to represent Heenara and Luck. She puts a circle around the two figures, and smiles at Luck. She reaches for their hands and clasps them together, pantomiming something like, Now you have Heenara all to yourself.

Heenara looks at Luck. They frown at one another and exchange a series of rapid sentences. She shakes her head and glances sideways at Lisa.

Luck picks up the stick. He draws, outside the circle Lisa has made but standing next to his own image, a figure of a man. He points at that figure and pronounces a name that sounds as if he's trying to say "Frederick" with a mouthful of stones. He draws another circle, now around this now man and himself, and overlapping Heenara's. Luck stands in the overlap of the two circles. Lisa smiles politely at the dirt diagram and raises her eyebrows. Heenara makes an exasperated sound. She draws a figure of the woman with complicated hair, next to her own image, and then a circle that encompasses the two of them, but not Luck. She pauses to see if Lisa understands. Then she erases the figure of her ex-girlfriend, leaving a blank space. She holds her two hands out to Lisa. She smiles at her left hand, which is cupped, as if holding something, and nods toward Luck. She shrugs sadly at the other, whose fingers are splayed open, empty.

Lisa takes a swallow of the plum wine. In the blank space left by the woman with complicated hair, she draws a woman with a backpack. Luck ducks his head, grinning into his wine. He kisses them both on the cheek and leaves the hut.

Heenara keeps her awake until sunrise. She performs a ritual involving a paste made of wine mixed into palmful of dirt gathered from under Lisa's sleeping mat. She hums a soulful tune and nakedly dances a series of steps around Lisa's front door. She removes Lisa's clothes and washes her with maternal tenderness from head to toe using a latherless soap that smells like oregano and fruit nectar. It leaves an oily film. Finally she hoists Lisa over her shoulder like a sack, drops her ungently onto the sleeping mat and pours the remaining wine over her torso, her legs, her shoulders and arms. They slide together with the wine as lubricant until it becomes sticky, whereupon Lisa demonstrates with her mouth one or two cleansing rituals commonly practiced among a certain tribe of humans she used to know.

When Heenara is asleep Lisa stands in the open doorway. In the flat tones of their urban language, the man Bennett had told her he was building a three-bedroom house in Westchester for himself and a woman named Julie. He said he admired Julie's devotion to transparency. Lisa's relationship with Bennett had long since ended; there was no particular reason for him to tell her all this. Still, months after he moved away from the city Lisa carried on interior dialogues with the memory of him. It was to be expected that he'd have identified someone new, but nevertheless the matter of Julie had startled her. Since her arrival in the village she hasn't had a single imaginary conversation with him. The stars above the village crowd the sky. How could there possibly be room for them all? How is it that they didn't smash into each other, in chaotic collisions of light and heat?

Lisa wakes up at dawn with Heenara pushing her gently off the mat. She accepts a bowl of hot tea. As soon as she's standing, Heenara pulls the mat from the floor and lays it outside, in the dirt. The plum wine has left a stain in outline of Lisa's body. Heenara sips tea in the yard. Villagers appear. They approach, smiling, slapping Heenara on the back and raising their eyebrows in the direction of Lisa's door. Through the cracks in the wall, Lisa watches.

A caravan of donkeys led by a couple of men in odd headgear arrives in the village. They pull packs off the animals and open their contents, spreading a blanket on the ground and displaying aluminum cookware, athletic socks, sewing needles. Lisa would like to have a necklace made of carved bone beads, but has nothing with which to trade. There was a time when she would purchase beautiful things. A set of vintage turquoise martini glasses. A distressed calfskin briefcase with copper buckles. Jade earrings set in Balinese silver. She waits for a feeling of longing to occur but the memory of these items is akin to a foreign object in her eye. How silly she used to be! Yet how comfortable.

One of the traders stares at her. Heenara says something sharp to him and he turns away.

The opening weeks of her relationship with Heenara are spent in a sexual frenzy broken up only by Heenara's perfunctory visits to Luck's hut. Upon her return Lisa smells him on Heenara's skin, which she finds not unpleasant. Beating her mat clean on the rocks at the stream, Lisa runs into him. He's polite but has a pained look that suggests his patience is wearing thin. She learns from Heenara that Luck's lover Frederick is away from the village with a group of hunters, tracking a herd of mountain goats across the plateau.

One evening Luck appears at her door. He's had a fair amount of plum wine. Her remedial knowledge of their language results in a distressing conversation in which she understands that Luck wants her to break up with Heenara. When he sees Lisa's tears he leaves and returns with Heenara, who rolls her eyes in the direction of the sheepish Luck and informs Lisa via their semi-efficient system of communication that it's time for Lisa to find a boyfriend.

Among the village inhabitants there is a specialist in such matters. She visits Lisa's hut and cheerfully submits her to a series of questions Lisa only halfway understands, having mostly to do with matters such as eyes, hair, and body type. She strikes Lisa as being awfully young for the job. Lisa defers to her judgment about borrowing a dress that displays her cleavage, and together they spend the following morning visiting a handful of potential boyfriends. Each of them is beautiful beyond belief. Their upper bodies trigger a hazy memory of men lifting weights in a gym located in the gay section of the city where she used to live. The men look at her as if she were some exquisite yet puzzling object they uncovered while digging a hole.

She finds herself judging them by the way they move around their huts. She finally settles on one whose name she mispronounces less comically than the others and who betrays his nervousness by splashing a bit of boiling water on his foot in the process of making her a cup of bitter tea. He's called Toruk, more or less, and she finds herself flirting uncontrollably with him, as if overcome by some Darwinian instinct to snag a hunter-gatherer of her own.

In the days following Bennett's revelations about Julie and Westchester, Lisa experienced an accelerated interest in her psyche by certain people in her life. Her mother; a previously indifferent co-worker; her gay boyfriend. They grilled her regarding what had occurred between her and Bennett and what had not; what was said and what was left unsaid. They berated her for her failure to expose herself, as is apparently standard practice in the pursuit of modern urban love. Such a fuss, Lisa thinks now. How did she endure it? Why didn't she leave the city so much earlier?

In preparation for her date with Toruk, Heenara coaches Lisa on the first-night ritual, the initiation of which turns out to be the responsibility of the aggressor, in this case Lisa. Teaching her the steps to the front-door dance and the nonsensical lyrics of the song that accompanies it, Heenara becomes teary and in need of assurance. It's possible Lisa is witnessing a temporary moment of emotional fallout brought on by culturally coerced nonmonogamy. Or maybe Heenara is preoccupied with something she can't translate—crop failure, perhaps a sick parent. Which would constitute a mystery in itself, Lisa realizes: she still hasn't encountered any old people. Heenara and Lisa get very drunk and make bittersweet, dramatic love until Lisa gets out of bed to vomit in the bushes behind her hut.

In the morning she awakes to Heenara's voice in the front yard. She goes outside. Heenara is talking to the trader who came to the village and stared at Lisa. She uses words Lisa more or less understands to explain the man has said that people in the town at the base of the mountain are asking about a woman with yellow hair. "A woman who is lost," she says.

Lisa shakes her head and says something like, "Not lost, me." Heenara smiles.

The man has brown teeth. He lets loose a current of words. He gestures in Lisa's direction. Heenara raises her voice and flaps her hand, shooing him from the yard. Lisa goes inside and pulls the hiking boots from her backpack. She runs after the man and gives them to him. She looks him carefully in the face. "Not lost, me," she says.

He takes the boots and nods. He doesn't meet her eye. Surely he understands, though, about payment in exchange for complicity. Lisa walks back to her hut. The trader will sell her boots for a nice amount of money. He'll feed his family for a month.

In the city at the bottom of the mountain there are people looking for her, probably, people paid by her mother. It's not too late to chase the trader. To erase any ambiguity regarding her desire for his silence. She should appeal to his love of homeland, his indigenous understanding that this is the place, not her city, where humans are meant to live.

Heenara has seen the exchange. She frowns, and goes inside. Slung by their laces over the trader's shoulder, Lisa's boots retreat down the mountain. She tries to make Heenara understand. But she lacks the words to explain that she no longer knows the difference between *lost* and *found*.

For the occasion of their first night together, Toruk has shaved his beard. As part of this procedure he has applied to the skin of his face a berry-scented oil that reminds Lisa of a sweet drink she often consumed as a child. He remains still, waiting for her to move toward him, and when she arrives at his bare chest he raises his arms as if to offer his underbelly. She reaches up to pull on his biceps, to place his arms around her waist, but he refuses to move them. She pulls harder, and he smiles at her and shakes his head. If necessary she could hang the entire weight of her body on these arms.

She performs the ritual to the best of her ability. Toruk smiles understandingly when she screws up the dance and also skips an entire verse of the song. In the washing of his skin she finds herself in a trance of sorts, focused and consumed by the task, unbothered by a soap that won't yield suds. She becomes giggly when the time comes for her to toss him into bed, unsure how to approach the feat of physically moving a mountain of muscle, but he solves the problem by throwing himself onto the mat with what appears to be a painful thud.

She pours the wine on him. Finally, he abandons his ritual passivity and pulls her sharply to the floor to land hard on his body, very nearly knocking her breath away. She is thrilled by the jolt of it, and by her own desire: she found it so rarely in the city.

In the morning she sleeps late. When she wakes up Toruk is glaring at her. She's forgotten to display the stained mat in his front yard. She's forgotten to receive congratulatory visitors. She doesn't know how to say I'm sorry in his language. She pouts in a shamefaced way and sucks his dick by way of apology.

Sometimes the man named Bennett used to step inside the shower. In the pink light he'd wash her hair. He'd ask if she was okay. When he performed these tender acts she was careful to maintain a neutral expression. Since her face was already wet she could cry without provoking questions as long as she kept her lip from trembling. She didn't want to explain her happiness to him. The joy she harbored was easily scared away; a timid, furry creature.

Heenara retreats to Luck's sleeping mat to wait out Lisa's infatuation with Toruk. After only two days, however, Frederick returns from the hunt, triumphant with goat meat and horny for Luck. Lisa is at the village well when the hunters return. Luck dashes across the dusty compound to slam into Frederick's body, their mouths joining in a display of sweaty lust. Everyone stops to watch.

Lisa runs into Heenara outside the shower hut. She cups her neck affectionately, but Heenara is stiff. Lisa pulls her by the hair into a shower stall and closes the woven straw curtain. She turns the warm water on their bodies and methodically works half her hand into Heenara's vagina. This, it turns out, was the right thing to do. Heenara is smug and satisfied.

Lisa finds herself unable to apply to her new life the wisdoms she knew in the old. For example: don't meet the eyes of strangers. Don't be tempted to take the local train; sit tight for the express. Walk at night to the Laundromat with your pepper spray ready, however do feel free to yell at men pissing against your building: no one with a limp penis in his hand is a threat. Expect that all lovers, eventually, will leave.

Lisa comes to the realization that on any given night, one-third of the huts in the village are empty. She speculates on the efficiency, resource-wise, of this arrangement. She wonders if this condition is related to the eerie absence in the village of anyone under the age of eighteen. One night she draws in the dirt floor of Toruk's hut a stick figure of a small person holding the hand of a larger person. She circles the child figure and says "Where?"

Given Toruk's tender laughter, Lisa's expression must reveal her fear of the question, and of what he might answer. He points to the hills. He talks, he smiles fondly, he says a lot of words. She doesn't need to understand their meaning to know the children have not, after all, been sold into slavery, or sacrificed to some grumpy god.

Slowly, Lisa's comprehension of the stream-over-rocks language gets better. She knows now, for example, that when Toruk looks pensively at the ceiling and utters a masculine yet lilting series of words, he's not making an observation on the vast and mysterious wonders of the universe. As a public works laborer of sorts—preparing communal garden plots, digging sewage canals—he turns out to be mostly preoccupied with moving piles of dirt from one end of the village to another. As for Lisa's own preoccupations, either Toruk doesn't know how to ask or he isn't especially interested.

As time passes, the domino effect created by the prolonged absence of Frederick the goat hunter becomes sorted out. Lisa settles into a routine with Heenara and

Toruk. They don't have anything so formal as a schedule of visits, but there emerges between them an understanding that things always even out, more or less.

On a calm morning with huge white clouds in the sky, Bennett arrives in the village, unshaven, dirty and limping. Behind him is the trader. Filling her water gourd at the well, Lisa spots him before he realizes it's her. When she approaches, he holds her and he cries. "I've been looking for you," he says. He is oblivious to the people staring.

"I'm fine," she says into his shirt. Underneath the old sweat he smells like Bennett.

Heenara appears, unsmiling, at Lisa's side. Lisa introduces him.

"You speak their language?" Bennett says.

"Not really." She shrugs. She shouldn't be proud of this. "What are you doing here?"

"Your mother asked me to come. She's going out of her mind—"

He turns to see why Lisa is looking over his shoulder. Toruk stands at the entrance to his hut, observing them. His arms are folded across his chest. She is surprised to notice he's not any taller than Bennett. Heenara removes the water gourd from Lisa's hand and gives it to Bennett for a drink. She takes his arm and walks them to Lisa's hut. She gives Lisa a look and comes inside with them.

"I'm sorry," Lisa says to Bennett.

"What were you thinking?" he says. "Did you lose your passport? Or something? Were you hurt? Are you sick?" He lowers his voice. He watches Heenara. "Are these people keeping you here?"

Heenara is banging around in Lisa's cooking area. Her cheeks are flushed. Lisa is overcome with loyalty toward her. "It's good here," she says.

"You've been living here? In this woman's hovel?" he says.

"Where's Julie?" she asks.

"Home. About ready to leave me over all this." He looks at Heenara, who is blowing earnestly on the fire. "What's going on, Lisa?"

"Go back," Lisa says. "Call my mother."

"And tell her what?"

"I don't know. Tell her not to worry."

"Tell me this is a joke," he says. "Is this some kind of joke?"

Bennett pitches an orange pup tent and for two days skulks around the edges of the village. He stakes out her movements, watching from behind his tent flap. Lisa brings him food, which he accepts wordlessly. The villagers stay clear of him. Apparently they don't know much about stalkers. Lisa's never had one before, and is disappointed hers is so benign.

It becomes colder at night. Toruk presents her with a finely woven goat wool blanket. During an afternoon of cleaning she discovers the backpack in the corner of her hut, behind a large pile of wool. She caresses the items inside the pack and thinks about the relative usefulness or frivolity of each. She boils water and prepares the freeze-dried chicken noodle soup. She gives a taste to Heenara, who finds it disgusting.

"I wish you wouldn't spit food on my floor," Lisa says in the stream-over-stones language.

"You call that food?" Heenara says.

Lisa recalls a brunch of salmon benedict and roasted rosemary potatoes at a sidewalk café on the Upper West Side.

"I love you," she says. It's possible she's now speaking English.

"I don't understand," Heenara says.

"Neither do I," Lisa replies.

Heenara wipes her thumb across Lisa's forehead, as if to rub out the worry.

Late one afternoon, it snows. The villagers quicken the pace of their work. Many are smiling in a distracted, anticipatory way, lifting their faces to the falling flakes. When it becomes dark, the temperature drops. Lisa approaches Bennett's campsite at the edge of the village and calls his name. He unzips the tent flap, sits back on his heels and gazes up at her.

"Why don't you come inside," she tells him.

"I've been squatting here for three days," Bennett says. "Not much to do."

"It's cold," Lisa says. "I'll heat some stew." She tightens Toruk's blanket around her shoulders.

Bennett stands, stretches his limbs. "I do have a few things to ask you about," he says.

The moon rises with characteristic drama over the eastern mountains. "It's pretty enough," Bennett says after a while. "I can see the appeal."

On the moonlit hillside to the north of the village, a line of people appear, making their way down the path. Lisa and Bennett wait for the group to approach. Snow falls thickly, coating rocks, everything.

The travelers are led by a woman with long gray hair and a thin neck. She leans hard on her walking stick, though her pace is steady. The children behind her seem as if they would break into a run if not for a duty to support teetering grandparents. A small group of women follows, carrying babies and toddlers in cloth slings. An ancient man lying in a litter is transported via the muscled shoulders of four very young men. At the rear of the line, attractive teenagers lead pack animals by their halters. Theatrically illuminated by an accommodating moon, the faces in the procession reveal fatigue and communion and anticipation of home.

"Wow," Bennett says. The spectacle passes them by. To the south, Lisa sees villagers wrapped in blankets and waiting in their doorways, each cupping with ritualistic tenderness a steaming bowl of tea. Light from cooking fires behind them creates a series of soft yellow squares on the ground.

From the little hill selected by Bennett three days before for its convenient view of village activity, Lisa witnesses the homecomings. Bennett remains heavily quiet. The boys carrying the old man stop at Toruk's hut and bring him inside. At Heenara's door, one of the women with an infant sling removes the baby from its pouch and hands it, squalling, to her. Their heads are thrown back in laughter. Together they drink from the bowl of tea. At each hut, couples reassemble themselves. One at a time the doors close, until every yellow square is extinguished.

Bennett sets his arm across Lisa's shoulders and guides her down the path to her hut. In the warm interior he ladles her stew into bowls. Through the walls of grass and mud comes the muted gurgle of families in conversation.

Junot Díaz

Junot Díaz (1968-) was born in Santo Domingo, Dominican Republic and is a Pulitzer prize winning author of fiction. His novel, The Brief Wondrous Life of Oscar Wao *(1997), and collection of short stories,* Drown *(1996), are both highly acclaimed. The short story "How to Date a Browngirl, Blackgirl, Whitegirl, or Halfie" is included in* Drown *and was first published in* The New Yorker *in 1995. Díaz teaches creative writing at the Massachusetts Institute of Technology and is the fiction editor for the* Boston Review.

How to Date a Browngirl, Blackgirl, Whitegirl, or Halfie

Wait for your brother and your mother to leave the apartment. You've already told them that you're feeling too sick to go to Union City to visit that tía who likes to squeeze your nuts. (He's gotten big, she'll say.) And even though your moms knows you ain't sick you stuck to your story until finally she said, Go ahead and stay, malcriado.

Clear the government cheese from the refrigerator. If the girl's from the Terrace stack the boxes behind the milk. If she's from the Park or Society Hill hide the cheese in the cabinet above the oven, way up where she'll never see. Leave yourself a reminder to get it out before morning or your moms will kick your ass. Take down any embarrassing photos of your family in the campo, especially the one with the half-naked kids dragging a goat on a rope leash. The kids are your cousins and by now they're old enough to understand why you're doing what you're doing. Hide the pictures of yourself with an Afro. Make sure the bathroom is presentable. Put the basket with all the crapped-on toilet paper under the sink. Spray the bucket with Lysol, then close the cabinet.

Shower, comb, dress. Sit on the couch and watch TV. If she's an outsider her father will be bringing her, maybe her mother. Neither of them want her seeing any boys from the Terrace—people get stabbed in the Terrace—but she's strong-headed and this time will get her way. If she's a white girl you know you'll at least get a hand job.

The directions were in your best handwriting, so her parents won't think you're an idiot. Get up from the couch and check the parking lot. Nothing. If the girl's local, don't sweat it. She'll flow over when she's good and ready. Sometimes she'll run into her other friends and a whole crowd will show up at your apartment and even though that means you ain't getting shit it will be fun anyway and

213

you'll wish these people would come over more often. Sometimes the girl won't flow over at all and the next day in school she'll say sorry, smile and you'll be stupid enough to believe her and ask her out again.

Wait and after an hour go out to your corner. The neighborhood is full of traffic. Give one of your boys a shout and when he says, Are you still waiting on that bitch? say, Hell yeah.

Get back inside. Call her house and when her father picks up ask if she's there. He'll ask, Who is this? Hang up. He sounds like a principal or a police chief, the sort of dude with a big neck, who never has to watch his back. Sit and wait. By the time your stomach's ready to give out on you, a Honda or maybe a Jeep pulls in and out she comes.

Hey, you'll say.

Look, she'll say. My mom wants to meet you. She's got herself all worried about nothing.

Don't panic. Say, Hey, no problem. Run a hand through your hair like the whiteboys do even though the only thing that runs easily through your hair is Africa. She will look good. The white ones are the ones you want the most, aren't they, but usually the out-of-towners are black, blackgirls who grew up with ballet and Girl Scouts, who have three cars in their driveways. If she's a halfie don't be surprised that her mother is white. Say, Hi. Her moms will say hi and you'll see that you don't scare her, not really. She will say that she needs easier directions to get out and even though she has the best directions in her lap give her new ones. Make her happy.

You have choices. If the girl's from around the way, take her to El Cibao for dinner. Order everything in your busted-up Spanish. Let her correct you if she's Latina and amaze her if she's black. If she's not from around the way, Wendy's will do. As you walk to the restaurant talk about school. A local girl won't need stories about the neighborhood but the other ones might. Supply the story about the loco who'd been storing canisters of tear gas in his basement for years, how one day the canisters cracked and the whole neighborhood got a dose of the military-strength stuff. Don't tell her that your moms knew right away what it was, that she recognized its smell from the year the United States invaded your island.

Hope that you don't run into your nemesis, Howie, the Puerto Rican kid with the two killer mutts. He walks them all over the neighborhood and every now and then the mutts corner themselves a cat and tear it to shreds, Howie laughing as the cat flips up in the air, its neck twisted around like an owl, red meat showing through the soft fur. If his dogs haven't cornered a cat, he will walk behind you and ask, Hey, Yunior, is that your new fuckbuddy?

Let him talk. Howie weighs about two hundred pounds and could eat you if he wanted. At the field he will turn away. He has new sneakers, and doesn't want them muddy. If the girl's an outsider she will hiss now and say, What a fucking asshole. A homegirl would have been yelling back at him the whole time, unless she was shy. Either way don't feel bad that you didn't do anything. Never lose a fight on a first date or that will be the end of it.

Dinner will be tense. You are not good at talking to people you don't know. A halfie will tell you that her parents met in the Movement, will say, Back then people thought it a radical thing to do. It will sound like something her parents made her memorize. Your brother once heard that one and said, Man, that sounds like a whole lot of Uncle Tomming to me. Don't repeat this.

Put down your hamburger and say, It must have been hard.

She will appreciate your interest. She will tell you more. Black people, she will say, treat me real bad. That's why I don't like them. You'll wonder how she feels about Dominicans. Don't ask. Let her speak on it and when you're both finished eating walk back into the neighborhood. The skies will be magnificent. Pollutants have made Jersey sunsets one of the wonders of the world. Point it out. Touch her shoulder and say, That's nice, right?

Get serious. Watch TV but stay alert. Sip some of the Bermúdez your father left in the cabinet, which nobody touches. A local girl may have hips and a thick ass but she won't be quick about letting you touch. She has to live in the same neighborhood you do, has to deal with you being all up in her business. She might just chill with you and then go home. She might kiss you and then go, or she might, if she's reckless, give it up, but that's rare. Kissing will suffice. A whitegirl might just give it up right then. Don't stop her. She'll take her gum out of her mouth, stick it to the plastic sofa covers and then will move close to you. You have nice eyes, she might say.

Tell her that you love her hair, that you love her skin, her lips, because, in truth, you love them more than you love your own.

She'll say, I like Spanish guys, and even though you've never been to Spain, say, I like you. You'll sound smooth.

You'll be with her until about eight-thirty and then she will want to wash up. In the bathroom she will hum a song from the radio and her waist will keep the beat against the lip of the sink. Imagine her old lady coming to get her, what she would say if she knew her daughter had just lain under you and blown your name, pronounced with her eighth-grade Spanish, into your ear. While she's in the bathroom call one of your boys and say, Lo hice, loco. Or just sit back on the couch and smile.

But usually it won't work this way. Be prepared. She will not want to kiss you. Just cool it, she'll say. The halfie might lean back, breaking away from you. She will cross her arms, say, I hate my tits. Stroke her hair but she will pull away. I don't like anybody touching my hair, she will say. She will act like somebody you don't know. In school she is known for her attention-grabbing laugh, as high and far-ranging as a gull, but here she will worry you. You will not know what to say.

You're the only kind of guy who asks me out, she will say. Your neighbors will start their hyena calls, now that the alcohol is in them. You and the blackboys.

Say nothing. Let her button her shirt, let her comb her hair, the sound of it stretching like a sheet of fire between you. When her father pulls in and beeps, let her go without too much of a good-bye. She won't want it. During the next hour the phone will ring. You will be tempted to pick it up. Don't. Watch the shows you want to watch, without a family around to debate you. Don't go downstairs. Don't fall asleep. It won't help. Put the government cheese back in its place before your moms kills you.

Alison Hawthorne Deming

Alison Hawthorne Deming (1946-) is a distinguished poet and essayist. Her books of poetry include Science and Other Poems *(1994),* The Monarchs: A Poem Sequence *(1997),* Genius Loci *(2005), and most recently,* Rope *(2009). She has also written several nonfiction books, including* The Edges of the Civilized World *(1998), which was a finalist for the PEN Center West Award. Deming teaches creative writing at the University of Arizona. The poem, "Persephone Speaks," was first published on Kore Press' blog in 2006 and along with "Zeus" is collected in* Rope.

Persephone Speaks

My father was the Big Guy
Generator
Energy Spill
My mother was Cereal
Corn
Matter Sink

Get real I used to tell them
Ditching their dream
That I would be
Forever daughter
Picking flowers in the meadow
While they made action movies
Out of everyone else's lives

What they wanted for me
Was never
What I wanted
So abduction is not quite the word
For what my lover did to me
For me is more like it

Oh beautiful sin of falling
Under the rhythm of his need
And finding I could answer
Stroke for stroke
Be bad and claim my loving
And find the pleasure good

How could I have known
The hunger would persist
Once I had left
My mother's threshing floor
My father's distant light

Pulled into the underworld
I forgot what lay above
The soil drying seedless
Unable to revive
Din of lamentation
Not even the gods could abide

My husband too is a god
He struts like a jaguar
His sex is an epic poem
He loves the dead
Because they tell no lies
And yield themselves
Completely to the future

When he fed me the pomegranate
That would keep me
Coming to his dark bed
I did say thank you
My goodness married
To the limbo night inside

Zeus

Quis multa gracilis te puer in rosa . . .
—Horace

When Zeus paced in front of the class,
professing how in a line of Horace
the words describing an embrace
modeled in form the action they
invoked—sense and syntax clenched
closer than rules for English allowed—
I got it. How close the poem was
to the growing tip of life. I knew then
language could reveal divine pleasure
in the human mind. Zeus had a pate

like the dome of St. Peter's Basilica.
He was Greek, though, not Roman—
his name rhymed with metropolis.
This was the summer of 1963 and I was
a junior in high school, studying fifth-year Latin
at Trinity College in Hartford, Connecticut,
the city of my birth, of my daughter's birth
two years later. I had wanted to study
sociology or psychology, a science to solve
the puzzle I felt myself to be. Everyone
may feel this way—we arrive
somehow whole and childhood breaks us
into pieces we spend our lives reassembling.
My parents said no. You can go if you take Latin.
No one cared about dead languages even then,
except the scholarship office which bought me
a ride out of the house of denials and into the "dorm"
on the "campus"—every word of the new world
springing from its burial on the page. It *was*
like sleeping in a starry field out in the open
after being confined too long in walls.
Zeus wore a gray suit to class
every humid Hartford day that summer.
I fell for my first radical there in the cafeteria,
an organizer for SNCC, who had traveled
to Americus, Georgia, to register black voters.
He wore the clothes he'd learned from the rural South—
Levi's and blue work shirt, smoked Pall Malls,
the red cellophane pack so attractive
in contrast with his blues. Black coffee,
New York Times—I read all his signs
and found another god in my desire. Call him
Zeus too, my own undressed imperative to know.

Olga Broumas

Olga Broumas (1949-) was born in Syros, Greece. She has taught at several colleges and universities, including Brandeis University. Her book, Beginning with O, *was the Yale Younger Poets selection in 1976. She has translated two works by the Greek poet Odysseas Elytis,* What I Love, *Selections and* The Little Mariner.

Translator's Note: What I Love *by Odysseas Elytis*

The Poetry of Odysseas Elytis has been a homeland to me since my arrival in this country in 1967. His song burns the senses as the Greek sun and sea burn daily and annually into the skin, and his dignity is of my people, joyous, active.

Elytis makes full use of the grammatical and syntactical fluidity of Greek for his word order, gender, mood, rhythm, tense, and regional evocation, and I have tried to honor his choices within the limits of English. Line by line, the poems nearly match their original.

I have chosen to give Elytis's *voice* in English, and being true to his voice is to create an English with an accent, idiosyncratic, true to the man whose sensibility is born of and flowers in a cultural and syntactical grammar foreign to a world shaped and expressed by English.

It is this world, for me best seen and sung in my time by Odysseas Elytis, that I wish especially to share here, *as is*, as the food is served in a taverna by the sea of Marathiás near my father's village, subject to the mood of the day and the region, not food made familiar for the foreigner at the urban strip.

The poet is known to his Greek and some of his international audience as Odysseas Elytis. He uses and prefers the contemporary form of Odysseas to the latinate Odysseus.

I am elated to have made of myself a home where his music may sing of itself again. And I want to thank Jane Miller, Rita Speicher, Sam Hamill, Tree Swenson, Stanley Kunitz, IKAROS, and, especially, Claire Broumas for their assistance and support.

Odysseas Elytis

Odysseas Elytis (1911-1996) is a Greek poet and the winner of the 1979 Nobel Prize in Literature. The Monogram *(1973) is one of his many publications, which also include Olga Broumas' translations,* What I Love, Selections *(1986) and* The Little Mariner *(1988).*

The Monogram

I'll mourn always – you hear me? – for you
alone, in Paradise.

I

Fate will turn elsewhere the engravings
Of the palm, like a key keeper
Some moment Time will acquiesce

How else, since people love each other

The sky will represent our guts
And innocence will smite the world
With black death's acrid sickle.

II

I mourn the sun and I mourn the years that come
Without us and I sing those others gone
If it's true

That bodies conspired with the boats struck sweetly
The guitars flickering under the waters
The *believe me* and the *don't*
Once in the air, once in the music

The two small animals, our hands
That looked to climb secretly one on the other
The pot of coolweed in the open yards
And the seas in pieces coming together
Over the dryrock, behind the fence
The anemone that sat in your hand
And trembled three times purple three days above the falls

If these are true I sing
The wooden beam and the square weaving

On the wall, the Mermaid with unplaited hair
The cat who saw us in the dark
Child with frankincense and red cross
In the hour of dusk by the unapproachable boulders
I mourn the garment I touched and the world came to me

III
This is how I speak for you and me

Because I love you and in love I know
Like a Full Moon to enter
From everywhere, for your small foot in the vast sheets
I unpetal jasmines – and I have the strength
Asleep, to blow and take you
Through luminous passages and the sea's secret arcades
Hypnotized trees silver with spiders

The waves have heard of you
How you caress, how you kiss
How you whisper *what* and *eh*
Around the neck the bay
Always we the light and shade

Always you little star and always I dark navigable
Always you the port and I the lantern at right
The wet mooring and the oar's shine
High in the house with the grape arbor
The tied roses, the water that cools
Always you the stone statue and always I shade that grows
The pulled shutter you, the wind that opens it I
Because I love you and I love you
Always you the coin and I the worship that cashes it:

So much the night, so much the howl in the wind
So much the dew in the air, so much for silence
Around us the despotic sea
Arc of the sky with stars
So much your least breath

That at last I've nothing left
In the four walls, the ceiling, the floor
To call on but you and my voice beats me
To smell of but you and people go wild
Because the untried and the from elsewhere brought
Is intolerable and it's early, do you hear me
It's early still in this world my love.

To speak about you and about me.

IV
It is still early in this world, do you hear me
The beasts have not been tamed, do you hear me
My spilled blood and the pointed, do you hear me
Knife
Like a ram running the skies
Snapping the stars' branches, do you hear me
It's me, do you hear me
I love you, do you hear me
I hold you and take you and dress you
In Ophelia's white bridal, do you hear me
Where do you leave me, where do you go and who, do you
hear me

Holds your hands over the floods

The enormous lianas and the volcanos' lavas
One day, do you hear me
Will bury us and the thousand later years, do you hear
Luminous will make of us strata, do you hear me
On which the heartlessness of, do you hear me
People will shine
And throw us a thousand pieces, do you hear
In the water one by one, do you hear
I cournt my bitter pebbles, do you hear me
And time is a large church, do you hear
Where sometimes the figures, do you hear me
Of Saints
Emit a real tear, do you hear me
The bells open on high, do you hear me
A passage deep for me to pass
The angels wait with candles and funereal psalms
I am not going anywhere, do you hear me
Either neither or together both, do you hear me

This flower of storm and, do you hear
Of love
We cut once and for all, do you hear me
And it can't flower otherwise, do you hear me
In another earth, another star, do you hear me
The soil is gone, the air is gone
That we touched, that same, do you hear me

And no gardener ever had the luck

From so much winter so much north wind, do you hear me
To pull a flower, only we, do you hear me
In the middle of the sea
From just the wanting of love, do you hear me
Raised a whole island, do you hear

With caves and coves and flowering gullies
Hear, hear
Who speaks to the waters and who cries – hear?
Who looks for the other, who shouts – hear?
It's me who shouts and it's me who cries, do you hear me
I love you, I love you, you hear me.

V

Of you I've spoken long ago
With wise nurses and veteran rebels
What gives you the sorrow of a beast
On your face the trembling water's reflection
And why am I meant to come near you
I who don't want love but want the wind
Want the uncovered standing sea's full gallop
And none had heard of you
Not the doubleroot and not the mushroom
In Crete's high places nothing
Of you but God accepted to guide my hand

A little here, a little there, carefully the whole circle
Of the beach, the face, the bay, the hair
Of the hill waving toward the left

Your body in the stance of the solitary plane tree
Eyes of pride and the transparent
Seafloor, in the house with the old screen
The yellow lace and cypresswood
I wait for you alone to first appear
High in the room or behind the flagstones
With the Saint's horse and the Easter egg

As if from a destroyed fresco
Large as small life wanted you
To fit inside a candle the stentorian volcanic flash

So no one might have seen hor heard
Anything in the deserts the ruined houses
About you, no the ancestor buried at yard's edge
Nor the old crome with all her herbs

About you only I, maybe, and the music
I chase from me but stronger it returns
For you the unformed twelve-year-old breast
Turned to the future with its red crater
For you the bitter odor like a pin
That in the body finds and pierces memory
And there's the soil, there doves, there our ancient earth.

VI

I've seen a lot and the earth, to my mind, is more beautiful
More beautiful in the golden vapors
The cutting stone, more beautiful
The isthmus purple and the roofs like waves
The rays more beautiful where without stepping you pass
Invincible like the goddess of Samothrace over the moun-
tainous sea

I've seen you so and it's enough
That all time's been absolved
In the small channel your passing leaves
Like a novice dolphin following

And playing with the white and the cyanic blue my soul!

Victory, victory where I've been beaten
Before love and with love
To passion flowers and mimosa
Go, go, even if I am lost

Alone, though the sun you hold is a newborn
Alone, though I'm the homeland that mourns
Though the word I sent to hold a laurel to you is
Alone, the wind strong and alone
In the blink of the dark seafloor the pebble
Paradise
The fisherman lifted and threw back again at Time.

VII

In Paradise I've sighted an island
Identical you and a house by the sea

With a big bed and a small door
I've thrown an echo to the deep
To see my self each morning waking

To see you half passing in the water
And weep for you half in Paradise.

Jane Miller and Olga Broumas

Jane Miller (1949-) is the author of several poetry collections, including the National Poetry Series selection, The Greater Leisures *(1983),* Memory at These Speeds: New and Selected Poems *(1996), and* A Palace of Pearls *(2005). Her collaboration with the poet Olga Broumas,* Black Holes, Black Stockings *(1985), is excerpted here and collected in* Memory at These Speeds. *More recently, Miller collaborated with the artist Beverley Pepper for the book* Midnights *(2008). She has taught at the University of Iowa Writers' Workshop, Goddard College, and currently teaches at the University of Arizona.*

Olga Broumas (1949-) was born in Syros, Greece. She has taught at several colleges and universities, including Brandeis University. Her book, Beginning with O, *was the Yale Younger Poets selection in 1976. She has translated two works by the Greek poet Odysseas Elytis,* What I Love, Selections *and* The Little Mariner.

Excerpts from Black Holes, Black Stockings

She liked to be in the middle. One of them was taken by how close her beat to the surface like a robin's and how she landed with a light touch. If the sheets were white and the sun glanced on them, blond had more red. Another was olive with almond eyes, who liked to wake slowly and fall back. She lay beside the row of windows and rolled out into the night on their long wooden oven spoons. Sometimes they came for the her and woke her, kissing the corners of her mouth. The long hairs in the bed, the very curly, the weighty and the subtle, lit an arabesque. When they were wet they were very very wet, and when they were dry they were funny. Excited, the candle burned like cry-breath. Who called out and where answered and when became thirsty. She reached for the lucky pitcher sailing across the sky. Tissue, tissue, kiss you.

Lizards and ants yes, mosquitos and flies no. yellowjackets yes, wasps gnats bumblebees no. Nightingales, swallows, woodchucks, dragonflies, fireflies yes. Mina birds usually. Kittens, puppies, guppies; pigeons, doves, yes. Owls, not usually. Nor do I like dogs in packs or frog-singing, mating in the fog with his camouflaged baritone. Buggers. Do flies bite? One mother is a bitch and the other pink and pert. They were here for a performance and tea, mothers of famous lovers. Serum is squeezed out of a bite, not without pain but the itch is gone; makes a funny mark where you've bleached your leg hair rather than shave. We all sang Try A Little Tenderness. Risk of pus. The countess invited her publisher and one mother a series of relatives. Split genes, clones, insomniacs, reptiles no. Fly-by-night, tea-for-two. One sang for mother, another recited. Goods for nothing, good for nothings: one loves two who loves three. I took each Polaroid into the sun: the countess and mother-in-mourning are dark against the great blue; the other mother and the countess again, impressionistic, fleeting; a third, of the four of them: daughters and mothers who had been—over-exposed in front of a bowl of wild strawberries bleeding together a little. Looking up I saw out of place on a fig tree limb a rather large mouse staring down the fabulous blouses of great beauties with a secret, mine, happy no matter, pulling it off. We spent the last hour of the night, at last, just looking at each other alone.

She rose from them, walked through the room, at the door bowed, and turned. It was her opportunity between formal goodbye and exit to judge the impression she had made, a demilitarized zone in which she was already assumed gone. Bowing, she kept her eyes up to fix the panorama and trick an accidental gaze into a matching bow. Taken by surprise and politeness, invariably he smiled into her closing eyes, eroticized, in her favor, where she left him. She had been presented by the minor official but it was the general with whom she had slept a month ago and to whom she had addressed her request, without looking at him in either case, the latter according to his preference, the former hers, as in wearing her hair severely back and off her neck—having discovered in a similarly critical situation with a gentleman of means that one is seen and not recognized if a great feature like the hair is hidden. And turned in her handwoven silk scarf embossed with an ancient script without a word, having chosen the few necessary ones which had been repeated twice, once for the general, in the straightforward manner he had asked her once for a certain act, and the second time that the general's audience might take in her beautiful white skin where the royal blue kimono cut away. An ivory sash swung at the slit if she gestured, which she reserved for when things were going well; they had. Her lover would be released from prison where he had been detained five months earlier for contraband and was sick from claustrophobia and filth. She had been allowed to visit him and was given a handmade Malay suit as she had been given her impeccable manner: from the poor, who accepted her generosity of spirit—and money when she had it—returning abundantly like the beloved silkworm.

> A gram. How much?
> Are you married?
> Yes.
> Is she?
> Of course.
> Where are your men?
> My husband is arriving later.
> Will he let you go?
> Of course.
> Where are we going?
> I will meet you here at 4 o'clock.
> How much?
> He will let you go?
> 4 o'clock.

She whispered *anemones* naming the flowers the boy had brought, a minor scene against the erotic masterpiece of the girl and her older lover Brando. We walked in in time for and accentuating the suddenness of their first intimacy in an unfurnished apartment. Driving home, after the movie, people we passed almost knew what they were doing in the back. The sunroof was open on the powdery sky and the narcissus from Tangiers smelled differently on each. One wore it like a light laugh surprising the air, the other like a vapor. I drove carefully exercising my hearing—I loved to hear first and see later and later still to touch. Taste, the darling of life, lay on her rosy couch on the other side of arrival, where we would fall as into a great beginning elsewhere, after acceleration, after light and sound. First it was like talc and then oily. I let myself take in from the back a finger, and there the darkness of all our colors lacing the room quickly magnetized in one spot like absence focused upon and enlarged—light, lightly. I was disappeared into an impersonal moment where the casual is sacrosanct; that anemone, for example, into which I was driven and from whose center I was pulled, into time, rested, ready to sleep.

In the film version she writes across his forehead in lipstick MINE. We drank cool liquid out of Chinese decanters at the villa under its long beams, under the overfed moon. We kept the inside cool like a cave and, very sober, waltzed to Vivaldi, missing the minor tones. I took her on the white wool rug protecting cold stone, two unmodified extremes, black and white marble. We were interrupted by a family, a husband and wife and wife's mother, to whom the house was to be shown. Had they not seemed tranquilized we could never have avoided being in the same room together sharing one blouse. Having come to say goodbye properly, the other, different and equally undemanding, never even saw the inside of the house. She drank three glasses of milk on the back veranda, peeling the croissant crust off the chocolate bread, and asked us to lie in the grass. For once the sun was directly overhead, neither casting shadow nor, where it did make shade of the overhang or leaves, distorting their proportions. We were one mouth unadorned, making an imprint. As lithographic ink is black before it is receptive to any other color, the most moving operation is that of the almost complete effacement of the first imprint.

Women who fly on separate planes to meet in strange cities, poppies with their black follicled centers, chicken eggs with a little blood on the shell like a stain on a sheet, the stain soaked through and left on the bedpad unwashed, print housedresses washed and, in the wind, torn at the hem; pneumatic alliances: the plane too low, a drinking glass pitched off a table, uncracked, but with its blow to the head, unmarked, bleeding inside a drop; bird coo, too regular, parrot trained to the French national anthem, bumblebee, its lion markings burned black, stabbing the window and otherwise horrible fly. Brain dust, spindletops blown in the air, brow furrowed with electric violin practice, seeds planted too close in a furrow, tomorrow, because of a dream; giving orders; taking orders; the wearing of black, the wearing of mirrored glasses; dust; haze; ants on a naked woman, lipstick on a man; with a penknife, manipulation of a developing Polaroid; periodic rinsing through the night of the menstrual sponge; the days and the nights sulphuric between golden and leafy, between the sun and the moon: discharge, between flights in an airport: dizziness; black, yellow, red; yolk, ink; the beautiful striations after the sun sets invisible, as without love.

the only cool day of summer
kids at bullfights
yellow and purple
green olives under an almond tree
a trapezoid smile
indoors without a flash
two aunts and an uncle
avocado vinaigrette
a bath with no hot water
a spoon and a fork
illuminated hands of a clock on its side
the hidden side of an arriving train
Paris at night
a face appearing at different windows of a big house
the last half of April and the first of May
one other

Remember how close we sat in Sifnos having dinner by the water? You said in your country once you put the table in the water. You began the meal, and then what a great idea to move it over a little, it would cool you, it was that calm. You rolled your pants to the knee and poured drinks all around, the fishbones back to the sea. Lizards climb the stone outside the kitchen by the sea. Weeds and flowers grow out of the stone; the relatives spill out of the kitchen. The daughter is well educated or about to be. She serves us with the happy face of one who is leaving. You lifted your skirt walking home in the dark over the pebbles to sit. One night we saw the only other lovers—they were both fair, she blond and he gray—and their eyes moved only to each other and the sea, these two destinations. Now the sea once in a while slips a wave up to their feet, because a boat passes or for no reason, now the yellow moon divides the sea into fields.

Blue of rainforest green, of moss, ultamarine of closed eyes, evening pearl, berry black, blue of earth cerulean in space, royal, prussian; porpoise blue and whale gray, slate blue of metal, enamel; iridescent trout, blue of fungus and mold; sky, pacific, mediterranean, aqua of translucent blues, blue stained with yellow; iris, silver, purple, rose blue, military, grape; in the shadow, violet or port; pool blue, quivering; church-stain, red madder, octopal; ice blue; blue of sighs, bluebird in twilight with a white stripe; polka dot, blood blue, nordic, light; diamond, meteor, parallel lines, density; powder, red, white and blue, blue concerto, island.

Barbara Cully

Barbara Cully (1955-) currently teaches composition and creative writing at the University of Arizona. She is the author of Desire Reclining *(2003),* Shoreline Series *(1997) and* The New Intimacy *(1997), which won the National Poetry Series Open Competition. She has received fellowships from the Arizona Commission on the Arts and has also taught at the Prague Summer Writers' Program. The poems here are from* The New Intimacy.

Maybe It's Cold Outside

. . . Later in the program a man returns to center stage, his face painted red singing Bellini's aria for a woman mourning her love as a lament over a dying flower: The modern piece is probably about AIDS. It is about a fist full of dirt falling from a man dropping to the boards in his underwear. The fact of loss is actually pervasive in dance right now, visible in ways a man wearing a T-shirt that says NOBODY KNOWS I'M GAY is visible in a crowd we might imagine would like to hurt him. (Will time bring these children anything good?) (The chorus says that when we get up we will bury our dead.) When the audience gets up, they are free to go to the bathroom, free to go back across the fields to have quick, muffled sex or to take their time. Maybe it's cold outside, or maybe two or three friends must be transported to the nearest medical facility. The (text) would like us to consider that all desires enter us as waters enter the ever-full and unmoved sea. The (text) would like us to consider woman the unfettered frost-foamed sea. The (text) would like us to consider that lasting peace is never achieved by one who is not complete unto himself, who still craves worldly things. The (text) would like us to consider woman a worldly thing. In a world where armed forces kill largely what they desire or resemble, sentimentality remains the shadow of cruelty, and— as for the targets—survival means a soul—a strong container in which silence can be churned. Did you (remember to) ask the pond where else we might find anything so pure, so transparent? We inhabited a planet—My love, small kisses—My love, energetic kisses and fucking were illegal. It wasn't an opera, but wherever we traveled the libretto read: At the end of the garden rocks a hammock and the water lilies of summer are gone.

In an Open View

While moonlight shines on the cars, the new paintings of imaginary women explode in renovated galleries. Here a palette of warm golds and browns enters a long period of downtown. Two women dressed alike arrange themselves like lovers outside the convenience store, and their love for one another is masked by the viewer's love for their teenage midriffs above equally white pairs of dreams.

They are in love with each other, but the shock of this castration nightmare is tempered by the cartoony certainty that they are too beautiful to carelessly come and go, intent upon a night alone, far away from the way men see women. Perhaps if we look more closely, there will be scars where the taller one's right eye should be just as the smaller's smile becomes a grimace.

Is the artist wrong to call attention so soon to girls in their transparent dresses, indolent and lascivious outside the Circle K on a desert night best left to the acceptable hungers and the insistent gods? Who is it who nestles in open view under the recently painted eaves?

What these swans want is hidden beneath a privacy so hallowed it is brilliant with Mediterranean apricots. When they wake up sprawling and full of wine, they are still in this world, fifteen and stabbed with sorrow.

4

Writing from the Borderlands

Beth Alvarado

There is a rock tower in northwestern New Mexico that bears the mark of many travelers. For thousands of years, people who have journeyed through this region have carved names, images, and symbols into the rock's surface, preserving their memory on the landscape. The rock tower is known as Inscription Rock, or *El Morro*. . . . The writing on Inscription Rock reminds us that many people—from the Ancient Anasazi to Spanish Conquistadores to White American settlers—have lived and moved here and have tried to make sense of what they have experienced here in various written forms. And in spite of the fences that today protect *El Morro* from further 'graffiti,' this rock still stands as a figurative as well as literal crossroads, as a cross-cultural marker, as an indicator of the rich history and heritage of the landscape that we now journey into—the American Southwest.

—Alesia Garcia and Maureen Salzer

The first time I encountered the landscape of the Sonoran desert, it seemed surreal, a vision from some science fiction movie: the saguaros were tall and forbidding, the spiny fingers of the ocotillo scratched at the sky, and the flat disks of the prickly pear were studded with spikes. The heat. As a native of Colorado, what can I say about the heat? I've seen rain turn to steam as soon as it hits the asphalt.

233

Summer air scorches the tissues in my lungs. My skin can tell the minute the thermometer climbs over one hundred. It seems unnatural. Of course, if you are from
here, or once you have spent time here, the desert can seem lush. Nothing is like
the velvet green of the mesquite in early spring; by April, the *palo verde* are
golden. You begin to believe what the desert dwellers tell you: there *are* seasons.
You can feel the subtle shift in the morning air as we enter autumn. In summer,
you feel rain long before you see clouds or smell the moisture.

My husband, who was born here and who works outside in the sun, no matter
how hot it gets, tells me there is a zen to surviving summer. I would like to believe
him. Instead, even after having lived here for three decades, I still move from air
conditioned house to air conditioned car to air conditioned building. Every summer, as I stand at the window and gaze at mountains flattened by the glare of a
relentless sun, I realize how dependent on technology we are. Electric pumps
deliver water from the rapidly shrinking aquifers that lie deep beneath the surface
of the earth. How long could we survive without that water? After all, every summer people die trying to cross the desert. There are portions of it where there is no
water, where daytime temperatures can reach 125 degrees in the shade, but even
here, in Tucson, we live in a place where we could not survive out of our own
resources, where the forces of nature—the heat and lack of water—could kill us.

The border between Mexico and the United States is another reality of this
part of the country and, again, it might be good to begin with our own experiences. When we imagine a border, we may visualize any number of things. We
may see ourselves sitting aboard a stopped train or bus, armed policemen walking
down the aisles, scrutinizing passengers' passports, speaking a language we don't
understand. Their gestures or facial expressions may make us feel nervous—no
matter that we've done nothing wrong. Or we may remember sitting in a long line
of cars while children try to sell us *chicle* (Chiclets gum), or while they ask to wash
the windshield, hoping we'll give them loose change. The border itself might be
clearly marked with a wall and armed men in trucks patrolling the tops of nearby
hills, or it might be marked by a small station house on a lonely highway, or there
may be nothing at all, not even a road sign, not even a piece of rusted barbed wire
or a line on the ground.

For instance, just last autumn, my brother-in-law Alfonso had been hunting
with his sons in the desert south of Arivaca. He asked a rancher how far it was to
the border, and the rancher told him six miles. Alfonso told me, "I remember,
when we stepped across this old fence, Gabriel asked me if it was the border and I
said, 'Nah.'" They continued on until they came to a canyon. At the bottom of it,
where the canyon widened, there were trees and a pond, the surface covered with
ducks. It was beautiful. They were going to start climbing down when Alfonso
noticed a tall tower that said, "Mexico." They had crossed the border without
knowing it. There they were, illegally in Mexico, with rifles. Had they been spotted by the authorities, they could have been thrown in jail. How long would they
have been there before the family was notified? Would they have been able to convince either the *Federales* or the U. S. Border Patrol that it was an innocent mistake? They quickly traveled north, back across the border, and as soon as they
crossed to this side they saw a deer. A buck. At least three points on his antlers.
But because he was on the other side, safe in Mexico, they couldn't shoot him.

When it is that easy to forget about the line between "here" and "there," the border may seem completely arbitrary. In her essay in this chapter, "The Home-land, *Aztlan, El Otro Mexico*," Gloria Anzaldua acknowledges that "Borders are set up to define the places that are safe and unsafe, to distinguish us from them. A border is a dividing line, a narrow strip along a steep edge." However, from her point of view, the border divides a people, a culture, a *pueblo*—tribes and fami-lies. She thinks of the border as being an "unnatural boundary," calling it an open wound, "*una herida abierta* where the Third World grates against the first and bleeds." Many of us would never think of the border in this way although, when the Berlin Wall divided West Berlin from East, Americans often lamented the fact that families had been divided. Further, when East Germans risked their lives to cross into the West, whether to reunite with family members or simply to find bet-ter opportunities, we found them heroic and supported their efforts to cross over to freedom. Many authors from the southwest, including Leslie Marmon Silko and Luis Alberto Urrea, compare the U.S./Mexican border to the Iron Curtain and the Gaza Strip, hoping, perhaps, that such analogies will provoke readers to re-see the border and re-think their assumptions about it.

While the border seems, at least geographically, fairly easy to define, "border-lands" is much more difficult. How far do the borderlands extend? Past Colorado? Is Los Angeles a part of them? Do we think of the area south of the border as being a part of our borderlands? In Spanish, the word for the border is *la frontera*. Annette Kolodny, a professor of American literature at the University of Arizona, builds on the work of two historians when she says that a frontier is not a "boundary or line, but . . . a territory or zone of interpenetration between . . . previously distinct societies" (Lamar and Thompson as cited in Kolodny 313). Because of the way we've been taught American history, we tend to think of the frontier in terms of expansion westward, of the white settlers displac-ing the Indians, but Kolodny notes that indigenous cultures and languages were coming together in both conflict and trade—and therefore were exchanging stories and knowledge—long before the Spanish Conquistadors and European-American settlers ever showed up. In fact, while there are 21 Native American tribes in Arizona today, Kolodny tells us that in precolonial North America there were 550 different languages in use north of the Rio Grande (314).

Because of this history, Kolodny argues that we need to think of *la frontera* as a "liminal landscape of changing meanings," and she and other literary scholars use the image of a "continuously unfolding palimpsest" in order to illustrate this view of the history of the region (315). As Garcia and Salzer explain it, a "palimpsest is a document that has been constructed in layers . . . The early writ-ing [on the wall or on the stone, like El Morro] may be completely or imperfectly covered up. It may, at times, begin to bleed through and color later inscriptions" (307). We've probably all heard the old saying that the conqueror gets to write history, but the image of history as a palimpsest complicates that idea. Even though we can't deny that conquest and colonialism took place here, and that we continue to be defined by that legacy of inequality and oppression, the palimpsest encourages us to look for the various stories and histories of this region and asks us to resist privileging one over the other. Further, it suggests that because older stories will "bleed through" the new layers, history cannot be completely erased.

Here, though, it seems important to note that in cultures that rely on oral story-telling, where there is no written record, the stories are always only one generation away from being lost.

While Kolodny describes what happened in history, Mary Louise Pratt, a professor of Spanish and Comparative Literature at Stanford, uses the term "Contact Zone" to describe "social places where cultures meet, clash, and grapple with each other, often in contexts of highly asymmetrical relations of power, such as colonialism, slavery, or their aftermaths as they are lived out in many parts of the world today" (34). In other words, the term "contact zone" acknowledges that this contact between cultures, this hybridizing process, is mutual and is still going on. For instance, we often hear Spanglish words and, if you go to the *Yaqui* deer dances here in Tucson, you can see that some dancers have integrated contemporary items like Burger King Crowns into their traditional costumes. San Xavier Mission, on the *Tohono O'Odahm* reservation south of Tucson, is another visual representation of the fusion of cultures: the architecture is obviously Spanish but, inside, the geometric designs reveal Native American influences.

Pratt also notes that, in texts created in the contact zones, we will often find stories that use more than one language, old stories retold in ways that question or critique the dominant culture, stories told in ways that appropriate or critique representations from both cultures, and stories that parody or redefine representations (37). In these narratives, people are redefining themselves as they clash or mingle with people from other cultures. Because texts from the contact zone call cultural assumptions into question, Pratt notes that they are often met with mis-comprehension or incomprehension.

The texts in this chapter contain many of the characteristics Pratt describes. As you read them, you will see that *la frontera* is a place not only where cultures and languages come together, but also where the past and present meet, where the surreal emerges from the real, and where the mythical world coexists with the physical. *La frontera* is a place where surprising things can happen. For instance, when my mother-in-law was a child, she heard stories about how Geronimo used to sneak into Tucson and play pool in the bars on Cushing Street. Meanwhile, the troops stationed at Fort Lowell were out scouring the desert for him. "*Se dice que los Apaches podrian correr todo el dia en el sol, sin agua, y podrian desaparecer en el desierto, como fantasmos.*" (They say that the Apaches could run all day in the sun, without water, and that they could disappear into the desert, like ghosts.) Likewise, many old Tucson families tell stories about Pancho Villa crossing the border at will, showing up at their great-grandmother's door for a midnight snack. In Kimi Eisle's essay, Mexican children and their parents tell stories of La Llorona and ask Eisle if it's true that there are vampires on this side of the line. In "Yellow Woman" by Leslie Silko, the character Silva may be a man or a spirit. Is he from this world or another? Can anyone know for sure?

As you read the selections in this chapter, consider yourself in a frontier, where reading is a way to encounter other cultures as well as other perspectives and realities. Even if you are from Tucson or from this region, you might think of yourself as a traveler, someone who is taking note of the place and the people who inhabit it and of the stories they tell. Because we often come away from our travels feeling as if *we* have been changed, you'll also want to take careful note of your interior landscape. You might write about passages where you connect with the authors and understand their points of view, but also note points where you feel tension or have strong reactions. What details stand out for you and why? How might someone else interpret them? In other words, you'll want to use your writer's journal to record your journey through this territory and to create a dialogue with the writers and characters you encounter.

Works Cited

Anzaldua, Gloria. *Borderlands/La Frontera: The New Mestiza*. San Francisco: Aunt Lute, 1987.

Garcia, Alesia and Maureen Salzer. "Introduction to 'Writing Southwestern Journeys'." *Writing as Re-Vision*, 1st Edition. Eds. Beth Alvarado and Barbara Cully. Needham Heights, MA: Simon and Schuster Education Group, 1996. 305–309.

Kolodny, Annette. "Letting Go Our Grand Obsessions: Notes Toward a New Literary History of the American Frontiers." *Writing as Re-Vision*, 1st Edition. 310–319.

Pratt, Mary Louise. "Arts of the Contact Zone." *Profession* 91, 33–40.

John Washington

John Washington (1981–) is the author of a few unpublished novels. He is currently in the MFA program at the U of A for fiction. He has published his nonfiction at wordriot.org *and* America, *a Romanian-American newspaper in Cleveland, Ohio, where he grew up.*

The New Colossus: Exploring the Idea of Border

It's a big donut over there when I see the fence. When I look across the fence I see a big donut.
   —Luis Ramos, 3/16/10, Nogales, Sonora, Mexico

In 2009 there were 213 migrant deaths in the deserts of Arizona[*].

The best way to spot a recently dumped migrant in Nogales, Sonora is by looking at the feet. None of the deportees wear shoelaces. Border Patrol agents confiscate them so they don't hang themselves in custody. Another sign of a dumped migrant in Nogales is a bad limp; a twisted ankle, sprained knee, cactus spines stuck in the skin, an infected wound, festering fungus, trench foot, or a spider or centipede bite. Some of the migrant feet are so swollen they don't fit back into shoes. And the shoes, often they're broken, the soles are split, worn through, busted in the heel.

And why are their feet so bad?

Because they've been walking. Many have traveled more than a thousand miles from their homes, walking for long stretches of that distance. Many have been lost in the desert for days, or even weeks, walking through their shoes.

I say dumped, the best way to spot a *dumped* migrant, because I've seen them "repatriated," and I know that repatriated is a kind euphemism for the way migrants are offloaded from government contracted busses, their belongings thrown in piles on the sidewalk—injured men and single women deposited into dark Nogales nights without a clue which way to turn or what to turn to. Dumped is the more accurate term. As is *dog-catcher* a better word than "Border Patrol truck." The trucks *look* like dog-catcher trucks. And the migrants are stuffed in the back-cabs sometimes a dozen or more at once, not unlike dogs, without AC, in the cold of winter or the dog-days of the summer. I remember

---

[*]In fiscal year 2010, as of this publication, there are already 85 bodies recovered from the desert, a 60% increase from last year. –www.derechoshumanosaz.net

meeting a few horseback BP agents a few years ago in a back-canyon of the Anza-Borrego desert in California. They kept referring to the *herding* and *prodding* of groups of migrants. They weren't ashamed, or seemed to think twice, of how they were describing the less-than humane treatment of persons. When people are treated like cattle you use cattle terms, naturally. When people are dumped you say they are dumped. You don't say "repatriated" when a single young woman is offloaded at two in the morning after having spent three nights sleeping on a jail floor without a proper meal and all of her personal belongings have been "lost" in her transfer between detention centers. You say she has been *dumped* and you are right to say it.

I know this, that migrants are dumped, dumped without shoelaces, dumped with bleeding and untreated feet, because I have been volunteering in Nogales off and on for the past year. As a volunteer and an EMT, I've been giving medical aid and food to migrants. I spent most of the summer of 2009 handing out socks, tending to blisters, sending victims to the hospital, dishing out rice and beans, listening to stories of broken families, dead friends, lost brothers, sisters, husbands, wives. I was there, in Nogales, with the humanitarian-aid organization called No More Deaths, because I believed in the group's mission, to "end death and suffering on the US-Mexico border," because I wanted to help. Because I thought I could help. Because I thought the migrants needed and deserved help. Because my own mother migrated from Romania to the United States in search of a better life, which she found, and which I think that everybody deserves a chance to seek. I was there because I believe, like some documents say, that all persons have the right to the pursuit of dignity, and happiness, and life. Because I believe it's not a crime for a person to be born in a place where this pursuit is not possible. Because I had (and still have) a jejune understanding of international economics that makes me believe that the over-extravagant American lifestyle is only possible because of the exploitation of the "third world." And because I don't think that the system of surfeit depending on suffering is fair. And because I don't want to live in a glass house, or in conditions, no matter how comfortable, which were built, and are only possible, because of the exploitation of persons.

But this doesn't matter. It doesn't matter what I want. No matter how many blisters I treat, how many new socks I trade for old fungal socks, no matter how many stories of abuse or terrible detention center conditions that I listen to, or report to the consulate, the migrants will keep coming. They'll keep coming north from southern Mexico to cross the border and get caught and then dumped back, busload after busload, day after day, dumped back into the streets of Nogales like unwanted scraps from a slaughterhouse. They will continue to be mishandled, herded, prodded, thrown in dog-catcher trucks and then dumped back into Mexico. The only way, I believe, that I can serve to stop the next blister from forming rather than merely treat the last one that popped, is to tell the story. Is to find the story. To understand the story.

This essay is not the story. It is only a beginning. It is only the beginning of the question that I believe needs to be asked, and hasn't yet been asked, not fully at least, not successfully.

But before the question can be asked, before it can even be posited, we need some perspective.

Glancing at a political map, it looks as if the countries are perfect—tidy pastel packages with thin black borderlines. A wallmap defines borders so cleanly that they can seem as if they are timeless, harmless thin skins stretched around countries. But a "clean" map, and the sense of nationhood, is a relatively recent concept, not even fully realized in Europe until the breakup of the Austro-Hungarian, Ottoman and Russian Empires after World War I. The last birth-period of nations was an era which, as John Torpey describes, "witnessed the end of dynastic states in Europe and the elimination of 'the easy-going' nations of the past in favor of . . . the 'crustacean type of nation,' which crabbily distinguished between 'us' and 'them'" (122). Historically, before the rise of nation-states, demarcated borders were much less common, were much less distinct than the international boundaries today. Even the legendary walls left by the Han and Roman empires are misperceived as hard limits of empire. As with Hadrian's Wall in England, it was less a clenched perimeter and more "a *spine* around which Roman control of the north of Britannia toughened and stabilized" (Schama 34). And even now, now that countries seem to be more neatly packaged than the empires of past, borders may still be more accurately thought of as spines of control, rather than impenetrable divisions. And though the effects of globalization have been tearing down these divisions, physical barrier borders are increasingly "replaced in both urgency and importance by problems of a new kind of frontiers—frontiers of ideological worlds" (Kristof 278). But if the trend for the absolute physical barricading of countries is to become, in some ways, more porous, borders are being reinforced or redrawn along increasingly divisive lines, as, for example, the "security fence" which still grows in violent fits and starts between Israel and the West Bank, or as small sections of "unclimbable fence" are constructed between the U.S. and Mexico. So while the secure barrier line between countries is in many places dissolving, the effects of "symbolic" or "ideological" border walls are taking on increasingly important and penetrating consequences, drawing definite lines between the "first" and "third" worlds, between subjugators and subjugated, between the privileged and the underprivileged, and between the franchised and the disenfranchised.

After some reflection, however, looking at a map, you might notice that many of the borderlines seem to be drawn rather haphazardly, or even, as Nick Megoran puts it in describing the Kyrgyzstan-Uzbekistan border, *maliciously* drawn. When you start noticing the awkward appendages of some nations, like the Caprivi strip of Namibia between Botswana and Zambia, or the Wakhan Corridor of Afghanistan, which reaches over the back of Pakistan for two hundred narrow miles to touch China, or the intermixed international archipelago of South Asia, where Vietnam, Thailand, Singapore, Malaysia, Indonesia and East Timor vie for island rights and struggle to set boundaries even in the unmarkable sea, or "Winston's Hiccup*," the strange Saudi bite out of Jordan, or the exclave American

---

*"I created Transjordan with the stroke of a pen on a Sunday afternoon in Cairo" –Winston Churchill, quoted by William F. Shughart II, *An analytical history of terrorism, 1945–2000* p. 42.

drop of Point Roberts hanging off Canadian land below the 49th parallel above Washington State, the borderlines begin to seem less geospatially natural, less timeless, less pre-ordained, and less simple. Upon close reflection, or even after just spending a few minutes with a world map, borderlines seem less systematic, less tidy, and more representations of the violent maneuvering of land and person, more the awkwardly hashed aftermath of war, political domination, and endless vying for control as is repeatedly emphasized in, for example, the Caucasus, where keeping track of newly formed ex-Soviet satellite countries like Dagestan, North Ossetia, Ingushetia, Georgia, Adygea, Karachay-Cherkessia seems like following a celebrity gossip column and yet wars are still being fought and bombs are exploding and people are dying and being threatened over the constant editing and re-editing of their borderlines. The borders serve, in this region as elsewhere, to continually instigate violence, murder, and fear.

The history of borders is a history of violence. Even many "peace treaties" (the Treaty of Westphalia in 1648, the "treaty" of Velasco in 1836 in which Santa Ana signed away Texas under the gun, or the series of Indian Appropriation Acts, a sort of pathetic culmination of Native American peace treaties, come to mind) which established, drew or redrew borders throughout history, have often been nothing but impetus to further fighting, domination, and the splitting of cultures and families.

Consider, for example, as another "peace" treaty, the border between India and Pakistan, drawn by Sir Cyril Radcliffe in 1947 during the dissolution of British Colonialism on the Indian subcontinent. Sir Cyril spent only a few weeks of his entire life in Asia, and his line is perhaps one of the most contested borders in the modern world, and yet is commonly known as "the line of control." Disputes over and across this Line of Control have sparked wars and violence since Sir Cyril's pen hit the paper in 1947, and as recently as the Mumbai Massacre of 2008. Also drawn by Sir Cyril is the eastern border between Bangladesh (once East Pakistan) and India, which is demarcated not by a borderline at all, but by a labyrinthine confusion of 198 enclaves (an enclave is a piece of a country entirely inside another country), counter-enclaves (a counter-enclave is an enclave within an enclave), and even a counter-counter-enclave, in which a little pocket of India sits in a little pocket of Bangladesh which sits in a bigger pocket of India which is entirely enisled in Bangladesh, and vice versa, and even vice-vice versa. One of the most diplomatically controversial Bangladeshi enclaves, the Dahagram/Angarpota enclave, surrounded by Indian territory, is a mere five hundred feet from the Bangladeshi mainland. You could almost pitch a baseball that far, and yet the Bangladeshi government can't access its own territory to build roads, schools, or even install electric lines. Nor can those living within the enclave visit their families in mainland Bangladesh without crossing two international boundaries. In initial years, those living within Dahagram/Angarpota could only cross the border during a short and unreliable three hour window. The near total lack of administration and the complete absence of governmental infrastructure (including roads, electricity, police, hospitals, bridges, schools) leaves the enclaved residents in an almost constant state of "insecurity, in terms of both the daily threat of violence and persistent concerns about land tenure, food security, and health." In many of the Indian enclaves surrounded by Bangladesh, "the residents are forced either to not educate (*sic*) their children or to establish residency in Bangladesh, often through illegal means" (Jones 29).

Forcing people to engage in illegal activity in order to survive, in order to properly educate their children, as in the enclaves of India/Bangladesh, may seem like a third-world anomaly of a border conflict, but even in the United States, when California Governor Pete Wilson passed Proposition 187 into law in 1994, undocumented migrants and their children were *de jure* prohibited from attending public schools or receiving medical care for anything except emergencies*. Many of the migrants who cross America's southern border, without adequate means for survival in their home country, are thus forced, if they work to feed their families, or want to send their children to school, into states of illegality. In Phoenix today, with the frightened atmosphere instituted by Sheriff Joe Arpaio and his trumpeting of the 287(g) bill (which grants local police officers the right to enforce immigration crimes), many migrants don't report crimes or even go to the hospital in fear that they will be deported. The border's legal lockdown and the implementation of programs like 287(g) do not to curb crime, instead, they perpetuate criminal activity, and worse, even criminalize survival. Robert Koulish reports in *Immigration and American Democracy* that in counties with 287(g), crime actually increases "because residents lose trust in police and fail to report crime" (137). UNC law professor Deborah Weismann finds that when local police start enforcing immigration law, battered migrant women often have to make the choice "between further domestic abuse and deportation" (Koulish 137). In other words, with the effects of 287(g), reporting a crime can become synonymous with becoming a criminal. The presence and penetration of the borderlines thus forces people even in Arizona into states of illegality not unlike the trapped, enclaved residents of Dahagram/Angarpota.

Though illegal immigration itself (entering without authorization) is criminal by legal standards, "the law suggests that it is [only] an administrative offense," and yet due to the public castigation of migrants, this "administrative offense" is being conflated into something akin to an aggravated felony (Koulish 39). This process of over-criminalization strips migrants of rights—including the legal right to due process. Everyday at the courthouse in downtown Tucson, migrants are prosecuted through Operation Streamline. They are sentenced en masse, as many as seventy or more migrants at a time, with insufficient legal counsel and the farcical rejection of due process. Not only is Streamline a humiliating, frightening, and traumatic experience for the migrants, not only does it dehumanize them, robbing them of their dignity or their right to due process, but it also, disastrously, devalues American ideals of justice and freedom. Likewise, Joe Arpaio's tent cities, where arrested migrants are paraded in striped prison uniforms, wear pink underwear, both men and women work in "voluntary" chain gangs and are forced to eat and

---

*The ACLU almost immediately challenged the law. Most of its provisions were deemed unconstitutional and were not implemented until Clinton's Welfare Reform Act slipped into law with some of Prop 187's same statues in 1996.

sleep in what feels like a Vietnam Prison camp*, set precedent that the United States government does not treat people with internationally standardized human rights.

But what strikes first, before the devaluation of American justice or the slack record of human rights, is the smell. The BO in the Tucson courthouse almost stings your eyes, unless that's the shock of seeing the line of chained men and women—shackled ankles, wrist and waist—hobbling in to the rhythm of their manacles like a line of slaves. Migrants aren't given a chance to shower before entering court. The women can't even brush the hair out of their eyes, or maneuver the awkward translator headphones on their heads, because their wrists are cuffed to their waist. When they do have to scratch their face, they cow over, steeply arching their back and pulling at their waist chains. To the question if they waive their right to an individual trial, most of the migrants answer the judge meekly a coerced "Sí" (which is obviously coached by the nodding lawyers) followed by the long chain of admitted pleas of "Cupable" or "Guilty." Some of the migrants, however, clearly do not understand the quickly translated legalese, and in the first few minutes of proceedings there are random answers from the migrants still seated in the back, or random and unasked for admissions of cupable. The repeated guilt, the antiquated scene reminiscent of a slave auction, and the clear and persistent confusion of many of the migrants*, makes one wonder exactly of what, besides being born on the wrong side of the border, these people are guilty.

Giving aid, medical care, and documenting abuses at migrant aid stations in Nogales, Sonora, I've heard countless stories of overcrowded jailhouses (not just Arpaio's tent cities) with men and women driven into cells like cattle, sometimes kept handcuffed for days, without even benches to sit on or floorspace to lie on. They are given water sometimes out of a single jug, fed very little, often nothing but crackers and kids-size juiceboxes. These details, the crackers and juiceboxes, or the racial intimidation and beatings by detention officers, are corroborated again and again by deported migrants: a small juicebox and a pack of crackers and a tonk on the head. One particularly disturbing reoccurring story is of migrants fed for days on little but still-frozen Burger King hamburger patties.

In the summer of 2009, I recall treating a man named Oscar Rojas. He was bit on the foot by a brown recluse, a dangerous spider he claimed to frequently see in detention center dining halls. The guards ignored his complaints for days until he finally succeeded in showing them the necrotic hole developing on the top of his

---

*"Arpaio makes inmates pay for their meals, which some say are worse than those for the guard dogs. Canines eat $1.10 worth of food a day, the inmate 90 cents, the sheriff says. 'I'm very proud of that too.'" –CNN.com *July 27, 1999.*

†On March 25th, one woman from Oaxaca, Juana Antonio Acevedo, for whom Spanish was a second language, had so much trouble understanding the Operation Streamline proceedings, even as her lawyer practically whispered her answers into her ear, that after the judge said, "I know that's a difficult question because you're from Mexico," Juana started weeping. The lawyer, kindly, gave her a handful of tissues. Juana, however, couldn't wipe her tears away as her hands were shackled to her belt-chain. She stood, bent over before the judge, trying to reach her face to her waist, and then the US Marshall escorted her to prison.

foot. A doctor performed a quick surgery, scrubbing the wound, then ICE (Immigration and Customs Enforcement) deported him with a bottle of saline solution and a package of bandages to self-care in the dusty Nogales streets. Having no family in or around Nogales, as is true of almost all migrants who cross the U.S.-Mexico border, he spent a couple of nights in a migrant shelter, and then moved into the streets to sleep in the cemetery. When I first saw him a few days after his deportation, he unwound a smelly rag of a bandage to reveal an infected, golfball size bloody scoop out of the top of his foot. These conditions, the spectacle of a Streamline courtroom constantly clanging with the body-chains of men and women being sentenced en-masse, serve not only as the administrative processing of charging defendants, but as a horrifying lesson of what it means, for some, to cross a border. In the summer of 2009, according to a report by No More Deaths, 32% of migrants reported verbal abuse (one out of every three) and 29% reported instances of physical abuse (NMD).

Many times, in Nogales, working with migrants, I awkwardly had to pat the shoulder of a grown man who broke down in front of me, reduced to tears like a child because of the gruesome trials he faced trying to find or keep work. I recall one migrant, a man named Guadalupe. He was from El Salvador, a diabetic, and was deported on a flight back to his home country, a not uncommon practice used to put a generous-seeming picture on a front page paper when Homeland Security is under budget at the end of the fiscal year. Guadalupe was chained–ankles, wrists and waist–only given two chances to use the bathroom during the long flight, and despite repeated requests of the guards, explaining that he was diabetic, he ended up pissing his own pants. He was a fifty-year-old man, shackled as if he were a rapist, humiliated like a child, dumped back into his own country with a piss stain down the front of his pants. This is what it means for some to cross a border.

For a proper understanding of the U.S.-Mexico divide, for a basic conception of what the border is that these people are crossing, we need first to consider the origins and history of the border.

In his precocious essay, *What Is a Nation?*, Ernest Renan wrote in 1882, that "forgetting, I would even go so far as to say historical error, is a crucial factor in the creation of a nation." To maintain a healthy, democratic nation, or, even more so, to maintain an unbiased understanding of the creation of a border between two nations, one must, according to the logic of Renan, *unforget*. In terms of the U.S.-Mexico border, you first must *un*forget that almost all of the American West (Arizona, New Mexico, Texas, California and parts of Nevada, Utah, Colorado and Wyoming) was forcibly taken from Mexico in 1848 in the U.S. Mexican War. This was an expansionist war. There was no threat of invasion, nor was their threat of terrorism (as contemporary American wars are justified). There was hardly even an underlying animosity. In his memoirs, Ulysses S. Grant famously called the Mexican War, "the most unjust war ever waged by a stronger against a weaker nation . . . an instance of a republic following the bad example of European monarchies . . ." (Grant 18). In Mexico, quite simply, the war is more accurately referred to as *la invasión estadounidense de México* (the U.S. invasion of Mexico). After the war Mexico lost nearly half of its territory. After the Gadsden Purchase, five years later in 1853, which swept up even more Mexican land (for railroad interests), including Tucson, into America's expanding pockets, the U.S. government has led a long and ambivalent campaign in its stance along the southern border.

Over the years U.S. legislation has encouraged migration, prohibited it, granted amnesty, and even gone so far as organizing mass deportations under unapologetically racist banners such as Operation Wetback in 1954. The first sign of wavering, however, came with another discriminatory ruling, the Chinese Exclusion Act, the first of a series of laws which were enacted in 1882. These acts, which weren't repealed until sixty-one years later, in 1943, were the first instances which "determined that Congress has the power to decide who can come to America, how long they can stay, and when they must leave*" (Koulish 31). But besides securing this exclusionary power as the sole say of Congress, the Chinese Exclusion Acts were in stark opposition to the Burlingame Treaty of 1868. This treaty, signed into law only fourteen years earlier and also directed at China, was written in a more universal language and granted the "inherent and inalienable right of man to change his home and allegiance, and . . . the mutual advantage of free migration" (Koulish 32). This legislative tergiversation on behalf of the U.S. government marked what would be a steady trend of contradictory rulings and messages to migrants, continuing even today as the Obama administration promises paths to legalization and billions of dollars to heighten border security and remove the aliens.

A few other key moments in history must be unforgotten to even begin to understand the current situation along the border. Though currently in the Arizona State Senate a bill (SB 1070) is being pushed to further criminalize companies for knowingly hiring illegal immigrants, in the 1940's and 50's during the Bracero Program (a government program that brought in temporary workers from Mexico), Congress passed what was known as the "Texas Proviso," which explicitly prohibited the prosecution of employers for hiring undocumented workers" (Massey 36). Of course a government, run at least theoretically by the people, has the right to change its stance about certain laws, but on no other issue except immigration has there been such consistent vagueness and double talk. This persistent waffling, promising amnesty at the same time as locking down the border, punishing people for taking jobs they were baited with, belittles and exploits an entire and substantive contingent of the population on which the U.S. economy remains dependent. The ambivalence sustains a metaphorical border, a border that divides an "us" from a "them," a them who then remain subjugated and susceptible to exploitation.

After this brief glance into the history and original politicking of the U.S.-Mexico border, let us now look at a paradigmatic example of how popular conceptions, or misconceptions, of migrants have infiltrated the American discourse.

---

*Congress still holds and wields this power. Until 1991, homosexuality was grounds for exclusion from admission to the United States under section 212(a)(4) of the Immigration and Nationality Act of 1965. Before the implementation of the Immigration Act of 1990, Congress officially excluded gays and lesbians as sexual deviants. Until 2009, testing positive for HIV was also grounds for exclusion.

Consider the debate over the "Illegal Alien Halloween Costume" which was sold by Targets and WalMarts for Halloween 2009. The costume was a Roswell looking alien mask, an oversized plastic green card with the words 'green card' printed on it, and an orange jumpsuit with the words ILLEGAL ALIEN printed across the chest. Besides the redundancy of writing the words 'green card' on a green card, or 'illegal alien' on the orange chest of someone wearing an alien mask, and besides the obvious associating of a civil offender with a dangerous, Alcatraz-like, violent criminal (a murderer or rapist), the costume is indicative of the illegal status that is doubly perpetuated by the oxymoron of an *illegal* alien holding a *legalizing* greencard. The implication is either that the green card is a forgery (that what you take for a *legal* migrant is only a costume of *legality*), or that even with a greencard, a "legalized" migrant still maintains an aura of illegality.

This aura of illegality is foisted on migrants not only along the border zones, but it is also burdened onto the daily life of many who look "illegal." Gloria Anzaldúa writes of the 1,950 mile wound, "una herida abierta," (the U.S.-Mexico border) "running down the length of [her] body." Likewise, Leslie Marmon Silko laments the lost freedom of traveling American highways in the border states if one even potentially looks like a migrant. Here, the international border and the feelings of anxiety, daily racial discrimination, and the fear of violence that accompany it are not only extending, but, using a vascular metaphor in the same vein as Anzaldúa, the borders are hemorrhaging ever deeper into American heartlands. Consider the swelling of borderlands as virtual fences* and increased surveillance advances centripetally inward. Michel Foucault refers to the ex-judicial restriction on a person, or the internalizations of illegality, as "carceral archipelagos," in which some people, in some places, are treated as illegal. And yet today there is hardly anywhere, excluding Iran, or maybe North Korea, where an American would be illegal. And yet to those born in Nogales, Tijuana, Ciudad Juarez, merely walking across the city reterms them as illegals. In fact, as with a friend of mine, Sal, who moved from Mexico to Phoenix with his parents when he was a baby, who was recently deported to Nogales when he was twenty for jaywalking, the only thing of which he was guilty, was existence.

A common response to hearing such a story is that unauthorized migrants should "get in line" for proper "legalizing" authorizations. However, according to a 2009 report by the Immigration Policy Center, unequivocally, **"there is no "line" for unauthorized migrants.** If you don't fit into one of the limited categories [advanced professional degree, kinship ties, etc.], you cannot qualify for permanent legal status" (emphasis not mine) (4).

While there are many government incentivized draws for migrants to cross the border, there are just as many or more borderlines in America that keep migrants

---

*In September, 2006. Boeing was awarded 2.5 billion dollar contract with Department of Homeland Security to create a virtual fence. Since 2005, the Border Patrol began using 14 million dollar drone aircrafts to patrol the border. Recently, in March of 2010, what seemed like positive news for the demilitarization of the border (the cutting of funding for the virtual fence), turns out to be a mere reallocation of funds for other types of border fortifications.

suppressed. When I cross or approach the U.S. Mexican border, for example, I become not just who I am, but I am reconsidered as an American citizen. Others, however, as they approach the same border, change from who they are to a non-citizen, or to an "illegal," and are thus subjected to states of great vulnerability. In effect, they lose their rights. When a black or Chinese student tried to leave his or her neighborhood in LA in the forties (as is unfortunately still often true today), he or she was often met with not only resistance, but even brutality. Aisha Sloan, in *Glass Houses*, points out that in Los Angeles there exist numerous borderwalls, enclaves and exclaves, dividing the city both by race and class. Consider, too, the many borders in the American heartlands between urban and suburban, between the new commercial centers and neglected ghettos. Or, internationally, in France, the eight-lane highway known as "the periph" that separates the Parisian ghettoes (where riots and immigrant-nativist violence erupted for weeks in 2005) and the clean City of Lights itself. Likewise, in Arizona, there are "borderwalls" between overlit, fountain burbling downtown Phoenix and the dim drug-addled neighborhoods in the immediate outskirts. In a preliminarily passed bill, sponsored by AZ Senator Russell Pearce in March of 2010, elementary schools will be forced to ask students the status of their citizenship. "The laws," Pearce said, directly referring even to schoolchildren, "are intended to make people fearful" (Howard Fischer). These laws, the flaunting of them, will serve not to unite citizens, but to divide classrooms and to engender fear and criminalize children.

In Postville, Iowa, even deeper into the hinterlands and the archetypal marrow of America, in May of 2008, 900 heavily armed ICE agents with Blackhawk helicopters raided a kosher meat factory and arrested over three hundred migrants in a single morning. The travesty there is not only that men and women—many of whom were the sole breadwinners for their families—were arrested and treated as if they were enemy combatants in a war zone, but that the pastoral, almost Arcadian ideal of Postville was a façade for terrible, exploitative working conditions. The factory ran something akin to a hard-labor camp, employing boys and girls as young as twelve and often forcing them to work twelve or more hours a day. Some of the women later confessed that they were repeatedly raped by their bosses. And, as they feared legal recourse (deportation), the rapes went unreported. The migrants were not only exploited for their sweat and blood labor, a border was not only constructed that let them be treated like indentured servants, or worse, but after their "time served," they were violently extirpated from their homes after years of living peacefully in the community.[*]

Despite the proclamation in the Universal Declaration of Human Rights, ratified by the United States, which dictates that, "Everyone is entitled to all the rights and freedoms set forth in this Declaration, without distinction of any kind, such as race, color, sex, language, religion, political or other opinion, national or social origin, property, birth or other status," the migrants in Iowa, and many of the migrants all over America, clearly are discriminated against just because of their national origin and birth status. Though they live and work in the country, and

---

[*]Agriprocessors, Inc. was charged with 9,311 counts of child labor violations. –abUSedthe postvilleraid.com.

are drawn or sometimes even forced into the country by economic policy, they are consistently underprivileged, and the path to citizenship, the path to economic and personal freedom, is often insurmountably complex and costly. One dismayingly anachronistic path to citizenship, however, is serving in the military. As Jacqueline Stevens notes: "An immigrant can be hired by one branch of government security to kill Iraquis but will be imprisoned by another branch of government security for picking a tomato" (29). Birth location is an act of nature, the distinction between citizenship and the granting of rights is a construct of government. Borderlines distinguish (even here in the United States) who has rights and who does not. Referring to Jefferson's most famous phrase ("all men are created equal") from the Declaration of Independence, Aviva Chomsky states the plight of immigrants quite frankly: "the suggestion that noncitizens, too, are created equal is virtually absent from the public sphere" (xxv).

During the summer of 2009 I spent many a Nogales evening sitting on the bare, littered slope of a barranca, overlooking a wide arroyo in which stretched the rusted border fence that represents the international divide between Mexico and the United States. I'd sit on the Mexican side with groups of migrants, coyotes (migrant guides or often the bosses of migrant guides who orchestrate border crossings), or fellow volunteers, or sometimes I'd go into the little clapboard "restaurant" which sat on the bank of the hill. Graciela, the purveyor, who built her shack herself, and serves Cokes and stew with tortillas to the men who wash windshields or sell papers in la linea, the line of vehicles waiting to cross into the U.S., would let us under her roof during a monsoon, or to escape the beat of the summer sun, and we would drink a soda or eat seeds and watch the strange play in the wide arroyo below. The borderfence was sturdy as far west as I could see, rising and dipping sinusoidally to the sunset, but against the bank where the Mariposa border crossing stands, and the tail of US I-19 becomes the mouth of Carretera Federal 19, there was a gaping hole in the border. The American Recovery and Reinvestment Act, the "stimulus package" of 2009, awarded Arizona 213 million dollars to make the Mariposa entry port "an object of national envy," and yet down in the ditch there was an obvious, lazy, yawning hole in the fence through which passed goats, dogs, and Mexicans (McCombs).

Everyday, from inside or next to Graciela's hut, we would watch migrants ducking over into *el otro lado*. And, on the other side, there was inevitably a Border Patrol truck, or two, waiting for them. The migrants would either jump and sprint, or bellycrawl and hide among the bushes and cacti, depending on weather[*], time of day, and if they were going solo or were being guided by a coyote and a lookout (usually a young man communicating to the coyote with a walkie-talkie cellphone). From where I sat, with the other volunteers, palateros, migrants, or coyotes, we would watch this demonic cat and mouse game, cheering or cringing as if it were a sporting event, spitting our seeds. But to the men and women bellycrawling under and around the snakes and razorwire, it was not a

---

[*]Especially during the summer monsoons, migrants took advantage of Border Patrol agents reluctance to get wet, and would, usually successfully, just jump and sprint. On a rainy day sometimes I would see migrants walking simply, indiscreetly, across the border.

game. Many of them had spent or lost their life-savings to reach that point, and were within moments of arrest and deportation. Many of them had families, husbands, wives, children and parents who depended on them and were struggling to survive. That the United States can spend 213 million dollars to renovate a bordergate, or fly drone aircraft over the borderlands, or subcontract Boeing for billions to build infrared virtual fence technology, and still neglect to fix a hole in a fence that I could patch in an hour after a trip to Home Depot, seems a sad metaphor for the absurdity of over-militarizing and overfunding a hole-riddled borderfence when the problem is perpetuated and double-downed by increasingly neoliberal political agreements by the national governments and the de facto draw of open and paying jobs in the U.S.. The border is much more than a single, ineffective wall, and yet the government insists on cementing the façade, on "sticking to its guns," which, sadly, seems the most apt metaphor. It is an example of how a faceless bureaucratic system can palpably impact and deface an individual: the rights and dignity of individual men and women trounced by a blind and insensitive economic machine. 213 million dollars and a hole in the fence. It is reminiscent of the oxymoronic employment of illegal migrants to renovate the borderfence in San Diego, for which a Californian fence-building firm paid 5 million dollars in fines in 2006 (Horsley).

The passing of the IRCA (Immigration Reform and Control Act) in 1986, which both granted amnesty and further tightened security, was another of the many confounding miscalculations which complicated rather than solved the "problem" of migration. The IRCA legalized 2.3 million migrants, and yet, the increased militarization along the border further marginalized and endangered the migrants who were drawn by both jobs and the promise of legalization. Though in 1994 the North American Free Trade Agreement (NAFTA), along similar ideological lines, opened gates to free trade, it slammed doors on the free movement of labor, and wrought nearly irrevocable havoc on the Mexican economy. Eula Biss notes in *A Letter to Mexico*, that NAFTA "in effect eroded many of the rights and protections provided by the Mexican constitution." The agricultural economy was where NAFTA hit Mexico the hardest: the price of tortillas doubled in the 1990s, "small farmers found it impossible to sell corn," and WalMart soon became Mexico's largest retailer (Bacon 6). In 1995, only a year after NAFTA, in a land long fed by corn, because of the abolishment of subsidizations for small farmers and the undercutting of price supports (in effect NAFTA outlawed the government from favoring the small farmer over the larger foreign corporation) Mexico became reliant for the first time on corn imported from the United States (Bacon 5). In the same year, as Biss also remarks, because of the international corporitization of Southern-Mexican farms, one million farmworkers lost their jobs (Chacon 121). That's about twice the population of Tucson, suddenly jobless, in a single year. As Immigration Reform is again pending, it seems absurd that none of the proposed legislation even touches on NAFTA, on the root cause of the problem, on the policy which, as Charles Bowden put it, has "launched [the] largest migration on earth."

These equivocations and political deflections underline how "U.S. policy toward Mexico is inherently self-contradictory, simultaneously promoting integration while insisting on separation" (Massey 83). The conflicting messages define and redefine migrants through a complex juridical gauntlet. The insistence on illegalizing a person, as Foucault argues, "is not intended to eliminate offences, but rather to distinguish them, to distribute them, to use them" (272). The question is to what ends– to "use them," or to "distinguish them," for what? The answer is clear: the sustained force of cheap illegal labor has been in place for almost a century. Over the last century the U.S. legal system has "persistently sought ways of accepting Mexicans as workers while limiting their claims as human beings" (Massey 105). There is no doubt that immigrant labor is a necessary component of the U.S. economic machine, that U.S. corporations want and need cheap immigrant labor. Steve Strifler poignantly exemplifies (and it's worth quoting in full) this fact in his book *Chicken, The Dangerous Transformation of America's Food*:

> The Justice Department claimed that fifteen Tyson Foods plants in nine states had conspired since 1994 to smuggle illegal immigrants across the Mexican border and set them up with counterfeit papers. According to the indictment, the hiring of illegal alien workers was condoned at the highest levels of management to meet production goals, cut costs, and maximize profits. Undocumented workers were preferred because their fear of deportation meant they would accept working conditions that U.S. employees would not. They would tolerate faster line speeds, take fewer bathroom breaks, and complain less to managers or government officials. They were also less likely to file workers' compensation claims or be absent from work. Fear of deportation produced the ideal worker. This sentiment is hardly unique to poultry. A supervisor at a meatpacking plant explained: "I don't want them after they've been here for a year and know how to get around. I want them right off the bus" (98).

It is clear, in this case and generally, that Mexican migrants, though turned away from the border by militarization and strict immigration laws, are also drawn across the border by economic policies, especially since the passage of NAFTA*. Since the annexation of Mexican land more than a hundred and fifty years ago, "it is not an exaggeration to suggest that the U.S. "standard of living" depends fundamentally on the existence of this low wage, migrant labor pool" (Chomsky Nogales 3) And today, as Aviva Chomsky continues, "Not a single U.S. citizen can go through a day without using or consuming the products of Mexican workers" (Nogales 3).

To understand the border between two countries is to understand much more than a physical wall. As Nick Megoran writes, in analyzing the political dispute at the Uzbekistan-Krygyzstan border, "the state border, although physically at the

---

*In 2008, the U.S. imported 234 billion dollars of goods from Mexico and exported 151 billion dollars of goods. –statistics from the State Department, http://www.state.gov/ r/pa/ei/bgn/35749.htm

extremities of the polity, can be at the heart of nationalist discourse about the meaning of the nation" (Megoran 44). If a border helps to define a people, how do we define a border? Sometimes, borders are not immediately recognizable. There are multiple borders in Tucson, Phoenix, and as Aisha Sloan elucidates, there are myriad borders in Los Angeles. There are borders within families, as Beth Alvarado describes the psychological, religious, national rift between sisters in *Emily's Exit*. There are borders between ways of talking and ways of thinking. And there are cultural borders which are formed, broken, and reformed, as, for example, the borders constructed for Muslims in France with the banning of the hijab, or in Switzerland with the recent banning of minarets. There is also a critical border in southern Mexico. While many Mexicans sacrifice to cross the border into the U.S., many Guatemalans, Hondurans and El Salvadorans sacrifice, pick up their lives and risk the same, or more, to cross into Mexico at its southern border.

When someone accuses you of "crossing the line," what line are they referring to, and who drew it?

The borders around the University of Arizona function, though on a much smaller and less consequential scale, to include and exclude types of people in a similar way that the U.S. Mexico border draws distinctions based on class and race. When someone "different-looking" than the typical student walks into the library, many act as if a border has been crossed. In the Police Beat in *The Daily Wildcat*, one often reads reports of suspicious characters, for which the police are called, that are described merely by appearance. One might argue that despite the fact that this is a partly (now less so) state-funded public university, dedicated to "serving the diverse citizens of Arizona and beyond," the University is for the students, and that a *non-student* does indeed cross the border when entering University grounds, but what if a student dressed like a homeless person? Would they, too, be crossing a line? Or what if a student wore a hijab? In Spring semester of 2010 a fellow student hung a confederate flag on a black female student's dorm room door. This gravely offensive, racist act, later investigated as a hate crime, attempted (and may even have succeeded) to draw a line, a line between white and black, a line that is crossed daily, and yet a line that is continually redrawn. The following relative silence and the lack of publicity that this act elicited is symptomatic of a disturbing apathy to a lingering racism. Consider how this prejudice, this exclusion, this line-drawing, whether on campus, in your neighborhood, or in your country, affects not only those excluded, but also those included. Consider how these "carceral archipelagos" are formed, and what it takes to form them, and what Tony can mean in Leslie Marmon Silko's, *Tony's Story*, when he says, "There's no place left to hide. It follows us everywhere." Eula Biss posits an abstract definition of a border: "the extreme limit of understanding." What are the implications of running up against the limits of understanding? Or how else can we define a border? How about: the extreme limit of compassion? Consider, for example, the shocking disparity between Miami, Florida, where an art museum is renovated for over 200 million dollars, and pre-quake Haiti, where in 2008 a neologism was coined–*asid batri*–which is used to refer to a hunger that feels like battery acid in the stomach* (Pogrebin). Or consider the ramshackle daily lives in "pig village" in the dumps of Tijuana which are within eyeshot of wealthy San Diego County. Or Ciudad Juarez, a city in atrophy, where there were 2,660 murders in 2009, one about every three hours consistently for an entire year, while El Paso snoozes a quick but dangerous swim across the river as one of the consistently safest cities in America†, and yet is one of the many U.S. cities consuming Mexican grown and trafficked drugs and which continues to help supply Mexico its firearms (*The Economist 34*). The American recession, as well, leaked directly into Ciudad Juarez, putting almost 80,000 young people (in a single city) out of work. The borderwall there is clearly a unidirectional membrane, prohibiting the passing of people and encouraging the free flow of capital.

    The point is not that the American political/economic machine is dependent on migrant labor and so should afford government services to these workers (though this seems only "fair"), for that idea relegates these people to a mechanism akin to a cog or a clutch in machinery, but rather, that there is an economically enforced subjugation imposed on actual persons, and we should promote and enact legislation for their rights not because of political-economical dependence or potential gain from them‡, but because they are *human beings*. The argument for human rights is falsely constructed if it is based on figures. It must, first, start with faces.

In the stories in this chapter there are walls between cultures, walls between the past and the present, and walls between the mythical and the real. Though a borderwall may be hard to define, it is imperative to consider how our borders also define us. Even if the trend continues that the hard walls between countries become more, especially economically, porous, as between the United States and Mexico, borderwalls are perhaps becoming more important to maintain some tangible and potentially exploitable other, more important as ideological frontiers that drive deep the division between first and third world persons.

A borderwall is a wound and a scar. It functions to define Mexico and the United States, yet it also serves to blur these distinctions. When Eula Biss crosses the border to Mexico, she is not only American, but, as she enters the bar in Las Salinas, she explains how her sense of identity is muddled: she becomes a gringa, she carries the weight of being an American that she didn't feel at home in San Diego. When a Mexican or a Honduran crosses over to the United States, is he or she still Mexican, or Honoduran? Maybe, but these migrants are also referred to by many other names,

---

*The Royal Carribean Cruise line resumed service to its Haitian resort in Labadee® (a private (and also trademarked) resort isolated from the rest of Haiti by a security fence), just five days after the earthquake on Jan. 12, 2010, where tourists were able to lounge on the beach with the famous "Labadoozie" cocktail (Stoll).

†According to the Houston Chronicle, (www.chron.com/disp/story/mpl/metropolitan/6162732.html), the murder rate of El Paso is less than one hundred times that of its sister city.

‡This the fact that "in an open letter 500 economists, including five Nobel Laureates, stated that "immigration is a gain for America and its citizens and the greatest anti-poverty program ever devised" (Navarro 378).

such as: illegals, aliens, illegal aliens, undocumented entrants, undocumented aliens (UDAs), alambristas (fence-climbers), braceros, entrants, refugees, illegal asylum seekers, mojados (wets in Spanish, in reference to crossing rivers to enter the U.S.), and, in common Border Patrol parlance, wets, wetbacks, tonks (in reference to the sound a flashlight makes when hit against a head), boys, bodies, quitters, and even, roadkill. These many names for someone who crosses a border are indicative of the insurmountable disconnect between national policy and an individual's struggle for dignity and survival. I do not suggest that a government supposedly representing a diverse 300-plus million people take into account each person, which under an enormous, representative "democracy" would be impossible, but that a national government should create and push policy towards protecting and securing individual liberty, rather than simply defining (illegal) and discarding.

There are debates all across the world as how to designate, include and exclude migrants. The word *alien* may be dehumanizing, but it is the legal standard. The word *illegal* may commonly imply a violent criminal, but would it be accurate to call an undocumented entrant (another unwieldy term) *legal*? How do these appellations shape and sway debates over immigration?

It was estimated in 2005 that there were 193 million migrants in the world and 38 million foreign born persons in the United States (Samers 21). There is not an easy solution to the economical conundrum of immigration. I find, though, that in current and currently proposed legislation, almost all of the arguments for immigration reform are economically structured, as if iron ore or cattle were being negotiated. Let us not forget the human element. People are not fungible. Politicians are not playing carbon cap and trade, they are toying with the lives of actual persons. These debates and appellations directly affect millions of lives, and not just those leaving their homes in search of work or better living conditions, but also those living those sought-after, "better" lives, that is, those already in the glass houses, that is, you and me. The common argument that "we can't take care of everybody" is moot here, for it is they, the undocumented, who, in providing labor for cheap goods and services, are sustaining our lifestyles, who are already taking care of us.

I think of Ignacio, a 57-year-old man I met in Nogales last summer. He told me his story of trying to cross the desert to reunite with his daughters in Atlanta. He had worked for over twenty years in Atlanta as a cook and a maintenance man and then crossed back to Mexico to see his dying mother. Unable to find legal or safe means to return to his family and life in Atlanta, Ignacio crossed the border close to Altar, Sonora. He got lost in the desert, spent days wandering, following cows to water tanks, drinking dirty water ("era puro lodo," Ignacio said to me, which I wrote down in my notebook) succumbing to bouts of diarrhea, vomiting, delirium. On the verge of giving up for good, he came across volunteers putting water out in the desert. They gave him food and drink. They wanted to call the Border Patrol to take him to the hospital, but, energized by clean water and food, Ignacio refused. He knew that accepting treatment would also be accepting deportation. He knew it would be years again without seeing his family. Ignacio continued walking that day, but never made it to his destination. He got lost again and the Border Patrol arrested him a few days later. They gave him basic treatment and then deported him, without a dime in his pocket, to Nogales, a city he had never been to in his life. When I first saw him, he had two badly sprained and swollen ankles, and he was as weak as a child from the dehydration and utter exhaustion. He could barely walk. At first, he seemed barely able to raise his eyes to meet mine.

This is what it means for some people to cross a border.

Asking migrants why they cross the border, why they leave their homes and family, the answer is almost always, in some form or another, to survive, to give their children or their spouses or themselves a fighting chance. I think of the poem by Emma Lazarus, inscribed on the Statue of Liberty, and I think if there are any who are tired and poor (those who are walking in the Arizona deserts right now, as I write this, those who are hiding behind a bush or sleeping in the dirt next to a cactus, as you read this), if there are any who deserve a lamp to light their way, it is these persons, the migrants, these who are discriminated against, abused, oppressed, these who are marginalized and starved by economic policies and border militarization, it is these persons who deserve justice and a break. These persons, who lend helping hands to us in so many ways in our daily life, it is these persons who deserve a helping hand now, from us.

After the bloody conquest of the native people, America has always been, as people say, a nation of immigrants. How, then, do we justify still blazoning Emma Lazarus' poem as national standard on the emblematic statue of America, and yet so violently mistreat and discard migrants like Ignacio?

> Not like the brazen giant of Greek fame,
> With conquering limbs astride from land to land;
> Here at our sea-washed, sunset gates shall stand
> A mighty woman with a torch, whose flame
> Is the imprisoned lightning, and her name
> Mother of Exiles. From her beacon-hand
> Glows world-wide welcome; her mild eyes command
> The air-bridged harbor that twin cities frame.
> "Keep, ancient lands, your storied pomp!" cries she
> With silent lips. "Give me your tired, your poor,
> Your huddled masses yearning to breathe free,
> The wretched refuse of your teeming shore.
> Send these, the homeless, tempest-tossed to me,
> I lift my lamp beside the golden door!"

> —"The New Colossus," by Emma Lazarus,
> as inscribed on the pedestal of the Statue of Liberty.

Works Cited

abUSed: The Postville Raid. Dir. Luis Argueta. Vivian Rivas, 2010.

Annerino, John. *Dead in their Tracks: Crossing America's Desert Borderlands in the New Era.* Tucson: University of Arizona Press, 2009.

Bacon, David. *Uprooted and Criminalized: The Impact of Free Markets on Migrants.* The Oakland Institute. Fall, 2008.

Bowden, Charles. "Law Enforcement and Border Security within Mexico." *The Diane Rehm Show*. NPR. 24 Mar. 2010.

Chacon, Justin Akers and Mike Davis. *No One is Illegal: Fighting Racism and State Violence on the U.S.-Mexico Border*. Chicago: Haymarket Books, 2006.

Chomsky, Aviva. *"They Take Our Jobs" and 20 Other Myths about Migration*. Boston: Beacon Press, 2007.

Chomsky, Aviva. "Today's Deportees." forthcoming from *Race/Ethnicity: Multidisciplinary Global Contexts*.

The Economist. "A 'Dying' City Protests." 20 Feb. 2010: 34.

Foucault, Michel. *Discipline and Punish: The Birth of the Prison*. New York: Vintage Books, 1977.

Grant, Ulyyses S. *Personal Memoirs of U. S. Grant*: 18. *Gutenberg.org* Project Gutenberg, 2009. Web. 22 Mar. 2010.

Horsley, Scott. "Border Fence Firm Snared for Hiring Illegal Workers." NPR.org. *NPR*. 14 Dec. 2006.

Howard Fischer Capitol Media Services. "Bill: Make Schools Ask if Kids Are in US Illegally." *Arizona Daily Star*. 30 Mar. 2010.

Immigration Policy Center. *Breaking Down the Problems: What's Wrong with Our Immigration System*. October, 2009.

Jones, Reece. "The Border Enclaves of India and Bangladesh: The Forgotten Lands." *Borderlines and Borderlands*. Eds. Alexander C. Diener and Joshua Hagen. New York: Rowman and Littlefield Publishers, Inc., 2010. 15–33.

Koulish, Robert. *Immigration and American Democracy: Subverting the Rule of Law*. New York: Routledge, 2010.

Kristof, Ladis. "The Nature of Frontiers and Boundaries," *Annals of the Association of American Geographers* 49, no. 3 (1959):278.

Massey, Douglass, Jorge Durand, and Nolan Malone. *Beyond Smoke and Mirrors: Mexican Immigration in an Era of Economic Integration*. New York: Russell Sage Foundation, 2002.

McCombs, Brady. "4-yr Effort to Make Entry Port an Object of National Envy." *Arizona Daily Star*. 31 Jan. 2010.

McCombs, Brady. "213 Deaths in Arizona Alone." *Arizona Daily Star*. 27 Dec. 2009.

Megoran, Nick. *The Uzbekistan-Krygyzstan Boundary: Stalin's Cartography, Post-Soviet Geography*. *Borderlines and Borderlands*. Eds. Alexander C. Diener and Joshua Hagen. New York: Rowman and Littlefield Publishers, Inc., 2010. 33–53

Navarro, Armando. *The Immigration Crisis: Nativism, Armed Vigilantism, and the Rise of a Countervailing Movement*. New York: Altamira Press, 2009.

Nevins, Joseph. *Dying to Live: A Story of U.S. Immigration in an Age of Global Apartheid*. San Francisco: City Lights Books, 2008.

Pogrebin, Robin. "Exiting MOMO Curator Heads for Miami." *The New York Times.* 5 Jan. 2006.

Renan, Ernest. "What is a Nation?" from *The Nationalism Project.* Eric G.E. Zuelow, 2007. (http://www.nationalismproject.org/what/renan.htm)

Samers, Michael. *Migration.* New York: Routledge, 2010.

Schama, Simon. *A History of Britain: At the Edge of the World? 3000BC – AD1603* New York: Hyperion, 2000.

Stevens, Jacqueline. *States without Nations: Citizenship for Mortals.* New York: Columbia University Press, 2010.

Stoll, Steven. "Toward a Second Haitian Revolution." *Harper's Magazine.* Apr. 2010. 7.

Strifler, Steve. *Chicken: The Dangerous Transformation of America's Food.* New Haven: Yale University Press, 2005.

Torpey, John. *The Invention of the Passport: Surveillance, Citizenship and the State.* Cambridge: Cambridge University Press, 2000.

Gloria Anzaldúa

Gloria Anzaldúa self-identifies as a Tejana, Chicana, feminist, lesbian, poet. She is widely known through her contributions to the anthologies of writing by radical women of color This Bridge Called My Back *and* Haciendo Caras/Making Face, Making Soul. *Her own collection,* Borderlands/La Frontera: The New Mestiza, *is a groundbreaking collection of essays and poetry because it represents one of the first books of feminist writing that discusses feminism from a Chicana point of view.*

In the preface to that book, Anzaldúa states, "The psychological borderlands, the sexual borderlands and the spiritual borderlands are not particular to the Southwest. In fact the Borderlands are physically present wherever two or more cultures edge each other, where people of different races occupy the same territory, where under, lower, middle and upper classes touch, where the space between two individuals shrinks with intimacy." In the piece below, the first chapter of Borderlands/La Frontera, *Anzaldúa uses the concept of Aztlán, what is known as the mythical Chicano homeland that is traditionally situated in the Southwest, to describe her understanding of borders from the literal United States/Mexico border to ethnic and racial borders to intellectual borders.*

The Homeland, Aztlán/El Otro Mexico

> *El otro México que acá hemos construido*
> *el espacio es lo que ha sido*
> *territorio nacional.*
> *Es del esfuerzo de todos nuestros hermanos*
> *y latinoamericanos que han sabido*
> *progresar.*
> —Los Tigres del Norte[1]

"The *Aztecas del norte* . . . compose the largest single tribe or nation of Anishinabeg (Indians) found in the United States today. . . . Some call themselves Chicanos and see themselves as people whose true homeland is Aztlán [the U.S. Southwest]."[2]

Wind tugging at my sleeve
feet sinking into the sand
I stand at the edge where earth touches ocean
where the two overlap
a gentle coming together
at other times and places a violent clash.

Across the border in Mexico
    stark silhouette of houses gutted by waves,
        cliffs crumbling into the sea,
            silver waves marbled with spume
                gashing a hole under the border fence.
                    Miro el mar atacar
                la cerca en Border Field Park
            con sus buchones de agua,
an Easter Sunday resurrection
of the brown blood in my veins.

Oigo el llorido del mar, el respiro del aire,
    my heart surges to the beat of the sea.
        In the gray haze of the sun
            the gulls' shrill cry of hunger,
                the tangy smell of the sea seeping into me.

            I walk through the hole in the fence
                to the other side.
        Under my fingers I feel the gritty wire
            rusted by 139 years
                of the salty breath of the sea.

Beneath the iron sky
Mexican children kick their soccer ball across,
run after it, entering the U.S.

        I press my hand to the steel curtain—
chainlink fence crowned with rolled barbed wire—
rippling from the sea where Tijuana touches San Diego
    unrolling over mountains
            and plains
            and deserts,
this "Tortilla Curtain" turning into *el Río Grande*
        flowing down to the flatlands
            of the Magic Valley of South Texas
    its mouth emptying into the Gulf.

1,950 mile-long open wound
            dividing a *pueblo*, a culture,
            running down the length of my body,
               staking fence rods in my flesh,

splits me   splits me
me raja   me raja

This is my home
this thin edge of
barbwire.

But the skin of the earth is seamless.
The sea cannot be fenced,
el mar does not stop at borders
To show the white man what she thought of his
arrogance,
Yemaya blew that wire fence down.

This land was Mexican once,
was Indian always
and is.
And   will be again.

Yo soy un puente tendido
del mundo gabacho al del mojado.
lo pasado me estirá pa' 'trás
y lo presente pa' 'delante.
Que la Virgen de Guadalupe me cuide
Ay ay ay, soy mexicana de este lado.

The U.S.-Mexican border es una herida abierta where the Third World grates against the first and bleeds. And before a scab forms it hemorrhages again, the lifeblood of two worlds merging to form a third country—a border culture. Borders are set up to define the places that are safe and unsafe, to distinguish us from them. A border is a dividing line, a narrow strip along a steep edge. A borderland is a vague and undetermined place created by the emotional residue of an unnatural boundary. It is in a constant state of transition. The prohibited and forbidden are its inhabitants. Los atravesados live here: the squint-eyed, the perverse, the queer, the troublesome, the mongrel, the mulato, the half-breed, the half dead; in short, those who cross over, pass over, or go through the confines of the "normal." Gringos in the U.S. Southwest consider the inhabitants of the borderlands transgressors, aliens—whether they possess documents or not, whether they're Chicanos, Indians or Blacks. Do not enter, trespassers will be raped, maimed, strangled, gassed, shot. The only "legitimate" inhabitants are those in power, the whites and those who align themselves with whites. Tension grips the inhabitants of the borderlands like a virus. Ambivalance and unrest reside there and death is no stranger.

In the fields, *la migra.* My aunt saying, "*No corran,* don't run. They'll think you're *del otro lado.*" In the confusion, Pedro ran, terrified of being caught. He couldn't speak English, couldn't tell them he was fifth generation American. *Sin papeles*—he did not carry his birth certificate to work in the fields. *La migra* took him away while we watched. *Se lo llevaron.* He tried to smile when he looked back at us, to raise his fist. But I saw the shame pushing his head down, I saw the terrible weight of shame hunch his shoulders. They deported him to Guadalajara by plane. The furthest he'd ever been to Mexico was Reynosa, a small border town opposite Hidalgo, Texas, not far from McAllen. Pedro walked all the way to the Valley. *Se lo llevaron sin un centavo al pobre. Se vino andando desde Guadalajara.*

During the original peopling of the Americas, the first inhabitants migrated across the Bering Straits and walked south across the continent. The oldest evidence of humankind in the U.S.—the Chicanos' ancient Indian ancestry—was found in Texas and has been dated to 35,000 B.C.[3] In the Southwest United States archeologists have found 20,000-year-old campsites of the Indians who migrated through, or permanently occupied, the Southwest, Aztlán—land of the herons, land of whiteness, the Edenic place of origin of the Azteca.

In 1000 B.C., descendants of the original Cochise people migrated into what is now Mexico and Central America and became the direct ancestors of many of the Mexican people. (The Cochise culture of the Southwest is the parent culture of the Aztecs. The Uto-Aztecan languages stemmed from the language of the Cochise people.)[4] The Aztecs (the Nahuatl word for people of Aztlán) left the Southwest in 1168 A.D.

> Now let us go,
>   *Tihueque, tihueque,*
> Vámonos, vámonos.
>   *Un pájaro cantó.*
> *Con sus ocho tribus salieron*
>   *de la "cueva del origen."*
> *Los aztecas siguieron al dios*
>   *Huitzilopochtli.*

Huitzilopochtli, the God of War, guided them to the place (that later became Mexico City) where an eagle with a writhing serpent in its beak perched on a cactus. The eagle symbolizes the spirit (as the sun, the father); the serpent symbolizes the soul (as the earth, the mother). Together, they symbolize the struggle between the spiritual/celestial/male and the underworld/earth/feminine. The symbolic sacrifice of the serpent to the "higher" masculine powers indicates that the patriarchal order had already vanquished the feminine and matriarchal order in pre-Columbian America.

At the beginning of the 16th century, the Spaniards and Hernán Cortéz invaded Mexico and, with the help of tribes that the Aztecs had subjugated, conquered it. Before the Conquest, there were twenty-five million Indian people in Mexico and the Yucatán. Immediately after the Conquest, the Indian population had been reduced to under seven million. By 1650, only one-and-a-half-million pure-blooded Indians remained. The *mestizos* who were genetically equipped to survive small pox, measles, and typhus (Old World diseases to which the natives had no immunity), founded a new hybrid race and inherited Central and South America.[5] *En 1521 nació una nueva raza, el mestizo, el mexicano* (people of mixed Indian and Spanish blood), a race that had never existed before. Chicanos, Mexican-Americans, are the offspring of those first matings.

Our Spanish, Indian, and *mestizo* ancestors explored and settled parts of the U.S. Southwest as early as the sixteenth century. For every gold-hungry *conquistador* and soul-hungry missionary who came north from Mexico, ten to twenty Indians and *mestizos* went along as porters or in other capacities.[6] For the Indians, this constituted a return to the place of origin, Aztlán, thus making Chicanos originally and secondarily indigenous to the Southwest. Indians and *mestizos* from central Mexico intermarried with North American Indians. The continual intermarriage between Mexican and American Indians and Spaniards formed an even greater *mestizaje*.

EL DESTIERRO/THE LOST LAND

> *Entonces corre la sangre*
> *no sabe el indio que hacer,*
> *le van a quitar su tierra,*
> *la tiene que defender,*
> *el indio se cae muerto,*
> *y el afuerino de pie.*
> *Levántate, Manquilef.*
>
> *Arauco tiene una pena*
> *más negra que su chamal,*
> *ya no son los españoles*
> *los que les hacen llorar,*
> *hoy son los propios chilenos*
> *los que les quitan su pan.*
> *Levántate, Pailahuan.*
> —Violeta Parra,
>   *"Arauco tiene una pena"*[7]

In the 1800s, Anglos migrated illegally into Texas, which was then part of Mexico, in greater and greater numbers and gradually drove the *tejanos* (native Texans of Mexican descent) from their lands, committing all manner of atrocities against them. Their illegal invasion forced Mexico to fight a war to keep its Texas territory. The Battle of the Alamo, in which the Mexican forces vanquished the whites, became, for the whites, the symbol for the cowardly and villainous character of the Mexicans. It became (and still is) a symbol that legitimized the white imperialist takeover. With the capture of Santa Anna later in 1836, Texas became a republic. *Tejanos* lost their land and, overnight, became the foreigners.

> *Y la mitad del terreno*
> *les vendió el traidor Santa Anna,*
> *con lo que se ha hecho muy rica*
> *la nación americana.*

> *¿Qué acaso no se conforman*
> *con el oro de las minas?*
> *Ustedes muy elegantes*
> *y aquí nosotros en ruinas.*
> *—from the Mexican corrido,*
> *"Del peligro de la Intervención"*[8]

In 1846, the U.S. incited Mexico to war. U.S. troops invaded and occupied Mexico, forcing her to give up almost half of her nation, what is now Texas, New Mexico, Arizona, Colorado and California.

With the victory of the U.S. forces over the Mexican in the U.S.-Mexican War, *los norteamericanos* pushed the Texas border down 100 miles from *el Río Nueces* to *el Río Grande*. South Texas ceased to be part of the Mexican state of Tamaulipas. Separated from Mexico, the Native Mexican-Texan no longer looked toward Mexico as home; the Southwest became our homeland once more. The border fence that divides the Mexican people was born on February 2, 1848 with the signing of the Treaty of Guadalupe Hidalgo. It left 100,000 Mexican citizens on this side, annexed by conquest along with the land. The land established by the treaty as belonging to Mexicans was soon swindled away from its owners. The treaty was never honored and restitution, to this day, has never been made.

> The justice and benevolence of God
> will forbid that . . . Texas should again
> become a howling wilderness
> trod only by savages, or . . . benighted
> by the ignorance and superstition,
> the anarchy and rapine of Mexican misrule
> The Anglo-American race are destined
> to be forever the proprietors of
> this land of promise and fulfillment.
> Their laws will govern it,
> their learning will enlighten it,
> their enterprise will improve it.
> Their flocks range its boundless pastures,
> for them its fertile lands will yield . . .
> luxuriant harvests. . . .
> The wilderness of Texas has been redeemed
> by Anglo-American blood & enterprise.
> —William H. Wharton[9]

The Gringo, locked into the fiction of white superiority, seized complete political power, stripping Indians and Mexicans of their land while their feet were still rooted in it. *Con el destierro y el exilo fuimos desuñados, destroncados, destripados*—we were jerked out by the roots, truncated, disemboweled, dispossessed, and separated from our identity and our history. Many, under the threat of Anglo terrorism, abandoned homes and ranches and went to Mexico. Some stayed and protested. But as the courts, law enforcement officials, and government officials not only ignored their pleas but penalized them for their efforts, *tejanos* had no other resource but armed retaliation.

After Mexican-American resisters robbed a train in Brownsville, Texas on October 18, 1915, Anglo vigilante groups began lynching Chicanos. Texas Rangers would take them into the brush and shoot them. One hundred Chicanos were killed in a matter of months, whole families lynched. Seven thousand fled to Mexico, leaving their small ranches and farms. The Anglos, afraid that the *mexicanos*[10] would seek independence from the U.S., brought in 20,000 army troops to put an end to the social protest movement in South Texas. Race hatred had finally fomented into an all out war.[11]

My grandmother lost all her cattle,
they stole her land.

"Drought hit South Texas," my mother tells me. "*La tierra se puso bien seca y los animales comenzaron a morirse de se'. Mí papá se murió de un* heart attack *dejando a mamá* pregnant *y con ocho huercos*, with eight kids and one on the way. *Yo fui la mayor, tenía diez años.* The next year the drought continued *y el ganado* got hoof and mouth. *Se cayeron* in droves *en las pastas y el* brushland, *panzas blancas* ballooning to the skies. *El siguiente año* still no rain. *Mi pobre madre viuda perdió* two-thirds of her *ganado*. A smart *gabacho* lawyer took the land away *mamá* hadn't paid taxes. *No hablaba inglés*, she didn't know how to ask for time to raise the money." My father's mother, Mama Locha, also lost her *terreno*. For a while we got $12.50 a year for the "mineral rights" of six acres of cemetery, all that was left of the ancestral lands. Mama Locha had asked that we bury her there beside her husband. *El cementerio estaba cercado.* But there was a fence around the cemetery, chained and padlocked by the ranch owners of the surrounding land. We couldn't even get in to visit the graves, much less bury her there. Today, it is still padlocked. The sign reads: "Keep out. Trespassers will be shot."

In the 1930s, after Anglo agribusiness corporations cheated the small Chicano landowners of their land, the corporations hired gangs of *mexicanos* to pull out the brush, chaparral and cactus and to irrigate the desert. The land they toiled over had once belonged to many of them, or had been used communally by them. Later the Anglos brought in huge machines and root plows and had the Mexicans scrape the land clean of natural vegetation. In my childhood I saw the end of dryland farming. I witnessed the land cleared; saw the huge pipes connected to underwater sources sticking up in the air.

As children, we'd go fishing in some of those canals when they were full and hunt for snakes in them when they were dry. In the 1950s I saw the land, cut up into thousands of neat rectangles and squares, constantly being irrigated. In the 340-day growth season, the seeds of any kind of fruit or vegetable had only to be stuck in the ground in order to grow. More big land corporations came in and bought up the remaining land.

To make a living my father became a sharecropper. Rio Farms Incorporated loaned him seed money and living expenses. At harvest time, my father repaid the loan and forked over 40% of the earnings. Sometimes we earned less than we owed, but always the corporations fared well. Some had major holdings in vegetable trucking, livestock auctions and cotton gins. Altogether we lived on three successive Rio farms; the second was adjacent to the King Ranch and included a dairy farm; the third was a chicken farm. I remember the white feathers of three thousand Leghorn chickens blanketing the land for acres around. My sister, mother and I cleaned, weighed and packaged eggs. (For years afterwards I couldn't stomach the sight of an egg.) I remember my mother attending some of the meetings sponsored by well-meaning whites from Rio Farms. They talked about good nutrition, health, and held huge barbeques. The only thing salvaged for my family from those years are modern techniques of food canning and a food-stained book they printed made up of recipes from Rio Farms' Mexican women. How proud my mother was to have her recipe for *enchiladas coloradas* in a book.

EL CRUZAR DEL MOJADO/ILLEGAL CROSSING

> *"Ahora sí ya tengo una tumba para llorar,"*
> *dice Conchita,* upon being reunited with
> her unknown mother just before the mother dies
> —from Ismael Rodríguez' film,
> *Nosotros los pobres*[12]

La crisis. Los gringos had not stopped at the border. By the end of the nineteenth century, powerful landowners in Mexico, in partnership with U.S. colonizing companies, had dispossessed millions of Indians of their lands. Currently, Mexico and her eighty million citizens are almost completely dependent on the U.S. market. The Mexican government and wealthy growers are in partnership with such American conglomerates as American Motors, IT&T and Du Pont which own factories called *maquiladoras*. One-fourth of all Mexicans work at *maquiladoras*: most are young women. Next to oil, *maquiladoras* are Mexico's second greatest source of U.S. dollars. Working eight to twelve hours a day to wire in backup lights of U.S. autos or solder miniscule wires in TV sets is not the Mexican way. While the women are in the *maquiladoras*, the children are left on their own. Many roam the street, become part of *cholo* gangs. The infusion of the values of the white culture, coupled with the exploitation by that culture, is changing the Mexican way of life.

The devaluation of the *peso* and Mexico's dependency on the U.S. have brought on what the Mexicans call *la crisis. No hay trabajo.* Half of the Mexican people are unemployed. In the U.S. a man or woman can make eight times what they can in Mexico. By March, 1987, 1,088 pesos were worth one U.S. dollar. I remember when I was growing up in Texas how we'd cross the border at Reynosa or Progreso to buy sugar or medicines when the dollar was worth eight *pesos* and fifty *centavos*.

La travesía. For many *mexicanos del otro lado*, the choice to stay in Mexico and starve or move north and live. *Dicen que cada mexicano siempre sueña de la conquista en los brazos de cuatro gringas rubias, la conquista del país poderoso del norte, los Estados Unidos. En cada Chicano y mexicano vive el mito del tesoro territorial perdido.* North Americans call this return to the homeland the silent invasion.

> *"A la cueva volverán"*
> —El Puma *en la canción "Amalia"*

South of the border, called North America's rubbish dump by Chicanos, *mexicanos* congregate in the plazas to talk about the best way to cross. Smugglers, *coyotes, pasadores, enganchadores* approach these people or are sought out by them. *"¿Qué dicen muchachos a echársela de mojado?"*

> "Now among the alien gods with
> weapons of magic am I."
> —Navajo protection song,
> sung when going into battle.[13]

We have a tradition of migration, a tradition of long walks. Today we are witnessing *la migración de los pueblos mexicanos,* the return odyssey to the historical/mythological Aztlán. This time, the traffic is from south to north.

El retorno to the promised land first began with the Indians from the interior of Mexico and the *mestizos* that came with the *conquistadores* in the 1500s. Immigration continued in the next three centuries, and, in this century, it continued with the *braceros* who helped to build our railroads and who picked our fruit. Today thousands of Mexicans are crossing the border legally and illegally; ten million people without documents have returned to the Southwest.

Faceless, nameless, invisible, taunted with "Hey cucaracho" (cockroach). Trembling with fear, yet filled with courage, a courage born of desperation. Barefoot and uneducated, Mexicans with hands like boot soles gather at night by the river where two worlds merge creating what Reagan calls a frontline, a war zone. The convergence has created a shock culture, a border culture, a third country, a closed country.

Without benefit of bridges, the *"mojados"* (wetbacks) float on inflatable rafts across *el Río Grande,* or wade or swim across naked, clutching their clothes over their heads. Holding onto the grass, they pull themselves along the banks with a prayer to *Virgen de Guadalupe* on their lips: *Ay virgencita morena, mi madrecita, dame tu bendición.*

The Border Patrol hides behind the local McDonalds on the outskirts of Brownsville, Texas or some other border town. They set traps around the river beds beneath the bridge.[14] Hunters in army-green uniforms stalk and track these economic refugees by the powerful nightvision of electronic sensing devices planted in the ground or mounted on Border Patrol vans. Cornered by flashlights, frisked while their arms stretch over their heads, *los mojados* are handcuffed, locked in jeeps, and then kicked back across the border.

One out of every three is caught. Some return to enact their rite of passage as many as three times a day. Some of those who make it across undetected fall prey to Mexican robbers such as those in Smugglers' Canyon on the American side of the border near Tijuana. As refugees in a homeland that does not want them, many find a welcome hand holding out only suffering, pain, and ignoble death.

Those who make it past the checking points of the Border Patrol find themselves in the midst of 150 years of racism in Chicano *barrios* in the Southwest and in big northern cities. Living in a no-man's-borderland, caught between being treated as criminals and being able to eat, between resistance and deportation, the illegal refugees are some of the poorest and the most exploited of any people in the U.S. It is illegal for Mexicans to work without green cards. But big farming combines, farm bosses and smugglers who bring them in make money off the "wetbacks"' labor—they don't have to pay federal minimum wages, or ensure adequate housing or sanitary conditions.

The Mexican woman is especially at risk. Often the *coyote* (smuggler) doesn't feed her for days or let her go to the bathroom. Often he rapes her or sells her into prostitution. She cannot call on county or state health or economic resources because she doesn't know English and she fears deportation. American employers are quick to take advantage of her helplessness. She can't go home. She's sold her house, her furniture, borrowed from friends in order to pay the *coyote* who charges her four or five thousand dollars to smuggle her to Chicago. She may work as a live-in maid for white, Chicano or Latino households for as little as $15 a week. Or work in the garment industry, do hotel work. Isolated and worried about her family back home, afraid of getting caught and deported, living with as many as fifteen people in one room, the *mexicana* suffers serious health problems. *Se enferma de los nervios, de alta presión.*[15]

La mojada, la mujer indocumentada, is doubly threatened in this country. Not only does she have to contend with sexual violence, but like all women, she is prey to a sense of physical helplessness. As a refugee, she leaves the familiar and safe homeground to venture into unknown and possibly dangerous terrain.

> This is her home
> this thin edge of
> barbwire.

Notes

1. Los Tigres del Norte is a *conjunto* band.
2. Jack D. Forbes, *Aztecas del Norte: The Chicanos of Aztlán.* (Greenwich, CT: Fawcett Publications, Premier Books, 1973), 13, 183; Eric R. Wolf, *Sons of Shaking Earth* (Chicago, IL: University of Chicago Press, Phoenix books, 1959), 32.
3. John R. Chávez, *The Lost Land: The Chicano Images of the Southwest* (Albuquerque, NM: University of New Mexico Press, 1984), 9.
4. Chávez, 9. Besides the Aztecs, the Ute, Gabrillino of California, Pima of Arizona, some Pueblo of New Mexico, Comanche of Texas, Opata of Sonora, Tarahumara of Sinaloa and Durango, and the Huichol of Jalisco speak Uto-Aztecan languages and are descended from the Cochise people.

5. Reay Tannahill, *Sex In History* (Briarcliff Manor, NY: Stein and Day/Publishers/ Scarborough House, 1980), 308.

6. Chávez, 21.

7. Isabel Parra, *El Libro Mayor de Violeta Parra* (Madrid, España: Ediciones Michay, S.A., 1985), 156–7.

8. From the Mexican *corrido*, *"Del peligro de la intervención,"* Vicente T. Mendoza, *El Corrido Mexicano* (México. D.F.: Fondo De Cultura Económica, 1954), 42.

9. Arnoldo De León, *They Called Them Greasers: Anglo Attitudes Toward Mexicans in Texas, 1821–1900* (Austin, TX: University of Texas Press, 1983), 2–3.

10. The Plan of San Diego, Texas, drawn up on January 6, 1915, called for the independence and segregation of the states bordering Mexico: Texas, New Mexico, Arizona, Colorado, and California. Indians would get their land back, Blacks would get six states from the south and form their own independent republic. Chávez, 79.

11. Jesús Mena, "Violence in the Rio Grande Valley," *Nuestro* (Jan./Feb. 1983), 41–42.

12. *Nosotros los pobres* was the first Mexican film that was truly Mexican and not an imitation European film. It stressed the devotion and love that children should have for their mother and how its lack would lead to the dissipation of their character. This film spawned a generation of mother-devotion/ ungrateful-sons films.

13. From the Navajo "Protection Song" (to be sung upon going into battle). George W. Gronyn, ed., *American Indian Poetry: The Standard Anthology of Songs and Chants* (New York, NY: Liveright, 1934), 97.

14. Grace Halsell, *Los ilegales,* trans. Mayo Antonio Sánchez (Editorial Diana Mexica, 1979).

15. Margarita B. Melville, "Mexican Women Adapt to Migration," *International Migration Review,* 1978.

Kimi Eisele

Kimi Eisele is a Tucson resident who received her Master of Arts in Geography at the University of Arizona where she also founded You Are Here: The Journal of Creative Geography. *This essay, "The Space in Between" is based on her master's degree project in which she held geography and art workshops with children in Nogales, Sonora in order to understand how they viewed their place in the world. Over a period of a year, she worked most extensively with about fifteen children, ages 8–12, from nine families. The Arizona-Sonora Desert Museum's "Sense of Place Project" funded her work. Eisele has written several essays on her experiences with the children in Nogales, Sonora and on the environmental issues their community faces. One of them, "The Other Side of the Wires," documents the health problems that can result from contaminated water. It was published in* Orion *magazine in Spring 2000; this essay was published in* Fourth Genre.

The Space in Between

Always it began with the drive down Highway 19, not a particularly exciting stretch of highway, but an access road of sorts, a gateway. I'd pass the Duvall copper mine to the west, blue and glowing; the spiky Santa Rita Mountains to the east; the senior citizen sprawl of Green Valley on both sides. The speeding and swerving shuttle vans from Phoenix would invariably pass me in my clunky truck.

The only peculiar thing about this highway was where it ended—at the southern edge of the United States. It steered me into Nogales, Arizona, pushed me under an overpass, and spilled me into Mexico. There, I'd feel either pleasantly received or violently accosted. This, I suppose, is the mercurial nature of borders.

If it was still early in the morning, the city cool and just waking up, I felt at ease. The foreignness was a rush. Suddenly I was in another language, and it changed everything. The movement was what I liked—a man towed a burro across the street, hunched *doñas* carried baskets of tortillas, old men stood eating stew on the corner. This was a part of the West that had not been paved over by wide slabs of asphalt. In some places, it wasn't paved at all. People did not hide inside homes. On the street, I could hear the tapping of women's feet on the pavement, the shouts of boys on their way to school, the trilling exchanges between mothers and babes.

But if it was hot, late, and I was in a hurry, the motion was what I most disliked. Buses pulled out in front of me. Potholes in the road compressed my spine. I swerved to miss mangy dogs. Everyone honked. Too often I smelled the sour stench of rotting fruit and sewage. I felt like a warrior on a mission to get through town. I could not fully enter the language, and my tongue stumbled.

Then there was the space in between. A friend in Tucson finally installed a new horn in the truck in an ingeniously Mexican style—I had to keep my eyes on the road and reach for a large white plastic button under the dash. Still, I was deeply satisfied with making my own noise and used little discretion. With the radio tuned to loud, bouncy *Norteño* music, I stared back at people. I gained full control of Spanish, and in it, I cursed eloquently. I relished the chaos.

I drove this stretch of highway into the city of Nogales, Sonora, mostly because I had to cross a line to get there. With this, there was an instinctual and endless fascination. And also, of course, a certain sort of privilege.

The trips I made were regular visits to a community called Colonia Solidaridad on the outskirts of the burgeoning Mexican border city of Nogales. There, I gathered together a group of children to find out what it meant to grow up right next to the world's most powerful country, my own. Over the course of several months, I asked children to describe to me, in words, drawings, and photographs, where they lived.

I picked the place because it was close and because it seemed an appropriate vantage point from which to understand something about the impacts of global economic change on Mexico in general and on its young people in particular. Since 1964, when the Mexican government lured foreign-owned assembly plants known as *maquiladoras* to its northern border through tax-incentives, people had left an ailing countryside and flocked to the border in search of more permanent work. And not just in the factories, but also as hot dog salesmen, chauffeurs, homebuilders, waiters, seamstresses, hairstylists, photographers, or merchants in the tourist district. Decades later the city still struggled to keep up. In Nogales, as in other border cities, houses of cardboard, shipping pallets, and aluminum are tacked together almost overnight. Solidaridad represents a fairly typical self-help neighborhood on the border. Today, over half of the houses there still do not have running water or plumbing. Water is delivered by a truck and poured into metal drums supplied by the factories. Garbage collection is sporadic at best, and when it rains, the refuse flows in rivers down gravel streets. Walls made of stacked tires hold up the hillsides.

Before I began to cross the border regularly, I heard stories about it. Some I read in the newspapers, some I watched on the local nightly news, some I heard on the streets. Most of these stories were about desperate souls who'd do anything to get north. There were the eight migrants who drowned in a drainage ditch, the seventeen who suffocated in an airless van en route to Phoenix, and the countless dry and desiccated bodies that end up in the deserts of the American Southwest.

I traveled to Solidaridad because I wanted to understand the other side of things in as many ways as possible. I wanted to revision the border, to understand what the line really separated. How does it define difference? What limits does it place on those who cannot cross it easily? On those who can? What would the present life of children reveal about the future of the border? How far north would children's imaginations wander? How far would my own imagination wander? These were the nagging questions. To answer them, I crossed again and again. Eventually, in the crossing, I learned to invert the world, to rearrange north and south.

Late one morning, after a walk through the neighborhood, twelve children didn't want to go home yet. We sat in the fifth-grade classroom, the one room I had been given the key to, a dim concrete room that often smelled of petrol, and told stories.

Suzi, at twelve, was the oldest of the group. She was tall with dark round eyes and a leftover scar from a cleft palate. Her hair, long and shiny and black, stood straight up in the front. I had seen her shower her entire head with hair spray. She wore mini-skirts and thick-soled shoes and liked to paint her nails sky blue.

"I know a story but I don't know where it's from," she said. "There once was a little girl whose mother told her to pay attention when she was speaking to her. The mother said, 'I don't know what's wrong with you. If you don't pay attention to me, the devil will get you and turn you to stone.' And the bad little girl didn't pay attention, so the devil grabbed her, and they say that he turned her to stone and that now every night, she opens one eye and lets out la Llorona."

"La Llorona!" Maria Fernanda said. "I know that story."

"So do I!" said Grillo, Suzi's eight-year-old brother.

I knew the story too. La Llorona—the woman who weeps. It's like a Grimm's fairy tale, a bit twisted, and everyone knows it. The versions of La Llorona are all slightly different, but at base, it's the story of a woman who long ago drowned her own children in a river. Now the woman wanders the banks of rivers everywhere, looking for her children, wailing.

"Any stories about the *border*?" I asked again.

Yesenia chimed in with a story about a man named Nahuatl. "He was a drunk and a wanderer and his mother said, 'You will travel the world for all your life.' They say that the devil told him if he didn't change when he was little, he would be cursed for his whole life. And I've seen him. My mother said he's not bad, he takes care of children, he's just cursed."

The children told tale after tale like these, never really answering my question. None mentioned anything about an uncle who headed for *"el Norte"* in the dead of night with only the clothes on his back. None spoke of treacherous river cross-ings. Of falsified passports, crooked *coyotes,* or flashflood drownings in storm drains—the kind of border stories I'd heard before, the kind I expected them to have heard too.

The tales they told were all of mother's curses and devils. Didactic stories, they scared children into paying attention and following orders. They modeled correct behavior, the way to find your right position in relation to others. They reminded me of fables and ghost stories. They were not about the border at all. It might as well not have existed.

One day Yesenia looked at me and said, "I thought Americans were bad until I met you." Then she cited the battle of Santa Anna, the Treaty of Guadalupe Hidalgo, and La Mesilla (the Gadsden Purchase), three events that in the 19th century significantly shrunk the territory of Mexico.

The teaching of history engenders nationalism, and the children in Solidaridad seemed full of it. On the fifth of May, the day that commemorates the 1862 Battle of Puebla when Mexico thwarted France's attempt to install a monarch, several children marched in the city parade. Both Yesenia and Blanca walked down the main street through town in their school uniforms. Amidst the crowd of people watching that day were many who visited parents, aunts and uncles, children, siblings, and spouses in the United States. Some of those watching could slip effortlessly between Spanish and English with perfectly trilled r's and hardened d's. Many bought sneakers, chicken, plastic dishes, and underwear regularly in Nogales, Arizona. Even more knew how to say "Hello" and "How much?" and sing the lyrics to "Hotel California."

The director of Solidaridad's school, Antonio Arán, told me that children are not taught much about the international border in the classroom. "The line marks the line of our work," he said. "We focus mostly on our own history. They don't know much about the United States, and there, you don't know much about us. That seems obvious because that line divides us for so many kilometers."

Almost 2,000 miles long, the border between Mexico and the United States stretches from the Gulf of Mexico to the Pacific, from eastern Texas and Tamaulipas to western California and Baja. Nogales, Sonora and its twin city, Nogales, Arizona, were officially founded in 1882 when the railroad from Guaymas met the line from Kansas City. Since then, goods and people have moved with varying degrees of ease across the border. In the 1920s, Prohibition and antigambling laws in the United States sent Americans on brief visits to the Mexican side where they could get their fill of alcohol, games, and women. Since then, tourism has been one of the economic mainstays of Mexico's northern frontier.

Despite a few setbacks brought about by economic hardships and recessions over the years, the Nogales tourist strip today still thrives. When I walked through it vendors persistently tried to sell me gold chains, cigars, ceramic suns, rugs, leather bags, baskets, tequila, fertility pills, and Viagra. Amidst the chaos, I spotted Nikes and Arizona license plates. I heard words in English.

In the 1980s, several journalists popularized the notion of the U.S.-Mexico border region as a "third country" between the two nations, a country with its own distinct culture. Perhaps, perhaps not—it depends on where you stand.

From the highest hill behind Solidaridad, I could look north to an American landscape. It was only American because I knew so. The mountains ahead were remarkably similar to those behind. If I descended the hill and wandered the streets of Solidaridad—where ramshackle houses were built and rebuilt daily, where tinny *Ranchera* music squeezed out of pocket radios, where on good days the smell of fresh tortillas swirled in the air—I was most certainly and fully in Mexico.

Figuring out what children in Solidaridad knew about the other side of the line, for me, bordered on an obsession. I finally got through, via television, to Lupita, a sharp 11-year-old girl with a propensity for asking questions repeatedly. "On TV, they say people in the United States are getting richer," she said.

"How do you imagine it there?" I asked.

"I imagine that it's a city with many buildings, that there's almost no garbage. And I imagine that there are only blondes. Well, some kids are the same as me."

Lupita told me she wanted to cross the border because of what they sell on the other side. "When I was very little we went, and there was a bicycle, very cheap, and my Papí said that someday he's going to buy it for me."

Nine-year-old Lucero also said she had seen the United States on television. "On TV, I have seen that they rob a lot, that there are a lot of *cholos*." Lucero had watched the home movies her aunt had brought from the U.S. side. "She videotapes when there is a party." Though it looks fun sometimes, Lucero said she would rather live in Nogales, Mexico. "There," she said, "there are no houses, only trailers."

The first time I asked Lucero's older sister Blanca what she imagined the other side is like, she gave me a blank stare. A moment later she looked up and said, "There's a pool."

Carmen, a mother of two, said, "[The other side] doesn't affect me at all. We don't go there."

"You've never wanted to go across to the other side""

"What you don't know, you don't want," Carmen said. Then she leaned over in her chair. "Is it true?" she whispered. "Is it true there are vampires there? On the other side?"

Sometimes on my way through town, I'd stop just south of the port of entry, in one of the tourist strip locales, a corner stall in an open-air market. There, the father of Josué, one of the kids I worked with, ran a small photography stand he inherited from his father. On Saturdays Josué and his three younger sisters sometimes assisted him.

On good days, Ricardo took as many as 40 photos a day of retirees, families, and fraternity boys who crossed the border for a day long "Mexican experience." In front of the camera, they'd don a sombrero and a colored shawl, some would mount María the burro and pose in front of a sanguine painting of the Mexican countryside titled with "Mexico 1999" or "2000" or "2001."

Josué had learned to say things in English like "Cahmon, meester," "Betty cheep" and "Tayka peecher!" Sometimes he got tips from the posers. He told me that someday he too wanted to be a photographer. With the camera I gave him, he took pictures of María the burro, the green hills outside of the neighborhood, and the inside of his house.

Josué's house was bigger and sturdier than other houses in Solidaridad. Built on two lots, it had cement walls, a full roof, glass windows, and steel doors. Inside were a cement floor, a living room, a kitchen, and a fully furnished separate bedroom, where the whole family slept. Sometimes, because of the extra space, I spent the night there on a spare sofa, which sagged, but gave me enough of a good night's sleep.

Josué's father told me his job was lucrative enough to earn him three times what he'd make in the factories. During the months I spent with the family, he finished the roof, purchased a new double bed, and gave new bicycles to Josué and his two sisters for Christmas.

In the evenings I helped Ricardo's wife, Rosario, with dinner. In the dark kitchen, I learned to flatten balls of flour, water, and lard into tortillas. Habitually, I steered the conversation toward the other side. "There, people live better for the comforts they have," Rosario said. "I've never tried to explain [the differences] to [my children]. It all really depends on each person. If God wanted me to be Mexican, then that's why I am Mexican and my children are Mexican. Maybe if he didn't plan that, we wouldn't live so humbly. We're Mexicans whether the country is strong or failing, but we have to look for the way to move forward here."

Ricardo told me he had no intention of ever moving his family north across the border. "I wouldn't leave here to go struggle in the United States," he said. "I realize that most leave behind their own property, their own house; they go, supposedly to work, to progress, but I don't call that progress to go to the United States and begin to pay rent. For me, it would be like starting over. Because here in Mexico, thanks to God, there's a little hill and you climb it and make your house of wood, but it's your own—the land and the house. We struggle with little problems, but it's our own."

One morning I asked the children to draw maps of their world. Met with confused stares, I explained it over and over. "Here. The place where you live. Your neighborhood." Slowly, they caught on. I held up a variety of different maps and applauded each effort.

Eventually Josué made two maps. The first showed a bird's-eye view of the school grounds and the route to his house. With a pencil he drew a roller-coaster-like line then colored in brown the space below it—the steep, dusty hills he walks over to get home. In the second map, drawn more hastily, Josué recorded both his house and the school, along with the hills, María the burro's house, and this time the border itself—a thick pencil line at the top of the page.

Blanca drew an irregular triangle shape. She colored in a one-inch brown stripe at the top and filled the rest in with orange. In the center of the line dividing the two colors, she drew a small gray square. Above Mexico she wrote "Los Estados Unidos." Inside the gray square she wrote "Sonora," and placed a small dot, which she labeled "Nogales."

I was still marveling at Blanca's sense of space and scale two weeks later when she drew another map, almost identical. When I suggested adding more details, she drew in two squares, one on each side of the country. In each she wrote "La Ley," the name of a local super-store with two Nogales locations.

Yesenia made a detailed map of her street. Meticulously, she drew a row of houses and behind several of them included the walls of tires built to hold up the eroding hillsides. She colored the hills beyond the neighborhood green and decorated them with tiny flower stickers. Lucero rendered two houses, labeled them "My house" and "My Nana's house," and connected them with a thick road. Other children drew floor plans of the interior of their houses, mostly one-room sketches crammed with beds, chairs, a refrigerator, and always, a television. My favorite included a single light bulb dangling by a wire from the ceiling.

Of all the information these maps revealed, the border was conspicuously absent from all but two. Only Blanca and Josué drew lines to signify it, though neither rendered anything on the other side.

When I asked the children to draw their visions of utopia, the perfect place, they drew pictures of large sturdy houses, green fields, castles, sports complexes, and pools—landscapes of wealth they had seen on TV, perhaps, or right in Nogales, where on the west side of town a neighborhood of large bright houses along paved streets looms over the self-help colonias that circle the city. From what I could see, there was nothing unequivocally American in their pictures. But I knew that as always, our world is as big or as small as our experience. The children's lack of curiosity and conceptual understanding of the border was likely the result of their youth and limited knowledge. Few had traveled to the states and towns their parents left years ago. Few had traveled across the border north.

The repeated blank stares, the simple drawings, and the silent answers to my diligent questions, revealed that for now at least the border was less of a boundary in the children's geography as it was in my own.

In April, a department at the University of Arizona in Tucson organized a meeting on border health and environmental issues. Representatives from organizations on both sides of the border, all the way across it, would meet for a long weekend in Tijuana, Baja California, Mexico. I rallied funds together to take three girls with me to present the project. We would drive on the Mexican side, a ten-hour journey, because none had a passport.

Two months ahead of time I talked to their parents, explained the trip, hoped that they'd trust me. The morning of our departure, I arrived in a large, white university van. Yesenia told me right away that Blanca wasn't allowed to go. When I walked up the hill, Blanca stepped out of the house. She told me it was because she couldn't miss her catechism class. She kicked the ground and never looked me in the eye. Her parents didn't come out of the house.

While we waited for Karla, the immediate substitute, Lupita's mother told me that she trusted me fully, but that Blanca's parents feared I might steal the girls and take them across the border to sell. I had heard this before. For a time, a popular rumor in the borderlands and throughout Latin America told that Americans, women especially, kidnapped children, carried them north, and sold off their organs to keep white babies alive.

The words crawled into my gut and lodged themselves there. Was this for real? After months of activities with these children, lunches in their house, long conversations with their parents, had I not won any trust? Was I still the same light-haired, blue-eyed foreigner to them that I had been when I first arrived? I went outside to wait. Though I fought hard against them, the tears came in torrents.

In her book *Translated Woman*, American anthropologist Ruth Behar documents the life history of a sixty-year-old Mexican woman from a small village and reflects on her own position as the collector and translator of a story told by a woman of a different race, class, and social position as her own. Lamenting the fact that many people in Mexico assumed things about her that were not true, that she was there to exploit them for instance, Behar gets the "gringa blues." Though she knew it was impossible, she wanted to be disconnected from associations that invariably linked her to the *other* side of the border.

That morning, the gringa blues overwhelmed me. Feeling foolish and fragile, I fought the urge to get back in the van, drive home, and stay there forever. In the moment, I arrived at the horrible realization that no matter what I did, no matter how much I gave, no matter how patient I was, no matter how close I became to the children and their families, I would always be someone else from somewhere else. South of the border, this simple fact would forever slant both the way I saw and the way I was seen.

Despite its beginnings, the trip was a stunning success. In Tijuana, the girls presented their photographs and stories confidently. The accolades poured in. Although they attended some of the other sessions, the girls spent most of the time riding the elevators, watching *telenovelas,* and taking baths. Every time I entered their room, one of them was in the bathtub. It was a new and wonderful phenomenon—to turn a knob and have water pour endlessly out of the faucet.

For a time, I worried that the luxury of that hotel room would raise their expectations about material comforts and set them up for disappointment. But after four long days the girls were more than ready to go home. To that, I could relate.

For many weeks, I made a habit out of buying *bolillos,* knobs of fresh bread, before I crossed back into Arizona. From time to time, I thought to buy watermelon and mangos, too, but then I remembered I couldn't carry produce into the United States. This law, like many of them, was so bizarre I often forgot it was one.

Depending on the hour I left Sonora, I either had little time to think or I was forced to meditate for thirty minutes or more. More often it was the latter, as the queue was usually long. If I was lucky, women sold fresh green corn tamales there and I could buy a dozen for half of what I paid for them in Tucson. Otherwise, I cursed the length of the wait and how arbitrary this boundary could seem. A cruel trick of politics, it was both convenient and inconvenient. It was, as one writer put it, "a word game." I tried continuously to crack it.

Often a man wearing alligator-skin boots and an oversized cowboy hat wound his way in and out of the traffic twirling a lasso. There was something patient and talented about him, and I gave him coins off my dashboard. Women with Mayan faces paced back and forth, their arms struggling to not to drop their wares—large plastic Tweety Birds and oversized crucifixes. On these crosses, Jesus was hard and lean and muscular; squiggles of dark red paint trailed down his arms.

I said the same thing every time: children, colonia, research project. Sometimes the customs agents or immigration officers pretended to be interested. But I was just one of thousands. Sometimes they smacked my tires, sometimes the dog came, panting, to smell circles around the truck.

I crossed the line easily. Still, there was another kind of toll. On either side, I stumbled into a confusing blend of relief and anxiety. I expected this in crossing from the United States to Mexico, where I could feel nervous, uncomfortable, foreign. I was not supposed to feel this upon returning.

In 1939 Graham Greene wrote, "The border means more than a customs house, a passport officer, a man with a gun. Over there everything is going to be different; life is never going to be quite the same again. . . . The atmosphere of the border—it is like starting over again, there is something about it like a good confession: poised for a few happy moments between sin and sin."

Leaving Mexico, I carried with me drawings, tape recordings, and undeveloped film. These items filled the room in my house I use as an office. Suddenly the whole house felt too big, too empty, too clean. I tried to compensate. I taped drawings of flowers and houses to the wall. When I sat at my desk I could read the sweet words written on them in Spanish with crayon, "I'll never forget you." Looking at these drawings, these words, gave me an uncomfortable comfort.

I sorted through the children's photographs and assembled them in a large three-ring binder. There was a stunning image of a girl looking out of a shop window, a contemplative boy sitting on boards in the schoolyard, a young boy's self-portrait with the Virgin and a lollipop. I showed these pictures to others and tried to deliver impressive statements about the children—how talented they were, how young, how challenged. I told the stories. Inevitably, things got lost in translation.

I eased back into my American life. I swam in a pool, made long-distance phone calls, read books, watched the news. The border got thicker. It became a broad barrier separating two worlds, indeed different from each other. I could still cross it whenever I want, but the consequences of doing so were greater than the ease in which I made the action. There grew in me a desire to remain poised on the line, in the space between.

Perhaps I could have done better to ignore the border, to disregard what lies beyond it. After all, to do that would be to do what the families of the children I know did. But to deny the border would be to ignore what I now know—that not all of the stories about what's on the other side are true. That not everyone is yearning to jump the fence, give up their identity in exchange for dollar bills. That the shiny country I call my own is not everyone's dream destination.

Though perhaps unpatriotic of me, I found it refreshing that the children in Solidaridad were not overflowing with knowledge nor longing to know more about the place where I come from. Despite what the media, the economists, and a century of cartographic projections would have me believe, my country is not the center of the world. Ultimately, the stories that children told and didn't tell shifted my view of the world.

Now, if someone were to ask me to draw a map of my own world, I would expand my range. I would still draw the adobe house I rent, the garden and mesquite trees, the train tracks, and the interstate highway. But on the lower half of the page, I would add an hour's worth of line, Highway 19, and I'd scribble in a few red-tailed hawks alongside it. I would intersect the page with a solid line, but I would leave a space for easy crossing. On the other side of that line, I would drag a road through traffic, across a set of train tracks, and through a series of neighborhoods. In one of them, I would draw a handful of pink cement buildings and a basketball court in a big lot. Around it, I'd put houses, and draw X's in ten of them. Then I would park a yellow truck next to the basketball court, get out, and greet a gathering of children who I hope would be there, waiting.

Eula Biss

Eula Biss teaches creative nonfiction at Northwestern University. Her book, Notes from No Man's Land: American Essays *(2009), won the Graywolf Press Nonfiction Prize, and includes the essay published here, "Letter to Mexico." She received her MFA in nonfiction writing from the University of Iowa and she is a founding editor of Essay Press, a new press dedicated to innovative nonfiction. Her essays have recently appeared in* The Best Creative Nonfiction *and the* Touchstone Anthology of Contemporary Nonfiction.

Letter to Mexico

I am sending you a photocopy of a passage from the book *Shame and Its Sisters*. This photocopy was sent to me not long after I returned from Mexico, by the man who was my traveling companion there. It begins, "If I wish to touch you but do not wish to be touched, I may feel ashamed."

If you were to ask me now, "Why did you go to Mexico?" I would not be able to answer you honestly. I might say that I went to learn a language I have been trying to learn for a decade and still cannot speak.

Shame and Its Sisters continues, "If I wish to look at you but you do not wish me to, I may feel ashamed . . . .If I wish to look at you and at the same time wish that you look at me, I can be shamed. If I wish to be close to you but you move away, I am ashamed."

As we drove across the border I saw a long line of people waiting to go to work in San Diego, their bicycles locked on the fence near customs. In the months before leaving for Mexico, I took a Spanish class at San Diego Community College taught by a woman who commuted from Tijuana. Sometimes, she told us in class, it took her more than two hours to get across the border. That Spanish class is the only course I have ever failed.

Once across the border, there was a wall of corrugated metal that we drove along, and razor wire, and a ditch, and a lone man carrying a plastic bag in the sun, and a sudden change in the surface of the landscape, which I did not anticipate, because San Diego and Tijuana are closer than sisters, almost two halves of the same city. But San Diego is green along the highways, and Tijuana is not. In San Diego, dusk brings the rhythmic sound of sprinklers, but here it does not.

The Colorado River is split down its deepest channel by the border. So much water is drawn off by both countries that the river rarely reaches the ocean anymore. Every day, a good part of Mexico's share of that water is used to cool the turbines at two new power plants in Mexicali. The plants are owned by American companies, and most of the power they generate is sold to California and Arizona. These power plants and two thousand maquiladoras, American-owned factories along the border, are the fruits of the North American Free Trade Agreement, which has been in effect for more than a decade. The ten-year reports on NAFTA reveal that Mexico, like the United States, now has a small number of billionaires. And the real wages for everyone else have fallen. One of the promises of NAFTA was that it would make Mexico more like the United States. And it did— in that it widened the gap between the richest people in Mexico and the poorest.

When we stopped, after driving south for an hour, in a very small town with one cantina, which was also a motel, I asked a woman standing by the bar, "*Por favor, necesitamos un cuarto para esta noche.*" It was a sentence I had repeated over and over to myself in the car until I could say it somewhat casually. The woman said, "Hold on honey," and pulled me by the arm up to the bartender, saying, "Ramón, this little girl doesn't speak English."

In La Salina that evening all the Americans were having their weekly potluck at the cantina. I would discover that beyond the guarded gate next to the cantina, the town of La Salina was inhabited almost exclusively by Americans. Ramón, the bartender, and Gustavo, the waiter, spoke English, and no one else, as far as I could tell, spoke Spanish. That night, while firecrackers popped outside on the beach and strains of "La Bamba" and "Achy Breaky Heart" pounded through the floor of my room, I realized that I could never leave my country. I could check out any time I liked, as the song goes, but I could never leave.

I woke up to the sound of a man throwing rocks at the streetlight that lighted the patio behind the cantina at night. It was the same streetlight that this man had boasted was illegally wired so that it ran off power stolen from Mexico. The Americans were going to have a bonfire, and they wanted the patio to be dark. After one of his rocks hit something beyond the wall, making a cracking sound, the man dropped the rocks and slunk away like a naughty boy.

When I first arrived in La Salina, I had the illusion that the Americans there were outlaws. I thought that I had stumbled upon a community of people who were wanted for serious crimes in the United States. I would later realize exactly how fanciful this idea was, and how ignorant of economics, but for a time this was how I would interpret the nightly fireworks and the stolen electricity and the fight in the bar and my sense that I was among cowboy impersonators and gold prospectors. It now seems unlikely to me that the Americans in La Salina were guilty of anything more than ordinary poverty and a distinctly American desire to live the good life. But they were indeed, in the tradition of the old West, prospectors.

Two men, in particular, were often talking loudly out on the patio about what they could build and what they could sell and what it would cost and what they would make. One of them, I gathered, owned the cantina, and the other seemed to have some interest in it. Their calculations were like NAFTA negotiations on a small scale, in that they were always banking on getting the cheapest possible materials and paying as little as possible for labor. But NAFTA wasn't designed to benefit small operations, and if these guys weren't rich already, they probably weren't going to be, no matter whom they cheated.

In Spanish, the word for "border" is *frontera*—sounding like the English word "frontier," which can mean "the border between two countries." Or, according to my dictionary, "the extreme limit of understanding."

In the cantina one evening, a Mexican man with a guitar was singing. I heard his voice through the floor of my room, and when I came down for dinner we talked a bit about his Hollywood ambitions. Later, he would suggest that I write the story of his life, but I would never see him again. "*Cucurrucucu*," he sang, "*paloma*." The song was about a dove who cries for her lost lover. "*Cucurru-cucu*," he sang, "*cucurrucucu, cucurrucucu, paloma, ya no llores*." I was slightly drunk on my second margarita and the song was bringing tears to my eyes when a gringo at the bar interrupted by shouting, "Hey, who wrote that?" The song was a folk song with no known author, but the man persisted, "Who wrote that?"

"A couple of pigeons," the singer said finally, still looking at his guitar, not the gringo.

I felt sick with hatred then for my own people. If you had asked me then why I hated them, I might have said that I hated them for being so loud and for being so drunk. But now I believe I hated them for suddenly being my people, not just other people. In the United States, it is very easy for me to forget that the people around me are my people. It is easy, with all our divisions, to think of myself as an outsider in my own country. I have been taught, and I have learned well, I realize now, to think of myself as distinctly different from other white folks—more educated, more articulate, less crude. But in Mexico these distinctions became as meaningless to me as they should have always been.

A few months before I left for Mexico, after having four teeth pulled in San Diego—which cost me my entire savings, because I had no dental insurance—I noticed, in the Laundromat that was a block from my apartment, a gum-ball machine that vended "hillbilly teeth." These were a complete set of rotted, crooked, blackened, partially missing teeth that you could put over your own, presumably healthier teeth as a joke. I watched a little black boy buy some hill-billy teeth for a quarter and walk away with a parody of the problems of rural whites—a parody of loss and decay. In that moment I felt for my people.

Now, remembering that moment, I am reminded of James Baldwin in France. "His past," Baldwin wrote of the black American expatriate, "he now realizes, has not been simply a series of ropes and bonfires and humiliations, but something vastly more complex, which, as he thinks painfully, 'It was much worse than that,' was also, he irrationally feels, something much better."

My past, I discovered in Mexico, was both simpler and more complicated than I had ever thought it to be. I had, very simply, enjoyed great privilege in life, and great opportunity. But it was much worse than that. I began to recognize at whose price I had enjoyed a comfortable life. This is not to say that I immediately understood the intricacies of international trade agreements—it is only to say that I felt a nameless, crushing remorse.

In La Salina, I sat at the bar with Americans whom I disdained for their greed and ignorance. But I was there for the same reason they were. Because in La Salina I could afford to stay on the beach for the money I made as a receptionist in San Diego.

"Why La Salina Del Mar?" asked an ad for lots and houses and condos that would soon be built on the hill next to La Salina.

- The closest reasonably priced lots in Mexico
- Building costs below current U.S. rates
- Access by modern dual highway
- Retirement living within everyone's reach

Retirement living within everyone's reach. Affordable oceanfront. Freedom and fireworks for all. This is what Mexico had to offer us. And we were happy to take it.

The beach in La Salina was a glorious beach. It smelled like gasoline and horse dung, and the Americans there were all fat and ravaged by sun and alcohol and cigarettes. Tattered blonds in T-shirts carried drinks to paunchy old men on the patio. There were dirty white towels, ants in the carpet, rust in the sink, ATVs roaring across the beach, dogs chasing the ATVs, and two giant, fanlike flying machines that buzzed back and forth above the surf all day. Horses strolled by as I stood on the balcony watching, girls on motorcycles tossed up sand, and some guys at the top of the beach hit golf balls and hooted.

During my time in Mexico, I would return to La Salina every weekend. And I would return with relief. I would swim in the ocean there, drink at the bar, read in my room, and stand on the balcony, watching the surf and a Jeep full of gringos that was about to topple into the surf. On an average day, the song "Hotel California" played about once an hour in the cantina at La Salina. I don't know who decided this, but old Ramón, who controlled what stations played silently on the TVs, certainly might have been responsible. He seemed nearly as weary as that song began to sound to me. In my most vivid memory of La Salina, I am standing in the shade of the cantina, on the patio outside the bar, feeling remorse, looking at the back of my companion's reddening neck where he sits reading in the sun with a gallon of water next to him, and the ocean far ahead of him, and I hear, in between the faint sounds of pool balls from inside, "They're livin' it up at the Hotel California . . . ."

"Hotel California" was a hit song the year I was born. It was playing on all the radios, and its lyrics now are the only photograph I have of the moment I was born into. "Mirrors on the ceiling," Don Henley sings, "the pink champagne on ice. And she said, 'We are all just prisoners here of our own device.' And in the master's chambers they gathered for the feast. They stab it with their steely knives but they just can't kill the beast."

Perhaps the story of Mexican immigrants coming to America for a better life has been told so many times that it has obscured the reality of American expatriates fleeing to Mexico for the life they have been promised but not delivered. And perhaps this is why, in the cantina in La Salina, the song "Hotel California" was so haunting to me. As I grew used to hearing it, it took on the kind of raw, heartbreaking humor that I found in the black boy buying hillbilly teeth from a gum-ball machine in the San Diego Laundromat. It was the same humor I found in the small statues of skeletons dressed as doctors that were sold in the tourist district of Ensenada. I bought one of these skeleton doctors for my father, a doctor, but later found it very difficult to explain to him why.

I stayed in the cantina at La Salina on weekends, but during the week, while I was taking Spanish classes in Ensenada, I stayed in the home of a Mexican family. The father was a doctor, like my father, and the mother taught at the Spanish school where I took classes. Their daughter had just returned from a semester abroad in Kansas, and their son led tours for Americans over where the cruise ships docked. The house they lived in was surrounded by a high cement wall, and the wall was topped with broken glass. If I had grown up in Mexico, I realized, I too would have grown up behind a wall. At meals, the mother reminded me how to say "napkin" and we talked of very little else because I lacked the words I needed to say anything meaningful. My companion initiated one halting conversation about the Zapatistas, which ended in us all staring at the television, where *Terminator* was playing with Spanish subtitles. One evening, the father forgot his keys and stood on the street, where he could just barely see me reading by the window above the wall, and he yelled for an hour before I realized that it was him yelling and that he was saying, in Spanish, "Child! Child! Open the door! Let me in!"

That phrase and my inability to hear it echo now through my memory of Mexico, along with the sounds of roosters and birds and the endless honks of the water truck as it made its morning rounds. In Ensenada, the horn of the water truck makes the high A of a violin tuning before a concert, giving the mornings there the sound of the moments before some grand concert of dogs and cars and metal on concrete. Outside my window, beyond the wall topped with broken glass, kids played in the dried-up canal, throwing rocks or riding bikes without seats down a sandy bank.

Walking the streets of Ensenada felt to me like walking along the edge of the ocean. I was confined to the shore there, even when I was not in the tourist district, where the cruise ships unloaded and middle-aged Americans periodically swarmed the bars and souvenir stands then receded like a tide. I was confined to the shore even in the alleys, even in the bodegas, even in the house where I slept. At first, I smiled eagerly and hopefully at everyone who looked at me on the street in Ensenada. Soon, when I was not looking at the ground, I looked at everyone the same way they looked at me, with a wary expressionlessness.

I would walk to school in the dust, on the broken sidewalks, through the stares, past the skinny dogs that stood up and followed me with their eyes before they lay back down. I would pass the truck piled high with bunches of clean radishes, where I would buy a *torta* for lunch and then wash my hands with the juice of a lime. I would pass shacks made of corrugated metal and lines of laundry and a row of pickle jars full of peaches and strawberries and mangos waiting to be poured over ice. I would read signs, and I would understand some of what I heard, but not all of it. Not nearly all of it.

Signs for candidates in the local elections were plastered all over the telephone poles, but I knew even less about local politics than I knew about national politics. I did not know then that NAFTA had in effect eroded many of the rights and protections provided by the Mexican constitution. I did not know that breaking strikes had become a common practice under NAFTA, even after the federal court ruled in 1999 that strikes were legal. I did not know, really, anything.

One afternoon in Ensenada, I stopped in a *farmacia*, where I picked up a Popsicle and some aspirin. The store was not in the tourist district, and it was empty in the afternoon heat. The girl at the register stood looking out the window with her shoulder to me, where I stood waiting at the counter. She was very still, and her long hair fluttered up in an arc every time the rotating fan turned in her direction. She would not look at me, even when I murmured, "Cuanto cuesta?" She would not look at me and would not say anything. Finally, I put down a bill, and she slapped down change, still not turning to face me. I left with tears in my eyes, holding, pathetically, a melting Popsicle.

The fact that I was hated in Baja California was not lost on me for a moment. At times, I cherished the delusion that I could blame the fact that I was hated on the loud and rowdy Americans who flooded the restaurants and bars in the tourist district with an alarming sense of ownership. But now I understand that they were just a way for me to think about American excesses. Most of the Americans in the bars were as damaged by those excesses as Mexico was.

In my mornings and afternoons of walking, I had plenty of time to think about being hated, and I often, after thinking on it for a while, concluded that I deserved to be hated. At times, I was as sure of this as I was sure I deserved the F that I had received in my Spanish class in San Diego, but I still did not understand exactly how personally implicated I should feel. I knew that my body and my presence there meant something, spoke something to everyone who saw me, but I did not know what. And I still do not know, but I suspect it was something about everything America was stealing from Mexico.

I was relieved of the sensation of being hated only when I went to La Salina for the weekends, where I could indulge in hating other Americans. Even after four weekends I could not admit that the hatred I felt for the Americans in the cantina at La Salina was the hatred I felt for myself—a punishment for being so ignorant of the world outside my country and for eating all the pomegranate seeds I had ever been offered. In all my time in La Salina, I managed never to exchange more than a few words with another American. I did not ask anyone how they got there, or why they lived there, or what they had left behind. I tried, for the most part, to talk only to Mexicans. And for the most part I failed.

In school in Ensenada I learned the words for many different kinds of food and some parts of the body. I did not learn how to say, "The excesses of my country are paid for by your country." But I learned to say, "I have a stomachache." And in one of my final lessons, I learned the construction *me da vergüenza*. Literally, "it gives me shame."

I would, while I was in Mexico, read over and over a letter that had been written to me by a woman I worked with in San Diego. For some time in San Diego after I quit my job as a reporter I worked only on my own writing. But after my teeth were pulled, I temped as a receptionist at a chemical factory in Chula Vista. I now understand, having learned a few things about NAFTA, why this factory was so close to the border and why they wanted a receptionist who could speak Spanish. But at the time I was happy to be entirely unaware of nearly everything that went on in the chemical factory. I spent my days there forwarding calls and printing a several-thousand-page document that needed to be printed one page at a time, for reasons I did not care to understand. From where I sat, I could see the sign that I drove past every morning on my way in to work:

WARNING

Beyond this point are chemicals known to the state of
California to be hazardous . . . .

I was supposed to be a bilingual receptionist, able to handle calls in both Spanish and English. Often, when I needed to speak more than a few words of Spanish on the phone I would panic and ask for help from Rosa, who worked across the office. In turn, Rosa would ask me to correct her English on memos and in letters. We spoke very haltingly in each other's languages of how difficult it is to learn a new language. I told her that I was going to go to Mexico so that I could learn faster. She told me she was sure that would help. On the day I left the factory, Rosa ran out into the parking lot as I was getting into my car and handed me a letter, then ran back inside.

> Dear Friend,
>   This is your last day working with our Company and I just want to tell you thank you for every thing, thank you for your help and Keep Smiling. You know what? Usually in this days the people don't pay attention to the small details but Keep Smiling no matter what happen and my best wishes for you, you are young and have a long live in front of you, you are very smart and I'm sure you can be true to all your goals, try to learn as more you can from the places and from the people that you meat. And don't forget that God have a special plans for you.
>
> Sincerely,
Rosa
>
>   P.D.T. You know what? When I came to this country I started working in a Restaurant washing Dishes, in a factory the worst work in all my life, Construction drywall with men, dirty clothes hard job, but you know what in my country I study Human resources in the University and all the times the only think that make my stand up is an ilution that one day every thing go better for me. And now this is not an excellent job but I'm happy.

I tried, several times, to answer this letter in Spanish. I sat and made two or three words with the help of my dictionary. "Querida Rosa," I always began. In the end, I never answered Rosa's letter, and I never heard from her again.

We joined the line, eventually, of cars leaving Mexico. The line was miles long, and the cars were mostly minivans and Jeeps and SUVs with California plates. Our enormous motorcade crawled past a man standing by the side of the road, holding up a giant plaster cast of *The Last Supper*. I did not understand, at first, that *The Last Supper* was for sale. I saw the gesture as some kind of beautiful protest.

At the next intersection, men with buckets washed windows, and I watched one man cross himself quickly after being paid with change. The road had become six lanes wide, all stopped with traffic. An Indian woman with long braids walked between the cars, selling peanuts, a baby bound to her body. All the people around the cars now were Indians, and they seemed to be streaming onto the highway directly from their fields of corn that no longer existed, still sun baked and dusty. A little girl ran between the cars, selling cigarettes, and a very small boy stood motionless between two lanes of traffic, holding out a plastic cup, vacant-faced as cars streamed around him.

On New Year's Day in 1994, the same day NAFTA was implemented, there was an uprising of Indian peasants in Chiapas. NAFTA, the Zapatista army declared, was a "death sentence" for the indigenous people of Mexico. While Clinton was promising that NAFTA would "lift all boats," the Zapatistas warned that NAFTA would bring falling prices for corn, falling wages for workers, and the loss of land to foreign investors. That is exactly what happened. Because Iowa corn imported into Mexico is heavily subsidized by the United States government, the price of corn in Mexico fell by half during the first ten years of NAFTA. More than a million farmers were displaced from their land and forced to migrate to the cities or the United States, where they became day laborers, picking U.S. crops.

Next to our car, all along the side of the road, men sold rugs printed with American flags and painted plaster statues of Woodstock, Spider-Man, and Betty Boop. In the traffic, men and women and children sold fried dough, crucifixes, Doritos, and Fritos. Little girls with braids and no front teeth raised their eyebrows and held out cups when our eyes met.

I watched all this and I felt pure despair. I put change in the cups and I felt despair.

It was getting dark and it began to rain as we approached the border. Two little girls near our car were singing. One absently fixed her sandal with her hand while she sang. She seemed to be in good spirits, despite the sudden cold. The heat was on in our car and the windows were fogging. Ahead of us, a man unrolled his window to give the girl two quarters. Without missing a beat, still stamping time with one foot, she handed one quarter to the girl next to her. Their voices rose above the sound of hundreds of motors idling and mingled with the fumes.

Luis Urrea

Luis Urrea (1955–) is a novelist, poet, and essayist. He is currently a professor of creative writing at the University of Illinois in Chicago. His major works include The Devil's Highway *(2004), a national best-seller and the winner of the Lannan Literary Award,* Nobody's Son: Notes from an American Life *(2002), and most recently the historical novel,* The Hummingbird's Daughter *(2005). This piece is an excerpt from his nonfiction book* Across the Wire *(1993).*

Sifting through the Trash

One of the most beautiful views of San Diego is from the summit of a small hill in Tijuana's municipal garbage dump. People live on that hill, picking through the trash with long poles that end in hooks made of bent nails. They scavenge for bottles, tin, aluminum, cloth; for cast-out beds, wood, furniture. Sometimes they find meat that is not too rotten to be cooked.

This view-spot is where the city drops off its dead animals—dogs, cats, sometimes goats, horses. They are piled in heaps six feet high and torched. In that stinking blue haze, amid nightmarish sculptures of charred ribs and carbonized tails, the garbage-pickers can watch the buildings of San Diego gleam gold on the blue coastline. The city looks cool in the summer when heat cracks the ground and flies drill into their noses. And in the winter, when windchill drops night temperatures into the low thirties, when the cold makes their lips bleed, and rain turns the hill into a gray pudding of ash and mud, and babies are wrapped in plastic trash bags for warmth, San Diego glows like a big electric dream. And every night on that burnt hill, these people watch.

In or near every Mexican border town, you will find trash dumps. Some of the bigger cities have more than one "official" dump, and there are countless smaller, unlicensed places piled with garbage. Some of the official dumps are quite large, and some, like the one outside Tecate, are small and well hidden. People live in almost every one of them.

Each *dompe* has its own culture, as distinct as the people living there. (*Dompe* is border-speak, a word in neither Spanish nor English. It is an attempt to put a North American word or concept—"dump"—into a Mexican context. Thus, "junkyard" becomes *yonke* and "muffler" becomes *mofle*.) Each of these *dompes* has its own pecking order. Certain people are "in." Some families become power brokers due to their relationships to the missionaries who invariably show up, bearing bags of old clothes and vanloads of food. Some *dompes* even have "mayors"; some have hired goons, paid off by shady syndicates, to keep the trash-pickers in line. It's a kind of illegal serfdom, where the poor must pay a ransom to the rich to pick trash to survive.

Then there are those who are so far "out" that the mind reels. In the Tijuana *dompe*, the outcasts were located along the western edge of the settlement in shacks and lean-tos, in an area known as "the pig village." This was where the untouchables of this society of untouchables slept, among the pigs awaiting slaughter.

I knew them all: the Serranos, the Cheese Lady, Pacha, Jesusita.

A Woman Called Little Jesus

It was raining. It had been raining for weeks, and the weather was unremittingly cold. The early-morning van-loadings were glum; all spring and summer and even into the fall, more volunteers than we'd known what to do with joined us for the weekly trips into Mexico. One day, we had over a hundred eager American kids loaded into buses ready to go forth and change the world. Now, though, as the late-winter/early-spring rain came, the group dwindled. Sometimes we were reduced to a small core of old-timers, six to ten at most.

When we pulled into the dump, the vans slid almost sideways in the viscous, slick mud. Windchill turned the air icy; there was no smoke to speak of that day, and the dogs were mostly hiding. Women awaiting food were lined up, covering their heads with plastic sheets. Even in this wind and wet they joked and laughed. This feature of the Mexican personality is often the cause of much misunderstanding—that if Mexicans are so cheerful, then they certainly couldn't be hungry or ill. It leads to the myth of the quaint and jovial peasant with a lusty, Zorba-like love affair with life. Like the myth of the lazy Mexican, sleeping his life away, it's a lie.

Perhaps the women laughed because they were simply relieved to be getting food. Perhaps they were embarrassed—Mexicans are often shamed by accepting help of any kind. When embarrassed or ashamed, they often overcompensate, becoming boisterous, seemingly carefree. Or maybe the poor don't feel the compunction to play the humble and quiet role we assign them in our minds.

As I climbed out of the van, Doña Araceli, the Cheese Lady, bustled over to me. We called her the Cheese Lady because she had taken to coming to the dump with globs of drippy white goat cheese wrapped in cloth. She sold it to the locals, and she always pressed a lump of it into my hands as a gift. Nobody in the crew had the guts to taste it. We'd pass the cheese around for a couple of hours, then unload it at an orphanage or a *barrio* in Tijuana.

Doña Araceli was extremely agitated. She had discovered a new family—a married couple, several children, including toddlers, and one daughter with an infant—and they had no house to stay in. They were very poor, she said, and in dire need of help.

One of our projects over the years was to build homes and churches for the poor. An associate of ours named Aubrey devised an ingeniously simple construction plan. He collected garage doors from houses being torn down or renovated; these doors, hammered to a simple wooden frame, made handy walls. Depending on how many doors were available, the new house could be as long or as wide as the builders chose. With saws and donated windows, Aubrey could modify the place and make it quite fancy. The roofs were either more garage doors, plywood, or two-by-six planks covered with plastic sheeting that was either carpet-tacked or stapled into place. Old carpets and plastic sheets were transformed into a quick floor. Once a month, we had a *dompe* workday: truckloads of youths armed with tools came in and began hammering, and in a matter of hours, they created a new building.

Doña Araceli wanted us to build this family a house right away. She said the mother was waiting to meet me. The woman's name was Jesusita. Little Jesus.

Jesusita shook my hand and called me *"Hermano"*—"Brother."

This is not a common Mexican greeting; it is used among Protestants as a shorthand for "fellow Christian." A "real" Mexican would never resort to such Protestant language (though it is a habit for Mexicans to call each other *"'mano,"* which is short for "brother" but actually takes the place of "pal" or "dude." Mexican linguistics are a delicate and confusing art: *mano* also means "hand"). The poor, however, deal with missionaries and soon learn to use the more religious term freely. It is often a manipulative thing. They are hoping you will assume they are *"Hallelujahs,"* too, and give them more goods than the rest. Consequently, Jesusita's *"Hermano"* didn't move me. I paid it no heed.

What really caught my eye instead was her face. She was small, a round woman with gray hair and the kind of face that retains a hint of young beauty under layers of pain and comfortless years. Her eyes, nestled in laugh lines, were a light, nutbrown color. She smiled easily. She wound her hair in twin braids and pinned it to the top of her head, framing her face. She made me feel happy, absurdly pleased, as though she were a long-lost aunt who had appeared with a plate of cookies.

Over the next year, as we got to be friends, she lavished me with bear hugs. Her head fit easily beneath my chin. On the day I met her, though, she cried.

"*Hermano*," she said, "*vinimos desde el sur, y no tenemos casa.*" (We came from the south, and we don't have a house.) "*Somos muchos, todos mis hijos, un nietito, y mi señor.*" (There are many of us, all my children, a little grandson, and my husband.)

"Help her, Luis!" cried Doña Araceli.

Jesusita's full name was María de Jesús. Mary of Jesus.

Requests for help were a constant; they were the rule. That Jesusita needed assistance didn't make her special, but something about her involved me right away. I suppose it is the thing we conveniently call "chemistry." Still, Jesusita was one face in a river of hundreds.

Everyone needed help. For example, there was the family recently arrived from near Guadalajara. They had no clothes except what they were wearing, and the children were so infected with scabies that their skin looked like old chewing gum. Scabies is a mange caused by a burrowing mite, a louse, that tunnels through your flesh, leaving eggs under your skin. You scratch and scratch, but can never quite get to the itch—the mites move in you at night. They like crotches and armpits. Scabies victims claw themselves raw. The kids didn't understand what was wrong with them. They all slept together, and the mites could easily move from body to body. Their beds were full of these mites; their clothes and under-wear were also infested. When we tried to explain what was causing their itch, they looked at us with disbelief and laughed.

The family was living in a shack on a hillside across the highway from the dump. It could be reached only after a long and confusing drive through crooked alleys and ridgetop dirtpaths. Lean-tos thrown together by junkies and winos sur-rounded their shack. You could smell the booze and urine coming through the slats. There was a small goat tied to a stake in the dirt, and no lights brightened the neighborhood save for small fires and the occasional flashlight. The men's voices were thick; they cursed and broke glass in the dark. In the shack hid Socorro, the thirteen-year-old daughter. The men wanted her. They'd come out after dark and storm the house, trying to break through the doors and walls to get to her. When I went up there one night, waving my flashlight in the dust clouds, I could hear them outside Socorro's door, howling.

Clearly, the Guadalajarans needed a new house. Everywhere we turned, some-one needed a new house. Jesusita's family would have to wait for theirs, though we committed to giving them assistance wherever it was possible. I told Jesusita to wait for us in her place down the hill, and we'd be down as soon as we could. She cried again and put her arms around me. "*Gracias, Luis*," she said. "*Gracias, Hermano Luis.*"

Fear

This is a record of a small event that happened on a typical spring day near the pig village.

I was unloading one of the vans—the huge Dodge we called "the White Elephant." Some of my friends were standing around the van with me—Doña Araceli, a Mixtec woman named Juanita, and a little girl named Negra. I noticed a woman standing in the distance, among the trash piles. I didn't recognize her. None of the dump people seemed to know her, either. We watched her lurch back and forth, spitting and waving her arms. She would occasionally glare at me, start toward me, then stop after a few steps and curse. Her face looked like a rubber mask: white creases and a red-slash mouth.

"Is she drunk?" said Juanita. I said something, no doubt a joke, and leaned into the van. I worked the box I was looking for free by shoving one of the heavy bags of beans out of the way. When I turned around, the woman was standing right beside me, staring into my face. She snarled.

I stumbled back from her. Her hair stood straight off her scalp as though she were taking a heavy charge of electricity through her feet. She was wheezing.

One of the women said, "She's crazy, *Hermano*."

"Fuck you," she snapped. Her voice was deep, like a man's voice. "*Vete a la chingada.*"

She leaned toward me. "We know you," she said. "We know who you are. We know what you're doing."

I laughed nervously. "What?" I said.

"You'll pay for this."

I put down my box. "I don't understand," I said.

She began to rasp obscenities in her man's voice. "We *know* you. We'll get you."

She spun around and jerked away from us, very fast. She stumbled over rocks in the road, but kept moving, shouting all the time, "*¡Vas a ver!* You'll see! We'll get you. We'll stop you."

She paused in front of Pacha's house at the top of the hill, gesturing at me and yelling her strange threats. The hair at the back of my neck began to rise.

"Is she drunk?" Juanita repeated.

The woman threw her head back and screamed.

Pacha

Pacha had startling eyes. They had a kind of gold-green edge; they had yellow flecks, like the eyes of a cat. They slanted up the slightest bit. If she'd lived anywhere but the Tijuana garbage dump, her eyes would have seemed like a movie star's.

She lived with a thin, dark man named José. He called himself her husband, though he was not the father of her children. His face was craggy and his teeth long, hidden by a thick black mustache. When he talked to you, he'd bob his head and grin. When either of them laughed, they'd cover their mouths with their hands. They were pagans when they came north, of full Indian blood, and not used to church services or ministers. Their marriage ceremony was more personal and private—José moved into Pacha's bed. He became her mate, and he remained faithful to her. It was a simple agreement, as firm as a wolf's.

José liked Jesus very much. When Pastor Von and his workers visited his house, José always asked Von to pray for him. We put our arms around each other and Von prayed and I translated and José kept saying, "Thank you, Jesus, for listening to me." He cried.

Pacha wouldn't come to the vans to get food. She said it embarrassed her to be begging and fighting with all those other women. I made it a habit to save her out a box of goods, and after the crowds dissipated a bit, I would take it up to her.

Her home was on a slope that swept down into the dump; hers was a long, meandering shack with a low roof and uneven walls. The entire house was at an angle. José designed it this way so that the rain, when it came, would flow through the house, under their bed, and down the hill. He was very proud of his ingenuity: he had built one of the dump's best-engineered houses. Those who built below him, on flatland or in hollows, found themselves in puddles of mud all winter.

Their floor was a conglomeration of carpet pieces and stray linoleum squares. José and Pacha pressed them into wet soil. The exterior walls were board. The interior walls were cardboard, with an occasional bit of wood—fruit crates, barrel slats. They sealed the gaps with plastic sheeting.

They did have one luxury: a bed. It was quite odd to look through a door and see a big bed with an iron bedframe and headboard. Often a bed was the only thing people in the dumps owned that was worth anything. Except for televisions.

You'd see little black and white TV sets scattered through the dump. There was no electricity, but there were wrecked cars in the *yonkes* in the valleys. The men took the car batteries and hooked the TV sets to them. Sometimes the TVs were balanced on huge oil cans—rusted Pemex, Opec barrels—which, when filled with paper and dung or twigs, served as stoves.

Pacha didn't have a television, but she did have oil barrels: she cooked in one of them. The other she used to store water. It was full of mosquito larvae wiggling like tiny fish. Its water was the color of blood.

Pacha's eldest daughter offered to pay me to smuggle her across the border. She was pregnant—her husband had gone across the wire and never come back. She watched for him on a neighbor's television. I told her I couldn't do it.

On New Year's morning, she had her baby in the free clinic in Tijuana. The nurse took the infant and dunked it in a tub of icy water. It had a heart attack and died. It was a girl.

Pacha got pregnant next. Her belly stuck out far and hard, like a basketball, from her small body. When we arrived at the dump, she stood in front of her house with José, pointed at me and laughed. They laughed a lot. She was furious with me if I didn't come up the hill right away to see her kids.

José had hurt his back. He could barely stand, much less work, and the days were hard for Pacha and her kids. They all had to take the trash-picking poles and work the mounds, supporting José, who would give out after a few hours.

When I took them the food, I'd pat that huge stomach and shout, "What are you doing in there!" They would laugh, and she would scold me for waking him up. It was José's first child with her, the seal of their marriage.

One day, when we drove over the hill, a crowd was there, milling. It was hot—the flies had hatched, and were forming clouds that swept out of the trash like black dust devils. The rain had been over for months, and the deep heat was on. I glanced at Pacha's house—nobody in front. Then I saw an old pickup truck coming up the hill. José was in the back with a group of men. They held cloudy bottles by the necks.

I waved at him, but he just looked at me as the truck went by, no emotion at all on his face.

As we were unloading the vans, one of Pacha's girls came to me and put her hand on my arm. "Luis," she said, quietly. "Mama's baby died."

I stared at her.

"Don José just took him away in the truck. His head was too big. He was all black."

I asked her if it had been born here.

She shook her head. "Free clinic," she said.

She stood calmly, watching me. "Mama needs you," she said.

I didn't want to go up there.

It was a terrible charade: Pacha was blushing and overly polite, as though caught in an embarrassment. I was pleasant, as though we were having tea and crumpets at the Ritz. Everything felt brittle, ready to shatter. She wore baggy green stretch pants and stood holding a salvaged aluminum kitchen chair.

"Poor José," she said, looking off. It was very dark in the house, and it smelled of smoke. "Poor José. It hurt him so much."

That look as he drove past, drunk: where was Jesus now?

"The baby wouldn't come out," she said. She looked at her feet. "The doctor got up under my *chi-chis* and pushed on him after I tried for a few hours."

"He sat on your abdomen?"

She nodded. "Sí. They got up on my chest and shoved on me. And then the doctor had to get down there and pull me open because the baby was black and we were both dying." She swayed. I jumped up and took her arm, trying to get her into the chair. "It hurts," she said. She smiled. "It's hard to sit." I got her down. "They stuck iron inside me. They pulled him out with tools, and I'm scared because I'm fat down there. I'm still all fat." She couldn't look at me; she bowed her head. "It's hard and swollen and I can't touch it."

I told her not to move and ran down the hill to get Dave, a medical student who was working with us. He grabbed a flashlight and followed me up.

Pacha repeated her story; I translated.

He said, "Tell her to pull the pants tight against her crotch so I can see the swelling."

She did it. He bent close. It looked like she had grown a set of testicles. He whistled.

"Think it's a hernia?" he asked.

"I don't know. Could be." Many of the women in the dump get hernias that are never treated—I knew one woman who had one for fifteen years until she asked one of us to look at it.

Dave said, "Tell her I have to feel it."

I told Pacha. She just looked at me. Brown eyes flecked with gold. "Anything you say." She nodded.

"Is she all right?" Dave asked.

"Yeah."

He handled her very tenderly; she winced, sucked air. "Feels bad," he said.

She kept her eyes on my face.

"We have to get her pants off, buddy."

"Wonderful, Dave."

"Culturally?" he asked.

"A disaster."

One of my aunts, when she was pregnant, was attended to by a male obstetrician. My uncle ordered him to stand outside a closed door—his nurse looked at my aunt and called out the details to him. My uncle hovered nearby to make sure there would be no outrage against her womanhood.

Dave stood there for a moment. "Too bad. We have to look."

"Pacha," I said. "The, ah, doctor needs to see it."

She nodded. She took her children outside and told them not to come back for a while. I held her hand and helped her into the bed.

José had designed a little paper alcove for the bed. Pictures of musicians, movie stars, and saints were pasted to the walls. A ragged curtain hung beside the bed for privacy.

"He was too big," she said, stretching out. "Too fat."

She worked the pants down around her hips. A strip of dirty elastic—perhaps torn out of an old girdle—was wrapped around her fallen belly to hold it up. She unwrapped herself. Her navel hung out like a fat thumb.

She undid some safety pins that held her underpants together. They were blue, lightly stained. A smell rose of warm bread and vinegar. Dave sat beside her. She stared into my eyes.

I looked away. I was embarrassed and nervous.

Dave handed me the flashlight and said, "Here. Illuminate it for me."

Her right side was thick and grotesque. The right labium was red. Bits of lint stuck to her. Every time he touched her, Pacha gasped.

"Blood," he said. "Tell her it's blood. No hernia." He smiled at her.

I translated.

She smiled a little bit, more with her eyes than her lips.

We put her to bed for several days—no more trash-picking. She needed to let the blood reabsorb. Dave gave her a battery of vitamins, some aspirin, put her on lots of fluids.

"*Ay, Luis,*" she said.

I stepped out of her home. The sky was black and brown—they were burning dogs at the end of the dump. It smelled like Hell. I took a deep breath and walked away.

Coffee

It was finally time to go down and see Jesusita.

We climbed into the four-wheel-drive Blazer and drove down the slippery hill. The dirt road was already so deep in mud that the truck couldn't make it. We had to abandon it and slog down. In places, the mud went higher than my knees.

Jesusita and some of her brood waited for us at the bottom of the hill. They led us to what seemed to be—for the dump, anyway—an especially luxurious house. It was a small American-style place with stucco walls and what appeared to be a real roof. It even had a porch. We were a little suspicious at first. The Cheese Lady had made such a fuss about this? Our opinions changed when we got inside. Half of the interior walls had fallen in, with the back walls sagging and open to the wind. The floor was raw, uncovered cement, and the whole house was awash in one or two inches of water. Only two areas remained recognizable as rooms. In what had clearly been a living room, on a sheet of plastic, were piled all of Jesusita's possessions—clothes, bundles—forming a small dry island. The family slept on this pile. The other room was a kitchen.

They had dragged the empty shell of a stove from the dump. A linoleum-and-aluminium table stood in the kitchen, too, with four unmatched chairs. On the counter, a few coffee cups, a pan, and the meager food supplies we had given Jesusita. Her husband arrived, took off his straw *vaquero* hat, shook our hands, and very formally and graciously invited us to sit and have a cup of coffee with him. He was an iron-backed man, not tall, but erect and strong; his hands were thick and solid as oak burls. He wore old cowboy boots and faded jeans and a white pearl-snap shirt. We learned that he was a horse-breaker from the interior of Mexico, a real cowboy who took pride in his talents.

Jesusita said, "He is the best horse-tamer in our region."

He shushed her—he never liked too much talk of home. His tightly curled hair was tinged gray and white. A small peppery mustache sketched itself across his upper lip. He referred to each of us as *"usted,"* the formal "you," and it was clear that he expected the same respect. The most lasting impression we took with us was one of dignity and pride.

Their children were remarkably attractive—several girls and two little boys. One of the girls, perhaps fifteen, had a baby. All their hair was shiny and black, and the girls wore it pulled back in loose ponytails.

Jesusita put wads of newspaper in the hollow stove and lit them. She heated water in the battered pan, and she made Nescafé instant coffee with it. It was clearly the last of their coffee, and she served it in four cups. We men sat at the table. Jesusita and the kids stood around us, watching us drink.

It was a lovely moment. The weak coffee, the formal and serious cowboy, the children, and Jesusita, hovering over us. She broke a small loaf of sweet bread into pieces and made us eat.

It was also a fearsome moment—the water was surely polluted, runoff from the miasma above. A great deal of disease infested the area from the constant flooding and the scattered bodies of dead animals. To refuse their hospitality would have been the ultimate insult, yet to eat and drink put us at risk. Von had the grim set in his lips that said, *Here we go again*, and with a glance at us, he took a sip. We drank. "*¡Ah!*" we exulted. "*¡Delicioso!*" Jesusita beamed. The cowboy nodded gravely, dipped his bit of sweet bread in his cup, and toasted us with it. Outside, the cold rain hammered down. Inside, we all shivered. We could find no way to get warm.

Leslie Marmon Silko

Leslie Marmon Silko, a Laguna Pueblo (New Mexico) woman whose heritage includes White and Mexican forebears, is best known for her novels Ceremony *and* Almanac of the Dead. *Her work stems from the Pueblo world of her childhood and is grounded in the oral tradition in which culture and values are maintained through story. Silko's political concerns range from local water rights issues to global concerns regarding the rights of indigenous peoples.*

In the essay below, Silko recounts an experience she and a companion had while driving home one evening from a poetry reading. As they drove south down a New Mexico state road, they were stopped by United States Border Patrol agents and questioned. Silko's experience inspired her to write about the meaning of borders, particularly the meaning of official borders as defined by the United States government and law enforcement in the Southwest. The piece was originally published in The Nation.

The Border Patrol State

I used to travel the highways of New Mexico and Arizona with a wonderful sensation of absolute freedom as I cruised down the open road and across the vast desert plateaus. On the Laguna Pueblo reservation, where I was raised, the people were patriotic despite the way the U.S. government had treated Native Americans. As proud citizens, we grew up believing the freedom to travel was our inalienable right, a right that some Native Americans had been denied in the early twentieth century. Our cousin, old Bill Pratt, used to ride his horse 300 miles overland from Laguna, New Mexico, to Prescott, Arizona, every summer to work as a fire lookout.

In school in the 1950s, we were taught that our right to travel from state to state without special papers or threat of detainment was a right that citizens under communist and totalitarian governments did not possess. That wide open highway told us we were U.S. citizens: we were free. . . .

Not so long ago, my companion Gus and I were driving south from Albuquerque, returning to Tucson after a book promotion for the paperback edition of my novel *Almanac of the Dead*. I had settled back and gone to sleep while Gus drove, but I was awakened when I felt the car slowing to a stop. It was nearly midnight on New Mexico State Road 26, a dark, lonely stretch of two-lane highway between Hatch and Deming. When I sat up, I saw the headlights and emergency flashers of six vehicles—Border Patrol cars and a van were blocking both lanes of

Reprinted from the *Nation*, October 1994, pp. 412–416.

the highway. Gus stopped the car and rolled down the window to ask what was wrong. But the closest Border Patrolman and his companion did not reply; instead, the first agent ordered us to "step out of the car." Gus asked why, but his question seemed to set them off. Two more Border Patrol agents immediately approached our car, and one of them snapped, "Are you looking for trouble?" as if he would relish it.

I will never forget that night beside the highway. There was an awful feeling of menace and violence straining to break loose. It was clear that the uniformed men would be only too happy to drag us out of the car if we did not speedily comply with their request (asking a question is tantamount to resistance, it seems). So we stepped out of the car and they motioned for us to stand on the shoulder of the road. The night was very dark, and no other traffic had come down the road since we had been stopped. All I could think about was a book I had read—*Nunca Más*—the official report of a human rights commission that investigated and certified more than 12,000 "disappearances" during Argentina's "dirty war" in the late 1970s.

The weird anger of these Border Patrolmen made me think about descriptions in the report of Argentine police and military officers who became addicted to interrogations, torture and the murder that followed. When the military and police ran out of political suspects to torture and kill, they resorted to the random abduction of citizens off the streets. I thought how easy it would be for the Border Patrol to shoot us and leave our bodies and car beside the highway, like so many bodies found in these parts and ascribed to "drug runners."

Two other Border Patrolmen stood by the white van. The one who had asked if we were looking for trouble ordered his partner to "get the dog," and from the back of the van another patrolman brought a small female German shepherd on a leash. The dog apparently did not heel well enough to suit him, and the handler jerked the leash. They opened the doors of our car and pulled the dog's head into it, but I saw immediately from the expression in her eyes that the dog hated them, and that she would not serve them. When she showed no interest in the inside of our car, they brought her around back to the trunk, near where we were standing. They half-dragged her up into the trunk, but still she did not indicate any stowed-away human beings or illegal drugs.

Their mood got uglier; the officers seemed outraged that the dog could not find any contraband, and they dragged her over to us and commanded her to sniff our legs and feet. To my relief, the strange violence the Border Patrol agents had focused on us now seemed shifted to the dog. I no longer felt so strongly that we would be murdered. We exchanged looks—the dog and I. She was afraid of what they might do, just as I was. The dog's handler jerked the leash sharply as she sniffed us, as if to make her perform better, but the dog refused to accuse us: She had an innate dignity that did not permit her to serve the murderous impulses of those men. I can't forget the expression in the dog's eyes; it was as if she were embarrassed to be associated with them. I had a small amount of medicinal marijuana in my purse that night, but she refused to expose me. I am not partial to dogs, but I will always remember the small German shepherd that night.

Unfortunately, what happened to me is an everyday occurrence here now. Since the 1980s, on top of greatly expanding border checkpoints, the Immigration and Naturalization Service and the Border Patrol have implemented policies that interfere with the rights of U.S. citizens to travel freely within our borders. I.N.S. agents now patrol all interstate highways and roads that lead to or from the U.S.-Mexico border in Texas, New Mexico, Arizona and California. Now, when you drive east from Tucson on Interstate 10 toward El Paso, you encounter an I.N.S. check station outside Las Cruces, New Mexico. When you drive north from Las Cruces up Interstate 25, two miles north of the town of Truth or Consequences, the highway is blocked with orange emergency barriers, and all traffic is diverted into a two-lane Border Patrol checkpoint—ninety-five miles north of the U.S.-Mexico border.

I was detained once at Truth or Consequences, despite my and my companion's Arizona driver's licenses. Two men, both Chicanos, were detained at the same time, despite the fact that they too presented ID and spoke English without the thick Texas accents of the Border Patrol agents. While we were stopped, we watched as other vehicles—whose occupants were white—were waved through the checkpoint. White people traveling with brown people, however, can expect to be stopped on suspicion they work with the sanctuary movement, which shelters refugees. White people who appear to be clergy, those who wear ethnic clothing or jewelry and women with very long hair or very short hair (they could be nuns) are also frequently detained; white men with beards or men with long hair are likely to be detained, too, because Border Patrol agents have "profiles" of "those sorts" of white people who may help political refugees. (Most of the political refugees from Guatemala and El Salvador are Native American or mestizo because the indigenous people of the Americas have continued to resist efforts by invaders to displace them from their ancestral lands.) Alleged increases in illegal immigration by people of Asian ancestry means that the Border Patrol now routinely detains anyone who appears to be Asian or part Asian, as well.

Once your car is diverted from the Interstate Highway into the checkpoint area, you are under the control of the Border Patrol, which in practical terms exercises a power that no highway patrol or city patrolman possesses: They are willing to detain anyone, for no apparent reason. Other law-enforcement officers need a shred of probable cause in order to detain someone. On the books, so does the Border Patrol; but on the road, it's another matter. They'll order you to stop your car and step out; then they'll ask you to open the trunk. If you ask why or request a search warrant, you'll be told that they'll have to have a dog sniff the car before they can request a search warrant, and the dog might not get there for two or three hours. The search warrant might require an hour or two past that. They make it clear that if you force them to obtain a search warrant for the car, they will make you submit to a strip search as well.

Traveling in the open, though, the sense of violation can be even worse. Never mind high-profile cases like that of former Border Patrol agent Michael Elmer, acquitted of murder by claiming self-defense, despite admitting that as an officer he shot an "illegal" immigrant in the back and then hid the body, which remained undiscovered until another Border Patrolman reported the event. (Last month, Elmer was convicted of reckless endangerment in a separate incident, for shooting at least ten rounds from his M-16 too close to a group of immigrants as they were crossing illegally into Nogales in March 1992). Or that in El Paso, a high school football coach driving a vanload of his players in full uniform was pulled over on the freeway and a Border Patrol agent put a cocked revolver to his head. (The football coach was Mexican-American, as were most of the players in his van; the incident eventually caused a federal judge to issue a restraining order against the Border Patrol.) We've a mountain of personal experiences like that which never make the newspapers. A history professor at U.C.L.A. told me she had been traveling by train from Los Angeles to Albuquerque twice a month doing research. On each of her trips, she had noticed that the Border Patrol agents were at the station in Albuquerque scrutinizing the passengers. Since she is six feet tall and of Irish and German ancestry, she was not particularly concerned. Then one day when she stepped off the train in Albuquerque, two Border Patrolmen accosted her, wanting to know what she was doing, and why she was traveling between Los Angeles and Albuquerque twice a month. She presented identification and an explanation deemed "suitable" by the agents, and was allowed to go about her business.

Just the other day, I mentioned to a friend that I was writing this article and he told me about his 73-year-old father, who is half Chinese and had set out alone by car from Tucson to Albuquerque the week before. His father had become confused by road construction and missed a turnoff from Interstate 10 to Interstate 25; when he turned around and circled back, he missed the turnoff a second time. But when he looped back for yet another try, Border Patrol agents stopped him and forced him to open his trunk. After they satisfied themselves that he was not smuggling Chinese immigrants, they sent him on his way. He was so rattled by the event that he had to be driven home by his daughter.

This is the police state that has developed in the southwestern United States since the 1980s. No person, no citizen, is free to travel without the scrutiny of the Border Patrol. In the city of South Tucson, where 80 percent of the respondents were Chicano or Mexicano, a joint research project by the University of Wisconsin and the University of Arizona recently concluded that one out of every five people there had been detained, mistreated verbally or nonverbally, or questioned by I.N.S. agents in the past two years.

Manifest Destiny may lack its old grandeur of theft and blood—"lock the door" is what it means now, with racism a trump card to be played again and again, shamelessly, by both major political parties. "Immigration," like "street crime" and "welfare fraud," is a political euphemism that refers to people of color. Politicians and media people talk about "illegal aliens" to dehumanize and demonize undocumented immigrants, who are for the most part people of color. Even in the days of Spanish and Mexican rule, no attempts were made to interfere with the flow of people and goods from south to north and north to south. It is the U.S. government that has continually attempted to sever contact between the tribal people north of the border and those to the south.[1]

Now that the "Iron Curtain" is gone, it is ironic that the U.S. government and its Border Patrol are constructing a steel wall ten feet high to span sections of the border with Mexico. While politicians and multinational corporations extol the virtues of NAFTA and "free trade" (in goods, not flesh), the ominous curtain is already up in a six-mile section at the border crossing at Mexicali; two miles are being erected but are not yet finished at Naco; and at Nogales, sixty miles south of Tucson, the steel wall has been all rubber-stamped and awaits construction likely to begin in March. Like the pathetic multimillion-dollar "antidrug" border surveillance balloons that were continually deflated by high winds and made only a couple of meager interceptions before they blew away, the fence along the border is a theatrical prop, a bit of pork for contractors. Border entrepreneurs have already used blowtorches to cut passageways through the fence to collect "tolls," and are doing a brisk business. Back in Washington, the I.N.S. announces a $300 million computer contract to modernize its record-keeping and Congress passes a crime bill that shunts $255 million to the I.N.S. for 1995, $181 million earmarked for border control, which is to include 700 new partners for the men who stopped Gus and me in our travels, and the history professor, and my friend's father, and as many as they could from South Tucson.

It is no use; borders haven't worked, and they won't work, not now, as the indigenous people of the Americas reassert their kinship and solidarity with one another. A mass migration is already under way; its roots are not simply economic. The Uto-Aztecan languages are spoken as far north as Taos Pueblo near the Colorado border, all the way south to Mexico City. Before the arrival of the Europeans, the indigenous communities throughout this region not only conducted commerce, the people shared cosmologies, and oral narratives about the Maize Mother, the Twin Brothers and their Grandmother, Spider Woman, as well as Quetzalcoatl the benevolent snake. The great human migration within the Americas cannot be stopped; human beings are natural forces of the Earth, just as rivers and winds are natural forces.

Deep down the issue is simple: The so-called "Indian Wars" from the days of Sitting Bull and Red Cloud have never really ended in the Americas. The Indian people of southern Mexico, of Guatemala and those left in El Salvador, too, are still fighting for their lives and for their land against the "cavalry" patrols sent out by the governments of those lands. The Americas are Indian country, and the "Indian problem" is not about to go away.

One evening at sundown, we were stopped in traffic at a railroad crossing in downtown Tucson while a freight train passed us, slowly gaining speed as it headed north to Phoenix. In the twilight I saw the most amazing sight: Dozens of human beings, mostly young men, were riding the train; everywhere, on flat cars, inside open boxcars, perched on top of boxcars, hanging off ladders on tank cars and between boxcars. I couldn't count fast enough, but I saw fifty or sixty people headed north. They were dark young men, Indian and mestizo; they were smiling and a few of them waved at us in our cars. I was reminded of the ancient story of Aztlán, told by the Aztecs but known in other Uto-Aztecan communities as well. Aztlán is the beautiful land to the north, the origin place of the Aztec people. I don't remember how or why the people left Aztlán to journey farther south, but the old story says that one day, they will return.

Note

1. The Treaty of Guadalupe Hidalgo, signed in 1848, recognizes the right of the Tohano O'Odom (Papago) people to move freely across the U.S.-Mexico border without documents. A treaty with Canada guarantees similar rights to those of the Iroquois nation in traversing the U.S.-Canada border.

Leslie Marmon Silko

Leslie Silko's story "Yellow Woman" is based on a female character from ancient Laguna stories. In the traditional stories, Yellow Woman has many, and sometimes contradictory, characteristics, from being loyal to being selfish to being a witch. The particular version that Silko re-tells here is based on the abduction stories; in those, a powerful, mythical male figure takes Yellow Woman away from her husband and children. The setting of Silko's version, though, is contemporary, and because it follows the woman's journey into adultery and myth and back again, the story focuses on her identity, her sexuality, and her relationships to family, community and tradition. In order to research stories about Yellow Woman, both traditional and contemporary, you might see Spider Woman's Granddaughters *by Paula Gunn Allen, which has a chapter on Yellow Woman stories.* Yellow Woman *by Leslie Silko, a book edited by Melody Graulich, is part of a series called* Women Writers: Text and Context; *it contains articles about the story as well as other sources, such as interviews with Silko.*

Yellow Woman

One

My thigh clung to his with dampness, and I watched the sun rising up through the tamaracks and willows. The small brown water birds came to the river and hopped across the mud, leaving brown scratches in the alkali-white crust. They bathed in the river silently. I could hear the water, almost at our feet where the narrow fast channel bubbled and washed green ragged moss and fern leaves. I looked at him beside me, rolled in the red blanket on the white river sand. I cleaned the sand out of the cracks between my toes, squinting because the sun was above the willow trees. I looked at him for the last time, sleeping on the white river sand.

I felt hungry and followed the river south the way we had come the afternoon before, following our footprints that were already blurred by the lizard tracks and bug trails. The horses were still lying down, and the black one whinnied when he saw me but he did not get up—maybe it was because the corral was made out of thick cedar branches and the horses had not yet felt the sun like I had. I tried to

Reprinted from *Storyteller*, (1981), by permission of Seaver Books.

look beyond the pale red mesas to the pueblo. I knew it was there, even if I could not see it, on the sand rock hill above the river, the same river that moved past me now and had reflected the moon last night.

The horse felt warm underneath me. He shook his head and pawed the sand. The bay whinnied and leaned against the gate trying to follow, and I remembered him asleep in the red blanket beside the river. I slid off the horse and tied him close to the other horse. I walked north with the river again, and the white sand broke loose in footprints over footprints.

"Wake up."

He moved in the blanket and turned his face to me with his eyes still closed. I knelt down to touch him.

"I'm leaving."

He smiled now, eyes still closed. "You are coming with me, remember?" He sat up now with his bare dark chest and belly in the sun.

"Where?"

"To my place."

"And will I come back?"

He pulled his pants on. I walked away from him, feeling him behind me and smelling the willows.

"Yellow Woman," he said.

I turned to face him. "Who are you?" I asked.

He laughed and knelt on the low, sandy bank, washing his face in the river. "Last night you guessed my name, and you knew why I had come."

I stared past him at the shallow moving water and tried to remember the night, but I could only see the moon in the water and remember his warmth around me.

"But I only said that you were him and that I was Yellow Woman—I'm not really her—I have my own name and I come from the pueblo on the other side of the mesa. Your name is Silva and you are a stranger I met by the river yesterday afternoon."

He laughed softly. "What happened yesterday has nothing to do with what you will do today, Yellow Woman."

"I know—that's what I'm saying—the old stories about the ka'tsina spirit and Yellow Woman can't mean us."

My old grandpa liked to tell those stories best. There is one about Badger and Coyote who went hunting and were gone all day, and when the sun was going down they found a house. There was a girl living there alone, and she had light hair and eyes and she told them that they could sleep with her. Coyote wanted to be with her all night so he sent Badger into a prairie-dog hole, telling him he thought he saw something in it. As soon as Badger crawled in, Coyote blocked up the entrance with rocks and hurried back to Yellow Woman.

"Come here," he said gently.

He touched my neck and I moved close to him to feel his breathing and to hear his heart. I was wondering if Yellow Woman had known who she was—if she knew that she would become part of the stories. Maybe she'd had another name that her husband and relatives called her so that only the ka'tsina from the north and the storytellers would know her as Yellow Woman. But I didn't go on; I felt him all around me, pushing me down into the white river sand.

Yellow Woman went away with the spirit from the north and lived with him and his relatives. She was gone for a long time, but then one day she came back and she brought twin boys.

"Do you know the story?"

"What story?" He smiled and pulled me close to him as he said this. I was afraid lying there on the red blanket. All I could know was the way he felt, warm, damp, his body beside me. This is the way it happens in the stories, I was thinking, with no thought beyond the moment she meets the ka'tsina spirit and they go.

"I don't have to go. What they tell in stories was real only then, back in time immemorial, like they say."

He stood up and pointed at my clothes tangled in the blanket. "Let's go," he said.

I walked beside him, breathing hard because he walked fast, his hand around my wrist. I had stopped trying to pull away from him, because his hand felt cool and the sun was high, drying the river bed into alkali. I will see someone, eventually I will see someone, and then I will be certain that he is only a man—some man from nearby—and I will be sure that I am not Yellow Woman. Because she is from out of time past and I live now and I've been to school and there are highways and pickup trucks that Yellow Woman never saw.

It was an easy ride north on horseback. I watched the change from the cottonwood trees along the river to the junipers that brushed past us in the foothills, and finally there were only piñons, and when I looked up at the rim of the mountain plateau I could see pine trees growing on the edge. Once I stopped to look down, but the pale sandstone had disappeared and the river was gone and the dark lava hills were all around. He touched my hand, not speaking, but always singing softly a mountain song and looking into my eyes.

I felt hungry and wondered what they were doing at home now—my mother, my grandmother, my husband, and the baby. Cooking breakfast, saying, "Where did she go?—maybe kidnapped," and Al going to the tribal police with the details: "She went walking along the river."

The house was made with black lava rock and red mud. It was high above the spreading miles of arroyos and long mesas. I smelled a mountain smell of pitch and buck brush. I stood there beside the black horse, looking down on the small, dim country we had passed, and I shivered.

"Yellow Woman, come inside where's it's warm."

Two

He lit a fire in the stove. It was an old stove with a round belly and an enamel coffeepot on top. There was only the stove, some faded Navajo blankets, and a bedroll and cardboard box. The floor was made of smooth adobe plaster, and there was one small window facing east. He pointed at the box.

"There's some potatoes and the frying pan." He sat on the floor with his arms around his knees pulling them close to his chest and he watched me fry the potatoes. I didn't mind him watching me because he was always watching me—he had been watching me since I came upon him sitting on the river bank trimming leaves from a willow twig with his knife. We ate from the pan and he wiped the grease from his fingers on his Levis.

"Have you brought women here before?" He smiled and kept chewing, so I said, "Do you always use the same tricks?"

"What tricks?" He looked at me like he didn't understand.

"The story about being a ka'tsina from the mountains. The story about Yellow Woman."

Silva was silent; his face was calm.

"I don't believe it. Those stories couldn't happen now," I said.

He shook his head and said softly, "But someday they will talk about us, and they will say, 'Those two lived long ago when things like that happened.'"

He stood up and went out. I ate the rest of the potatoes and thought about things—about the noise the stove was making and the sound of the mountain wind outside. I remembered yesterday and the day before, and then I went outside.

I walked past the corral to the edge where the narrow trail cut through the black rim rock. I was standing in the sky with nothing around me but the wind that came down from the blue mountain peak behind me. I could see faint mountain images in the distance miles across the vast spread of mesas and valleys and plains. I wondered who was over there to feel the mountain wind on those sheer blue edges—who walks on the pine needles in those blue mountains.

"Can you see the pueblo?" Silva was standing behind me.

I shook my head. "We're too far away."

"From here I can see the world." He stepped out on the edge. "The Navajo reservation begins over there." He pointed to the east. "The Pueblo boundaries are over here." He looked below us to the south, where the narrow trail seemed to come from. "The Texans have their ranches over there, starting with that valley, the Concho Valley. The Mexicans run some cattle over there too."

"Do you ever work for them?"

"I steal from them," Silva answered. The sun was dropping behind us and shadows were filling the land below. I turned away from the edge that dropped forever into the valleys below.

"I'm cold," I said; "I'm going inside," I started wondering about this man who could speak the Pueblo language so well but who lived on a mountain and rustled cattle. I decided that this man Silva must be Navajo, because Pueblo men didn't do things like that.

"You must be a Navajo."

Silva shook his head gently. "Little Yellow Woman," he said, "you never give up, do you? I have told you who I am. The Navajo people know me, too." He knelt down and unrolled the bedroll and spread the extra blankets out on a piece of canvas. The sun was down, and the only light in the house came from outside—the dim orange light from sundown.

I stood there and waited for him to crawl under the blankets.

"What are you waiting for?" he said, and I lay down beside him. He undressed me slowly like the night before beside the river—kissing my face gently and running his hands up and down my belly and legs. He took off my pants and then he laughed.

"Why are you laughing?"

"You are breathing so hard."

I pulled away from him and turned my back to him.

He pulled me around and pinned me down with his arms and chest. "You don't understand, do you, little Yellow Woman? You will do what I want."

And again he was all around me with his skin slippery against mine, and I was afraid because I understood that his strength could hurt me. I lay underneath him and I knew that he could destroy me. But later, while he slept beside me, I touched his face and I had a feeling—the kind of feeling for him that overcame me that morning along the river. I kissed him on the forehead and he reached out for me.

When I woke up in the morning he was gone. It gave me a strange feeling because for a long time I sat there on the blankets and looked around the little house for some object of his—some proof that he had been there or maybe that he was coming back. Only the blankets and the cardboard box remained. The .30–.30 that had been leaning in the corner was gone, and so was the knife I had used the night before. He was gone, and I had my chance to go now. But first I had to eat, because I knew it would be a long walk home.

I found some dried apricots in the cardboard box, and I sat down on a rock at the edge of the plateau rim. There was no wind and the sun warmed me. I was surrounded by silence. I drowsed with apricots in my mouth, and I didn't believe that there were highways or railroads or cattle to steal.

When I woke up, I stared down at my feet in the black mountain dirt. Little black ants were swarming over the pine needles around my foot. They must have smelled the apricots. I thought about my family far below me. They would be wondering about me, because this had never happened to me before. The tribal police would file a report. But if old Grandpa weren't dead he would tell them what happened—he would laugh and say, "Stolen by a ka'tsina, a mountain spirit. She'll come home—they usually do." There are enough of them to handle things. My mother and grandmother will raise the baby like they raised me. Al will find someone else, and they will go on like before, except that there will be a story about the day I disappeared while I was walking along the river. Silva had come for me; he said he had. I did not decide to go. I just went. Moonflowers blossom in the sand hills before dawn, just as I followed him. That's what I was thinking as I wandered along the trail through the pine trees.

It was noon when I got back. When I saw the stone house I remembered that I had meant to go home. But that didn't seem important any more, maybe because there were little blue flowers growing in the meadow behind the stone house and the gray squirrels were playing in the pines next to the house. The horses were standing in the corral, and there was a beef carcass hanging on the shady side of a big pine in front of the house. Flies buzzed around the clotted blood that hung from the carcass. Silva was washing his hands in a bucket full of water. He must have heard me coming because he spoke to me without turning to face me.

"I've been waiting for you."

"I went walking in the big pine trees."

I looked into the bucket full of bloody water with brown-and-white animal hairs floating in it. Silva stood there letting his hand drip, examining me intently.

"Are you coming with me?"

"Where?" I asked him.

"To sell the meat in Marquez."

"If you're sure it's O.K."

"I wouldn't ask you if it wasn't," he answered.

He sloshed the water around in the bucket before he dumped it out and set the bucket upside down near the door. I followed him to the corral and watched him saddle the horses. Even beside the horses he looked tall, and I asked him again if he wasn't Navajo. He didn't say anything; he just shook his head and kept cinching up the saddle.

"But Navajos are tall."

"Get on the horse," he said, "and let's go."

The last thing he did before we started down the steep trail was to grab the .30–30 from the corner. He slid the rifle into the scabbard that hung from his saddle.

"Do they ever try to catch you?" I asked.

"They don't know who I am."

"Then why did you bring the rifle?"

"Because we are going to Marquez where the Mexicans live."

Three

The trail leveled out on a narrow ridge that was steep on both sides like an animal spine. On one side I could see where the trail went around the rocky gray hills and disappeared into the southeast where the pale sandrock mesas stood in the distance near my home. On the other side was a trail that went west, and as I looked far into the distance I thought I saw the little town. But Silva said no, that I was looking in the wrong place, that I just thought I saw houses. After that I quit looking off into the distance; it was hot and the wildflowers were closing up their deep-yellow petals. Only the waxy cactus flowers bloomed in the bright sun, and I saw every color that a cactus blossom can be; the white ones and the red ones were still buds, but the purple and the yellow were blossoms, open full and the most beautiful of all.

Silva saw him before I did. The white man was riding a big gray horse, coming up the trail toward us. He was traveling fast and the gray horse's feet sent rocks rolling off the trail into the dry tumbleweeds. Silva motioned for me to stop and we watched the white man. He didn't see us right away, but finally his horse whinnied at our horses and he stopped. He looked at us briefly before he loped the gray horse across the three hundred yards that separated us. He stopped his horse in front of Silva, and his young fat face was shadowed by the brim of his hat. He didn't look mad, but his small, pale eyes moved from the blood-soaked gunny sacks hanging from my saddle to Silva's face and then back to my face.

"Where did you get the fresh meat?" the white man asked.

"I've been hunting," Silva said, and when he shifted his weight in the saddle the leather creaked.

"The hell you have, Indian. You've been rustling cattle. We've been looking for the thief for a long time."

The rancher was fat, and sweat began to soak through his white cowboy shirt and the wet cloth stuck to the thick rolls of belly fat. He almost seemed to be panting from the exertion of talking, and he smelled rancid, maybe because Silva scared him.

Silva turned to me and smiled. "Go back up the mountain, Yellow Woman."

The white man got angry when he heard Silva speak in a language he couldn't understand. "Don't try anything, Indian. Just keep riding to Marquez. We'll call the state police from there."

The rancher must have been unarmed because he was very frightened and if he had a gun he would have pulled it out then. I turned my horse around and the rancher yelled, "Stop!" I looked at Silva for an instant and there was something ancient and dark—something I could feel in my stomach—in his eyes, and when I glanced at his hand I saw his finger on the trigger of the .30–30 that was still in the saddle scabbard. I slapped my horse across the flank and the sacks of raw meat swung against my knees as the horse leaped up the trail. It was hard to keep my balance, and once I thought I felt the saddle slipping backward; it was because of this that I could not look back.

I didn't stop until I reached the ridge where the trail forked. The horse was breathing deep gasps and there was a dark film of sweat on its neck. I looked down in the direction I had come from, but I couldn't see the place. I waited. The wind came up and pushed warm air past me. I looked up at the sky, pale blue and full of thin clouds and fading vapor trails left by jets.

I think four shots were fired—I remember hearing four hollow explosions that reminded me of deer hunting. There could have been more shots after that, but I couldn't have heard them because my horse was running again and the loose rocks were making too much noise as they scattered around his feet.

Horses have a hard time running downhill, but I went that way instead of uphill to the mountain because I thought it was safer. I felt better with the horse running southeast past the round gray hills that were covered with cedar trees and black lava rock. When I got to the plain in the distance I could see the dark green patches of tamaracks that grew along the river; and beyond the river I could see the beginning of the pale sandrock mesas. I stopped the horse and looked back to see if anyone was coming; then I got off the horse and turned the horse around, wondering if it would go back to its corral under the pines on the mountain. It looked back at me for a moment and then plucked a mouthful of green tumbleweeds before it trotted back up the trail with its ears pointed forward, carrying its head daintily to one side to avoid stepping on the dragging reins. When the horse disappeared over the last hill, the gunny sacks full of meat were still swinging and bouncing.

Four

I walked toward the river on a wood-hauler's road that I knew would eventually lead to the paved road. I was thinking about waiting beside the road for someone to drive by, but by the time I got to the pavement I had decided it wasn't very far to walk if I followed the river back the way Silva and I had come.

The river water tasted good, and I sat in the shade under a cluster of silvery willows. I thought about Silva, and I felt sad at leaving him; still, there was something strange about him, and I tried to figure it out all the way back home.

I came back to the place on the river bank where he had been sitting the first time I saw him. The green willow leaves that he had trimmed from the branch were still lying there, wilted in the sand. I saw the leaves and I wanted to go back to him—to kiss him and to touch him—but the mountains were too far away now. And I told myself, because I believe it, he will come back sometime and be waiting again by the river.

I followed the path up from the river into the village. The sun was getting low, and I could smell supper cooking when I got to the screen door of my house. I could hear their voices inside—my mother was telling my grandmother how to fix the Jell-O and my husband, Al, was playing with the baby. I decided to tell them that some Navajo had kidnapped me, but I was sorry that old Grandpa wasn't alive to hear my story because it was the Yellow Woman stories he liked to tell best.

Beth Alvarado

Beth Alvarado's story collection, Not a Matter of Love, *won the Many Voices Prize from New Rivers Press in 2006. Her essays and stories have appeared many journals, most recently* Ploughshares, Cimarron Review, Seattle Review, Third Coast, *and* Dedicated to the People of Darfur: Writings on Fear, Risk, and Hope. *A graduate of Stanford University and the University of Arizona, she is the fiction editor of* Cutthroat: A Journal of the Arts *and teaches at the University of Arizona in Tucson.*

Emily's Exit

My older sister Emily practiced suffering as if it were an art form. She liked the clean lines of pain and would often lie, arms folded over her chest, as if she were dead or dying. Long hair held back by a wide black headband, a large silver cross on her chest, she looked like nothing so much as a nun, although if you'd asked her, she would have said that Catholicism was corrupt. No mystery or mysticism for her. No metaphors, thank you. The word of God was in the Bible and all you had to do was believe it.

Even her bedroom was spare and fundamental, a line drawing in progress. Danish, that's what she liked. When she was eighteen, Emily had insisted our mother remove all the antiques she'd spent years refinishing—cherry dresser, four poster bed, oak rolltop desk—and replace them with the sparest, geometric furniture she could find until all of Emily's room had sharp edges. Light wood, sculptural shapes, tubular lamps, a woven mat to cover the wooden floor. Blinds, not curtains. No comfort. When I looked in her room, I froze. I felt like I was in some icy Ingmar Bergman film—white, black, and tan with a few red accents pulsing.

Emily lying straight-backed on her hard bed, arms folded across her chest. Was she asleep or pretending? Her bed was never rumpled. Perhaps she slept without breathing, I always wondered. Above the bed, one of her own drawings, as simple as the sparest Matisse. A few curved lines suggesting a face, crescent-moon eyes, lifted, of course, toward the Lord. Two lines, which were hands pressed together in prayer, intersecting two shorter lines, which were lips, also pressed together. A cross. Silencing her.

"Emily?"

This was the last time I would see her before she disappeared.

"Emily?"

She opened her eyes.

"Dinner's ready."

Little did I know she was emptying herself to see if God would enter.

Of course, my vision of her is tainted and diminished by time, reduced to the most essential details. She disappeared into the Sonoran Desert to the south of us when I was sixteen. She was twenty and headed, I guess, for her own brand of sainthood. Why else make the trek across the desert in June?

Emily knew the desert. Perhaps the geometry of it appealed to her. The sloping curve of hills on the horizon, angular volcanic outcroppings to the west, the smooth disks of the prickly pear, phallus of saguaro, the long skinny fingers of the ocotillo, crooked elbows of cholla. Everything pierced by spikes and thorns. Earth, caliche, hard and parched, dry sand, no water, that was the desert to the south of here. Forbidding and hostile. It was not the lush desert full of mesquite and palo verde we grew up in. No. That would've been too easy for Emily.

And June? In other parts of the country, June might be June moon spoon, long walks in the pastoral twilight, damp evening air cool and fragrant with alfalfa, but June in Arizona is one word: hot. Hold your hand over the burner to feel the way the sun sears the skin at noon. Waves of heat radiate up from the asphalt, even from bare earth. Dry June air bakes the tissues of your lungs when you inhale. June light bleaches the color out of the mountains and sky; even mesquite leaves fade to a dull gray and wilt. Midnight is a dark furnace. Everything, everyone waits for the clouds to build in the sky, for the monsoon rains, for relief. June is stasis. Limbo. Only the cicadas, in their incessant chirping, move.

They say the Apache could run through the desert all day without water. They'd disappear into it, then reappear like a mirage. That was how I imagined Emily's exit. She just began walking into the wilderness of the desert and, as she walked, she slowly faded until she disappeared altogether. Like a camera trick. Fade out. Perhaps she held a small, blue stone in her mouth and from it sprang forth a trickle of cool water, a miracle stone, that's what she would have needed.

But it couldn't have been easy. Emily was no Apache. She knew the gruesome details, how every summer, poor Mexicans fried to death in the desert: their thirst compelling them to drink their own urine, the sun so hot it boiled their brains inside their skulls, their tongues swollen black, their bones eventually picked clean and bleached white. Surely the irony of her crossing, of going against traffic, occurred to her.

When Emily disappeared, my mother, an ex-hippie who wore Birkenstock sandals with wool socks no matter what the season, occasion, or rest of her outfit demanded, became a Buddhist. It was the only way she could deal with it, she said. Emily's room became a shrine where my mother would retreat when she was feeling stressed. I'd hear the bell and know a clear space was opening up in her heart, a space she was making calm and quiet so she could get a transmission from Emily.

After a few months of not-knowing, my mother decided to build a garden for meditation in the back yard. Maybe she thought it was too difficult for Emily's spirit to come in through the walls of the house. At any rate, she mortared stones together to make a small pool and fountain; she made a tiny shrine on one side of the pool and planted small palms, weird cacti that looked like they were from outer space, and other geometric plants Emily would have liked. It had the same ascetic quality as Emily's room and often, when I stood in the window of our air-conditioned house and watched my mother meditate in her garden, it would occur to me that Emily was more real to her than I was. I was the child who was never missed and not grieved, who paled in her physical realness while Emily began to glow incandescently in her absence.

Shortly after the garden was built, Emily began to visit our mother in the middle of the night, like a vision. She'd float through the air to her, surrounded like *la Virgen de Guadalupe* with tongues of light, and then pause right before my mother's eyes and say, "I am whole."

"I swear," my mother used to say to me the next morning over coffee and a bagel, her eyes moist with gratitude for Emily's thoughtfulness, "it wasn't a dream. It was her and there was this glowing light all around her. It wasn't a dream, it was her spirit, she came to me, and I was filled with warmth and a feeling of complete well-being."

One morning, after the umpteenth vision, I couldn't help it. I said, "Maybe she said, 'I'm a *whore*,' not I'm *whole*. That's why she has to keep coming back. Because you don't listen. You never listen."

My mother was not amused. "That's it," she glared at me. "You've always been jealous."

But jealousy wasn't my problem and she knew it. Emily and I had always been on two different trajectories. For as long as I could remember, Emily had tortured herself by trying to figure out what God wanted from her. She couldn't even eat a candy bar without His blessing. Okay, that might be an exaggeration, but if one could flagellate the spirit; that's what Emily did. Lying still on her bed, she took out some interior cat-o'-ninetails and flailed away. What had she said that might offend the Lord that day? What were her impure thoughts? What scripture should she turn to? And when she had driven her own voice from inside her head and another voice entered, she was never sure if it was the voice of God or the devil.

On those days, she was so weak she could scarcely crawl from bed. We would bring her water, juice, vegetable broth, lift her head to help her drink. My mother bought air purifiers, removed yet more objects from the room, drew the blinds lest the light motes contained something undetectable by anything less sensitive than Emily's spirit. The doctors were perplexed, one specialist said perhaps she was allergic to certain chemicals or gasses in the atmosphere around her, but I knew it was paralysis. Emily wanted so badly to believe God had chosen her that she would bring suffering upon herself to prove it.

The way I tortured myself was much simpler. I carved the names of boys I liked into my thigh with a razor blade. If Emily's domain was the spirit, mine was the flesh.

Not long after my mother had finished building her shrine, we got a visit from Emily's boyfriend. He wanted to know if we'd heard from her. Rick—that was his name—was a revelation. We hadn't known Emily had a boyfriend, for one thing, and for another, I would have thought, had she had one, his name would've been Meshack or Esau or Obediah or one of those other so-and-so-begat-so-and-so names. But, no, he was *Rick*, a regular guy, baseball cap, majoring in business management, drove a little red truck and ate at McDonald's. They'd met one another at church, so he was a Christian but, as he would later tell me, not devout enough for her.

His appearance was, in some ways, a setback for my mother. At that point, we didn't know Emily had disappeared into the desert. My mother had assumed, wrongly, that either Emily had finally been overcome by passion and run off with the love of her life—as my mother had done at her age, mistaking the summer of love for the real thing—or that she had run off with a group of evangelists and was trailing some preacher around the country, much in the same way my mother had trailed the Grateful Dead. Either way, my mother had cherished the idea that Emily was following, if only vaguely, in her footsteps and was off on a trek to find herself.

Rick's appearance disabused her of the first notion and of some others as well. It seems my sister not only had a secret amour (sans sex, of course) but she had invented a secret life (sans my mother and me). She'd told everyone at church that her parents were missionaries in Indochina and she had grown up there surrounded by infidels. She'd told Rick my mother was her crazy sinning aunt and her parents had sent her here to save her soul. She had never mentioned me: I was not a sister left back on some island, nor was I the sinning aunt's sinning daughter. I did not exist in her invented universe. I was not even worth a lie.

What was it that plunged my mother into despair? That she didn't know Emily? The thought that the heart and mind of her own flesh and blood was foreign to her? This was Emily, the daughter she had created inside herself when everyone was advising an abortion; Emily, her oldest, the one she had sacrificed her own hopes and education for. To hear her tell it, she had given up everything: Emily's father because he was dealing, peace marches, smoking dope, dropping acid, grooving with the Dead and the Airplane (because, after all, she had lived in the Haight). No, that scene was getting too weird, violent, and so she had opted for motherhood as activism, nurturing life in a world bent on destroying it. And now, now, not only was Emily foreign and mysterious, but closed. Willfully closed. My mother's heart was broken. The ringing of the bell in Emily's room didn't help. The cooing of the mourning dove in the garden didn't heal. The space cleared in her heart was not expectant. It was empty.

While my mother was busy retreating inside herself, trying to undo the knots of Emily's betrayal, I was busy snooping. The advent of Rick motivated me to search even harder for the elusive journal I was sure Emily had kept. Sure enough, I finally found it stashed in a box marked "Fishing Gear" on the top shelf in the storage room. In excruciating detail, her love aflame: Rick's eyes locking on hers when she was supposed to be deep in prayer; in meetings, his hand brushing against hers made spasms in her heart; the heat from his breath as he sang hymns was like the summer wind. Who could have known Emily was filled with such passion? The problem was, she wanted to be filled with *com*passion, in the Biblical sense, as in filled with the passion of Christ.

She asked God for a sign. She emptied her heart, her mind, for God—but Rick kept entering. His voice, his smell, his skin. He was distracting her from Christ. His reassurances of love and fidelity were like whispers from the devil himself. And when she gave in, let him hold her, felt the heat of his body through his shirt, felt his breath in her hair, his lips on her forehead, then she knew she couldn't trust him. Every molecule in her body was saying yes. Sin, sin, sin. It was so clear. Rick was the way of sin, and everyone knew what the wages of sin were.

No wonder she took off through the desert: she wanted to deny the body, to scourge it with heat and thirst, to vaporize her flesh and become air, spirit.

But if the desert was Emily's test, then I was Rick's. It was inevitable that, under the blade of my razor, little bloody *Ricks* would begin blossoming on my thighs before I went to bed each night.

Only when María showed up did we realize what had really happened to Emily. In Spanish, sprinkled with equal parts Spanglish and broken English, María told us that Emily had been found lying in the desert hills near the small town of Magdalena in Sonora, Mexico. She was past delirious—in fact, they'd thought she was dead at first—her lips so parched they were cracked open, her body temperature off the thermometer. And, sure enough, María said, when Emily woke up, she was *muy disorientado*. Knew not where she was, nor who she was, nor why she didn't know. When she opened her eyes, it was as if she were still asleep or dreaming. She didn't seem to see anyone who was in the room, was staring instead at some interior apparition. She didn't seem to hear or understand what anyone said to her and, when she tried to speak, all that came out was fragments of prayers. It was as if *she* were not there. María was sure she was possessed. "*No hay nadia pa'dentro,*" she said. "Very creepy."

Emily had been taken by the men who found her in the hills to the hacienda where María worked. It was owned by a strange *rubia*, or blonde woman, the daughter of a wealthy Spaniard who was not all there herself. In fact, according to María, this woman was *muy loca*. It happened when she lost both of her children in a car accident. They were on their way to visit her when their car rolled three times, killing them both instantly. After a period of intense grief, where *la señora* shut herself up in one wing of the house and refused to see anyone, she emerged dressed all in white and like *la llorona* herself, floated down the halls of the hacienda in an unworldly calm. She had the bodies of both children exhumed and, just as Father Kino's bones lie in a glass case in the town square of Magdalena, the partially decomposed bodies—María shivered and crossed herself—of *los niños de la señora* lie in their own glass cases in the central courtyard of the hacienda.

As soon as Emily had recovered, every morning she and *la señora* would kneel and pray before the caskets of the dead children. This alarmed María so much that she went through Emily's things, found her I.D. and decided she must find out if she had a family.

"If you don't go down there, she will be lost to you." That's what she told my mother. "*La señora* keeps her up late at night, every night, praying. When she starts to fall asleep, she wakes her up. Sometimes she doesn't let her eat. They spend all day together, sitting in the garden, reading the Bible, praying in the chapel. Always your daughter has to stay at *la señora's* side." She shook her head and whispered. "Sometimes she opens the glass and makes your daughter kiss her daughter's hand. *Aye, Díos mío.*" She crossed herself. "It isn't natural."

No surprise, then, when my mother loaded María and a few of her things into her old Volvo and headed for Magdalena. I immediately called Rick and told him I had news about Emily and, *voila!*, he hopped in his little red truck and was standing on my doorstep in no time.

He had on a white tee shirt, blue jeans, no baseball cap. His hair was cut short and I knew, under the palm of my hand, just what his head would feel like. His eyes were hazel and while, on the way over, they may have been visualizing Emily, once I opened the front door and smiled at him, he only had eyes for me—and, in them, I could see: I was as luscious as a peach.

Now I am not saying Rick was a man of few convictions and I am not saying I seduced him because Emily had erased me. Both of those things may be true, of course, to some extent, but all I know is what happened. Not why. All I know is that I stepped forward. I put my hand on his cheek and I said, "Rick. I don't think Emily's coming back."

"Where is she?" he asked and, as I watched his lips move, I could see why he had become her personal demon.

"Over the edge," I told him. "For sure."

I took his hand and led him into the house, taking him on a little impromptu tour. First we visited Emily's room. We sat on her hard bed and I told him all about the crazy *señora* in Magdalena and how Emily was kissing the bony hand of a dead girl.

He seemed sad. Still, I wanted him to sit there for a moment, in that room, so he could clearly remember the facts of Emily, her arid surfaces, the edges of her fear. The way she would never be able to give in to this messy life.

Then I led him into my room. The soft rumpled bed, the feather pillows you could plump up and then sink into, the fat plum-colored comforter, the window full of green leaves and sunlight. We sat next to each other on the bed. He sighed. I put my arm around him. "I'm sorry," I told him.

I put the palm of my hand against his head and rubbed his skull. I loved the downy texture of his hair, the bristles on his cheek where he hadn't shaved yet. I knew his chest would be smooth, there would be a line of hair above his belly button.

He looked at me. "She was so pure of heart," he said, but he didn't mean it. That's not why he was sad.

I just smiled. I put my other hand on his knee.

"I'm not," I said.

As if it were a sigh, we fell back onto the bed together. For a while we just lay there. We sighed. We were quiet. Emily had left an absence in each of us.

Then he leaned over me and said, "I know you're not Emily. I'm glad."

He kissed me and I put my arms around his neck and felt myself rise to meet him. We began comforting each other over the loss of her, and while it healed me (in certain ways) to feel him as she never would, I was also thinking how she was right: two people can't complete one another. One person can't fill the holes in another's heart. For an instant, I became her and I was terrified by her knowledge: nothing could ever fill my essential alone-ness.

My mother returned without her, just as I had predicted she would. She said the hacienda was a beautiful place, an oasis set back in the hills of the desert. The high white walls had disturbed her, at first, because it looked like a fortress, a fortress from which Emily would never escape. But then, she sat me down and took both my hands in hers. "It isn't a matter of escape," she said. In a way, my mother's worst fear had come true. Emily was not herself. Maybe the heat had boiled her brain, maybe she had hit her head when she fell from exhaustion, but she no longer spoke much English. She was wan and timid as if she were much younger in some ways, but her eyes seemed ancient, my mother said, they shone with fever or with some unworldy wisdom.

"She is not the same person," my mother shrugged. "I don't know. Maybe she saw something or something happened in the desert that changed her. But," and here she covered her heart with her hand, "she barely recognized me. It was as if she hadn't seen me for years. For us, it's been months. For her, a lifetime."

She went on to tell me that when she first arrived, Emily had seemed frightened of her. She'd clung to *la señora* as if she were a child. When my mother held out a picture of me, Emily had smiled and said I was pretty. *Simpatica*. But when my mother asked her if she wanted to come home, she started quaking and crying. She seemed to believe that if she stepped over the threshold of the hacienda, out into the desert, she would fall off the face of the earth and go straight to hell.

"There was nothing I could do to reassure her," my mother said. She said Beatrice, that was *la señora's* name, could not reassure Emily either, and so my mother had come home alone.

My mother had said nothing about the dead children in the courtyard. And she never did. Ever. She retreated into her room and grieved. For a few months afterwards, she toyed with the idea of visiting again, of sending psychiatrists to Mexico, doctors, priests, preachers. Who could best untangle the mysteries of Emily's mind? My mother couldn't decide. She seemed to lose her will. She spent hours in Emily's room, hours in the garden. She turned inward, like Emily had, trusting that some vision would come and liberate her from her own indecision.

Finally, on the anniversary of Emily's exit, she showed me a picture taken in the garden of the hacienda. It was true, Emily's eyes burned with a fever I'd never seen in them. She was a different version of herself, at once paler and yet more intense, as if the flame of her spirit was consuming her flesh from the inside. Then my mother showed me photographs of the *retablos* Emily had been painting for *la señora*. They were beautiful, not the primitives that most *retablos* were. Instead, in hers, the Madonna and Child had delicate faces, elongated bodies, gauzy, ethereal gowns. They were otherworldly, Byzantine in their simplicity and grace.

She said, "Emily has chosen."

Of all the things in the Bible, the Song of Solomon was the only book I ever liked. Sometimes, in the afternoons when Rick and I were in my room, I would look out the window and see my mother in her garden and realize she was turning ever more inward, seeking some sort of Nirvana which was *in* this world although not *of* it. Then I would think of Emily, how she had entered another world altogether.

Sometimes, when Rick touched me or as my hands wandered over him, I would remember phrases. It was as if his body held a kind of Braille that only my fingers could read and I'd remember the song: this is my beloved, this is my friend, his mouth is most sweet, his eyes as doves, his cheeks a bed of spices, his lips like lilies. And I'd think how it was true, our bed was green. And how, if there was a God, He had made the fruits of this world so sweet, so sweet it was some kind of sin, maybe the worst kind of sin, to turn your back on them too soon.

Richard Shelton

Richard Shelton was born in 1933 in Boise, Idaho, though he has lived in Southern Arizona since 1956. Much of his writing reflects his impressions of the Sonoran Desert. Shelton has written several books of poetry and his work has been translated into Spanish, French, Swedish, Polish and Japanese. Going Back to Bisbee, *published in 1992, won the Western States Book Award for creative non-fiction. Shelton is a Regent Professor at the University of Arizona. Since 1974 he has been the director of a creative writing workshop at Arizona State Prison in Florence, Arizona; in the twenty-one years he has been working at the prison eight books of poetry, written by inmates, have been published.*

The Bus to Veracruz

The mail is slow here. If I died, I wouldn't find out about it for a long time. Perhaps I am dead already. At any rate, I am living in the wrong tense of a foreign language and have almost no verbs and only a few nouns to prove I exist. When I need a word, I fumble among the nouns and find one, but so many are similar in size and color. I am apt to come up with *caballo* instead of *caballero,* or *carne* instead of *casa.* When that happens, I become confused and drop the words. They roll across the tile floor in all directions. Then I get down on my hands and knees and crawl through a forest of legs, reaching under tables and chairs to retrieve them. But I am no longer embarrassed about crawling around on the floor in public places. I have come to realize that I am invisible most of the time and have been since I crossed the border.

All the floors are tile. All the tiles are mottled with the same disquieting pattern in one of three muddy colors—shades of yellow, purple, or green. They make me think of dried vomit, desiccated liver, and scum on a pond. The floor of my room is dried vomit with a border of scum on a pond, and like most of the floors it has several tiles missing, which is a great blessing to me. These lacunae are oases in the desert where I can rest my eyes. The nausea from which I suffer so much of the time is not caused by food or water, but by the floors. I know this because when I sit in the town square, which is covered with concrete of no particular color, the nausea subsides.

The town is small, although larger than it would seem to a visitor—if there are any visitors—and remote. It has no landing field for even small planes, and the nearest railroad is almost one hundred kilometers to the east. The only bus goes to Veracruz. Often I stop at the bus terminal to ask about the bus to Veracruz. The

Reprinted from *The Other Side of the Story,* (1987), by permission of the author.

floor of the bus terminal is scum on a pond with a border of desiccated liver, but there are many tiles missing. The terminal is always deserted except for Rafael and Esteban, sometimes sitting on the bench inside, sometimes lounging just outside the door. They are young, barefoot, and incredibly handsome. I buy them Cocas from the machine, and we have learned to communicate in our fashion. When I am with them, I am glad to be invisible, glad that they never look directly at me. I could not bear the soft vulnerability of those magnificent eyes.

"When does the bus leave for Veracruz?" I ask them. I have practiced this many times and am sure I have the right tense. But the words rise to the ceiling, burst, and fall as confetti around us. A few pieces catch in their dark hair and reflect the light like jewels. Rafael rubs his foot on the floor. Esteban stares out the filthy window. Are they sad, I wonder, because they believe there is no bus to Veracruz or because they don't know when it leaves.

"Is there a bus to Veracruz?" Suddenly they are happy again. Their hands fly like vivacious birds. "*¡Sí, hay! ¡Por supuesto, Señor! ¡Es verdad!*" They believe, truly, in the bus to Veracruz. Again I ask them when it leaves. Silence and sadness. Rafael studies on the tiles on the floor if it contains the answer. Esteban turns back to the window, I buy them *Cocas* from the machine and go away.

Once a week I stop at the post office to get my mail from the ancient woman in the metal cage, and each week I receive one letter. Actually, the letters are not mine, and the ancient woman has probably known this for a long time, but we never speak of it and she continues to hand me the letters, smiling and nodding in her coquettish way, eager to please me. Her hair is braided with colored ribbons, and her large silver earrings jingle when she bobs her head, which she does with great enthusiasm when I appear. I could not estimate how old she is. Perhaps even she has forgotten. But she must have been a great beauty at one time. Now she sits all day in the metal cage in the post office, a friendly apparition whose bright red lipstick is all the more startling because she has no teeth.

The first time I entered the post office, it was merely on an impulse to please her. I was expecting no mail, since no one knew where I was. But each time I passed, I had seen her through the window, seated in her metal cage with no customers to break the monotony. She always smiled and nodded at me through the window, eager for any diversion. Finally one day I went in on the pretext of calling for my mail, although I knew there would be none. To avoid the confusion which my accent always causes, I wrote my name on a slip of paper and presented it to her. Her tiny hands darted among the pigeonholes, and to my astonishment she presented me with a letter which was addressed to me in care of general delivery. She was so delighted with her success that I simply took the letter and went away, unwilling to disillusion her.

As soon as I opened the letter, the mystery was solved. My name is fairly common. The letter was intended for someone else with the same name. It was written on blue paper, in flawless Palmer Method script, and signed by a woman. It was undated and there was no return address. But it was in English, and I read it shamelessly, savoring each phrase. I rationalized by convincing myself that the mail was so slow the man to whom the letter had been written was probably already dead and could not object to my reading his mail. But I knew before I finished the letter that I would return to the post office later on the chance there might be others. She loved him. She thought he was still alive.

Since then I have received one letter each week, to the enormous delight of my ancient friend in the post office. I take the letters home and steam them open, careful to leave no marks on the delicate paper. They are always from the same woman, and I feel by now that I know her. Sometimes I dream about her, as if she were someone I knew in the past. She is blond and slender, no longer young but far from old. I can see her long, graceful fingers holding the pen as she writes, and sometimes she reaches up to brush a strand of hair away from her face. Even that slight gesture has the eloquence of a blessing.

When I have read each letter until I can remember it word for word, I reseal it, Then, after dark, I take it back to the post office by a circuitous route, avoiding anyone who might be on the street at that hour. The post office is always open, but the metal cage is closed and the ancient one is gone for the night. I drop the letter into the dead letter box and hurry away.

At first I had no curiosity about what happened to the letters after they left my hands. Then I began to wonder if they were destroyed or sent to some central office where, in an attempt to locate the sender and return them, someone might discover that they had been opened. Still later, the idea that some nameless official in a distant city might be reading them became almost unbearable to me. It was more and more difficult to remember that they were not my letters. I could not bear to think of anyone else reading her words, sensing her hesitations and tenderness. At last I decided to find out.

It took months of work, but with practice I became clever at concealing myself in shadowy doorways and watching. I have learned that once each week a nondescript man carrying a canvas bag enters the post office through the back door, just as the ancient woman is closing her metal cage for the night. She empties the contents of the dead letter box into his canvas bag, and he leaves by the door he came in. The man then begins a devious journey which continues long into the night. Many nights I have lost him and have had to begin again the following week. He doubles back through alleys and down obscure streets. Several times he enters deserted buildings by one door and emerges from another. He crosses the cemetery and goes through the Cathedral.

But finally he arrives at his destination—the bus terminal. And there, concealed behind huge doors which can be raised to the ceiling, is the bus to Veracruz. The man places his canvas bag in the luggage compartment, slams the metal cover with a great echoing clang, and goes away.

And later, at some unspecified hour, the bus to Veracruz rolls silently out of the terminal, a luxury liner leaving port with all its windows blazing. It has three yellow lights above the windshield and three gold stars along each side. The seats are red velvet and there are gold tassels between the windows. The dashboard is draped with brocade in the richest shades of yellow, purple, and green; and on this altar is a statue of the Virgin, blond and shimmering. Her slender fingers are extended to bless all those who ride the bus to Veracruz, but the only passenger is an ancient woman with silver earrings who sits by the window, nodding and smiling to the empty seats around her. There are two drivers who take turns during the long journey. They are young and incredibly handsome, with eyes as soft as the wings of certain luminous brown moths.

The bus moves through sleeping streets without making a sound. When it gets to the highway, it turns toward Veracruz and gathers speed. Then nothing can stop it: not the rain, nor the washed-out bridges, nor the sharp mountain curves, nor the people who stand by the road to flag it down.

I believe in the bus to Veracruz. And someday, when I am too tired to struggle any longer with the verbs and nouns, when the ugliness and tedium of this place overcome me, I will be on it. I will board the bus with my ticket in my hand. The doors of the terminal will rise to the ceiling, and we will move out through the darkness, gathering speed, like a great island of light.

Luci Tapahonso

Luci Tapahonso grew up in Shiprock, New Mexico, in the Navajo Nation. She has published five books of poetry: One More Shiprock Night, Seasonal Woman, A Breeze Swept Through, The Women Are Singing, *and* Blue Horses Rush In. *Tapahonso currently teaches here at the University of Arizona. Her work is anchored in the land she shares with her people and in Navajo traditions.*

In her short essay, "A Sense of Myself," Tapahonso explores her relationship to both the Navajo and English languages. Her poetry also reflects her awareness of the interfaces always present between Indian and non-Indian worlds. In her short story, "What I Am," she explores her connection to her mother, grandmother, and her great-grandmother, whom she knew only through stories.

A Sense of Myself

Earlier this year, as I was driving to a poetry reading in southern Colorado, I was trying to remember a certain part of a song that I wanted to sing that evening.

In the last part of the song, there were a few notes that seemed to dip and lower, then the song repeated itself again. I felt I had to get that tiny part accurate before it was sung in public. I asked my father if he remembered it and he did. He was sitting in the back seat and looking out at the mountains, then leaning forward towards me to listen as I sang. He sang it over and over again. After a half-hour or so, I finally learned it right and we sang it all the way into Durango where I was to read.

Before the reading, I asked my father if he thought I should sing that particular song as it was attached to the poem. He said, "If you know the song and like it when you sing, then sing it. It's your song. The English in the poems, though, is not yours. You are only borrowing that. Once you read it to others, it becomes theirs also. You are responsible for what that may create. You should be careful with that particular use of English."

He is right in that the language I have chosen to write in and express myself with is not truly mine. I have adopted it and learned to use it for myself. Because I was born into and come out of an oral culture, I learned early that the use of words involves responsibility and respect for oneself. A person is known primarily by his use of language and song. One's family and upbringing are reflected in the way he or she talks among others. So one does not act alone in the use of words or songs; it always involves his parents, his family and distant relatives. In telling me this again, in English no less, my father was essentially saying, "Remember you

Reprinted from *Dine Be'iina: A Journal of Navajo Life* 1, no. 1, pp. 372–373, (1987).

are talking for us all, the things you write will come back to us, because you are part of us. We are together whole."

And so it is in this way of learning and being spoken to, that I have come to see my work as not even really being mine but as an outlet for those whom I belong to. So that I do not write alone and I am responsible and held accountable for what I write in terms of my history, my family and myself.

It is this sense of having "borrowed" that increases the value of the language for me. In Navajo, there is a song or oration that goes with every activity in daily life. To use these out of context, whether carelessly or in jest, is frowned upon greatly. As I write in English, I am aware of how this particular line or feeling would be in Navajo first so that I am translating roughly into English the song or the prayer, the story that accompanies whatever I happen to be writing about. Thus it becomes important for my work to carry the "rhythm" or the "feeling" of the story or event as it would if I were sitting at my mother's kitchen table telling about the event.

After the reading that night, it was snowing as we drove home. As we neared Shiprock, the snow started to thin out, becoming lighter and clearer. "It was like this the night your sister was born," my mother said and she went on to tell about that night and why this sister possessed this or that characteristic because of her birth-night long ago. In my mother's telling of that event, the weather that night became synonymous with my sister's birth in my mind and the songs she sang immediately after will remember that.

It has been that way my whole life, and my sense of language, my awareness of words becomes entangled with songs, memories, history and the land. It is not separate—the borrowing of English—from the way I would use it in Navajo. My sense of poetics, in this case, becomes a sense of myself.

What I Am

Nineteen hundred thirty-five. Kinɫichíí'nii Bitsí waited, looking across the snow-covered desert stretching out before her. Snow was falling lightly and the desert was flat and white. From where she stood at the foothills of the Carriso Mountains, she could see for miles.

She would see him when he approached—a small, dark speck on the vast whiteness, moving slowly, but closer. Her son, Prettyboy, tall and lanky on the sure-footed horse. She would see him.

All evening, she kept watch, stepping out every once in a while. He had gone to visit some relatives at Little Shiprock and should have returned by now. It had begun snowing early and continued into the evening. She knew Prettyboy had

Reprinted from *Saani Dahataal: The Women Are Singing*, (1993), by permission of University of Arizona Press. Copyright © 1993 by Luci Tapahonso.

started home before the storm and would be arriving soon. She kept watch, looking out on the horizon.

In those days, hogans had no windows so she stood at the front door, a shawl around her shoulders. Only her eyes were uncovered as she squinted, looking out into the desert night. "Nihimá, deesk'aaz. Our mother, it's cold," her children called her inside. She would come in for a while, then go back out to watch for him again. All evening she waited, and her children urged her not to worry. He would be home soon they said. She continued watching for him, insisting that she wasn't cold.

Finally, she saw him, a dark speck on the horizon. She rushed in and stirred up the fire, heated up the stew, and put on a fresh pot of coffee. She heated up the grease for frybread. He came in, damp and cold with snow. They laughed because his eyebrows were frozen white. "Tell us everything about your trip," they said to him. "Tell us about your trip." While he ate, he talked about the relatives he visited and the news that he had heard. He said the horse seemed to know the way by itself through the snow and wind. He kept his head down most of the way, he said. The snow was blowing and it was hard to see. The family finally went to bed, relieved that Prettyboy was safely home. Outside the wind blew and the snow formed drifts around the hogan.

In the morning, KinLichíi'nii Bitsí was sick—feverish and dizzy. She didn't get up and they fed her blue corn mush and weak Navajo tea to drink. She slept most of the day and felt very warm. Her family began to worry. The nearest medical doctor was in Shiprock, fifty miles to the east. On horseback, it was a full day's journey. Even then, the doctor was at the agency only two days a week, and they couldn't remember which days he was there. A medicineman lived nearby on the mountainside, and they decided to wait until morning to go over there and alert him, if they had to. She would get better, they said, and they prayed and sang songs for strength and for the children. Very late that night, she became very ill and talked incessantly about her children and grandchildren.

She died before morning, and Prettyboy went out into the snow and blowing wind to tell other relatives who lived at distances from the hogan of KinLichíi'nii Bitsí. People gathered quickly despite the snow; they came from all around to help out with the next four days.

Nineteen hundred sixty-eight. The granddaughter of KinLichíi'nii Bitsí said:

My Uncle Prettyboy died today, and we went over to his house. His aunt, my grandma, was sweeping out her hogan next door and scolding the young people for not helping out. They were listening to the radios in their pickups and holding hands. You know, they are teenagers. My grandma is 104 years old. My real grandma, KinLichíi'nii Bitsí, would have been 106 if she hadn't died in the 1930s. I know a lot about her through stories they told me. I know how she was. I think I'm like her in some ways.

At Prettyboy's house, his wife and children were sitting in the front room, and people came in and spoke to them quietly. They were crying and crying; sometimes loudly, sometimes sobbing. In the kitchen, and outside over open fires, we were cooking and preparing food for everyone who had come following his death.

Prettyboy was a tall man and he died of cancer. It was awful because he didn't even smoke. But he had worked in the uranium mines near Red Valley, like many other Navajo men, and was exposed to radioactive materials.

Last week when we were hoeing in the field, my mother told me, "Having a mother is everything. Your mother is your home. When children come home, the mother is always ready with food, stories, and songs for the little ones. She's always happy to see her children and grandchildren."

She had always told me this as I was growing up. That day when we were hoeing corn, I asked her, "Tell me about my grandmother and how you knew something was wrong that time. Tell me the story, shima."

She told me, saying:

That night Prettyboy was coming home, I knew something was wrong. The wind blew hard and roared through the tall pine trees. We lived in the mountains at Oak Springs, ten miles above where my mother lived. We were just married then. Our first baby, your oldest sister, was a month old.

That night the dogs started barking wildly and loudly; they were afraid of something. Then they stopped suddenly. Your father and I looked at each other across the room. Then we heard the coyotes barking and yelping outside. He opened the door and they were circling the hogan, running around and around, yelping the whole time. Your father grabbed the rifle and shot at the coyotes, but he missed each time. He missed. He had been a sharpshooter in the army, and he couldn't shoot them. Finally, they ran off, and we were both afraid. We talked and prayed into the night. We couldn't go anywhere. The snow was deep, and even the horses would have a hard time.

In the morning, I went out to pray and I saw my brother, Prettyboy, riding up to our hogan. He was still far away, but even then, I knew something had happened. I tried not to cry, but I knew in my bones something had happened. My brother would not ride out in that weather just to visit. Even though the sun was out, the snow was frozen, and the wind blew steadily. I held the baby and prayed, hoping I was wrong.

Finally, as he came up to our hogan, I went out and I could see that he was crying. He wasn't watching where he was going. The horse led my brother who was crying. I watched him, and then he saw me. I called out, "Shínaaí, my older brother!" He got off the horse and ran to me, crying out, "Shideezhí, nihimá adin. My younger sister, our mother's gone!" My heart fell. We cried. The wind stopped blowing and we went inside.

I held my baby girl and told her she would not see her grandmother. Neither would our other children. My mother died, and I realized that she was my home. She had always welcomed us, and since I was the youngest, she called me "baby." "Even if you are a grandmother, you will be my baby always," she often said to me.

When my mother told this story, we always cried. Even if I had known Kin-Lichíi'nii Bitsî, I couldn't love her more than I do now—knowing her only through stories and my mother's memory.

My grandmother had talked to my father about a week before she died. She told him, "Take care of her. She is my youngest, my baby. I trust you, and I have faith that you will care for her as I have all these years. She is my baby, but she knows what to do. Listen to her and remember that a woman's wisdom is not foolish. She knows a lot, because I have raised her to be a good and kind person."

My father listened, and he treats my mother well. He listens to her and abides by her wishes.

Nineteen hundred eighty-seven. The great-granddaughter of KinLichíi'nii Bitsí said:

Early in the morning, we went out to pray. The corn pollen drifted into the swimming pool, becoming little specks of yellow on the blue water. The water lapped quietly against the edges. We prayed and asked the holy ones and my ancestors who died before to watch over me.

I was going so far away to Europe. What a trip it would be. My grandma called the evening before I left and said, "Remember who you are. You're from Oak Springs, and all your relatives are thinking about you and praying that you will come back safely. Do well on your trip, my little one." I was nervous and couldn't sleep. I felt like changing my mind, but my mother had already spent all that money. She promised she wouldn't cry at the airport, then she did. I know that my little sister teased her about it.

I put the bag of pollen in my purse. At La Guardia Airport, I went to the bathroom and tasted some. My mother, I thought, my grandmother, help me. Everything was confusing and loud, so many people smoking and talking loudly. I wanted my mother's soft, slow voice more than anything. I was the only Indian in the group, and no one knew how I felt. The other girls were looking at boys and giggling.

At least I had the corn pollen. I was afraid they would arrest me at customs for carrying an unknown substance, but they didn't. I knew I was meant to go to Paris.

I prayed on top of the Eiffel Tower, and the pollen floated down to the brick plaza below. I was so far away from home, so far above everything. The tower swayed a bit in the wind. I never missed Indians until I went abroad. I was lonely to see an Indian the whole time. People thought I was "neat"—being a "real" Indian. They asked all kinds of questions and wanted to learn Navajo. It was weird to be a "real" Indian. All along, I was just regular, one of the bunch, laughing with relatives and friends, mixing Navajo and English. We were always telling jokes about cowboys, computer warriors, and stuff.

It was while I stood on top of the Eiffel Tower that I understood that who I am is my mother, her mother, and my great-grandmother, KinLichíi'nii Bitsí. It was she who made sure I got through customs and wasn't mugged in Paris. When I returned, my grandmother was at the airport. She hugged me tightly. My mother stood back, then came forward and held me. I was home.

Helena María Viramontes

Helena María Viramontes is a professor of creative writing at Cornell University. Her first collection of short stories received wide acclaim for its representations of the lives of Mexican-American women in nontraditional roles.

The Moths, Viramontes's most widely anthologized short story, is an excellent example of how she pushes the boundaries of Chicana identity and challenges popular stereotypes about Mexican-American women.

The Moths

I was fourteen years old when Abuelita requested my help. And it seemed only fair. Abuelita had pulled me through the rages of scarlet fever by placing, removing and replacing potato slices on the temples of my forehead; she had seen me through several whippings, an arm broken by a dare jump off Tío Enrique's toolshed, puberty, and my first lie. Really, I told Amá, it was only fair.

Not that I was her favorite granddaughter or anything special. I wasn't even pretty or nice like my older sisters and I just couldn't do the girl things they could do. My hands were too big to handle the fineries of crocheting or embroidery and I always pricked my fingers or knotted my colored threads time and time again while my sisters laughed and called me bull hands with their cute waterlike voices. So I began keeping a piece of jagged brick in my sock to bash my sisters or anyone who called me bull hands. Once, while we all sat in the bedroom, I hit Teresa on the forehead, right above her eyebrow and she ran to Amá with her mouth open, her hand over her eye while blood seeped between her fingers. I was used to the whippings by then.

I wasn't respectful either. I even went so far as to doubt the power of Abuelita's slices, the slices she said absorbed my fever. "You're still alive, aren't you?" Abuelita snapped back, her pasty gray eye beaming at me and burning holes in my suspicions. Regretful that I had let secret questions drop out of my mouth, I couldn't look into her eyes. My hands began to fan out, grow like a liar's nose until they hung by my side like low weights. Abuelita made a balm out of dried moth wings and Vicks and rubbed my hands, shaped them back to size and it was the strangest feeling. Like bones melting. Like sun shining through the darkness of your eyelids. I didn't mind helping Abuelita after that, so Amá would always send me over to her.

Reprinted from *The Moths and Other Stories*, (1995), by permission of Arte Publico Press.

In the early afternoon Amá would push her hair back, hand me my sweater and shoes, and tell me to go to Mama Luna's. This was to avoid another fight and another whipping, I knew. I would deliver one last direct shot on Marisela's arm and jump out of our house, the slam of the screen door burying her cries of anger, and I'd gladly go help Abuelita plant her wild lilies or jasmine or heliotrope or cilantro or hierbabuena in red Hills Brothers coffee cans. Abuelita would wait for me at the top step of her porch holding a hammer and nail and empty coffee cans. And although we hardly spoke, hardly looked at each other as we worked over root transplants, I always felt her gray eye on me. It made me feel, in a strange sort of way, safe and guarded and not alone. Like God was supposed to make you feel.

On Abuelita's porch, I would puncture holes in the bottom of the coffee cans with a nail and a precise hit of a hammer. This completed, my job was to fill them with red clay mud from beneath her rose bushes, packing it softly, then making a perfect hole, four fingers round, to nest a sprouting avocado pit, or the spidery sweet potatoes that Abuelita rooted in mayonnaise jars with toothpicks and daily water, or prickly chayotes that produced vines that twisted and wound all over her porch pillars, crawling to the roof, up and over the roof, and down the other side, making her small brick house look like it was cradled within the vines that grew pear-shaped squashes ready for the pick, ready to be steamed with onions and cheese and butter. The roots would burst out of the rusted coffee cans and search for a place to connect. I would then feed the seedlings with water.

But this was a different kind of help, Amá said, because Abuelita was dying. Looking into her gray eye, then into her brown one, the doctor said it was just a matter of days. And so it seemed only fair that these hands she had melted and formed found use in rubbing her caving body with alcohol and marihuana, rubbing her arms and legs, turning her face to the window so that she could watch the Bird of Paradise blooming or smell the scent of clove in the air. I toweled her face frequently and held her hand for hours. Her gray wiry hair hung over the mattress. Since I could remember, she'd kept her long hair in braids. Her mouth was vacant and when she slept, her eyelids never closed all the way. Up close, you could see her gray eye beaming out the window, staring hard as if to remember everything. I never kissed her. I left the window open when I went to the market.

Across the street from Jay's Market there was a chapel. I never knew its denomination, but I went in just the same to search for candles. I sat down on one of the pews because there were none. After I cleaned my fingernails, I looked up at the high ceiling. I had forgotten the vastness of these places, the coolness of the marble pillars and the frozen statues with blank eyes. I was alone. I knew why I had never returned.

That was one of Apá's biggest complaints. He would pound his hands on the table, rocking the sugar dish or spilling a cup of coffee and scream that if I didn't go to mass every Sunday to save my goddamn sinning soul, then I had no reason to go out of the house, period. Punto final. He would grab my arm and dig his nails into me to make sure I understood the importance of catechism. Did he make himself clear? Then he strategically directed his anger at Amá for her lousy ways of bringing up daughters, being disrespectful and unbelieving, and my older sisters would pull me aside and tell me if I didn't get to mass right this minute, they were all going to kick the holy shit out of me. Why am I so selfish? Can't you see what it's doing to Amá, you idiot? So I should wash my feet and stuff them in my black Easter shoes that shone with Vaseline, grab a missal and veil, and wave good-bye to Amá.

I would walk slowly down Lorena to First to Evergreen, counting the cracks on the cement. On Evergreen I would turn left and walk to Abuelita's. I liked her porch because it was shielded by the vines of the chayotes and I could get a good look at the people and car traffic on Evergreen without them knowing. I would jump up the porch steps, knock on the screen door as I wiped my feet and call Abuelita? mi Abuelita? As I opened the door and stuck my head in, I would catch the gagging scent of toasting chile on the placa. When I entered the sala, she would greet me from the kitchen, wringing her hands in her apron. I'd sit at the corner of the table to keep from being in her way. The chiles made my eyes water. Am I crying? No, Mama Luna, I'm sure not crying. I don't like going to mass, but my eyes watered anyway, the tears dropping on the tablecloth like candle wax. Abuelita lifted the burnt chiles from the fire and sprinkled water on them until the skins began to separate. Placing them in front of me, she turned to check the menudo. I peeled the skins off and put the flimsy, limp looking green and yellow chiles in the molcajete and began to crush and crush and twist and crush the heart out of the tomato, the clove of garlic, the stupid chiles that made me cry, crushed them until they turned into liquid under my bull hand. With a wooden spoon, I scraped hard to destroy the guilt, and my tears were gone. I put the bowl of chile next to a vase filled with freshly cut roses. Abuelita touched my hand and pointed to the bowl of menudo that steamed in front of me. I spooned some chile into the menudo and rolled a corn tortilla thin with the palms of my hands. As I ate, a fine Sunday breeze entered the kitchen and a rose petal calmly feathered down to the table.

I left the chapel without blessing myself and walked to Jay's. Most of the time Jay didn't have much of anything. The tomatoes were always soft and the cans of Campbell soups had rusted spots on them. There was dust on the tops of cereal boxes. I picked up what I needed: rubbing alcohol, five cans of chicken broth, a big bottle of Pine Sol. At first Jay got mad because I thought I had forgotten the money. But it was there all the time, in my back pocket.

When I returned from the market, I heard Amá crying in Abuelita's kitchen. She looked up at me with puffy eyes. I placed the bags of groceries on the table and began putting the cans of soup away. Amá sobbed quietly. I never kissed her. After a while, I patted her on the back for comfort. Finally: "¿Y mi Amá?" she asked in a whisper, then choked again and cried into her apron.

Abuelita fell off the bed twice yesterday, I said, knowing that I shouldn't have said it and wondering why I wanted to say it because it only made Amá cry harder. I guess I became angry and just so tired of the quarrels and beatings and unanswered prayers and my hands just there hanging helplessly by my side. Amá looked at me again, confused, angry, and her eyes were filled with sorrow. I went outside and sat on the porch swing and watched the people pass. I sat there until she left. I dozed off repeating the words to myself like rosary prayers: when do you stop giving when do you start giving when do you . . . and when my hands fell from my lap, I awoke to catch them. The sun was setting, an orange glow, and I knew Abuelita was hungry.

There comes a time when the sun is defiant. Just about the time when moods change, inevitable seasons of a day, transitions from one color to another, that hour or minute or second when the sun is finally defeated, finally sinks into the realization that it cannot with all its power to heal or burn, exist forever, there comes an illumination where the sun and earth meet, a final burst of burning red orange fury reminding us that although endings are inevitable, they are necessary for rebirths, and when that time came, just when I switched on the light in the kitchen to open Abuelita's can of soup, it was probably then that she died.

The room smelled of Pine Sol and vomit and Abuelita had defecated the remains of her cancerous stomach. She had turned to the window and tried to speak, but her mouth remained open and speechless. I heard you, Abuelita, I said, stroking her cheek, I heard you. I opened the windows of the house and let the soup simmer and overboil on the stove. I turned the stove off and poured the soup down the sink. From the cabinet I got a tin basin, filled it with lukewarm water and carried it carefully to the room. I went to the linen closet and took out some modest bleached white towels. With the sacredness of a priest preparing his vestments, I unfolded the towels one by one on my shoulders. I removed the sheets and blankets from her bed and peeled off her thick flannel nightgown. I toweled her puzzled face, stretching out the wrinkles, removing the coils of her neck, toweled her shoulders and breasts. Then I changed the water. I returned to towel the creases of her stretch-marked stomach, her sporadic vaginal hairs, and her sagging thighs. I removed the lint from between her toes and noticed a mapped birthmark on the fold of her buttock. The scars on her back which were as thin as the life lines on the palms of her hands made me realize how little I really knew of Abuelita. I covered her with a thin blanket and went into the bathroom. I washed my hands, and turned on the tub faucets and watched the water pour into the tub with vitality and steam. When it was full, I turned off the water and undressed. Then, I went to get Abuelita.

She was not as heavy as I thought and when I carried her in my arms, her body fell into a V, and yet my legs were tired, shaky, and I felt as if the distance between the bedroom and bathroom was miles and years away. Amá, where are you?

I stepped into the bathtub one leg first, then the other. I bent my knees slowly to descend into the water slowly so I wouldn't scald her skin. There, there, Abuelita, I said, cradling her, smoothing her as we descended, I heard you. Her hair fell back and spread across the water like eagle's wings. The water in the tub overflowed and poured onto the tile of the floor. Then the moths came. Small, gray ones that came from her soul and out through her mouth fluttering to light, circling the single dull light bulb of the bathroom. Dying is lonely and I wanted to go to where the moths were, stay with her and plant chayotes whose vines would crawl up her fingers and into the clouds; I wanted to rest my head on her chest with her stroking my hair, telling me about the moths that lay within the soul and slowly eat the spirit up; I wanted to return to the waters of the womb with her so that we would never be alone again. I wanted. I wanted my Amá. I removed a few strands of hair from Abuelita's face and held her small light head within the hollow of my neck. The bathroom was filled with moths, and for the first time in a long time I cried, rocking us, crying for her, for me, for Amá, the sobs emerging from the depths of anguish, the misery of feeling half born, sobbing until finally the sobs rippled into circles and circles of sadness and relief. There, there, I said to Abuelita, rocking us gently, there, there.

Aisha Sabatini Sloan

Aisha Sabatini Sloan (1981–) was born in Los Angeles. She received her MFA in creative writing from the University of Arizona and holds an MA in Studio Art and Cultural Studies from the Gallatin School for Individualized Study at New York University. She currently teaches composition classes as an adjunct in Arizona, and is working on two essay collections. A hypertext version of this essay with photographs was published as "How to Draw a Glass Mountain: Los Angeles and the Architecture of Segregation" in the web-based journal Terrain.org in 2010. This version, "What They Say about Glass Houses," is the first chapter of her book-length manuscript, An Ethnography of Satellites.

What They Say about Glass Houses

In the City of Angels, you can live in a hillside house where the courtyard juts into the sky and spills out over a precipice. There are walls made out of glass, creating the illusion that what lies outside—trees, a thousand city lights, or the yellow desert hills—is a part of your own, personal living room. Houses manage to encapsulate a sense of spareness and solitude in the midst of a city with almost ten million inhabitants.

I grew up a few miles south of Los Angeles's famous, snaking east/west artery, Sunset Boulevard—down the hill from the types of celebrity homes that best demonstrate a classic Los Angeles aesthetic. Brentwood, a wealthy enclave between UCLA and the Santa Monica beach, is home to some of the earliest examples of modern architecture. Our apartment is on the second floor of a brown, two-story building just on the borderline between Brentwood and West Los Angeles. It is not encased with glass or particularly chic, but there are jade plants, pollution-pink sunsets and olive trees outside our windows. Before the cream-colored condominiums arrived, anyway.

I am meeting someone up the street from the apartment where I grew up, at a coffee shop that stands on an odd block: outdoor seating spills out onto a concrete triangle that sticks out between San Vicente Boulevard and Gorham like a peninsula. Some time before the café arrived, there was an Italian restaurant that fared poorly after one of its waiters was found murdered alongside Nicole Brown Simpson just a few blocks away. Today, espresso machines reflect light with the sophistication of a black-and-white photograph in the noisy coffee bar. The bright, blue day makes a lovely backdrop for the coral trees that stand parallel to the café's wall of north-facing windows. While tapping on a window pane with her fingernail, an elderly lady once told me that when she first moved west, this part of the city consisted of little more than a grove of orange trees.

329

The person I am meeting is a friend of my father's. We are getting together for the first time without him. Before coming to join me at a table that sits in the sun-lit crease between two window-covered walls, she stops at the counter to order a drink. Her back is recently broken, and she wears a strict, white brace outside of her clothing. She speaks warmly with the barista—a skinny playwright with black-rimmed glasses who has tattoos on his arms and a Spanish accent. I assume she comes here often, because they laugh easily and he refuses to let her pay for her drink. When she arrives she places a book newly checked out from the library on the table in front of her. Her skin is the color of a wilted chrysanthemum. We have both ordered hot tea, despite the eighty-degree day outside. She says, "I enjoy living in California. I enjoy the anonymity of it."

I. Architecture as Therapy

According to the 2003 book *LA's Early Moderns,* the modern architects who brought the spare, glass walls style of living to Los Angeles in the 1920's and 30's saw the promise of architecture as revolutionary. It held the key to physical and emotional health. California architect Irving Gill was not only concerned with bringing more of what nature had to offer into people's daily lives, he also felt that there was a morality inherent to his chosen field—architecture had the potential to do social good. He chose materials that were cheap and widely available, and used them efficiently. He sought to make good housing accessible to the wealthy and the working class alike, building at one point a barracks for Mexican workers and their families, and at another housing for Native Americans in an Indian Resettlement area. Some prefabricated homes could be purchased and assembled by unskilled workmen in less than a week's time.

In 1945, *Art and Architecture Magazine* sponsored a Case Study House Program, inviting architects to build six model homes intended to bring the most innovative ideals of architecture—as seen in the German Bauhaus movement and the work of American architect Philip Johnson—to everyday citizens. Many of these designs, created by Richard Neutra and the inventers Charles and Ray Eames, were phenomenona of resourcefulness and odd beauty. But for the thousands of soldiers returning from World War II, and a majority of home builders who sought to house them, these modern visions (made with glass, steel and plastic) seemed freakish—not to mention threatening. Boxy, uniform suburban tract homes sprouted up in the valley instead, bringing residents farther and farther away from the city's riverside areas, like South Central Los Angeles.

At around the same time that the modernists attempted to revolutionize the architectural landscape of Los Angeles, educators were trying to account for increasing diversity in city schools. In a 2000 article in the *Annals of the Association of American Geographers*, Laura Pulido writes that Latino, Chinese, African American and Caucasian students spent their childhoods together in elementary school classrooms. Pulido notes that some teachers even created curricula that honored the backgrounds of a diverse student body—long before the civil rights era prompted the establishment of ethnic studies departments in universities. These diverse populations were composed of working class families who lived along the Los Angeles River, where one could find industrial work and affordable housing.

But schools were not exactly or always havens of progressive ideals. Teachers pushed minority students to prepare for work as plumbers and construction workers like their fathers. Despite laws intended to keep kids in school, the Depression, World War II and other factors forced children from less affluent families out of school and into the workforce. By the time children of this era reached adolescence, they were again surrounded by people who looked just like them. Because neighborhoods were usually composed of one ethnic group, white residents were able to modify policies that dictated which neighborhoods were eligible to attend the best schools, making it less and less likely that Caucasian children would mix with minorities. Black students, like would-be mayor Tom Bradley, had to lie about their residence if they wanted to get a good education.

Some blacks sought to move into neighborhoods with better facilities and higher home values, but housing restrictions prevented this. A 1998 article by John Sides in the *Pacific Historical Review* points out that if African Americans—many of whom had moved recently from the south—were able to find a loophole and buy or rent in a mostly white neighborhood, they could expect to meet with hostility, expressed through burning crosses, vigilante groups and what has become known as an infamous system of racist police brutality. Los Angeles began to be separated by hard-drawn geographical lines, which kept the city color-coded.

Though a close friend of his, the woman I have come to meet is not my father's age—much younger. She explains to me that she met my dad at the OJ Simpson trial; he used his press pass to get her a seat inside. My father enjoys making connections with people. Almost every book he owns has a phone number written inside of it. Brief outings with him often involve half-hour conversations with so-and-so at Starbucks about their granddaughter's decision to return to Russia. He has a near-superstitious sense of allegiance to this cast of strangers orbiting through his life. He will say of someone I've barely met, "Annie was on my mind the other day. I kept calling only to find that she died last week." Or, "we've got to do something to keep the city from reclaiming Mr. Collins' firehouse." When he met the friend I am now here to see, he found out that she was very sick, and living far away from her family. He began to take her on errands to various medical appointments, and called to check on her periodically. She became a kind of daughter to him, and remains so. For the longest time, I felt suspicious of her voice on the phone, which sounded sultry and withdrawn.

During our conversation, she references Israel and Jerry Springer, and explains what it feels like to almost die. She cries. Against my expectations, she chuckles often, and looks at me the way that people do when they share a secret. She says, "I think the more in harmony you are with yourself, the better chance you have." Her words become a soundtrack for the broken city whose shadows, truck sounds, bodies and light loop around us. I imagine Los Angeles as an anxious patient who hovers, pacing—eager to consult with this woman who has managed to survive a life of incessant fragmentation.

II. Painters and Housewives

The artist David Hockney first came to Los Angeles in 1963. He loved to go downtown, where the streets were seedy and the gay bars flourished; though his art for the most part focused on the lives of the very rich. The people in his paintings tended to live in the same houses that the Modernists had created as symbols of democracy.

It was in the early 1960's that Hockney began to paint one subject for which he'd eventually become renowned: the swimming pool. The challenge fascinated him. He writes, "It is a formal problem to represent water, to describe water, because it can be anything—it can be any color, it's moveable, it has no set visual description." The painter also depicted another transparent surface that has come, partly due to his influence, to define the houses of Los Angeles: glass. In a 2006 article in the *Los Angeles Times,* Christopher Hawthorne concludes, "glass walls have become for Los Angeles a modern version of the classical column: an architectural building block that's both timeless and intrinsically wedded to the culture of the city."

A working class Brit, Hockney was initially flabbergasted by the wealth of the people whose homes he turned into icons of his new city. In one portrait called *Beverly Hills Housewife*, a white woman with blonde hair stands hesitantly near the center of the painting, wearing what looks to be a nightgown. She gazes toward the left, her back facing a glass window that stretches across the entire wall of her house. The flat rectangles of open space that can be seen behind her are typical features on these steel framed, prefab houses. A zebra print lounge chair and modern sculpture decorate the otherwise spare interior, and a short palm tree stands with the lady outside. The 12′, two-paneled canvas was painted in a tiny studio in Santa Monica, where the artist had little room to step back from the picture while he painted it. The seam running vertically through the middle of the image, where the two canvases come together, resembles the seam of two windows meeting.

What, one wonders, has caught the attention of the pink-clad housewife? Or are we to take her pose as contemplative—even bored? The painting was completed in 1966, one year after the Watts Riots. It would be nice to think that she could hear something in the distance, the sound of shouting and fire truck sirens blaring across town.

When Martin Luther King Jr., Bayard Rustin and Andrew Young walked through Watts after the six days of rioting in 1965, they were met by the proud shouts of young men: "We won! We won!" According to a 1971 study published in the *American Journal of Sociology*, when the incredulous civil rights leaders asked why, the young men responded, "We made them pay attention to us!" This study, titled "Black Invisibility, the Press, and the LA Riot," notes that there had been a stark lack of information about the city's black community. Much of what was printed about African Americans was related either to entertainment or crime. It is perhaps, then, not surprising that the Watts riots resonated differently for whites than it did for blacks. Racially exclusive housing was pervasive in the 1940's and 50's, preventing people of color from living in certain areas. This changed with the Rumsford Fair Housing act in 1963, but not long after that, the city voted for a proposition to reinstate them. Though the Watts riots had other causes—anger over poorly kept schools and facilities, and the daily threat of being pulled over, frisked, questioned, arrested, abused and in rare cases killed by police—this change in legislation could not have helped.

Instead of receding back into their assigned territory in silence, the black community of South Los Angeles erupted in frustration. The 1971 study notes that more than half of the blacks surveyed after the Watts riots claimed that they hoped the incident would alert a sense of awareness, even sympathy towards these unfair conditions. However, the majority of whites surveyed—over seventy percent—interpreted the violence as a warning, a threat to their own safety. The riot simply "increased the gap between races and hurt the Negro cause." The study concludes, "preoccupied with their own interests, even the most liberal of whites have been easily distracted from the faint signals emanating from the ghetto."

On a 2005 episode of the radio show *This American Life*, an advertising firm debates whether or not a soda commercial should include images of young African Americans in a swimming pool. They wonder: do black people swim? A test group of African Americans respond in a unanimous protest: black people do not swim. According even to our own imaginations, the image of the swimming pool does not reflect back a black population.

Hockney notes, "the look of swimming pool water is controllable—and its dancing rhythms reflect not only the sky but because of its transparency, the depth of the water as well."

My father's friend discusses the time she first met her own father, when he was dying. No one had ever explained that he was black, which was why she looked different from the rest of her family, except through hints. One stepbrother gave reason for her darker complexion by saying "there was a nigger in the haystack somewhere." When she says of this remark, "this is how they describe where I came from," I try to visualize the encounter with her half-siblings in the hospital. Her heart must have shot through her chest like an epileptic's. A once invisible heritage was suddenly endowed with limbs and faces and eyes, all in mourning, near to her for the first time. Here was palpability where a nasty near-silence had been.

She says, "my great grandmother on my mother's side was full-blooded Cherokee; her husband was full-blooded Irish. Neither one of them spoke English. So she didn't even communicate with her own children verbally. She didn't want them to learn her language. She thought it'd be too difficult for them. So they grew up thinking that their mother was strange, weird, alien."

She comments, of her step-father, "I think his mom is Mexican, but they never talk about that."

I am sitting with my back to the windows, facing her. It has always baffled me that something as invisible as a window can cast its own, bizarre shadow—insinuating the hidden chaos of its composition. The shadow of two windows meeting can slice a line straight through you. Sipping tea, my father's friend gazes out at the street behind me. She says, "I always knew that I was an outsider. Not just in the way I look but, the way I see the world."

III. An Aerial Perspective

When I was growing up, there was a poster of a 1986 color etching by Richard Diebenkorn called *Green* hanging in the kitchen. It is from his "Ocean Park" series, which comprises over one hundred prints made while he worked in a studio in the West Los Angeles neighborhood of Venice Beach. The images are abstract, with blue, green, white, red and yellow shapes intersecting or overlapping, and lightly sketched lines visible underneath. They are not unlike blueprints, a kind of cartography—the aerial view of a landscape that has been divided into sections. In an interview for the Smithsonian, Diebenkorn laments, "it's one thing that's always missing for me in abstract painting, that I don't have this kind of dialogue between something that can be, elements that can be wildly different and can be at war . . . or in extreme conflict." Though the *Ocean Park* series immediately resonates as a depiction of the city, the lines that seem to delineate sectors, districts, communities and neighborhoods from each other are drained of sociopolitical significance: a civic vision with the serene soundtrack of ocean surf and sea gulls. The city becomes a series of benign shapes pretty enough to hang on a gallery wall.

In a 1996 article on the Los Angeles Police Department, Steve Herbert notes, "while discussing the possibility of hostile action, the sergeant repeatedly mentions the 'vermin' that plague Los Angeles, the various people who 'don't have a life.'" The article goes on to say that "immoral areas are referred to as 'dirty' and in need of police territorial action. In these areas, which are likely to be heavily populated by minorities, officers believe that violence is an inherent part of life and thus that it must be met with violence. Space is thereby purified of its moral pollution and a sense of order is restored."

The writer Mike Davis published the seminal book *City of Quartz* just two years before the Rodney King Riots of 1992. In it, he points out that police in Los Angeles had been encouraged to run rampant in poor minority areas, committing acts of violence in the name of the law. Black men in police custody were in danger of dying from "accidental" choke-hold killings, which were at one point blamed on the anatomy of the victim and not the police officer involved. In 1988, eighty-eight police officers raided the 3900 block near Exposition Park, in search of gangs and weapons. Before taking thirty-two people into captivity, the officers "spray painted walls with slogans, such as 'LAPD rules,'" and "punched and kicked" at residents. They threw "washing machines into bathtubs, pouring bleach over clothes, smashing walls and furniture with sledge hammers and axes, and ripping an outside stairwell away from one building." Most bizarrely, the residents held in captivity were forced to whistle the theme song to *The Andy Griffith Show* while being beaten with fists and flashlights. While a small quantity of drugs was recovered, no gangs or weapons were found.

Davis notes that green spaces like Elysian Park were not just patrolled, but "occupied" by police. In a number of incidents, black and Latino children and young men attempting to enjoy open spaces, entertainment centers and ballparks were frisked, "forced to kiss concrete," arrested and taunted with statements about how the area they'd trespassed upon was "for rich white people" only.

These incidents were a response to a shocking increase in gang activity that was beginning to spread through the city. But they may also be an explanation as to why, to the horror of Charlton Heston, the rapper Ice-T wrote the following lines:

> I got my black shirt on
> I got my black gloves on
> I got my ski mask on
> This shit's been too long
> I got my twelve gauge sawed off
> I got my headlights turned off
> I'm bout to bust some shots off
> I'm bout to dust some cops off.

This song, *Cop Killa*, became an anthem for some blacks, who clearly felt that they were under siege—whether they were in their own homes, or dared venture beyond them.

My father's friend remembers of the Mexicans, "they picked cherries and apples;" and of the Japanese, "there were internment camps where I grew up." Of her stepbrother, she remembers, he "used to do things like bomb the synagogues and stuff like that . . . they would make their own pipe bombs."

She remembers of her childhood, "we never talked about anything."

IV. Simulated Cityscapes

After the riots of 1992, architects set out to build City Walk, one in a series of contained entertainment centers that would pop up around the city's more affluent areas. Chris Welsch of *The Star Tribune* writes, "MCA Inc. built a two block long outdoor city, a place where tourists and Los Angelenos would feel safe, where they would not have to deal with panhandlers, drive-by shootings, knife-fights or any other urban hassles." In his book, Mike Davis is eager to point out that violence, especially gang-related, very rarely occurred across ethnic, socioeconomic and community lines, but the fantasy of gang warfare was now part of the Los Angeles image. This image was propagated by the likes of Dennis Hopper's 1988 film *Colors*, and by the lyrics of rap artists who either romanticized or participated in the rampant gang warfare that began to bring Southern Los Angeles to its knees. People who had never set foot in the famed Compton began to discuss that neighborhood's warring gangs, the Bloods and Crypts, as though they were a common feature of any Southern California neighborhood.

The Star Tribune article continues, "as diners enjoy sushi or gourmet pizza, the rumble of explosions and distant gunfire can be heard. Not real danger, though. It's manufactured for tourists in Universal Studios theme park nearby." True danger, in the form of "gangsters and rowdy teens," is deterred by a $6 parking fee and City Walk's tight security.

The creators of City Walk tried especially hard to make sure that visitors were able to enjoy all the pleasures of Los Angeles in this simulacrum of a city. One store went so far as to install an artificial ocean, where a constant crowd of watchers can peer into the enclosed tank in order to enjoy as the "small waves splash against the wall." Sections of the city began to fossilize their boundaries, preferring to be trapped inside glass-encased environments, not unlike snakes at a zoo.

City Walk emerges out of a cultural psychology that Thomas Pynchon seems to lampoon in the California novel, *Vineland*. One character wishes to start an amusement park with "automatic-weapon firing ranges, paramilitary fantasy adventures, gift shops and food courts and videogames for kids." A game called "Scum of the City" would give all visitors the chance "to wipe from the world images of assorted urban undesirables, including pimps, perverts, drug dealers and muggers, all carefully multiracial so as to offend everybody, in an environment of dark alleys, lurid neon, and piped-in saxophone music."

My father's friend is sick all the time. It is part of her father's genetic gift. She has survived cancer more than once. She explains, "I feel like there's some big lesson in the last few years that I haven't been getting, because I keep having all this crap happening to me. But I just think that in a way I hadn't been humiliated enough, lost enough . . . and now I really believe in the way the world works. I think that everything we go through is something that we were supposed to learn. And if we didn't learn it that time around, then we are given another opportunity."

V. Frank Gehry and the Post-Modern Approach to Social Strife

When I was a teenager, my parents warned me to be very careful on an afternoon outing with my friend to Venice Beach. My father explained that I might unwittingly anger a female gang member who would be all set to fight me, having pregreased her face with Vasoline and hidden razor blades under her hair or tongue. Without seeming to stir the wrath of anyone, we enjoyed a stroll along the beach while eating French fries and ice cream, watching street performers against an ocean backdrop. My parents are not the only ones whose vision of Venice Beach—designed by Abbot Kinney to resemble Venice, Italy—is somewhat bloodied.

Venice Beach is one of the only wealthy areas of Los Angeles that openly embraces the glamorous image of violence that the city as a whole has inherited. In a 1990 article, Ann Bergren notes that the area's Gold's Gym, which was established across the street from a lushly painted restaurant and gourmet ice creamery, looks like it inhabits a building that was originally created for a light-industrial factory—when in reality the gym is its first occupant. The critic goes on to say that "the development of Venice, California depends not on erasing the ghetto, but on maintaining it as a marketable material and style."

In his coffee table book, *Venice, CA: Art + Architecture in a Maverick Community,* Michael Webb writes, "residents chat with friends and neighbors as they walk or bike around, coexisting with a hood in which gangs face off and bullets fly." Some of the multi-million dollar homes in which these residents live were built by the most prominent architect of the Los Angeles metropolitan area: Frank Gehry.

While Gehry's designs embrace the motif of glass walls so treasured by his modern predecessors, other materials and other intentions play a role as well. In a 1987 article for *Design Quarterly*, he playfully mocks the conservative ideals of his wealthy clientele: "I became interested in chain link fencing not because I like it but because I don't. The culture seems to produce it and absorb it in a mindless way, and when I proposed to use it in a way that was decorative or sculptural, people became very upset. There was a discrepancy: people may have had it around their tennis courts, around their swimming pools, or around their back-yards, where it was only chain link. But if I proposed to use it as a screen in front of their house, they were annoyed and confused."

Gehry's friends love to point out his social conscience, his ability to draw attention to the rough edges of an urban environment rather than escape it. And he has even taken this aesthetic to his own Santa Monica home, which is covered with chained link fencing and corrugated aluminum siding. Not visible to the passerby is the window "made by taking a hammer and banging a hole and then gluing a piece of glass on it." The notion of breaking or questioning barriers has obviously entered into Gehry's mind. But his manner of cleaning up the mess that causes such fracture seems more like an inside joke than a preventative measure.

A client who embraces the architect's aesthetic and sense of humor is the director of the film *Colors* about gang warfare in Los Angeles, Dennis Hopper. From the outside, Hopper's home is a squat quadrilateral structure of corrugated aluminum, surrounded by a very tongue-in-check white picket fence. But, as shown in Michael Webb's coffee table book, inside are loft-sized spaces, feeding into a courtyard with a pool where prominent art pieces are displayed with a frequency that just borders on chaotic. Alongside the photographs, the director brags in a clean, tasteful font, "The gangs know where I live but so far they haven't bothered me—though they've taken the back gate off its hinges to let me know they are there . . . I heard one guy going by and telling his friends: 'He's a crazy man, an OG [old gangster]. You want to live in a prison like that?'" It is not just a corrugated wall that protects people like Hopper from his gangster friends. The Los Angeles Police Department patrols Venice Beach with tenacity. We are supposed to laugh at the notion of this multi-millionaire being referred to as a prisoner in his own home. Webb adds, "behind the wall, the OG is at peace, savoring his cigar beside the pool." But I don't find any of this particularly funny.

Hopper's backdrop combines luxury and a mythology of violence, and is all the more attractive for this fusion of opposites. But if he tires of these so-called gangsters taking his gate of its hinges, Hopper has the resources to make a home somewhere else.

My father's friend remarks of whites who marched and protested in the Civil Rights Movement, "You have to remember. People can go home."

One of Gehry's earlier designs is the 1984 Frances Howard Goldwyn Regional Branch Library in Hollywood, which utilizes the motif of a fortress—and the building is, in fact, under high security. In *City of Quartz,* Mike Davis describes the library as having "fifteen–foot security walls of stucco-covered concrete block . . . anti-graffiti barricades covered in ceramic tile . . . sunken entrance protected by ten-foot steel stacks . . . stylized sentry boxes perched precariously on each side." In one photograph, a man who looks to be homeless sits outside of the building, dwarfed by the jail-like wall behind him, which protects him from the books inside. Or vice versa.

In a 1996 article for *The Journal of Architectural Education,* Gerard Gutenschwager warns that post-modern architectural designs such as these may be "represented as playful—but they are engaged in a dangerous game . . . resting as they do on the edge of the abiding existential dilemma, they're always in danger of (unknowingly) leading or accompanying society into fascism on the one side or chaos on the other." In other words, when people pass by Gehry's designs and see these structures, which suggest an environment of incessant violence, is he really helping us to eradicate the cause of violence and poverty, or is he encouraging a sense of separation and fear that prevents people from noticing a real city with real problems and actual pain? Gutenschwager continues, "Discovering ambiguity does not excuse one from acting, however tenuously, in relation to those actual problems of repression."

Essayist Joan Didion once wrote, "The public life of liberal Hollywood comprises a kind of dictatorship of good intentions, a social contract in which actual and irreconcilable disagreement is as taboo as failure or bad teeth."

My father's friend, whose grandfather was "very much a Southern white guy," begins to cry when she says "I've seen a lot of changes in people who have had a son or a daughter come home with a biracial kid. It's just different for people when they see someone who is black or mixed. And they hold it and they love it, and they change its diapers, and they see that it is a human being."

She compares her life to the Fellini film, *La Strada,* but reminds me of a character created by another Italian director. In Michelangelo Antonioni's film *Red Desert,* a housewife played by Monica Vitti lives near an industrial plant in the North Italian town of Ravenna. One gets the impression that she identifies with her natural surroundings in a way that others don't. She is crazy, wakes with nightmares, while others seem unaffected by the yellow smoke plumes that come out of the factories around them. When she was a child, swimming on the beach, she could hear a voice singing when she put her ear close to the ground. She feels herself a part of the things around her. The concept of separate selves befuddles her.

One night, she wanders out to a dock, and meets a sailor. She tells him,

> At times, I feel separated.
> Not from my husband, no.
> The bodies . . . are separated.
> If you pinch me, you don't suffer.

What was I saying?
Oh yes. I have been sick, but I must not think of it.
That is, I have to think that all that happens to me . . .
is my life.
That's it.
I'm sorry.
Forgive me.

Perhaps Antonioni's sad protagonist can offer some wisdom into what is truly polluting the city of Los Angeles. The bodies . . . are separated. If you pinch me, you don't suffer.

VI. Glass Mountains

David Hockney was once asked to illustrate some stories from Grimm's fairy tails. One in particular captured the artist's imagination. In it, a king builds a glass mountain, and announces that he will give his daughter away to the man who can climb it without falling. Hockney says, "I loved the idea of finding how you draw a glass mountain."

In a 2008 article, Mike Bochm of the *Los Angeles Times* describes the walk to Frank Gehry's long awaited Disney Concert Hall in Downtown Los Angeles as grueling. Before public transit was established, those who couldn't afford to drive or pay for parking at the hall had to "essay a steep, sweat inducing grade that calls to mind the myth of Sisyphus."

Contrary to popular belief, Los Angeles is not a fairytale.

My father's friend notes, "I think, um, I think when you don't deal with the myth but you deal with the person, human being, then you go a long way toward conquering those stereotypes. Which, I mean, governments have known that forever. That's why they have mythified, they are always dealing with stereotypical images. When you are talking about destroying people, you are talking about savages or . . . infidels. When you see someone as a person, it's much more difficult to think about destroying them."

VII. Glass Walls are Still Walls

Once lined with historic jazz venues and African American families, South Los Angeles' Central Avenue is now home to a mostly Latino population. The area still battles with poverty, homelessness and poorly kept facilities. But after the riots of 1992, the city allowed for a fourteen acre patch of land in South Central to be utilized as a community plot for planting everything from banana trees, papaya trees, corn and cabbage. It became the largest urban community garden in the world.

In a documentary called, *The Garden*, director Scott Hamilton Kennedy follows this group of three hundred and forty seven farmers and their families as they fight eviction. While the likes of Daryl Hannah, Danny Glover, Antonio Villaraigosa and the Annenburg Foundation have all pledged support, and the farmers have raised more than an unfathomable 16 million dollars to buy the land, ultimately, the white property owner says that he will not sell it. The farmers have conducted themselves through the course of their legal battle in a manner that the property owner swears is not in keeping with American ideals. He specifies: they never said "thank you" to him for letting them exist there so long in the first place. And so the bulldozers arrive.

Throughout the film, there are some allusions on the part of African Americans to resentment over a mostly Latino group of gardeners claiming that they represent the "community." There is talk of tension between the black and the brown.

My father's friend exclaims, "I get a lot of crap from people who are Latino who think that I'm trying to pretend that I'm not Mexican; I've had problems with white folks who think that I'm, that I should act more white, and . . . dark skinned women have actively shown a lot of prejudice against me, as much as whites."

She says, "We're very territorial. We don't want to share our tables with someone we've never seen before."

At first glance one might think that her body is so busted because it is weak; but I suspect that it is broken because she has been walking into walls since the day she was born.

This city teems with diversity. Looking at it, walking through it, you wouldn't think that its infrastructure has long been rooted in division. Subtle cues, transparent as the wall in front of you, reinforce the inclination to remain distant. Some people see racism only as screamed epithets and burning objects or hanging bodies. But more often it is quiet as glass. It is the quiet separateness, the one masquerading as a peaceful silence, of which we must be weary. It takes an action to break it.

In a 2009 *New York Times* article, Nicolai Ouroussoff writes that Frederick Law Olmsted Jr., whose father designed New York's Central Park, once "proposed digging up parts of the Los Angeles river's concrete bed and transforming its banks into a necklace of parks that would provide green space for some of the city's poorest neighborhoods. Almost seventy years later, the Los Angeles City Council, prodded by a mix of local advocates and architects, revived that vision." Perhaps instead of conveying the illusion of openness through see-through surfaces, Los Angeles will some day open itself, unblocking areas that have been walled off by glass, freeways, fences, cement and stereotypes.

My new friend, my somewhat sister, is about to leave the café. Outside, the soft brown curls of her hair will start to melt downward from the heat. She will stand on the island in the middle of the intersection with her hand against a coral tree and squint into the sun while a breeze eases the creases from her forehead. If she's lucky, she won't have to wait very long for the Santa Monica bus. "I feel like a dog," she says. "I live the same day over and over again. I don't have a horizon out there." She reincarnates like a perennial flower, incessantly grazing death and emerging anew, bewildered and suspicious. Not everyone, not every city, has been granted the opportunity to start over after catastrophe hits. To see misfortune as a lesson and be changed by it.

She says, "I would rather have someone look at me and see someone who is akin to the more disadvantaged. I think that you have to elevate the lowest of . . . whoever you are. I think you have to reach out to . . . whomever is struggling the most. And until you have helped that person, you haven't done shit."

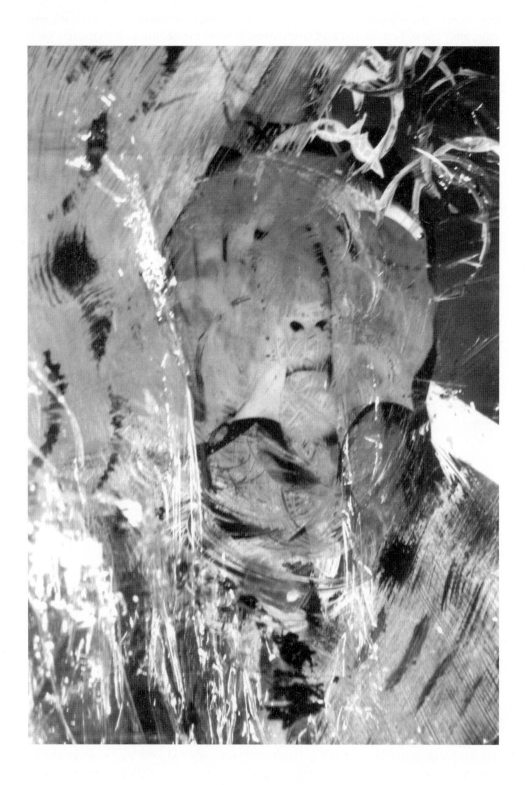

5

Writing as Social Witness

Beth Alvarado

> What we ask of writers is that they guarantee the survival of what we call *human* in a world where everything appears inhuman
>
> —*Italo Calvino*

The problem for every writer—whether that writer is a published author or a student; an essayist, novelist, poet, or journalist—is the same: what do you have to say? what has happened that compels you to speak in the first place? how do you translate your experiences and observations into language? how do you not only communicate with your readers but move them, affect them, *change* them in some way?

Just as we learn to listen before we learn to speak, every writer begins as a reader and, as readers, we are sometimes fortunate enough to read something that encourages us to write. For instance, the first time I read James Baldwin's story, "Sonny's Blues," I remember thinking, "Yes, I've heard this voice before." It was a familiar voice even though James Baldwin was an African-American man writing in New York City in the 1950's and I was a young mother, in Tucson, in 1980, who was feeling trapped at home with two small children. Too, Baldwin was writing from the point of view of a narrator who feels helpless in the face of his younger brother's addiction to heroin; I also knew how it felt to love someone who was an addict, to be able to see beyond the "addict" to the person inside, and yet to be unable to reach him because I was unable to break through the silence between us and speak.

The selections in this chapter all attempt to break through some sort of silence, usually the silence that is caused by extreme experiences. Sam Hamill's essay "The Necessity to Speak," which begins the chapter, documents the way that silence allows the violence in our lives to make this an "inhuman" world and argues that each of us must speak out in order to empower ourselves and make the world more humane. In his discussion, Hamill also points out the ways that issues which are often considered public or political—addiction, rape, battering, imprisonment, discrimination, war—are also intensely private; but, just as social forces shape our lives, he argues, so do our private acts and beliefs shape society. In this way, he elaborates on Calvino's statement and sets up the primary theme of this chapter: the responsibility of the artist, and of the individual, to "bear witness" to our shared social lives.

The idea of witness is best understood, perhaps, when we consider writing about war. In Carolyn Forché's essay, "Against Forgetting," where she discusses how wars and political oppression have shaped the work of other poets, she argues that a poem may be the only "witness" to an event, the only evidence that an atrocity has occurred and, further, that poems written by victims of the Holocaust, for instance, bear witness to the fact that *individuals* were murdered in the death camps. These poems individualize the lives of the victims in the same way that Tim O'Brien's short story "How to Tell a True War Story" recreates one soldier's experience in Vietnam.

Baldwin draws our attention to this tension between the "individual" and the "universal" in his essay "The Uses of the Blues." He is ostensibly talking about the blues but may as well be discussing fiction when he says, "Consider some of the things the blues are about. They're about work, love, death, floods, lynchings; in fact, a series of disasters which can be summed up under the arbitrary heading, 'Facts of Life.'" In a sense, he is saying that fiction is about what we do, think and feel, about our everyday lives and struggles but, when he, an African-American male, includes "lynching" as a "fact of life," he is also making a political statement about how our private lives are shaped by social problems.

Of course, some of the worlds we'll read about in this chapter are so foreign or so removed in time—the war poems, for instance—that we won't "see" ourselves at ali, at least not at first glance. And some of them are so inhumane and so depressing, we wonder how anyone could have survived them and why, after surviving, they would choose to write about them. Baldwin, in his essay, seems to believe that writing not only gives us insight into our own lives but that it can help us survive emotionally and spiritually. Still, Celan survived the concentration camps and wrote poetry only to take his own life years after the war. O'Brien, in his article, "The Vietnam in Me," admits that he often still feels suicidal and, in one of his short stories, says that he is "Tim trying to save Timmy's life with a story." In this way, breaking silence seems to be a necessary act, even if the solace is only temporary for the writer, even if the story never reaches a reader.

Forché acknowledges that reading literature of witness is disturbing; she says the reader "has to be willing to accept the trauma" the poem creates. For instance, she says of Celan's "Death Fugue": "to enter the poem, either in the original or in this translation, is to enter the world of death." In this way, she argues, the poem becomes not only "evidence" of an event but an "event" that the reader experiences vicariously through language. This, she argues, is what poetry of witness is all about: the attempt "at such translation, an attempt to mark, to change, to impress, but never to leave things as they are."

So now, we could conclude, both the writer and the reader have been marked by history, but what can the reader do in response to this trauma?

Baldwin suggests that singing (or writing) the blues and listening to (or reading about) them are equally cathartic. For instance, in "Sonny's Blues," as the older brother listens to his younger brother play the blues, he thinks, "while the tale of how we suffer, and how we are delighted, and how we may triumph is never new, it always must be heard. There isn't any other tale to tell, it's the only light we've got in all this darkness." Here, not only is the brother getting some comfort from listening but he is also telling us this tale. The listener has become the speaker.

Like the older brother, we can listen and we can speak. Baldwin suggests that the power of the blues—or of writing or of any form of expression—depends on the listener and on the listener's response as much as it does on the artist and further, that because the blues arise out of shared experiences, they can help strengthen bonds between people. Literature can also provide a kind of conversation between the writer and readers and among readers and, in so doing, create a sense of community. In this way, reading and writing are a reciprocal process. Once we begin putting our own words down on the page, we become much better readers; once we enter the conversation, we discover we have all kinds of things to say.

I hope that, as you read these selections, you will begin to think about both how and why they "speak" to us—or, perhaps, about how and why some of them fail to impress us. And, in thinking about these writers and what they have to say, in thinking about how their worlds influenced them and about their projects as people who have decided to break silence, I hope you will also think about the ways in which you enter into this community of writers and readers. What does their work mean to you? Does it help you see the world or your own experiences in another way? Does it make you think about what it means to be human, about what gives our lives meaning? These are large, philosophical questions, questions that people have been trying to answer for centuries, but they are exactly the types of questions that literature, especially literature born of extremity, prompts us to ask.

Sam Hamill

Sam Hamill was born in 1942, perhaps in Northern California. He was abandoned in Northern Utah and spent the years during World War II in an orphanage before being adopted by a Utah farm family. His adolescent years are marked by time spent in and out of jails and on the streets until his late teens, when he joined the United States Marine Corps in order to eradicate his juvenile record and visit Japan. While in the Marine Corps, serving in Okinawa, Hamill began to study Zen Buddhist literature. He became a social activist and campaigned against the Vietnam War in the 1960s. Hamill is a poet and translator of extraordinary range who has taught in prisons, public schools and universities. He is the recipient of many prestigious awards, a longtime editor of Copper Canyon Press and author of A Poet's Work: The Other Side of Poetry *(1990), the collection from which the following essay is taken.*

The Necessity to Speak

One must understand what fear means: what it implies and what it rejects. It implies and rejects the same fact: a world where murder is legitimate, and where human life is considered trifling. . . . All I ask is that, in the midst of a murderous world, we agree to reflect on murder and to make a choice. After that, we can distinguish those who accept the consequences of being murderers themselves or the accomplices of murderers, and those who refuse to do so with all their force and being. Since this terrible dividing line does actually exist, it will be a gain if it be clearly marked.
—Albert Camus, *Neither Victims Nor Executioners*

And yet we go on living closed lives, pretending we are not each personally responsible for the deaths we buy and sell. We go on living our sheltered lives among the potted plants and automobiles and advertising slogans. We don't want to know what the world is like, we can't bear very much reality.

The man in prison remembers. The man who's been in prison remembers. Cesare Pavese brings the message home most forcefully: "The lonely man, who's been in prison, goes back to prison every time he eats a piece of bread." The woman who was battered remembers. The woman who was raped will never forget. The convict and the ex-con, the rape victim, the battered child—each, reading these words, will remember.

I teach creative writing in the prisons because I have been in prison. Writing is a form of human communication expressing ideas regarding the human condition.

Because writing creates emotion in the audience, the writer's responsibility is enormous. Arousing passion, exploring the grief of loss, making another laugh, showing someone how to care—these are the concerns of the writer, and they do not come free of responsibility. But the creative writing itself is only a by-product. What I teach cannot be simply stated.

The women I have escorted to shelters where they can be protected from the rage of sick men have also been my friends and my students and my teachers. Three of every four of these victims, men and women, will return—the men will go back to prison, and the women will return to battering relationships. The battered child will grow into the child batterer.

There are presently fifteen hundred men on Death Row in the United States. There are over two hundred in Florida alone, and they are let out of their cells twice per week for a quick shower, and once per week for one hour of exercise. Ninety-two percent of these men were battered children. They have had a lengthy schooling. But they are beginning to understand how we as a society establish acceptable levels of violence. We pay the bill for murder in Nicaragua. We say the $27 million we send there this year, like the $40 million we sent last year, is for "humanitarian purposes," and we tell ourselves the money is not for murder. We weep for the battered woman, but we are stingy when it comes time to pay for groceries and bandages at the shelter. The victim of rape earns our sympathy. But we discipline our children with a belt or a stick or a fist. The battered woman learns that violence is one of the forms love takes. The battered child learns that there are two possibilities in human life: one can remain the victim, or one can seize power and become the executioner. The mother who was battered typically understands that the only condition worse than being a victim is to become an executioner.

The convict writes himself out of prison, he writes his brothers out of prison. The battered woman makes peace in the world with tender words chosen with deep care.

A true poet, someone once said, is often faced with the difficult task of telling people what they already know and do not want to hear. Sharon Olds, in *The Dead and the Living* (Alfred A. Knopf, 1983), writes of being a victim of domestic violence herself, and her poems are painful to read, very painful, but beautiful because they are true.

> When Mother divorced you, we were glad. She took it and
> took it, in silence, all those years and then
> kicked you out, suddenly, and her
> kids loved it.

We can't bear very much reality. When the rape victim cries out for help, we are frozen. Our emotions are mute. We are seized as though we are catatonic. We have not been taught how to properly express our feelings. We find poetry embarrassing.

A critic writing of Kenneth Rexroth's love poems in the *New York Times* declares, "Rexroth has issued a volume of breasts-and-thighs poems. What would I say, should I chance to meet his wife in public?" The poet Deena Metzger makes a beautiful, joyous poster of herself, naked, arms outstretched, following a radical mastectomy of her left breast. We are embarrassed by her naked body and by her joy, but mostly we are embarrassed because we do not know how or what to think confronted by that long ragged scar. Our vocabulary of the emotions has become critically impoverished.

Veterans returning from Viet Nam often found it impossible to discuss what transpired there. Delayed Stress Syndrome has probably taken as many American lives as Agent Orange. And yet, in high schools today, no one has heard of My Lai. Unless we learn to articulate our own emotions, we cannot prevent other My Lais and other Viet Nams from recurring, nor will we ever properly address the domestic violence so common in the American home.

"All wisdom," Kung-fu Tze says, "is rooted in learning to call things by the right name."

I became a conscientious objector while serving in the U.S. Marine Corps. I am proud of my decision to practice non-cooperation, and I am shamed by my complicity. In the vocabulary of human emotions, the terms "guilt" and "innocence" are insufficient. Like "right" and "wrong," they reject compassionate wisdom.

Once each month the recruiters for the business of death are permitted into our high schools to recruit more cannon fodder. There is no voice for non-violence inside those same institutions; the children who listen and enlist are being trained to become both victims and executioners. And we are all co-conspirators. Our silence grants permission to the military to establish all critical vocabulary pertaining to the armed forces. The *armed forces* are precisely what that name implies: a resort to armed force, a complete collapse of compassionate communication.

The battering of women and children is the most common felony committed in the United States. No one knows how often it happens because it is so rarely reported. But every cop on a beat will tell you that the most feared call of all is the domestic dispute. One never knows what to expect. It kills more cops than dope-dealers and bank robbers combined.

When James Cagney shoves half a grapefruit in a woman's face, we all laugh and applaud. Nobody likes an uppity woman. And a man who is a man, when all else fails, asserts his "masculinity." It is easy to learn to be a man. I learned to be a batterer without ever thinking about it. That's the way we learn. When I was an adolescent, it was taken for granted that real men sometimes had to slap their women around. Just like John Wayne did to Maureen O'Hara in the movies. How very often in our movies and popular fiction the assaulted woman falls in love with the assaulting "hero."

The man who slips off his belt to spank his naughty child is about to commit felony assault. If he behaves like this toward any other human being but those of his immediate family, he is locked up for the protection of society. The child is about to get a practical lesson in adult behavior when reason breaks down. This incident, repeated over the years, will help to form the growing child's sense of justice, it will inform the definition of compassion. The father will say, "I'm sorry I have to do this. It will hurt me more than it hurts you." Because this father believes himself a good man, a kind and compassionate father. But the child won't believe a word of it. The child fears the wound. The child has learned that might makes right, that parents sometimes lie, and that there are acceptable limits of violence.

If a belt is acceptable, why not a stick? If a stick is acceptable, why not a baseball bat? If broken bones are unacceptable, what about cuts or welts or bruises?

The first duty of the writer is the rectification of names—to name things properly, for, as Kung-fu Tze said, "All wisdom is rooted in learning to call things by the right name."

"The names of things bring them closer," Robert Sund wrote. This applies to the terrible as well as to the sublime. The writer learns from the act of writing. "I write to find out what's on my mind," Gary Snyder once said. What the writer invents is its own reality.

The writer is aware that verbs show action and that precision in the use of nouns and verbs frees one from the muddiness of most modifiers. The writer accepts responsibility for every implication derived from what is stated. The writer is also eternally vulnerable.

The writer *is* the battered woman in her blossoming pain; the writer *is* the lonely face behind the steel door; the writer *is* the good man with the belt wrapped around his fist. Before the first word is written, the writer is a witness who struggles not to flinch, not to look away.

We hear all around us our language being de-valued. Our president tells us that a missile with one thousand times the power of the bomb we dropped on Hiroshima is a "peacekeeper." We remember the bitter irony with which Colt named its pistol the Peacemaker. Our president tells us that $27 million is being sent to aid one side of a civil war in Nicaragua, but that the money won't be used for military purposes. The writer is in the service of the language. The writer is accountable.

We live in a culture in which "real men" don't often touch and often don't even like to be touched. Touch is a primary language in the discourse of emotions. There is eighteen square feet of skin on the average human being, and that skin holds about five million sensory perceptors. A University of Wisconsin study determined that denial of touch in young monkeys resulted in deformation in the cerebellum. D. H. Lawrence, in a story called "You Touched Me!," describes how simple human physical contact can restore the health of a life. Our president is a tough guy. He shakes hands, presumably with a firm grip, but he doesn't hug the foreign dignitaries. John Wayne didn't hug. Sylvester Stallone, Hollywood's male role model for our children, doesn't touch much.

We are embarrassed when the poet weeps publicly during the recitation of a poem. The physical expression of emotion makes many people uncomfortable. I was taught as a child—like most of my contemporaries—that men should not express emotion.

Men envy women their friendships with other women. Men secretly wish they, too, could have friends like that. Men have learned that ours is a lonely and insular country. We think poetry is about emotions. We are dead wrong. Poetry is not *about*. Take the rhyme out of poetry, and there is still poetry; take the rhythm out of it, and there is still poetry; take even the words themselves away, and poetry remains, as Yang Wan-li said a thousand years ago. The poet identifies a circumstance in which the poetry reveals itself. The poet is the vehicle used by poetry so that *it* can touch us. From the inside out. The words are only the frame which focuses the epiphany we name poetry. We say the poem touches us, sometimes even deeply. We often say the poet is a bit touched. Adrienne Rich dreams of a common language.

In the language of violence all argument is solipsistic. Those who pay tithing at the altar of violence are afraid: they fear the here-and-now and they fear the here-after, but most of all, they fear the truth of knowledge. Knowledge is the loss of innocence. How desperately we want our innocence. How desperately we protect the innocence of our children! Our children don't know what has happened. They have never heard of Auschwitz or Treblinka, they have never heard of Canyon de Chelly. They do not know that it was their European-immigrant great-great-grandfathers who invented scalp-taking, they have never dreamed of the tortured flesh that has subtly informed our attitudes since those long-ago trials in Salem. They do not know that German death camps were modeled on U.S. camps, our own nineteenth-century Final Solution to "the Indian problem."

The past we name History. Out of it, today. Every day there are people who die to know. Every day, people die because they know. In El Salvador, in Chile, in the Philippines, in Korea, Nicaragua, and Lebanon. In the U.S.S.R. and in the U.S. of A.

And the murderers, the dirty little dictators who order the heads brought in upon a platter? Our money sustains their power. Just as our indifference permits gangs to run our prisons where men also die for knowing and for speaking up. Just as we continue to permit the deaths of 2500 women per year at the hands of their "lovers," one every three-and-a-half hours, and just as we permit a woman to be battered senseless every eighteen seconds of every day in this country.

And our money brings us television to distract us from what we know we are responsible for but do not want to know. It is difficult to explain things to our children. It is convenient to declare international conflict too large, too ugly, or too confusing to explain. And we likewise declare the personal too embarrassing. How else do we account for the fact that ten percent of all teenage girls get pregnant? We perform forty-five abortions per every thousand teenage girls every year, or about one out of every twenty-five girls. One in three sixteen-year-old girls is sexually active and knows almost nothing about birth control. Her seventeen-year-old lover knows nothing, typically, or doesn't care. Our silence contributes to the shame and misery of these girls and to the deaths of millions of unborn children.

We warn our daughters lest they become "loose" with their affections. We don't want them to care for the wrong people. We don't want to wound them with the knowledge that womankind has been singled out for special suffering throughout history, so we protect them from *her-story*. We persuade ourselves that perhaps, if we don't talk about sex, sexual involvement won't happen too soon. And perhaps, if we don't think about our daughters loving a batterer, that won't happen either. Our silence grants violence permission. We sacrifice our daughters to protect our own beloved innocence. In the language of violence, every speech is a solipsism and silence a conspirator.

* * *

The true poet gives up the self. The *I* of my poem is not *me*. It is the first person impersonal, it is permission for you to enter the experience which we name Poem.

Although the poem itself is often a "given" thing, in the justice of poetry we often earn the gift in some way. The disciplining of the self helps the poet clarify the experience so that the experience itself may be yours with as little superficial clutter as possible. The true poet asks for nothing "in return" because the poem itself is given to the poet who, in turn, gives it away and gives it away again. The poet is grateful for the opportunity to serve.

The poet wants neither fame nor money, but simply to be of use.

I am not the *I* of my poem. But I am responsible for the poem and, therefore, for that *I*. The poet invents a being, and that being, man or woman, stands before the world, naked and feeling. Thus, the poet who invents the persona of the poem is reflected similarly "undressed," and we say, "This poet takes risks," because there is neither false modesty nor the arrogance of exhibitionism, but the truth of human experience as it is, all somehow beyond the mere words of the poem.

The poet may speak for the speechless, for the suffering and the wounded. The poet may be a conscience, walking. The poet honors the humble most of all because poetry is gift-giving. The poet adores the erotic because in a world of pain there is charity and hope and because the poet aspires to a condition of perpetual vulnerability.

But there are poets who murder and poets who lie. Dante placed the corrupters of language in the seventh circle of Hell, and there are poets among them. Christopher Marlowe was an assassin.

I was strapped belly-down with webbing ripped from beds in a prison for the young, my face in a pillow to muffle my screams, my mouth gagged with my own socks—I was gang-raped by I-don't-know-how-many boys, ice-picked in the face, and left, presumably to die, alone all night before the guards discovered me, bloody and crazed. Fourteen years old and in the custody of the State. It has been thirty years, and I remember it like yesterday at noon. Out of my own guilt and shame over having been raped, out of my own guilt and shame over having been a batterer, out of my own silence over these terrible events, I began to articulate needs; out of defining my own needs, I discovered a necessity for believing that justice is possible; out of a commitment to a sense of justice, I found it necessary, essential, to bear witness.

Some of my students are women who begin writing because a writing class is permission to speak, which they do not have at home. Some of these women are battered because they have taken my class. Some have been battered when their "lovers" discovered that I talk about violence and responsibility in class. One of the kindest women I have ever known was murdered by her husband because he feared she would tell the truth. Our last conversation took place over a leisurely brunch; we discussed the origins and history of Kuan Yin, bodhisattva of compassion.

We are all impoverished by our silence.

There are more men in prison in the United States than there are people in South Dakota. Many of these men are eager to work, eager to learn, and dream of learning another way of life. They exist in a moment-to-moment despair that is utterly beyond the comprehension of anyone who has not been there.

The history of our prisons is a study of cruelty and stupidity so savage and so constant that almost no one wants to know a thing about it. Poor men go to prison. Men from minority races go to prison. But batterers come from every station, even from Reagan's Administration. The rich are as likely to commit sexual violence as are the poor. The batterer cannot name his fear, the thing inside that makes him strike out blindly at the very things he loves. It is his own inability to articulate his needs, his own speechlessness, that makes him crazy. Because he has been denied his language, he cannot name things clearly; because he cannot name, he cannot see what frightens him so terribly; therefore, the fear is invisible and is everywhere and consumes him.

Only when those of us who have overcome the terrible cycle of violence bear witness can we demonstrate another possibility. Because I have been both victim and executioner, I am able to speak from the bleak interior, and, perhaps, bring a little light into a vast darkness. An apology from a reformed batterer means nothing. The only conceivable good that can come from my confession is that of example for other sick men, a little hope for change amidst the agony of despair.

She took a class in creative writing. There was much talk of naming things correctly: objects, feelings, acts, deeds. And each time there was talk, there was also responsibility. "You will be held accountable," she was told, "just as you will be expected to hold others accountable."

And then one night it happened. She got home a little late from class. He was drunk. She tried to be especially nice, she tried to calm and soothe him. But his voice got louder and louder. He screamed. He grabbed her by the throat and shook her like a rag. And then he hit her. He hit her hard.

And then he apologized. He begged her not to leave. She was crumpled in a corner, her lip bleeding, her whole body trembling out of control. He got her a wet towel and tried to touch her face. She turned her face away and held up her hands for protection. Tears streamed down his face. He begged her not to go, he swore he'd never do that again, he swore he'd gone crazy. She knew it would happen again. It had *already* happened again.

She went that night to the shelter. She spent weeks talking to a counselor every day. She was lucky. She didn't have children. He didn't find her. She was lucky to be alive. For a while, she hated men. She hated being a victim. But she made friends in the shelter. Later, she made more friends outside. And through friendship, learned to love. True love is not without its own accountability.

The violence we learn at home we take with us everywhere we go. It shapes the way we look at a man or a woman, it colors our foreign policy and our tax structure. It is outright theft to pay a woman fifty-eight cents on the dollar we pay a man for doing the same job; it is economic violence.

In Viet Nam, the soldiers, those young men conscripted or enlisted from our high schools and colleges to do our killing for us, called the enemy "Gook," an epithet first used in Nicaragua in the 1920s, China in the 1930s, Japan in the

1940s, and in the Philippines since the 1940s, because that removed an element of the enemy's humanity, making it more like killing a thing than murdering a man, a woman, or a child.

I see them every day, the wounded women in the supermarket or in the bookstore, the children beaten to a whimper until all life has grayed in them. I've learned to recognize Fear's signature scrawled across their faces. The way one learns to recognize a man who walks with a "prison shuffle."

It is essential to make it clear that these things are personal. Our nuclear arms have 180,000 times the blast of the charge that leveled Hiroshima forty years ago. Our ability to deliver death is so unspeakably potent that it is far beyond the range of all human imagination. And we add to that arsenal every day. Nothing will change until we demolish the "we-and-they" mentality. We are human, and therefore all human concerns are ours. And those concerns are personal. "Everywhere we go," George Seferis said, "we walk on the faces of the dead."

Children in our public schools are paddled, whipped, slapped, locked in closets, lockers, and bathrooms—all quite legally. Every fourth homosexual male in a U.S. high school is the victim of a major assault during his tenure. Virtually all of them are victims of harassment. Homophobia is so rampant in our culture that it is common to see people fly into a rage over the mere sight of a gay couple holding hands in public. We excuse racism, sexism, homophobia—all the mindless violence of others—by refusing to make a *personal* issue of the problem.

We lend a helping hand to the mugger when we don't educate our children (of both sexes) about self-defense; we lend a hand to the rapist when we don't readily discuss rape. Our silence grants permission to the child molester. Because we have not learned how to name things properly, the batterer beats his child or lover in public, and we stand to one side, crippled inside, fearful and guilty.

If we really do believe that felony assault has no place in the home, we must encourage all victims to name names, to come forward and bear witness. We must find a way to save the victims. And we must find a way to save the executioners, as well.

There is a way. I know. Poetry has been a means for me, a way to find my way out of Hell. But it takes an iron will or a deeply spiritual conviction not unlike that of many poets toward poetry, the way James Wright spoke with compassion for drunkards and murderers, the way Richard Hugo testified on behalf of the dying farm towns and lonely saloons of the Northwest, or the way we might learn from Denise Levertov how to accept the loss of our mothers or to accept responsibility for our own violent realpolitik or for a marriage that was "good in its time" after that time has passed.

There *is* a third way. It begins with the end of lies and silence about violence. It begins with accepting responsibility for our own words and deeds. It begins with searching one's own heart for the compassionate justice which is located *only* there. It begins with the articulation of one's truest and deepest response to a world where, as Camus said, murder is legitimate and human life is considered trifling. Only from such a profoundly articulated *No!* can we hope to achieve a final, irrefutable affirmation of the human soul.

Raymond Carver

Raymond Carver was born in 1938 in a logging town in Oregon; his father was a laborer and his mother a housewife. After graduating from high school, Carver worked as a gas station attendant, a janitor, and a manual laborer in order to support his wife and children. In 1958 he enrolled in a creative writing course where he gained direction as a writer. In 1963 he received his A.B. from California State University Humboldt and in 1966 earned an MFA from the Iowa Writer's Workshop. Carver divorced his first wife in 1983. In 1988 shortly before he died of lung cancer, he married poet Tess Gallagher, his companion for almost a decade and who, like Carver, grew up poor in the Pacific Northwest.

Carver's first collection of short stories, Will You Please Be Quiet, Please?, *was nominated for a National Book Award in 1976. Later collections,* Cathedral *(1984) and* Where I'm Calling From *(1988) were both nominated for the Pulitzer Prize for Fiction in 1985 and 1989, respectively. Carver's frank depiction of the working class comes from his own experiences and critics' response to this depiction initially surprised Carver: In an interview with Bruce Weber of the* New York Times, *Carver discloses, "Until I started reading these reviews of my work, praising me, I never felt the people I was writing about were so bad. . . . The waitress, the bus driver, the mechanic, the hotel keeper. God, the country is filled with these people. They're good people. People doing the best they could." Carver's subject subsequently caught the eye of film director, Robert Altman, who adapted several of his short stories, including "So Much Water So Close to Home," for the film* Short Cuts.

So Much Water So Close to Home

My husband eats with good appetite but he seems tired, edgy. He chews slowly, arms on the table, and stares at something across the room. He looks at me and looks away again. He wipes his mouth on the napkin. He shrugs and goes on eating. Something has come between us though he would like me to believe otherwise.

"What are you staring at me for?" he asks. "What is it?" he says and puts his fork down.

"Was I staring?" I say and shake my head stupidly, stupidly.

The telephone rings. "Don't answer it," he says.

Reprinted from *Furious Seasons*, (1976).

"It might be your mother," I say. "Dean—it might be something about Dean."

"Watch and see," he says.

I pick up the receiver and listen for a minute. He stops eating. I bite my lip and hang up.

"What did I tell you?" he says. He starts to eat again, then throws the napkin onto his plate. "Goddamn it, why can't people mind their own business? Tell me what I did wrong and I'll listen! It's not fair. She was dead, wasn't she? There were other men there besides me. We talked it over and we all decided. We'd only just got there. We'd walked for hours. We couldn't just turn around, we were five miles from the car. It was opening day. What the hell, I don't see anything wrong. No, I don't. And don't look at me that way, do you hear? I won't have you passing judgment on me. Not you."

"You know," I say and shake my head.

"What do I know, Claire? Tell me. Tell me what I know. I don't know anything except one thing: you hadn't better get worked up over this." He gives me what he thinks is a *meaningful* look. "She was dead, dead, dead, do you hear?" he says after a minute. "It's a damn shame, I agree. She was a young girl and it's a shame, and I'm sorry, as sorry as anyone else, but she was dead, Claire, dead. Now let's leave it alone. Please, Claire. Let's leave it alone now."

"That's the point," I say. "She was dead. But don't you see? She needed help."

"I give up," he says and raises his hands. He pushes his chair away from the table, takes his cigarettes and goes out to the patio with a can of beer. He walks back and forth for a minute and then sits in a lawn chair and picks up the paper once more. His name is there on the first page along with the names of his friends, the other men who made the "grisly find."

I close my eyes for a minute and hold onto the drainboard. I must not dwell on this any longer. I must get over it, put it out of sight, out of mind, etc., and "go on." I open my eyes. Despite everything, knowing all that may be in store, I rake my arm across the drainboard and send the dishes and glasses smashing and scattering across the floor.

He doesn't move. I know he has heard, he raises his head as if listening, but he doesn't move otherwise, doesn't turn around to look. I hate him for that, for not moving. He waits a minute, then draws on his cigarette and leans back in the chair. I pity him for listening, detached, and then settling back and drawing on his cigarette. The wind takes the smoke out of his mouth in a thin stream. Why do I notice that? He can never know how much I pity him for that, for sitting still and listening, and letting the smoke stream out of his mouth. . . .

He planned his fishing trip into the mountains last Sunday, a week before the Memorial Day weekend. He and Gordon Johnson, Mel Dorn, Vern Williams. They play poker, bowl, and fish together. They fish together every spring and early summer, the first two or three months of the season, before family vacations, little league baseball, and visiting relatives can intrude. They are decent men, family men, responsible at their jobs. They have sons and daughters who go to school with our son, Dean. On Friday afternoon these four men left for a three-day fishing trip to the Naches River. They parked the car in the mountains and hiked several miles to where they wanted to fish. They carried their bedrolls, food and cooking utensils, their playing cards, their whiskey. The first evening at the river, even before they could set up camp, Mel Dorn found the girl floating face down in the river, nude, lodged near the shore in some branches. He called the other men and they all came to look at her. They talked about what to do. One of the men—Stuart didn't say which—perhaps it was Vern Williams, he is a heavy-set, easy man who laughs often—one of them thought they should start back to the car at once. The others stirred the sand with their shoes and said they felt inclined to stay. They pleaded fatigue, the late hour, the fact that the girl "wasn't going anywhere." In the end they all decided to stay. They went ahead and set up the camp and built a fire and drank their whiskey. They drank a lot of whiskey and when the moon came up they talked about the girl. Someone thought they should do something to prevent the body from floating away. Somehow they thought that this might create a problem for them if it floated away during the night. They took flashlights and - stumbled down to the river. The wind was up, a cold wind, and waves from the river lapped the sandy bank. One of the men, I don't know who, it might have been Stuart, he could have done it, waded into the water and took the girl by the fingers and pulled her, still face down, closer to shore, into shallow water, and then took a piece of nylon cord and tied it around her wrist and then secured the cord to tree roots, all the while the flashlights of the other men played over the girl's body. Afterward, they went back to camp and drank more whiskey. Then they went to sleep. The next morning, Saturday, they cooked breakfast, drank lots of coffee, more whiskey, and then split up to fish, two men upriver, two men down.

That night, after they had cooked their fish and potatoes and had more coffee and whiskey, they took their dishes down to the river and rinsed them off a few yards from where the body lay in the water. They drank again and then they took out their cards and played and drank until they couldn't see the cards any longer. Vern Williams went to sleep, but the others told coarse stories and spoke of vulgar or dishonest escapades out of their past, and no one mentioned the girl until Gordon Johnson, who'd forgotten for a minute, commented on the firmness of the trout they'd caught, and the terrible coldness of the river water. They stopped talking then but continued to drink until one of them tripped and fell cursing against the lantern, and then they climbed into their sleeping bags.

The next morning they got up late, drank more whiskey, fished a little as they kept drinking whiskey. Then, at one o'clock in the afternoon, Sunday, a day earlier than they'd planned, they decided to leave. They took down their tents, rolled their sleeping bags, gathered their pans, pots, fish, and fishing gear, and hiked out. They didn't look at the girl again before they left. When they reached the car they drove the highway in silence until they came to a telephone. Stuart made the call to the sheriff's office while the others stood around in the hot sun and listened. He gave the man on the other end of the line all of their names—they had nothing to hide, they weren't ashamed of anything—and agreed to wait at the service station until someone could come for more detailed directions and individual statements.

He came home at eleven o'clock that night. I was asleep but woke when I heard him in the kitchen. I found him leaning against the refrigerator drinking a can of beer. He put his heavy arms around me and rubbed his hands up and down my back, the same hands he'd left with two days before, I thought.

In bed he put his hands on me again and then waited, as if thinking of something else. I turned slightly and then moved my legs. Afterward, I know he stayed awake for a long time, for he was awake when I fell asleep; and later, when I stirred for a minute, opening my eyes at a slight noise, a rustle of sheets, it was almost daylight outside, birds were singing, and he was on his back smoking and looking at the curtained window. Half-asleep I said his name, but he didn't answer. I fell asleep again.

He was up this morning before I could get out of bed to see if there was anything about it in the paper, I suppose. The telephone began to ring shortly after eight o'clock.

"Go to hell," I heard him shout into the receiver. The telephone rang again a minute later, and I hurried into the kitchen. "I have nothing else to add to what I've already said to the sheriff. That's right!" He slammed down the receiver.

"What is going on?" I said, alarmed.

"Sit down," he said slowly. His fingers scraped, scraped against his stubble of whiskers. "I have to tell you something. Something happened while we were fishing." We sat across from each other at the table, and then he told me.

I drank coffee and stared at him as he spoke. Then I read the account in the newspaper that he shoved across the table:

"... unidentified girl eighteen to twenty-four years of age ... body three to five days in the water ... rape a possible motive ... preliminary results show death by strangulation ... cuts and bruises on her breasts and pelvic area ... autopsy ... rape, pending further investigation."

"You've got to understand," he said. "Don't look at me like that. Be careful now, I mean it. Take it easy, Claire."

"Why didn't you tell me last night?" I asked.

"I just ... didn't. What do you mean?" he said.

"You know what I mean," I said. I looked at his hands, the broad fingers, knuckles covered with hair, moving, lighting a cigarette now, fingers that had moved over me, into me last night.

He shrugged. "What difference does it make, last night, this morning? It was late. You were sleepy, I thought I'd wait until this morning to tell you." He looked out to the patio: a robin flew from the lawn to the picnic table and preened its feathers.

"It isn't true," I said. "You didn't leave her there like that?"

He turned quickly and said, "What'd I do? Listen to me carefully now, once and for all. Nothing happened. I have nothing to be sorry for or feel guilty about. Do you hear me?"

I got up from the table and went to Dean's room. He was awake and in his pajamas, putting together a puzzle. I helped him find his clothes and then went back to the kitchen and put his breakfast on the table. The telephone rang two or three more times and each time Stuart was abrupt while he talked and angry when he hung up. He called Mel Dorn and Gordon Johnson and spoke with them, slowly, seriously, and then he opened a beer and smoked a cigarette while Dean ate, asked him about school, his friends, etc., exactly as if nothing had happened.

Dean wanted to know what he'd done while he was gone, and Stuart took some fish out of the freezer to show him.

"I'm taking him to your mother's for the day," I said.

"Sure," Stuart said and looked at Dean who was holding one of the frozen trout. "If you want to and he wants to, that is. You don't have to, you know. There's nothing wrong."

"I'd like to anyway," I said.

"Can I go swimming there?" Dean asked and wiped his fingers on his pants.

"I believe so," I said. "It's a warm day so take your suit, and I'm sure your grandmother will say it's okay."

Stuart lighted a cigarette and looked at us.

Dean and I drove across town to Stuart's mother's. She lives in an apartment building with a pool and a sauna bath. Her name is Catherine Kane. Her name, Kane, is the same as mine, which seems impossible. Years ago, Stuart has told me, she used to be called Candy by her friends. She is a tall, cold woman with white-blonde hair. She gives me the feeling that she is always judging, judging. I explain briefly in a low voice what has happened (she hasn't yet read the newspaper) and promise to pick Dean up that evening. "He brought his swimming suit," I say. "Stuart and I have to talk about some things," I add vaguely. She looks at me steadily from over her glasses. Then she nods and turns to Dean, saying "How are you, my little man?" She stoops and puts her arms around him. She looks at me again as I open the door to leave. She has a way of looking at me without saying anything.

When I return home Stuart is eating something at the table and drinking beer. . . .

After a time I sweep up the broken dishes and glassware and go outside. Stuart is lying on his back on the grass now, the newspaper and can of beer within reach, staring at the sky. It's breezy but warm out and birds call.

"Stuart, could we go for a drive?" I say. "Anywhere."

He rolls over and looks at me and nods. "We'll pick up some beer," he says. "I hope you're feeling better about this. Try to understand, that's all I ask." He gets to his feet and touches me on the hip as he goes past. "Give me a minute and I'll be ready."

We drive through town without speaking. Before we reach the country he stops at a roadside market for beer. I notice a great stack of papers just inside the door. On the top step a fat woman in a print dress holds out a licorice stick to a little girl. In a few minutes we cross Everson Creek and turn into a picnic area a few feet from the water. The creek flows under the bridge and into a large pond a few hundred yards away. There are a dozen or so men and boys scattered around the banks of the pond under the willows, fishing.

So much water so close to home, why did he have to go miles away to fish?

"Why did you have to go there of all places?" I say.

"The Naches? We always go there. Every year, at least once." We sit on a bench in the sun and he opens two cans of beer and gives one to me. "How the hell was I to know anything like that would happen?" He shakes his head and shrugs, as if it had all happened years ago, or to someone else. "Enjoy the afternoon, Claire. Look at this weather."

"They said they were innocent."

"Who? What are you talking about?"

"The Maddox brothers. They killed a girl named Arlene Hubly near the town where I grew up, and then cut off her head and threw her into the Cle Elum River. She and I went to the same high school. It happened when I was a girl."

"What a hell of a thing to be thinking about," he says. "Come on, get off it. You're going to get me riled in a minute. How about it now? Claire?"

I look at the creek. I float toward the pond, eyes open, face down, staring at the rocks and moss on the creek bottom until I am carried into the lake where I am pushed by the breeze. Nothing will be any different. We will go on and on and on and on. We will go on even now, as if nothing had happened. I look at him across the picnic table with such intensity that his face drains.

"I don't know what's wrong with you," he says. "I don't—"

I slap him before I realize. I raise my hand, wait a fraction of a second, and then slap his cheek hard. This is crazy, I think as I slap him. We need to lock our fingers together. We need to help one another. This is crazy.

He catches my wrist before I can strike again and raises his own hand. I crouch, waiting, and see something come into his eyes and then dart away. He drops his hand. I drift even faster around and around in the pond.

"Come on, get in the car," he says. "I'm taking you home."

"No, no," I say, pulling back from him.

"Come on," he says. "Goddamn it."

"You're not being fair to me," he says later in the car. Fields and trees and farmhouses fly by outside the window. "You're not being fair. To either one of us. Or to Dean, I might add. Think about Dean for a minute. Think about me. Think about someone else besides your goddamn self for a change."

There is nothing I can say to him now. He tries to concentrate on the road, but he keeps looking into the rearview mirror. Out of the corner of his eye, he looks across the seat to where I sit with my knees drawn up under my chin. The sun blazes against my arm and the side of my face. He opens another beer while he drives, drinks from it, then shoves the can between his legs and lets out breath. He knows. I could laugh in his face. I could weep.

Stuart believes he is letting me sleep this morning. But I was awake long before the alarm sounded, thinking, lying on the far side of the bed, away from his hairy legs and his thick, sleeping fingers. He gets Dean off for school, and then he shaves, dresses, and leaves for work. Twice he looks into the bedroom and clears his throat, but I keep my eyes closed.

In the kitchen I find a note from him signed "Love." I sit in the breakfast nook in the sunlight and drink coffee and make a coffee ring on the note. The telephone has stopped ringing, that's something. No more calls since last night. I look at the paper and turn it this way and that on the table. Then I pull it close and read what it says. The body is still unidentified, unclaimed, apparently unmissed. But for the last twenty-four hours men have been examining it, putting things into it, cutting, weighing, measuring, putting back again, sewing up, looking for the exact cause and moment of death. Looking for evidence of rape. I'm sure they hope for rape. Rape would make it easier to understand. The paper says the body will be taken to Keith & Keith Funeral Home pending arrangements. People are asked to come forward with information, etc.

Two things are certain: 1) people no longer care what happens to other people; and 2) nothing makes any real difference any longer. Look at what has happened. Yet nothing will change for Stuart and me. Really change, I mean. We will grow older, both of us, you can see it in our faces already, in the bathroom mirror, for instance, mornings when we use the bathroom at the same time. And certain things around us will change, become easier or harder, one thing or the other, but nothing will ever really be any different. I believe that. We have made our decisions, our lives have been set in motion, and they will go on and on until they stop. But if that is true, then what? I mean, what if you believe that, but you keep it covered up, until one day something happens that should change something, but then you see nothing is going to change after all. What then? Meanwhile, the people around you continue to talk and act as if you were the same person as yesterday, or last night, or five minutes before, but you are really undergoing a crisis, your heart feels damaged. . . .

The past is unclear. It's as if there is a film over those early years. I can't even be sure that the things I remember happening really happened to me. There was a girl who had a mother and father—the father ran a small cafe where the mother acted as waitress and cashier—who moved as if in a dream through grade school and high school and then, in a year or two, into secretarial school. Later, much later—what happened to the time in between?—she is in another town working as a receptionist for an electronics parts firm and becomes acquainted with one of the engineers who asks her for a date. Eventually, seeing that's his aim, she lets him seduce her. She had an intuition at the time, an insight about the seduction that later, try as she might, she couldn't recall. After a short while they decide to get married, but already the past, her past, is slipping away. The future is something she can't imagine. She smiles, as if she has a secret, when she thinks about the future. Once, during a particularly bad argument, over what she can't now remember, five years or so after they were married, he tells her that someday this affair (his words: "this affair") will end in violence. She remembers this. She files this away somewhere and begins repeating it aloud from time to time. Sometimes she spends the whole morning on her knees in the sandbox behind the garage playing with Dean and one or two of his friends. But every afternoon at four o'clock her head begins to hurt. She holds her forehead and feels dizzy with the pain. Stuart asks her to see a doctor and she does, secretly pleased at the doctor's solicitous attention. She goes away for a while to a place the doctor recommends. Stuart's mother comes out from Ohio in a hurry to care for the child. But she, Claire, spoils everything and returns home in a few weeks. His mother moves out of the house and takes an apartment across town and perches there, as if waiting. One night in bed when they are both near sleep, Claire tells him that she heard some women patients at the clinic discussing fellatio. She thinks this is something he might like to hear. Stuart is pleased at hearing this. He strokes her arm. Things are going to be okay, he says. From now on everything is going to be different and better for them. He has received a promotion and a substantial raise. They've even bought another car, a station wagon, her car. They're going to live in the here and now. He says he feels able to relax for the first time in years. In the dark, he goes on stroking her arm. . . . He continues to bowl and play cards regularly. He goes fishing with three friends of his.

That evening three things happen: Dean says that the children at school told him that his father found a dead body in the river. He wants to know about it.

Stuart explains quickly, leaving out most of the story, saying only that, yes, he and three other men did find a body while they were fishing.

"What kind of body?" Dean asks. "Was it a girl?"

"Yes, it was a girl. A woman. Then we called the sheriff." Stuart looks at me.

"What'd he say?" Dean asks.

"He said he'd take care of it."

"What did it look like? Was it scary?"

"That's enough talk," I say. "Rinse your plate, Dean, and then you're excused."

"But what'd it look like?" he persists. "I want to know."

"You heard me," I say. "Did you hear me, Dean? Dean!" I want to shake him. I want to shake him until he cries.

"Do what your mother says," Stuart tells him quietly. "It was just a body, and that's all there is to it."

I am clearing the table when Stuart comes up behind and touches my arm. His fingers burn. I start, almost losing a plate.

"What's the matter with you?" he says, dropping his hand. "Claire, what is it?"

"You scared me," I say.

"That's what I mean. I should be able to touch you without you jumping out of your skin." He stands in front of me with a little grin, trying to catch my eyes, and then he puts his arm around my waist. With his other hand he takes my free hand and puts it on the front of his pants.

"Please, Stuart." I pull away and he steps back and snaps his fingers.

"Hell with it then," he says. "Be that way if you want. But just remember."

"Remember what?" I say quickly. I look at him and hold my breath.

He shrugs. "Nothing, nothing," he says.

The second thing that happens is that while we are watching television that evening, he in his leather recliner chair, I on the sofa with a blanket and magazine, the house quiet except for the television, a voice cuts into the program to say that the murdered girl has been identified. Full details will follow on the eleven o'clock news.

We look at each other. In a few minutes he gets up and says he is going to fix a nightcap. Do I want one?

"No," I say.

"I don't mind drinking alone," he says. "I thought I'd ask."

I can see he is obscurely hurt, and I look away, ashamed and yet angry at the same time.

He stays in the kitchen a long while, but comes back with his drink just when the news begins.

First the announcer repeats the story of the four local fishermen finding the body. Then the station shows a high school graduation photograph of the girl, a dark-haired girl with a round face and full, smiling lips. There's a film of the girl's parents entering the funeral home to make the identification. Bewildered, sad, they shuffle slowly up the sidewalk to the front steps to where a man in a dark suit stands waiting, holding the door. Then, it seems as if only seconds have passed, as

361

if they have merely gone inside the door and turned around and come out again, the same couple is shown leaving the building, the woman in tears, covering her face with a handkerchief, the man stopping long enough to say to a reporter, "It's her, it's Susan. I can't say anything right now. I hope they get the person or persons who did it before it happens again. This violence. . . ." He motions feebly at the television camera. Then the man and woman get into an old car and drive away into the late afternoon traffic.

The announcer goes on to say that the girl, Susan Miller, had gotten off work as a cashier in a movie theater in Summit, a town 120 miles north of our town. A green, late-model car pulled up in front of the theater and the girl, who according to witnesses looked as if she'd been waiting, went over to the car and got in, leading the authorities to suspect that the driver of the car was a friend, or at least an acquaintance. The authorities would like to talk to the driver of the green car.

Stuart clears his throat, then leans back in the chair and sips his drink.

The third thing that happens is that after the news Stuart stretches, yawns, and looks at me. I get up and begin making a bed for myself on the sofa.

"What are you doing?" he says, puzzled.

"I'm not sleepy," I say, avoiding his eyes. "I think I'll stay up a while longer and then read something until I fall asleep."

He stares as I spread a sheet over the sofa. When I start to go for a pillow, he stands at the bedroom door, blocking the way.

"I'm going to ask you once more," he says. "What the hell do you think you're going to accomplish by this?"

"I need to be by myself tonight," I say. "I need to have time to think."

He lets out breath. "I'm thinking you're making a big mistake by doing this. I'm thinking you'd better think again about what you're doing. Claire?"

I can't answer. I don't know what I want to say. I turn and begin to tuck in the edges of the blanket. He stares at me a minute longer and then I see him raise his shoulders. "Suit yourself then. I could give a fuck less what you do," he says. He turns and walks down the hall scratching his neck.

This morning I read in the paper that services for Susan Miller are to be held in Chapel of the Pines, Summit, at two o'clock the next afternoon. Also, that police have taken statements from three people who saw her get into the green Chevrolet. But they still have no license number for the car. They are getting warmer, though, and the investigation is continuing. I sit for a long while holding the paper, thinking, then I call to make an appointment at the hairdresser's.

I sit under the dryer with a magazine on my lap and let Millie do my nails.

"I'm going to a funeral tomorrow," I say after we have talked a bit about a girl who no longer works there.

Millie looks up at me and then back at my fingers. "I'm sorry to hear that, Mrs. Kane. I'm real sorry."

"It's a young girl's funeral," I say.

"That's the worst kind. My sister died when I was a girl, and I'm still not over it to this day. Who died?" she says after a minute.

"A girl. We weren't all that close, you know, but still."

"Too bad. I'm real sorry. But we'll get you fixed up for it, don't worry. How's that look?"

"That looks . . . fine, Millie, did you ever wish you were somebody else, or else just nobody, nothing, nothing at all?"

She looks at me. "I can't say I ever felt that, no. No, if I was somebody else I'd be afraid I might not like who I was." She holds my fingers and seems to think about something for a minute. "I don't know, I just don't know. . . . Let me have your other hand now, Mrs. Kane."

At eleven o'clock that night I make another bed on the sofa and this time Stuart only looks at me, rolls his tongue behind his lips, and goes down the hall to the bedroom. In the night I wake and listen to the wind slamming the gate against the fence. I don't want to be awake, and I lie for a long while with my eyes closed. Finally I get up and go down the hall with my pillow. The light is burning in our bedroom and Stuart is on his back with his mouth open, breathing heavily. I go into Dean's room and get into bed with him. In his sleep he moves over to give me space. I lie there for a minute and then hold him, my face against his hair.

"What is it, Mama?" he says.

"Nothing, honey. Go back to sleep. It's nothing, it's all right."

I get up when I hear Stuart's alarm, put on coffee and prepare breakfast while he shaves.

He appears in the kitchen doorway, towel over his bare shoulder, appraising.

"Here's coffee," I say. "Eggs will be ready in a minute."

He nods.

I wake Dean and the three of us have breakfast. Once or twice Stuart looks at me as if he wants to say something, but each time I ask Dean if he wants more milk, more toast, etc.

"I'll call you today," Stuart says as he opens the door.

"I don't think I'll be home today," I say quickly. "I have a lot of things to do today. In fact, I may be late for dinner."

"All right. Sure." He moves his briefcase from one hand to the other. "Maybe we'll go out for dinner tonight? How would you like that?" He keeps looking at me. He's forgotten about the girl already. "Are you all right?"

I move to straighten his tie, then drop my hand. He wants to kiss me goodbye. I move back a step. "Have a nice day then," he says finally. He turns and goes down the walk to his car.

I dress carefully. I try on a hat that I haven't worn in several years and look at myself in the mirror. Then I remove the hat, apply a light makeup, and write a note for Dean.

> *Honey, Mommy has things to do this afternoon, but will be home later. You are to stay in the house or in the back/yard until one of us comes home.*
>
> *Love*

I look at the word "Love" and then I underline it. As I am writing the note I realize I don't know whether *back yard* is one word or two. I have never considered it before. I think about it and then I draw a line and make two words of it.

I stop for gas and ask directions to Summit. Barry, a forty-year-old mechanic with a mustache, comes out from the restroom and leans against the front fender while the other man, Lewis, puts the hose into the tank and begins to slowly wash the windshield.

"Summit," Barry says, looking at me and smoothing a finger down each side of his mustache. "There's no best way to get to Summit, Mrs. Kane. It's about a two-, two-and-a-half-hour drive each way. Across the mountains. It's quite a drive for a woman. Summit? What's in Summit, Mrs. Kane?"

"I have business," I say, vaguely uneasy. Lewis has gone to wait on another customer.

"Ah. Well, if I wasn't tied up there—" he gestures with his thumb toward the bay—"I'd offer to drive you to Summit and back again. Road's not all that good. I mean it's good enough, there's just a lot of curves and so on."

"I'll be all right. But thank you." He leans against the fender. I can feel his eyes as I open my purse.

Barry takes the credit card. "Don't drive it at night," he says. "It's not all that good a road, like I said. And while I'd be willing to bet you wouldn't have car trouble with this, I know this car, you can never be sure about blowouts and things like that. Just to be on the safe side I'd better check these tires." He taps one of the front tires with his shoe. "We'll run it onto the hoist. Won't take long."

"No, no, it's all right. Really, I can't take any more time. The tires look fine to me."

"Only takes a minute," he says. "Be on the safe side."

"I said no. No! They look fine to me. I have to go now. Barry. . . ."

"Mrs. Kane?"

"I have to go now."

I sign something. He gives me the receipt, the card, some stamps. I put everything into my purse. "You take it easy," he says. "Be seeing you."

As I wait to pull into the traffic, I look back and see him watching. I close my eyes, then open them. He waves.

I turn at the first light, then turn again and drive until I come to the highway and read the sign: SUMMIT 117 MILES. It is ten-thirty and warm.

The highway skirts the edge of town, then passes through farm country, through fields of oats and sugar beets and apple orchards, with here and there a small herd of cattle grazing in open pastures. Then everything changes, the farms become fewer and fewer, more like shacks now than houses, and stands of timber replace the orchards. All at once I'm in the mountains and on the right, far below, I catch glimpses of the Naches River.

In a little while I see a green pickup truck behind me, and it stays behind me for miles. I keep slowing at the wrong times, hoping it will pass, and then increasing my speed, again at the wrong times. I grip the wheel until my fingers hurt. Then on a clear stretch he does pass, but he drives along beside for a minute, a crew-cut man in a blue workshirt in his early thirties, and we look at each other. Then he waves, toots the horn twice, and pulls ahead of me.

I slow down and find a place, a dirt road off of the shoulder. I pull over and turn off the ignition. I can hear the river somewhere down below the trees. Ahead of me the dirt road goes into the trees. Then I hear the pickup returning.

I start the engine just as the truck pulls up behind me. I lock the doors and roll up the windows. Perspiration breaks on my face and arms as I put the car in gear, but there is no place to drive.

"You all right?" the man says as he comes up to the car. "Hello. Hello in there." He raps the glass. "You okay?" He leans his arms on the door and brings his face close to the window.

I stare at him and can't find any words.

"After I passed I slowed up some," he says. "But when I didn't see you in the mirror I pulled off and waited a couple of minutes. When you still didn't show I thought I'd better drive back and check. Is everything all right? How come you're locked up in there?"

I shake my head.

"Come on, roll down your window. Hey, are you sure you're okay? You know it's not good for a woman to be batting around the country by herself." He shakes his head and looks at the highway, then back at me. "Now come on, roll down the window, how about it? We can't talk this way."

"Please, I have to go."

"Open the door, all right?" he says, as if he isn't listening. "At least roll the window down. You're going to smother in there." He looks at my breasts and legs. The skirt has pulled up over my knees. His eyes linger on my legs, but I sit still, afraid to move.

"I want to smother," I say. "I am smothering, can't you see?"

"What in the hell?" he says and moves back from the door. He turns and walks back to his truck. Then, in the side mirror, I watch him returning, and I close my eyes.

"You don't want me to follow you toward Summit or anything? I don't mind. I got some extra time this morning," he says.

I shake my head.

He hesitates and then shrugs. "Okay, lady, have it your way then," he says. "Okay."

I wait until he has reached the highway, and then I back out. He shifts gears and pulls away slowly, looking back at me in his rearview mirror. I stop the car on the shoulder and put my head on the wheel.

The casket is closed and covered with floral sprays. The organ begins soon after I take a seat near the back of the chapel. People begin to file in and find chairs, some middle-aged and older people, but most of them in their early twenties or even younger. They are people who look uncomfortable in their suits and ties, sport coats and slacks, their dark dresses and leather gloves. One boy in flared pants and a yellow short-sleeved shirt takes the chair next to mine and begins to bite his lips. A door opens at one side of the chapel and I look up and for a minute the parking lot reminds me of a meadow. But then the sun flashes on car windows. The family enters in a group and moves into a curtained area off to the side. Chairs creak as they settle themselves. In a few minutes a slim, blond man in a dark suit stands and asks us to bow our heads. He speaks a brief prayer for us, the living, and when he finishes he asks us to pray in silence for the soul of Susan Miller, departed. I close my eyes and remember her picture in the newspaper and on television. I see her leaving the theater and getting into the green Chevrolet.

Then I imagine her journey down the river, the nude body hitting rocks, caught at by branches, the body floating and turning, her hair streaming in the water. Then the hands and hair catching in the overhanging branches, holding, until four men come along to stare at her. I can see a man who is drunk (Stuart?) take her by the wrist. Does anyone here know about that? What if these people knew that? I look around at the other faces. There is a connection to be made of these things, these events, these faces, if I can find it. My head aches with the effort to find it.

He talks about Susan Miller's gifts: cheerfulness and beauty, grace and enthusiasm. From behind the closed curtain someone clears his throat, someone else sobs. The organ music begins. The service is over.

Along with the others I file slowly past the casket. Then I move out onto the front steps and into the bright, hot afternoon light. A middle-aged woman who limps as she goes down the stairs ahead of me reaches the sidewalk and looks around, her eyes falling on me. "Well, they got him," she says. "If that's any consolation. They arrested him this morning. I heard it on the radio before I came. A guy right here in town. A longhair, you might have guessed." We move a few steps down the hot sidewalk. People are starting cars. I put out my hand and hold on to a parking meter. Sunlight glances off polished hoods and fenders. My head swims. "He's admitted having relations with her that night, but he says he didn't kill her." She snorts. "They'll put him on probation and then turn him loose."

"He might not have acted alone," I say. "They'll have to be sure. He might be covering up for someone, a brother, or some friends."

"I have known that child since she was a little girl," the woman goes on, and her lips tremble. "She used to come over and I'd bake cookies for her and let her eat them in front of the TV." She looks off and begins shaking her head as the tears roll down her cheeks.

Stuart sits at the table with a drink in front of him. His eyes are red and for a minute I think he has been crying. He looks at me and doesn't say anything. For a wild instant I feel something has happened to Dean, and my heart turns.

"Where is he?" I say. "Where is Dean?"

"Outside," he says.

"Stuart, I'm so afraid, so afraid," I say, leaning against the door.

"What are you afraid of, Claire? Tell me, honey, and maybe I can help. I'd like to help, just try me. That's what husbands are for."

"I can't explain," I say. "I'm just afraid. I feel like, I feel like, I feel like. . . ."

He drains his glass and stands up, not taking his eyes from me. "I think I know what you need, honey. Let me play doctor, okay? Just take it easy now." He reaches an arm around my waist and with his other hand begins to unbutton my jacket, then my blouse. "First things first," he says, trying to joke.

"Not now, please," I say.

"Not now, please," he says, teasing. "Please nothing." Then he steps behind me and locks an arm around my waist. One of his hands slips under my brassiere.

"Stop, stop, stop," I say. I stamp on his toes.

And then I am lifted up and then falling. I sit on the floor looking up at him and my neck hurts and my skirt is over my knees. He leans down and says, "You go to hell then, do you hear, bitch? I hope your cunt drops off before I touch it again." He sobs once and I realize he can't help it, he can't help himself either. I feel a rush of pity for him as he heads for the living room.

He didn't sleep at home last night.

This morning, flowers, red and yellow chrysanthemums. I am drinking coffee when the doorbell rings.

"Mrs. Kane?" the young man says, holding his box of flowers.

I nod and pull the robe tighter at my throat.

"The man who called, he said you'd know." The boy looks at my robe, open at the throat, and touches his cap.

He stands with his legs apart, feet firmly planted on the top step. "Have a nice day," he says.

A little later the telephone rings and Stuart says, "Honey, how are you? I'll be home early, I love you. Did you hear me? I love you, I'm sorry, I'll make it up to you. Goodbye, I have to run now."

I put the flowers into a vase in the center of the dining room table and then I move my things into the extra bedroom.

Last night, around midnight, Stuart breaks the lock on my door. He does it just to show me that he can, I suppose, for he doesn't do anything when the door springs open except stand there in his underwear looking surprised and foolish while the anger slips from his face. He shuts the door slowly, and a few minutes later I hear him in the kitchen prying open a tray of ice cubes.

I'm in bed when he calls today to tell me that he's asked his mother to come stay with us for a few days. I wait a minute, thinking about this, and then hang up while he is still talking. But in a little while I dial his number at work. When he finally comes on the line I say, "It doesn't matter, Stuart. Really, I tell you it doesn't matter one way or the other."

"I love you," he says.

He says something else and I listen and nod slowly. I feel sleepy. Then I wake up and say, "For God's sake, Stuart, she was only a child."

Andrew Foster Altschul

Andrew Foster Altschul's short fiction, essays, and political commentaries have appeared in several publications and anthologies such as, Best New American Voices *and* O. Henry Prize Stories. *His novels include* Lady Lazarus *(2008) and* Deus Ex Machina *(2010). He currently lives in San Francisco and is the books editor of the web-based magazine,* The Rumpus. *He also directs the Center for Literary Arts at San Jose State University.*

A New Kind of Gravity

Around one in the morning I go out to the alley with Horace to bum a cigarette and trade the evening's tragedies. I'll pick him up at his cage in the basement, rap on the reinforced glass, point to the clock over his head. We check the monitors to make sure all's clear, no belligerent drunks or clever husbands waiting in ambush. Mattie would fire us both in about a minute and a half if she knew we did this. If she looked back at the night's security tapes, saw the steel door propped open with a brick, the two of us leaning against the outside wall like we were on school recess—she'd have no choice, everyone knows that.

"Play with your own life if you want to," she said when she hired me. She looked me in the eye, shook my hand, but didn't raise her voice. "Don't fuck with someone else's. That's our rule here." Mattie always says things that way—real plain, like she's just talking. But Mattie's never just talking.

I tried to laugh about it with Horace once, my first week on the job, trying to get chummy with the other guard. I did a pretty good impression of Mattie's monotone, her cold half-smile, the way she presses her palms together when she's lecturing you. Horace didn't think it was so funny. He unbuttoned his uniform and showed me the thick, brown scar where a husband had knifed him on the sidewalk at eight in the morning and taken his keys. Mattie shot the guy in the vestibule, then gave them both first aid until the ambulance came.

It's not that we can't smoke in the building—nicotine practically holds this place together. There are meeting rooms on the second and fourth floors with big, industrial ash cans that are always overflowing. There's the dingy third-floor kitchen, and there's the roof. But to get there you have to walk down those sad hallways, posters of Paris and the Grand Canyon, "One day at a time" in flowing letters across a sunrise. You can hear the women in their rooms, praying or sobbing or talking in their sleep, yelling at their children or reading bedtime stories. Some of the rooms are dead silent. The meeting room walls are cluttered with photocollages and news clippings and needlepoint, third-grade spelling tests and divorce papers and Spanish prayers. Me and Horace like it better out in the alley, where it's just the Dumpsters and the weather, a few minutes of bare freedom.

The women don't come out here. They don't stand on the roof or stroll in the city park or take their kids to Little League practice. Some of them can't even hold jobs anymore, haven't left the building in two, three, ten weeks. When they do leave, we usually don't see them again for a while, until they come back with their noses broken or their elbows dislocated or worse.

"Look at them," Horace says out in the alley. He doesn't have to look up to know they're there—sleepless faces in the windows above, staring out at the shabby buildings, jealously watching us smoke outside. "Pathetic," he says. "Pathetic specimens."

Horace is on a roll. Sometimes you'd think he hated the women, the way he talks. But he's been here six years. I've helped him and Mattie wrestle a body-builder into a four-point restraint, the guy so amped you could smell the crystal. I saw Horace's face while we held the husband down, howling into the concrete. I don't have to ask whose side he's on.

Tonight he's worked up because he saw on the log that Lucille Johnson checked back in. "You explain it to me, Charlie," he says, blowing out the smoke like it insulted him. "You tell me why a woman like that ought to be coming and going from here, wasting her life in this place. Don't she have brothers? Don't she have a father? And nobody doing shit."

Horace gets especially enraged by black women at Skyer House. He says it's a private thing, the community ought to take care of it. "Woman in my neighborhood gets beat up like that she's not gonna need no safehouse. She's not gonna need no restraining order," he says. He flicks his cigarette across the alley, where it bursts into a small orange shower against the Dumpster. "That kinda shit only gonna happen once. You know why?"

I've heard this speech a hundred times. "Because black men know how to treat their women?" I say.

Horace gives a sour laugh. "Black men know how to treat animals," he says. He crosses his arms and nods. I grind out my cigarette with the toe of my shoe.

"Get back?" I suggest, checking my watch. There's a 1:30 A.M. rerun of *The Honeymooners* that I don't want to miss.

"Talk about humane," he's growling as we head for the door. "I'll show you some fucking humanity."

I kick the doorstop away and try not to look up—even though I know I will, even though I know who I'll see when I do: a seven-year-old girl in Wonder Woman pajamas, waving at me from the fourth-floor window. I wave back, point to my watch and pantomime sleep, but Camila only stares from behind the bullet-proof glass. It's the same every night: I trudge upstairs to my cage in the lobby, and in the monitors I can still see her standing there, a tiny figure looking at the place I've left, while I triple-check the doors and clean my gun and wonder if the day will come when I'll have to kill her father to keep her safe.

The doorbell chimes at seven in the morning and I don't even need to check the monitors to know what's out there: a husband on the front stoop, fidgeting with his clothes, trying not to eyeball the camera. He'll be freshly shaved, maybe wearing a tie. He'll definitely have flowers, red roses from the Korean shop on the corner—they do a hell of a business. Some of these husbands are big, real big; some of them aren't. Some of them look like the bottom of the barrel, some look like accountants. But when they walk past you, you get the same feeling, like a smell they give off, like something hot and rotten has been packed inside them, crammed down into a space too small to hold it in.

Soon there are footsteps clicking down the stairs and April Pittelli floats past the cage in her best dress and an hour's worth of makeup. She's wearing a big smile, despite her swollen jaw, glowing like a teenager getting picked up for the prom—she's leaving, she says, we can give her bed to someone who really needs it. It's what she always says. She stops to give me a hug before I buzz her out. In the monitors, I watch them embrace, her husband crying, smothering her in kisses. They hold hands as they walk away.

The first time I had to let one of the women go, I started arguing with her, incredulous. Mattie shook her head at me from across the lobby. "It's not your decision," she said later. "No one can take care of them but themselves."

It's true. You can't stop them. Even the fourth or fifth time—when they've come back to lay low awhile, let their bones heal, their hair grow back—when that door chimes they practically fly down the stairs. The caseworkers talk about how scared the women are, how they go back because they don't know what else to do, or they can't support themselves, or for the kids. But it's the smile that gets me, the way they throw open that door and fall into their husbands' arms. You'd think they really believed this time would be different. You might as well tear up the restraining orders in their file, shower them like ticker tape out the second-story window, make a big celebration out of it.

But then you'd just have to call the courthouse for new copies in a week or ten days, when she comes back in a squad car with cigarette burns on her arms or a high wheeze from broken ribs or, worse, injuries you can't see, whatever spirit she'd had left replaced by shaking hands and a self-loathing so deep she won't find the bottom for months.

When Mariana came back the first time, wearing a neck brace and gripping Camila's hand so tight the little girl was trying to pry it off, I opened the door and put an arm around her to bring her inside. She closed her eyes for a second, and I thought she might cry on my shoulder, but then she pulled away and yanked her daughter up the stairs and disappeared. Mattie called me into her office a minute later and gave me another warning. There's no such thing as positive male attention here, she said, slicing the air with clasped hands. You open the door, you close the door. You see a raised hand, you grab it. You see a knife, you shoot it. These women are not your friends, she said. They're not your girlfriends. They're sick. And let me tell you, you don't want to catch what they've got.

For a while it seemed every woman I dated had an ex who hit. For some it was unpredictable, a kind of reflex—the hard shove in the middle of a fight, the drink thrown against the wall; for others it would be premeditated, methodical. It started with Teresa, my old fiancée. Soon after she moved in with me, she told me about her ex, how he used to cry while he wrapped a towel around his fist so he wouldn't bruise her. She sat on the edge of the bed, her back to me, and I held a pillow over my face while she told me how sorry he'd feel afterward, how she believed it was a different person, like something taking over his body.

He put her in the emergency room once, she said, and when she came home the next morning she found him in the bathtub—he had shaved his head and was trying to slash his wrists. When I asked why she didn't let him do it, she closed her eyes and twisted her mouth into a smile, as if there were some things about love I just couldn't understand.

I heard so many of these stories they stopped surprising me. I didn't know what it was about me that attracted women who'd been with such people. I'd have dreams about running into the guy on the street, smashing his face into the pavement. This was when I still worked at the mall, I'd find myself taking it out on some stupid shoplifter, pinning him to the wall by his neck.

What got me was that they all went back. Maybe they'd go into counseling or quit drinking together, but it didn't make a difference, after the first hit it wouldn't stop. None of these assholes went to jail. No one pressed charges. Teresa's ex was the only one who even got arrested, and that was because he pulled the phone out of the wall when she tried to call 911. Apparently pulling the phone out of the wall is a federal offense.

The last thing Horace and I do each morning is put the kids on the bus. The counselors bring them down the back stairs and they file past Horace's cage with their book bags and lunch boxes, when we see the bus pull up in the monitors we stand outside the steel doors and the kids pass between us. It's almost like any other bus stop, just a bunch of kids going to school—except that these kids barely make a sound, they don't tease each other or complain, and they need two men with guns to make sure they get on the bus all right.

Sometimes a father will be out in the alley, but usually he'll just call to his kid and wave. "Tell your mother I love her" is what they usually say. We have lines painted on the pavement at 100 feet and 200 feet, so they can see exactly where they'll be violating their order. Sometimes, watching a father out of the corner of my eye, I catch myself hoping he'll cross the line, give me a reason.

Horace says he's never seen a problem at the bus. The fathers know there's not much to gain here, what with the mother locked inside and armed guards and all. He says they just come to feel like fathers for a few minutes. Maybe they hope their kid will wave. Maybe they think their kid will run over to them, crying, "Daddy, Daddy!" We have to stop them if they do.

I've worked out a deal with Camila's caseworker where I'm allowed to pat her on the head before she gets on the bus. She used to run over to me and hug my legs—her caseworker watching, alarmed, I stood there and tried to gently pry her away. Now I'm allowed to say, "Have a good day at school," and she's allowed to blow me a kiss.

Last week her father showed up in the alley. I knew he was there because Camila walked out the door and froze and immediately started to cry. "Camila," he shouted. "*Te quiero*, Camilita. *Tu mamá, dile que le amo.*" The caseworker had to carry her onto the bus. I turned to see a middle-aged guy in cords and a fisherman's sweater. I figured I'd get some kind of dirty look or Spanish curses, but he wasn't even looking at me. He just stared at the bus pulling away and gnawed miserably at his thumbnail.

In the evenings things are more informal. From eight o'clock, when I come on, until ten, all the women are in meetings. The night counselors are supposed to plan activities for the kids, but mostly they have them do their homework or watch TV. I sit in my cage with the day's logs and drink coffee, read up on any new residents or watch *Wheel of Fortune* on the little black-and-white. Eventually, out of the corner of my eye, I'll see half of a face and a few strands of hair peek around the corner of the stairwell. I'll pretend not to notice, looking over the notes on the console, and she'll sneak down the last stairs to spring up at the door of the cage.

"Boo!" she yells, and I pretend to fall out of my chair.

"You shouldn't sneak up on a man with a gun," I said to her once, thinking that was kind of funny, but I could see from her face that it wasn't. Another time I put my hands in the air and said, "Please, don't hurt me!" like it was a stickup. That wasn't funny either. You really have to watch yourself.

Camila brings her homework downstairs and I let her sit in my chair and swivel around and I help her with math. She has her times tables down cold, but she's completely blocked on long division. Last night I had to tell her again that it doesn't always come out even, that sometimes there's a remainder.

"This is stupid," she said, shoving the book onto the floor. She started pressing buttons on my console and I could hear the electric lock on the front door clicking in and out. I quickly checked the monitors, which thankfully were clear, but I still didn't want her fooling with the doors. I picked up the book and the pencil and put them back in front of her, but she didn't stop.

"Camila, you can't touch those," I said, and when she kept doing it I reached out and put my hands over hers—so gently I didn't even breathe—and moved her arms away. "We have to keep the doors locked," I said, rolling the chair back.

"Why?" she said.

"That's the rule. That way everyone's safe."

"But what if someone wants to come in?" she said.

I pointed to the monitors and said anyone who wants to come in can talk to me through the intercom. She knows all this. We've been through it before. She said she wanted to go outside and use the intercom. She wanted me to buzz her inside. When I said no, she said I should go outside and she would buzz me in. She wanted to make sure it wasn't broken,

"I'm not allowed to go outside," I told her.

"You'd get in trouble?"

"I'd get in trouble."

"You'd get a *castigo*?" she asked. I didn't know what that meant, so I just nodded.

We finished the last problem and I told Camila it was time to brush her teeth. The groups were letting out upstairs, the women spilling out of the meeting rooms, zooming on caffeine and affirmations.

"My daddy wants to visit me," she said, erasing and carefully rewriting her name in the exercise book, brushing eraser shavings all over my console. "He said he wants to take us home."

"You saw your father today?" I asked, trying to sound casual.

"He said he wants to see my room."

I took a deep breath. I'd have to tell her caseworker. Her father's order says he can't come to her school, but they just don't have the staff to keep a lid on these things. Last month one of our first-graders was taken right out of PE. He was missing for almost a week until they found him, in a motel with his father, two towns away. They were just watching TV and ordering pizzas, like they couldn't think of what else to do.

"He says you won't let him visit me," Camila said.

I pictured her father behind me in the alley while Camila got on the bus. I wondered how many mornings he'd been out there, watching, what it would feel like to see your daughter grab a stranger's leg when you called her. I made myself stop thinking about it—Mattie says the worst thing you can do is let yourself identify with these people.

"I can only let in the people they tell me to," I said, taking back my chair. I tried to say it the way Mattie says it, slow and reassuring. "It's so everyone can be safe."

She crossed her arms in the door and glared. "My daddy loves me."

I pretended to straighten some papers, checked the monitors again. I could see the women in the upstairs hallways, leaning against the walls, on line at the pay phones—waiting to call their husbands, to cup the receiver for their allotted fifteen minutes, whisper how much they miss them.

"I know," I said.

"He does."

I saw Mariana in the third-floor stairwell, on her way down. She couldn't have been more than twenty-five, but she looked much older. Her hair was pulled back tightly and she walked with a stoop, her head tilted to one side like she was listening for something. She never talks to any of the other women. Camila stood in the door of the cage and scowled.

"You're stupid," she finally said.

"You need to be careful with Camila Lopez," Mattie said over the phone. She usually checks in around eleven. Now that I'm on nights, I only see her at our monthly supervisions, or when something is really wrong. "Young girls like her behave in very sexualized ways around men. It's how they get attention."

"Sexualized?" I said, too loud. I tried to laugh. "I'm helping her with long division, for Christ's sake."

"Don't be defensive. I'm not accusing you of anything. You're not trained to see these things. You don't know the things I know."

I knew where she was headed. Horace and I are allowed to see the court orders, so we know who can do what—but only caseworkers can read the files. We hear a lot of stuff, but there's always more. I stared at the monitors, at the washed-out olive world surrounding Skyer House, while Mattie talked about positive reinforcement, appropriate buffer zones, and nonverbal cues. I could feel that tightness creeping back, that heat on the back of my neck. At my first weekly supervision, almost a year ago, I told Mattie how angry it made me to think of what these women had been through, what the kids had been through. I twisted a paper clip until it left dark indentations in my fingertips and said if a husband tried anything while I was around he'd end up in worse shape than his wife.

Mattie put down my folder and told me to take the next week off to decide whether this was the right job for me. There was nothing angry or disappointed in the way she said it, but nothing encouraging either.

"It's better if you don't care so much," she said. "We don't need another Rambo. That's why most of them are here in the first place."

Out in the alley, I asked Horace if he thought there was anything weird about how Camila hugs me or asks me to pick her up. He propped a foot against the wall and blew smoke up toward the windows.

"Someone gotta treat these kids like kids," he said. "Else they grow up thinking everyone's just as fucked up as their mother and father. Thinking one minute you hug someone, next minute they punch you in the gut."

"Kids are naturally affectionate. You don't want to discourage that," I said, but it came out sounding a lot like a question.

A light drizzle pattered against the Dumpsters and our breath came out in orange clouds. The alley smelled of burned rubber, like someone had just peeled out around the corner. "You ask me, they should lock both of them up, the mother and the father," Horace said. "You let your kid see that kind of shit, see you putting up with it, now what kind of damn message is that?

"It's weakness," he said on the way inside, gearing up for another one of his rants. "Nothing makes someone want to victimize you more than you being a victim already. They can smell it. Like a shark smells blood a mile away. There's no blood, you can swim right next to a shark and he just leave you alone. But show him you weak . . . ," he said and shut the door to his cage. I watched him sit on his chair and cross his arms, his mouth still moving, the raspy, hollow sound of his voice through the two-way speaker.

Upstairs, I checked all the doors and windows and put on *The Honeymooners*—Ralph steamed again, Alice shaking her fist in his face. I watched Camila in the monitor, her back to the camera as she stared out the meeting room window. Some nights she stands there for hours, wrapped in her Wonder Woman cape. Maybe she's worried that her father will come to get her. Or maybe she's hoping he will. In the months before Teresa moved out I used to stand at our kitchen window, watching the street. Sometimes I'd see her ex, driving slowly past the building, squinting up at the windows; by the time I got down there he was always gone. Other times, waiting for her to come home, I'd sit with the light off and pray for her car to appear.

After the kids got on the bus I went home and pulled down the shade and slept through the morning. I had the dream again, the one I've been having for months: I'm up on the fourth floor and I've found a room I've never been in. The windows are open, long curtains fluttering, and I don't know if someone's gotten in or gotten out. I rush downstairs but can't make it fast enough, moving in that excruciating slow motion. That's when I usually wake up, but this time there was more. This time it was Mariana's father down on the street, and then Mattie was shouting at me from the bottom of the stairs and I couldn't find my gun. "It's the end of the week!" she kept yelling, as though this kind of thing shouldn't be happening, and I fumbled at my holster, trying to make it to the bottom but there were so many stairs, my feet so heavy I knew I'd never make a difference.

Mariana's been talking to her husband again, hanging off the fourth-floor pay phone every night this week. Her caseworker got it from the night counselor, though Mariana still denies it in their sessions.

"It's the old pattern," says the caseworker, shrugging as the school bus pulls away. "She doesn't really have anyone else, no skills, no experience being on her own. It's either go back to her husband or go back to El Salvador." She looks up at the brick wall and bulletproof windows, the crumpled gray sky. "Or stay here."

He's coming to Camila's school every morning, says the caseworker, giving her notes to bring to her mother. This is how it happened last time, she says. She's called the school, the police; no one acts very concerned.

"There's gotta be something you can do," I say. She looks at me like I have three heads. "She can't just go back. I mean, there's a little girl involved."

"I'm aware of that, Charlie," she says.

"Maybe I should ride the bus with them," I say. "Make sure they get in the school all right."

She looks at her hands. "The school has security guards."

"Hell of a job they're doing."

"I'm just saying."

She leans against the wall, looks at me over her glasses. She's my age, or maybe a little younger, with a face that would be pretty if she let it, if she didn't pull her hair back so tight, if she smiled once in a while. Her nose looks like it was broken once. When she talks, her eyes don't blink.

"There must be something we can do," I say.

"We're doing it," she sighs, and goes right into the spiel. "We're giving her choices. We're giving her a place she can be safe, for as long as she needs it."

"What about Camila's choices?" I say, as quietly as I can manage.

The caseworker doesn't answer. It's not really a fair question. She pats me on the arm and walks inside. I can tell by the set of her shoulders how tired she is. I try to imagine her outside of Skyer House—walking in the park or driving, or maybe out on a date, sipping a drink, hair down around her shoulders. But all I can see is that exhausted expression, the lines at the corners of her eyes deepening each day. I picture my own face, shaving in the bathroom mirror. Behind me, my silent apartment, the empty refrigerator and broken stereo, one side of the closet bare where Teresa used to hang her clothes.

I got my job at the shelter when Mattie fired the previous guard, a kid named Trevor. She never told me what he actually did to get fired, but she said she'd always known he wouldn't last. In supervision he'd snicker and talk about irony. It was ironic that so many of the women hung crucifixes in their rooms, he told Mattie. It was ironic that their husbands were out there, living normal lives, while these women were locked up like criminals. It wasn't that he didn't have sympathy for them, she said. Just that he saw them as unwitting, the helpless butts of a cruel joke.

But cheap ironies abound at Skyer House and Mattie won't permit you to underestimate the women. "It's mutually assured destruction—just like the bombs," she once told me. We'd just watched an ambulance pull away; one of the women had swallowed a bottle of pills and collapsed at meeting. You can't stop people from fucking up their own lives, Mattie said. You can't even really stop them from fucking up someone else's, if that's what they want to do. All you can do is give them choices, offer them some scaled-down version of freedom, then stand back and cover your ears when they still decide to push the button.

"Now I'm going to stand there and wave and then you press this button to let me back in," I tell her. I make her point to the button three times, until I'm convinced she knows the right one. "No playing around," I say. "I wave, you push."

But Camila wants me to talk to her on the intercom. She says I have to ask permission.

"No. You just press the button. That's it."

She crosses her arms and spins around and around in the chair. "But you have to pretend I don't know you. You have to ask if you can come in," she says. She stops spinning and puts her arms around my waist. "Please?"

I glance up at the monitors. The meeting room doors are still closed, the sidewalks and the alley all empty. Horace is in the third-floor kitchen, taking his first break. "You can't ever tell anyone," I say, showing her how to key the intercom. "I'll get in big trouble."

"Okay."

"Promise?" She nods solemnly.

As I'm opening the front door, I turn back to look at her—sitting in my chair, staring at the console, her lips pursed in concentration. Outside on the stoop, I wait for a few seconds and wave to the camera, press the doorbell, grasp the handle. After a moment, the speaker crackles, but there's no voice. It crackles again, just the tail end of whatever Camila tried to say.

"It's Charlie," I tell the speaker, smiling for the camera. That's when I realize I left my keys in the cage. "Can I come in please?"

There's another crackle of the speaker, a quick clicking in and out of the lock, too fast for me to pull it open. I look up into the camera and wait, and she does it again—in and out—not holding the button long enough to open the door.

"Camila, no messing around," I whisper into the speaker. "Open the door now." But when it crackles again I can hear her laughing, saying my name. The lock keeps clicking, too fast, she's playing with that button like a damned video game, like this whole thing is just a game. Then it stops clicking altogether.

For a moment it's quiet outside Skyer House. The front of the building is patterned with lit windows—if someone looks out and sees me standing here, if they tell Mattie about it tomorrow, I can kiss my job good-bye. "Camila, open this door," I say, trying to keep my voice down, yanking on the reinforced steel. "Open the damn door, or you'll get a *castigo*." I'm starting to sweat. There's still no response, another minute I'm standing out there like a fool, then the lock buzzes steadily and I'm back inside.

"Camila," I'm saying, throwing open the vestibule door, ready to pick her up out of my chair and send her upstairs. But Mariana is standing in front of my cage, holding her daughter tightly by the arm. Camila is bawling, hiding her face against her mother's hip, holding the hem of Mariana's sweatshirt in one hand and hitting her other fist against her mother's leg. She turns to look at me, her face red and miserable, and cries harder.

"She just wanted to see how the door worked," I say, a little out of breath, feeling like I should apologize for something. Mariana looks at the floor, still gripping Camila's shoulder. Her sweatshirt hangs nearly to her knees, over old jeans. She looks so young—she could be anyone, a college girl in a dorm, or someone's little sister. Above her head, the monitors are gray and empty.

"She is a very bad girl," Mariana says quietly. Camila hiccups and sniffles. "She doesn't listen to me, she doesn't listen to her father."

"It was my fault," I say, scanning the console, the inside of the cage. "I shouldn't have let her do it."

"*Disculpe,*" Mariana says. "I keep her in the room. She will not bother you."

"It's okay," I say. "It's no big deal." I reach out to put my hand on Camila's head, but she hides behind her mother. Mariana raises her eyes, and for just a second I can imagine her as a young girl, back in El Salvador, before all this. Then I imagine her upstairs on the fourth floor, in the small room she shares with her daughter, staring out at the alley and wondering what the hell happened.

"She's a good girl," I tell Mariana, who blinks at me from the door of my cage. "She's very nice. Just like her mother."

For a second she looks like she's going to smile. But then, just as quickly, she lowers her eyes and slides past me. She mutters another apology and guides Camila to the stairs; I sit back in my chair, watch them move through the monitors, climbing back up to the fourth floor, where they'll be safe for the rest of the night.

The next night the front-door chime sounds as Horace and I are heading out for our smoke. I freeze up for a second, sure that it's Camila's father. I have to grind my teeth and tell my feet to follow Horace back to his cage. I have to remind myself that I'm a professional, I'm not paid to understand.

But the guy outside is white, in his thirties, jeans and a dress shirt. He stands there with his hands in his pockets, whistling at the sky. Through the monitors he seems almost friendly, like an insurance agent; if you saw this guy in the supermarket you wouldn't think twice. He's no one we've seen before, probably the husband of a new client, just testing the waters, seeing how much we'll let him get away with.

Horace keys the intercom. "Sorry, we didn't order no pizza," he says.

"I want to see my wife," the guy says. He looks right into the camera, leans forward so his face grows large in the monitor, breaks up into green pixels. His pupils are shrunken to pinheads.

"Visiting hours are over," Horace tells him. "You got two minutes to find somewhere else to be." He keeps his voice even but firm, exactly the way we were taught. He's really good at it—I've seen him put a guy in an armlock while the wife clawed at Horace's face, drawing blood, all without raising his voice. I don't know how you do that, how you lock those feelings away. I wonder if it comes out when he gets home, if the walls of his house have big divots in the plaster where he punches them, like mine do.

"You've got two minutes to go fuck yourself," the guy snarls into the camera. "She's my fucking wife, you piece of shit."

The clock on Horace's console reads 1:08 A.M. and I take out the incident log to start a report. Horace leans back and crosses his arms, trying to wait him out.

You never want to get into it with a husband—especially when he's flying on something, like this guy. You keep it friendly as long as you can, let him know the limits, and hope he'll show some good sense and let it go. That almost never happens.

The husband hits the chime again, mashing the button and shouting into the intercom. Any minute now, the women will start coming out of their rooms. We'll see them in the monitors—nightgowned ghosts drifting through the hallways. The chime only sounds in our cages, but somehow they just know. It's like a sixth sense.

"Don't make me call the police," Horace says, rolling his eyes. "Make a better decision than that."

"I'm gonna decide to bust down this door and kick your ass," says the husband. He starts pounding against the door, slamming into it with his shoulder. "You hear me, fuckhead?" he screams, pointing his finger into the camera. "When I get in there I'm gonna rip off your head and shit down your neck. I want to see my fucking wife!"

"Two points for the shit-down-the-neck comment," I say. "This one's creative."

"Yeah, he a real poet," Horace says, reaching for the phone. There are women in the halls now, whispering among themselves, shooing their children back into the rooms. This will be over in five minutes when the police arrive. The only thing to worry about is whether the husband will catch a glimpse of his wife or not. If his wife goes to the window, and her husband looks up and sees her, all bets are off. I've seen a 140-pound husband throw off three cops after seeing his wife in the window. I've seen a guy make it halfway up to the third floor by scaling the front of the building—his wife beating against the glass, trying to put her arms around him. I couldn't stop thinking it wasn't human, that normal people don't behave like this. I watched him in the monitors, clinging to the bricks until the fire department came, his wife being restrained by the counselors—they weren't human, they were more like moths hurling themselves against a lightbulb, some frantic, uncontrollable instinct driving them.

This is what Teresa wouldn't say to me, why she couldn't stop going back to her ex, time after time. It's not something that can be explained. It's a force of nature. We were together for two years, and she said she loved me, but I never felt it. They were just words when she said them to me. They had no force.

The cops finally pull up, and after the obligatory struggle—the husband spits in one of their faces, they slam him onto the hood of the crusier, his legs wild and rubbery as they cuff him—things are under control. Horace and I flip a coin to see who'll go calm the women. I lose, and climb the stairs to the second floor, where they're still whispering in the hall and peering out the windows. Lucille Johnson is on the phone already, slapping her hand against the wall, her face smeared with cold cream. I tell them everything's all right, to go back to bed. I keep my hands open at my sides, like Mattie showed me. I maintain acceptable distance. These women know me, know I'd never hurt them, but it's not a question of what they know. I speak quietly, and do my best not to look at the open bathrobes, the thin nightgowns and worn sweatpants, the shy smile of a woman who leans against the wall and tries to hide the cast on her wrist.

"Who was it, Charlie?" they ask, their eyes nervous, excited. They grab my arms and ask, "Is he going to come back? Where's Mattie?" I don't know whose husband it was, but it seems like she might have slept through it. If not, if she saw her husband downstairs, it could be an even longer night than it's already been.

When I've finally gotten everyone out of the hallways I remember the cigarette in my shirt pocket. Mattie will review tonight's security tapes, so I open the door to the fourth-floor meeting room, look for a pack of matches. As soon as I walk in I can feel the cold breeze—someone left a window open again—and I'm halfway across the room before I notice Mariana standing in the dark, her nightgown camouflaging her against the curtains. She's standing in the same spot Camila always stands in, holding her arms around herself, her cheek damp and reddish-silver from the streetlights.

"Are you okay?" I ask quietly. I start to reach out to touch her shoulder but think better of it. Mariana just nods. "It's over," I tell her. "There's nothing to be scared of."

I shut the window and look for a blanket or a robe to put around her, but there's nothing. There's the faintest of reflections in the glass, doubling her face, and the large darkness looming behind her is just me.

"Do you need anything?" I ask. "Is there any way I can help?" As I'm saying it I can hear Mattie's voice in my head, but I just don't believe what she says. I don't believe you can help another human being by not helping them. It makes no goddamn sense.

"You are very nice," Mariana says, her voice barely audible. Her eyes are swollen from crying, the light on her face makes her look girlish and innocent. "Camila, she likes you. She says you are very intelligent."

"She's the smart one," I tell her. "She really is a bright little girl."

Mariana still won't look at me. "It is from her father. He is very intelligent."

I know I shouldn't say anything but I can't help it. "I don't think he's very smart," I tell her.

She starts to say something but stops, and that's when I see that she's holding something, a picture frame that she's pressing to her belly, the fabric of her nightgown taut against her body. I don't have to look to know what that photo is. There's no sound in the room, only the rise and fall of her chest, a siren somewhere in the city, as she holds it out to me.

"I was only seventeen years old," she says, handing me her wedding photo. Her eyes are dark and liquid, her hair tucked behind one small, ringless ear. And as we stare at each other I realize that she hadn't been scared by the commotion outside. She wasn't frightened—she was crying because it wasn't her husband, because he wasn't the one who tried to force his way inside and take her home. She pushes the frame to me, her gaze finally meeting mine, and her need for me to look at that photo, to see in it what she sees, is a tangible force between us, a new kind of gravity, bodies that somehow repel and attract each other at the same time. I look at the security camera in the corner, the little red light blinking slowly, I take her wrists and gently push them away, her skin warm on my hands, my knuckles brushing the fabric of her nightgown.

I open my mouth and all that comes out, whispered, is "Camila." We're standing much closer than we should be, something pushing us even closer, I should take my hands away but I don't. We both take a breath, and I don't know whether in the next instant I'm going to lean down and press my lips to hers or take her small, pale neck between my hands. I don't know what comes over me, but the image is so clear, so imminent that I snatch my hands away and take a step back, the frame falls at Mariana's feet and shatters.

"Don't move," I tell her, awake now, bending to grab the frame, collecting the shards in the palm of my hand. "Stay here. I can't see it all, dammit," I tell Mariana whose bare toes are inches from my fingers. "Just hang on, I'll carry you out or something."

There are already faces in the doorway, drawn to the sound of violence. I'm on my hands and knees, running my fingertips over the carpet, invisible splinters burrowing into my skin. Mariana snatches the frame out of my hand and then, despite my warnings, walks right past me in her bare feet. I want to reach up and grab her arm, pull her back, ask why she would do such a thing. But I keep my eyes on the carpet, scrounging around stupidly, all I see is a flutter of cotton, the flash of her calves as she pulls the door shut behind her.

A few days later, Camila doesn't come down to the school bus with the others. Horace and I stand in the sunshine, a fragile, early-spring morning, and I watch the kids' faces file past. When the bus door closes, I raise an eyebrow to the caseworker, who shrugs and turns away, heads upstairs before I can catch her.

"Smoke?" Horace says, reaching into his pocket. He casually moves between me and the door. The bus turns out of the alley, sunlight warbling off the back windows.

"I think I'll go see what's wrong with Camila," I tell him, but he grabs my elbow as I try to move past.

"Have a cigarette first," he says. "You go in a few minutes." His hand on my arm is friendly but firm, his expression studiously neutral. I know that expression, have seen it on my own face, practiced it in mirrors.

"What's going on?" I say.

Horace looks past me. "What do you mean?"

By the time I'm halfway up the stairs I can hear Mattie's voice in the front hallway and I know something terrible has happened. I take the stairs two at a time, hands clenched, wondering how I could have missed it. At the top of the stairs I nearly barrel into the four people standing outside my cage.

"Good morning, Charlie," says Mattie, taking a half-step forward to look me in the eyes. "Can you wait in my office a moment, please?"

Before I can say anything, Camila runs to me and wraps her arms around my leg, pressing her face into my thigh. Her mother calls to her, but she holds on to me, sniffling into my leg. Her father says nothing, frowning and watching her over his mustache, holding Mariana's hand. Mariana says something in Spanish and he nods. He's shorter than his wife, wearing freshly ironed black pants and a collared shirt. Mariana clutches the roses to her chest. Her suitcase sits by the door, Camila's small backpack slumped on top of it.

"Camila, *ven*," says Mariana, her voice steadier than I've heard it.

Mattie says my name again, but I don't look at her. My hand rests on Camila's head, stroking her hair.

"*Hija, ven,*" says the husband. Camila looks up at me, wanting me to tell her what to do, but I won't take my eyes off her father. Finally, she lets go and straggles back to her parents. Her father crouches to whisper in her ear. She shakes her head, but he turns her around, urges her back to me.

"He said thank you for being my friend," she translates. Mattie has her hands on her hips, watching me intently, but no one can control what's about to happen, least of all me.

"Tell him I'm not his friend," I say.

Camila starts to giggle. "No, stupid," she says. "*My* friend. Me."

Mariana starts to say something, but I've already taken a step forward, drawn myself up—it's like I can see it happening, like I'm watching the whole thing, that fucking animal shrinking away from me, trying to get his arms up, but not in time, and the sting of his face against my open hand sends a shiver through me, the sharp smack ringing in the air as he half-twirls, slides against the wall, stumbles over his wife's suitcase and sprawls to the floor. Then I'm standing over him, just waiting for him to get up, just waiting, Camila is crying, everyone shouting, but it all seems to come from somewhere else. For that instant it's just me and him, staring at each other, one of us stronger than the other, locked in a moment of perfect communication.

"Now you done it," says a voice behind me, there are arms wrapping me into a bear hug, Horace nearly lifts me off the ground, pushes me against the far wall. He stands inches from me, containing me without anger, Mattie shaking her head and Mariana sheltering her sobbing daughter, the roses strewn across the floor.

"Stand right there," Horace says quietly, barring an arm against my chest. "Don't you move." He reaches around and undoes my belt, removes the holster, faces peering from the top of the stairs, tense voices whispering. I stand with my palms flat against the wall, my throat so tight I can't swallow, while Camila's father picks himself up and smooths out his clothes, reaches for his wife's arm. It's hard to tell who's leaning on whom.

Mattie opens the door and the lobby floods with sunshine. Mariana picks up her howling daughter, her husband's arm around both of them as they walk out of Skyer House. Over her mother's shoulder, Camila looks at me one last time, her face smeared with tears, her eyes wide open and afraid.

The door swings shut and Horace backs off, still wary, ready to tackle me if I try to go after them. "Shit, Charlie, what in hell are you thinking," he says, trying to make eye contact. His voice sounds like it's coming through a tunnel. "You know that motherfucker just gonna take it out on her."

There's noise in the stairwell, women applauding, hooting and calling down congratulations. "You're my hero, Charlie!" comes Lucille Johnson's voice. I walk back to my cage—slowly, hands in the air so Horace will know I'm not a danger anymore. I sit at the console and find them in the monitors, watch them move from camera to camera, Camila's face buried in her mother's shoulder, her father's arm across Mariana's back. The image skips from one monitor to the next, the angle changing as a new camera picks them up, so for a second it almost looks like they're coming back.

Soon they've passed beyond the cameras. I can see Mattie on the stoop, catching her breath, waiting to come inside and fire me. I can hear her doing it, that businesslike voice telling me it's for the good of the shelter. I can't blame her. I've given her no choice.

She'll say it's for my own good, too. She'll smile weakly and suggest I think about getting counseling. She'll say it's up to me to decide what to do now. Then she'll ask for my keys and tell me never to come back.

But first she'll bring me into her office and close the door, and from a desk drawer she'll take out the tape from the other night. She'll ask me if I know what's on that tape and I'll nod, unable to speak. She'll put the tape in the player and let herself out, leaving me alone in her tidy, windowless office. And while she's upstairs, setting everything back to normal, I'll watch that tape again and again, sit right up close to the monitor and stare at the grainy image of a man—standing outside the shelter, coming in the door. I'll keep hitting the rewind button, watching him forward and backward, and wonder if that's what I really look like in the flat gray world outside the door.

Kate Braverman

Kate Braverman (1950-) is a poet and fiction writer. Her novels include Lithium for Medea *(1979),* Palm Latitudes *(1988),* Wonders of the West *(1993), and* The Incantation of Frida K *(2001). Her memoir,* Frantic Transmissions to and from Los Angeles: An Accidental Memoir *(2006), won the Graywolf Prize for Creative Non-Fiction. Her short story, "Tall Tales from the Mekong Delta," appeared in the* Norton Anthology of Short Fiction. *She has previously taught creative writing at California State University, Los Angeles and now lives in Santa Fe, New Mexico.*

Tall Tales from the Mekong Delta

It was in the fifth month of her sobriety. It was after the hospital. It was after her divorce. It was autumn. She had even stopped smoking. She was wearing pink acrobic pants, a pink T-shirt with KAUAI written in lilac across the chest, and tennis shoes. She had just come from the gym. She was walking across a parking lot bordering a city park in West Hollywood. She was carrying cookies for the AA meeting. She was in charge of bringing the food for the meeting. He fell into step with her. He was short, fat, pale. He had bad teeth. His hair was dirty. Later, she would freeze his frame in her mind and study it. She would say he seemed frightened and defeated and trapped, "cagey" was the word she used to describe his eyes, how he measured and evaluated something in the air between them. The way he squinted through hazel eyes, it had nothing to do with the sunlight.

"I'm Lenny," he said, extending his hand. "What's your name?"

She told him. She was holding a bag with packages of cookies in it. After the meeting, she had an appointment with her psychiatrist, then a manicure. She kept walking.

"You a teacher? You look like a teacher," he said.

"I'm a writer," she told him. "I teach creative writing."

"You look like a teacher," Lenny said.

"I'm not just a teacher," she told him. She was annoyed.

"Okay. You're a writer. And you're bad. You're one of those bad girls from Beverly Hills. I've had my eye on you," Lenny said.

She didn't say anything. He was wearing blue jeans, a black leather jacket zipped to his throat, a long red wool scarf around his neck, and a Dodgers baseball cap. It was too hot a day for the leather jacket and scarf. She didn't find that detail significant. It caught her attention, she touched it briefly and then let it go. She looked but did not see. They were standing on a curb. The meeting was in a community room across the boulevard. She wasn't afraid yet.

"You do drugs? What do you do? Drink too much?" he asked.

"I'm a cocaine addict," she told him.

"Me too. Let's see your tracks. Show me your tracks." Lenny reached out for her arm.

"I don't have any now." She glanced at her arm. She extended her arm into the yellow air between them. The air was already becoming charged and disturbed. "They're gone."

"I see them," Lenny told her, inspecting her arm, turning it over, holding it in the sunlight. He touched the part of her arm behind her elbow where the vein rose. "They're beautiful."

"But there's nothing there," she said.

"Yeah, there is. There always is if you know how to look," Lenny told her. "How many people by the door? How many steps?"

He was talking about the door across the boulevard. His back was turned. She didn't know.

"Four steps," Lenny said. "Nine people. Four women. One odd man. I look. I see."

She was counting the people on the steps in front of the meeting. She didn't say anything.

"Let's get a coffee later. That's what you do, right? You can't get a drink? You go out for coffee?" Lenny was studying her face.

"I don't think so," she said.

"You don't think so? Come on. I'll buy you coffee. You can explain AA to me. You like that Italian shit? That French shit? The little cups?" Lenny was staring at her.

"No, thank you. I'm sorry," she said. He was short and fat and sweating. He looked like he was laughing at her with his eyes.

"You're sorry. I'll show you sorry. Listen. I know what you want. You're one of those smart-ass teachers from Beverly Hills," Lenny said.

"Right," she said. She didn't know why she bothered talking to him.

"You want to get in over your head. You want to see what's on the other side. I'll show you. I'll take you there. It'll be the ride of your life," Lenny said.

"Goodbye," she answered.

Lenny was at her noon meeting the next day. She saw him immediately as she walked through the door. She wondered how he knew that she would be there. As she approached her usual chair, she saw a bouquet of long-stemmed pink roses.

"You look beautiful," Lenny said. "You knew I'd be here. That's why you put that crap on your face. You didn't have that paint on yesterday. Don't do that. You don't need that. Those whores from Beverly Hills need it. Not you. You're a teacher. I like that. Sit down." He picked the roses up. "Sit next to me. You glad to see me?"

"I don't think so." She sat down. Lenny handed the roses to her. She put them on the floor.

"Yeah. You're glad to see me. You were hoping I'd be here. And here I am. You want me to chase you? I'll chase you. Then I'll catch you. Then I'll show you what being in over your head means." Lenny was smiling.

She turned away. When the meeting was over, she stood up quickly and began moving, even before the prayer was finished. "I have to go," she said softly, over her shoulder. She felt she had to apologize. She felt she had to be careful.

"You don't have to go," Lenny said. He caught up with her on the steps. "Yeah. Don't look surprised. Lenny's fast, real fast. And you're lying. Don't ever lie to me. You think I'm stupid? Yeah, you think Lenny's stupid. You think you can get away from me? You can't get away. You got an hour. You don't pick that kid up from the dance school until four. Come on. I'll buy you coffee."

"What are you talking about?" She stopped. Her breath felt sharp and fierce. It was a warm November. The air felt like glass.

"I know all about you. I know your routine. I been watching you for two weeks. Ever since I got to town. I saw you my first day. You think I'd ask you out on a date and not know your routine?" Lenny stared at her.

She felt her eyes widen. She started to say something but she changed her mind.

"You live at the top of the hill, off of Doheny. You pick up that kid, what's her name, Annie something? You pick her up and take her to dance school. You get coffee next door. Table by the window. You read the paper. Then you go home. Just the two of you. And that Mex cleaning lady. Maria. That her name? Maria? They're all called Maria. And the gardener Friday afternoons. That's it." Lenny lit a cigarette.

"You've been following me?" She was stunned. Her mouth opened.

"Recon," Lenny said.

"I beg your pardon?"

"In Nam. We called it recon. Fly over, get a lay of the land. Or stand behind some trees. Count the personnel. People look but they don't see. I'll tell you about it. Get coffee. You got an hour. Want to hear about Vietnam? I got stories. Choppers? I like choppers. You can take your time, aim. You can hit anything, even dogs. Some days we'd go out just aiming at dogs. Or the black market? Want to hear about that? Profiteering in smack? You're a writer, right? You like stories. I got some tall tales from the Mekong Delta for you, sweetheart. Knock your socks off. Come on" He reached out and touched her arm. "Later you can have your own war stories. I can be one of your tall tales. I can be the tallest."

The sun was strong. The world was washed with white. The day seemed somehow clarified. He was wearing a leather jacket and shaking. It occurred to her that he was sick.

"Excuse me. I must go," she said. "If you follow me, I shall have someone call the police."

"Okay. Okay. Calm down," Lenny was saying behind her. "I'll save you a seat tomorrow, okay?"

She didn't reply. She sat in her car. It was strange how blue the sky seemed, etched with the blue of radium or narcotics. Or China blue, perhaps. Was that a color? The blue of the China Sea? The blue of Vietnam. When he talked about Asia, she could imagine that blue, luminescent with ancient fever, with promises and bridges broken, with the harvest lost in blue flame. Always there were barbarians, shooting the children and dogs.

She locked her car and began driving. It occurred to her, suddenly, that the Chinese took poets as concubines. Their poets slept with warlords. They wrote with gold ink. They ate orchids and smoked opium. They were consecrated by nuance, by birds and silk and the ritual birthdays of gods and nothing changed for a thousand years. And afternoon was absinthe yellow and almond, burnt orange and chrysanthemum. And in the abstract sky, a litany of kites.

She felt herself look for him as she walked into the meeting the next day at noon. The meeting was in the basement of a church. Lenny was standing near the coffeepot with his back to the wall. He was holding two cups of coffee as if he was expecting her. He handed one to her.

"I got seats," he said. He motioned for her to follow. She followed. He pointed to a chair. She sat in it. An older woman was standing at the podium, telling the story of her life. Lenny was wearing a white warm-up suit with a green neon stripe down the sides of the pants and the arms of the jacket. He was wearing a baseball cap. His face seemed younger and tanner than she had remembered.

"Like how I look? I look like a lawyer on his way to tennis, right? I even got a tan. Fit right in. Chameleon Lenny. The best, too." He lit a cigarette. He held the pack out to her.

She shook her head, no. She was staring at the cigarette in his mouth, in his fingers. She could lean her head closer, part her lips, take just one puff.

"I got something to show you," Lenny said.

The meeting was over. They were walking up the stairs from the basement of the church. The sun was strong. She blinked in the light. It was the yellow of a hot autumn, a yellow that seemed amplified and redeemed. She glanced at her watch.

"Don't do that," Lenny said. He was touching the small of her back with his hand. He was helping her walk.

"What?"

"Looking at that fucking watch all the time. Take it off," Lenny said.

"My watch?" She was looking at her wrist as if she had never seen it before.

"Give it here, come on." Lenny put his hand out. He motioned with his fingers. She placed her watch in the palm of his hand.

"That's a good girl," Lenny was saying. "You don't need it. You don't have to know what time it is. You're with me. Don't you get it? You're hungry, I feed you. You're tired, I find a hotel You're in a structured environment now. You're protected. I protect you. It doesn't matter what time it is." He put her watch in his pocket. "Forget it. I'll buy you a new one. A better one. That was junk. I was embarrassed for you to wear junk like that. Want a Rolex?"

"You can't afford a Rolex," she said. She felt intelligent. She looked into his face.

"I got a drawerful," Lenny told her. "I got all the colors. Red. Black. Gold."

"Where?" She studied his face. They were walking on a side street, in Hollywood. The air was a pale blue, bleeding into the horizon, taking the sky.

"In the bank," Lenny said. "In the safety deposit with everything else. All the cash that isn't buried." Lenny smiled.

"What else?" She put her hands on her hips.

"Let's go for a ride," Lenny said.

They were standing at the curb. They were two blocks from the church. A motorcycle was parked there. Lenny took out a key.

"Get on," he said.

"I don't want to get on a motorcycle." She was afraid.

"Yes, you do," Lenny told her. "Sit down on it. Wrap your arms around me. Just lean into me. Nothing else. You'll like it. You'll be surprised. It's a beautiful day. It looks like Hong Kong today. Want to go to the beach? Want lunch? I know a place in Malibu. You like seafood? Crab? Scampi? Watch the waves?" Lenny was doing something to the motorcycle. He looked at her face.

"No," she said.

"How about Italian? I got a place near the Marina. Owner owes for ten kilos. We'll get a good table. You like linguini?" Lenny sat down on the motorcycle.

She shook her head, no.

"Okay. You're not hungry. You're skinny. You should eat. Come on. We'll go around the block. Get on. Once around the block and I'll bring you back to the church." Lenny reached out his hand through the warm white air.

She looked at his hand and how the air seemed blue near his fingers. It's simply a blue glaze, she was thinking. In Malibu, in Hilo, in the China Sea, forms of blue, confusion and remorse, a dancing dress, a daughter with a mouth precisely your own and it's done, all of it.

Somewhere it was carnival night in the blue wash of a village on the China Sea. On the river, boats passed with low-slung antique masts sliding silently to the blue of the ocean, to the inverted delta where the horizon concluded itself in a rapture of orchid and pewter. That's what she was thinking when she took his hand.

She did not see him for a week. She changed her meeting schedule. She went to women's meetings in the Pacific Palisades and the Valley. She went to meetings she had never been to before. She trembled when she thought about him.

She stopped her car at a red light. It occurred to her that it was an early afternoon autumn in her thirty-eighth year. Then she found herself driving to the community center. The meeting was over. There was no one left on the street. Just one man, sitting alone on the front steps, smoking. Lenny looked up at her and smiled.

"I was expecting you," Lenny said. "I told you. You can't get away from me."

She could feel his eyes on her face, the way when she lived with a painter, she had learned to feel lamplight on her skin. When she had learned to perceive light as an entity. She began to cry.

"Don't cry," Lenny said, his voice soft. "I can't stand you crying. Let's make up. I'll buy you dinner."

"I can't." She didn't look at him.

"Yeah. You can. I'll take you someplace good. Spago? You like those little pizzas with the duck and shit? Lobster? You want the Palm? Then Rangoon Racket Club? Yeah. Don't look surprised. I know the places. I made deals in all those places. What did you think?" He was lighting a cigarette and she could feel his eyes on her skin.

She didn't say anything. They were walking across a parking lot. The autumn made everything ache. Later, it would be worse. At dusk, with the subtle irritation of lamps.

"Yeah. I know what you think. You think Lenny looks like he just crawled out from a rock. This is a disguise. Blue jeans, sneakers. I fit right in. I got a gang of angry Colombians on my ass. Forget it." Lenny stared at her. "You got a boyfriend?"

"What's it to you?"

"What's it to me? That's sharp. I want to date you. I probably want to marry you. You got a boyfriend, I got to hurt him." Lenny smiled.

"I can't believe you said that." She put her hands on her hips.

"You got a boyfriend? I'm going to cut off his arm and beat him with it. Here. Look at this." He was bending over and removing something from his sock. He held it in the palm of his hand.

"Know what this is?" Lenny asked.

She shook her head, no.

"It's a knife, sweetheart," Lenny said.

She could see that now, even before he opened it. A pushbutton knife. Lenny was reaching behind to his back. He was pulling out something from behind his belt, under his shirt. It was another knife.

"Want to see the guns?"

She felt dizzy. They were standing near her car. It was early in December. The Santa Anas had been blowing. She felt that it had been exceptionally warm for months.

"Don't get in the car," Lenny said. "I can't take it when you leave. Stay near me. Just let me breathe the same air as you. I love you."

"You don't even know me," she said.

"But you know me. You been dreaming me. I'm your ticket to the other side, remember?" Lenny had put his knives away. "Want to hear some more Nam stories? How we ran smack into Honolulu? You'll like this. You like the dope stories. You want to get loaded?"

She shook her head, no.

"You kidding me? You don't want to get high?" Lenny smiled.

"I like being sober," she said.

"Sure," Lenny said. "Let me know when that changes. One phone call. I got the best dope in the world."

They were standing in front of her car. The street beyond the parking lot seemed estranged, the air was tarnished. She hadn't thought about drugs in months. Lenny was handing her something, thin circles of metal. She looked down at her hand. Two dimes seemed to glare in her palm.

"For when you change your mind," Lenny said. He was still smiling.

They were sitting on the grass of a public park after a meeting. Lenny was wearing Bermuda shorts and a green T-shirt that said CANCÚN. They were sitting in a corner of the park with a stucco wall behind them.

"It's our anniversary," Lenny told her. "We been in love four weeks."

"I've lost track of time," she said. She didn't have a watch anymore. The air felt humid, green, stalled. It was December in West Hollywood. She was thinking that the palms were livid with green death. They could be the palms of Vietnam.

"I want to fuck you," Lenny said. "Let's go to your house."

She shook her head, no. She turned away from him. She began to stand up.

"Okay. Okay. You got the kid. I understand that. Let's go to a hotel. You want the Beverly Wilshire? I can't go to the Beverly Hills Hotel. I got a problem there. What about the Four Seasons? You want to fuck in the Four Seasons?"

"You need to get an AIDS test," she said.

"Why?" Lenny looked amused.

"Because you're a heroin addict. Because you've been in jail," she began.

"Who told you that?" Lenny sat up.

"You told me," she said. "Terminal Island. Chino. Folsom? Is is true?"

"Uh-huh," Lenny said. He lit a cigarette. "Five years in Folsom. Consecutive. Sixty months. I topped out."

She stared at him. She thought how easy it would be, to reach and take a cigarette. Just one, once.

"Means I finished my whole sentence. No time off for good behavior. Lenny did the whole sixty." He smiled. "I don't need an AIDS test."

"You're a heroin addict. You shoot cocaine. You're crazy. Who knows what you do or who you do it with?" She was beginning to be afraid.

"You think I'd give you a disease?" Lenny looked hurt.

Silence. She was looking at Lenny's legs, how white the exposed skin was. She was thinking that he brought his sick body to her, that he was bloated, enormous with pathology and bad history, with jails and demented resentments.

"Listen. You got nothing to worry about. I don't need a fucking AIDS test. Listen to me. Are you hearing me? You get that disease, I take care of you. I take you to Bangkok. I keep a place there, on the river. Best smack in the world. Fifty cents. I keep you loaded. You'll never suffer. You start hurting, I'll take you out. I'll kill you myself. With my own hands. I promise," Lenny said.

Silence. She was thinking that he must be drawn to her vast emptiness, could he sense that she was aching and hot and always listening? There is always a garish carnival across the boulevard. We are born, we eat and sleep, conspire and mourn, a birth, a betrayal, an excursion to the harbor, and it's done. All of it, done.

"Come here." Lenny extended his arm. "Come here. You're like a child. Don't be afraid. I want to give you something."

She moved her body closer to his. There are blue enormities, she was thinking, horizons and boulevards. Somewhere, there are blue rocks and they burn.

"Close your eyes," Lenny said. "Open your mouth."

She closed her eyes. She opened her mouth. There was something pressing against her lip. Perhaps it was a flower.

"Close your mouth and breathe," Lenny said.

It was a cigarette. She felt the smoke in her lungs. It had been six months since she smoked. Her hand began to tremble.

"There," Lenny was saying. "You need to smoke. I can tell. It's okay. You can't give up everything at once. Here. Share it. Give me a hit."

They smoked quietly. They passed the cigarette back and forth. She was thinking that she was like a sacked capital. Nothing worked in her plazas. The palm trees were on fire. The air was smoky and blue. No one seemed to notice.

"Sit on my lap. Come on. Sit down. Closer. On my lap," Lenny was saying. "Good. Yeah. Good. I'm not going to bite you. I love you. Want to get married?

Want to have a baby? Closer. Let me kiss you. You don't do anything. Let me do it. Now your arms. Yeah. Around my neck. Tighter. Tighter. You worried? You got nothing to worry about. You get sick, I keep you whacked on smack. Then I kill you. So what are you worried? Closer. Yeah. Want to hear about R and R in Bangkok? Want to hear about what you get for a hundred bucks on the river? You'll like this. Lean right up against me. Yeah. Close your eyes."

"Look. It's hot. You want to swim. You like that? Swimming? You know how to swim?" Lenny looked at her. "Yeah? Let's go. I got a place in Bel Air."

"You have a place in Bel Air?" she asked. It was after the meeting. It was the week before Christmas. It was early afternoon.

"Guy I used to know. I did a little work for him. I introduced him to his wife. He owes me some money. He gave me the keys." Lenny reached in his pocket. He was wearing a white-and-yellow warm-up suit. He produced a key ring. It hung in the hot air between them. "It's got everything there. Food. Booze. Dope. Pool. Tennis court. Computer games. You like that? Pac Man?"

She didn't say anything. She felt she couldn't move. She lit a cigarette. She was buying two packages at a time again. She would be buying cartons soon.

"Look. We'll go for a drive. I'll tell you some more war stories. Come on. I got a nice car today. I got a brand-new red Ferrari. Want to see it? Just take a look. One look. It's at the curb. Give me your hand." Lenny reached out for her hand.

She could remember being a child. It was a child's game in a child's afternoon, before time or distance were factors. When you were told you couldn't move or couldn't see. And for those moments you are paralyzed or blind. You freeze in place. You don't move. You feel that you have been there for years. It does not occur to you that you can move. It does not occur to you that you can break the rules. The world is a collection of absolutes and spells. You know words have a power. You are entranced. The world is a soft blue.

"There. See. I'm not crazy. A red Ferrari. A hundred forty grand. Get in. We'll go around the block. Sit down. Nice interior, huh? Nice stereo. But I got no fuck-ing tapes. Go to the record store with me? You pick out the tapes, okay? Then we'll go to Bel Air. Swim a little. Watch the sunset. Listen to some music. Want to dance? I love to dance. You can't get a disease doing that, right?" Lenny was hold-ing the car door open for her.

She sat down. The ground seemed enormous. It seemed to leap up at her face.

"Yeah. I'm a good driver. Lean back. Relax. I used to drive for a living," Lenny told her.

"What did you drive? A bus?" She smiled.

"A bus? That's sharp. You're one of those sharp little Jewish girls from Bev-erly Hills with a cocaine problem. Yeah. I know what you're about. All of you. I drove some cars on a few jobs. Couple of jewelry stores, a few banks. Now I fly," Lenny said.

Lenny turned the car onto Sunset Boulevard. In the gardens of the houses behind the gates, everything was in bloom. Patches of color slid past so fast she thought they might be hallucinations. Azaleas and camellias and hibiscus. The green seemed sullen and half asleep. Or perhaps it was opiated, dazed, exhausted from pleasure.

"You fly?" she repeated.

"Planes. You like planes? I'll take you up. I got a plane. Company plane," Lenny told her. "It's in Arizona."

"You're a pilot?" She put out her cigarette and immediately lit another.

"I fly planes for money. Want to fly? I'm going next week. Every second Tuesday. Want to come?" Lenny looked at her.

"Maybe," she said. They had turned on a street north of Sunset. They were winding up a hill. The street was narrow. The bougainvillea was a kind of net near her face. The air smelled of petals and heat.

"Yeah. You'll come with me. I'll show you what I do. I fly over a stretch of desert looks like the moon. There's a small manufacturing business down there. Camouflaged. You'd never see it. I drop some boxes off. I pick some boxes up. Three hours' work. Fifteen grand," Lenny said. "Know what I'm talking about?"

"No."

"Yeah. You don't want to know anything about this. Distribution," Lenny said. "That's federal."

"You do that twice a month?" she asked. They were above Sunset Boulevard. The bougainvillea was a magenta web. There were sounds of birds and insects. They were winding through pine trees. "That's 30,000 dollars a month."

"That's nothing. The real money's the Bogotá run," Lenny said. "Mountains leap up out of the ground, out of nowhere. The Bogotá run drove me crazy. Took me a month to come down. Then the Colombians got mad. You know what I'm talking about?"

"No."

"That's good. You don't want to know anything about the Colombians," Lenny said again.

She was thinking about the Colombians and Bogotá and the town where Lenny said he had a house, Medellín. She was thinking they would have called her *gitana*, with her long black hair and bare feet. She could have fanned herself with handfuls of 100-dollar bills like a green river. She could have borne sons for men crossing borders, searching for the definitive run, the one you don't return from. She would dance in bars in the permanently hot nights. They would say she was intoxicated with grief and dead husbands. Sadness made her dance. When she thought about this, she laughed.

The driveway seemed sudden and steep. They were approaching a walled villa. Lenny pushed numbers on a console. The gate opened.

He parked the red Ferrari. He opened the car door for her. She followed him up a flight of stone steps. The house looked like a Spanish fortress.

A large Christmas wreath with pine cones and a red ribbon hung on the door. The door was unlocked. The floor was tile. They were walking on an Oriental silk carpet, past a piano, a fireplace, a bar. There were ceiling-high glass cabinets in which Chinese artifacts were displayed, vases and bowls and carvings. They were walking through a library, then a room with a huge television, stereo equipment, a pool table. She followed him out a side door.

The pool was built on the edge of the hill. The city below seemed like a sketch for a village, something not quite formed beneath the greenery. Pink and yellow roses had been planted around two sides of the pool. There were beds of azaleas with ferns between them and red camellias, yellow lilies, white daisies, and birds-of-paradise.

"Time to swim," Lenny said.

She was standing near the pool, motionless. "We don't have suits," she said.

"Don't tell nobody, okay?" Lenny was pulling his shirt over his head. He stared at her, a cigarette in his mouth. "It's private. It's walled. Just a cliff out here. And Bernie and Phyllis aren't coming back. Come on. Take off your clothes. What are you? Scared? You're like a child. Come here. I'll help you. Daddy'll help you. Just stand near me. Here. See? Over your head. Over baby's head. Did that hurt? What's that? One of those goddamn French jobs with the hooks in front? You do it. What are you looking at? I put on a few pounds. Okay? I'm a little out of shape. I need some weights. I got to buy some weights. What are you? Skinny? You're so skinny. You one of those vomiters? I'm not going to bite. Come here. Reach down. Take off my necklace. Unlock the chain. Yeah. Good. Now we swim."

The water felt strange and icy. It was nothing like she expected. There were shadows on the far side of the pool. The shadows were hideous. There was nothing ambiguous about them. The water beneath the shadows looked remote and troubled and green. It looked contaminated. The more she swam, the more the infected blue particles clustered on her skin. There would be no way to remove them.

"I have to leave," she said.

The sun was going down. It was an unusual sunset for Los Angeles, red and protracted. Clouds formed islands in the red sky. The sprinklers came on. The air smelled damp and green like a forest. There were pine trees beyond the rose garden. She thought of the smell of camp at nightfall, when she was a child.

"What are you? Crazy? You kidding me? I want to take you out," Lenny said. He got out of the pool. He wrapped a towel around his waist. Then he wrapped a towel around her shoulders. "Don't just stand there. Dry off. Come on. You'll get sick. Dry yourself."

He lit a cigarette for her. "You want to get dressed up, right? I know you skinny broads from Beverly Hills. You want to get dressed up. Look. Let me show you something. You'll like it. I know. Come on." He put out his hand for her. She took it.

They were walking up a marble stairway to the bedroom. The bedroom windows opened onto a tile balcony. There were sunken tubs in the bathroom. Everything was black marble. The faucets were gold. There were gold chandeliers hanging above them. Every wall had mirrors bordered by bulbs and gold. Lenny was standing in front of a closet.

"Pick something out. Go on. Walk in. Pink. You like pink? No. You like it darker. Yeah. Keep walking. Closet big as a tennis court. They got no taste, right? Looks like Vegas, right? You like red? No. Black. That's you. Here. Black silk." Lenny came out of the closet. He was holding an evening gown. "This your size? All you skinny broads wear the same size."

Lenny handed the dress to her. He stretched out on the bed. "Yeah. Let go of the towel. That's right. Only slower."

He was watching her. He lit a cigarette. His towel had come apart. He was holding something near his lap. It was a jewelry box.

"After you put that crap on your face, the paint, the lipstick, we'll pick out a little something nice for you. Phyllis won't need it. She's not coming back. Yeah." Lenny laughed. "Bernie and Phyllis are entertaining the Colombians by now. Give those boys from the jungle something to chew on. Don't look like that. You like diamonds? I know you like diamonds."

Lenny was stretched out on the bed. The bed belonged to Bernie and Phyllis but they weren't coming back. Lenny was holding a diamond necklace out to her. She wanted it more than she could remember wanting anything.

"I'll put it on you. Come here. Sit down. I won't touch you. Not unless you ask me. I can see you're all dressed up. Just sit near me. I'll do the clasp for you," Lenny offered.

She sat down. She could feel the stones around her throat, cool, individual, like the essence of something that lives in the night. Or something more ancient, part of the fabric of the night itself.

"Now you kiss me. Come on. You want to. I can tell. Kiss me. Know what this costs?" Lenny touched the necklace at her throat with his fingertips. He studied the stones. He left his fingers on her throat. "Sixty, seventy grand maybe. You can kiss me now."

She turned her face toward him. She opened her lips. Outside, the Santa Ana winds were startling, howling as if from a mouth. The air smelled of scorched lemons and oranges, of something delirious and intoxicated. When she closed her eyes, everything was blue.

She didn't see him at her noon meeting the next day or the day after. She thought, Well, that's it. She wasn't sorry. She got a manicure. She went to her psychiatrist. She began taking a steam bath after her aerobics class at the gym. She went Christmas shopping. She bought her daughter a white rabbit coat trimmed with blue fox. She was spending too much money. She didn't care.

It was Christmas Eve when the doorbell rang. There were carols on the radio. She was wearing a silk robe and smoking. She told Maria that she could answer the door.

"You promised never to come here." She was angry. "You promised to respect my life. To recognize my discrete borders."

"Discrete borders?" Lenny repeated. "I'm in serious trouble. Look at me. Can't you see there's something wrong? You look but you don't see."

There was nothing unusual about him. He was wearing blue jeans and a black leather jacket. He was carrying an overnight bag. She could see the motorcycle near the curb. Maybe the Colombians had the red Ferrari. Maybe they were chewing on that now. She didn't ask him in.

"This is it," Lenny was saying. He brushed past her and walked into the living room. He was talking quickly. He was telling her what had happened in the desert, what the Colombians had done. She felt like she was being electrocuted, that her hair was standing on end. It occurred to her that it was a sensation so singular that she might come to enjoy it. There were small blue wounded sounds in the room now. She wondered if they were coming from her.

"I disappear in about five minutes." Lenny looked at her. "You coming?"

She thought about it. "I can't come, no," she said finally. "I have a child."

"We take her," Lenny offered.

She shook her head, no. The room was going dark at the edges, she noticed. Like a field of blue asters, perhaps. Or ice when the sun strikes it. And how curious the blue becomes when clouds cross the sun, when the blue becomes broken, tawdry.

"I had plans for you. I was going to introduce you to some people. I should of met you fifteen years ago. I could have retired. Get me some ice," Lenny said. "Let's have a drink."

"We're in AA. Are you crazy?" She was annoyed.

"I need a drink. I need a fix. I need an automatic weapon. I need a plane," he said. He looked past her to the den. Maria was watching television and wrapping Christmas presents.

"You need a drink, too," Lenny said. "Don't even think about it. The phone. You're an accessory after the fact. You can go to jail. What about your kid then?"

They were standing in her living room. There was a noble pine tree near the fireplace. There were wrapped boxes beneath the branches. Maria asked in Spanish if she needed anything. She said not at the moment. Two glasses with ice, that was all.

"Have a drink," Lenny said. "You can always go back to the meetings. They take you back. They don't mind. I do it all the time. All over the world. I been doing it for ten years."

"I didn't know that." she said. It was almost impossible to talk. It occurred to her that her sanity was becoming intermittent, like a sudden stretch of intact road in an abandoned region. Or radio music, blatant after months of static.

"Give me the bottle. I'll pour you one. Don't look like that. You look like you're going down for the count. Here." Lenny handed the glass to her. She could smell the vodka. "Open your mouth, goddamn it."

She opened her mouth. She took a sip. Then she lit a cigarette.

"Wash the glass when I leave," Lenny said. "They can't prove shit. You don't know me. You were never anywhere. Nothing happened. You listening? You don't look like you're listening. You look like you're on tilt. Come on, baby. Listen to Daddy. That's good. Take another sip."

She took another sip. Lenny was standing near the door. "You're getting off easy, you know that? I ran out of time. I had plans for you," he was saying.

He was opening the door. "Some ride, huh? Did Daddy do like he said? Get you to the other side? You catch a glimpse? See what's there? I think you're starting to see. Can't say Lenny lied to you, right?"

She took another sip. "Right," she agreed. When this glass was finished she would pour another. When the bottle was empty, she would buy another.

Lenny closed the door. The night stayed outside. She was surprised. She opened her mouth but no sound came out. Instead, blue things flew in, pieces of glass or tin, or necklaces of blue diamonds, perhaps. The air was the blue of a pool when there are shadows, when clouds cross the turquoise surface, when you suspect something contagious is leaking, something camouflaged and disrupted. There is only this infected blue enormity elongating defiantly. The blue that knows you and where you live and it's never going to forget.

Sherman Alexie

Sherman Alexie (b. 1966), a Spokane/Coeur d'Alene Indian, is the author of several novels, collections of poetry, and a collection of short stories, The Lone Ranger and Tonto Fistfight in Heaven *(1993). He adapted some of the stories from that collection into a screenplay, and the result was the award-winning movie* Smoke Signals. *Alexie's stories are fun and easy to read, yet carry complex messages about the nature of reservation life and the grim reality of alcoholism, loss of tradition, and the history of oppression that Native Americans have faced. Although often set on the Spokane Indian Reservation, his work has implications for all of us, particularly in considering our place in American society, the distances that separate us from each other, and the ties that bind us together. Survival, forgiveness, resistance, community, humor, and mythmaking are important themes for Alexie, who writes, "Survival = Anger x Imagination. Imagination is the only weapon on the reservation."*

Because My Father Always Said He Was the Only Indian Who Saw Jimi Hendrix Play "The Star-Spangled Banner" at Woodstock

During the sixties, my father was the perfect hippie, since all the hippies were trying to be Indians. Because of that, how could anyone recognize that my father was trying to make a social statement?

But there is evidence, a photograph of my father demonstrating in Spokane, Washington, during the Vietnam war. The photograph made it onto the wire service and was reprinted in newspapers throughout the country. In fact, it was on the cover of *Time*.

In the photograph, my father is dressed in bell-bottoms and flowered shirt, his hair in braids, with red peace symbols splashed across his face like war paint. In his hands my father holds a rifle above his head, captured in that moment just before he proceeded to beat the shit out of the National Guard private lying prone on the ground. A fellow demonstrator holds a sign that is just barely visible over my father's left shoulder. It read MAKE LOVE NOT WAR.

Reprinted from *The Lone Ranger and Tonto Fistfight in Heaven*, (1994), by permission of Grove/Atlantic, Inc.

The photographer won a Pulitzer Prize, and editors across the country had a lot of fun creating captions and headlines. I've read many of them collected in my father's scrapbook, and my favorite was run in the *Seattle Times*. The caption under the photograph read DEMONSTRATOR GOES TO WAR FOR PEACE. The editors capitalized on my father's Native American identity with other headlines like ONE WARRIOR AGAINST WAR and PEACEFUL GATHERING TURNS INTO NATIVE UPRISING.

Anyway, my father was arrested, charged with attempted murder, which was reduced to assault with a deadly weapon. It was a high-profile case so my father was used as an example. Convicted and sentenced quickly, he spent two years in Walla Walla State Penitentiary. Although his prison sentence effectively kept him out of the war, my father went through a different kind of war behind bars.

"There was Indian gangs and white gangs and black gangs and Mexican gangs," he told me once. "And there was somebody new killed every day. We'd hear about somebody getting it in the shower or wherever and the word would go down the line. Just one word. Just the color of his skin. Red, white, black, or brown. Then we'd chalk it up on the mental scoreboard and wait for the next broadcast."

My father made it through all that, never got into any serious trouble, somehow avoided rape, and got out of prison just in time to hitchhike to Woodstock to watch Jimi Hendrix play "The Star-Spangled Banner."

"After all the shit I'd been through," my father said, "I figured Jimi must have known I was there in the crowd to play something like that. It was exactly how I felt."

Twenty years later, my father played his Jimi Hendrix tape until it wore down. Over and over, the house filled with the rockets' red glare and the bombs bursting in air. He'd sit by the stereo with a cooler of beer beside him and cry, laugh, call me over and hold me tight in his arms, his bad breath and body odor covering me like a blanket.

Jimi Hendrix and my father became drinking buddies. Jimi Hendrix waited for my father to come home after a long night of drinking. Here's how the ceremony worked:

1. I would lie awake all night and listen for the sounds of my father's pickup.

2. When I heard my father's pickup, I would run upstairs and throw Jimi's tape into the stereo.

3. Jimi would bend his guitar into the first note of "The Star-Spangled Banner" just as my father walked inside.

4. My father would weep, attempt to hum along with Jimi, and then pass out with his head on the kitchen table.

5. I would fall asleep under the table with my head near my father's feet.

6. We'd dream together until the sun came up.

The days after, my father would feel so guilty that he would tell me stories as a means of apology.

"I met your mother at a party in Spokane," my father told me once. "We were the only two Indians at the party. Maybe the only two Indians in the whole town. I thought she was so beautiful. I figured she was the kind of woman who could make buffalo walk on up to her and give up their lives. She wouldn't have needed to hunt. Every time we went walking, birds would follow us around. Hell, tumbleweeds would follow us around."

Somehow my father's memories of my mother grew more beautiful as their relationship became more hostile. By the time the divorce was final, my mother was quite possibly the most beautiful woman who ever lived.

"Your father was always half crazy," my mother told me more than once. "And the other half was on medication."

But she loved him, too, with a ferocity that eventually forced her to leave him. They fought each other with the kind of graceful anger that only love can create. Still, their love was passionate, unpredictable, and selfish. My mother and father would get drunk and leave parties abruptly to go home and make love.

"Don't tell your father I told you this," my mother said. "But there must have been a hundred times he passed out on top of me. We'd be right in the middle of it, he'd say *I love you*, his eyes would roll backwards, and then out went his lights. It sounds strange, I know, but those were good times."

I was conceived, during one of those drunken nights, half of me formed by my father's whiskey sperm, the other half formed by my mother's vodka egg. I was born a goofy reservation mixed drink, and my father needed me just as much as he needed every other kind of drink.

One night my father and I were driving home in a near blizzard after a basketball game, listening to the radio. We didn't talk much. One, because my father didn't talk much when he was sober, and two, because Indians don't need to talk to communicate.

"Hello out there, folks, this is Big Bill Baggins, with the late-night classics show on KROC, 97.2 on your FM dial. We have a request from Betty in Tekoa. She wants to hear Jimi Hendrix's version of 'The Star-Spangled Banner' recorded live at Woodstock."

My father smiled, turned the volume up, and we rode down the highway while Jimi led the way like a snowplow. Until that night, I'd always been neutral about Jimi Hendrix. But, in that near-blizzard with my father at the wheel, with the nervous silence caused by the dangerous roads and Jimi's guitar, there seemed to be more to all that music. The reverberation came to mean something, took form and function.

That song made me want to learn to play guitar, not because I wanted to be Jimi Hendrix and not because I thought I'd ever play for anyone. I just wanted to touch the strings, to hold the guitar tight against my body, invent a chord, and come closer to what Jimi knew, to what my father knew.

"You know," I said to my father after the song was over, "my generation of Indian boys ain't ever had no real war to fight. The first Indians had Custer to fight. My great-grandfather had World War I, my grandfather had World War II, you had Vietnam. All I have is video games."

My father laughed for a long time, nearly drove off the road into the snowy fields.

"Shit," he said. "I don't know why you're feeling sorry for yourself because you ain't had to fight a war. You're lucky. Shit, all you had was that damn Desert Storm. Should have called it Dessert Storm because it just made the fat cats get fatter. It was all sugar and whipped cream with a cherry on top. And besides that, you didn't even have to fight it. All you lost during that war was sleep because you stayed up all night watching CNN."

We kept driving through the snow, talked about war and peace.

"That's all there is," my father said. "War and peace with nothing in between. It's always one or the other."

"You sound like a book," I said.

"Yeah, well, that's how it is. Just because it's in a book doesn't make it not true. And besides, why the hell would you want to fight a war for this country? It's been trying to kill Indians since the very beginning. Indians are pretty much born soldiers anyway. Don't need a uniform to prove it."

Those were the kinds of conversations that Jimi Hendrix forced us to have. I guess every song has a special meaning for someone somewhere. Elvis Presley is still showing up in 7-11 stores across the country, even though he's been dead for years, so I figure music just might be the most important thing there is. Music turned my father into a reservation philosopher. Music had powerful medicine.

"I remember the first time your mother and I danced," my father told me once. "We were in this cowboy bar. We were the only real cowboys there despite the fact that we're Indians. We danced to a Hank Williams song. Danced to that real sad one, you know. 'I'm So Lonesome I Could Cry.' Except your mother and I weren't lonesome or crying. We just shuffled along and fell right goddamn down into love."

"Hank Williams and Jimi Hendrix don't have much in common," I said.

"Hell, yes, they do. They knew all about broken hearts," my father said.

"You sound like a bad movie."

"Yeah, well, that's how it is. You kids today don't know shit about romance. Don't know shit about music either. Especially you Indian kids. You all have been spoiled by those drums. Been hearing them beat so long, you think that's all you need. Hell, son, even an Indian needs a piano or guitar or saxophone now and again."

My father played in a band in high school. He was the drummer. I guess he'd burned out on those. Now, he was like the universal defender of the guitar.

"I remember when your father would haul that old guitar out and play me songs," my mother said. "He couldn't play all that well but he tried. You could see him thinking about what chord he was going to play next. His eyes got all squeezed up and his face turned all red. He kind of looked that way when he kissed me, too. But don't tell him I said that."

Some nights I lay awake and listened to my parents' lovemaking. I know white people keep it quiet, pretend they don't ever make love. My white friends tell me they can't even imagine their own parents getting it on. I know exactly what it sounds like when my parents are touching each other. It makes up for knowing exactly what they sound like when they're fighting. Plus and minus. Add and subtract. It comes out just about even.

Some nights I would fall asleep to the sounds of my parents' lovemaking. I would dream Jimi Hendrix. I could see my father standing in the front row in the dark at Woodstock as Jimi Hendrix played "The Star-Spangled Banner." My mother was at home with me, both of us waiting for my father to find his way back home to the reservation. It's amazing to realize I was alive, breathing and wetting my bed, when Jimi was alive and breaking guitars.

I dreamed my father dancing with all these skinny hippie women, smoking a few joints, dropping acid, laughing when the rain fell. And it did rain there. I've seen actual news footage. I've seen the documentaries. It rained. People had to share food. People got sick. People got married. People cried all kinds of tears.

But as much as I dream about it, I don't have any clue about what it meant for my father to be the only Indian who saw Jimi Hendrix play at Woodstock. And maybe he wasn't the only Indian there. Most likely there were hundreds but my father thought he was the only one. He told me that a million times when he was drunk and a couple hundred times when he was sober.

"I was there," he said. "You got to remember this was near the end and there weren't as many people as before. Not nearly as many. But I waited it out. I waited for Jimi."

A few years back, my father packed up the family and the three of us drove to Seattle to visit Jimi Hendrix's grave. We had our photograph taken lying down next to the grave. There isn't a gravestone there. Just one of those flat markers.

Jimi was twenty-eight when he died. That's younger than Jesus Christ when he died. Younger than my father as we stood over the grave.

"Only the good die young," my father said.

"No," my mother said. "Only the crazy people choke to death on their own vomit."

"Why you talking about my hero that way?" my father asked.

"Shit," my mother said. "Old Jesse WildShoe choked to death on his own vomit and he ain't anybody's hero."

I stood back and watched my parents argue. I was used to these battles. When an Indian marriage starts to fall apart, it's even more destructive and painful than usual. A hundred years ago, an Indian marriage was broken easily. The woman or man just packed up all their possessions and left the tipi. There were no arguments, no discussions. Now, Indians fight their way to the end, holding onto the last good thing, because our whole lives have to do with survival.

After a while, after too much fighting and too many angry words had been exchanged, my father went out and bought a motorcycle. A big bike. He left the house often to ride that thing for hours, sometimes for days. He even strapped an old cassette player to the gas tank so he could listen to music. With that bike, he learned something new about running away. He stopped talking as much, stopped drinking as much. He didn't do much of anything except ride that bike and listen to music.

Then one night my father wrecked his bike on Devil's Gap Road and ended up in the hospital for two months. He broke both his legs, cracked his ribs, and punctured a lung. He also lacerated his kidney. The doctors said he could have died easily. In fact, they were surprised he made it through surgery, let alone survived those first few hours when he lay on the road, bleeding. But I wasn't surprised. That's how my father was.

And even though my mother didn't want to be married to him anymore and his wreck didn't change her mind about that, she still came to see him every day. She sang Indian tunes under her breath, in time with the hum of the machines hooked into my father. Although my father could barely move, he tapped his finger in rhythm.

When he had the strength to finally sit up and talk, hold conversations, and tell stories, he called for me.

"Victor," he said. "Stick with four wheels."

After he began to recover, my mother stopped visiting as often. She helped him through the worst, though. When he didn't need her anymore, she went back to the life she had created. She traveled to powwows, started to dance again. She was a champion traditional dancer when she was younger.

"I remember your mother when she was the best traditional dancer in the world," my father said. "Everyone wanted to call her sweetheart. But she only danced for me. That's how it was. She told me that every other step was just for me."

"But that's only half of the dance," I said.

"Yeah," my father said. "She was keeping the rest for herself. Nobody can give everything away. It ain't healthy."

"You know," I said, "sometimes you sound like you ain't even real."

"What's real? I ain't interested in what's real. I'm interested in how things should be."

My father's mind always worked that way. If you don't like the things you remember, then all you have to do is change the memories. Instead of remembering the bad things, remember what happened immediately before. That's what I learned from my father. For me, I remember how good the first drink of that Diet Pepsi tasted instead of how my mouth felt when I swallowed a wasp with the second drink.

Because of all that, my father always remembered the second before my mother left him for good and took me with her. No. I remembered the second before my father left my mother and me. No. My mother remembered the second before my father left her to finish raising me all by herself.

But however memory actually worked, it was my father who climbed on his motorcycle, waved to me as I stood in the window, and rode away. He lived in Seattle, San Francisco, Los Angeles, before he finally ended up in Phoenix. For a while, I got postcards nearly every week. Then it was once a month. Then it was on Christmas and my birthday.

On a reservation, Indian men who abandon their children are treated worse than white fathers who do the same thing. It's because white men have been doing that forever and Indian men have just learned how. That's how assimilation can work.

My mother did her best to explain it all to me, although I understood most of what happened.

"Was it because of Jimi Hendrix?" I asked her.

"Part of it, yeah," she said. "This might be the only marriage broken up by a dead guitar player."

"There's a first time for everything, enit?"

"I guess. Your father just likes being alone more than he likes being with other people. Even me and you."

Sometimes I caught my mother digging through old photo albums or staring at the wall or out the window. She'd get that look on her face that I knew meant she missed my father. Not enough to want him back. She missed him just enough for it to hurt.

On those nights I missed him most I listened to music. Not always Jimi Hendrix. Usually I listened to the blues. Robert Johnson mostly. The first time I heard Robert Johnson sing I knew he understood what it meant to be Indian on the edge of the twenty-first century, even if he was black at the beginning of the twentieth. That must have been how my father felt when he heard Jimi Hendrix. When he stood there in the rain at Woodstock.

Then on the night I missed my father most, when I lay in bed and cried, with that photograph of him beating that National Guard private in my hands, I imagined his motorcycle pulling up outside. I knew I was dreaming it all but I let it be real for a moment.

"Victor," my father yelled. "Let's go for a ride."

"I'll be right down. I need to get my coat on."

I rushed around the house, pulled my shoes and socks on, struggled into my coat, and ran outside to find an empty driveway. It was so quiet, a reservation kind of quiet, where you can hear somebody drinking whiskey on the rocks three miles away. I stood on the porch and waited until my mother came outside.

"Come on back inside," she said. "It's cold."

"No," I said. "I know he's coming back tonight."

My mother didn't say anything. She just wrapped me in her favorite quilt and went back to sleep. I stood on the porch all night long and imagined I heard motorcycles and guitars, until the sun rose so bright that I knew it was time to go back inside to my mother. She made breakfast for both of us and we ate until we were full.

James Baldwin

James Baldwin (1924–1987) was born and raised in New York City. He graduated from De Witt Clinton High School in 1942. After high school, he was variously employed as a handyman, dishwasher, waiter and office boy. In 1948 Baldwin moved to France because he felt artistically inhibited as a gay, black man in the United States. In France, he was able to write critically about race, sexual identity and social injustice in America, producing his first two novels Go Tell It on the Mountain *(1953) and* Giovanni's Room *(1956), and a collection of essays,* Notes of a Native Son *(1955). Nearly a decade later, Baldwin returned to New York where he became a national figure in the civil rights movement. Later, he returned to St. Paul de Vence, France, where he continued to live and write until his death of cancer in 1987. The short story* Sonny's Blues *was written in 1955.*

Sonny's Blues

I read about it in the paper, in the subway, on my way to work. I read it, and I couldn't believe it, and I read it again. Then perhaps I just stared at it, at the newsprint spelling out his name, spelling out the story. I stared at it in the swinging lights of the subway car, and in the faces and bodies of the people, and in my own face, trapped in the darkness which roared outside.

It was not to be believed and I kept telling myself that, as I walked from the subway station to the high school. And at the same time I couldn't doubt it. I was scared, scared for Sonny. He became real to me again. A great block of ice got settled in my belly and kept melting there slowly all day long, while I taught my classes algebra. It was a special kind of ice. It kept melting, sending trickles of ice water all up and down my veins, but it never got less. Sometimes it hardened and seemed to expand until I felt my guts were going to come spilling out or that I was going to choke or scream. This would always be at a moment when I was remembering some specific thing Sonny had once said or done.

When he was about as old as the boys in my classes his face had been bright and open, there was a lot of copper in it; and he'd had wonderfully direct brown eyes, and great gentleness and privacy. I wondered what he looked like now. He had been picked up, the evening before, in a raid on an apartment downtown, for peddling and using heroin.

I couldn't believe it: but what I mean by that is that I couldn't find any room for it anywhere inside me. I had kept it outside me for a long time. I hadn't wanted to know. I had had suspicions, but I didn't name them, I kept putting them away. I told myself that Sonny was wild, but he wasn't crazy. And he'd always been a good boy, he hadn't ever turned hard or evil or disrespectful, the way kids can, so quick, so quick, especially in Harlem. I didn't want to believe that I'd ever see my brother going down, coming to nothing, all that light in his face gone out, in the condition I'd already seen so many others. Yet it had happened and here I was, talking about algebra to a lot of boys who might, every one of them for all I knew, be popping off needles every time they went to the head.[1] Maybe it did more for them than algebra could.

I was sure that the first time Sonny had ever had horse,[2] he couldn't have been much older than these boys were now. These boys, now, were living as we'd been living then, they were growing up with a rush and their heads bumped abruptly against the low ceiling of their actual possibilities. They were filled with rage. All they really knew were two darknesses, the darkness of their lives, which was now closing in on them, and the darkness of the movies, which had blinded them to that other darkness, and in which they now, vindictively, dreamed, at once more together than they were at any other time, and more alone.

When the last bell rang, the last class ended, I let out my breath. It seemed I'd been holding it for all that time. My clothes were wet—I may have looked as though I'd been sitting in a steam bath, all dressed up, all afternoon. I sat alone in the classroom a long time. I listened to the boys outside, downstairs, shouting and cursing and laughing. Their laughter struck me for perhaps the first time. It was not the joyous laughter which—God knows why—one associates with children. It was mocking and insular, its intent to denigrate. It was disenchanted, and in this, also, lay the authority of their curses. Perhaps I was listening to them because I was thinking about my brother and in them I heard my brother. And myself.

One boy was whistling a tune, at once very complicated and very simple, it seemed to be pouring out of him as though he were a bird, and it sounded very cool and moving through all that harsh, bright air, only just holding its own through all those other sounds.

I stood up and walked over to the window and looked down into the courtyard. It was the beginning of the spring and the sap was rising in the boys. A teacher passed through them every now and again, quickly, as though he or she couldn't wait to get out of that courtyard, to get those boys out of their sight and off their minds. I started collecting my stuff. I thought I'd better get home and talk to Isabel.

The courtyard was almost deserted by the time I got downstairs. I saw this boy standing in the shadow of a doorway, looking just like Sonny. I almost called his name. Then I saw that it wasn't Sonny, but somebody we used to know, a boy from around our block. He'd been Sonny's friend. He'd never been mine, having been too young for me, and, anyway, I'd never liked him. And now, even though he was a grown-up man, he still hung around that block, still spent hours on the street corners, was always high and raggy. I used to run into him from time to time and he'd often work around to asking me for a quarter or fifty cents. He always had some real good excuse, too, and I always gave it to him, I don't know why.

But now, abruptly, I hated him. I couldn't stand the way he looked at me, partly like a dog, partly like a cunning child. I wanted to ask him what the hell he was doing in the school courtyard.

He sort of shuffled over to me, and he said, "I see you got the papers. So you already know about it."

"You mean about Sonny? Yes, I already know about it. How come they didn't get you?"

He grinned. It made him repulsive and it also brought to mind what he'd looked like as a kid. "I wasn't there. I stay away from them people."

"Good for you." I offered him a cigarette and I watched him through the smoke. "You come all the way down here just to tell me about Sonny?"

"That's right." He was sort of shaking his head and his eyes looked strange, as though they were about to cross. The bright sun deadened his damp dark brown skin and it made his eyes look yellow and showed up the dirt in his kinked hair. He smelled funky. I moved a little away from him and I said, "Well, thanks. But I already know about it and I got to get home."

"I'll walk you a little ways," he said. We started walking. There were a couple of kids still loitering in the courtyard and one of them said goodnight to me and looked strangely at the boy beside me.

"What're you going to do?" he asked me. "I mean, about Sonny?"

"Look. I haven't seen Sonny for over a year. I'm not sure I'm going to do anything. Anyway, what the hell *can* I do?"

"That's right," he said quickly, "ain't nothing you can do. Can't much help old Sonny no more, I guess."

It was what I was thinking and so it seemed to me he had no right to say it.

"I'm surprised at Sonny, though," he went on—he had a funny way of talking, he looked straight ahead as though he were talking to himself—"I thought Sonny was a smart boy, I thought he was too smart to get hung."

"I guess he thought so too," I said sharply, "and that's how he got hung. And how about you? You're pretty goddamn smart, I bet."

Then he looked directly at me, just for a minute. "I ain't smart," he said. "If I was smart, I'd have reached for a pistol a long time ago."

"Look. Don't tell *me* your sad story, if it was up to me, I'd give you one." Then I felt guilty—guilty, probably, for never having supposed that the poor bastard *had* a story of his own, much less a sad one, and I asked, quickly, "What's going to happen to him now?"

He didn't answer this. He was off by himself some place.

"Funny thing," he said, and from his tone we might have been discussing the quickest way to get to Brooklyn, "when I saw the papers this morning, the first thing I asked myself was if I had anything to do with it. I felt sort of responsible."

I began to listen more carefully. The subway station was on the corner, just before us, and I stopped. He stopped, too. We were in front of a bar and he ducked slightly, peering in, but whoever he was looking for didn't seem to be there. The juke box was blasting away with something black and bouncy and I half watched the barmaid as she danced her way from the juke box to her place behind the bar. And I watched her face as she laughingly responded to something someone said to her, still keeping time to the music. When she smiled one saw the little girl, one sensed the doomed, still-struggling woman beneath the battered face of the semi-whore.

"I never *give* Sonny nothing," the boy said finally, "but a long time ago I come to school high and Sonny asked me how it felt." He paused, I couldn't bear to watch him, I watched the barmaid, and I listened to the music which seemed to be causing the pavement to shake. "I told him it felt great." The music stopped, the barmaid paused and watched the juke box until the music began again. "It did."

All this was carrying me some place I didn't want to go. I certainly didn't want to know how it felt. It filled everything, the people, the houses, the music, the dark, quicksilver barmaid, with menace; and this menace was their reality.

"What's going to happen to him now?" I asked again.

"They'll send him away some place and they'll try to cure him." He shook his head. "Maybe he'll even think he's kicked the habit. Then they'll let him loose"— he gestured, throwing his cigarette into the gutter. "That's all."

"What do you mean, that's *all*?"

But I knew what he meant.

"I *mean,* that's *all*." He turned his head and looked at me, pulling down the corners of his mouth. "Don't you know what I mean?" he asked, softly.

"How the hell *would* I know what you mean?" I almost whispered it, I don't know why.

"That's right," he said to the air, "how would *he* know what I mean?" He turned toward me again, patient and calm, and yet I somehow felt him shaking, shaking as though he were going to fall apart. I felt that ice in my guts again, the dread I'd felt all afternoon; and again I watched the barmaid, moving about the bar, washing glasses, and singing. "Listen. They'll let him out and then it'll just start all over again. That's what I mean."

"You mean—they'll let him out. And then he'll just start working his way back in again. You mean he'll never kick the habit. Is that what you mean?"

"That's right," he said, cheerfully. "*You* see what I mean."

"Tell me," I said at last, "why does he want to die? He must want to die, he's killing himself, why does he want to die?"

He looked at me in surprise. He licked his lips. "He don't want to die. He wants to live. Don't nobody want to die, ever."

Then I wanted to ask him—too many things. He could not have answered, or if he had, I could not have borne the answers. I started walking. "Well, I guess it's none of my business."

"It's going to be rough on old Sonny," he said. We reached the subway station. "This is your station?" he asked. I nodded. I took one step down. "Damn!" he said, suddenly. I looked up at him. He grinned again. "Damn it if I didn't leave all my money home. You ain't got a dollar on you, have you? Just for a couple of days, is all."

All at once something inside gave and threatened to come pouring out of me. I didn't hate him any more. I felt that in another moment I'd start crying like a child.

"Sure," I said. "Don't sweat." I looked in my wallet and didn't have a dollar, I only had a five. "Here," I said. "That hold you?"

He didn't look at it—he didn't want to look at it. A terrible closed look came over his face, as though he were keeping the number on the bill a secret from him and me. "Thanks," he said, and now he was dying to see me go. "Don't worry about Sonny. Maybe I'll write him or something."

"Sure," I said. "You do that. So long."

"Be seeing you," he said. I went on down the steps.

And I didn't write Sonny or send him anything for a long time. When I finally did, it was just after my little girl died, he wrote me back a letter which made me feel like a bastard.

Here's what he said:

> Dear brother,
>
> You don't know how much I needed to hear from you. I wanted to write you many a time but I dug how much I must have hurt you and so I didn't write. But now I feel like a man who's been trying to climb up out of some deep, real deep and funky hole and just saw the sun up there, outside. I got to get outside.
>
> I can't tell you much about how I got here. I mean I don't know how to tell you. I guess I was afraid of something or I was trying to escape from something and you know I have never been very strong in the head (smile). I'm glad Mama and Daddy are dead and can't see what's happened to their son and I swear if I'd known what I was doing I would never have hurt you so, you and a lot of other fine people who were nice to me and who believed in me.
>
> I don't want you to think it had anything to do with me being a musician. It's more than that. Or maybe less than that. I can't get anything straight in my head down here and I try not to think about what's going to happen to me when I get outside again. Sometime I think I'm going to flip and *never* get outside and sometime I think I'll come straight back. I tell you one thing, though, I'd rather blow my brains out than go through this again. But that's what they all say, so they tell me. If I tell you when I'm coming to New York and if you could meet me, I sure would appreciate it. Give my love to Isabel and the kids and I was sure sorry to hear about little Gracie. I wish I could be like Mama and say the Lord's will be done, but I don't know it seems to me that trouble is the one thing that never does get stopped and I don't know what good it does to blame it on the Lord. But maybe it does some good if you believe it.
>
> Your brother,
> Sonny

Then I kept in constant touch with him and I sent him whatever I could and I went to meet him when he came back to New York. When I saw him many things I thought I had forgotten came flooding back to me. This was because I had begun, finally, to wonder about Sonny, about the life that Sonny lived inside. This life, whatever it was, had made him older and thinner and it had deepened the distant stillness in which he had always moved. He looked very unlike my baby brother. Yet, when he smiled, when we shook hands, the baby brother I'd never known looked out from the depths of his private life, like an animal waiting to be coaxed into the light.

"How you been keeping?" he asked me.

"All right. And you?"

"Just fine." He was smiling all over his face. "It's good to see you again."

"It's good to see you."

The seven years' difference in our ages lay between us like a chasm: I wondered if these years would ever operate between us as a bridge. I was remembering, and it made it hard to catch my breath, that I had been there when he was born; and I had heard the first words he had ever spoken. When he started to walk, he walked from our mother straight to me. I caught him just before he fell when he took the first steps he ever took in this world.

"How's Isabel?"

"Just fine. She's dying to see you."

"And the boys?"

"They're fine, too. They're anxious to see their uncle."

"Oh, come on. You know they don't remember me."

"Are you kidding? Of course they remember you."

He grinned again. We got into a taxi. We had a lot to say to each other, far too much to know how to begin.

As the taxi began to move, I asked, "You still want to go to India?"

He laughed. "You still remember that. Hell, no. This place is Indian enough for me."

"It used to belong to them," I said.

And he laughed again. "They damn sure knew what they were doing when they got rid of it."

Years ago, when he was around fourteen, he'd been all hipped on the idea of going to India. He read books about people sitting on rocks, naked, in all kinds of weather, but mostly bad, naturally, and walking barefoot through hot coals and arriving at wisdom. I used to say that it sounded to me as though they were getting away from wisdom as fast as they could. I think he sort of looked down on me for that.

"Do you mind," he asked, "if we have the driver drive alongside the park? On the west side—I haven't seen the city in so long."

"Of course not," I said. I was afraid that I might sound as though I were humoring him, but I hoped he wouldn't take it that way.

So we drove along, between the green of the park and the stony, lifeless elegance of hotels and apartment buildings, toward the vivid, killing streets of our childhood. These streets hadn't changed, though housing projects jutted up out of them now like rocks in the middle of a boiling sea. Most of the houses in which we had grown up had vanished, as had the stores from which we had stolen, the basements in which we had first tried sex, the rooftops from which we had hurled tin cans and bricks. But houses exactly like the houses of our past yet dominated the landscape, boys exactly like the boys we once had been found themselves smothering in these houses, came down into the streets for light and air and found themselves encircled by disaster. Some escaped the trap, most didn't. Those who got out always left something of themselves behind, as some animals amputate a leg and leave it in the trap. It might be said, perhaps, that I had escaped, after all, I was a school teacher; or that Sonny had, he hadn't lived in Harlem for years. Yet, as the cab moved uptown through streets which seemed, with a rush, to darken with dark people, and as I covertly studied Sonny's face, it came to me that what we both were seeking through our separate cab windows was that part of ourselves which had been left behind. It's always at the hour of trouble and confrontation that the missing member aches.

We hit 110th Street and started rolling up Lenox Avenue. And I'd known this avenue all my life, but it seemed to me again, as it had seemed on the day I'd first heard about Sonny's trouble, filled with a hidden menace which was its very breath of life.

"We almost there," said Sonny.

"Almost." We were both too nervous to say anything more.

We live in a housing project. It hasn't been up long. A few days after it was up it seemed uninhabitably new, now, of course, it's already rundown. It looks like a parody of the good, clean, faceless life—God knows the people who live in it do their best to make it a parody. The beat-looking grass lying around isn't enough to make their lives green, the hedges will never hold out the streets, and they know it. The big windows fool no one, they aren't big enough to make space out of no space. They don't bother with the windows, they watch the TV screen instead. The playground is most popular with the children who don't play at jacks, or skip rope, or roller skate, or swing, and they can be found in it after dark. We moved in partly because it's not too far from where I teach, and partly for the kids; but it's really just like the houses in which Sonny and I grew up. The same things happen, they'll have the same things to remember. The moment Sonny and I started into the house I had the feeling that I was simply bringing him back into the danger he had almost died trying to escape.

Sonny has never been talkative. So I don't know why I was sure he'd be dying to talk to me when supper was over the first night. Everything went fine, the oldest boy remembered him, and the youngest boy liked him, and Sonny had remembered to bring something for each of them; and Isabel, who is really much nicer than I am, more open and giving, had gone to a lot of trouble about dinner and was genuinely glad to see him. And she's always been able to tease Sonny in a way that I haven't. It was nice to see her face so vivid again and to hear her laugh and watch her make Sonny laugh. She wasn't, or, anyway, she didn't seem to be, at all uneasy or embarrassed. She chatted as though there were no subject which had to be avoided and she got Sonny past his first, faint stiffness. And thank God she was there, for I was filled with that icy dread again. Everything I did seemed awkward to me, and everything I said sounded freighted with hidden meaning. I was trying to remember everything I'd heard about dope addiction and I couldn't help watching Sonny for signs. I wasn't doing it out of malice. I was trying to find out something about my brother. I was dying to hear him tell me he was safe.

"Safe!" my father grunted, whenever Mama suggested trying to move to a neighborhood which might be safer for children. "Safe, hell! Ain't no place safe for kids, nor nobody."

He always went on like this, but he wasn't, ever, really as bad as he sounded, not even on weekends, when he got drunk. As a matter of fact, he was always on the lookout for "something a little better," but he died before he found it. He died suddenly, during a drunken weekend in the middle of the war, when Sonny was fifteen. He and Sonny hadn't ever got on too well. And this was partly because Sonny was the apple of his father's eye. It was because he loved Sonny so much and was frightened for him, that he was always fighting with him. It doesn't do any good to fight with Sonny. Sonny just moves back, inside himself, where he can't be reached. But the principal reason that they never hit it off is that they were so much alike. Daddy was big and rough and loud-talking, just the opposite of Sonny, but they both had—that same privacy.

Mama tried to tell me something about this, just after Daddy died. I was home on leave from the army.

This was the last time I ever saw my mother alive. Just the same, this picture gets all mixed up in my mind with pictures I had of her when she was younger. The way I always see her is the way she used to be on a Sunday afternoon, say, when the old folks were talking after the big Sunday dinner. I always see her wearing pale blue. She'd be sitting on the sofa. And my father would be sitting in the easy chair, not far from her. And the living room would be full of church folks and relatives. There they sit, in chairs all around the living room, and the night is creeping up outside, but nobody knows it yet. You can see the darkness growing against the windowpanes and you hear the street noises every now and again, or maybe the jangling beat of a tambourine from one of the churches close by, but it's real quiet in the room. For a moment nobody's talking, but every face looks darkening, like the sky outside. And my mother rocks a little from the waist, and my father's eyes are closed. Everyone is looking at something a child can't see. For a minute they've forgotten the children. Maybe a kid is lying on the rug, half asleep. Maybe somebody's got a kid in his lap and is absentmindedly stroking the kid's head. Maybe there's a kid, quiet and big-eyed, curled up in a big chair in the corner. The silence, the darkness coming, and the darkness in the faces frightens the child obscurely. He hopes that the hand which strokes his forehead will never stop—will never die. He hopes that there will never come a time when the old folks won't be sitting around the living room, talking about where they've come from, and what they've seen, and what's happened to them and their kinfolk.

But something deep and watchful in the child knows that this is bound to end, is already ending. In a moment someone will get up and turn on the light. Then the old folks will remember the children and they won't talk any more that day. And when light fills the room, the child is filled with darkness. He knows that every time this happens he's moved just a little closer to that darkness outside. The darkness outside is what the old folks have been talking about. It's what they've come from. It's what they endure. The child knows that they won't talk any more because if he knows too much about what's happened to *them,* he'll know too much too soon, about what's going to happen to *him.*

The last time I talked to my mother, I remember I was restless. I wanted to get out and see Isabel. We weren't married then and we had a lot to straighten out between us.

There Mama sat, in black, by the window. She was humming an old church song, *Lord, you brought me from a long ways off.* Sonny was out somewhere. Mama kept watching the streets.

"I don't know," she said, "if I'll ever see you again, after you go off from here. But I hope you'll remember the things I tried to teach you."

"Don't talk like that," I said, and smiled. "You'll be here a long time yet."

She smiled, too, but she said nothing. She was quiet for a long time. And I said, "Mama, don't you worry about nothing. I'll be writing all the time, and you be getting the checks. . . ."

"I want to talk to you about your brother," she said, suddenly. "If anything happens to me he ain't going to have nobody to look out for him."

"Mama," I said, "ain't nothing going to happen to you *or* Sonny. Sonny's all right. He's a good boy and he's got good sense."

"It ain't a question of his being a good boy," Mama said, "nor of his having good sense. It ain't only the bad ones, nor yet the dumb ones that gets sucked under." She stopped, looking at me. "Your Daddy once had a brother," she said, and she smiled in a way that made me feel she was in pain. "You didn't never know that, did you?"

"No," I said, "I never knew that," and I watched her face.

"Oh, yes," she said, "your Daddy had a brother." She looked out of the window again. "I know you never saw your Daddy cry. But *I* did—many a time, through all these years."

I asked her, "What happened to his brother? How come nobody's ever talked about him?"

This was the first time I ever saw my mother look old.

"His brother got killed," she said, "when he was just a little younger than you are now. I knew him. He was a fine boy. He was maybe a little full of the devil, but he didn't mean nobody no harm."

Then she stopped and the room was silent, exactly as it had sometimes been on those Sunday afternoons. Mama kept looking out into the streets.

"He used to have a job in the mill," she said, "and, like all young folks, he just liked to perform on Saturday nights. Saturday nights, him and your father would drift around to different places, go to dances and things like that, or just sit around with people they knew, and your father's brother would sing, he had a fine voice, and play along with himself on his guitar. Well, this particular Saturday night, him and your father was coming home from some place, and they were both a little drunk and there was a moon that night, it was bright like day. Your father's brother was feeling kind of good, and he was whistling to himself, and he had his guitar slung over his shoulder. They was coming down a hill and beneath them was a road that turned off from the highway. Well, your father's brother, being always kind of frisky, decided to run down this hill, and he did, with that guitar banging and clanging behind him, and he ran across the road, and he was making water behind a tree. And your father was sort of amused at him and he was still coming down the hill, kind of slow. Then he heard a car motor and that same minute his brother stepped from behind the tree, into the road, in the moonlight. And he started to cross the road. And your father started to run down the hill, he says he don't know why. This car was full of white men. They was all drunk, and when they seen your father's brother they let out a great whoop and holler and they aimed the car straight at him. They was having fun, they just wanted to scare him, the way they do sometimes, you know. But they was drunk. And I guess the boy, being drunk, too, and scared, kind of lost his head. By the time he jumped it was too late. Your father says he heard his brother scream when the car rolled over him, and he heard the wood of that guitar when it give, and he heard them strings go flying, and he heard them white men shouting, and the car kept on a-going and it ain't stopped till this day. And, time your father got down the hill, his brother weren't nothing but blood and pulp."

Tears were gleaming on my mother's face. There wasn't anything I could say.

"He never mentioned it," she said, "because I never let him mention it before you children. Your Daddy was like a crazy man that night and for many a night thereafter. He says he never in his life seen anything as dark as that road after the lights of that car had gone away. Weren't nothing, weren't nobody on that road, just your Daddy and his brother and that busted guitar. Oh, yes. Your Daddy never did really get right again. Till the day he died he weren't sure but that every white man he saw was the man that killed his brother."

She stopped and took out her handkerchief and dried her eyes and looked at me.

"I ain't telling you all this," she said, "to make you scared or bitter or to make you hate nobody. I'm telling you this because you got a brother. And the world ain't changed."

I guess I didn't want to believe this. I guess she saw this in my face. She turned away from me, toward the window again, searching those streets.

"But I praise my Redeemer," she said at last, "that He called your Daddy home before me. I ain't saying it to throw no flowers at myself, but, I declare, it keeps me from feeling too cast down to know I helped your father get safely through this world. Your father always acted like he was the roughest, strongest man on earth. And everybody took him to be like that. But if he hadn't had me there—to see his tears!"

She was crying again. Still, I couldn't move. I said, "Lord, Lord, Mama, I didn't know it was like that."

"Oh, honey," she said, "there's a lot that you don't know. But you are going to find out." She stood up from the window and came over to me. "You got to hold on to your brother," she said, "and don't let him fall, no matter what it looks like is happening to him and no matter how evil you gets with him. You going to be evil with him many a time. But don't you forget what I told you, you hear?"

"I won't forget," I said. "Don't you worry, I won't forget. I won't let nothing happen to Sonny."

My mother smiled as though she were amused at something she saw in my face. Then, "You may not be able to stop nothing from happening. But you got to let him know you's *there.*"

Two days later I was married, and then I was gone. And I had a lot of things on my mind and I pretty well forgot my promise to Mama until I got shipped home on a special furlough for her funeral.

And, after the funeral, with just Sonny and me alone in the empty kitchen, I tried to find out something about him.

"What do you want to do?" I asked him.

"I'm going to be a musician," he said.

For he had graduated, in the time I had been away, from dancing to the juke box to finding out who was playing what, and what they were doing with it, and he had bought himself a set of drums.

"You mean, you want to be a drummer?" I somehow had the feeling that being a drummer might be all right for other people but not for my brother Sonny.

"I don't think," he said, looking at me very gravely, "that I'll ever be a good drummer. But I think I can play a piano."

I frowned. I'd never played the role of the older brother quite so seriously before, had scarcely ever, in fact, *asked* Sonny a damn thing. I sensed myself in the presence of something I didn't really know how to handle, didn't understand. So I made my frown a little deeper as I asked: "What kind of musician do you want to be?"

He grinned. "How many kinds do you think there are?"

"Be *serious,*" I said.

He laughed, throwing his head back, and then looked at me. "I *am* serious."

"Well, then, for Christ's sake, stop kidding around and answer a serious question. I mean, do you want to be a concert pianist, you want to play classical music and all that, or—or what?" Long before I finished he was laughing again. "For Christ's *sake,* Sonny!"

He sobered, but with difficulty. "I'm sorry. But you sound so—*scared!*" and he was off again.

"Well, you may think it's funny now, baby, but it's not going to be so funny when you have to make your living at it, let me tell you *that.*" I was furious because I knew he was laughing at me and I didn't know why.

"No," he said, very sober now, and afraid, perhaps, that he'd hurt me, "I don't want to be a classical pianist. That isn't what interests me. I mean"—he paused, looking hard at me, as though his eyes would help me to understand, and then gestured helplessly, as though perhaps his hand would help—"I mean, I'll have a lot of studying to do, and I'll have to study *everything,* but, I mean, I want to play *with*—jazz musicians." He stopped. "I want to play jazz," he said.

Well, the word had never before sounded as heavy, as real, as it sounded that afternoon in Sonny's mouth. I just looked at him and I was probably frowning a real frown by this time. I simply couldn't see why on earth he'd want to spend his time hanging around nightclubs, clowning around on bandstands, while people pushed each other around a dance floor. It seemed—beneath him, somehow. I had never thought about it before, had never been forced to, but I suppose I had always put jazz musicians in a class with what Daddy called "good-time people."

"Are you *serious*?"

"Hell, *yes,* I'm serious."

He looked more helpless than ever, and annoyed, and deeply hurt.

I suggested, helpfully: "You mean—like Louis Armstrong?"

His face closed as though I'd struck him. "No. I'm not talking about none of that old-time, down home crap."

"Well, look, Sonny, I'm sorry, don't get mad. I just don't altogether get it, that's all. Name somebody—you know, a jazz musician you admire."

"Bird."

"Who?"

"Bird! Charlie Parker!³ Don't they teach you nothing in the goddamn army?"

I lit a cigarette. I was surprised and then a little amused to discover that I was trembling. "I've been out of touch," I said. "You'll have to be patient with me. Now. Who's this Parker character?"

"He's just one of the greatest jazz musicians alive," said Sonny, sullenly, his hands in his pockets, his back to me. "Maybe *the* greatest," he added, bitterly, "that's probably why *you* never heard of him."

"All right," I said, "I'm ignorant. I'm sorry. I'll go out and buy all the cat's records right away, all right?"

"It don't," said Sonny, with dignity, "make any difference to me. I don't care what you listen to. Don't do me no favors."

I was beginning to realize that I'd never seen him so upset before. With another part of my mind I was thinking that this would probably turn out to be one of those things kids go through and that I shouldn't make it seem important by pushing it too hard. Still, I didn't think it would do any harm to ask: "Doesn't all this take a lot of time? Can you make a living at it?"

He turned back to me and half leaned, half sat, on the kitchen table. "Everything takes time," he said, "and—well, yes, sure, I can make a living at it. But what I don't seem to be able to make you understand is that it's the only thing I want to do."

"Well, Sonny," I said, gently, "you know people can't always do exactly what they *want* to do—"

"*No,* I don't know that," said Sonny, surprising me. "I think people *ought* to do what they want to do, what else are they alive for?"

"You getting to be a big boy," I said desperately, "it's time you started thinking about your future."

"I'm thinking about my future," said Sonny, grimly. "I think about it all the time."

I gave up. I decided, if he didn't change his mind, that we could always talk about it later. "In the meantime," I said, "you got to finish school." We had already decided that he'd have to move in with Isabel and her folks. I knew this wasn't the ideal arrangement because Isabel's folks are inclined to be dicty⁴ and they hadn't especially wanted Isabel to marry me. But I didn't know what else to do. "And we have to get you fixed up at Isabel's."

There was a long silence. He moved from the kitchen table to the window. "That's a terrible idea. You know it yourself."

"Do you have a *better* idea?"

He just walked up and down the kitchen for a minute. He was as tall as I was. He had started to shave. I suddenly had the feeling that I didn't know him at all.

He stopped at the kitchen table and picked up my cigarettes. Looking at me with a kind of mocking, amused defiance, he put one between his lips. "You mind?"

"You smoking already?"

He lit the cigarette and nodded, watching me through the smoke. "I just wanted to see if I'd have the courage to smoke in front of you." He grinned and blew a great cloud of smoke to the ceiling. "It was easy." He looked at my face. "Come on, now. I bet you was smoking at my age, tell the truth."

I didn't say anything but the truth was on my face, and he laughed. But now there was something very strained in his laugh. "Sure. And I bet that ain't all you was doing."

He was frightening me a little. "Cut the crap," I said. "We already decided that you was going to go and live at Isabel's. Now what's got into you all of a sudden?"

"*You* decided it," he pointed out. "*I* didn't decide nothing." He stopped in front of me, leaning against the stove, arms loosely folded. "Look, brother. I don't want to stay in Harlem no more, I really don't." He was very earnest. He looked at me, then over toward the kitchen window. There was something in his eyes I'd never seen before, some thoughtfulness, some worry all his own. He rubbed the muscle of one arm. "It's time I was getting out of here."

"Where do you want to *go*, Sonny?"

"I want to join the army. Or the navy, I don't care. If I say I'm old enough, they'll believe me."

Then I got mad. It was because I was so scared. "You must be crazy. You god-damn fool, what the hell do you want to go and join the *army* for?"

"I just told you. To get out of Harlem."

"Sonny, you haven't even finished *school*. And if you really want to be a musician, how do you expect to study if you're in the *army*?"

He looked at me, trapped, and in anguish. "There's ways. I might be able to work out some kind of deal. Anyway, I'll have the G.I. Bill when I come out."

"*If* you come out." We stared at each other. "Sonny, please. Be reasonable. I know the setup is far from perfect. But we got to do the best we can."

"I ain't learning nothing in school," he said. "Even when I go." He turned away from me and opened the window and threw his cigarette out into the narrow alley. I watched his back. "At least, I ain't learning nothing you'd want me to learn." He slammed the window so hard I thought the glass would fly out, and turned back to me. "And I'm sick of the stink of these garbage cans!"

"Sonny," I said, "I know how you feel. But if you don't finish school now, you're going to be sorry later that you didn't." I grabbed him by the shoulders. "And you only got another year. It ain't so bad. And I'll come back and I swear I'll help you do *whatever* you want to do. Just try to put up with it till I come back. Will you please do that? For me?"

He didn't answer and he wouldn't look at me.

"Sonny. You hear me?"

He pulled away. "I hear you. But you never hear anything *I* say."

I didn't know what to say to that. He looked out of the window and then back at me. "OK," he said, and sighed. "I'll try."

Then I said, trying to cheer him up a little, "They got a piano at Isabel's. You can practice on it."

And as a matter of fact, it did cheer him up for a minute. "That's right," he said to himself. "I forgot that." His face relaxed a little. But the worry, the thoughtfulness, played on it still, the way shadows play on a face which is staring into the fire.

But I thought I'd never hear the end of that piano. At first, Isabel would write me, saying how nice it was that Sonny was so serious about his music and how, as soon as he came in from school, or wherever he had been when he was supposed to be at school, he went straight to that piano and stayed there until suppertime. And, after supper, he went back to that piano and stayed there until everybody went to bed. He was at the piano all day Saturday and all day Sunday. Then he bought a record player and started playing records. He'd play one record over and over again, all day long sometimes, and he'd improvise along with it on the piano. Or he'd play one section of the record, one chord, one change, one progression, then he'd do it on the piano. Then back to the record. Then back to the piano.

Well, I really don't know how they stood it. Isabel finally confessed that it wasn't like living with a person at all, it was like living with sound. And the sound didn't make any sense to her, didn't make any sense to any of them—naturally. They began, in a way, to be afflicted by this presence that was living in their home. It was as though Sonny were some sort of god, or monster. He moved in an atmosphere which wasn't like theirs at all. They fed him and he ate, he washed himself, he walked in and out of their door; he certainly wasn't nasty or unpleasant or rude, Sonny isn't any of those things; but it was as though he were all wrapped up in some cloud, some fire, some vision all his own; and there wasn't any way to reach him.

At the same time, he wasn't really a man yet, he was still a child, and they had to watch out for him in all kinds of ways. They certainly couldn't throw him out. Neither did they dare to make a great scene about that piano because even they dimly sensed, as I sensed, from so many thousands of miles away, that Sonny was at that piano playing for his life.

But he hadn't been going to school. One day a letter came from the school board and Isabel's mother got it—there had, apparently, been other letters but Sonny had torn them up. This day, when Sonny came in, Isabel's mother showed him the letter and asked where he'd been spending his time. And she finally got it out of him that he'd been down in Greenwich Village, with musicians and other characters, in a white girl's apartment. And this scared her and she started to scream at him and what came up, once she began—though she denies it to this day—was what sacrifices they were making to give Sonny a decent home and how little he appreciated it.

Sonny didn't play the piano that day. By evening, Isabel's mother had calmed down but then there was the old man to deal with, and Isabel herself. Isabel says she did her best to be calm but she broke down and started crying. She says she just watched Sonny's face. She could tell, by watching him, what was happening with him. And what was happening was that they penetrated his cloud, they had reached him. Even if their fingers had been a thousand times more gentle than human fingers ever are, he could hardly help feeling that they had stripped him naked and were spitting on that nakedness. For he also had to see that his presence, that music, which was life or death to him, had been torture for them and that they had endured it, not at all for his sake, but only for mine. And Sonny couldn't take that. He can take it a little better today than he could then but he's still not very good at it and, frankly, I don't know anybody who is.

The silence of the next few days must have been louder than the sound of all the music ever played since time began. One morning, before she went to work, Isabel was in his room for something and she suddenly realized that all of his records were gone. And she knew for certain that he was gone. And he was. He went as far as the navy would carry him. He finally sent me a postcard from some place in Greece and that was the first I knew that Sonny was still alive. I didn't see him any more until we were both back in New York and the war had long been over.

He was a man by then, of course, but I wasn't willing to see it. He came by the house from time to time, but we fought almost every time we met. I didn't like the way he carried himself, loose and dreamlike all the time, and I didn't like his friends, and his music seemed to be merely an excuse for the life he led. It sounded just that weird and disordered.

Then we had a fight, a pretty awful fight, and I didn't see him for months. By and by I looked him up, where he was living, in a furnished room in the Village, and I tried to make it up. But there were lots of other people in the room and Sonny just lay on his bed, and he wouldn't come downstairs with me, and he treated these other people as though they were his family and I weren't. So I got mad and then he got mad, and then I told him that he might just as well be dead as live the way he was living. Then he stood up and he told me not to worry about him any more in life, that he *was* dead as far as I was concerned. Then he pushed me to the door and the other people looked on as though nothing were happening, and he slammed the door behind me. I stood in the hallway, staring at the door. I heard somebody laugh in the room and then the tears came to my eyes. I started down the steps, whistling to keep from crying, I kept whistling to myself, *You going to need me, baby, one of these cold, rainy days.*

I read about Sonny's trouble in the spring. Little Grace died in the fall. She was a beautiful little girl. But she only lived a little over two years. She died of polio and she suffered. She had a slight fever for a couple of days, but it didn't seem like anything and we just kept her in bed. And we would certainly have called the doctor, but the fever dropped, she seemed to be all right. So we thought it had just been a cold. Then, one day, she was up, playing, Isabel was in the kitchen fixing lunch for the two boys when they'd come in from school, and she heard Grace fall down in the living room. When you have a lot of children you don't always start running when one of them falls, unless they start screaming or something. And, this time, Grace was quiet. Yet, Isabel says that when she heard that *thump* and then that silence, something happened in her to make her afraid. And she ran to the living room and there was little Grace on the floor, all twisted up, and the reason she hadn't screamed was that she couldn't get her breath. And when she did scream, it was the worst sound, Isabel says, that she'd ever heard in all her life, and she still hears it sometimes in her dreams. Isabel will sometimes wake me up with a low, moaning, strangling sound and I have to be quick to awaken her and hold her to me and where Isabel is weeping against me seems a mortal wound.

I think I may have written Sonny the very day that little Grace was buried. I was sitting in the living room in the dark, by myself, and I suddenly thought of Sonny. My trouble made his real.

One Saturday afternoon, when Sonny had been living with us, or, anyway, been in our house, for nearly two weeks, I found myself wandering aimlessly about the living room, drinking from a can of beer, and trying to work up the courage to search Sonny's room. He was out, he was usually out whenever I was home, and Isabel had taken the children to see their grandparents. Suddenly I was standing still in front of the living room window, watching Seventh Avenue. The idea of searching Sonny's room made me still. I scarcely dared to admit to myself what I'd be searching for. I didn't know what I'd do if I found it. Or if I didn't.

On the sidewalk across from me, near the entrance to a barbecue joint, some people were holding an old-fashioned revival meeting. The barbecue cook, wearing a dirty white apron, his conked[5] hair reddish and metallic in the pale sun, and a cigarette between his lips, stood in the doorway, watching them. Kids and older people paused in their errands and stood there, along with some older men and a couple of very tough-looking women who watched everything that happened on the avenue, as though they owned it, or were maybe owned by it. Well, they were watching this, too. The revival was being carried on by three sisters in black, and a brother. All they had were their voices and their Bibles and a tambourine. The brother was testifying[6] and while he testified two of the sisters stood together, seeming to say, amen, and the third sister walked around with the tambourine outstretched and a couple of people dropped coins into it. Then the brother's testimony ended and the sister who had been taking up the collection dumped the coins into her palm and transferred them to the pocket of her long black robe. Then she raised both hands, striking the tambourine against the air, and then against one hand, and she started to sing. And the two other sisters and the brother joined in.

It was strange, suddenly, to watch, though I had been seeing these meetings all my life. So, of course, had everybody else down there. Yet, they paused and watched and listened and I stood still at the window. "*Tis the old ship of Zion,*" they sang, and the sister with the tambourine kept a steady, jangling beat, "*it has rescued many a thousand!*" Not a soul under the sound of their voices was hearing this song for the first time, not one of them had been rescued. Nor had they seen much in the way of rescue work being done around them. Neither did they especially believe in the holiness of the three sisters and the brother, they knew too much about them, knew where they lived, and how. The woman with the tambourine, whose voice dominated the air, whose face was bright with joy, was divided by very little from the woman who stood watching her, a cigarette between her heavy, chapped lips, her hair a cuckoo's nest, her face scarred and swollen from many beatings, and her black eyes glittering like coal. Perhaps they both knew this, which was why, when, as rarely, they addressed each other, they addressed each other as Sister. As the singing filled the air the watching, listening faces underwent a change, the eyes focusing on something within; the music seemed to soothe a poison out of them; and time seemed, nearly, to fall away from the sullen, belligerent, battered faces, as though they were fleeing back to their first condition, while dreaming of their last. The barbecue cook half shook his head and smiled, and dropped his cigarette and disappeared into his joint. A man fumbled in his pockets for change and stood holding it in his hand impatiently, as though he had just remembered a pressing appointment further up the avenue. He looked furious. Then I saw Sonny, standing on the edge of the crowd. He was carrying a wide, flat notebook with a green cover, and it made him look, from where I was standing, almost like a schoolboy. The coppery sun brought out the copper in his skin, he was very faintly smiling, standing very still. Then the singing stopped, the tambourine turned into a collection plate again. The furious man dropped in his coins and vanished, so did a couple of the women, and Sonny dropped some change in the plate, looking directly at the woman with a little smile. He started across the avenue, toward the house. He has a slow, loping walk, something like the way Harlem hipsters walk, only he's imposed on this his own half-beat. I had never really noticed it before.

I stayed at the window, both relieved and apprehensive. As Sonny disappeared from my sight, they began singing again. And they were still singing when his key turned in the lock.

"Hey," he said.

"Hey, yourself. You want some beer?"

"No. Well, maybe." But he came up to the window and stood beside me, looking out. "What a warm voice," he said.

They were singing *If I could only hear my mother pray again!*

"Yes," I said, "and she can sure beat that tambourine."

"But what a terrible song," he said, and laughed. He dropped his notebook on the sofa and disappeared into the kitchen. "Where's Isabel and the kids?"

"I think they went to see their grandparents. You hungry?"

"No." He came back into the living room with his can of beer. "You want to come some place with me tonight?"

I sensed, I don't know how, that I couldn't possibly say no. "Sure. Where?"

He sat down on the sofa and picked up his notebook and started leafing through it. "I'm going to sit in with some fellows in a joint in the Village."

"You mean, you're going to play, tonight?"

"That's right." He took a swallow of his beer and moved back to the window. He gave me a sidelong look. "If you can stand it."

"I'll try," I said.

He smiled to himself and we both watched as the meeting across the way broke up. The three sisters and the brother, heads bowed, were singing *God be with you till we meet again.* The faces around them were very quiet. Then the song ended. The small crowd dispersed. We watched the three women and the lone man walk slowly up the avenue.

"When she was singing before," said Sonny, abruptly, "her voice reminded me for a minute of what heroin feels like sometimes—when it's in your veins. It makes you feel sort of warm and cool at the same time. And distant. And—and sure." He sipped his beer, very deliberately not looking at me. I watched his face. "It makes you feel—in control. Sometimes you've got to have that feeling."

"Do you?" I sat down slowly in the easy chair.

"Sometimes." He went to the sofa and picked up his notebook again. "Some people do."

"In order," I asked, "to play?" And my voice was very ugly, full of contempt and anger.

"Well"—he looked at me with great, troubled eyes, as though, in fact, he hoped his eyes would tell me things he could never otherwise say—"they *think* so. And *if* they think so—!"

"And what do *you* think?" I asked.

He sat on the sofa and put his can of beer on the floor. "I don't know," he said, and I couldn't be sure if he were answering my question or pursuing his thoughts. His face didn't tell me. "It's not so much to *play*. It's to *stand* it, to be able to make it at all. On any level." He frowned and smiled: "In order to keep from shaking to pieces."

"But these friends of yours," I said, "they seem to shake themselves to pieces pretty goddamn fast."

"Maybe." He played with the notebook. And something told me that I should curb my tongue, that Sonny was doing his best to talk, that I should listen. "But of course you only know the ones that've gone to pieces. Some don't—or at least they haven't *yet* and that's just about all *any* of us can say." He paused. "And then there are some who just live, really, in hell, and they know it and they see what's happening and they go right on. I don't know." He sighed, dropped the notebook, folded his arms. "Some guys, you can tell from the way they play, they on something *all* the time. And you can see that, well, it makes something real for them. But of course," he picked up his beer from the floor and sipped it and put the can down again, "they *want* to, too, you've got to see that. Even some of them that say they don't—*some*, not all."

"And what about you?" I asked—I couldn't help it. "What about you? Do *you* want to?"

He stood up and walked to the window and remained silent for a long time. Then he sighed. "Me," he said. Then: "While I was downstairs before, on my way here, listening to that woman sing, it struck me all of a sudden how much suffering she must have had to go through—to sing like that. It's *repulsive* to think you have to suffer that much."

I said: "But there's no way not to suffer—is there, Sonny?"

"I believe not," he said and smiled, "but that's never stopped anyone from trying." He looked at me. "Has it?" I realized, with this mocking look, that there stood between us, forever, beyond the power of time or forgiveness, the fact that I had held silence—so long!—when he had needed human speech to help him. He turned back to the window. "No, there's no way not to suffer. But you try all kinds of ways to keep from drowning in it, to keep on top of it, and to make it seem— well, like *you*. Like you did something, all right, and now you're suffering for it. You know?" I said nothing. "Well you know," he said, impatiently, "why *do* people suffer? Maybe it's better to do something to give it a reason, *any* reason."

"But we just agreed," I said, "that there's no way not to suffer. Isn't it better, then, just to—take it?"

"But nobody just takes it," Sonny cried, "that's what I'm telling you! *Everybody* tries not to. You're just hung up on the *way* some people try—it's not *your* way!"

The hair on my face began to itch, my face felt wet. "That's not true," I said, "that's not true. I don't give a damn what other people do, I don't even care how they suffer. I just care how *you* suffer." And he looked at me. "Please believe me," I said, "I don't want to see you—die—trying not to suffer."

"I won't," he said, flatly, "die trying not to suffer. At least, not any faster than anybody else."

"But there's no need," I said, trying to laugh, "is there? in killing yourself."

I wanted to say more, but I couldn't. I wanted to talk about will power and how life could be—well, beautiful. I wanted to say that it was all within; but was it? or, rather, wasn't that exactly the trouble? And I wanted to promise that I would never fail him again. But it would all have sounded—empty words and lies.

So I made the promise to myself and prayed that I would keep it.

"It's terrible sometimes, inside," he said, "that's what's the trouble. You walk these streets, black and funky and cold, and there's not really a living ass to talk to, and there's nothing shaking, and there's no way of getting it out—that storm inside. You can't talk it and you can't make love with it, and when you finally try to get with it and play it, you realize *nobody's* listening. So *you've* got to listen. You got to find a way to listen."

And then he walked away from the window and sat on the sofa again, as though all the wind had suddenly been knocked out of him. "Sometimes you'll do *anything* to play, even cut your mother's throat." He laughed and looked at me. "Or your brother's." Then he sobered. "Or your own." Then: "Don't worry. I'm all right now and I think I'll *be* all right. But I can't forget—where I've been. I don't mean just the physical place I've been, I mean where I've *been*. And *what* I've been."

"What have you been, Sonny?" I asked.

He smiled—but sat sideways on the sofa, his elbow resting on the back, his fingers playing with his mouth and chin, not looking at me. "I've been something I didn't recognize, didn't know I could be. Didn't know anybody could be." He stopped, looking inward, looking helplessly young, looking old. "I'm not talking about it now because I feel *guilty* or anything like that—maybe it would be better if I did, I don't know. Anyway, I can't really talk about it. Not to you, not to anybody," and now he turned and faced me. "Sometimes, you know, and it was actually when I was most *out* of the world, I felt that I was in it, that I was *with* it, really, and I could play or I didn't really have to *play*, it just came out of me, it was there. And I don't know how I played, thinking about it now, but I know I did awful things, those times, sometimes, to people. Or it wasn't that I *did* anything to them—it was that they weren't real." He picked up the beer can; it was empty; he rolled it between his palms: "And other times—well, I needed a fix, I needed to find a place to lean, I needed to clear a space to *listen*—and I couldn't find it, and I—went crazy, I did terrible things to *me*, I was terrible *for* me." He began pressing the beer can between his hands, I watched the metal begin to give. It glittered, as he played with it like a knife, and I was afraid he would cut himself, but I said nothing. "Oh well. I can never tell you. I was all by myself at the bottom of something, stinking and sweating and crying and shaking, and I smelled it, you know? *my* stink, and I thought I'd die if I couldn't get away from it and yet, all the same, I knew that everything I was doing was just locking me in with it. And I didn't know," he paused, still flattening the beer can, "I didn't know, I still *don't* know, something kept telling me that maybe it was good to smell your own stink, but I didn't think that *that* was what I'd been trying to do—and—who can stand it?" and he abruptly dropped the ruined beer can, looking at me with a small, still smile, and then rose, walking to the window as though it were the lodestone rock. I watched his face, he watched the avenue. "I couldn't tell you when Mama died— but the reason I wanted to leave Harlem so bad was to get away from drugs. And then, when I ran away, that's what I was running from—really. When I came back, nothing had changed, *I* hadn't changed, I was just—older." And he stopped, drumming with his fingers on the windowpane. The sun had vanished, soon darkness would fall. I watched his face. "It can come again," he said, almost as though speaking to himself. Then he turned to me. "It can come again," he repeated. "I just want you to know that."

"All right," I said, at last. "So it can come again, All right."

He smiled, but the smile was sorrowful. "I had to try to tell you," he said.

"Yes," I said. "I understand that."

"You're my brother," he said, looking straight at me, and not smiling at all.

"Yes," I repeated, "yes. I understand that."

He turned back to the window, looking out. "All that hatred down there," he said, "all that hatred and misery and love. It's a wonder it doesn't blow the avenue apart."

We went to the only nightclub on a short, dark street, downtown. We squeezed through the narrow, chattering, jam-packed bar to the entrance of the big room, where the bandstand was. And we stood there for a moment, for the lights were very dim in this room and we couldn't see. Then, "Hello, boy," said a voice and an enormous black man, much older than Sonny or myself, erupted out of all that atmospheric lighting and put an arm around Sonny's shoulder. "I been sitting right here," he said, "waiting for you."

He had a big voice, too, and heads in the darkness turned toward us.

Sonny grinned and pulled a little away, and said, "Creole, this is my brother. I told you about him."

Creole shook my hand. "I'm glad to meet you, son," he said, and it was clear that he was glad to meet me *there*, for Sonny's sake. And he smiled, "You got a real musician in *your* family," and he took his arm from Sonny's shoulder and slapped him, lightly, affectionately, with the back of his hand.

"Well. Now I've heard it all," said a voice behind us. This was another musician, and a friend of Sonny's, a coal-black, cheerful-looking man, built close to the ground. He immediately began confiding to me, at the top of his lungs, the most terrible things about Sonny, his teeth gleaming like a lighthouse and his laugh coming up out of him like the beginning of an earthquake. And it turned out that everyone at the bar knew Sonny, or almost everyone; some were musicians, working there, or nearby, or not working, some were simply hangers-on, and some were there to hear Sonny play. I was introduced to all of them and they were all very polite to me. Yet, it was clear that, for them, I was only Sonny's brother. Here, I was in Sonny's world. Or, rather: his kingdom. Here, it was not even a question that his veins bore royal blood.

They were going to play soon and Creole installed me, by myself, at a table in a dark corner. Then I watched them, Creole, and the little black man, and Sonny, and the others, while they horsed around, standing just below the bandstand. The light from the bandstand spilled just a little short of them and, watching them laughing and gesturing and moving about, I had the feeling that they, nevertheless, were being most careful not to step into that circle of light too suddenly; that if they moved into the light too suddenly, without thinking, they would perish in flame. Then, while I watched, one of them, the small black man, moved into the light and crossed the bandstand and started fooling around with his drums. Then—being funny and being, also, extremely ceremonious—Creole took Sonny by the arm and led him to the piano. A woman's voice called Sonny's name and a few hands started clapping. And Sonny, also being funny and being ceremonious, and so touched, I think, that he could have cried, but neither hiding it nor showing it, riding it like a man, grinned, and put both hands to his heart and bowed from the waist.

Creole then went to the bass fiddle and a lean, very bright-skinned brown man jumped up on the bandstand and picked up his horn. So there they were, and the atmosphere on the bandstand and in the room began to change and tighten. Someone stepped up to the microphone and announced them. Then there were all kinds of murmurs. Some people at the bar shushed others. The waitress ran around, frantically getting in the last orders, guys and chicks got closer to each other, and the lights on the bandstand, on the quartet, turned to a kind of indigo. Then they all looked different there. Creole looked about him for the last time, as though he were making certain that all his chickens were in the coop, and then he— jumped and struck the fiddle. And there they were.

All I know about music is that not many people ever really hear it. And even then, on the rare occasions when something opens within, and the music enters, what we mainly hear, or hear corroborated, are personal, private, vanishing evocations. But the man who creates the music is hearing something else, is dealing with the roar rising from the void and imposing order on it as it hits the air. What is evoked in him, then, is of another order, more terrible because it has no words, and triumphant, too, for that same reason. And his triumph, when he triumphs, is ours. I just watched Sonny's face. His face was troubled, he was working hard, but he wasn't with it. And I had the feeling that, in a way, everyone on the bandstand was waiting for him, both waiting for him and pushing him along. But as I began to watch Creole, I realized that it was Creole who held them all back. He had them on a short rein. Up there, keeping the beat with his whole body, wailing on the fiddle, with his eyes half closed, he was listening to everything, but he was listening to Sonny. He was having a dialogue with Sonny. He wanted Sonny to leave the shoreline and strike out for the deep water. He was Sonny's witness that deep water and drowning were not the same thing—he had been there, and he knew. And he wanted Sonny to know. He was waiting for Sonny to do the things on the keys which would let Creole know that Sonny was in the water.

And, while Creole listened, Sonny moved, deep within, exactly like someone in torment. I had never before thought of how awful the relationship must be between the musician and his instrument. He has to fill it, this instrument, with the breath of life, his own. He has to make it do what he wants it to do. And a piano is just a piano. It's made out of so much wood and wires and little hammers and big ones, and ivory. While there's only so much you can do with it, the only way to find this out is to try; to try and make it do everything.

And Sonny hadn't been near a piano for over a year. And he wasn't on much better terms with his life, not the life that stretched before him now. He and the piano stammered, started one way, got scared, stopped; started another way, panicked, marked time, started again; then seemed to have found a direction, panicked again, got stuck. And the face I saw on Sonny I'd never seen before. Everything had been burned out of it, and, at the same time, things usually hidden were being burned in, by the fire and fury of the battle which was occurring in him up there.

Yet, watching Creole's face as they neared the end of the first set, I had the feeling that something had happened, something I hadn't heard. Then they finished, there was scattered applause, and then, without an instant's warning, Creole started into something else, it was almost sardonic, it was *Am I Blue*.[7] And, as though he commanded, Sonny began to play. Something began to happen. And Creole let out the reins. The dry, low, black man said something awful on the drums, Creole answered, and the drums talked back. Then the horn insisted, sweet and high, slightly detached perhaps, and Creole listened, commenting now and then, dry, and driving, beautiful and calm and old. Then they all came together again, and Sonny was part of the family again. I could tell this from his face. He seemed to have found, right there beneath his fingers, a damn brand-new piano. It seemed that he couldn't get over it. Then, for awhile, just being happy with Sonny, they seemed to be agreeing with him that brand-new pianos certainly were a gas.

Then Creole stepped forward to remind them that what they were playing was the blues. He hit something in all of them, he hit something in me, myself, and the music tightened and deepened, apprehension began to beat the air. Creole began to tell us what the blues were all about. They were not about anything very new. He and his boys up there were keeping it new, at the risk of ruin, destruction, madness, and death, in order to find new ways to make us listen. For, while the tale of how we suffer, and how we are delighted, and how we may triumph is never new, it always must be heard. There isn't any other tale to tell, it's the only light we've got in all this darkness.

And this tale, according to that face, that body, those strong hands on those strings, has another aspect in every country, and a new depth in every generation. Listen, Creole seemed to be saying, listen. Now these are Sonny's blues. He made the little black man on the drums know it, and the bright, brown man on the horn. Creole wasn't trying any longer to get Sonny in the water. He was wishing him Godspeed. Then he stepped back, very slowly, filling the air with the immense suggestion that Sonny speak for himself.

Then they all gathered around Sonny and Sonny played. Every now and again one of them seemed to say, amen. Sonny's fingers filled the air with life, his life.

But that life contained so many others. And Sonny went all the way back, he really began with the spare, flat statement of the opening phrase of the song. Then he began to make it his. It was very beautiful because it wasn't hurried and it was no longer a lament. I seemed to hear with what burning he had made it his, with what burning we had yet to make it ours, how we could cease lamenting. Freedom lurked around us and I understood, at last, that he could help us to be free if we would listen, that he would never be free until we did. Yet, there was no battle in his face now. I heard what he had gone through, and would continue to go through until he came to rest in earth. He had made it his: that long line, of which we knew only Mama and Daddy. And he was giving it back, as everything must be given back, so that, passing through death, it can live forever. I saw my mother's face again, and felt, for the first time, how the stones of the road she had walked on must have bruised her feet. I saw the moonlit road where my father's brother died. And it brought something else back to me, and carried me past it. I saw my little girl again and felt Isabel's tears again, and I felt my own tears begin to rise. And I was yet aware that this was only a moment, that the world waited outside, as hungry as a tiger, and that trouble stretched above us, longer than the sky.

Then it was over. Creole and Sonny let out their breath, both soaking wet, and grinning. There was a lot of applause and some of it was real. In the dark, the girl came by and I asked her to take drinks to the bandstand. There was a long pause, while they talked up there in the indigo light and after awhile I saw the girl put a Scotch and milk on top of the piano for Sonny. He didn't seem to notice it, but just before they started playing again, he sipped from it and looked toward me, and nodded. Then he put it back on top of the piano. For me, then, as they began to play again, it glowed and shook above my brother's head like the very cup of trembling.[8]

1957

Notes

1. Lavatory.
2. Heroin.
3. Charlie ("Bird") Parker (1920–1955), brilliant saxophonist and innovator of jazz; working in New York in the mid-1940s, he developed, with Dizzy Gillespie and others, the style of jazz called "bebop." He was a narcotics addict.
4. Snobbish, bossy.
5. Processed: straightened and greased.
6. Publicly professing belief.
7. A favorite jazz standard, brilliantly recorded by Billie Holiday.
8. See Isaiah 51:17, 22–23: "Awake, awake, stand up, O Jerusalem, which hast drunk at the hand of the Lord the cup of his fury; thou hast drunken the dregs of the cup of trembling, and wrung them out. . . . Behold, I have taken out of thine hand the cup of trembling, even the dregs of the cup of my fury; thou shalt no more drink it again: But I will put it into the hand of them that afflict thee; . . ."

Aisha Sabatini Sloan

Aisha Sabatini Sloan (1981-) was born in Los Angeles. She received her MFA in creative writing from the University of Arizona and holds an MA in Studio Art and Cultural Studies from the Gallatin School for Individualized Study at New York University. She currently teaches composition classes as an adjunct in Arizona, and is working on two essay collections. "Birth of the Cool," was first published in the web-based magazine, Identity Theory, *in 2009.*

Birth of the Cool

Los Angeles glinted like an Austrian crystal through the windows of my mother's Toyota Corolla. "Why can't daddy and I be white like you?" I whined. We were on the freeway. Gray paths snaked their way towards the ocean. Green signs held a collection of numbers and letters, some of which indicated that we were almost home. My mother said, "I love your coloring. I wish I had skin the same color as you." The word *glint* comes from the Middle English *glent*, and it is of Scandinavian origin. My origin is Italian and Black—brown Afro's on either side.

At the time I had a boyfriend, and he was blonde. We had recently gotten married during a free period at our preschool, which was owned by an energetic Indian woman named Hapi. She called the school Happyland. Alec had lifted some sort of fabric off of my forehead so that we could kiss. I was four and brown and curly. Something about this romance made me regret myself, my appearance. If he said something to make me feel that way, I have forgotten what it was.

Los Angeles glints because of the way sunlight illuminates the smog that hangs in the polluted air. Blonde hair also glints. Brown, curly hair, for the most part, absorbs things. Like tangles and curious fingers. What I didn't take into consideration during this brooding moment of self-hatred was that Alec's little sister was brown like me. Adopted perhaps. Los Angeles was like that – multicolored. I grew up in a wealthy, Westside neighborhood and attended schools dreamt up by former hippies. The city's racial metaphor for me felt like a pot of soup with a nice, chef salad, something casual and light and accompanied by a glass of iced tea. But this didn't prevent me from getting upset about race.

Thelonious Sphere Monk was born in Rocky Mount, North Carolina, in what some people have called "1918, question mark?" He would eventually study music at Julliard, travel the world, and live on in history as a founder of Be-bop whose piano improvisation was a cold, crazed shiver of genius. His face appears on a pin I once bought from a jewelry case in southeastern Alaska. Outside, the tide brought coldness from the ice-blue glacier across Kachemak Bay onto a beach littered with driftwood. Which is to say, his influence has permeated the globe.

I imagine him as a five-year-old boy, standing on a porch of peeling blue paint, prophetic. He closes his eyes and sees images of his future flash before him: a glacier, a cactus, the Berlin wall. Then he opens them and sees the green hot South. He looks down on his skin, forty-two years before the Civil Rights Act. The journey from this small boy's present to the life he would lead seems enormous and impossible.

My girlfriend recently described Monk's piano playing with her hands. "You know how he goes over it, and you know what he's *not* playing, but he doesn't give it to you?" Her hands move around and establish an invisible area, then trip over it. "And he goes over it, and around it, and you want it so bad . . . or you don't? And finally he gives it to you. Or he doesn't." It strikes me to think of this man, alive in the long, pale hands of a twenty-five-year old. Her fingers pantomime his jazz in the dry Tucson morning, underneath chirping birds. Long, skinny branches with thin thorns make shadows on the patio floor.

My father's mother, Argusta, was born in Alabama. Her family lived next door to a white family, and all the children played together. The father of the neighboring family was a violent man when he drank, and his children would often run to my great-grandparent's house for safekeeping. They hid in the attic for hours. My great grandmother made sure they were safe, then took out her bible and waited downstairs for their father to arrive. "I know what you're going to say," he would moan, as she pushed him down and began to recite passages. Argusta and my great aunt Cora May waited near the train tracks for their neighbors after school on cold winter days, so that they could all walk home together, as their parents had commanded.

One of the girls in the white family was nicknamed "Nig." Eventually, she grew up and got married. She came back home one day to show off her new husband, and bumped into my grandmother, who went into a fit of nostalgia. "Nig! How you been!" She screamed, and gave her old friend a huge hug. The husband went into a rage. He demanded that my grandmother get away from his wife, and how dare she address her that way? "What did you do?" I ask my grandmother on the phone. "I just laughed. I know it wasn't funny, but I couldn't help myself. He was making such a fuss."

My grandmother told me this story one recent afternoon. I was preparing to make dinner for company. "What chu makin'?" She asked. This is a question my mother asks me incessantly too, minus the southern twang. All of our conversations are often devoted to the preparation and consumption of meals. Every day my mother calls her mother-in-law in Detroit to chat on her way to work while slowly creeping along the 10 freeway towards downtown L.A. "Your mamma made pork roast last night," my grandmother will inform me when we talk later on in the day. "I'd give anything for one of her salads."

On the Internet, there is footage of Thelonious Monk playing a concert in Berlin. When you look at his face, he shows you nothing. His expression pretends to cover his interior life, but this is only a farce, because what's inside him comes spilling out onto the piano keys, along with the sweat dripping off his hot, dark face. He wore a round, half-sphere shaped hat, which often had a button on the top. He was known for his suits. Is it just my imagination, or do people tend to call well-dressed black men "dapper"? His face and movements projected an air of mystery, as if to say, "There is more of me. You think you've got it, but you can't have it."

I have rented Clint Eastwood's documentary on the artist, "Straight No Chaser." In one scene Monk stands in front of a door marked "Gentlemen." He begins to spin circles in place. Then he stops, takes a drag from his cigarette and says, "I do that on the street. Somebody else do that, they'd put him in a straight jacket. Oh that Thelonious Monk, he's craaazy." Someone is laughing in the background. It is rare that Monk's mumbles clear the way for distinguishable words and phrases in the landscape of his language. Sometimes he would get up in the middle of a concert to spin in circles while somebody else was playing. It's possible that he was actually bi-polar, but something about Monk's persona seems purposefully insolent. Childish. And in a way, *black*. A woman I know once described a film director by saying, "he has the most bizarre outlook on life that I've encountered in a long time. He has such innocence, but it's such a black innocence. Childishness about him." This idea seems relevant here. It is childish to spin around in a circle on stage when you are the featured performer of a concert, and it is bizarre, but in what way is it innocent?

My parents met in Detroit, in the public library where they both worked. My father called the circulation desk that she was manning and told her to look up to where he was standing several feet away. Their first date was to go to a friend's barbeque.

Several dates later, they were at a restaurant for dinner. A man flashed a gun at them, and said something about interracial couples. He and my father began an argument that eventually led them outside. My father removed the gun from the man's possession, a tiny pistol. When my parents moved to Los Angeles in the 1970's, the two of them would go to the movies and wait for black women to tusk their tongues as they passed, calling my father a sell-out with their narrowed eyelids and not looking my mother in the eye at all.

But I was rarely the target of overt racism during my childhood. There was the one time when, on a class trip to Catalina Island, a group of friends and I sat down with a kid from another school group. He lost a game of "Go Fish" and called me a nigger. "Why don't you go back to Africa with Martin Luther King?" he asked. Because my friends and I were smart enough to see the nonsense in his slander, and laughed about it, I was fine. I collected my playing cards from him and my friends and I plotted to step on his toes at various points during the remainder of the boat ride.

What hurt about the experience was not his limp attempt at hatred, though. What bothered me was the loaded silence surrounding the issue. Three of my teachers, all of them white, sat in a booth within earshot of his tirade. I later told them what happened, and they said, "Yes, we heard. It seemed like you had everything under control." The fact that they hadn't said anything to me about it afterwards made me feel strangely abandoned. Did they think this happened to me all the time? I had never been called that word before, and I wanted an adult to acknowledge its power and *then* dismiss it. Silence was a common way of handling the issue of race for most of the politically correct people I grew up around. But small questions would emerge like bright green pricks of grass out of the quiet. "Why is your mom white?" kids always, eventually, muttered—a sentence I always anticipated and always felt like a slap. There is no simple answer to this question, which is profoundly philosophical if you think about it.

When I was ten, a kid in my class did not like my curly hair, despite the fact that my mother had spent an hour combing, moussing and decorating it with ribbon. It hung in shiny ringlets to my shoulders. He made a sour face and asked, "Why is your hair like that?" Every day for the next four years I wore it in a tight bun. Some might call me oversensitive.

During one period, later in my life, I listened to Billie Holiday sing "In My Solitude" over and over again, until her particular timing and the sweet croon of her inflection sewed the song onto my body. I can't pull on the melody without disturbing the sadness that it helped me survive. My first experience of heartbreak was nothing compared with what, of her life, Holiday was infusing into her music. In his essay, "The Uses of the Blues," James Baldwin describes the time when someone asked Miles Davis why he was giving money to Holiday, when he knew she'd just spend it on heroin. Davis replied, "Baby, have you ever been sick?" The songs that Billie Holiday sings are draped in the biography of her own sadness, which is tugged on and burdened by the added sadness that her singing evokes in other people.

One of Monk's better-known compositions is called "Epistrophy," a play on the word *epistrophe*, which is pronounced the same way. Epistrophe is a figure of speech, opposite of *anaphora*. It describes the repetition of the same word or words at the end of successive phrases, clauses or sentences. It is meant to create emphasis on the repeated word or phrase. In one video recording of Thelonious Monk in Berlin, he plays the Ellington standard, "In My Solitude," which immediately brings Holiday's voice to my mind. Towards the end of the song, he avoids playing the low note, which is supposed to punctuate the end of each line. This way, the most powerful part of this profoundly sad song is suspended in high notes. The pause of silence where a note should be feels like a comma, or an ellipsis, and he leaves us to fill in the blank. This way, the most emotionally conclusive moment of the line is left hanging, bringing to mind a singer too distraught to finish her sentences. If he were a singer, at this point in the song he would be saying:

I sit in my –	[chair]
And filled with de –	[spair]
There's no one could be so –	[sad]
With gloom every –	[where]
I sit and I –	[stare]
I know that I'll soon go –	[mad]

On that last line, instead of pausing or playing the note that evokes the word "mad," he waits for the time of the word to pass, then shoves two discordant notes together, off to the side, capturing the pitch of crazy without leaving enough space for a word.

In "Straight No Chaser," Monk's agent tells a story about the musician being interviewed by a reporter. The reporter asks, "What kind of music do you like?" and Monk replies, "I like all kinds of music." The reporter asks, "Do you like Country music?" And Monk does not say anything. The reporter tries again. "Did you . . . do you like country music?" Monk looks at his agent and says, "I think the fella's hard of hearing."

I went to an elementary school with about five black kids, total, and I was one of three in my class. A girl named Erica, who lived in the wealthy, majority black neighborhood of Leimert Park, was more of an acquaintance than a good friend, but we bonded. I spent a lot of energy making sure that everyone knew that just because I was one of two black girls, I was not necessarily interested in the only black boy in our class, a nice kid named Robert. Which is to say, I was a bit of a shit.

Despite this, I was not ignorant or disdainful of my own blackness. One day during P.E. class, Erica and I were across the playground from each other. As had happened on numerous occasions prior, our P.E. teacher, who was white, began calling my name to Erica, who pretended that she could not hear her until finally announcing, "I AM EH-REE-KA!" back. "That's it!" we told each other afterwards. We arranged for an appointment with the principal to discuss the dismissal of the already unpopular P.E. instructor, due to ignorance, bigotry, and discrimination. The principal humored us for a half hour, and we bragged to our parents about our political activities, but no one was fired.

One afternoon at Erica's house, I sat at the kitchen table while she sat on her father's lap. "You ever give your daddy sugar?" he asked me.

"No." I said.

"Why not?" he prodded. The moment pauses, clicks and glints in my memory. "He's diabetic."

I sat confused as he and Erica spent the next two minutes laughing so hard they drooled. "What's so funny?" I asked. A glint is a spatially localized brightness. Her father caught his breath. "I don't mean *sugar*, I mean, do you ever give him love? Give him hugs and kisses?" I was black enough to get pissed off at my P.E. teacher, but not quite black enough to know how to talk right around *real* black people.

Thelonious Monk was born cool. After all, his *given* middle name is Sphere. But his childish, bizarre behavior is both black and *un*innocent because he participates in a larger tradition in which absurdity is a means of social protest. In other words, his innocence is feigned. By spinning around in a circle onstage, he is escaping what must have been at that time a stultifying, deracinated social role – as a black man and a musician – with unpredictability. Rather than make an appointment with the principal in order to communicate, "fuck you" to his P.E. teacher, he stands in silence at the sound of the wrong name as it is shouted across the playground. He dances in place, sings a song, does cartwheels – anything that is not what the woman is asking for. He lets the P.E. teacher yell her voice hoarse until she is able to realize her own mistake. If she walks away thinking that he is insolent, deaf or an idiot, she is walking away believing a lie. And that lack of truth is what will hurt her, not him, in the greater scheme of things.

At another point in Eastwood's documentary, Monk walks into a recording studio. A short, white record producer approaches him, sort of grabs at him in an attempt at greeting, and says "don't be jivin' me man!" after which point he laughs hysterically. Monk is as still as a vase of flowers. The producer asks, "Where'd you get that hat?" and Monk replies,

"Oh yeah. That was given to me in Poland."

"Where?"

"Poland."

I cringe as I watch the producer dance around the room in a strained attempt to be similar to Monk, or to the other blacks or jazz musicians he's encountered. The result is, though unintentional, a near-minstrel show of dissonance. But Monk's worldliness tucks itself into his own personal sphere of sophistication, into the inaudible soup of his speech, where the producer can't touch him. He chuckles underneath his breath. During some songs, he leaves a lit cigarette on the keys. When Monk plays "In My Solitude," the perspiration on his face reflects the light. To glint is to throw a brief glance at something, or to take a brief look. It also means to be shiny, as if wet. To glisten. To be looked upon by light.

Monk litters quiet moments throughout his music like a breadcrumb path of crystals for us to follow. Where one might expect emphasis, he leaves us with silence, generating an exaggerated sense of loss. We fill in the missing beat, note or word with a manifestation of our own longing. He makes the act of listening into an exchange or conversation. Like a church congregation, we say "chair," "despair," "sad," "where," "stare," and "mad" as if on cue, tripping off the edge of his melody, where he refuses to give us the comfort of an ending we anticipate. This is a form of communication that goes against the notion of communication altogether, a kind of induction of silence into language. By doing this, he suggests that we know *it*—we know this thing we are missing—already. We can put our hands around the space that it inhabits.

When I was in high school, I watched a lot of documentaries on cable television while making collages in my room. One day *Straight No Chaser* came on. What I remember from that first time watching, are the times when Thelonious Monk was in the airport or on an airplane. At one point, he is sitting between a woman and his wife on a plane to London, and sunlight streams through the window. He is busy shuffling something, then he sits back, his eyes drift toward the camera, and he smiles, happy to be watched, perhaps aware of the audience beyond the cameraman. At that moment in his life, he was already starting to unravel. His son said, "He may pace for a few days, and then he'd get exhausted." And, "It's a startling thing to look your father in the eye and to realize he doesn't exactly know who you are." Only once did Monk mention anything about his own madness. In a cab in New York with his patroness and friend, Baroness Pannonica de Koenigswarter he said, "I think there's something wrong with me." When I listen to his music I picture him pacing across the gate of an airport. A blue shadow loping across a screen of black and white.

I went to college in Minnesota, and my father came to visit one winter. We drove to a gas station just outside of St. Paul where you could pay after you pumped. "Can you imagine that in Detroit?" My dad asked. "Brothers be standing on the corner saying, 'They're giving gas away for free!'" My father saves black-talk for only the funniest of jokes. I mostly hear it as he bellows on the phone with his best friend, Rodney, who still lives in Detroit. He will laugh so hard he'll fall out of the kitchen chair. I always wanted to tell him a joke that funny, and relished in these moments of uncontrolled joy. At that moment in Minnesota, I laughed until I spit. We were listening to "Ruby, My Dear" from a *Best of Thelonious Monk* album. The newly setting sun streaked the sky pink, and the horizon was blue and long. Pinpricks of snow reflected light in the soft landscape around us like scattered crystals. Brightness is defined as the location of a visual perception along the black-to-white continuum. Between blackness and whiteness, brightness holds clues about what connects one side to the other. "These niggers is crazy," my father said, when he finally caught his breath. "They givin' this shit away for free and they don't even know it." I put the track on repeat until we got to where we were going.

Joyce Carol Oates

Joyce Carol Oates (b. 1938) is a writer, critic, and professor at Princeton University. She majored in English at Syracuse University and received an MA from the University of Wisconsin in 1961. After she discovered by chance that a story she'd written had been noted in the honor roll of The Best American Short Stories, *she put together her first book of stories,* By the North Gate, *in 1963. Today, she has published nearly 70 books, including* Heat and Other Stories *(1991),* Haunted: Tales of the Grotesque *(1994), and* Will You Always Love Me? *(1996). First published in* Epoch *in 1966, "Where Are You Going, Where Have You Been?" also appeared in the* Best American Short Stories *of 1967 and* Prize Stories: The O'Henry Awards 1968. *Additionally, it was made into the film* Smooth Talk. *Oates based this story on an article in* Life *magazine about a serial murderer in Tucson, Arizona, known as "The Pied Piper of Tucson."*

Where Are You Going, Where Have You Been?

For Bob Dylan

Her name was Connie. She was fifteen and she had a quick nervous giggling habit of craning her neck to glance into mirrors, or checking other people's faces to make sure her own was all right. Her mother, who noticed everything and knew everything and who hadn't much reason any longer to look at her own face, always scolded Connie about it. "Stop gawking at yourself, who are you? You think you're so pretty?" she would say. Connie would raise her eyebrows at these familiar complaints and look right through her mother, into a shadowy vision of herself as she was right at that moment: she knew she was pretty and that was everything. Her mother had been pretty once too, if you could believe those old snapshots in the album, but now her looks were gone and that was why she was always after Connie.

"Why don't you keep your room clean like your sister? How've you got your hair fixed—what the hell stinks? Hair spray? You don't see your sister using that junk."

Her sister June was twenty-four and still lived at home. She was a secretary in the high school Connie attended, and if that wasn't bad enough—with her in the

Reprinted from *The Wheel of Love,* (1970), John Hawkins & Associates, Inc..

same building—she was so plain and chunky and steady that Connie had to hear her praised all the time by her mother and her mother's sisters. June did this, June did that, she saved money and helped clean the house and cooked and Connie couldn't do a thing, her mind was all filled with trashy daydreams. Their father was away at work most of the time and when he came home he wanted supper and he read the newspaper at supper and after supper he went to bed. He didn't bother talking much to them, but around his bent head Connie's mother kept picking at her until Connie wished her mother was dead and she herself was dead and it was all over. "She makes me want to throw up sometimes," she complained to her friends. She had a high, breathless, amused voice which made everything she said a little forced, whether it was sincere or not.

There was one good thing: June went places with girl friends of hers, girls who were just as plain and steady as she, and so when Connie wanted to do that her mother had no objections. The father of Connie's best girl friend drove the girls the three miles to town and left them off at a shopping plaza, so that they could walk through the stores or go to a movie, and when he came to pick them up again at eleven he never bothered to ask what they had done.

They must have been familiar sights, walking around that shopping plaza in their shorts and flat ballerina slippers that always scuffed the sidewalk, with charm bracelets jingling on their thin wrists; they would lean together to whisper and laugh secretly if someone passed by who amused or interested them. Connie had long dark blond hair that drew anyone's eye to it, and she wore part of it pulled up on her head and puffed out and the rest of it she let fall down her back. She wore a pullover jersey blouse that looked one way when she was at home and another way when she was away from home. Everything about her had two sides to it, one for home and one for anywhere that was not home: her walk that could be childlike and bobbing, or languid enough to make anyone think she was hearing music in her head, her mouth which was pale and smirking most of the time, but bright and pink on these evenings out, her laugh which was cynical and drawling at home—"Ha, ha, very funny"—but high-pitched and nervous anywhere else, like the jingling of the charms on her bracelet.

Sometimes they did go shopping or to a movie, but sometimes they went across the highway, ducking fast across the busy road, to a drive-in restaurant where older kids hung out. The restaurant was shaped like a big bottle, though squatter than a real bottle, and on its cap was a revolving figure of a grinning boy who held a hamburger aloft. One night in midsummer they ran across, breathless with daring, and right away someone leaned out a car window and invited them over, but it was just a boy from high school they didn't like. It made them feel good to be able to ignore him. They went up through the maze of parked and cruising cars to the bright-lit, fly-infested restaurant, their faces pleased and expectant as if they were entering a sacred building that loomed out of the night to give them what haven and what blessing they yearned for. They sat at the counter and crossed their legs at the ankles, their thin shoulders rigid with excitement and listened to the music that made everything so good: the music was always in the background like music at a church service, it was something to depend upon.

A boy named Eddie came in to talk with them. He sat backwards on his stool, turning himself jerkily around in semi-circles and then stopping and turning again, and after a while he asked Connie if she would like something to eat. She said she did and so she tapped her friend's arm on her way out—her friend pulled her face up into a brave droll look—and Connie said she would meet her at eleven, across the way. "I just hate to leave her like that," Connie said earnestly, but the boy said that she wouldn't be alone for long. So they went out to his car and on the way Connie couldn't help but let her eyes wander over the windshields and faces all around her, her face gleaming with the joy that had nothing to do with Eddie or even this place; it might have been the music. She drew her shoulders up and sucked in her breath with the pure pleasure of being alive, and just at that moment she happened to glance at a face just a few feet from hers. It was a boy with shaggy black hair, in a convertible jalopy painted gold. He stared at her and then his lips widened into a grin. Connie slit her eyes at him and turned away, but she couldn't help glancing back and there he was still watching her. He wagged a finger and laughed and said, "Gonna get you, baby," and Connie turned away again without Eddie noticing anything.

She spent three hours with him, at the restaurant where they ate hamburgers and drank Cokes in wax cups that were always sweating, and then down an alley a mile or so away, and when he left her off at five to eleven only the movie house was still open at the plaza. Her girl friend was there, talking with a boy. When Connie came up the two girls smiled at each other and Connie said, "How was the movie?" and the girl said, "*You* should know." They rode off with the girl's father, sleepy and pleased, and Connie couldn't help but look at the darkened shopping plaza with its big empty parking lot and its signs that were faded and ghostly now, and over at the drive-in restaurant where cars were still circling tirelessly. She couldn't hear the music at this distance.

Next morning June asked her how the movie was and Connie said, "So-so."

She and that girl and occasionally another girl went out several times a week that way, and the rest of the time Connie spent around the house—it was summer vacation—getting in her mother's way and thinking, dreaming, about the boys she met. But all the boys fell back and dissolved into a single face that was not even a face, but an idea, a feeling, mixed up with the urgent insistent pounding of the music and the humid night air of July. Connie's mother kept dragging her back to the daylight by finding things for her to do or saying suddenly, "What's this about the Pettinger girl?"

And Connie would say nervously, "Oh, her. That dope." She always drew thick clear lines between herself and such girls, and her mother was simple and kindly enough to believe her. Her mother was so simple, Connie thought, that it was maybe cruel to fool her so much. Her mother went scuffling around the house in old bedroom slippers and complained over the telephone to one sister about the other, then the other called up and the two of them complained about the third one. If June's name was mentioned her mother's tone was approving, and if Connie's name was mentioned it was disapproving. This did not really mean she disliked Connie and actually Connie thought that her mother preferred her to June because she was prettier, but the two of them kept up a pretense of exasperation, a sense that they were tugging and struggling over something of little value to either of them. Sometimes, over coffee, they were almost friends, but something would come up—some vexation that was like a fly buzzing suddenly around their heads—and their faces went hard with contempt.

One Sunday Connie got up at eleven—none of them bothered with church—and washed her hair so that it could dry all day long, in the sun. Her parents and sister were going to a barbecue at an aunt's house and Connie said no, she wasn't interested, rolling her eyes, to let mother know just what she thought of it. "Stay home alone then," her mother said sharply. Connie sat out back in a lawn chair and watched them drive away, her father quiet and bald, hunched around so that he could back the car out, her mother with a look that was still angry and not at all softened through the windshield, and in the back seat poor old June all dressed up as if she didn't know what a barbecue was, with all the running yelling kids and the flies. Connie sat with her eyes closed in the sun, dreaming and dazed with the warmth about her as if this were a kind of love, the caresses of love, and her mind slipped over onto thoughts of the boy she had been with the night before and how nice he had been, how sweet it always was, not the way someone like June would suppose but sweet, gentle, the way it was in movies and promised in songs; and when she opened her eyes she hardly knew where she was, the back yard ran off into weeds and a fenceline of trees and behind it the sky was perfectly blue and still. The asbestos "ranch house" that was now three years old startled her—it looked small. She shook her head as if to get awake.

It was too hot. She went inside the house and turned on the radio to drown out the quiet. She sat on the edge of her bed, barefoot, and listened for an hour and a half to a program called XYZ Sunday Jamboree, record after record of hard, fast, shrieking songs she sang along with, interspersed by exclamations from "Bobby King": "An' look here you girls at Napoleon's—Son and Charley want you to pay real close attention to this song coming up!"

And Connie paid close attention herself, bathed in a glow of slow-pulsed joy that seemed to rise mysteriously out of the music itself and lay languidly about the airless little room, breathed in and breathed out with each gentle rise and fall of her chest.

After a while she heard a car coming up the drive. She sat up at once, startled, because it couldn't be her father so soon. The gravel kept crunching all the way in from the road—the driveway was long—and Connie ran to the window. It was a car she didn't know. It was an open jalopy, painted a bright gold that caught the sun opaquely. Her heart began to pound and her fingers snatched at her hair, checking it, and she whispered "Christ. Christ," wondering how bad she looked. The car came to a stop at the side door and the horn sounded four short taps as if this were a signal Connie knew.

She went into the kitchen and approached the door slowly, then hung out the screen door, her bare toes curling down off the step. There were two boys in the car and now she recognized the driver: he had shaggy, shabby black hair that looked crazy as a wig and he was grinning at her.

"I ain't late, am I?" he said.

"Who the hell do you think you are?" Connie said.

"Toldja I'd be out, didn't I?"

"I don't even know who you are."

She spoke sullenly, careful to show no interest or pleasure, and he spoke in a fast bright monotone. Connie looked past him to the other boy, taking her time. He had fair brown hair, with a lock that fell onto his forehead. His sideburns gave him a fierce, embarrassed look, but so far he hadn't even bothered to glance at her. Both boys wore sunglasses. The driver's glasses were metallic and mirrored everything in miniature.

"You wanta come for a ride?" he said.

Connie smirked and let her hair fall loose over one shoulder.

"Don'tcha like my car? New paint job," he said. "Hey."

"What?"

"You're cute."

She pretended to fidget, chasing flies away from the door.

"Don'tcha believe me, or what?" he said.

"Look, I don't even know who you are," Connie said in disgust.

"Hey, Ellie's got a radio, see. Mine's broke down." He lifted his friend's arm and showed her the little transistor the boy was holding, and now Connie began to hear the music. It was the same program that was playing inside the house.

"Bobby King?" she said.

"I listen to him all the time. I think he's great."

"He's kind of great," Connie said reluctantly.

"Listen, that guy's *great*. He knows where the action is."

Connie blushed a little, because the glasses made it impossible for her to see just what this boy was looking at. She couldn't decide if she liked him or if he was just a jerk, and so she dawdled in the doorway and wouldn't come down or go back inside. She said, "What's all that stuff painted on your car?"

"Can'tcha read it?" He opened the door very carefully, as if he was afraid it might fall off. He slid out just as carefully, planting his feet firmly on the ground, the tiny metallic world in his glasses slowing down like gelatine hardening and in the midst of it Connie's bright green blouse. "This here is my name, to begin with," he said. ARNOLD FRIEND was written in tar-like black letters on the side, with a drawing of a round grinning face that reminded Connie of a pumpkin, except it wore sunglasses. "I wanta introduce myself, I'm Arnold Friend and that's my real name and I'm gonna be your friend, honey, and inside the car's Ellie Oscar, he's kinda shy." Ellie brought his transistor up to his shoulder and balanced it there. "Now these numbers are a secret code, honey," Arnold Friend explained. He read off the numbers 33, 19, 17 and raised his eyebrows at her to see what she thought of that, but she didn't think much of it. The left rear fender had been smashed and around it was written, on the gleaming gold background: DONE BY CRAZY WOMAN DRIVER. Connie had to laugh at that. Arnold Friend was pleased at her laughter and looked up at her. "Around the other side's a lot more—you wanta come and see them?"

"No."

"Why not?"

"Why should I?"

"Don'tcha wanta see what's on the car? Don'tcha wanta go for a ride?"

"I don't know."

"Why not?"

"I got things to do."

"Like what?"

"Things."

He laughed as if she had said something funny. He slapped his thighs. He was standing in a strange way, leaning back against the car as if he were balancing himself. He wasn't tall, only an inch or so taller than she would be if she came down to him. Connie liked the way he was dressed, which was the way all of them dressed: tight faded jeans stuffed into black, scuffed boots, a belt that pulled his waist in and showed how lean he was, and a white pull-over shirt that was a little soiled and showed the hard small muscles of his arms and shoulders. He looked as if he probably did hard work, lifting and carrying things. Even his neck looked muscular. And his face was a familiar face, somehow: the jaw and chin and cheeks slightly darkened, because he hadn't shaved for a day or two, and the nose long and hawk-like, sniffing as if she were a treat he was going to gobble up and it was all a joke.

"Connie, you ain't telling the truth. This is your day set aside for a ride with me and you know it," he said, still laughing. The way he straightened and recovered from his fit of laughing showed that it had been all fake.

"How do you know what my name is?" she said suspiciously.

"It's Connie."

"Maybe and maybe not."

"I know my Connie," he said, wagging his finger. Now she remembered him even better, back at the restaurant, and her cheeks warmed at the thought of how she sucked in her breath just at the moment she passed him—how she must have looked to him. And he had remembered her. "Ellie and I come out here especially for you," he said. "Ellie can sit in back. How about it?"

"Where?"

"Where what?"

"Where're we going?"

He looked at her. He took off the sunglasses and she saw how pale the skin around his eyes was, like holes that were not in shadow but instead in light. His eyes were like chips of broken glass that catch the light in an amiable way. He smiled. It was as if the idea of going for a ride somewhere, to some place, was a new idea to him.

"Just for a ride, Connie sweetheart."

"I never said my name was Connie," she said.

"But I know what it is. I know your name and all about you, lots of things," Arnold Friend said. He had not moved yet but stood still leaning back against the side of his jalopy. "I took a special interest in you, such a pretty girl, and found out all about you like I know your parents and sister are gone somewheres and I know where and how long they're going to be gone, and I know who you were with last night, and your best friend's name is Betty. Right?"

He spoke in a simple lilting voice, exactly as if he were reciting the words to a song. His smile assured her that everything was fine. In the car Ellie turned up the volume on his radio and did not bother to look around at them.

"Ellie can sit in the back seat," Arnold Friend said. He indicated his friend with a casual jerk of his chin, as if Ellie did not count and she could not bother with him.

"How'd you find out all that stuff?" Connie said.

"Listen: Betty Schultz and Tony Fitch and Jimmy Pettinger and Nancy Pettinger," he said, in a chant. "Raymond Stanley and Bob Hutter—"

"Do you know all those kids?"

"I know everybody."

"Look, you're kidding. You're not from around here."

"Sure."

"But—how come we never saw you before?"

"Sure you saw me before," he said. He looked down at his boots, as if he were a little offended. "You just don't remember."

"I guess I'd remember you," Connie said.

"Yeah?" He looked up at this, beaming. He was pleased. He began to mark time with the music from Ellie's radio, tapping his fists lightly together. Connie looked away from his smile to the car, which was painted so bright it almost hurt her eyes to look at it. She looked at that name, ARNOLD FRIEND. And up at the front fender was an expression that was familiar—MAN THE FLYING SAUCERS. It was an expression kids had used the year before, but didn't use this year. She looked at it for a while as if the words meant something to her that she did not yet know.

"What're you thinking about? Huh?" Arnold Friend demanded. "Not worried about your hair blowing around in the car, are you?"

"No."

"Think I maybe can't drive good?"

"How do I know?"

"You're a hard girl to handle. How come?" he said. "Don't you know I'm your friend? Didn't you see me put my sign in the air when you walked by?"

"What sign?"

"My sign." And he drew an X in the air, leaning out toward her. They were maybe ten feet apart. After his hand fell back to his side the X was still in the air, almost visible. Connie let the screen door close and stood perfectly still inside it, listening to the music from her radio and the boy's blend together. She stared at Arnold Friend. He stood there so stiffly relaxed, pretending to be relaxed, with one hand idly on the door handle as if he were keeping himself up that way and had no intention of ever moving again. She recognized most things about him, the tight jeans that showed his thighs and buttocks and the greasy leather boots and the tight shirt, and even that slippery friendly smile of his, that sleepy dreamy smile that all the boys used to get across ideas they didn't want to put into words. She recognized all this and also the singsong way he talked, slightly mocking, kidding, but serious and a little melancholy, and she recognized the way he tapped one fist against the other in homage to the perpetual music behind him. But all these things did not come together.

She said suddenly, "Hey, how old are you?"

His smile faded. She could see then that he wasn't a kid, he was much older—thirty, maybe more. At this knowledge her heart began to pound faster.

"That's a crazy thing to ask. Can'tcha see I'm your own age?"

"Like hell you are."

"Or maybe a coupla years older, I'm eighteen."

"Eighteen?" she said doubtfully.

He grinned to reassure her and lines appeared at the corners of his mouth. His teeth were big and white. He grinned so broadly his eyes became slits and she saw how thick the lashes were, thick and black as if painted with a black tar-like material. Then he seemed to become embarrassed, abruptly, and looked over his shoulder at Ellie. "*Him,* he's crazy," he said. "Ain't he a riot, he's a nut, a real character." Ellie was still listening to the music. His sunglasses told nothing about what he was thinking. He wore a bright orange shirt unbuttoned halfway to show his chest, which was a pale, bluish chest and not muscular like Arnold Friend's. His shirt collar was turned up all around and the very tips of the collar pointed out past his chin as if they were protecting him. He was pressing the transistor radio up against his ear and sat there in a kind of daze, right in the sun.

"He's kinda strange," Connie said.

"Hey, she says you're kinda strange! Kinda strange!" Arnold Friend cried. He pounded on the car to get Ellie's attention. Ellie turned for the first time and Connie saw with shock that he wasn't a kid either—he had a fair, hairless face, cheeks reddened slightly as if the veins grew too close to the surface of his skin, the face of a forty-year-old baby. Connie felt a wave of dizziness rise in her at this sight and she stared at him as if waiting for something to change the shock of the moment, make it all right again. Ellie's lips kept shaping words, mumbling along with the words blasting his ear.

"Maybe you two better go away," Connie said faintly.

"What? How come?" Arnold Friend cried. "We come out here to take you for a ride. It's Sunday." He had the voice of the man on the radio now. It was the same voice, Connie thought. "Don'tcha know it's Sunday all day and honey, no matter who you were with last night today you're with Arnold Friend and don't you forget it!—Maybe you better step out here," he said, and this last was in a different voice. It was a little flatter, as if the heat was finally getting to him.

"No. I got things to do."

"Hey."

"You two better leave."

"We ain't leaving until you come with us."

"Like hell I am—"

"Connie, don't fool around with me. I mean—I mean, don't fool *around,*" he said, shaking his head. He laughed incredulously. He placed his sunglasses on top of his head, carefully, as if he were indeed wearing a wig, and brought the stems down behind his ears. Connie stared at him, another wave of dizziness and fear rising in her so that for a moment he wasn't even in focus but was just a blur, standing there against his gold car, and she had the idea that he had driven up the driveway all right but had come from nowhere before that and belonged nowhere and that everything about him and even the music that was so familiar to her was only half real.

"If my father comes and sees you—"

"He ain't coming. He's at a barbecue."

"How do you know that?"

"Aunt Tillie's. Right now they're—uh—they're drinking. Sitting around," he said vaguely, squinting as if he were staring all the way to town and over to Aunt Tillie's back yard. Then the vision seemed to clear and he nodded energetically. "Yeah. Sitting around. There's your sister in a blue dress, huh? And high heels, the poor sad bitch—nothing like you, sweetheart! And your mother's helping some fat woman with the corn, they're cleaning the corn—husking the corn—"

"What fat woman?" Connie cried.

"How do I know what fat woman. I don't know every goddamn fat woman in the world!" Arnold Friend laughed.

"Oh, that's Mrs. Hornby. . . . Who invited her?" Connie said. She felt a little light-headed. Her breath was coming quickly.

"She's too fat. I don't like them fat. I like them the way you are, honey," he said, smiling sleepily at her. They stared at each other for a while, through the screen door. He said softly, "Now what you're going to do is this: you're going to come out that door. You're going to sit up front with me and Ellie's going to sit in the back, the hell with Ellie, right? This isn't Ellie's date. You're my date. I'm your lover, honey."

"What? You're crazy—"

"Yes, I'm your lover. You don't know what that is but you will," he said. "I know that too. I know all about you. But look: it's real nice and you couldn't ask for nobody better than me, or more polite. I always keep my word. I'll tell you how it is, I'm always nice at first, the first time. I'll hold you so tight you won't think you have to try to get away or pretend anything because you'll know you can't. And I'll come inside you where it's all secret and you'll give in to me and you'll love me—"

"Shut up! You're crazy!" Connie said. She backed away from the door. She put her hands against her ears as if she'd heard something terrible, something not meant for her. "People don't talk like that, you're crazy," she muttered. Her heart was almost too big now for her chest and its pumping made sweat break out all over her. She looked out to see Arnold Friend pause and then take a step toward the porch lurching. He almost fell. But, like a clever drunken man, he managed to catch his balance. He wobbled in his high boots and grabbed hold of one of the porch posts.

"Honey?" he said. "You still listening?"

"Get the hell out of here!"

"Be nice, honey. Listen."

"I'm going to call the police—"

He wobbled again and out of the side of his mouth came a fast spat curse, an aside not meant for her to hear. But even this "Christ!" sounded forced. Then he began to smile again. She watched this smile come, awkward as if he were smiling from inside a mask. His whole face was a mask, she thought wildly, tanned down onto his throat but then running out as if he had plastered make-up on his face but had forgotten about his throat.

"Honey—? Listen, here's how it is. I always tell the truth and I promise you this: I ain't coming in that house after you."

"You better not! I'm going to call the police if you—if you don't—"

"Honey," he said, talking right through her voice, "honey, I'm not coming in there but you are coming out here. You know why?"

She was panting. The kitchen looked like a place she had never seen before, some room she had run inside but which wasn't good enough, wasn't going to help her. The kitchen window had never had a curtain, after three years, and there were dishes in the sink for her to do—probably—and if you ran your hand across the table you'd probably feel something sticky there.

"You listening, honey? Hey?"

"—going to call the police—"

"Soon as you touch the phone I don't need to keep my promise and can come inside. You won't want that."

She rushed forward and tried to lock the door. Her fingers were shaking. "But why lock it," Arnold Friend said gently, talking right into her face. "It's just a screen door. It's just nothing." One of his boots was at a strange angle, as if his foot wasn't in it. It pointed out to the left, bent at the ankle. "I mean, anybody can break through a screen door and glass and wood and iron or anything else if he needs to, anybody at all and specially Arnold Friend. If the place got lit up with a fire, honey, you'd come running out into my arms, right into my arms an' safe at home—like you knew I was your lover and'd stopped fooling around, I don't mind a nice shy girl but I don't like no fooling around." Part of those words were spoken with a slight rhythmic lilt, and Connie somehow recognized them—the echo of a song from last year, about a girl rushing into her boy friend's arms and coming home again—

Connie stood barefoot on the linoleum floor, staring at him. "What do you want?" she whispered.

"I want you," he said.

"What?"

"Seen you that night and thought, that's the one, yes sir. I never needed to look any more."

"But my father's coming back. He's coming to get me. I had to wash my hair first—" She spoke in a dry, rapid voice, hardly raising it for him to hear.

"No, your daddy is not coming and yes, you had to wash your hair and you washed it for me. It's nice and shining and all for me. I thank you, sweetheart," he said, with a mock bow, but again he almost lost his balance. He had to bend and adjust his boots. Evidently his feet did not go all the way down; the boots must have been stuffed with something so that he would seem taller. Connie stared out at him and behind him at Ellie in the car, who seemed to be looking off toward Connie's right, into nothing. This Ellie said, pulling the words out of the air one after another as if he were just discovering them, "You want me to pull out the phone?"

"Shut your mouth and keep it shut," Arnold Friend said, his face red from bending over or maybe from embarrassment because Connie had seen his boots. "This ain't none of your business."

"What—what are you doing? What do you want?" Connie said. "If I call the police they'll get you, they'll arrest you—"

"Promise was not to come in unless you touch that phone, and I'll keep that promise," he said. He resumed his erect position and tried to force his shoulders back. He sounded like a hero in a movie, declaring something important. He spoke too loudly and it was as if he were speaking to someone behind Connie. "I ain't made plans for coming in that house where I don't belong but just for you to come out to me, the way you should. Don't you know who I am?"

"You're crazy," she whispered. She backed away from the door but did not want to go into another part of the house, as if this would give him permission to come through the door. "What do you. . . . You're crazy, you. . . ."

"Huh? What're you saying, honey?"

Her eyes darted everywhere in the kitchen. She could not remember what it was, this room.

"This is how it is, honey: you come out and we'll drive away, have a nice ride. But if you don't come out we're gonna wait till your people come home and then they're all going to get it."

"You want that telephone pulled out?" Ellie said. He held the radio away from his ear and grimaced, as if without the radio the air was too much for him.

"I toldja shut up, Ellie," Arnold Friend said, "You're deaf, get a hearing aid, right? Fix yourself up. This little girl's no trouble and's gonna be nice to me, so Ellie keep to yourself, this ain't your date—right? Don't hem in on me, don't hog, don't crush, don't bird dog, don't trail me," he said in a rapid, meaningless voice, as if he were running through all the expressions he'd learned but was no longer sure which one of them was in style, then rushing on to new ones, making them up with his eyes closed. "Don't crawl under my fence, don't squeeze in my chipmunk hole, don't sniff my glue, suck my popsicle, keep your own greasy fingers on yourself!" He shaded his eyes and peered in at Connie, who was backed against the kitchen table. "Don't mind him, honey, he's just a creep. He's a dope. Right? I'm the boy for you and like I said, you come out here nice like a lady and give me your hand, and nobody else gets hurt, I mean, your nice old bald-headed daddy and your mummy and your sister in her high heels. Because listen: why bring them in this?"

"Leave me alone," Connie whispered.

"Hey, you know that old woman down the road, the one with the chickens and stuff—you know her?"

"She's dead!"

"Dead? What? You know her?" Arnold Friend said.

"She's dead—"

"Don't you like her?"

"She's dead—she's—she isn't here any more—"

"But don't you like her, I mean, you got something against her? Some grudge or something?" Then his voice dipped as if he were conscious of rudeness. He touched the sunglasses on top of his head as if to make sure they were still there. "Now you be a good girl."

"What are you going to do?"

"Just two things, or maybe three," Arnold Friend said. "But I promise it won't last long and you'll like me that way you get to like people you're close to. You will. It's all over for you here, so come on out. You don't want your people in any trouble, do you?"

She turned and bumped against a chair or something, hurting her leg, but she ran into the back room and picked up the telephone. Something roared in her ear, a tiny roaring, and she was so sick with fear that she could do nothing but listen to it—the telephone was clammy and very heavy and her fingers groped down to the dial but were too weak to touch it. She began to scream into the phone, into the roaring. She cried out, she cried for her mother, she felt her breath start jerking back and forth in her lungs as if it were something Arnold Friend was stabbing her with again and again with no tenderness. A noisy sorrowful wailing rose all about her and she was locked inside it the way she was locked inside this house.

After a while she could hear again. She was sitting on the floor, with her wet back against the wall.

Arnold Friend was saying from the door, "That's a good girl. Put the phone back."

She kicked the phone away from her.

"No, honey. Pick it up. Put it back right."

She picked it up and put it back. The dial tone stopped.

"That's a good girl. Now you come outside."

She was hollow with what had been fear but what was now just an emptiness. All that screaming had blasted it out of her. She sat, one leg cramped under her, and deep inside her brain was something like a pinpoint of light that kept going and would not let her relax. She thought, I'm not going to see my mother again. She thought, I'm not going to sleep in my bed again. Her bright green blouse was all wet.

Arnold Friend said, in a gentle-loud voice that was like a stage voice, "The place where you came from ain't there any more, and where you had in mind to go is cancelled out. This place you are now—inside your daddy's house—is nothing but a cardboard box I can knock down any time. You know that and always did know it. You hear me?"

She thought, I have got to think. I have got to know what to do.

"We'll go out to a nice field, out in the country here where it smells so nice and it's sunny," Arnold Friend said. "I'll have my arms tight around you so you won't need to try to get away and I'll show you what love is like, what it does. The hell with this house! It looks solid all right," he said. He ran a fingernail down the screen and the noise did not make Connie shiver, as it would have the day before. "Now put your hand on your heart, honey. Feel that? That feels solid too but we know better. Be nice to me, be sweet like you can because what else is there for a girl like you but to be sweet and pretty and give in?—and get away before her people come back?"

She felt her pounding heart. Her hands seemed to enclose it. She thought for the first time in her life that it was nothing that was hers, that belonged to her, but just a pounding, living thing inside this body that wasn't hers either.

"You don't want them to get hurt," Arnold Friend went on. "Now get up, honey. Get up all by yourself."

She stood.

"Now turn this way. That's right. Come over to me—Ellie, put that away, didn't I tell you? You dope. You miserable creepy dope," Arnold Friend said. His words were not angry but only part of an incantation. The incantation was kindly. "Now come out through the kitchen to me honey and let's see a smile, try it, you're a brave sweet little girl and now they're eating corn and hotdogs cooked to bursting over an outdoor fire, and they don't know one thing about you and never did and honey you're better than them because not one of them would have done this for you."

Connie felt the linoleum under her feet; it was cool. She brushed her hair back out of her eyes. Arnold Friend let go of the post tentatively and opened his arms for her, his elbows pointing up toward each other and his wrist limp, to show that this was an embarrassed embrace and a little mocking, he didn't want to make her self-conscious.

She put out her hand against the screen. She watched herself push the door slowly open as if she were safe back somewhere in the other doorway, watching this body and this head of long hair moving out into the sunlight where Arnold Friend waited.

"My sweet little blue-eyed girl," he said in a half-sung sigh that had nothing to do with her brown eyes but was taken up just the same by the vast sunlit reaches of the land behind him and on all sides of him, so much land that Connie had never seen before and did not recognize except to know that she was going to it.

[1966]

Jo Ann Beard

Jo Ann Beard is an essayist and author of the collection, "The Boys of My Youth" (1999). She is a graduate of the Nonfiction Writing Program at the University of Iowa and received a Whiting Foundation Award in 1997. Her essay, "The Fourth State of Matter," was first published in The New Yorker *in 1996 and was included in* Best American Essays, *1997. She lives in New York state.*

The Fourth State of Matter

The collie wakes me up about three times a night, summoning me from a great distance as I row my boat through a dim, complicated dream. She's on the shoreline, barking. Wake up. She's staring at me with her head slightly tipped to the side, long nose, gazing eyes, toenails clenched to get a purchase on the wood floor. We used to call her the face of love.

She totters on her broomstick legs into the hallway and over the doorsill into the kitchen, makes a sharp left at the refrigerator—careful, almost went down—then a straightaway to the door. I sleep on my feet in the cold of the doorway, waiting. Here she comes. Lift her down the two steps. She pees and then stands, Lassie in a ratty coat, gazing out at the yard.

In the porch light the trees shiver, the squirrels turn over in their sleep. The Milky Way is a long smear on the sky, like something erased on a blackboard. Over the neighbor's house, Mars flashes white, then red, then white again. Jupiter is hidden among the anonymous blinks and glitterings. It has a moon with sulfur-spewing volcanoes and a beautiful name: Io. I learned it at work, from the group of men who surround me there. Space physicists, guys who spend days on end with their heads poked through the fabric of the sky, listening to the sounds of the universe. Guys whose own lives are ticking like alarm clocks getting ready to go off, although none of us are aware of it yet.

The dog turns and looks, waits to be carried up the two steps. Inside the house she drops like a shoe onto her blanket, a thud, an adjustment. I've climbed back under my covers already but her leg's stuck underneath her, we can't get comfortable. I fix the leg, she rolls over and sleeps. Two hours later I wake up and she's gazing at me in the darkness. The face of love. She wants to go out again. I give her a boost, balance her on her legs. Right on time: 3:40 A.M.

There are squirrels living in the spare bedroom upstairs. Three dogs also live in this house, but they were invited. I keep the door of the spare bedroom shut at all times, because of the squirrels and because that's where the vanished husband's belongings are stored. Two of the dogs—the smart little brown mutt and the Labrador—spend hours sitting patiently outside the door, waiting for it to be opened so they can dismantle the squirrels. The collie can no longer make it up the stairs, so she lies at the bottom and snores or stares in an interested manner at the furniture around her.

I can take almost anything at this point. For instance, that my vanished husband is neither here nor there; he's reduced himself to a troubled voice on the telephone three or four times a day.

Or that the dog at the bottom of the stairs keeps having mild strokes, which cause her to tilt her head inquisitively and also to fall over. She drinks prodigious amounts of water and pees great volumes onto the folded blankets where she sleeps. Each time this happens I stand her up, dry her off, put fresh blankets underneath her, carry the peed-on blankets down to the basement, stuff them into the washer and then into the dryer. By the time I bring them back upstairs they are needed again. The first few times this happened, I found the dog trying to stand up, gazing with frantic concern at her own rear. I praised her and patted her head and gave her treats until she settled down. Now I know whenever it happens, because I hear her tail thumping against the floor in anticipation of reward. In retraining her I've somehow retrained myself, bustling cheerfully down to the basement, arms drenched in urine, the task of doing load after load of laundry strangely satisfying. She is Pavlov and I am her dog.

I'm fine about the vanished husband's boxes stored in the spare bedroom. For now, the boxes and the phone calls convince me, that things could turn around at any moment. The boxes are filled with thirteen years of his pack-ratness: statistics textbooks that still harbor an air of desperation; smarmy suit coats from the Goodwill; various old Halloween masks and one giant black papier-mâché thing he made that was supposed to be Elvis's hair but didn't turn out. A collection of ancient Rolling Stones T-shirts. You know he's turning over a new leaf when he leaves the Rolling Stones behind.

What I can't take is the squirrels. They come alive at night, throwing terrific parties in the spare bedroom, making thumps and crashes. Occasionally a high-pitched squeal is heard amid bumps and the sound of scrabbling toenails. I've begun sleeping downstairs, on the blue vinyl dog couch, the sheets slipping off, my skin stuck to the cushions. This is an affront to the two younger dogs, who know the couch belongs to them; as soon as I settle in, they creep up and find their places between my knees and elbows.

I'm on the couch because the dog on the blanket gets worried at night. During the day she sleeps the catnappy sleep of the elderly, but when it gets dark her eyes open and she is agitated, trying to stand whenever I leave the room, settling down only when I'm next to her. We are in this together, the dying game, and I read for hours in the evening with one foot on her back, getting up only to open a new can of beer or take blankets to the basement. At some point I stretch out on the vinyl couch and close my eyes, one hand hanging down, touching her side. By morning the dog arm has become a nerveless club that doesn't come around until noon. My friends think I'm nuts.

One night, for hours, the dog won't lie down. I call my office pal, Mary, and wake her up. "*I'm weary*," I say, in italics.

Mary listens, sympathetic, on the other end. "Oh my God," she finally says. "*What* are you going to do?"

I calm down immediately. "Exactly what I'm doing," I tell her. The dog finally parks herself with a thump on the stack of damp blankets. She sets her nose down and tips her eyes up to watch me. We all sleep then, for a bit, while the squirrels sort through the boxes overhead and the dog on the blanket keeps nervous watch.

I've called in tired to work. It's midmorning and I'm shuffling around in my long underwear, smoking cigarettes and drinking coffee. The whole house is bathed in sunlight and the faint odor of used diapers. The dogs are being mild-mannered and charming; I nudge the collie with my foot.

"Wake up and smell zee bacons," I say. She lifts her nose groggily and falls back asleep. I get ready for the office.

"I'm leaving and I'm never coming back," I say while putting on my coat. I use my mother's aggrieved, underappreciated tone. The little brown dog transfers her gaze from me to the table, the last place she remembers seeing toast. The Labrador, who understands English, begins howling miserably. She wins the toast sweepstakes and is chewing loudly when I leave, the little dog barking ferociously at her.

At the office, there are three blinks on the answering machine, the first from a scientist who speaks very slowly, like a kindergarten teacher, asking about reprints. "What am I, the village idiot?" I ask the room, taking down his number in large backward characters. The second and third blinks are from my husband, the across-town apartment dweller.

The first of his calls makes my heart lurch in a hopeful way. "I have to talk to you right *now*," he says grimly. "Where *are* you? I can never find you."

"Try calling your own house," I say to the machine. In his second message he has composed himself.

"I'm *fine* now," he says firmly. "Disregard previous message and don't call me back, please; I have meetings." Click, dial tone, rewind.

My leaping heart settles back into its hole in my chest. I say "Damn it" out loud, just as Chris strides into the office.

"What?" he asks defensively. He tries to think if he's done anything wrong recently. He checks the table for work; things are in good shape. A graduate student, Gang Lu, stops by to drop off some reports. Chris and I have a genial relationship these days, reading the paper together in the mornings, congratulating ourselves on each issue of the journal. It's a space-physics monthly, and he's the editor and I'm the managing editor. I know nothing about the science part; my job is to shepherd the manuscripts through the review process and create a journal out of the acceptable ones.

Christoph Goertz. He's hip in a professorial, cardigan/jeans kind of way. He's tall and lanky and white-haired, forty-seven years old, with an elegant trace of accent from his native Germany. He has a great dog, a giant black outlaw named Mica, who runs through the streets of Iowa City at night inspecting garbage cans. She's big and friendly but a bad judge of character, and frequently runs right into the arms of the dogcatcher. Chris is always bailing her out.

"They don't understand dogs," he says.

I spend more time with Chris than I ever did with my husband. The morning I told him I was being dumped he was genuinely perplexed. "He's leaving *you*?" he asked.

Chris was drinking coffee, sitting at his table in front of the blackboard. Behind his head was a chalk drawing of a hip, professorial man holding a coffee cup. It was a collaborative effort; I had drawn the man and Chris framed him, using blue chalk and a straightedge. The two-dimensional man and the three-dimensional man stared at me intently.

"He's leaving *you*?" And for an instant I saw myself from their vantage point across the room—Jo Ann—and a small bubble of self-esteem percolated up from my depths. Chris shrugged. "You'll do fine," he said.

During my current turmoils I've come to think of work as my own kind of Zen practice, the constant barrage of paper hypnotic and soothing. Chris lets me work an eccentric schedule; in return I update his publications list for him and listen to stories about outer space.

Besides being an editor and a teacher, he's the head of a theoretical-plasma-physics team made up of graduate students and research scientists. He travels all over the world telling people about the magnetospheres of various planets, and when he comes back he brings me presents—a small bronze box from Africa with an alligator embossed on the top, a big piece of amber from Poland with the wings of flies preserved inside it, and, once, a set of delicate, horrifying bracelets made from the hide of an elephant.

Currently he is obsessed with the dust in the plasma of Saturn's rings. Plasma is the fourth state of matter. You've got your solid, your liquid, your gas, and then your plasma. In outer space there's the plasmasphere and the plasmapause. I avoid the math when I can and put a layperson's spin on these things.

"Plasma is blood," I told him.

"Exactly," he agreed, removing the comics page and handing it to me.

This is the kind of conversation we mostly have around the office, but today he's caught me at a weak moment, tucking my heart back inside my chest. I decide to be cavalier.

"I wish my *dog* was out tearing up the town and my *husband* was home sleeping on a blanket," I say.

Chris is neutral about my marriage problems, but he thinks the dog thing has gone far enough. "Why are you letting this go on?" he asks solemnly.

"I'm not *letting* it, that's why," I tell him. There are stacks of manuscripts everywhere, and he has all the pens over on his side of the room. "It just *is*, is all. Throw me a pen." He does, I miss it, stoop to pick it up, and when I straighten up again I might be crying.

"You have control over this," he explains in his professor voice. "You can decide how long she suffers."

This makes my heart pound. Absolutely not, I cannot do it. And then I weaken and say what I really want: for her to go to sleep and not wake up, just slip out of her skin and into the other world.

"Exactly," he says.

I have an ex-beauty queen coming over to get rid of the squirrels for me. She has long red hair and a smile that can stop trucks. I've seen her wrestle goats, scare off a giant snake, and express a dog's anal glands, all in one afternoon. I told her on the phone that a family of squirrels is living in the upstairs of my house.

"They're making a monkey out of me," I said.

So Caroline climbs into her car and drives across half the state, pulls up in front of my house, and gets out carrying zucchini, cigarettes, and a pair of big leather gloves. I'm sitting outside with my old dog, who lurches to her feet, staggers three steps, sits down, and falls over. Caroline starts crying.

"Don't try to give me zucchini," I say.

We sit companionably on the front stoop for a while, staring at the dog and smoking cigarettes. One time I went to Caroline's house and she was nursing a dead cat that was still breathing. At some point that afternoon, I saw her spoon baby food into its mouth, and as soon as she turned away the whole puréed mess plopped back out. A day later she took it to the vet and had it euthanized. I remind her of this.

"You'll do it when you do it," she says firmly.

I pick the collie up like a fifty-pound bag of sticks and feathers, stagger inside, place her on the damp blankets, and put the two other nutcases in the back yard. From upstairs comes a crash and a shriek. Caroline stares up at the ceiling.

"It's like having the Wallendas stay at your house," I say cheerfully. All of a sudden I feel fond of the squirrels and fond of Caroline and fond of myself for heroically calling her to help me. The phone rings four times. It's the husband, and his voice over the answering machine sounds frantic. He pleads with whoever Jo Ann is to pick up the phone.

"Please? I think I might be freaking out," he says. "Am I ruining my life here, or what? Am I making a *mistake*? Jo?" He breathes raggedly and sniffs into the receiver for a moment, then hangs up with a muffled clatter.

Caroline stares at the machine as if it's a copperhead.

"Holy fuckoly," she says, shaking her head. "You're *living* with this crap?"

"He wants me to reassure him that he's strong enough to leave me," I tell her. "Else he won't have fun on his bike ride. And guess what? I'm too tired to." But now I can see him in his dank little apartment, wringing his hands and staring out the windows. In his rickety dresser is the new package of condoms he accidentally showed me last week.

Caroline lights another cigarette. The dog pees and thumps her tail.

I need to call him back because he's suffering.

"You call him back and I'm forced to kill you," Caroline says. She exhales smoke and points to the phone. "That is evil shit."

I tend to agree. It's blanket time. I roll the collie off onto the floor and put the fresh blankets down, roll her back. Caroline has put on the leather gloves, which go all the way to her elbows. She's staring at the ceiling with determination.

The plan is that I'm supposed to separate one squirrel from the herd and get it in a corner. Caroline will take it from there. But when I'm in the room with her and the squirrels are running around, all I can do is scream. I'm not afraid of them, but my screaming button is on and the only way to turn it off is to leave the room.

"How are you doing?" I ask from the other side of the door. I can hear Caroline crashing around and swearing. The door opens and she falls out into the hall with a gray squirrel stuck to her glove. She clatters down the stairs and out the front door, and returns looking triumphant.

The collie appears at the foot of the stairs with her head cocked and her ears up. For an instant she looks like a puppy, then her feet start to slide. I run down and catch her and carry her upstairs so she can watch the show. The squirrels careen around the room, tearing the ancient wallpaper off the walls. The last one is a baby, so we keep it for a few minutes, looking at its little feet and its little tail. We show it to the collie, who stands up immediately and tries to get it.

Caroline patches the hole where they got in, cutting the wood with a power saw down in the basement. She comes up wearing a tool belt and lugging a ladder. I've seen a scrapbook of photos of her wearing evening gowns with a banner across her chest and a crown on her head. Curled hair, lipstick. She climbs down and puts the tools away. We eat nachos.

"I only make food that's boiled or melted these days," I tell her.

"I know," she replies.

The phone rings again, but whoever it is hangs up.

"Is it him?" she asks.

"Nope."

Caroline gestures toward the sleeping collie and remarks that it seems like just two days ago that she was a puppy.

"She was never a puppy," I tell her. "She's always been older than me."

When they say goodbye, Caroline holds the collie's long nose in one hand and kisses her on the forehead; the collie stares back at her gravely. Caroline is crying when she leaves, a combination of squirrel adrenaline and sadness. I cry, too, although I don't feel particularly bad about anything. I hand her the zucchini through the window and she pulls away from the curb.

The house is starting to get dark in that early-evening twilit way. I turn on lights and go upstairs. The black dog comes with me and circles the squirrel room, snorting loudly, nose to floor. There is a spot of turmoil in an open box—they made a nest in some disco shirts from the seventies. I suspect that's where the baby one slept. The mean landlady has evicted them.

Downstairs, I turn the lights back off and let evening have its way with me. Waves of pre-nighttime nervousness are coming from the collie's blanket. I sit next to her in the dimness, touching her ears, and listen for feet at the top of the stairs.

They're speaking in physics, so I'm left out of the conversation. Chris apologetically erases one of the pictures I've drawn on the blackboard and replaces it with a curving blue arrow surrounded by radiating chalk waves of green.

"If it's plasma, make it in red," I suggest. We're all smoking semi-illegally in the journal office with the door closed and the window open. We're having a plasma party.

"We aren't discussing *plasma*," Bob Smith says condescendingly. A stocky, short-tempered man, he's smoking a horrendously smelly pipe. The longer he stays in here, the more it feels as if I'm breathing small daggers in through my nose. He and I don't get along; each of us thinks the other needs to be taken down a peg. Once we had a hissing match in the hallway which ended with him suggesting that I could be fired, which drove me to tell him that he was *already* fired, and both of us stomped into our offices and slammed our doors.

"I had to fire Bob," I tell Chris later.

"I heard," he says. Bob is his best friend. They spend at least half of each day standing in front of blackboards, writing equations and arguing about outer space. Then they write theoretical papers about what they come up with. They're actually quite a big deal in the space-physics community, but around here they're just two guys who keep erasing my pictures.

Someone knocks on the door and we put our cigarettes out. Bob hides his pipe in the palm of his hand and opens the door.

It's Gang Lu, the doctoral student. Everyone lights up again. Gang Lu stands stiffly talking to Chris, while Bob holds a match to his pipe and puffs fiercely; nose daggers waft up and out, right in my direction. I give him a sugary smile and he gives me one back. Unimaginable, really, that less than two months from now one of his colleagues from abroad, a woman with delicate, birdlike features, will appear at the door to my office and identify herself as a friend of Bob's. When she asks, I take her down the hall to the room with the long table and then to his empty office. I do this without saying anything, because there's nothing to say, and she takes it all in with small, serious nods until the moment she sees his blackboard covered with scribbles and arrows and equations. At that point her face loosens and she starts to cry in long ragged sobs. An hour later, I go back and the office is empty. When I erase the blackboard finally, I can see where she laid her hands carefully, where the numbers are ghostly and blurred.

Bob blows his smoke discreetly in my direction and waits for Chris to finish talking to Gang Lu, who is answering questions in a monotone—yes or no or I don't know. Another Chinese student, Linhua Shan, lets himself in after knocking lightly. He nods and smiles at me and then stands at a respectful distance, waiting to ask Chris a question.

It's like a physics conference in here. I wish they'd all leave so I can make my usual midafternoon spate of personal calls. I begin thumbing through papers in a businesslike way.

Bob pokes at his pipe with a paper clip. Linhua Shan yawns hugely and then looks embarrassed. Chris erases what he put on the blackboard and tries unsuccessfully to redraw my pecking parakeet. "I don't know how it goes," he says to me.

Gang Lu looks around the room with expressionless eyes. He's sick of physics and sick of the buffoons who practice it. The tall glacial German, Chris, who tells him what to do; the crass idiot Bob, who talks to him as if he is a dog; the student Shan, whose ideas about plasma physics are treated with reverence and praised at every meeting. The woman who puts her feet on the desk and dismisses him with her eyes. Gang Lu no longer spends his evenings in the computer lab down the hall, running simulations and thinking about magnetic forces and invisible particles; he now spends them at the firing range, learning to hit a moving target with the gun he purchased last spring. He pictures himself holding the gun with both hands, arms straight out and steady; Clint Eastwood, only smarter.

He stares at each person in turn, trying to gauge how much respect each of them has for him. One by one. Behind black-rimmed glasses, he counts with his eyes. In each case the verdict is clear: not enough.

The collie fell down the basement stairs. I don't know if she was disoriented and was looking for me or what. But when I was at work she used her long nose like a lever and got the door open and tried to go down there, except her legs wouldn't do it and she fell. I found her sleeping on the concrete floor in an unnatural position, one leg still awkwardly resting on the last step. I repositioned the leg and sat down and petted her. We used to play a game called Maserati, where I'd grab her long nose like a gearshift and put her through all the gears—first second third fourth—until we were going a hundred miles an hour through town. She thought it was funny.

Friday, I'm at work, but this morning there's not much to do, and every time I turn around I see her sprawled, eyes mute, leg bent upward. We're breaking each other's heart. I draw a picture of her on the blackboard using brown chalk. I make X's where her eyes should be. Chris walks in with the morning paper and a cup of coffee. He looks around the clean office.

"Why are you here when there's no work to do?" he asks.

"I'm hiding from my life, what else?" This sounds perfectly reasonable to him. He gives me part of the paper.

His mother is visiting from Germany; she's a robust woman of eighty who is depressed and hoping to be cheered up. In the last year she has lost her one-hundred-year-old mother and her husband of sixty years. She can't be really cheered up, but she likes going to art galleries, so Chris has been driving her around the Midwest, to our best cities, showing her what kind of art Americans like to look at.

"How's your mom?" I ask him.

He shrugs and makes a flat-handed "so-so" motion.

We read, smoke, drink coffee, and yawn. I decide to go home.

"Good idea," he says.

It's November 1, 1991, the last day of the first part of my life. Before I leave, I pick up the eraser and stand in front of the collie's picture on the blackboard, thinking. I can feel Chris watching me, drinking his coffee. His long legs are crossed, his eyes are mild. He has a wife named Ulrike, a daughter named Karein, and a son named Göran. A dog named Mica. A mother named Ursula. A friend named me.

I erase the X's.

Down the hall, Linhua Shan feeds numbers into a computer and watches as a graph is formed. The computer screen is brilliant blue, and the lines appear in red and yellow and green. Four keystrokes and the green becomes purple, the blue background fades to the azure of a summer sky. The wave lines arc over it, crossing against one another. He asks the computer to print, and while it chugs along he pulls up a golf game on the screen and tees off.

One room over, at a desk, Gang Lu works on a letter to his sister in China. *The study of physics is more and more disappointing*, he tells her. *Modern physics is self-delusion*, and *All my life I have been honest and straightforward, and I have most of all detested cunning, fawning sycophants and dishonest bureaucrats who think they are always right in everything.* Delicate Chinese characters all over a page. She was a kind and gentle sister, and he thanks her for that. He's going to kill himself. *You yourself should not be too sad about it, for at least I have found a few traveling companions to accompany me to the grave.* Inside the coat on the back of his chair are a .38-caliber handgun and a .22-caliber revolver. They're heavier than they look and weigh the pockets down. *My beloved second elder sister, I take my eternal leave of you.*

The collie's eyes are almond-shaped; I draw them in with brown chalk and put a white bone next to her feet.

"That's better," Chris says kindly.

Before I leave the building I pass Gang Lu in the hallway and say hello. He has a letter in his hand and he's wearing his coat. He doesn't answer, and I don't expect him to. At the end of the hallway are the double doors leading to the rest of my life. I push them open and walk through.

Friday afternoon seminar, everyone is glazed over, listening as someone at the head of the long table explains something unexplainable. Gang Lu stands up and leaves the room abruptly, goes down one floor to see if the department chairman, Dwight, is sitting in his office. He is. The door is open. Gang Lu turns, walks back up the stairs, and enters the seminar room again. Chris Goertz is sitting near the door and takes the first bullet in the back of the head. There is a loud popping sound and then blue smoke. Linhua Shan gets the second bullet in the forehead; the lenses of his glasses shatter. More smoke and the room rings with the popping. Bob Smith tries to crawl beneath the table. Gang Lu takes two steps, holds his arms straight out, and levels the gun with both hands. Bob looks up. The third bullet in the right hand, the fourth in the chest. Smoke. Elbows and legs, people trying to get out of the way and then out of the room.

Gang Lu walks quickly down the stairs, expelling spent cartridges and loading new ones. From the doorway of Dwight's office: the fifth bullet in the head, the sixth strays, the seventh also in the head. A slumping. More smoke and ringing. Through the cloud an image comes to him—Bob Smith, hit in the chest, hit in the hand, still alive. Back up the stairs. Two scientists, young men, crouch over Bob, loosening his clothes, talking to him. From where he lies, Bob can see his best friend still sitting upright in a chair, head thrown back at an unnatural angle. Everything is broken and red. The two young scientists leave the room at gunpoint. Bob closes his eyes. The eighth and ninth bullets in his head. As Bob dies, Chris Goertz's body settles in his chair, a long sigh escapes his throat. Reload. Two more for Chris, one for Linhua Shan. Exit the building, cross two streets and the green, into the second building and up the stairs.

The administrator, Anne Cleary, is summoned from her office by the receptionist. She speaks to him for a few minutes, he produces a gun and shoots her in the face. The receptionist, a young student working as a temp, is just beginning to stand when he shoots her. He expels the spent cartridges in the stairwell, loads new ones. Reaches the top of the steps, looks around. Is disoriented suddenly. The ringing and the smoke and the dissatisfaction of not checking all the names off the list. A slamming and a running sound, the shout of police. He walks into an empty conference room, takes off his coat, folds it carefully, and puts it over the back of a chair. Checks his watch: twelve minutes since it began. Places the barrel against his right temple. Fires.

The first call comes at four o'clock. I'm reading on the bench in the kitchen, one foot on a sleeping dog's back. It's Mary, calling from work. There's been some kind of disturbance in the building, a rumor that Dwight was shot; cops are running through the halls carrying rifles. They're evacuating the building and she's coming over. Dwight, a tall, likable oddball who cut off his ponytail when they made him chair of the department. Greets everyone with a famous booming hello in the morning; studies plasma, just like Chris and Bob. Chris lives two and a half blocks from the physics building; he'll be home by now if they've evacuated. I dial his house and his mother answers. She tells me that Chris won't be home until five, and then they're going to a play. Ulrike, her daughter-in-law, is coming back from a trip to Chicago and will join them. She wants to know why I'm looking for Chris—isn't he where I am?

No, I'm at home and I just had to ask him something. Could he please call me when he comes in.

She tells me that Chris showed her a drawing I made of him sitting at his desk behind a stack of manuscripts. She's so pleased to meet Chris's friends, and the Midwest is lovely, really, except it's very brown, isn't it?

It *is* very brown. We hang up.

The Midwest is very brown. The phone rings. It's a physicist. His wife, a friend of mine, is on the extension. Well, he's not sure, but it's possible that I should brace myself for bad news. I've already heard, I tell him—something happened to Dwight. There's a long pause, and then his wife says, "Jo Ann. It's possible that Chris was involved."

I think she means Chris shot Dwight. "No," she says gently. "Killed, too."

Mary is here. I tell them not to worry and hang up. I have two cigarettes going. Mary takes one and smokes it. She's not looking at me. I tell her about the phone call.

"They're out of it," I say. "They thought Chris was involved."

She repeats what they said: "I think you should brace yourself for bad news." Pours whiskey into a coffee cup.

For a few minutes I can't sit down, I can't stand up. I can only smoke. The phone rings. Another physicist tells me there's some bad news. He mentions Chris and Bob and I tell him I don't want to talk right now. He says O.K. but to be prepared because it's going to be on the news any minute. It's 4:45.

"Now they're trying to stir Bob into the stew," I tell Mary. She nods; she's heard this, too. I have the distinct feeling there is something going on that I can either understand or not understand. There's a choice to be made.

"I don't understand," I tell Mary.

We sit in the darkening living room, smoking and sipping our cups of whiskey. Inside my head I keep thinking, Uh-oh, over and over. I'm rattled; I can't calm down and figure this out.

"I think we should brace ourselves in case something bad has happened," I say to Mary. She nods. "Just in case. It won't hurt to be braced." I realize that I don't know what "braced" means. You hear it all the time, but that doesn't mean it makes sense. Whiskey is supposed to be bracing, but what it is is awful. I want either tea or beer, no whiskey. Mary nods again and heads into the kitchen.

Within an hour there are seven women in the dim living room, sitting. Switching back and forth between CNN and the local news reports. There is something terrifying about the quality of the light and the way voices are echoing in the room. The phone never stops ringing, ever since the story hit the national news. Physics, University of Iowa, dead people. Names not yet released. Everyone I've ever known is checking in to see if I'm still alive. California calls, New York calls, Florida calls, Ohio calls twice. My husband is having a party and all his guests call, one after another, to ask how I'm doing. Each time, fifty times, I think it might be Chris and then it isn't.

It occurs to me once that I could call his house and talk to him directly, find out exactly what happened. Fear that his mother would answer prevents me from doing it. By this time I am getting reconciled to the fact that Linhua Shan, Gang Lu, and Dwight Nicholson were killed. Also an administrator and her office assistant. The Channel 9 newswoman keeps saying there are five dead and two in critical condition. The names will be released at nine o'clock. Eventually I sacrifice all of them except Chris and Bob; *they* are the ones in critical condition, which is certainly not hopeless. At some point I go into the study to get away from the terrible dimness in the living room—all those eyes, all that calmness in the face of chaos. The collie tries to stand up, but someone stops her with a handful of Fritos.

The study is small and cold after I shut the door, but more brightly lit than the living room. I can't remember what anything means. The phone rings and I pick up the extension and listen. My friend Michael is calling from Illinois for the second time. He asks Shirley if I'm holding up O.K. Shirley says it's hard to tell. I go back into the living room.

The newswoman breaks in at nine o'clock, and of course they drag it out as long as they can. I've already figured out that if they go in alphabetical order Chris will come first: Goertz, Lu, Nicholson, Shan, Smith. His name will come on first. She drones on, dead University of Iowa professors, lone gunman named Gang Lu.

Gang Lu. Lone gunman. Before I have a chance to absorb that, she says, The dead are.

Chris's picture.

Oh no, oh God. I lean against Mary's chair and then leave the room abruptly. I have to stand in the bathroom for a while and look at myself in the mirror. I'm still Jo Ann, white face and dark hair. I have earrings on, tiny wrenches that hang from wires. In the living room she's pronouncing all the other names. The two critically wounded are the administrator and her assistant, Miya Rodolfo-Sioson. The administrator is already dead for all practical purposes, although they won't disconnect the machines until the following afternoon. The student receptionist will survive but will never again be able to move much more than her head. She was in Gang Lu's path and he shot her and the bullet lodged in the top of her spine and she will never dance or walk or spend a day alone. She got to keep her head but lost her body. The final victim is Chris's mother, who will weather it all with a dignified face and an erect spine, then return to Germany and kill herself without further words or fanfare.

I tell the white face in the mirror that Gang Lu did this, wrecked everything and murdered all those people. It seems as ludicrous as everything else. I can't get my mind to work right. I'm still operating on yesterday's facts; today hasn't jelled yet. "It's a good thing none of this happened," I say to my face. A knock on the door, and I open it.

Julene's hesitant face. "She wanted to come visit you," she tells me. I bring the collie in and close the door. We sit by the tub. She lifts her long nose to my face and I take her muzzle and we move through the gears slowly—first second third fourth—all the way through town, until what happened has happened and we know it has happened. We return to the living room. The second wave of calls is starting to come in, from people who just saw the faces on the news. Shirley screens. A knock comes on the door. Julene settles the dog down again on her blanket. It's the husband at the door, looking distraught. He hugs me hard, but I'm made of cement, arms stuck in a down position.

The women immediately clear out, taking their leave, looking at the floor. Suddenly it's only me and him, sitting in our living room on a Friday night, just like always. I realize it took courage for him to come to the house when he did, facing all those women who think he's the Antichrist. The dogs are crowded against him on the couch and he's wearing a shirt I've never seen before. He's here to help me get through this. Me. He knows how awful this must be. Awful. He knows how I felt about Chris. Past tense. I have to put my hands over my face for a minute.

We sit silently in our living room. He watches the mute television screen and I watch him. The planes and ridges of his face are more familiar to me than my own. I understand that he wishes even more than I do that he still loved me. When he looks over at me, it's with an expression I've seen before. It's the way he looks at the dog on the blanket.

I get his coat and follow him out into the cold November night. There are stars and stars and stars. The sky is full of dead men, drifting in the blackness like helium balloons. My mother floats past in a hospital gown, trailing tubes. I go back inside where the heat is.

The house is empty and dim, full of dogs and cigarette butts. The collie has peed again. The television is flickering "Special Report" across the screen and I turn it off before the pictures appear. I bring blankets up, fresh and warm from the dryer.

After all the commotion the living room feels cavernous and dead. A branch scrapes against the house, and for a brief instant I feel a surge of hope. They might have come back. And I stand at the foot of the stairs staring up into the darkness, listening for the sounds of their little squirrel feet. Silence. No matter how much you miss them. They never come back once they're gone.

I wake her up three times between midnight and dawn. She doesn't usually sleep this soundly, but all the chaos and company in the house tonight have made her more tired than usual. The Lab wakes and drowsily begins licking her lower region. She stops and stares at me, trying to make out my face in the dark, then gives up and sleeps. The brown dog is flat on her back with her paws limp, wedged between me and the back of the couch.

I've propped myself so I'll be able to see when dawn starts to arrive. For now there are still planets and stars. Above the black branches of a maple is the Dog Star, Sirius, my personal favorite. The dusty rings of Saturn. Io, Jupiter's moon.

When I think I can't bear it for one more minute I reach down and nudge her gently with my dog arm. She rises slowly, faltering, and stands over me in the darkness. My peer, my colleague. In a few hours the world will resume itself, but for now we're in a pocket of silence. We're in the plasmapause, a place of equilibrium, where the forces of the earth meet the forces of the sun. I imagine it as a place of stillness, where the particles of dust stop spinning and hang motionless in deep space.

Around my neck is the stone he brought me from Poland. I hold it out. *Like this?* I ask. Shards of fly wings, suspended in amber.

Exactly, he says.

Carolyn Forché

Carolyn Forché (1950-) writes and translates poetry. Her first poetry collection, Gathering the Tribes *(1976), was chosen for the Yale Younger Poets Series. Forché edited the anthology,* Against Forgetting: Twentieth-Century Poetry of Witness *(1993) and the collection,* El Salvador: Work of Thirty Photographers *(1983). Her other books of poetry include* The Country between Us *(1981), in which "The Colonel" appears;* The Angel of History *(1994); and* Blue Hour *(2003). Forché has taught at several universities and now holds the Lannan Chair in Poetry at Georgetown University and is the acting director of the Lannan Center for Poetry and Poetics.*

Introduction to Against Forgetting: *Twentieth Century Poetry of Witness* The Colonel

In 1944, the Hungarian poet Miklós Radnóti was sent to a forced-labor camp in what became Yugoslavia. While there, he was able to procure a small notebook, in which he wrote his last ten poems, along with the following message in Hungarian, Croatian, German, French, and English: " . . . [this] contains the poems of the Hungarian poet Miklós Radnóti . . . to Mr. Gyula Ortutay, Budapest University lecturer . . . . Thank you in advance."

When it was clear that they would be defeated, the Germans decided to evacuate the camp and return the workers to Hungary. Radnóti, assuming that the first column would be the safest, volunteered for the march and recorded it in his poetry. Once in Hungary, the soldiers in charge, unable to find hospital room for these prisoners, took Radnóti and twenty-one others to a mass grave and executed them. Had Radnóti not volunteered to return to Hungary, he might have been saved by Marshal Tito's partisans. However, the story does not end—as millions of such stories ended—with execution and the anonymity of a mass grave. After the war was over, Radnóti's wife was among those who found and exhumed the mass grave in the village of Abda. The coroner's report for corpse #12 read: A visiting card with the name Dr. Miklós Radnóti printed on it. An ID card stating the mother's name as Ilona Grosz. Father's name illegible. Born in Budapest, May 5, 1909. Cause of death: shot in the nape. In the back pocket of the trousers a small notebook was found soaked in the fluids of the body and blackened by wet earth. This was cleaned and dried in the sun.

Radnóti's final poems are represented in this anthology, along with the poems of 144 other significant poets who endured conditions of historical and social

458

extremity during the twentieth century—through exile, state censorship, political persecution, house arrest, torture, imprisonment, military occupation, warfare, and assassination. Many poets did not survive, but their works remain with us as poetic witness to the dark times in which they lived.

This attempt to assemble such work in a single volume is the result of a thirteen-year effort to understand the impress of extremity upon the poetic imagination. My own journey began in 1980, upon my return from El Salvador—where I had worked as a human rights activist—and led me through the occupied West Bank, Lebanon, and South Africa. Something happened along the way to the introspective poet I had been. My new work seemed controversial to my American contemporaries, who argued against its "subject matter," or against the right of a North American to contemplate such issues in her work, or against any mixing of what they saw as the mutually exclusive realms of the personal and the political. Like many other poets, I felt that I had no real choice regarding the impulse of my poems, and had only to wait, in meditative expectancy. In attempting to come to terms with the question of poetry and politics, and seeking the solace of poetic camaraderie, I turned to the works of Anna Akhmatova, Yannis Ritsos, Paul Celan, Federico García Lorca, Nazim Hikmet, and others. I began collecting their work, and soon found myself a repository of what began to be called "the poetry of witness." In thinking about these poems, I realized that the arguments about poetry and politics had been too narrowly defined. Regardless of "subject matter," these poems bear the trace of extremity within them, and they are, as such, evidence of what occured. They are also poems which are as much "about" language as are poems that have no subject other than language itself.

This anthological history of our century begins with the genocide of the Armenians and follows extremity in its various forms. The volume is arranged in sections according to regions and major events, with historical headnotes. Within each section, poets appear in chronological order by date of birth, with biographical notes to illuminate the experience of extremity for each poet, and a selection of poetry from available works in the English originals or in translation. The criteria for inclusion were these: poets must have personally endured such conditions; they must be considered important to their national literatures; and their work, if not in English, must be available in a quality translation. The necessarily brief biographies included here provide information relevant to the poets' experience of extremity. In instances where it was possible to place poets in more than one section, they appear according to their first significant experience of this kind, even though their poems might reflect later experiences as well. Finally, not all poems address extreme conditions, nor do all appear relevant in terms of their subject matter. I was interested in what these poets wrote, regardless of the explicit content.

This collection reflects the abundance of works in translation from European languages, but unfortunately underscores the scarcity of works translated from Asian and African literatures. In addition, fewer women poets seem to have survived the horrors of our century than their male counterparts, and many fewer have been translated. Despite these limitations, the present volume makes available only about one quarter of the material I was able to gather. It is, however, not my intention to propose a canon of such works; this is, rather, a poetic memorial to those who suffered and resisted through poetry itself.

Poetry of witness presents the reader with an interesting interpretive problem. We are accustomed to rather easy categories: we distinguish between "personal" and "political" poems—the former calling to mind lyrics of love and emotional loss, the latter indicating a public partisanship that is considered divisive, even when necessary. The distinction between the personal and the political gives the political realm too much and too little scope; at the same time, it renders the personal too important and not important enough. If we give up the dimension of the personal, we risk relinquishing one of the most powerful sites of resistance. The celebration of the personal, however, can indicate a myopia, an inability to see how larger structures of the economy and the state circumscribe, if not determine, the fragile realm of individuality.

We need a third term, one that can describe the space between the state and the supposedly safe havens of the personal. Let us call this space "the social." As North Americans, we have been fortunate: wars for us (provided we are not combatants) are fought elsewhere, in other countries. The cities bombed are other people's cities. The houses destroyed are other people's houses. We are also fortunate in that we do not live under martial law; there are nominal restrictions on state censorship; our citizens are not sent into exile. We are legally and juridically free to choose our associates, and to determine our communal lives. But perhaps we should not consider our social lives as merely the products of our choice: the social is a place of resistance and struggle, where books are published, poems read, and protest disseminated. It is the sphere in which claims against the political order are made in the name of justice.

By situating poetry in this social space, we can avoid some of our residual prejudices. A poem that calls on us from the other side of a situation of extremity cannot be judged by simplistic notions of "accuracy" or "truth to life." It will have to be judged, as Ludwig Wittgenstein said of confessions, by its consequences, not by our ability to verify its truth. In fact, the poem might be our only evidence that an event has occurred: it exists for us as the sole trace of an occurrence. As such, there will be nothing for us to base the poem on, no independent account that will tell us whether or not we can see a given text as being "objectively" true. Poem as trace, poem as evidence. Radnóti's final notebook entry, dated October 31, 1944, read:

> I fell beside him; his body turned over,
> already taut as a string about to snap.
> Shot in the back of the neck. That's how you too will end,
> I whispered to myself; just lie quietly.
> Patience now flowers into death.
> *Der springt noch auf*, a voice said above me.
> On my ear, blood dried, mixed with filth.

This verse describes the death of his fellow prisoner Miklós Lorsi, a violinist, and remains the only trace of his dying.

Miklós Radnóti's poems evade easy categories. They are not merely personal, nor are they, strictly speaking, political. What is one to make of the first lines of "Forced March"?:

> The man who, having collapsed, rises, takes steps, is insane;
> he'll move an ankle, a knee, an errant mass of pain,
> and take to the road again . . .

The poem becomes an apostrophe to a fellow marcher, and so it is not only a record of experience but an exhortation and a plea against despair. It is not a cry for sympathy but a call for strength. The hope that the poem relies on, however, is not "political" as such: it is not a celebration of solidarity in the name of a class or common enemy. It is not partisan in any accepted sense. It opposes the dream of future satisfaction to the reality of current pain. One could argue that it uses the promise of personal happiness against a politically induced misery, but it does so in the name of the poet's fellows, in a spirit of communality.

We all know that atrocities have taken place on an unprecedented scale in the last one hundred years. Such monstrous acts have come to seem almost normal. It becomes easier to forget than to remember, and this forgetfulness becomes our defense against remembering—a rejection of unnecessary sentimentality, a hard-headed acceptance of "reality." Modernity, as twentieth-century German Jewish philosophers Walter Benjamin and Theodor Adorno argued, is marked by a superstitious worship of oppressive force and by a concomitant reliance on oblivion. Such forgetfulness, they argue, is willful and isolating: it drives wedges between the individual and the collective fate to which he or she is forced to submit. These poems will not permit us diseased complacency. They come to us with claims that have yet to be filled, as attempts to mark us as they have themselves been marked.

How do these poems try to remind us? The musical title of Holocaust survivor Paul Celan's "Todesfugue"—his "Death Fugue"—warns us that the poem will not represent the world "directly." And indeed it begins on the unexplained (and ultimately irreducible) vehicle of metaphor: "Black milk of daybreak we drink it at evening." There is no mention of who this "we" might be or what the milk is, nor is there any need to be explicit: the poem works through repetition and suggests meaning through juxtaposition. There are, of course, hints: the poem mentions Jews, and calls death "a master from Deutschland." In John Felstiner's translation, the German remains, and it remains out of terror. The German of the camps was an alien tongue, spoken gutturally to those who frequently knew no German, and who would have to construct its meaning out of their own fear and for their own survival. This poem, written by a Romanian Jew in France in German, is itself evidence of the experience it describes. "*Meister*" in German is not merely "master": in fact, *Herr* serves as Lord and Master as well. *Meister* also denotes mastery of a craft, the acceptance into a guild; to enter the poem, either in the original or in this translation, is to enter the world of death, to become a member of a guild whose language the poem can neither translate nor deny.

It is impossible to translate Celan into an accessible English, an English of contemporary fluency. Rather, to encompass Celan, we might have to translate English into him, that is, denature our language just as he denatured German. Benjamin argued that a poem brought into a new language had to transform that language: a good translation would enrich its adoptive tongue as it had changed the linguistic world of its original. Perhaps all the poems in this anthology—even those written in English—are attempts at such translation, an attempt to mark, to change, to impress, but never to leave things as they are.

To talk about a poem as the sole trace of an event, to see it in purely evidentiary terms, is perhaps to believe our own figures of speech too rigorously. If, as Benjamin indicates, a poem is *itself* an event, a trauma that changes both a common language and an individual psyche, it is a specific kind of event, a specific kind of trauma. It is an experience entered into voluntarily. Unlike an aerial attack, a poem does not come at one unexpectedly. One has to read or listen, one has to be willing to accept the trauma. So, if a poem is an event and the trace of an event, it has, by definition, to belong to a different order of being from the trauma that marked its language in the first place.

Not surprisingly, a large number of poems in this selection, written in conditions of extremity, rely on the immediacies of direct address. There are few writings as intimate as a letter to a spouse. Nazim Hikmet, the Turkish Communist who spent a large portion of his adult life in prison, writes from solitary confinement:

> It's spring outside, my dear wife, spring.
> Outside on the plain, suddenly the smell
> of fresh earth, birds singing, etc.
> It's spring, my dear wife,
> the plain outside sparkles . . .
> And inside the bed comes alive with bugs,
> the water jug no longer freezes.

The poem depends on bare-boned simplicity, for it marks the difference between inside and outside, between prison and the world, through small, disturbing details. Spring on the outside is easily evoked by cliché, so Hikmet can cut his list short with an offhand "etc." On the inside, however, spring is measured in the resurgence of lice and the lack of ice in the water jug. Of course, the fact that the jug freezes indicates just how cold the cell is. And so, while Hikmet is willing to greet the spring, he does so in terms of prison's stark dichotomies. Life there seems to consist of two seasons: the frozen and the verminridden. In spring, on the outside and the inside, a man dreams of freedom. How does the poet know this? From experience. It is difficult to read these lines. Does Hikmet only retrieve the "demon called freedom" from memory, or does the demon possess him, even now, in solitary confinement? I am inclined to favor the second reading (although both are possible), because in this way the final lines of the poem have an added pathos. Out in the yard, in the sun, the poet rests his back against a wall:

> For a moment no trap to fall into,
> no struggle, no freedom, no wife.
> Only earth, sun and me . . .
> I am happy.

The demon of freedom, like the pull of a wife, is a torment to a man in solitary, who is alone and most distinctly unfree. Happiness comes to the prisoner when he can forget his privations, his situation, and the claims of the outside. The contentment he feels might be viewed as a victory for his humanity, for his perseverance, but it contains a negative judgment as well. It is bought at a very dear price: the fleeting forgetfulness of who and where he is.

The epistolary mode, while intimate and private, is also deeply public. It has always been the poetry of the middle style, of a conscientious communality, an attempt to speak for more than one and to engage all others. So it is when Bertolt Brecht addresses *die Nachgeborenen*, the generations that come after him. His poem is a self-laceration ("To sleep I lay down among murderers") but also a demand for humility from the future:

> Remember
> When you speak of our failings
> The dark time too
> Which you have escaped.

These lines might be read as an attempt at exculpation, but such a reading does not do justice to the rest of the poem. Brecht writes to the future to remind it of the ease of moral disaster and ethical complacency.

More modern, perhaps, than the traditional letter or address, is the postcard. Pithier than the letter, the postcard as it appears in this anthology is freighted with irony. Radnóti writes:

> Bloody saliva hangs on the mouths of the oxen.
> Blood shows in every man's urine.
> The company stands in wild knots, stinking.
> Death blows overhead, revolting.

This card is not backed by a picture: it is itself a picture. Its brevity cuts to the horror of the situation. If extremity produces a new kind of postcard, it can only view the traditional cards with a mixture of nostalgia and mockery. So Günter Eich's "Old Postcards" from before the war are shadowed by the war itself. The carnival atmosphere of the eighth postcard is undercut by the final figure, where the Renaissance staircase becomes an unspecified but evidently determinate number of prisoners' steps. The odd current of distress that runs through the poem, the hint of conflict and the motifs of war, leads to the final card:

> Fine,
> fine.
> But when the war is over
> we'll go to Minsk
> and pick up Grandmother.

Let us assume that the war in question is either World War I or World War II. (We can make this presumption from the reference to Sedan Day, a now-forgotten German holiday to commemorate defeat of the French in the Franco-Prussian War.) The card seems to assure us of a German victory over the Russians, hence the writer's ability to pick up Grandmother in the city of Minsk. At the time of writing the poem, however, it would be impossible to "pick up Grandmother" in the Russian city: the course of history has made such ease of travel impossible. Hence the postcard comes to us (readers from the Cold War) as news from another time as well as another place: a time in which the world was so different as to be another place altogether. The poem also comments ironically on a certain chauvinism, and the belief in German military superiority and territorial hegemony. The victory that the poem indicates was nothing more than a vicious and dangerous dream.

It should come as no surprise that poets who urgently desire to influence a public have also used the news media as models, even if somewhat negative ones. Thus the Polish poet Zbigniew Herbert sends his "Report from the Besieged City," a fabular place that is an "everywhere." His is an "objective" report, a product of willed disinterest:

> I avoid any commentary I keep a tight hold on my emotions I write about
>   the facts only they it seems are appreciated in foreign markets

There is despair in this flatness of tone: markets define the news, not the experience of the besieged. Foreigners want to hear nothing but the facts because they do not wish to be disturbed by their complicity in the sufferings of the city. In a similar way, writing about Vietnam, John Balaban explodes the myth of the impartiality of the media in "News Update," in which he celebrates the sometimes partisan heroism of the journalist (which does not make the news) and the silly stories that seem—to editors at least—worthy of public attention. In these two poems, Herbert and Balaban use the news media to stress the importance of poetry: what comes to us in the newspapers and on television is not necessarily factual, nor is it necessarily cogent. Determined by the market and by the tender conscience of the distant consumer, the news is is a degenerate form of art, neither wholly fact nor wholly fiction, never true to objective truth or subjective reality. The demands of modernist literary communication, with its stress on close reading, irony, and the fiction of textual depth, open up more complex visions of historical circumstance than are otherwise available.

Postcards, letters, and reports on the news—all these are communal forms, ways of writing that stress the interpersonal aspects of poetry, the public side of literature. They underline the collective urgency that propels a literature of the social. In Latin America we find the *testimonio*, the act of judicial witness. Bearing witness in such a poem becomes literal: the poet imagines himself or herself in a court of law. The *testimonio* casts a large shadow in this anthology (and on my conception of the poetry of extremity). In an age of atrocity, witness becomes an imperative and a problem: how does one bear witness to suffering and before what court of law? Such is the dilemma of Ariel Dorfman, in "Vocabulary":

> But how can I tell their story
> if I was not there?

The poet claims he cannot find the words to tell the story of people who have been tortured, raped, and murdered. Nevertheless, it is vitally important that the story be told. Who shall tell it? The poet answers:

Let them speak for themselves.

It is not callousness that prompts Dorfman to write this line, but a sense that the story belongs to those who have undergone the extremity, and should not be determined, as in Herbert's poem, by foreign readers. Humility brings the poet before an ethical tribunal, a place where the writer must recognize the claims of difference, the otherness of others, and the specificities of their experience. Witness, in this light, is problematic: even if one has witnessed atrocity, one cannot necessarily speak *about* it, let alone *for* it.

The gap between self and other opens up the problem of relativism that has bedeviled modern philosophy, politics, and poetry. Respect for otherness seems always to release the specter of an infinite regress. The language of religion therefore becomes quite important in this supposedly secular century, for religion traditionally makes claims for universality and unimpeachable truth. Furthermore, some of the most flagrant forms of institutionalized violence in our era have been directed toward specific religions (during the Holocaust) or against religion in general (as in the Soviet Union and in Eastern Europe). Anna Akhmatova composes in the language of Christianity in her poem "Requiem," and even the title of this attack on both Stalinism and war becomes an act of protest, a religious form of memory that seeks to sanctify the dead and ease them on their way into the afterlife. Where Stalin erased the past and the present for the supposed good of the future, the poet asks the past and the present to stake a claim on that future:

> This woman is sick to her marrow-bone
> this woman is utterly alone,
>
> with husband dead, with son away
> in jail. Pray for me. Pray.

The appeal for prayer is both a request for help and a stroke against solitude: to pray for this woman is to express sympathy, to establish a communality through the medium of religion. It is to give help in the only way left to the powerless. Where there is nothing else, there is prayer.

If religion can provide a countersolidarity to the enforced communalism of the Stalinist era, it can also lend meaning to the desperate experiences of that time. The death of the son in Akhmatova's poem becomes a form of crucifixion: the apparent meaninglessness of terror is transfigured when it is mapped onto the story of Christ's Passion. Furthermore, it transforms that story by giving a special place to the Virgin Mary. Akhmatova's poem enters into a discreet dialogue with Christianity, a mutually informing interchange of meaning and pathos that indicates an enduring place for the explanatory possibility of religion: its ability to speak about us and to include us.

In countries where religion has been more firmly institutionalized, more central to the workings of the state, its conventions could provide an ironic counterpoint to the official version of extreme events. Wilfred Owen, himself killed in World War I, writes an anthem, a hymn of national praise and victory, for "doomed youth." Bells rung for the newly dead, prayers, candles—all the ritual accounterments of mourning—have been superseded by the realities of modern warfare:

> No mockeries now for them; no prayers nor bells;
> Nor any voice of mourning save the choirs,—
> The shrill, demented choirs of wailing shells . . .

The dead are mourned not by human song, but by the cacophony of new technologies and armaments. The comforts of religion seem to have no place in this poem. They only remind us of the lack of comfort of the present.

Religion in an age of atrocity, as Owen's anthem indicates, can itself bear a heavy responsibility for suffering. For Owen, the difficulty arises from the marriage of religion and the state, of the belligerent and nationalistic aspect of the very notion of the anthem itself. For other writers, religious qualms arise from the sheer prevalence of evil in this century, from the assault on theodicy that genocide, torture, and imposed misery present. This is perhaps most evident in the writings of Jewish poets, like Paul Celan and Edmond Jabès, where the reality of the Shoah (the Hebrew term for what is known as the Holocaust) seems to come into direct conflict with the traditional mission of the Jews. In "There Was Earth Inside Them" Celan writes of people who do not praise the Creator because He had willed their abjection. This refusal—apparently natural enough—leads to silence:

> They dug and heard nothing more;
> they did not grow wise, invented no song,
> thought up for themselves no language.
> They dug.

Theology, poetry, and words are all bound together—their antithesis, it seems, is the wormlike act of digging. The poem ends oddly, with an invocation to an absent other and the apparent inclusion of the poet among the silent diggers:

> O one, o none, o no one, o you
> Where did the way lead when it led nowhere?
> O you dig and I dig, and I dig towards you,
> and on our finger the ring awakes.

That "you" is both God and a loved one, God seen as a loved one and the loved one seen as God. The way to nowhere turns, through a difficult act of dialectics, into a road to somewhere, where the "no one" becomes a "someone" and that someone becomes a "you." Through this leap, the ring is not on one finger but on "our" finger: the same finger on different hands, or the one finger on a collective hand. It awakes because it has been asleep: the covenant, the troth, has been repledged. So for Celan (following perhaps the poetic precedent of Friedrich Hölderlin) the apparent absence of the Almighty leads us back to His presence. His absence is the mark of His presence. Divine absence in our time has two forms. One is the threat of the abyss, of the Death of God heralded by Nietzsche, and the other is the new technology of death presented by the death camps. To think religion through is to rediscover the holy in-between and in-spite-of this double negation, as Jabès has written: "I write in function of two limits. / On that side, there is the void. / On this side, the horror of Auschwitz."

The peculiar paradox, the insistence on God's existence in the face of His apparent disappearance, derives from the Kabbalah, the tradition of Jewish mysticism, in which the world in its imperfection is created by God's recession: He draws a curtain of darkness down before Himself in order to allow light to appear, darkness serving as the necessary foil for illumination. This thought rests at the center of Jabès's poetry, which turns on paradox and contradiction. Jabès writes in the final volume of his long work on the Shoah, *The Book of Questions*:

> [G-d] is image in the absence of images, language in the absence
> of language, point in the absence of points.

The counterintuitive thrust of this thought leads to the imperative (in "Notebook II") that we have to "take the contradictions into our keeping, / At the edge of Emptiness." This is a religious thought without irony because it stems from a religion based on the indispensability of irony, of dialectic and dialogue. There is a secular version of this theology, figured in the rhetorical trope of prosopopeia, where an absent other is given voice, invoked, engaged in conversation. Milosz summons forth the dead in his early poem "Dedication":

> You whom I could not save
> Listen to me.

In contradistinction to Milosz's later work, however, these dead are not desired. They are a burden:

> They used to pour on graves millet or poppy seeds
> To feed the dead who would come disguised as birds.
> I put this book here for you, who once lived
> So that you should visit us no more.

Milosz calls up the departed only to banish them again. His poetry is both a magical way of bringing the dead to life and a talisman against that life. He can only create the new by expelling the old through a ritual act.

The poetry of witness frequently resorts to paradox and difficult equivocation, to the invocation of what is *not* there as if it *were*, in order to bring forth the real. That it must defy common sense to speak of the common indicates that traditional modes of thought, the purview of common sense, no longer *make* sense, or only make sense if they are allowed to invert themselves. In the face of our increasingly unreal reality, then, fabulation, the writing of the blatantly fictitious, becomes the recourse of those who would describe the everyday. This is the basis for the Polish poet Aleksandr Wat's bleak parable in "Imagerie d'Epinal" where a young girl, given a lollipop by her father's executioner, carries his head in a parade:

> With that pole she marched in a parade on a sunny,
> populous road,
> under her school placard:
>   "Happiness to all—death to enemies . . . "

It is clear here that the slogans of repression and enforced solidarity are the expressions of absurdity, the voice of the fictional. Surrealism in this circumstance marks not only the utopian desire for secular transfiguration but also the attempt to come to terms with an untransfigured world. Fabulation and the surreal are also good ways of masking intent, of circumventing the censor's stricture.

Irony, paradox, and surrealism, for all the interpretive difficulties they present, might well be both the answer and a restatement of Adorno's often quoted and difficult contention that to write poetry after Auschwitz is barbaric. Adorno wrote this just after World War II, and in the context of the essay in which it appears, his indictment extends to all forms of art. Art, Adorno felt, rested on the social inequities and objectifying tendencies that made Fascism not only possible but inevitable. Auschwitz, then, was contiguous with all the ornaments of Western art, for it stood as the culmination of culture where culture turned into its opposite. While the language of the everyday might appeal to Hikmet and Radnóti, it may not present an adequate language for *witness* in situations where the quotidian has been appropriated by oppressive powers. The colonization of language by the state renders that language inaccessible to a poetry that wants to register its protest against such depredations. The accepted languages of art might not be adequate either, for the sphere of art is frequently the first to be attacked: Hitler banished the work of the expressionists and celebrated Wagner. Socialist realism displaced all other forms of aesthetic expression under Stalinism.

The ultimate example of the cross-fertilization of culture and barbarity took place at Auschwitz, where the Jews were forced to play chamber music for their executioners. Art in such a world carries with it a dangerous complicity which it can neither refute nor ignore. Adorno did not wish to banish art from an ideal republic. He wanted art to become conscious of the sins it had to suffer and withstand. A better expression of his understanding of the task of poetry comes in an aphorism from his book *Minima Moralia*:

> . . . there is no longer beauty or consolation except in the gaze
> falling on horror, withstanding it, and in unalleviated conscious-
> ness of negativity holding fast to the possibility of what is better.

In such a world poetry will yearn after truth through indirection—will speak, in the terms Jabès used to describe Celan, in wounded words. Jabès also maintains: "To Adorno . . . I say that we must write. But we cannot write as before." When we find eclogues by Miklós Radnóti, elegies by Johannes Bobrowski, and ballads by Ondra Lysohorsky, we are also forced to notice that these forms have been modified and transformed. Let us take another example, Robert Desnos's "Ars Poetica":

> Across the snout
> Picked up in the mud and slime

> Spit out, vomited, rejected—
> I am the verse witness of my master's breath—
> Left over, cast off, garbage
> Like the diamond, the flame, and the blue of the sky
> Not pure, not virgin
> But fucked to the core
> fucked, pricked, sucked, ass fucked, raped
> I am the verse witness of my master's breath . . .

This is not the language of the "sweet and the useful," the *dulce et utile* that Horace prescribed. On the contrary, Desnos has written his own poetics of extremity, of situations where diamonds, flames, and the sky are reduced to refuse. Poetry, in order to be the witness of lived experience, of breath, will have to resort to a language more suitable to the time. The violence of Desnos's language, his willful assault on decorum, and his scabrous use of slang all attest to the violence of the age. In fact, Desnos choose to leave the trace of extraliterary force by violating the codes of the literary. Thus Orpheus is turned into a "coldblooded fucker." He has been translated—as has poetry itself—into a wild, nasty, and demotic modernity.

Extremity, as we have seen, demands new forms or alters older modes of poetic thought. It also breaks forms and creates forms from these breaks. The fragment is not new to poetry: it has a venerable history. Nor is it limited to the poetry of witness. Fragmentation is a standard feature of literary modernism. But the fragment gains urgency in the aftermath of extremity. It might well be the feature that binds this anthology together. Lines of poetry can be grammatical fragments, as in Desnos's poem. Poems themselves can be fragments. Or rather, they can be collections of fragments that indicate a whole, or a narrative that cannot be written. Dorfman's stuttering "Vocabulary" tells of the inability to tell a story. It evokes the story but leaves it unfinished, omits the details and the denouement. As in Eich's postcards, the reader is strangely aware of what has been left out, what cannot or has not been said. The French call this procedure *recit éclaté*—shattered, exploded, or splintered narrative. The story cannot travel over the chasm of time and space. Violence has rendered it unspeakable.

The psychiatrist Dore Laub has found that in the oral testimony of survivors of the Shoah, their accounts fragment as they approach the core of the trauma. The narrative of trauma is itself traumatized, and bears witness to extremity by its inability to articulate directly or completely. Hence the reduction of a century to a series of staccato images in Adonis's "Mirror for the Twentieth Century":

> A coffin bearing the face of a boy
> A book
>
> Written on the belly of a crow
> A wild beast hidden in a flower
>
> A rock
> Breathing with the lungs of a lunatic:
>
> This is it
> This is the Twentieth Century.

Our age lacks the structure of a story. Or perhaps it would be closer to Adonis's poem to say that narrative implies progress and completion. The history of our time does not allow for any of the bromides of progress, nor for the promise of successful closure. That this history can be retold in scattered images (while eluding them) indicates that the age repeats the same story over and over again, marking an infernal return of the same. In "Lines for Translation into Any Language," the contemporary British poet James Fenton offers the same bleak analysis: the story of war, of a shantytown in a cemetery and the plight of a noncombatant, has been broken down into discrete sections that can exist on their own or be organized into a narrative which seems to imply connections it does not state. The darkness of the vision is made clear by its title. The situation the poem describes can happen anywhere: it is not limited in time or space. For Fenton, as for Adonis, the tale of our time is one of infinite repetition.

The fact that extremity can be translated the world over—that institutionalized suffering has been globalized—means that fragmentation might also be global—that displacement has been rendered universal. Exile in this anthology is as much a linguistic condition as it is a question of citizenship. At the most obvious level, we find a number of poets writing in languages that are alien to the nation in which they write. Brecht wrote German poems in the United States. Milosz writes polish poems in Berkeley, California. Vallejo wrote Spanish in Paris, and Faiz wrote in Urdu in the Arabic world. More interesting perhaps is a different kind of linguistic exile, where one comes to write in a foreign language or in a language that history has rendered foreign. We can compare here the different experiences of two Romanian Jews rendered homeless by World War II and its aftermath. Dan Pagis's native language was German. Pagis spent three years in a concentration camp and emigrated to Israel, where he became a leading Hebrew poet. His Hebrew was the result of history, of displacement—it was the very mark of his exile, a notion that is given great poignancy in his little graffiti poem "Written in Pencil in a Sealed Boxcar:"

> here in this carload
> i am eve
> with my able son
> if you see my other son
> cain son of man
> tell him that i

The language and the characters of the Bible have been translated into modern Europe: their Hebrew is the reason for their destruction.

For Celan, the task was different. He wrote in his native German in France. This first alienation from his language—the daily experience of his alterity, his foreignness—was augmented by his fractured use of that language. He attempted to purify the tongue, render up its Nazi contamination, mark it historically. His quest led him to write in a fragmented, idiosyncratic dialect of his own construction, whose grammar was as tortured as its words were often new. Thus he was exiled within his own mother tongue, and used his mother tongue to register that exile.

A similar sense of exile, of linguistic alienation, can be seen in writers like Quincy Troupe, who write some of their poetry in the vocabulary of Black English and seek to create their own poetic idioms:

> eye use to write poems about burning
> down the motherfucking country for crazy
> horse, geronimo & malcolm king
> x, use to (w)rite about stabbing white folks
> in their air-conditioned eyeballs with ice picks . . .

The thematized violence of Troupe's rejection of white America is repeated in the idiosyncrasies of spelling which seek to make visible the aural puns of the language, to uncover a depth in English which he can inhabit without undue self-sacrifice.

If modernity has established the norm of individual integrity which Troupe seeks to maintain, it should be obvious from much of the poetry in this anthology that the experience of this century has done much to undermine this norm. In *The Body in Pain*, Elaine Scarry has written eloquently about the way that torture seeks to destroy the language and the world of his victim; the way it tries to unmake the victim's ability to objectify himself or herself in language. Thus when we come across a poem in this book where the poet addresses himself or herself, this form of apostrophe speaks from and against a violent self-alienation, of a self-alienation born of violence. Claribel Alegría addresses her childhood self in "From the Bridge":

> Don't come any closer
> there's a stench of carrion
> surrounding me.

What separates the poet from the girl is precisely that smell of all the deaths the adult has witnessed, all the injustice the adult has seen. Similarly, Angel Cuadra writes of an inner split:

> The common man I might have been
> reproaches me now,
> blaming me for his ostracism
> his solitary shadow,
> his silent exile.

In this poem, "In Brief," the unimportant man the poet could have become is compared with the poet that the man has become. It would seem that Cuadra confronts himself with the possibility of a life not lived alone, not lived in exile. Had he not been a poet, the logic goes, he would not be ostracized. But as the poem unfolds, Cuadra claims that there is no difference between the common man and the poet. It is not poetry that has banished him from Cuba, nor is it fame that has made him an exile. It is exile that has alienated himself from himself, and its violence that has split him asunder. The "I" that speaks the poem, that begins and ends it, is a protest against such violence, and attempt to redeem speech from the silence of pain, and integrity from the disintegrating forces of extremity.

The poetry of witness reclaims the social from the political and in so doing defends the individual against illegitimate forms of coercion. It often seeks to register through indirection and intervention the ways in which the linguistic and moral universes have been disrupted by events. When I began this project. I was hard pressed to find a significant poet who could not be included, who in some important way or another did *not* bear witness to the ravages of our time. But clearly it was impossible to contemplate a book of such length. I was therefore forced to develop criteria for inclusion that would do justice to the poets I would necessarily have to exclude, criteria that would begin to describe the trajectory of our modernity. I decided to limit the poets in the anthology to those for whom the social had been irrevocably invaded by the political in ways that were sanctioned neither by law nor by the fictions of the social contract. The writers I have chosen are those for whom the normative promises of the nation-state have failed. They have not been afforded the legal or the physical protections that the modern state is supposed to lend its citizens, nor have they been able to enjoy the solidarity that the concept of the nation is supposed to provide. If my selection seems to include an inordinate number of writers whose human rights have been abused, it is because those rights, in the tradition of political theory, were supposed to police the boundries between the government and personal self-determination, between citizenship and autonomy.

For decades, American literary criticism has sought to oppose "man" and "society," the individual against the communal, alterity against universality. Perhaps we can learn from the practice of the poets in this anthology that these are not oppositions based on mutual exclusion but are rather dialectical complementaries that invoke and pass through each other. Extremity is born of the simplifying desire to split these dyads into separate parts. It is the product of the drive to expunge one category in the name of another, to sacrifice the individual on the alter of the communal or vice versa. The poetry of witness is itself born in dialectical opposition to the extremity that has made such witness necessary. In the process, it restores the dynamic structure of dialectics.

Because the poetry of witness marks a resistance to false attempts at unification, it will take many forms. It will be impassioned or ironic. It will speak in the language of the common man or in an esoteric language of paradox or literary privilege. It will curse and it will bless; it will blaspheme against or ignore the holy. Its protest might rest on an odd grammatical inversion, on a heady peroration to an audience, or on a bizarre flight of fancy. It can be partisan in a limited sense but is more often partisan in the best of senses, that is, it speaks for what might, with less than crippling irony be called "the party of humanity." I do not mean this in an unreflective way, as a celebration of some my thological "inherent" goodness in man's "innate" nature. Rather, I take the partisanship of humanity as a rejection of unwarranted pain inflicted on some humans by others, of illegitimate domination. I am guided in this by Hannah Arendt's meditation on the self-justifications of collaboration with oppression, on the claim that the resistance of the single individual does not count in the face of the annihilating superiority of totalitarian regimes which make all resistance disappear into "holes of oblivion":

The holes of oblivion do not exist. Nothing human is that perfect and there are simply too many people in the world to make oblivion possible. One man will always be left alive to tell the story . . . the lesson of such stories is simple and within everybody's grasp. Politically speaking, it is that under conditions of terror, most people will comply but *some people will not . . . .* Humanly speaking, no more is required, and no more can reasonably be asked, for this planet to remain a place fit for human habitation.

The resistance to terror is what makes the world habitable: the protest against violence will not be forgotten and this insistent memory renders life possible in communal situations. As Desnos wrote in a poem called "Epitaph":

> You who are living, what have you done with these treasures?
> Do you regret the time of my struggle?
> Have you raised your crops for a common harvest?
> Have you made my town a richer place?

If we have not, if we do not, what, in the end, have we become? And if we do not, what, in the end, shall we be?

Carolyn Forché

The Colonel

What you have heard is true. I was in his house. His wife carried a tray of coffee and sugar. His daughter filed her nails, his son went out for the night. There were daily papers, pet dogs, a pistol on the cushion beside him. The moon swung bare on its black cord over the house. On the television was a cop show. It was in English. Broken bottles were embedded in the walls around the house to scoop the kneecaps from a man's legs or cut his hands to lace. On the windows there were gratings like those in liquor stores. We had dinner, rack of lamb, good wine, a gold bell was on the table for calling the maid. The maid brought green mangoes, salt, a type of bread. I was asked how I enjoyed the country. There was a brief commercial in Spanish. His wife took everything away. There was some talk then of how difficult it had become to govern. The parrot said hello on the terrace. The colonel told it to shut up, and pushed himself from the table. My friend said to me with his eyes: say nothing. The colonel returned with a sack used to bring groceries home. He spilled many human ears on the table. They were like dried peach halves. There is no other way to say this. He took one of them in his hands, shook it in our faces, dropped it into a water glass. It came alive there. I am tired of fooling around he said. As for the rights of anyone, tell your people they can go fuck themselves. He swept the ears to the floor with his arm and held the last of his wine in the air. Something for your poetry, no? he said. Some of the ears on the floor caught this scrap of his voice. Some of the ears on the floor were pressed to the ground.

May 1978

Reprinted from *The Country Between Us*, (1980), HarperCollins.

Sharon Olds

Sharon Olds (b. 1942) is a poet who holds degrees from Stanford University (BA) and Columbia (Ph.D.). She is currently an associate professor at New York University and acting director of the graduate program in Creative Writing. She has published numerous collections of poetry including Satan Says *(1980),* The Gold Cell *(1987), and* Blood, Tin, Straw *(1999). Her poetry often challenges conventions and asks the reader to do the same.*

On the Subway

The boy and I face each other.
His feet are huge, in black sneakers
laced with white in a complex pattern like a
set of intentional scars. We are stuck on
opposite sides of the car, a couple of
molecules stuck in a rod of light
rapidly moving through darkness. He has the
casual cold look of a mugger,
alert under hooded lids. He is wearing
red, like the inside of the body
exposed. I am wearing dark fur, the
whole skin of an animal taken and
used. I look at his raw face,
he looks at my fur coat, and I don't
know if I am in his power—
he could take my coat so easily, my
briefcase, my life—
or if he is in my power, the way I am
living off his life, eating the steak
he does not eat, as if I am taking
the food from his mouth. And he is black
and I am white, and without meaning or
trying to I must profit from his darkness,
the way he absorbs the murderous beams of the
nation's heart, as black cotton
absorbs the heat of the sun and holds it. There is
no way to know how easy this

white skin makes my life, this
life he could take so easily and
break across his knee like a stick the way his
own back is being broken, the
rod of his soul that at birth was dark and
fluid and rich as the heart of a seedling
ready to thrust up into any available light.

Audre Lorde

Audre Lorde (1934–1992) was born in New York City to parents who had immigrated from Grenada. Lorde earned a B.A. from Hunter College and a Masters of Library Science from Columbia University and later taught English at John Jay College of Justice in New York and Hunter College. Although as a young woman, Lorde married a man and had two children, she was an outspoken lesbian whose bravery and audacity both shocks and enthralls her readers. Lorde's work is often anthologized and widely celebrated for its honesty, directness, and strength. Although Lorde is best known for her poetry, she published in several genres. In 1980, Lorde published The Cancer Journals, *a blend of essays, journal entries, and memoir that offers a painful account of Lorde's battle with breast cancer. In it, she writes, "I have been wanting to write a piece of meaning words on cancer as it affects my life and my consciousness as a woman, a black lesbian feminist mother lover poet all I am." In 1984, she published* Sister Outsider: Essays and Speeches, *a collection of her non-poetry that spans two decades and addresses a wide range of social issues. Her poetry and prose have earned her many honors, including two National Book Awards. She died of cancer on November 11, 1992.*

A Litany for Survival

For those of us who live at the shoreline
standing upon the constant edges of decision
crucial and alone
for those of us who cannot indulge
the passing dreams of choice
who love in doorways coming and going
in the hours between dawns
looking inward and outward
at once before and after
seeking a now that can breed
futures
like bread in our children's mouths
so their dreams will not reflect
the death of ours;

Reprinted from *The Black Unicorn*, (1978), W.W. Norton & Company.

For those of us
who were imprinted with fear
like a faint line in the center of our foreheads
learning to be afraid with our mother's milk
for by this weapon
this illusion of some safety to be found
the heavy-footed hoped to silence us
For all of us
this instant and this triumph
We were never meant to survive.

And when the sun rises we are afraid
it might not remain
when the sun sets we are afraid
it might not rise in the morning
when our stomachs are full we are afraid
of indigestion
when our stomachs are empty we are afraid
we may never eat again
when we are loved we are afraid
love will vanish
when we are alone we are afraid
love will never return
and when we speak we are afraid
our words will not be heard
nor welcomed
but when we are silent
we are still afraid.

So it is better to speak
remembering
we were never meant to survive.

Michael Lassell

Michael Lassell (b. 1947) often writes about life as a gay man. He speaks bravely about sexuality and vulnerability. His work expresses his anger, his loss, and his hope in the face of hopelessness. In a review of his book The Hard Way *(1995), Philip Gambone praises Lassell's writing because it embodies "his humanity—his bruised and burning embrace of life." His other works include* Poems for Lost and Un-lost Boys *(1985),* Decade Dance *(1990), and* Eros in Boystown *(1996). He has been a recipient of a Lambda Literary Award and is currently the articles director for* Metropolitan Home.

How to Watch Your Brother Die

When the call comes, be calm.
Say to your wife, "My brother is dying. I have to fly
to California."
Try not to be shocked that he already looks like
a cadaver.
Say to the young man sitting by your brother's side,
"I'm his brother."
Try not to be shocked when the young man says,
"I'm his lover. Thanks for coming."

Listen to the doctor with a steel face on.
Sign the necessary forms.
Tell the doctor you will take care of everything.
Wonder why doctors are so remote.

Watch the lover's eyes as they stare into
your brother's eyes as they stare into
space.
Wonder what they see there.
Remember the time he was jealous and
opened your eyebrow with a sharp stick.
Forgive him out loud
even if he can't
understand you.

Reprinted from *Decade Dance*, (1990), by permission of the author.

Realize the scar will be
all that's left of him.

Over coffee in the hospital cafeteria
say to the lover, "You're an extremely good-looking
young man."
Hear him say,
"I never thought I was good enough looking to
deserve your brother."

Watch the tears well up in his eyes. Say,
"I'm sorry. I don't know what it means to be
the lover of another man."
Hear him say,
"It's just like a wife, only the commitment is
deeper because the odds against you are so much
greater."
Say nothing, but
take his hand like a brother's.

Drive to Mexico for unproven drugs that might
help him live longer.
Explain what they are to the border guard.
Fill with rage when he informs you,
"You can't bring those across."
Begin to grow loud.
Feel the lover's hand on your arm
restraining you. See in the guard's eye
how much a man can hate another man.
Say to the lover. "How can you stand it?"
Hear him say, "You get used to it."
Think of one of your children getting used to
another man's hatred.

Call your wife on the telephone. Tell her,
"He hasn't much time.
I'll be home soon." Before you hang up say,
"How could anyone's commitment be deeper than
a husband and wife?" Hear her say,
"Please. I don't want to know all the details."

When he slips into an irrevocable coma,
hold his lover in your arms while he sobs,
no longer strong. Wonder how much longer
you will be able to be strong.
Feel how it feels to hold a man in your arms
whose arms are used to holding men.
Offer God anything to bring your brother back.
Know you have nothing God could possibly want.

Curse God, but do not
abandon Him.

Stare at the face of the funeral director
when he tells you he will not
embalm the body for fear of
contamination. Let him see in your eyes
how much a man can hate another man.

Stand beside a casket covered in flowers,
white flowers. Say,
"Thank you for coming," to each of several hundred men
who file past in tears, some of them
holding hands. Know that your brother's life
was not what you imagined. Overhear two
mourners say, "I wonder who'll be next?" and
"I don't care anymore,
as long as it isn't you."

Arrange to take an early flight home.
His lover will drive you to the airport.
When your flight is announced say,
awkwardly, "If I can do anything, please
let me know." Do not flinch when he says,
"Forgive yourself for not wanting to know him
after he told you. He did."
Stop and let it soak in. Say,
"He forgave me, or he knew himself?"
"Both," the lover will say, not knowing what else
to do. Hold him like a brother while he
kisses you on the cheek. Think that
you haven't been kissed by a man since
your father died. Think,
"This is no moment not to be strong."

Fly first class and drink Scotch. Stroke
your split eyebrow with a finger and
think of your brother alive. Smile
at the memory and think
how your children will feel in your arms,
warm and friendly and without challenge.

Mark Doty

Mark A. Doty (b. 1953) is the son of an army engineer and grew up in a succession of suburbs in Tennessee, Florida, southern California, and Arizona. Since the publication of his first volume of verse, Turtle, Swan, *in 1987, Mark Doty has become recognized as one of the most accomplished poets in America. Doty's work transcends the category of "gay poetry" to appeal to a diverse cross-section of readers. Fittingly, Doty has won a number of prestigious literary awards for his poetry and his two memoirs, including the* Whiting Writer's Award, *the T. S. Eliot Prize, the National Poetry Series, and the* Los Angeles Times *Book Award.*

Charlie Howard's Descent

Between the bridge and the river
he falls through
a huge portion of night;
it is not as if falling

is something new. Over and over
he slipped into the gulf
between what he knew and how
he was known. What others wanted

opened like an abyss: the laughing
stock-clerks at the grocery, women
at the luncheonette amused by his gestures.
What could he do, live

with one hand tied
behind his back? So he began to fall
into the star-faced section
of night between the trestle

and the water because he could not meet
a little town's demands,
and his earrings shone and his wrists
were as limp as they were.

I imagine he took the insults in
and made of them a place to live;

Reprinted from *Turtle Swan*, (1987), by permission of David R. Godine, Publisher, Inc. Copyright © 1987 by Mark Doty.

we learn to use the names
because they are there,

familiar furniture: *faggot*
was the bed he slept in, hard
and white, but simple somehow,
queer something sharp

but finally useful, a tool,
all the jokes a chair,
stiff-backed to keep the spine straight,
a table, a lamp. And because

he's fallen for twenty-three years,
despite whatever awkwardness
his flailing arms and legs assume
he is beautiful

and like any good diver
has only an edge of fear
he transforms into grace.
Or else he is not afraid,

and in this way climbs back
up the ladder of his fall,
out of the river into the arms
of the three teenage boys

who hurled him from the edge—
really boys now, afraid,
their fathers' cars shivering behind them,
headlights on—and tells them

it's all right, that he knows
they didn't believe him
when he said he couldn't swim,
and blesses his killers

in the way that only the dead
can afford to forgive.

Tim O'Brien

Tim O'Brien (b. 1946) graduated summa cum laude *from Mac-alester College (B.A. 1968) and did graduate study at Harvard University. O'Brien was drafted into the United States Army to serve in the Vietnam War. In his two years of service he was promoted to sergeant and received a Purple Heart. In 1973 he published his first book,* If I Die in a Combat Zone, Box Me Up and Ship Me Home, *a synthesis of autobiography and fiction. His third novel* Going after Cacciato (1978) *won the National Book Award and is considered to be one of the best books by a U.S. veteran about the Vietnam War. In "How to Tell a True War Story," which is from his collection* The Things They Carried, *and in his recent novel* In The Lake of the Woods, *O'Brien continues to blur distinctions between autobiography, fiction and history. His article, "The Vietnam in Me," was published in the* New York Times Magazine *in 1994.*

How to Tell a True War Story

This is true.

I had a buddy in Vietnam. His name was Bob Kiley, but everybody called him Rat.

A friend of his gets killed, so about a week later Rat sits down and writes a letter to the guy's sister. Rat tells her what a great brother she had, how together the guy was, a number one pal and comrade. A real soldier's soldier, Rat says. Then he tells a few stories to make the point, how her brother would always volunteer for stuff nobody else would volunteer for in a million years, dangerous stuff, like doing recon or going out on these really badass night patrols. Stainless steel balls, Rat tells her. The guy was a little crazy, for sure, but crazy in a good way, a real daredevil, because he liked the challenge of it, he liked testing himself, just man against gook. A great, great guy, Rat says.

Anyway, it's a terrific letter, very personal and touching. Rat almost bawls writing it. He gets all teary telling about the good times they had together, how her brother made the war seem almost fun, always raising hell and lighting up villes and bringing smoke to bear every which way. A great sense of humor, too. Like the time at this river when he went fishing with a whole damn crate of hand grenades. Probably the funniest thing in world history, Rat says, all that gore, about twenty zillion dead gook fish. Her brother, he had the right attitude. He knew how to have a good time. On Halloween, this real hot spooky night, the

Reprinted from *The Things They Carried*, (1991), Houghton Mifflin Company.

dude paints up his body all different colors and puts on this weird mask and hikes over to a ville and goes trick-or-treating almost stark naked, just boots and balls and an M-16. A tremendous human being, Rat says. Pretty nutso sometimes, but you could trust him with your life.

And then the letter gets very sad and serious. Rat pours his heart out. He says he loved the guy. He says the guy was his best friend in the world. They were like soul mates, he says, like twins or something, they had a whole lot in common. He tells the guy's sister he'll look her up when the war's over.

So what happens?

Rat mails the letter. He waits two months. The dumb cooze never writes back.

A true war story is never moral. It does not instruct, nor encourage virtue, nor suggest models of proper human behavior, nor restrain men from doing the things they have always done. If a story seems moral, do not believe it. If at the end of a war story you feel uplifted, or if you feel that some small bit of rectitude has been salvaged from the larger waste, then you have been made the victim of a very old and terrible lie. There is no rectitude whatsover. There is no virtue. As a first rule of thumb, therefore, you can tell a true war story by its absolute and uncompromising allegiance to obscenity and evil. Listen to Rat Kiley. Cooze, he says. He does not say bitch. He certainly does not say woman, or girl. He says cooze. Then he spits and stares. He's nineteen years old—it's too much for him—so he looks at you with those big sad gentle killer eyes and says *cooze*, because his friend is dead, and because it's so incredibly sad and true: she never wrote back.

You can tell a true war story if it embarrasses you. If you don't care for obscenity, you don't care for the truth; if you don't care for the truth, watch how you vote. Send guys to war, they come home talking dirty.

Listen to Rat: "Jesus Christ, man, I write this beautiful fuckin' letter, I slave over it, and what happens? The dumb cooze never writes back."

The dead guy's name was Curt Lemon. What happened was, we crossed a muddy river and marched west into the mountains, and on the third day we took a break along a trail junction in deep jungle. Right away, Lemon and Rat Kiley started goofing. They didn't understand about the spookiness. They were kids; they just didn't know. A nature hike, they thought, not even a war, so they went off into the shade of some giant trees—quadruple canopy, no sunlight at all—and they were giggling and calling each other yellow mother and playing a silly game they'd invented. The game involved smoke grenades, which were harmless unless you did stupid things, and what they did was pull out the pin and stand a few feet apart and play catch under the shade of those huge trees. Whoever chickened out was a yellow mother. And if nobody chickened out, the grenade would make a light popping sound and they'd be covered with smoke and they'd laugh and dance around and then do it again.

It's all exactly true.

It happened, to *me*, nearly twenty years ago, but I still remember that trail junction and the giant trees and a soft dripping sound somewhere beyond the trees. I remember the smell of moss. Up in the canopy there were tiny white blossoms, but no sunlight at all, and I remember the shadows spreading out under the trees where Curt Lemon and Rat Kiley were playing catch with smoke grenades. Mitchell Sanders sat flipping his yo-yo. Norman Bowker and Kiowa and Dave Jensen were dozing, or half-dozing, and all around us were those ragged green mountains.

Except for the laughter things were quiet.

At one point, I remember, Mitchell Sanders turned and looked at me, not quite nodding, as if to warn me about something, as if he already *knew,* then after a while he rolled up his yo-yo and moved away.

It's hard to tell you what happened next.

They were just goofing. There was a noise, I suppose, which must've been the detonator, so I glanced behind me and watched Lemon step from the shade into bright sunlight. His face was suddenly brown and shining. A handsome kid, really. Sharp gray eyes, lean and narrow-waisted, and when he died it was almost beautiful, the way the sunlight came around him and lifted him up and sucked him high into a tree full of moss and vines and white blossoms.

In any war story, but especially a true one, it's difficult to separate what happened from what seemed to happen. What seems to happen becomes its own happening and has to be told that way. The angles of vision are skewed. When a booby trap explodes, you close your eyes and duck and float outside yourself. When a guy dies, like Curt Lemon, you look away and then look back for a moment and then look away again. The pictures get jumbled; you tend to miss a lot. And then afterward, when you go to tell about it, there is always that surreal seemingness, which makes the story seem untrue, but which in fact represents the hard and exact truth as it *seemed.*

In many cases a true war story cannot be believed. If you believe it, be skeptical. It's a question of credibility. Often the crazy stuff is true and the normal stuff isn't, because the normal stuff is necessary to make you believe the truly incredible craziness.

In other cases you can't even tell a true war story. Sometimes it's just beyond telling.

I heard this one, for example, from Mitchell Sanders. It was near dusk and we were sitting at my foxhole along a wide muddy river north of Quang Ngai. I remember how peaceful the twilight was. A deep pinkish red spilled out on the river, which moved without sound, and in the morning we would cross the river and march west into the mountains. The occasion was right for a good story.

"God's truth," Mitchell Sanders said. "A six-man patrol goes up into the mountains on a basic listening-post operation. The idea's to spend a week up there, just lie low and listen for enemy movement. They've got a radio along, so if they hear anything suspicious—anything—they're supposed to call in artillery or gunships, whatever it takes. Otherwise they keep strict field discipline. Absolute silence. They just listen."

Sanders glanced at me to make sure I had the scenario. He was playing with his yo-yo, dancing it with short, tight little strokes of the wrist.

His face was blank in the dusk.

"We're talking regulation, by-the-book LP. These six guys, they don't say boo for a solid week. They don't got tongues. *All* ears."

"Right," I said.

"Understand me?"

"Invisible."

Sanders nodded.

"Affirm," he said. "Invisible. So what happens is, these guys get themselves deep in the bush, all camouflaged up, and they lie down and wait and that's all they do, nothing else, they lie there for seven straight days and just listen. And man, I'll tell you—it's spooky. This is mountains. You don't *know* spooky till you been there. Jungle, sort of, except it's way up in the clouds and there's always this fog—like rain, except it's not raining—everything's all wet and swirly and tangled up and you can't see jack, you can't find your own pecker to piss with. Like you don't even have a body. Serious spooky. You just go with the vapors—the fog sort of takes you in. . . . And the sounds, man. The sounds carry forever. You hear stuff nobody should *ever* hear."

Sanders was quiet for a second, just working the yo-yo, then he smiled at me.

"So, after a couple days the guys start hearing this real soft, kind of wacked-out music. Weird echoes and stuff. Like a radio or something, but it's not a radio, it's this strange gook music that comes right out of the rocks. Faraway, sort of, but right up close, too. They try to ignore it. But it's a listening post, right? So they listen. And every night they keep hearing this crazyass gook concert. All kinds of chimes and xylophones. I mean, this is wilderness—no way, it can't be real—but there it *is*, like the mountains are tuned in to Radio fucking Hanoi. Naturally they get nervous. One guy sticks Juicy Fruit in his ears. Another guy almost flips. Thing is, though, they can't report music. They can't get on the horn and call back to base and say, 'Hey, listen, we need some firepower, we got to blow away this weirdo gook rock band.' They can't do that. It wouldn't go down. So they lie there in the fog and keep their mouths shut. And what makes it extra bad, see, is the poor dudes can't horse around like normal. Can't joke it away. Can't even talk to each other except maybe in whispers, all hush-hush, and that just revs up the willies. All they do is listen."

Again there was some silence as Mitchell Sanders looked out on the river. The dark was coming on hard now, and off to the west I could see the mountains rising in silhouette, all the mysteries and unknowns.

"This next part," Sanders said quietly, "you won't believe."

"Probably not," I said.

"You won't. And you know why?" He gave me a tired smile. "Because it happened. Because every word is absolutely dead-on true."

Sanders made a little sound in his throat, like a sigh, as if to say he didn't care if I believed it or not. But he did care. He wanted me to feel the truth, to believe by the raw force of feeling. He seemed sad, in a way.

"These six guys," he said, "they're pretty fried out by now, and one night they start hearing voices. Like at a cocktail party. That's what it sounds like, this big swank gook cocktail party somewhere out there in the fog. Music and chitchat and stuff. It's crazy, I know, but they hear the champagne corks. They hear the actual martini glasses. Real hoity-toity, all very civilized, except this isn't civilization. This is Nam.

"Anyway, the guys try to be cool. They just lie there and groove, but after a while they start hearing—you won't believe this—they hear chamber music. They hear violins and cellos. They hear this terrific mama-san soprano. Then after a while they hear gook opera and a glee club and the Haiphong Boys Choir and a barbershop quartet and all kinds of weird chanting and Buddha-Buddha stuff. And the whole time, in the background, there's still that cocktail party going on. All these different voices. Not human voices, though. Because it's the mountains. Follow me? The rock—it's *talking*. And the fog, too, and the grass and the goddamn mongooses. Everything talks. The trees talk politics, the monkeys talk religion. The whole country. Vietnam. The place talks. It talks. Understand? Nam—it truly *talks*.

"The guys can't cope. They lose it. They get on the radio and report enemy movement—a whole army, they say—and they order up the firepower. They get arty and gunships. They call in air strikes. And I'll tell you, they fuckin' crash that cocktail party. All night long, they just smoke those mountains. They make jungle juice. They blow away trees and glee clubs and whatever else there is to blow away. Scorch time. They walk napalm up and down the ridges. They bring in the Cobras and F-4s, they use Willie Peter and HE and incendiaries. It's all fire. They make those mountains burn.

"Around dawn things finally get quiet. Like you never even *heard* quiet before. One of those real thick, real misty days—just clouds and fog, they're off in this special zone—and the mountains are absolutely dead-flat silent. Like Brigadoon—pure vapor, you know? Everything's all sucked up inside the fog. Not a single sound, except they still *hear* it.

"So they pack up and start humping. They head down the mountain, back to base camp, and when they get there they don't say diddly. They don't talk. Not a word, like they're deaf and dumb. Later on this fat bird colonel comes up and asks what the hell happened out there. What'd they hear? Why all the ordnance? The man's ragged out, he gets down tight on their case. I mean, they spent six trillion dollars on firepower, and this fatass colonel wants answers, he wants to know what the fuckin' story is.

"But the guys don't say zip. They just look at him for a while, sort of funny like, sort of amazed, and the whole war is right there in that stare. It says everything you can't ever say. It says, man, you got *wax* in your ears. It says, poor bastard, you'll never know—wrong frequency—you don't *even* want to hear this. Then they salute the fucker and walk away, because certain stories you don't ever tell."

You can tell a true war story by the way it never seems to end. Not then, not ever. Not when Mitchell Sanders stood up and moved off into the dark.

It all happened.

Even now, at this instant, I remember that yo-yo. In a way, I suppose, you had to be there, you had to hear it, but I could tell how desperately Sanders wanted me to believe him, his frustration at not quite getting the details right, not quite pinning down the final and definitive truth.

And I remember sitting at my foxhole that night, watching the shadows of Quang Ngai, thinking about the coming day and how we would cross the river and march west into the mountains, all the ways I might die, all the things I did not understand.

Late in the night Mitchell Sanders touched my shoulder.

"Just came to me," he whispered. "The moral, I mean. Nobody listens. Nobody hears nothin'. Like that fatass colonel. The politicians, all the civilian types. Your girlfriend. My girlfriend. Everybody's sweet little virgin girlfriend. What they need is to go out on LP. The vapors, man. Trees and rocks—you got to *listen* to your enemy."

And then again, in the morning, Sanders came up to me. The platoon was preparing to move out, checking weapons, going through all the little rituals that preceded a day's march. Already the lead squad had crossed the river and was filing off toward the west.

"I got a confession to make," Sanders said. "Last night, man, I had to make up a few things."

"I know that."

"The glee club. There wasn't any glee club."

"Right."

"No opera."

"Forget it, I understand."

"Yeah, but listen, it's still true. Those six guys, they heard wicked sound out there. They heard sound you just plain won't believe."

Sanders pulled on his rucksack, closed his eyes for a moment, then almost smiled at me.

I knew what was coming but I beat him to it.

"All right," I said, "what's the moral?"

"Forget it."

"No, go ahead."

For a long while he was quiet, looking away, and the silence kept stretching out until it was almost embarrassing. Then he shrugged and gave me a stare that lasted all day.

"Hear that quiet, man?" he said. "That quiet—just listen. There's your moral."

In a true war story, if there's a moral at all, it's like the thread that makes the cloth. You can't tease it out. You can't extract the meaning without unraveling the deeper meaning. And in the end, really, there's nothing much to say about a true war story, except maybe "Oh."

True war stories do not generalize. They do not indulge in abstraction or analysis.

For example: War is hell. As a moral declaration the old truism seems perfectly true, and yet because it abstracts, because it generalizes, I can't believe it with my stomach. Nothing turns inside.

It comes down to gut instinct. A true war story, if truly told, makes the stomach believe.

This one does it for me. I've told it before—many times, many versions—but here's what actually happened.

We crossed the river and marched west into the mountains. On the third day, Curt Lemon stepped on a booby-trapped 105 round. He was playing catch with

Rat Kiley, laughing, and then he was dead. The trees were thick; it took nearly an hour to cut an LZ for the dustoff.

Later, higher in the mountains, we came across a baby VC water buffalo. What it was doing there I don't know—no farms or paddies—but we chased it down and got a rope around it and led it along to a deserted village where we set for the night. After supper Rat Kiley went over and stroked its nose.

He opened up a can of C rations, pork and beans, but the baby buffalo wasn't interested.

Rat shrugged.

He stepped back and shot it through the right front knee. The animal did not make a sound. It went down hard, then got up again, and Rat took careful aim and shot off an ear. He shot it in the hindquarters and in the little hump at its back. He shot it twice in the flanks. It wasn't to kill; it was to hurt. He put the rifle muzzle up against the mouth and shot the mouth away. Nobody said much. The whole platoon stood there watching, feeling all kinds of things, but there wasn't a great deal of pity for the baby water buffalo. Curt Lemon was dead. Rat Kiley had lost his best friend in the world. Later in the week he would write a long personal letter to the guy's sister, who would not write back, but for now it was a question of pain. He shot off the tail. He shot away chunks of meat below the ribs. All around us there was the smell of smoke and filth and deep greenery, and the evening was humid and very hot. Rat went to automatic. He shot randomly, almost casually, quick little spurts in the belly and butt. Then he reloaded, squatted down, and shot it in the left front knee. Again the animal fell hard and tried to get up, but this time it couldn't quite make it. It wobbled and went down sideways. Rat shot it in the nose. He bent forward and whispered something, as if talking to a pet, then he shot it in the throat. All the while the baby buffalo was silent, or almost silent, just a light bubbling sound where the nose had been. It lay very still. Nothing moved except the eyes, which were enormous, the pupils shiny black and dumb.

Rat Kiley was crying. He tried to say something, but then cradled his rifle and went off by himself.

The rest of us stood in a ragged circle around the baby buffalo. For a time no one spoke. We had witnessed something essential, something brand-new and profound, a piece of the world so startling there was not yet a name for it.

Somebody kicked the baby buffalo.

It was still alive, though just barely, just in the eyes.

"Amazing," Dave Jensen said. "My whole life, I never seen anything like it."

"Never?"

"Not hardly. Not once."

Kiowa and Mitchell Sanders picked up the baby buffalo. They hauled it across the open square, hoisted it up, and dumped it in the village well.

Afterward, we sat waiting for Rat to get himself together.

"Amazing," Dave Jensen kept saying. "A new wrinkle. I never seen it before."

Mitchell Sanders took out his yo-yo. "Well, that's Nam," he said. "Garden of Evil. Over here, man, every sin's real fresh and original."

How do you generalize?

War is hell, but that's not the half of it, because war is also mystery and terror and adventure and courage and discovery and holiness and pity and despair and longing and love. War is nasty; war is fun. War is thrilling; war is drudgery. War makes you a man; war makes you dead.

The truths are contradictory. It can be argued, for instance, that war is grotesque. But in truth war is also beauty. For all its horror, you can't help but gape at the awful majesty of combat. You stare out at tracer rounds unwinding through the dark like brilliant red ribbons. You crouch in ambush as a cool, impassive moon rises over the nighttime paddies. You admire the fluid symmetries of troops on the move, the harmonies of sound and shape and proportion, the great sheets of metal-fire streaming down from a gunship, the illumination rounds, the white phosphorous, the purply orange glow of napalm, the rocket's red glare. It's not pretty, exactly. It's astonishing. It fills the eye. It commands you. You hate it, yes, but your eyes do not. Like a killer forest fire, like cancer under a microscope, any battle or bombing raid or artillery barrage has the aesthetic purity of absolute moral indifference—a powerful, implacable beauty—and a true war story will tell the truth about this, though the truth is ugly.

To generalize about war is like generalizing about peace. Almost everything is true. Almost nothing is true. At its core, perhaps, war is just another name for death, and yet any soldier will tell you, if he tells the truth, that proximity to death brings with it a corresponding proximity to life. After a firefight, there is always the immense pleasure of aliveness. The trees are alive. The grass, the soil—everything. All around you things are purely living, and you among them, and the aliveness makes you tremble. You feel an intense, out-of-the-skin awareness of your living self—your truest self, the human being you want to be and then become by the force of wanting it. In the midst of evil you want to be a good man. You want decency. You want justice and courtesy and human concord, things you never knew you wanted. There is a kind of largeness to it, a kind of godliness. Though it's odd, you're never more alive than when you're almost dead. You recognize what's valuable. Freshly, as if for the first time, you love what's best in yourself and in the world, all that might be lost. At the hour of dusk you sit at your foxhole and look out on a wide river turning pinkish red, and at the mountains beyond, and although in the morning you must cross the river and go into the mountains and do terrible things and maybe die, even so, you find yourself studying the fine colors on the river, you feel wonder and awe at the setting of the sun, and you are filled with a hard, aching love for how the world could be and always should be, but now is not.

Mitchell Sanders was right. For the common soldier, at least, war has the feel—the spiritual texture—of a great ghostly fog, thick and permanent. There is no clarity. Everything swirls. The old rules are no longer binding, the old truths no longer true. Right spills over into wrong. Order blends into chaos, love into hate, ugliness into beauty, law into anarchy, civility into savagery. The vapors suck you in. You can't tell where you are, or why you're there, and the only certainty is overwhelming ambiguity.

In war you lose your sense of the definite, hence your sense of truth itself, and therefore it's safe to say that in a true war story nothing is ever absolutely true.

Often in a true war story there is not even a point, or else the point doesn't hit you until twenty years later, in your sleep, and you wake up and shake your wife and start telling the story to her, except when you get to the end you've forgotten the point again. And then for a long time you lie there watching the story happen in your head. You listen to your wife's breathing. The war's over. You close your eyes. You smile and think, Christ, what's the point?

This one wakes me up.

In the mountains that day, I watched Lemon turn sideways. He laughed and said something to Rat Kiley. Then he took a peculiar half step, moving from shade into bright sunlight, and the booby-trapped 105 round blew him into a tree. The parts were just hanging there, so Dave Jensen and I were ordered to shinny up and peel him off. I remember the white bone of an arm. I remember pieces of skin and something wet and yellow that must've been the intestines. The gore was horrible, and stays with me, but what wakes me up twenty years later is Dave Jensen singing "Lemon Tree" as we threw down the parts.

You can tell a true war story by the questions you ask. Somebody tells a story, let's say, and afterward you ask, "Is it true?" and if the answer matters, you've got your answer.

For example, we've all heard this one. Four guys go down a trail. A grenade sails out. One guy jumps on it and takes the blast and saves his three buddies.

Is it true?

The answer matters.

You'd feel cheated if it never happened. Without the grounding reality, it's just a trite bit of puffery, pure Hollywood, untrue in the way all such stories are untrue. Yet even if it did happen—and maybe it did, anything's possible—even then you know it can't be true, because a true war story does not depend upon that kind of truth. Absolute occurrence is irrelevant. A thing may happen and be a total lie; another thing may not happen and be truer than the truth. For example: four guys go down a trail. A grenade sails out. One guy jumps on it and takes the blast, but it's a killer grenade and everybody dies anyway. Before they die, though, one of the dead guys says, "The fuck you do *that* for?" and the jumper says, "Story of my life, man," and the other guy starts to smile but he's dead.

That's a true story that never happened.

Twenty years later, I can still see the sunlight on Lemon's face. I can see him turning, looking back at Rat Kiley, then he laughed and took that curious half step from shade into sunlight, his face suddenly brown and shining, and when his foot touched down, in that instant, he must've thought it was the sunlight that was killing him. It was not the sunlight. It was a rigged 105 round. But if I could ever get the story right, how the sun seemed to gather around him and pick him up and lift him into a tree, if I could somehow recreate the fatal whiteness of that light, the quick glare, the obvious cause and effect, then you would believe the last thing Curt Lemon believed, which for him must've been the final truth.

Now and then, when I tell this story, someone will come up to me afterward and say she liked it. It's always a woman. Usually it's an older woman of kindly temperament and humane politics. She'll explain that as a rule she hates war stories; she can't understand why people want to wallow in blood and gore. But this one she liked. The poor baby buffalo, it made her sad. Sometimes, even, there are little tears. What I should do, she'll say, is put it all behind me. Find new stories to tell.

I won't say it but I'll think it.

I'll picture Rat Kiley's face, his grief, and I'll think, *You dumb cooze.*

Because she wasn't listening.

It *wasn't* a war story. It was a *love* story.

But you can't say that. All you can do is tell it one more time, patiently, adding and subtracting, making up a few things to get at the real truth. No Mitchell Sanders, you tell her. No Lemon, no Rat Kiley. No trail junction. No baby buffalo. No vines or moss or white blossoms. Beginning to end, you tell her, it's all made up. Every goddamn detail—the mountains and the river and especially that poor dumb baby buffalo. None of it happened. *None* of it. And even if it did happen, it didn't happen in the mountains, it happened in this little village on the Batangan Peninsula, and it was raining like crazy, and one night a guy named Stink Harris woke up screaming with a leech on his tongue. You can tell a true war story if you just keep on telling it.

And in the end, of course, a true war story is never about war. It's about sunlight. It's about the special way that dawn spreads out on a river when you know you must cross the river and march into the mountains and do things you are afraid to do. It's about love and memory. It's about sorrow. It's about sisters who never write back and people who never listen.

The Vietnam in Me

LZ Gator, Vietnam, February 1994

I'm home, but the house is gone. Not a sandbag, not a nail or a scrap of wire. On Gator, we used to say, the wind doesn't blow, it sucks. Maybe that's what happened—the wind sucked it all away. My life, my virtue.

In February 1969, 25 years ago, I arrived as a young, terrified pfc. on this lonely little hill in Quang Ngai Province. Back then, the place seemed huge and imposing and permanent. A forward firebase for the Fifth Battalion of the 46th infantry, 198th Infantry Brigade, LZ Gator was home to 700 or 800 American soldiers, mostly grunts. I remember a tar helipad, a mess hall, a medical station, mortar and artillery emplacements, two volleyball courts, numerous barracks and offices and supply depots and machine shops and entertainment clubs. Gator was our castle. Not safe, exactly, but far preferable to the bush. No land mines here. No paddies bubbling with machine-gun fire.

Maybe once a month, for three or four days at a time, Alpha Company would return to Gator for stand-down, where we took our comforts behind a perimeter of bunkers and concertina wire. There were hot showers and hot meals, ice chests

Reprinted from the *New York Times Magazine*, October 2, 1994, pp. 48–57, by permission of The New York Times Company. Copyright © 2001 by the New York Times Company.

packed with beer, glossy pinup girls, big, black Sony tape decks booming "We gotta get out of this place" at decibels for the deaf. Thirty or 40 acres of almost-America. With a little weed and a lot of beer, we would spend the days of stand-down in flat-out celebration, purely alive, taking pleasure in our own biology, kidneys and livers and lungs and legs, all in their proper alignments. We could breathe here. We could feel our fists uncurl, the pressures approaching normal. The real war, it seemed, was in another solar system. By day, we'd fill sandbags or pull bunker guard. In the evenings, there were outdoor movies and sometimes live floor shows—pretty Korean girls breaking our hearts in their spangled miniskirts and high leather boots—then afterward we'd troop back to the Alpha barracks for some letter writing or boozing or just a good night's sleep.

So much to remember. The time we filled a nasty lieutenant's canteen with mosquito repellent; the sounds of choppers and artillery fire; the slow dread that began building as word spread that in a day or two we'd be heading back to the bush. Pinkville, maybe. The Batangan Peninsula. Spooky, evil places where the land itself could kill you.

Now I stand in this patch of weeds, looking down on what used to be the old Alpha barracks. Amazing, really, what time can do. You'd think there would be *something* left, some faint imprint, but LZ (Landing Zone) Gator has been utterly and forever erased from the earth. Nothing here but ghosts and wind

At the foot of Gator, along Highway 1, the little hamlet of Nuoc Man is going bonkers over our arrival here. As we turn and walk down the hill, maybe 200 people trail along, gawking and chattering, the children reaching out to touch our skin. Through our interpreter, Mrs. Le Hoai Phuong, I'm told that I am the first American soldier to return to this place in the 24 years since Gator was evacuated in 1970. In a strange way, the occasion has the feel of a reunion—happy faces, much bowing. "Me Wendy," says a middle-aged woman. Another says, "Flower." Wendy and Flower: G.I. nicknames retrieved from a quarter-century ago.

An elderly woman, perhaps in her late 70's, tugs at my shirt and says, "My name Mama-san."

Dear God. We should've bombed these people with love.

Cambridge, Mass., June 1994

Last night suicide was on my mind. Not whether, but how. Tonight it will be on my mind again. Now it's 4 A. M., June the 5th. The sleeping pills have not worked. I sit in my underwear at this unblinking fool of a computer and try to wrap words around a few horrid truths.

I returned to Vietnam with a woman whose name is Kate, whom I adored and have since lost. She's with another man, seven blocks away. This I learned yesterday afternoon. My own fault, Kate would say, and she would be mostly right. Not entirely. In any case, these thoughts are probably too intimate, too awkward and embarrassing for public discussion. But who knows? Maybe a little blunt human truth will send you off to church, or to confession, or inside yourself.

Not that it matters. For me, with one eye on these smooth yellow pills, the world must be written about as it is or not written about at all.

LZ Gator, February 1994

By chance, Kate and I have arrived in Nuoc Man on a day of annual commemoration, a day when the graves of the local war dead are blessed and repaired and decorated and wept over.

The village elders invite us to a feast, a picnic of sorts, where we take seats before a low lacquered table at an outdoor shrine. Children press up close, all around. The elders shoo them away, but the shooing doesn't do much. I'm getting nervous. The food on display seems a bit exotic. Not to my taste. I look at Kate, Kate looks at me. "Number one chop-chop," an old woman says, a wrinkled, gorgeous, protective, scarred, welcoming old woman. "Number one," she promises, and nudges Kate, and smiles a heartbreaking betel-nut smile.

I choose something white. Fish, I'm guessing. I have eaten herring; I have enjoyed herring. This is not herring.

There are decisions to be made.

The elders bow and execute chewing motions. Do not forget: our hosts are among the maimed and widowed and orphaned, the bombed and rebombed, the recipients of white phosphorus, the tenders of graves. Chew, they say, and by God I chew.

Kate has the good fortune to find a Kleenex. She's a pro. She executes a polite wiping motion and it's over for her. Eddie Keating, the *Times* photographer whose pictures accompany this text, tucks his portion between cheek and gum, where it remains until the feast concludes. Me—I imagine herring. I remember Sunday afternoons as a boy, the Vikings on TV, my dad opening up the crackers and creamed herring, passing it out at half-time. Other flashes too. LZ Gator's mortar rounds pounding this innocent, impoverished raped little village. Eight or nine corpses piled not 50 yards from where we now sit in friendly union. I prepare myself. Foul, for sure, but things come around. Nuoc Man swallowed plenty.

The Song Tra Hotel, Quang Ngai City, February 1994

It's late in the evening. The air-conditioner is at full Cuban power. Kate's eyes sparkle, she's laughing. "Swallowed!" she keeps saying.

In 1969, when I went to war, Kate was 3 years old. Kennedy, Johnson, Nixon, McNamara, Bunker, Rogers, Bundy, Rusk, Abrams, Rostow—for her, these names are like the listings on a foreign menu. Some she recognizes not at all, some she recalls from books or old television clips. But she never tasted the dishes. She does not know ice cream from Brussels sprouts. Three years old—how could she? No more than I could know the Southern California of her own youth.

Still it was Kate who insisted we come here. I was more than reluctant—I was petrified. I looked for excuses. Bad dreams and so on. But Kate's enthusiasm won me over; she wanted to share in my past, the shapes of things, the smells and sunlight.

As it turns out, the sharing has gone both ways. In any other circumstances, I would have returned to this country almost purely as a veteran, caught up in memory, but Kate's presence has made me pay attention to the details of here and now, a Vietnam that exists outside the old perimeter of war. She takes delight in things alive: a chicken wired to someone's bicycle, an old woman's enormous fingernails, an infant slung casually on the hip of a tiny 7-year-old girl. Kate has the eyes and spirit of an adventurer, wide open to the variety of the world and these qualities have pushed me toward some modest adventurism of my own.

Now I watch her fiddle with the air-conditioner. "Swallowed!" she keeps saying.

Later in the night, as on many other nights, we talk about the war. I try to explain—ineptly, no doubt—that Vietnam was more than terror. For me, at least, Vietnam was partly love. With each step, each light-year of a second, a foot soldier is always almost dead, or so it feels, and in such circumstances you can't *help* but love. You love your mom and dad, the Vikings, hamburgers on the grill, your pulse, your future—everything that might be lost or never come to be. Intimacy with death carries with it a corresponding new intimacy with life. Jokes are funnier, green is greener. You love the musty morning air. You love the miracles of your own enduring capacity for love. You love your friends in Alpha Company— a kid named Chip, my buddy. He wrote letters to my sister, I wrote letters to his sister. In the rear, back at Gator, Chip and I would go our separate ways, by color, both of us ashamed but knowing it had to be that way. In the bush, though, nothing kept us apart. "Black and White" we were called. In May of 1969, Chip was blown high into a hedge of bamboo. Many pieces. I loved the guy, he loved me. I'm alive. He's dead. An old story, I guess.

Cambridge, June 1994

It's 5:25 in the morning, June 7. I have just taken my first drug of the day, a prescription drug, Oxazepam, which files the edge off anxiety. Thing is, I'm not anxious. I'm slop. This is despair. This is a valance of horror that Vietnam never approximated. If war is hell what do we call hopelessness?

I have not killed myself. That day, this day, maybe tomorrow. Like Nam, it goes.

For some time, years in fact, I have been treated for depression, $8,000 or $9,000 worth. Some of it has worked. Or was working. I had called back to memory—not to memory, exactly, but to significance—some pretty painful feelings of rejection as a child. Chubby and friendless and lonely. I had come to acknowledge, more or less, the dominant principle of love in my life, how far I would go to get it, how terrified I was of losing it. I have done bad things for love, bad things to stay loved. Kate is one case. Vietnam is another. More than anything, it was this desperate love craving that propelled me into a war I considered mistaken, probably evil. In college, I stood in peace vigils. I rang doorbells for Gene McCarthy, composed earnest editorials for the school newspaper. But when the draft notice arrived after graduation, the old demons went to work almost instantly. I thought about Canada. I thought about jail. But in the end I could not bear the prospect of rejection: by my family, my country, my friends, my hometown. I would risk conscience and rectitude before risking the loss of love.

I have written some of this before, but I must write it again. I was a coward. I went to Vietnam.

My Lai, Quang Ngai Province, February 1994

Weird, but I know this place. I've been here before. Literally, but also in my nightmares.

One year after the massacre, Alpha Company's area of operations included the village of My Lai 4, or so it was called on American military maps. The Vietnamese call it Thuan Yen, which belongs to a larger hamlet called Tu Cung, which in turn belongs to an even larger parent village called Son My. But names are finally irrelevant. I am just here.

Twenty-five years ago, knowing nothing of the homicides committed by American troops on the morning of March 16, 1968, Alpha Company walked through and around this hamlet on numerous occasions. Now, standing here with Kate, I can't recognize much. The place blends in with all the other poor, scary, beleaguered villes in this area we called Pinkville. Even so, the feel of the place is as familiar as the old stucco house of my childhood. The clay trails, the cow dung, the blank faces, the unknowns and unknowables. There is the smell of sin here. Smells of terror, too, and enduring sorrow.

What happened briefly, was this. At approximately 7:30 on the morning of March 16, 1968, a company of roughly 115 American solders were inserted by helicopter just outside the village of My Lai. They met no resistance. No enemy. No incoming fire. Still, for the next four hours, Charlie Company killed whatever could be killed. They killed chickens. They killed dogs and cattle. They killed people too. Lots of people. Women, infants, teen-agers, old men. The United States Army's Criminal Investigation Division compiled a list of 343 fatalities and an independent Army inquiry led by Lieut. Gen. William R. Peers estimated that the death count may have exceeded 400. At the Son My Memorial a large tablet lists 504 names. According to Col. William Wilson, one of the original Army investigators, "The crimes visited on the inhabitants of Son My Village included individual and group acts of murder, rape, sodomy, maiming, assault on noncombatants and the mistreatment and killing of detainees."

The testimony of one member of Charlie Company, Salvadore LaMartina, suggests the systematic, cold-blooded character of the slaughter.

Q: Did you obey your orders?
A: Yes, sir.
Q: What were your orders?
A: Kill anything that breathed.

Whether or not such instructions were ever directly issued is a matter of dispute. Either way, a good many participants would later offer the explanation that they were obeying orders, a defense explicitly prohibited by the Nuremberg Principles and the United States Army's own rules of war. Other participants would argue that the civilians at My Lai were themselves Vietcong. A young soldier named Paul Meadlo, who was responsible for numerous deaths on that bright March morning, offered this appalling testimony:

Q: What did you do?
A: I held my M-16 on them.
Q: Why?
A: Because they might attack.
Q: They were children and babies?

A: Yes.
Q: And they might attack? Children and babies?
A: They might've had a fully loaded grenade on them. The mothers might have throwed them at us.
Q: Babies?
A: Yes. . . .
Q: Were the babies in their mothers' arms?
A: I guess so.
Q: And the babies moved to attack?
A: I expected at any moment they were about to make a counterbalance.

Eventually, after a cover-up that lasted more than a year and after the massacre made nationwide headlines, the Army's Criminal Investigation Division produced sufficient evidence to charge 30 men with war crimes. Of these, only a single soldier, First Lieut. William Laws Calley Jr., was ever convicted or spent time in prison. Found guilty of the premeditated murder of "not less than" 22 civilians, Calley was sentenced to life at hard labor, but after legal appeals and sentence reductions, his ultimate jail time amounted to three days in a stockade and four and a half months in prison.

In some cases, judicial action was never initiated; in other cases, charges were quietly dropped. Calley aside, only a handful of men faced formal court-martial proceedings, either for war crimes or for subsequent cover-up activities, with the end result of five acquittals and four judicially ordered dismissals. Among those acquitted was Capt. Ernest Medina, who commanded Charlie Company on the morning of March 16, 1968.

All this is history. Dead as those dead women and kids. Even at the time, most Americans seemed to shrug it off as a cruel, nasty, inevitable consequence of war. There were numerous excuses, numerous rationalizations. Upright citizens decried even the small bit of justice secured by the conviction of Lieutenant Calley. Now, more than 25 years later, the villainy of that Saturday morning in 1968 has been pushed off to the margins of memory. In the colleges and high schools I sometimes visit, the mention of My Lai brings on null stares, a sort of puzzlement, disbelief mixed with utter ignorance.

Evil has no place, it seems, in our national mythology. We erase it. We use ellipses. We salute ourselves and take pride in America the White Knight, America the Lone Ranger, America's sleek laser-guided weaponry beating up on Saddam and his legion of devils.

It's beginning to rain when Kate and I sit down to talk with two survivors of the slaughter here. Mrs. Ha Thi Quy is a woman of 69 years. Her face is part stone, part anguish as she describes through an interpreter the events of that day. It's hard stuff to hear. "Americans came here twice before," Mrs. Quy says. "Nothing bad happened, they were friendly to us. But on that day the solders jumped out of their helicopters and immediately began to shoot. I prayed, I pleaded." As I take notes, I'm recalling other prayers, other pleadings. A woman saying "No VC, no VC," while a young lieutenant pistol-whipped her without the least expression on his face, without the least sign of distress or moral uncertainty.

Mad Mark, we called him. But he wasn't mad. He was numb. He'd lost himself. His gyroscope was gone. He didn't know up from down, good from bad.

Mrs. Quy is crying now. I can feel Kate crying off to my side, though I don't dare look.

"The Americans took us to a ditch. I saw two soldiers with red faces—sunburned—and they pushed a lot of people into the ditch. I was in the ditch. I fell down and many fell on top of me. Soldiers were shooting. I was shot in the hip. The firing went on and on. It would stop and then start again and then stop." Now I hear Kate crying, not loud just a certain breathiness I've come to recognize. This will be with us forever. This we'd have.

My notes take a turn for the worse. "I lay under the dead in the ditch. Around noon, when I heard no more gunfire, I came out of the ditch and saw many more. Brains, pieces of body. My house was burned. Cattle were shot. I went back to the ditch. Three of my four children were killed."

I'm exhausted when Mrs. Quy finishes. Partly it's the sheer magnitude of horror, partly some hateful memories of my own.

I can barely wire myself together as Mrs. Truong Thi Le, another survivor, recounts those four hours of murder. Out of her family of 10, 9 died that day. "I fell down," Mrs. Le tells us. "But I was not shot. I lay with three other bodies on me, all blood. Did not move at all. Pretended dead. Saw newborn baby near a woman. Woman died. Infant still alive. Soldiers came up. Shot baby."

Outside, the rain has let up. Kate, Eddie and I take a walk through the hamlet. We stare at foundations where houses used to stand. We admire a harsh, angular, defiant, beautiful piece of sculpture, a monument to the murdered.

Mrs. Quy accompanies us for a while. She's smiling, accommodating. Impossible, but she seems to like us.

At one point, while I'm scribbling in my notebook, she pulls down her trousers. She shows Kate the scarred-over bullet hole in her hip.

Kate nods and makes sounds of sympathy. What does one say? Bad day. World of hurt.

Now the rain is back, much harder. I'm drenched, cold and something else. Eddie and I stand at the ditch where maybe 50, maybe 80, maybe 100 innocent human beings perished. I watch Eddie snap his pictures.

Here's the something else: I've got the guilt chills.

Years ago, ignorant of the massacre, I hated this place, and places much like it. Two miles away, in an almost identical hamlet, Chip was blown into his hedge of bamboo. A mile or so east, Roy Arnold was shot dead, I was slightly wounded. A little farther east, a kid named McElhaney died. Just north of here, on a rocky hillside, another kid, named Slocum, lost his foot to a land mine. It goes on.

I despised everything—the soil, the tunnels, the paddies, the poverty and myself. Each step was an act of the purest self-hatred and self-betrayal, yet, in truth, because truth matters, my sympathies were rarely with the Vietnamese. I was mostly terrified. I was lamenting in advance my own pitiful demise. After fire fights, after friends died there was also a great deal of anger—black, fierce, hurting anger—the kind you want to take out on whatever presents itself. This is not to justify what occurred here. Justifications are empty and outrageous. Rather, it's to say that I more or less understand what happened on that day in March 1968, how it happened, the wickedness that soaks into your blood and heats up and starts to sizzle. I know the boil that precedes butchery. At the same time, however, the men in Alpha Company did not commit murder. We did not turn our machine guns on civilians; we did not cross that conspicuous line between rage and homicide. I know what occurred here, yes, but I also feel betrayed by a nation that so widely shrugs off barbarity, by a military judicial system that treats murderers and common soldiers as one and the same.

Apparently we're all innocent—those who exercise moral restraint and those who do not, officers who control their troops and officers who do not. In a way, America has declared *itself* innocent.

I look away for a time, and then look back.

By most standards, this is not much of a ditch. A few feet deep, a few feet wide. The rain makes the greenish brown water bubble like a thousand tiny mouths.

The guilt has turned to a gray, heavy sadness. I have to take my leave but don't know how.

After a time, Kate walks up, hooks my arm, doesn't say anything, doesn't have to, leads me into a future that I know will hold misery for both of us. Different hemispheres, different scales of atrocity. I don't want it to happen. I want to tell her things and be understood and live happily ever after. I want a miracle. That's the final emotion. The terror at this ditch, the certain doom, the need for God's intervention.

Cambridge, June 1994

I've been trying to perform good deeds. I bought a Father's Day card three days early. I made appointments for a physical exam, dental work, a smoke-ender's program. I go for walks every day. I work out, draw up lists, call friends, visit lawyers, buy furniture, discharge promises, keep my eyes off the sleeping pills. The days are all right.

Now the clock shows 3:55 A.M. I call NERVOUS and listen to an automated female voice confirm it. The nights are not all right.

I write these few words, which seem useless, then get up and pull out an album of photographs from the Vietnam trip. The album was Kate's parting gift. On the cover she inserted a snapshot that's hard to look at but harder still to avoid. We stand on China Beach near Danang. Side by side, happy as happy will ever be, our fingers laced in a fitted, comfortable, half-conscious way that makes me feel a gust of hope. It's a gust though, here and gone.

Numerous times over the past several days, at least a dozen, this piece has come close to hyperspace. Twice it lay at the bottom of a wastebasket. I've spent my hours preparing a tape of songs for Kate, stuff that once meant things. Corny songs, some of them. Happy songs, love-me songs.

Today, scared stiff, I deposited the tape on her doorstep. Another gust of hope, then a whole lot of stillness.

The Song Tra Hotel, Quang Ngai City, February 1994

Kate's in the shower, I'm in history. I sit with a book propped up against the air-conditioner, underlining sentences, sweating out my own ignorance.

Twenty-five years ago, like most other grunts in Alpha Company, I knew next to nothing about this place—Vietnam in general, Quang Ngai in particular. Now I'm learning. In the years preceding the murders at My Lai, more than 70 percent of the villages in this province had been destroyed by air strikes, artillery fire, Zippo lighters, napalm, white phosphorus, bulldozers, gunships and other such means. Roughly 40 percent of the population had lived in refugee camps, while civilian casualties in the area were approaching 50,000 a year. These numbers, reported by the journalist Jonathan Schell in 1967, were later confirmed as substantially correct by Government investigators. Not that I need confirmation. Back in 1969 the wreckage was all around us, so common it seemed part of the geography, as natural as any mountain or river. Wreckage was the rule. Brutality was S.O.P. Scalded children, pistol-whipped women, burning hootches, free-fire zones, body counts, indiscriminate bombing and harassment fire, villages in ash, M-60 machine guns hosing down dark green tree lines and any human life behind them.

In a war without aim, you tend not to aim. You close your eyes, close your heart. The consequences become hit or miss in the most general sense.

With so few military targets, with an enemy that was both of and among the population, Alpha Company began to regard Quang Ngai itself as the true enemy—the physical place, the soil and paddies. What had started for us as a weird, vicious little war soon evolved into something far beyond vicious, a hopped-up killer strain of nihilism, waste without want, aimlessness of deed mixed with aimlessness of spirit. As Schell wrote after the events at My Lai, "There can be no doubt that such an atrocity was possible only because a number of other methods of killing civilians and destroying their villages had come to be the rule, and not the exception, in our conduct of the war."

I look up from my book briefly, listen to Kate singing in the shower. A doctoral candidate at Harvard University, smart and sophisticated, but she's also fluent in joy, attuned to the pleasures and beauty of the world. She knows the lyrics to "Hotel California," start to finish, while here at the air-conditioner I can barely pick out the simplest melodies of Vietnam, the most basic chords of history. It's as if I never heard the song, as if I'd gone to war in some mall or supermarket. I discover that Quang Ngai Province was home to one of Vietnam's fiercest, most recalcitrant, most zealous revolutionary movements. Independent by tradition, hardened by poverty and rural isolation, the people of Quang Ngai were openly resistant to French colonialism as far back as the 19th century and were among the first to rebel against France in the 1930's. The province remained wholly under Vietminh control throughout the war against France; it remained under Vietcong control, at least by night, throughout the years of war against America. Even now, in the urbane circles of Hanoi and Ho Chi Minh City, the people of Quang Ngai are regarded as a clan of stubborn country bumpkins, coarse and insular, willfully independent, sometimes defiant of the very Government they had struggled to install.

"Like a different country," our interpreter told us after a long, frustrating session with representatives of the Quang Ngai People's Committee. "These people I don't like much, very crude, very difficult. I think you had horrible bad luck to fight them."

At noon, by appointment, a Vietnamese journalist named Pham Van Duong knocks on our door. It's a secret meeting of sorts. Nothing illegal—a couple of writers, a couple of beers—but I've still got the buzz of some low-level paranoia. Earlier in the day, our joint request for this interview had been denied by a stern, rather enigmatic functionary of the People's Committee. Impossible, we were told. Not on the schedule. The official offered little sympathy for our interpreter's reminder that schedules are man-made, that blocks of time appeared wide open. Logic went nowhere. Bureaucratic scowls, stare-into-space silence. A few minutes later, just outside the provincial offices, we quietly huddled to make our own unsanctioned arrangements.

Now, as Mr. Duong sits down and accepts a beer, I'm feeling the vigilant, slightly illicit anxiety of a midday drug buy. Kate locks the door; I close the drapes. Ridiculous, or almost ridiculous but for the first 10 minutes I sit picturing prison food, listening for footsteps in the hallway. Our interpreter explains to Mr. Duong that I will happily guard his identity in any written account of this conversation.

Mr. Duong snorts at the suggestion. "Only a problem in Quang Ngai," he says. "Officials in Hanoi would be glad for our talking. They wish good relations with America—good new things to happen. Maybe I get a medal. Sell the medal, buy Marlboros."

We click beer bottles. For the next two hours we chat about books, careers, memories of war. I ask about My Lai. Mr. Duong looks at the wall. There is a short hesitation—the hesitation of tact, I suppose. He was 8 years old when news of the massacre reached his village nearby. He recalls great anger among his relatives and friends, disgust and sadness, but no feelings of shock or surprise. "This kind of news came often," he says. "We did not then know the scale of the massacre, just that Americans had been killing people. But killing was everywhere."

Two years later, Mr. Duong's brother joined the 48th Vietcong Battalion. He was killed in 1972.

"My mother fainted when she heard this. She was told that his body had been buried in a mass grave with seven comrades who died in the same attack. This made it much worse for my mother—no good burial. After liberation in 1975, she began to look for my brother's remains. She found the mass grave 20 kilometers south of Quang Ngai City. She wished to dig, to rebury my brother, but people told her no, don't dig and in the beginning she seemed to accept this. Then the Americans returned to search for their own missing, and my mother became very angry. *Why them? Not me?* So she insisted we dig. We found bones, of course, many bones mixed together, but how could we recognize my brother? How could anyone know? But we took away some bones in a box. Reburied them near our house. Every day now, my mother passes by this grave. She feels better, I think. Better at least to tell herself *maybe*."

Kate looks up at me. She's silent, but she knows what I'm thinking. At this instant, a few blocks away, an American M.I.A. search team is headquartered at the Quang Ngai Government guesthouse. With Vietnamese assistance, this team and others like it are engaged in precisely the work of Mr. Duong's mother, digging holes, picking through bones, seeking the couple thousand Americans still listed as missing.

Which is splendid.

And which is also utterly one-sided. A perverse and outrageous double standard.

What if things were reversed? What if the Vietnamese were to ask us, or to require us, to locate and identify each of their own M.I.A.'s? Numbers alone make it impossible: 100,000 is a conservative estimate. Maybe double that. Maybe triple. From my own sliver of experience—one year at war, one set of eyes—I can testify to the lasting anonymity of a great many Vietnamese dead. I watched napalm turn villages into ovens. I watched burials by bulldozer. I watched bodies being flung into trucks, dumped into wells, used for target practice, stacked up and burned like cordwood.

Even in the abstract, I get angry at the stunning, almost cartoonish narcissism of American policy on this issue. I get angrier yet at the narcissism of an American public that embraces and breathes life into the policy—so arrogant, so ignorant, so self-righteous, so wanting in the most fundamental qualities of sympathy and fairness and mutuality. Some of this I express aloud to Mr. Duong, who nods without comment. We finish off our beers. Neither of us can find much to say. Maybe we're both back in history, snagged in brothers and bones. I feel hollow. So little has changed it seems, and so much will always be missing.

Cambridge, June 1994

June 11, I think—I'm too tired to find a calendar. Almost 5 A.M. In another hour it'll be 5:01. I'm on war time, which is the time we're all on at one point or another: when fathers die, when husbands ask for divorce, when women you love are fast asleep beside men you wish were you.

The tape of songs did nothing. Everything will always do nothing.

Kate hurts, too, I'm sure, and did not want it this way. I didn't want it either. Even so, both of us have to live in these slow-motion droplets of now, doing what we do, choosing what we choose, and in different ways both of us are now responsible for the casualty rotting in the space between us.

If there's a lesson in this, which there is not, it's very simple. You don't have to be in Nam to be in Nam.

The Batangan Peninsula, Quang Ngai Province, February 1994

The Graveyard we called it. Littered with land mines, almost completely defoliated, this spit of land jutting eastward into the South China Sea was a place Alpha Company feared the way others might fear snakes, or the dark, or the bogyman. We lost at least three men here; I couldn't begin to count the arms and legs.

Today our little caravan is accompanied by Mr. Ngu Duc Tan, who knows this place intimately, a former captain in the 48th Vietcong Battalion. It was the 48th that Alpha Company chased from village to village, paddy to paddy, during my entire tour in Vietnam. Chased but never found. They found us: ambushes, sniper fire, nighttime mortar attacks. Through our interpreter, who passes along commodious paragraphs in crisp little packets, Mr. Tan speaks genially of military tactics while we make the bumpy ride out toward the Batangan. "U.S. troops not hard to see, not hard to fight," he says. "Much noise, much equipment. Big columns. Nice green uniforms." Sitting ducks, in other words, though Mr. Tan is too polite to express it this way. He explains that the United States Army was never a primary target. "We went after Saigon puppet troops, what you called ARVN. If we beat them, everything collapse, the U.S. would have nothing more to fight for. You brought many soldiers, helicopters, bombs, but we chose not to fight you, except sometimes. America was not the main objective."

God help us, I'm thinking, if we *had* been. All those casualties. All that blood and terror. Even at this moment, more than half a lifetime later, I remember the feel of a bull's-eye pinned to my shirt, a prickly when-will-it-happen sensation, as if I alone had been the main objective.

Meanwhile, Kate is taking her own notes, now and then asking questions through the interpreter. She's better than I am at human dynamics, more fluid and spontaneous, and after a time she gets Mr. Tan to display a few war scars—arms, legs, hands, cheek, chest, skull. Sixteen wounds altogether. The American war, he says, was just one phase in his career as a soldier which began in 1961 and encompassed combat against the South Vietnamese, Khmer Rouge and Chinese.

Talk about bad dreams. One year gave me more than enough to fill up the nights.

My goal on the Batangan peninsula was to show Kate one of the prettiest spots on earth. I'm looking for a lagoon, a little fishing village, an impossibly white beach along the South China Sea.

First, though, Mr. Tan attends to his own agenda. We park the van in one of the inland hamlets, walk without invitation into a small house, sit down for lunch with a man named Vo Van Ba. Instantly, I'm thinking herring. Kate and Eddie have the sense to decline, to tap their stomachs and say things like "Full, full, thanks, thanks." Cans are opened. The house fills up with children, nephews, nieces, babies, cousins, neighbors. There are flies, too. Many, many flies. Many thousand.

Mr. Tan and Mr. Ba eat lunch with their fingers, fast and hungry, chatting amiably while our interpreter does her best to put the gist of it into English. I'm listening hard, chewing hard. I gather that these two men had been comrades of a sort during the war. Mr. Ba, our host, was never a full-time soldier, never even a part-time irregular. As I understand it, he belonged to what we used to call the VC infrastructure, offering support and intelligence to Mr. Tan and his fighting troops.

I lean forward, nod my head. The focus, however, is on the substance I'm swallowing, its remarkable texture, the flies trying to get at it. For five years, Mr. Ba explains, he lived entirely underground with a family of eight. Five years, he repeats. Cooking, bathing, working, sleeping. He waits for the translation, waits a bit longer, then looks at me with a pair of silvery, burned-out, cauterized, half-blind, underground eyes. "You had the daylight, but I had the earth." Mr. Ba turns to Mr. Tan. After a second he chuckles. "Many times I might reach up and take this man's leg. Many times. Very easy. I might just pull him down to where the war was."

We're on foot now. Even at 59, Mr. Tan moves swiftly, with the grace and authority of a man who once led solders in combat. He does not say much. He leads us toward the ocean, toward the quaint fishing village I'm hoping to show Kate, but along the way there is one last item Mr. Tan wishes to show me. We move down a trail through two or three adjacent hamlets, seem to circle back for a time, end up in front of another tiny house.

Mr. Tan's voice goes into command tone—two or three sharp, snapping words. A pair of boys dart into the house. No wasted time, they come out fast, carrying what's left of a man named Nguyen Van Ngu. They balance this wreckage on a low chair. Both legs are gone at the upper-upper thigh. We shake hands. Neither of us knows what to say—there is nothing worth saying—so for a few minutes we exchange stupidities in our different languages, no translator available to wash away the helplessness. We pose for photographs. We try for smiles.

Mr. Tan does not smile. He nods to himself—maybe to me. But I get the point anyway. Here is your paradise. Here is your pretty little fishing village by the sea.

Two minutes later, we're on the beach. It *is* beautiful, even stunning. Kate wades out into the water. She's surrounded by kids. They giggle and splash her, she splashes back, and I stand there like an idiot, grinning, admiring the view, while Mr. Tan waits patiently in the shade.

Cambridge, July 1994

Outside, it's the Fourth of July. Lovely day, empty streets. Kate is where Kate is, which is elsewhere, and I am where I am, which is also elsewhere. Someday, no doubt, I'll wish happiness for myself, but for now it's still war time, minute to minute. Not quite 11 A.M. Already I've been out for two walks, done the laundry, written a few words, bought groceries, lifted weights, watched the Fourth of July sunlight slide across my street-side balcony.

And Kate?

The beach, maybe? A backyard cookout?

The hardest part, by far, is to make the bad pictures go away. On war time, the world is one long horror movie, image after image, and if it's anything like Vietnam, I'm in for a lifetime of wee-hour creeps.

Meanwhile, I try to plug up the leaks and carry through on some personal resolutions. For too many years I've lived in paralysis—guilt, depression, terror, shame—and now it's either move or die. Over the past weeks, at profound cost, I've taken actions with my life that are far too painful for any public record. But at least the limbo has ended. Starting can start.

There's a point here: Vietnam, Cambridge, Paris, Neptune—these are states of mind. Minds change.

My Khe, Quang Ngai Province, February 1994

There is one piece of ground I wish to revisit above all others in this country. I've come . . . prepared with a compass, a military map, grid coordinates, a stack of after-action reports recovered from a dusty box in the National Archives.

We're back near Pinkville, a mile or so east of My Lai. We are utterly lost, the interpreter, the van driver, the People's Committee representative, Eddie, Kate, me. I unfold the map and place a finger on the spot I'm hoping to find. A group of villagers puzzle over it. They chatter among themselves—arguing, it seems—then one of them points west, another north, most at the heavens.

Lost, that was the Vietnam of 25 years ago. The war came at us as a blur, raw confusion, and my fear now is that I would not recognize the right spot even while standing on it.

For well over an hour we drive from place to place. We end up precisely where we started. Once more, everyone spills out of the van. The thought occurs to me that this opportunity may never come again. I find my compass, place it on the map and look up for a geographical landmark. A low green hill rises to the west— not much, just a hump on the horizon.

I'm no trailblazer; but this works. One eye on the compass, one eye on some inner rosary, I lead our exhausted column 200 yards eastward, past a graveyard and out along a narrow paddy lake, where suddenly the world shapes itself exactly as it was shaped a quarter-century ago—the curvatures, the tree lines, the precise angles and proportions. I stop there and wait for Kate. *This* I dreamed of giving her. *This* I dreamed of sharing.

Our fingers lock, which happens without volition, and we stand looking out on a wide and very lovely field of rice. The sunlight gives it some gold and yellow. There is no wind at all. Before us is how peace would be defined in a dictionary for the speechless. I don't cry. I don't know what to do. At one point I hear myself talking about what happened here so long ago, motioning out at the rice, describing chaos and horror beyond anything I would experience until a few months later. I tell her how Paige lost his lower leg, how we had to probe for McElhaney in the flooded paddy, how the gunfire went on and on, how in the course of two hell-on-earth hours we took 13 casualties.

I doubt Kate remembers a word. Maybe she shouldn't. But I do hope she remembers the sunlight striking that field of rice. I hope she remembers the feel of our fingers. I hope she remembers how I fell silent after a time, just looking out at the golds and yellows, joining the peace, and how in those fine sunlit moments, which were ours, Vietnam took a little Vietnam out of me.

Ho Chi Minh City, February 1994

We hate this place.

Even the names—Saigon, Ho Chi Minh City. A massive identity crisis. Too loud, too quiet. Too alive, too dead.

For all the discomforts of Quang Ngai Province, which were considerable, Kate and I had taken pleasure in those qualities of beauty and equanimity that must have vanished from Saigon when the first oil barge steamed into port.

But we give it our best. An hour in the Chinese market district which is like an hour in combat. Two hours at the old presidential palace—as tawdry and corrupt as its former inhabitants. We risk periodic excursions into streets where the American dollar remains more valuable than oxygen, of which there is precious little. Maybe we've hit some interior wall. Maybe it's the diesel-heat. We visit a war-crimes museum, the old American Embassy and order lunch by way of room service. Western pop music blares at full volume from Government loudspeakers just outside our hotel. For hours, even with earplugs, we listen to "As Tears Go By" and "My Way." What happened to Ho Chi Minh? What happened to revolution? All we've heard comes from the Beatles.

In mid-afternoon, the music ceases. We go out for a short walk, do some shopping, then retreat to the rooftop swimming pool of the Rex Hotel. It could as well be Las Vegas. We don't say so, not directly, but both Kate and I are ready to evacuate, we're humming "We gotta get out of this place." Pretty soon we'll be singing it over loudspeakers.

For now, Kate lounges at the pool. She writes postcards. She catches me watching. She snaps pictures to show her children someday.

Bruce Weigl

American poet Bruce Weigl (b. 1949) served in the First Air Cavalry of the Vietnam War during 1967 and 1968. He has written many books of poetry and received several awards. Weigl has returned to Vietnam two times. On his second visit, in 1990, he went with fellow writers Larry Heineman and Tim O'Brien, whose work also appears in this chapter.

What Saves Us

We are wrapped around each other
in the back of my father's car parked
in the empty lot of the high school
of our failures, sweat on her neck
like oil. The next morning I would leave
for the war and I thought I had something
coming for that, I thought to myself
that I would not die never having
been inside her body. I lifted
her skirt above her waist like an umbrella
blown inside out by the storm. I pulled
her cotton panties up as high
as she could stand. I was on fire. Heaven
was in sight. We were drowning
on our tongues and I tried
to tear my pants off when she stopped
so suddenly we were surrounded
only by my shuddering
and by the school bells
grinding in the empty halls.
She reached to find something,
a silver crucifix on a silver chain,
the tiny savior's head
hanging, and stakes through his hands and his feet.
She put it around my neck and held me
so long my heart's black wings were calmed.
We are not always right
about what we think will save us.
I thought that dragging the angel down that night

Reprinted from *What Saves Us*, (1992), by permission of Northwestern University.

would save me, but I carried the crucifix in my pocket
and rubbed it on my face and lips
nights the rockets roared in.
People die sometimes so near you,
you feel them struggling to cross over,
the deep untangling, of one body from another.

The Way of Tet

Year of the monkey, year of the human wave,
the people smuggled weapons in caskets through the city
in long processions undisturbed
and buried them in Saigon graveyards.
At the feet of their small Buddhas
weary bar girls burned incense
before the boy soldiers arrived
to buy them tea and touch them
where they pleased. Twenty years
and the feel of a girl's body
so young there's no hair
is like a dream, but living is a darker thing,
the iron burning bee who drains the honey,
and he remembers her
twisting in what evening
light broke into the small room in the shack
in the labyrinth of shacks
in the alley where the lost and corrupted kept house.
He undressed her for the last time,
each piece of clothing
a sacrifice she surrendered to the war
the way the world had become.
Tomorrow blood would run in every province.
Tomorrow people would rise from tunnels everywhere
and resurrect something ancient from inside them,
and the boy who came ten thousand miles to touch her
small self lies beside the girl whose words he can't understand,
their song a veil between them.

She is a white bird in the bamboo, fluttering.
She is so small he imagines

he could hold all of her
in his hands and lift her to the black
sky beyond the illumination round's white light
where she would fly from her life
and the wounds from the lovers would heal,
the broken skin grow back.
But he need only touch her, only
lift the blanket from her shoulders
and the automatic shape of love unfolds,
the flare's light burning down on them,
lost in a wave that arrives
after a thousand years of grief
at their hearts.

Song of Napalm

for my wife

After the storm, after the rain stopped pounding,
we stood in the doorway watching horses
walk off lazily across the pasture's hill.
We stared through the black screen,
our vision altered by the distance
so I thought I saw a mist
kicked up around their hooves when they faded
like cut-out horses
away from us.
The grass was never more blue in that light, more
scarlet; beyond the pasture
trees scraped their voices into the wind, branches
crisscrossed the sky like barbed wire
but you said they were only branches.

Okay. The storm stopped pounding.
I am trying to say this straight: for once
I was sane enough to pause and breathe
outside my wild plans and after the hard rain
I turned my back on the old curses. I believed
they swung finally away from me . . .

But still the branches are wire
and thunder is the pounding mortar,
still I close my eyes and see the girl
running from her village, napalm
stuck to her dress like jelly,
her hands reaching for the no one
who waits in waves of heat before her.

So I can keep on living,
so I can stay here beside you,
I try to imagine she runs down the road and wings
beat inside her until she rises
above the stinking jungle and her pain
eases, and your pain, and mine.

But the lie swings back again.
The lie works only as long as it takes to speak
and the girl runs only as far
as the napalm allows
until her burning tendons and crackling
muscles draw her up
into that final position
burning bodies so perfectly assume. Nothing
can change that, she is burned behind my eyes
and not your good love and not the rain-swept air
and not the jungle-green
pasture unfolding before us can deny it.

Brian Turner

Brian Turner's (1967–) debut book of poems, Here, Bullet, *received the Beatrice Hawley Award in 2005. He is a contributor to* The New York Times' *blog,* Home Fires, *which features the writing of men and women who have returned from wartime service in the United States military. He is the recipient of the 2009–2010 Amy Lowell Traveling Scholarship and teaches at Sierra Nevada College.*

What Every Soldier Should Know

> To yield to force is an act of necessity, not of will;
> it is at best an act of prudence.
>
> —Jean-Jacques Rousselau

If you hear gunfire on a Thursday afternoon,
it could be for a wedding, or it could be for you.

Always enter a home with your right foot;
the left is for cemeteries and unclean places.

O-guf! Tera armeek is rarely useful.
It means *Stop! Or I'll shoot.*

Sabah el khair is effective.
It means *Good Morning.*

Inshallah means *Allah be willing.*
Listen well when it is spoken.

You will hear the RPG coming for you.
Not so the roadside bomb.

There are bombs under the overpasses,
in trashpiles, in bricks, in cars.

There are shopping carts with clothes soaked
in foogas, a sticky gel of homemade napalm.

Parachute bombs and artillery shells
sewn into the carcasses of dead farm animals.

Graffiti sprayed onto the overpasses:
I will kell you, American.

Men wearing vests rigged with explosives
walk up, raise their arms and say *Inshallah.*

There are men who earn eighty dollars
to attack you, five thousand to kill.

Small children who will play with you,
old men with their talk, women who offer chai—

and any one of them
may dance over your body tomorrow.

Here, Bullet

If a body is what you want,
then here is bone and gristle and flesh.
Here is the clavicle-snapped wish,
the aorta's opened valves, the leap
thought makes at the synaptic gap.
Here is the adrenaline rush you crave,
that inexorable flight, that insane puncture
into heat and blood. And I dare you to finish
what you've started. Because here, Bullet,
here is where I complete the word you bring
hissing through the air, here is where I moan
the barrel's cold esophagus, triggering
my tongue's explosives for the rifling I have
inside of me, each twist of the round
spun deeper, because here, Bullet,
here is where the world ends, every time.

AB Negative (The Surgeon's Poem)

Thalia Fields lies under a gray ceiling of clouds,
just under the turbulence, with anesthetics
dripping from an IV into her arm,

and the flight surgeon says *The shrapnel*
cauterized as it traveled through her
here, breaking this rib as it entered,
burning a hole through the left lung
to finish in her back, and all of this
she doesn't hear, except perhaps as music—
that faraway music of people's voices
when they speak gently and with care,
a comfort to her on a stretcher
in a flying hospital en route to Landstuhl,
just under the rain at midnight, and Thalia
drifts in and out of consciousness
as a nurse dabs her lips with a moist towel,
her palm on Thalia's forehead, her vitals
slipping some, as burned flesh gives way
to the heat of blood, the tunnels within
opening to fill her, just enough blood
to cough up and drown in; Thalia
sees shadows of people working
to save her, but cannot feel their hands,
cannot hear them any longer,
and when she closes her eyes
the most beautiful colors rise in darkness,
tangerine washing into Russian blue,
with the droning engine humming on
in a dragonfly's wings, island palms
painting the sky an impossible hue
with their thick brushes dripping green . . .
a way of dealing with the fact
that Thalia Fields is gone, long gone,
about as far from Mississippi
as she can get, ten thousand feet above Iraq
with a blanket draped over her body
and an exhausted surgeon in tears,
his blooded hands on her chest, his head
sunk down, the nurse guiding him
to a nearby seat and holding him as he cries,
though no one hears it, because nothing can be heard

where pilots fly in blackout, the plane
like a shadow guiding the rain, here
in the droning engines of midnight.

Night in Blue

At seven thousand feet and looking back, running lights
blacked out under the wings and America waiting,
a year of my life disappears at midnight,
the sky a deep viridian, the houselights below
small as match heads burned down to embers.

Has this year made me a better lover?
Will I understand something of hardship,
of loss, will a lover sense this
in my kiss or touch? What do I know
of redemption or sacrifice, what will I have
to say of the dead—that it was worth it,
that any of it made sense?
I have no words to speak of war.
I never dug the graves in Talafar.
I never held the mother crying in Ramadi.
I never lifted my friend's body
when they carried him home.

I have only the shadows under the leaves
to take with me, the quiet of the desert,
the low fog of Balad, orange groves
with ice forming on the rinds of fruit.
I have a woman crying in my ear
late at night when the stars go dim,
moonlight and sand as a resonance
of the dust of bones, and nothing more.

Author Index

Title Index